The Continuing City

The Continuing City

Urban Morphology
in Western Civilization

James E. Vance, Jr.

The Johns Hopkins University Press
Baltimore and London

The Continuing City: Urban Morphology in Western Civilization is a completely revised edition of *This Scene of Man: The Role and Structure of the City in the Geography of Western Civilization,* which was published in 1977 by Harper's College Press as part of the Harper & Row Series in Geography, Donald W. Meinig, Advisor.

Frontispiece is used courtesy of the Uffizi Gallery, Florence, Italy.

The Johns Hopkins University Press, 2715 North Charles Street, Baltimore, Maryland 21218-4319
The Johns Hopkins Press Ltd., London

LIBRARY OF CONGRESS CATALOGING-IN-PUBLICATION DATA
Vance, James E.
  The continuing city : urban morphology in Western civilization / James E. Vance, Jr.
      p.   cm.
  Rev. ed. of: This scene of man. c1977.
  Includes bibliographical references.
  ISBN 0-8018-3801-0 (alk. paper). — ISBN 0-8018-3802-9 (pbk. :alk. paper)
  1. Cities and towns—History.   2. Civilization, Occidental.
I. Vance, James E.   This scene of man.   II. Title.
HT111.V289   1990
307.76´09—dc20   89-37341 CIP

A catalog record of this book is available from the British Library.

For Jean and Tiffany, who helped me to see the pattern in this "mighty maze" by encouragement in times of doubt and query in those of unwarranted certainty; and for Zeb, whose example of fortitude was to me as invaluable as his company.

Contents

Preface   ix

Preface to the Original Edition   xiii

1   Introduction: Urban Morphogenesis   3

2   The Gods Look Down: The Classical City   41

3   The Disintegration into Feudalism and the Dawn
of Freedom   79

4   The Expression of Liberalism: The Face of the
Medieval City   111

5   A Town for Everyman: The Late-Medieval Bastide   173

6   The Prince's Capital and the Merchant's Town   207

7   The Revolution of Economy and Evolution of the City:
Urban Morphogenesis in the Industrial Age   283

8   Urban Form in the Modern World: The Emergence of the
Complex City, 1845–1945   363

9   Urban Morphogenesis since 1945: The Rise of the
Complex City   457

Index   521

Preface

In the thirteen years between the publication of the original edition of this work (*This Scene of Man: The Role and Structure of the City in the Geography of Western Civilization* [New York: Harper's College Press, Harper and Row, 1977]) and the issuance of this considerably revised edition, more than simple revisions of this work have occurred. It was always my intention to think about cities as permanently in harness with another central aspect of Western civilization, an ever-evolving technology and geography of transportation. Much as I have always seen this yoking as indispensable to the understanding of the geography of either in turn, my analytical abilities fifteen years ago did not seem up to attempting an evolutionary and genetic study of the two in harness. For that reason I began my search for the relationship by first looking at cities. With that in hand, I then sought the same goals with respect to transportation, publishing an even more detailed book on the evolutionary technology and geographical pattern of human movement (*Capturing the Horizon: The Historical Geography of Transportation* [New York: Harper and Row, 1986]). This second pillar provided the frame to support a more complex edifice. In the revision here presented it has been possible in the last two chapters to attempt a brief interactive statement on transportation-settlement relationships employing processes in transportation evolution delineated only after the work on cities was first published.

It has proved possible at this time to bring together these intellectual siblings. When the revision here presented was begun, it was Paul Lee of Littlefield, Adams and Company who encouraged me in the task, but the stock market collapse of October 1987 made it impossible for a successor company to execute that role in the undertaking. Happy circumstance brought the manuscript to the attention of George Thompson at the Johns Hopkins University Press. At exactly the same time in the fall of 1987, the then recent sale of old and respectable Harper and Row to a foreign publishing company led to the near stillbirth of *Capturing the Horizon* when its production was stopped six months before the reviews were published. Only the prompt and vigorous search for the printers' films by Logan Campbell, who had been a friend of the book at Harper's, made it possible for the Johns Hopkins University Press to reissue *Capturing the Horizon* at the same time that this revision of *This Scene of Man* is being published. It is my earnest hope that a few may thus be encouraged to read as a pair these conceptually related books.

Any product, such as this, that has evolved over a period of nearly four decades owes a great deal to others, most notably to students and colleagues. In this I have been extremely fortunate in having been able to work with doctoral students of quick intelligence and questioning minds. All of these deserve thanks, and some should be singled out for acknowledgment of contributions they may not be particularly aware of having made. In particular I owe a complex and very real debt to Roger Barnett of the University of the Pacific, as well as considerable thanks to Charles S. Sargent of Arizona State University, Elizabeth Kates Burns of that same institution, Christopher Winters of the University of Chicago Library, Willard Tim Chow, formerly planning director of the City of Honolulu, William Code of the University of Western Ontario, William Brown of the Evergreen State College, Lynn Rosenvall of the University of Calgary, Richard Foster of the University of Manitoba, and Brian Godfrey of Vassar College, and a peculiar appreciation to Martyn Bowden of Clark University, as constructive a gadfly as any teacher could logically expect. Among my current students Christopher McGee, Alastair Shedden, and Piper Gaubatz have been equally stimulating and have continued to convince me that teaching can truly be the most satisfying of occupations.

Among my colleagues several stand out for their long and patient assistance in sorting out my ideas through the logic and directness of their thoughts. To J. B. Jackson I owe so many intellectual debts that they cannot be specified. I wish to express thanks to Peter Hall, formerly of the University of Reading and now of Berkeley, for a quarter-century of most pleasant and productive discussion of the matter of cities and the transportation that makes them work; to Peter Haggett of the University of Bristol, for both stimulation and a most necessary questioning of my ideas over a period that began when we were both much younger than now; to Yola Verhasselt of the Vrije Universiteit, Brussels, for making Belgian cities intelligible to me; and particularly to Walter Hardwick of the University of British Columbia, for some understanding of the fascinating comparative study of cities and for my standing as at least a part-time resident of Canada's westernmost frontier town.

In the course of a book as evolutionary as this, several editors have played a large and most necessary role. Donald Meinig of Syracuse, as contributing editor for geography to Harper and Row, was midwife to its birth, godfather to its existence, and savior in its regeneration. His initial criticisms were correctly stern and truly welcome. Raleigh Wilson of the then Harper's College Press deserves to be numbered among the historic mentors and trainers of editorial history, those persons who know that authors, like prize fighters, succeed best with plenty of regimen mixed with ultimate freedom of expression. And to George Thompson, the editor of this volume, go most sincere thanks for being fully equal to his predecessors. He has shown in complete measure that peculiarly selfless dedication to another's success that dignifies his calling.

Several authors and their publishers have been very generous in allowing me to quote extensively from their work. I particularly wish to thank the following: Duke University Press for permission to quote almost in its entirety Zelia Nuttal's translation of the town-planning portions of the Spanish Laws of the Indies; Harvard University Press for the quotation of the town-planning provisions of Morris Hicky Morgan's translation of Vitruvius; Harcourt Brace Jovanovich, Inc., for the right to quote Henri Pirenne's *Economic and Social History of Medieval Europe*; and Stanford University Press for the use of descriptive passages from Henderson and Chaloner's translation of Friedrich Engels, *The Condition of the Working Class in England*. For use of illustrative material I am particularly grateful to John Rogers Flather of Lowell; to the Lowell Historical Society; to Margaret Philbrick of Sheffield, Massachusetts; to the Waltham Public Library, Waltham; the late Professor H. J. Dyos, Leicester; and the firm of Ray Delvert, Villeneuve-sur-Lot, France. Finally, I wish to express appreciation for the kindness and assistance of several research libraries over a period of nearly ten years, specifically the Public Record Office, London; the Birmingham Reference Library; the Wellesley College Library; Miss Marion Henderson and the Clark University Library; and the Environmental Design Library and the Library Photo Service, Berkeley.

In the preparation of the original manuscript there are those whose careful efforts would remain unknown if I were not to acknowledge them here. To the late Miss Agnes Lincoln of the geography department in Berkeley go my thanks for her help in organizing, and to a considerable degree executing, the typing of the original manuscript. In that work Linda Yemoto and Natalia Vonnegut were invaluable. To Gail Larrick I wish to express particular thanks for her exemplary editorial assistance, and for her patience when faced by my sometimes ancient practices. Ken Burke was, in the original edition, unfailing in his wisdom as to the production of a book that both pleased the eye and avoided the ponderous quality of a manuscript.

The preparation of this revised edition has been far more than incidental in its demands. Completely set in new type and possessed of new and reordered illustrations as well as new chapters, it has required that the editing process be repeated. Mary Yates has proved the ideal of copy editors, the source of all the author lacks, careful in the extreme but quick-witted and wise. In preparing the manuscript in Berkeley Natalia Vonnegut was, as before, of great help, though now she is leader of the team. Charles Hadenfeldt was comprehensive and concerned in transforming the seeming chaos of a revision combined with new material into the electronic order of disks and then printed pages. I thank him for his skill but even more for his very personal participation. Doty Valrey has been helpful in the typing of the manuscript.

Since the original edition was published I must record the death of one to whom I wish to express particular thanks for all that he contributed by starting me along the path that led, with many shifts in course, to this book, even though the pursuit of the continuing city would never have been his objective. Raymond Murphy was a great teacher in a quite exceptional way. He had an unusual awareness of the weight of the dead hand of scholasticism, as well as a great wisdom in encouraging the individual to use the strongest scholarly weapon, personal geographical curiosity. For all that he gave me I wish both to thank and to remember him.

To all of these I wish to express my sincere thanks for their contributions while shielding them from any responsibility for blots on the page, which are always put there by the writer.

Preface to the Original Edition

Urbanization has been such a central aspect of Western civilization that the forces affecting cities are nearly as diverse as those shaping culture itself. To attempt to survey all that has been written about the Western city would be as foolish as it is impossible; there is a certain intellectual isostasy at work, which means that as fact is piled up, some of it will disappear below the base plane and the heights of understanding will not necessarily be greatly increased. In writing this book I have sought to provide neither a survey of Western cities nor a simple geography of their location. Instead, my purpose has been to search out two aspects of Western urbanization: the evolution of the role and purpose of cities in Western society, and the processes used by that society to create and transform the physical fabric of those cities. These two concerns are the elements in a study of urban morphogenesis wherein the actual process may explain the shaping of the city, but a rational observer seeks to understand the forces creating the process itself.

Urban morphogenesis, though ever expressed in city form, is best seen as a set of processes in times of fundamental transformation of that morphology. For the Western city we may begin the story with the initiation of urbanization of a complex sort, rather than the narrow purpose found in the oldest religious and administrative towns, which came when economic activity gained a full role in the support of cities. Archaic Greece around the beginning of the first millennium B.C. experienced this increasing complexity in individual settlements as well as the formation of the first "system of cities" wherein it was possible to perceive the existence of general rather than idiographic processes. Since that time periods of initiation or transformation have occurred with a certain inexorability: the Roman city succeeded on the Greek; the barbarians' attempt to embrace the late imperial Roman cities fatally disrupted their support, bringing a break in urban evolution; the return of an economic purpose around the beginning of the second millennium of our era shaped the medieval city, which had several expressions, the most interesting of which for Americans was the bastidal new towns of the thirteenth and fourteenth centuries; the subsequent economic "revolution," the commercial one of the sixteenth century and the industrial one of the nineteenth century, transformed the medieval town into the modern city. Through all of this transformation certain processes persisted, but their nature and impact were periodically readjusted as the role that cities were asked to play changed.

A wide variety of literature must lie behind a book of this sort, so wide in fact that it is impracticable to present a bibliography of contributive works. And a list of works cited can be handled efficiently in the footnotes, which are fully indexed. In order that this book might lead students into a further investigation of the work cited, I have tried to do two things. In those cases where I felt that the work had a literary as well as an informational contribution to make—as in Pirenne's analysis of the medieval city or Engels's description of Manchester in the early Industrial Era—I have quoted extensively in the hope of engaging the reader's attention enough to cause a further reading of the work. And I have sought where possible to use specific references still in print, and preferably available in paperback editions. In this way I believe individuals and colleges can gain easy access to these supporting volumes.

Because this book represents a summation of my temporary conclusions on urban morphogenesis after some forty years of thinking, teaching, and writing, I have had to cite my own work extensively. I do not view my words as either definitive or conclusive; rather, the problem is that urban morphogenesis has been little pursued by others until recently, and my words in a number of instances must stand not merely as the initial statements but still as the only statements.

Preface to the
Original Edition

The Continuing City

Introduction

<hr>
<hr>

Urban Morphogenesis

1

Cities are culture and geography's largest artifact, the product of a very complex play of greatly varied forces. No book could possibly consider all that shapes a city. My concern is with the physical form and structure of the city, its morphology. I shall extend morphology to include not only form and structure but also the actual physical expression of that form, and the manner, by chance or by consistent practice, in which the various physical components are related to each other in a system of form interaction.

Winston Churchill asserted that we shape our houses but then they shape us. Without interpreting that view to imply a rigid, simplistic environmental determinism, I argue that they do indeed shape us more than most social scientists and normative economic and social geographers would allow. To a very great extent, geographers in recent decades seem to have rejected a rigid environmental determinism only to become dominated by behavioral explanations of economic and social process. Arising from a long-felt craving for some sort of normative process, some modern expression of the law of symmetry, to explain the indigestible wealth of fact, this emphasis has become so strong as to result in a near abandonment of any real concern for the study of morphology and the delineation of its physical processes.

My purpose is to steer a sound course between a too simple belief in physical determinism and an equally too simple belief in a normative geography of institutional process. By its approach to the study of the origin and evolution of the morphology of cities, this book seeks to fill a particular void. It organizes the truths of morphology in such a way as to show the pattern throughout history and the interaction of the processes of morphological evolution with those of other institutional processes.

Covering a range of history from ancient Greece to the present, this book must make use of data that have not been systematically collected and deal with some rarely considered processes. Morphological geography is not a practice, nor does a canon of morphological process exist. A single author, however deep his concern and long his effort, cannot overcome all the neglect of the past. At best he can hope to pioneer in a new field before any further time is lost.

Learning and Teaching in City Form

The mortality of persons contrasts sharply with the immortality of cities. We must distinguish between the way that human beings transfer their learning to other generations and the way that transfer of experience and accomplishment is made through cities. Throughout human history nearly until the advent of European settlement in the New World, most people's ideas disappeared at their death. Although they lived in a literate culture, most people were illiterate. In any event, manuscript writing was so narrowly available that the probability of loss of ideas with the passage of time was very high indeed. To take a specifically germane case, we have left to us only

The William Carson House, Eureka, California, one of the great American houses, must certainly have had some impact on the family living in it.

one work of Roman origin that gives in any detail the thinking of those great city builders, or their conceptions and designs for the urban places that were both the instrument of Roman imperialism and the centers of that culture. We must depend on Vitruvius, author of the *Ten Books of Architecture* written in the time of Augustus, for all the literary knowledge that we have of this most important of urban epochs, for which only a modest amount of epigraphic evidence from inscriptions and other durable writings has survived the erosion of time. Trajan's column in Rome might be considered yet another "written" record with its scenes of bridge building and other construction activities. Even so, the record is meager; yet we know far more about Roman cities than we do about some far more recent construction. How have we learned so much on an essentially unrecorded subject? We know about Rome and its cities because we have looked at, observed, and analyzed those places in their physical remains.

In the study of cities the immortality of the places is a boon to us, if we will let it be. But the physical remains of the past tend to be viewed only as works of "art," and thus as a concern of aesthetics. Certainly Greek kraters are art, but they are also revealing documents telling us of daily life, though often life caricatured as a contemporary Walter Mitty would have perceived it. Given a larger physical creation, such as the apartmented houses of Ostia Antica, we can learn a great deal that is unfiltered by literary or artistic selection.

The record is incomplete—few records are not—so we must develop some system for filling the gaps by logical inference and extension. Not only

Urban
Morphogenesis

must we learn from a relatively uncommon system of teaching, reading the evidence of urban activity from the forms that are created to serve it, but we must also drop the dogma that cities can be understood and studied only in terms of human institutions. Our physical works are more enduring than many of our social and economic processes, so we must accept that the physical inheritance from the past belongs in any analysis fully as much as contemporary institutional practices.

Class and the City

The particular approach normally taken in scholarship toward physical evidence, rather than literary records, has ruled that tangible things must be "high art," "masterpieces," or at the very least "polite" rather than "vernacular" creations. The tattered papers of the common folk may have come to be prized by historians—though they seldom were a century ago—but their physical possessions and housing are only now gaining the interest they deserve in a democratic society. The elitist bias of history in general, and of architectural history in particular, has meant that far less attention has been given to the physical accommodation, daily life, and sincere thoughts of the average family than has been lavished on the sometime vacuous observations of the well-to-do. We find studies of European cities that leave us with no inkling of how most people lived, nor any understanding of the social and economic context that explains the only too real historical background of Marxist thought.

The purpose of this book is not philistinism, the rejection of the deliberately beautiful and intellectual, but we must remember that gold is an uncommon element and that life in the palace or the monastery was an unusual occupation even during the Middle Ages. In cities, notably, a vital existence derived at least initially and dominantly from production and trade. The situation could not have been otherwise, because most of the beauty subsequently introduced into human life and much of the general intellectual advance came as a charge on the merchants' and master artisans' enlarging purses. In simple truth, far more cathedrals were paid for by the everyday world than by royal patrons. Even if we seek to understand high art and architecture and the intellectual climate of a time, we must pay attention to the total system that produced the more specialized product.

Changes in Morphogenesis

The study of process always poses a real problem: how can a continuous force be captured for observation and analysis? We may have to start with rather scant, or gross, phenomena, leading to a statement of basic process relationships, and hope as more information is made available to refine that statement. We must draw a contrast between the workings of physical science and those of urban morphology. In physical science a fairly small number of absolute, or nearly absolute, properties can be used to explain physical and chemical phenomena. This is not the case in matters of human beings, whose systems are multiple and far more historically relative. Be-

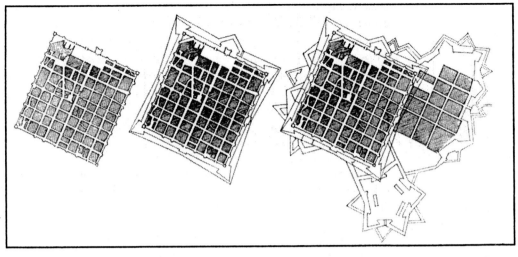

The growth of Turino from Roman times on, as shown in these diagrams, clearly demonstrates the complexity of morphogenetic processes. (Drawings from Steen Eiler Rasmussen, Cities and Buildings; *used by permission of the author.)*

cause culture is a conditional equilibrium, or even a periodic chaos, different systems are at work at different times. As we shall see, the reason the Romans set up their cities the way they did was quite different from the reason our forebears shaped the post–Civil War city, and we shape the complex place in which we live. Human beings reshape the "laws" of social and economic behavior in different eras of history in a way that nature does not.

But are there any eternal verities in the matter of cities? Certainly some biological and psychological human qualities persist: the simple scale of the human body gives a certain quality to people's homes; even though we must stoop to enter a Roman house, we need not crawl to do so. So much attention has been given to the biological and psychological conditions that they will be considered only as they bear upon the other eternal verity of the city, the physical form. That form persists for one of several reasons. The first would be the simple fact that the properties of the physical world are basically unchanging; stones are stable entities save under unfortunate and unusually destructive forces. The raw materials available for the making of cities changed little from the time of Pericles, who died in 429 B.C., to that of President Grant, who died in A.D. 1885. Thus, the plasma of cities has been transformed more often in the last century than in all previous urban history. City form—morphology—tends to change less rapidly than many human institutions because it is nongenerational, lacking the definite life span of the human organism. Although few seventeenth-century buildings remain in North America, and fairly few even in most Old World areas, their death was slow, overlapping the new construction that normally followed precedent in material and design to a degree sufficient to perpetuate the basic elements of form. The housing-tract structure of today is close in form to the houses of colonial America, though the religion and sexual mores of the two times differ greatly.

The structure and form of the city is to a very appreciable degree innate rather than conferred by immediate circumstance. In the long run changes

Urban
Morphogenesis

occur, but they come in a historical rather than a topical time span, and the process of adjustment is one of evolution, not of revolution. Thus, human culture is a conservative force at work in the morphogenesis of cities. Political and economic institutions may change, but such rapid transformations do not, in any automatic way, remake cities. A good test of this notion is found in Eastern Europe. There, most human institutions have been radically transformed since 1945, yet Sofia, Warsaw, Budapest, and Prague would be basically familiar to the resurrected resident of the presocialist 1930s. In truth, Marxist economics, education, social organization, and opposition to formal religion are practiced but, as I have noted elsewhere, no clear Marxist land-assignment system exists, and only a peculiar reversion to the most capitalist of times in early modern Chicago colors the architecture.[1]

The Time Sequence

Given the staged quality of urban history, we may treat the long range of time covered in this book in three fundamental eras—classical, medieval, and modern—with times of cultural and morphological transition standing dominant between them. We could begin with the earliest glimmering of urbanization, with the origin of cities. The intellectual problem we face is that of explaining a total change in human institutions and practices, if we assume that our origin was evolutionary rather than instantaneous. How did the human species become social in the peculiar way that it is, and how did it turn from what seems certain wandering and dispersed settlement to fixed and urban living? Because this problem is so clearly one of theories of culture, it will be left to other works. An extensive anthropological and geographical literature focuses on the origin of cities, so we may leave the specification of the evidence and its intellectual explanation to those immersed in the concern. We may simply take as given the existence of cities and begin our story with two reasonable conditions. The first is that urban history is essentially continuous from that time to the present; the second is that the culture with which we concern ourselves, that of the West, is the containing geographical milieu.

Any considerable body of evidence that can be brought to bear on the question of the morphogenesis of the Western city commences with the Greek city-states as they began to develop in the earlier part of the first millennium before Christ. Although great changes took place as those settlements grew and were transformed over a period of nearly fifteen hundred years, and fundamental differences arose between Greek and Roman towns, a basic consistency in cities of the Classical Era until they were atrophied by the barbarian invasions of the West allows us to treat them as a unified intellectual study. Not all the boundaries are neat. In the eastern reaches of the Roman Empire, the death of the classical world was a lingering one, and we may with considerable justice call it total only when the Turks captured

1. James E. Vance, Jr., "Land Assignment in the Precapitalist, Capitalist, and Postcapitalist City," *Economic Geography* 47 (1971): 101–20.

Constantinople in 1453. By then in the West a whole successor era, that of the Middle Ages, had passed and we may think of 1453, in a symbolic fashion, as the beginning of modern times. In that year the French finally pushed the English out of the area of French speech, save for a few more years in the curiosity that became the Channel Islands and Calais. This change encouraged the development of political, economic, and social policies that may be summed up under the name of mercantilism, and that led directly to the creation of the Industrial Era, in which we remain to this day.

In the West the atrophy of the classical city was sharp in form and narrow in time. Within several hundred years the direction of evolution was reversed and the Roman institutions were first disintegrated and then replaced. Form was borrowed from the Roman past—in a most significant decision, the then universal church placed its capital in Rome, not Jerusalem. In the West no essentially continuous practice of urban life and process of urbanization existed; thus, the "Dark Ages" stand as a striking period of urban transformation. When, around the end of the first Christian millennium, city filling began again in the West, it was for a purpose and in a social structure vastly different from that of the Roman cities whose physical cells it often occupied. The replacement element was as different from the Roman as is the silica from the carbon in a petrified log: dominion and tribute were the practices of Rome, whereas trade and craftsmanship were those of the true medieval city. Yet the continuity of cities was maintained; many of the public components of the physical structure of the medieval city were borrowed fairly directly from Rome, the Christian basilica being a case in point. The Middle Ages were a time of urbanization as vital and puissant as that of senatorial Rome, and distinctly medieval forms and structures soon developed within cities. The most commonly known was that of the Gothic church, whose form and functions would have been both unnecessary and misunderstood among the people of the classical Mediterranean. And in the layout of the town a surpassingly important contrast was introduced: the city's form sprang from its subjugation to the needs of its citizens rather than its gods, as had been the case in Rome.

The discontinuity at the end of the Middle Ages was more biological than functional. The onset of catastrophic plagues in the fourteenth century simply forced a grim effort to hold what ground had already been won in social and economic development. For two centuries the cities became tempering vessels in which durability of purpose was tested and, when present, strengthened. The weak and irresolute sought refuge in the countryside, to flood back into the city only with the onset of the modern era that came into existence when the nation-states emerged as successors to the weakened political power of the cities.

An interregnum occurred in the power of the city. When the nation-state came to stand as the successor to the powerful cities of the Middle Ages in most of Western Europe, the city was systematically reduced in power and the countryside was elevated, as a conscious policy of the newly strengthened monarchies. The locus of political domination swung clearly to the landed aristocracy in the centralized states—in England, France, and Spain. Only in a land of cities such as Holland were the worst excesses of

Urban
Morphogenesis

9

rural domination avoided to maintain some democratic balance in government. Thus, the discontinuity between the medieval city and that of the Industrial Era was at first a biological attack and then a shifting of the political balance in such a way that the city for several centuries lost its former power. Only when the city produced a new and again vital purpose, as the instrument of national economic policies, did it regain the powerful role it had held when economy of any wide interest was mainly restricted to the medieval city.

The city stands in Western civilization as the major expression of a continuous urban tradition. Starting in the middle of the sixteenth century, cities reattained critical importance in social and economic institutions, only to be delayed in the full enjoyment of political institutions in many places, most notably in Britain, until the nineteenth century. Perhaps most important, the city became the instrument for European domination of the world and for the first approximation of a world economy. The New Lands of the world were planted with European migrants, first in trading towns and then in the spreading rural settlements that ultimately, save in South Africa, destroyed any appreciable survival of the indigenous culture.

Cities represented the first points of attachment of the New Lands to Western civilization. They were the places to which the planted settlers first came and the centers out of which settlement spread to tap the resources of those generally thinly populated areas. And as the economies of the planted regions grew, they expanded in integration with the economies of the homeland. Where the area to be dominated economically was more densely settled, the practice may not have been that of seizing political sovereignty in a total sense; many areas were left as colonies and protectorates. But the instrument of attachment remained the "colonial city" planted by the "colonial power," as was the case with Britain at Bombay, Singapore, and, in a different sense, Hong Kong. When the colonial overlordship ended, the planted form of Western urbanism remained and became the model for city development, even when it was locally originated and encouraged. In these ways the city form that emerged with the quickening of industrial activity— first in England and the Low Countries, spreading subsequently to France and the United States and ultimately to all of the Western countries—came to be spread far more widely in the world than the specific culture that produced it.

Space within Cities

We seek an understanding of cities and the role they play by looking within them to see how people have used them and what physical demands have been made on them, and by asking what this tells us about the location of these, the largest intimately integrated institutions and the greatest of human physical artifacts. An equally significant question can be answered only from within: what is the structure of the city even after its location has been explained in broader terms?

Other academic disciplines have been concerned with questions internal to the city, but none has a responsibility for the physical build of the place. Historians have recently increased their attention to cities, and a new urban history is emerging that seeks to understand the nature of the proletarian citizen as well as the civic leader. Sociologists have always been most concerned with city people because in urban environments social institutions are most readily observed and compared and the social processes are most clearly perceived in research. Economists have always made an important, but largely unglamorous, study of land economics, to which in recent years have been added subfields—welfare and consumer economics—that are heavily urban in their interests. But none of these other studies concerns itself with the physical form of the city.

Architectural history and the practice of city planning, with attention to its history, might be thought to look at form. However, a kindly scrutiny of those fields shows that, much as they are concerned with the physical features of the city, they are not concerned with settlements, either as a totality or in an organic evolutionary way. Architectural history has mainly concerned itself with "high architecture," as expressed in great buildings built by practicing architects and normally quite deliberately expressive of the concerns of a small, highly self-conscious elite. Thus, from that most admirable discipline we have gained a much better understanding of the impact of educated taste and architectural technology than of actual city form. The history of city planning, as opposed to the professional practice of city planning, has been almost exclusively concerned with preconceived design in towns, and most heavily with the utopian or ideal cities, most of which never were transferred from paper onto the ground.

We are fundamentally concerned here with space *within* cities, even though much city planning was contemporaneous with early landscape planning. From the work of others we now have views as to "social space" within the city, the land economics of urban activities, and the design concept of space in art, architecture, landscape architecture, and preconceived planning. Their undertakings are not insignificant or invalid, but in our terms they are insufficient to encompass the total morphology of the city. Expressed another way, a reality of space exists within cities just as do the realities of social interaction and economic activity. If one concentrates on society, then social institutions and social space suffice to provide the substance of understanding. But if one looks at space as a reality, as a force operating independently of institutions, and as a medium for people to use in expressing many institutionally derived objectives, then a great interest and real need arises to look at space *tout à fait*. It might be argued that space is always dependent on people and their society or economy, that it is constantly relative to those institutions and is thereby subservient to their processes. The evidence does not support such a position. Economics presents the strongly held principle of "distance decay" in social questions; one of the fundamental explanations of the operation of innovation and the diffusion of ideas is the contagion theory, which holds that ideas and practices will diffuse if peoples are in contact but will fail to do so if empty space intervenes.

We shall look at space for its own sake, and specifically its expression in cities, which we call urban morphology. To do that, we need tools, so we shall explore the concepts of urban morphogenesis that might be used in that task.

The Concept of Normative Structure

In geography, the interest has been in the location of cities and other social and economic phenomena in broad-scale space, and an earnest effort has been made to determine a normative geographical structure for those activities. Walter Christaller's proposal of a central-place hierarchical arrangement of towns was such an undertaking, as have been proposals of "market potential," "population potential," and even "rank-size rule" ordering of towns in space. The basic assumption in all of this work is that natural order awaits discovery. Because the human mind can deal effectively only with a very modest set of causes, the practice has been to assign causation to one or two major forces, leaving most of the others to secondary consideration. Christaller argued three basic points: (1) the natural, universal distribution of population is dispersed in the countryside; (2) to gain goods and services beyond their shared capacity to produce them, people must physically converge on towns where centralized goods and services are to be had; and (3) such physical convergence is greatly influenced by the growing burden of increasing distance, to the point that eventually new central-places will be set up in some sort of hierarchical relation to all other central-places in order to be nearer to the most distant customers of the original place. The assumption behind this theory is that the understanding of this interrelated set of external processes furnishes us with the perception and explanation of a natural order of city siting and use.

Later, we will examine both the assumptions and the reality of this theory, but now let us use it as an example of the way assumptions of normative process have been employed to seek order and understanding in a factually complex world. We may argue that no innate quality of normality forbids its expression within as well as outside cities. Thus, we may seek to state such process theories in an internally viewed urban morphogenesis, as well as in the much more widely sought theories of regional relationship.

In seeking an understanding of normative structure within cities, two real problems arise, those of excessive particularization and excessive aggregation. An instance of the first is found when considering the residential unit—the house in most of human history, and the apartment of late. The housing unit may be defined as the basic physical unit or cell of urban morphology, as has been done by general historians and by those concerned with architecture in particular. The main difficulty comes when we try to determine how typical their description of a particular building is for all the buildings of the city. We have tended to gain an exaggerated view of past housing conditions by a heavy reliance on the writing of a small literate elite. In the same way, those outside the United States gained a most elevated view of the physical possessions of ordinary Americans during the Great Depression of the 1930s when their view of housing was based on the American movies so widely seen in that era. But historical records are not socially or economically balanced. The rich and powerful are far more likely to survive in records than the relatively poor and powerless mass of the population. The most extreme examples of a time have a way of becoming the prime examples of history. If we look at any one building as the example of a time, we must try to see how well it represents the norm we seek.

The problem of aggregation shows up in the tendency to take some reasonable norm and make of it reality. Three examples—one from the Classical Era, another from the late Middle Ages, and the third from modern America—give a clear view of the difficulty. In many textbooks of planning and architecture, three illustrations will be reproduced that have become so widely presented as to be taken as representative truth. The first shows a Roman military camp, the *castrum*, either as a theoretical construction or in some actual occurrence. Normally, a careful selection has been made from among the hundreds of *castra* that were built so the "example" will most simply, and perfectly, reproduce the theory as expounded by masters of Roman centuriation. Thus, the prime example becomes the norm. This practice also shows up when an author wishes to talk about the fascinating towns, or bastides, that were founded in the Middle Ages. The practice is to reproduce the ground plan of Monpazier in the Agenais of southwestern France to represent the bastides. In 1986 France issued a large, handsome stamp honoring the bastide and, sure enough, it shows Monpazier's town square and *cornières*. Again, perfection of the plan rather than the representative quality of Monpazier settles the choice. Finally, textbooks usually show some plan for a grid-pattern town in the American Middle West and leave in our minds the notion that all is symmetry, order, proportion, and uniformity there.

The difficulty in each of these examples is that the medium gives an erroneous message. Most Roman cities were laid out according to principles whose nature will be considered in the next chapter. Subsequently, the medieval bastides had principles at work during their construction that made them towns of rather democratic proportion in land assignment. And the Middle Western town was orderly only on the first map filed in the county courthouse. But great physical variety existed even within this general conceptual agreement.

When we look at these towns on the ground we find, for example, that the Roman *castrum* pattern for a settlement was a religious and military conception far more than it was the actual plan for development. Places of Roman origin share certain qualities, but their common elements come from an adherence to principles rather than to a rigid plan. A city is an organism that evolves as all organisms do, in response to genetic signals—concepts of what a city should do and how it should interact in its parts—such as those that make all men or women basically alike but infinitely different one from another. In a world of three billion people, no two are really identical. In the same way, city building responds to "genetic" signals but never produces identical products. Thus, to take Monpazier as what "the bastide" was when it was built is no service to truth. I have on occasion wished that Monpazier would disappear into separate pieces in a hundred museums so that no one would ever again think of it as whole, the substance of an aggregate reality.

If our interest is in hypothesized normative process or abstract form for

Urban
Morphogenesis

13

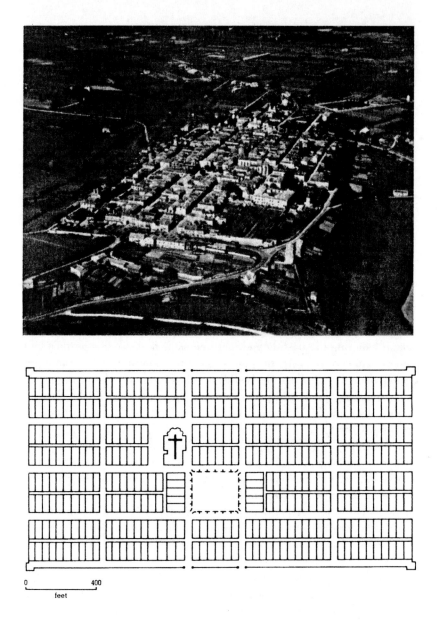

its own sake, the use of the ideal is of some value. If we seek to understand something less neat and far less abstract, we should eschew the ideal and look at the human world with the wondrous variety the quality of humanness implies. We can thus work inductively from the detail to a state of generalization of process. We take account of variety to begin with, rather than argue that a simple normative process has, by corruption, produced the vast variety of the world. In the deductive approach, which envisages normative processes shaping cities, all variation stands either as an a priori result of some presumptive relationship or as static introduced by imperfect human rationality. In the inductive approach, the generalization is always a posteriori, first taking into account the conditions found in cities and then dealing in a rational balancing with the seemingly contradictory conditions, ultimately arriving at an inductive generalization or statement of process that is fundamentally inclusive of diversity.

Idiograph and Induction

The effort to synthesize the numerous studies made of individual cities is far from new. Within the field of geography, the tendency has been toward the study of the concrete and the hitherto unknown or undescribed. Each part has been assumed to be a component of a more universally interesting whole. With few exceptions, the part has turned out to be an idiograph, complete in itself and of specific meaning only to the precise subject of the study. Thus, newer city monographs have collected on shelves as did the classical regional monographs of the French school during the Third Republic: an impressive collection of scholarship, but hardly the skeleton of a broader truth.

The failure of local, idiographic studies to advance broad understanding rather than local knowledge encouraged a complete shift in the viewpoint on cities. Instead of building up from the parts, it was argued that understanding would come from soaring above and projecting downward on local reality a natural order that had been arrived at a priori and from which explanation of the local pattern could be gained deductively. Not only did this elevated viewpoint hold out hope for a success that had not come with idiographic collections, but it was much more economical and less confusing. No longer were facts of equal importance; only those related to the deductive system need be considered. If from them a plausible fit with the theory could be established, then the other facts were not equal facts, but rather lesser realities that could be disregarded as not contributing any percentage of cause to the pattern proved from above.

But by deductive reasoning we know little about the processes shaping cities. We have found that by soaring above, we can see only certain things. The censuses of various nations have for many scholars become the view of the ground, and those things not collected by enumerators are not part of the picture. Unfortunately for our present interests, census enumerators have never turned any attention on the subject of urban morphology.

But even if the census sufficed, which it certainly does not, we have a much more fundamental reason for eschewing the soaring deduction: its use depends on standardization of data and procedure. In those terms local studies have little use; historical facts, whose survival is greatly adventitious, have almost none. To attempt to shape an understanding of urban morphology over the long life of the Western city, we must deal with diverse materials and sources seemingly too unstandard to be handled by most deductive systems. Thus, it is useful to propose an inductive approach to the considerable body of facts derived from locally based and formally unrelated studies.

Urban
Morphogenesis

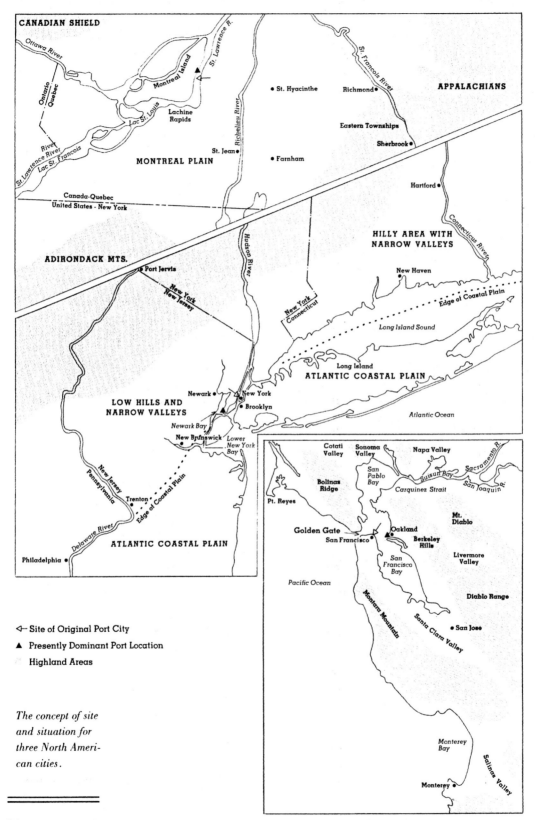

The concept of site
and situation for
three North Ameri-
can cities.

◁— Site of Original Port City

▲   Presently Dominant Port Location

    Highland Areas

Site and Situation

Not all local fact is grist for a larger mill; some items are simply unique. Even so, the response of the whole local system to that unusual fact may be in itself a great help in discerning how the more widely shared elements of morphogenesis work, particularly with regard to the physical site of the city. While the focus of urban studies lay on the local, the great tendency was to simplify the notion of location into a supposed dichotomy of site and situation; *site* was the physical nature of the ground on which the city was built, and *situation* was the assumed wider interconnections of the city and its surrounding area. This analytical device held a truth of a somewhat overly simple sort. Cities do have a fundament, which today tends to be rather too much belittled in our overfocus on social and economic institutions. San Francisco gains much of its character from its most eccentric site, as do New York City and Montréal. And who would argue that the etiolate image of Indianapolis is not in large part an outgrowth of its two-dimensional site? Thus, truth in siting is too often disregarded today.

Situation, the other component of the classic dichotomy of city location, has fitted somewhat better into the highly statistical study of modern cities, for implied in it is the notion of economic location, which the census data measure better than geographical location. Yet even in this regard, much needs be dealt with as a local matter. Looking again at San Francisco, New York City, and Montréal, we find the situations of the three are in one way similar: each is at the estuarine outlet of a major river system, and each was the entrepôt settlement from which a great valley—the Central Valley of California, the Hudson, and the St. Lawrence—was tied in with a larger economic world. This original situation can be considered fundamental to the founding of the town. Coming up to the present, the pattern is not shared. Montréal still has its initial situation in large measure, but New York is far less influenced by its river system and San Francisco little indeed. In fact the port function of San Francisco is a pale shadow of what it was when the place was founded. We need, then, to study cities and their situation, so that we may deal with either persisting original conditions or their virtual destruction and replacement. This inductive study is essential, and national standardization on the present is a camouflage of truth.

Stages of Truth

Because morphology can be immortal, though it often is not, we must take account of the past even to understand the narrowly defined present. To hold that the past is precept and continuous is a truism. Nevertheless, these patent truths force upon us the resolution of several methodological problems. If the precept of the present is continuous, how then can we most validly study it? The problem arises because of the discontinuous record we inherit, and because even if we could follow the development of cities continuously over a three-thousand-year period, the effort would overtax our abilities. We need an economy of effort and of attention, as well as a system that allows us to cantilever across gorges of unrecorded evidence.

Attention to the stage of morphogenesis becomes both a convenient and a necessary tool. If we know that a city was founded at a particular time—a fact more likely to survive the destruction of record than some others—and we know the form of town that existed at that time, we are in a position to draw certain inferences as to the philosophy and motivation of the founders. If we find a shared philosophy, as we do in the bastides of the Middle Ages or the towns of the nineteenth-century Middle West, we can establish certain processes that were at work. We can then reason from that establishment to a general morphogenetic process, with its associated physical build of city in response to determinate conditions. What we talk about is *stage* rather than *time;* the bastides were built mainly from the middle of the twelfth to the middle of the fourteenth century, whereas the Middle Western towns came largely in the nineteenth, but each was an initial state.

Time does have an impact. Certainly the rapidity with which a carpet of new towns spread across the Middle West was much greater than the slower progress of the bastidors across the devastated areas of Europe during the Middle Ages. And the easier flow of information in the last century as opposed to eight hundred years ago meant that the pattern in America was more consistent. But we should not become deterministic on the matter of the diffusion of information and ideas, for much of the greater consistency in America was the result of a rapid spread under a single political control, as opposed to the great political fragmentation of medieval Europe.

To point up precisely what is meant by *stage*, we may define by exclusion. Stage is not chronological time, it is morphological time. In the initial stage, we may make two assumptions: (1) the form of the town will tend most clearly and simply to reflect the purpose for which the settlement was established, and (2) the most obvious expression of the practices will then be used in town building. This will be true whether we consider the Greek *polis* or the English New Town of the postwar years. And as the town comes to undertake several different functions, the evidence becomes more mixed. For example, Bath in England was originally laid out by the Romans as a watering place, a literal bath, so it had a fairly obvious conformity to the special needs of that purpose. In the intervening two millennia Bath has been used for many purposes—abbey of the Middle Ages, local market town, show ring of Society during the Restoration, and home of the Admiralty in wartime, just to mention a few. Each of these activities has left its mark, some more than others. The Romans gave that particular cast to the place that is always allowed to the founder; the eighteenth-century peacocks of Beau Nash built so extravagantly that their tracks are still clearly in evidence; the Admiralty during World War II made less of a splash, perhaps because it was so far from its accustomed habitat.

From the successive transformations of Bath, and any other city that has lived very long, clear stages in use are obvious, but such clear relics of that use do not always remain. We know fairly well what the Romans did at Bath from the way they built, and we know what the empty Society of the eighteenth century did there because their buildings and street layouts remain until today. But the reuse made of the Roman buildings throughout the Middle Ages and the reoccupation of the buildings of regal Bath between the eighteenth century and today are not so clearly shown on the ground. Thus, for evidence on those scores we turn to places with clearer relics from which we may gain a much better understanding of shifts in urban processes. From those other examples we may project into a city such as Bath, where the evidence may be obscure, some understanding of what was happening at a particular time. Such a procedure has pitfalls and we must make certain assumptions as to the universality of particular conditions, but when we have fragmentary contemporaneous evidence from the place or observations from a succeeding time that seem to confirm our view of what was going on during the evidentiary gap, our risk in assumptions is reasonable.

We should be clear in our minds that an early, or even initial, stage can be a very durable attribute of morphology. Street plans are laid down on the ground to survive truly incredible destruction and adversity. Turin and Chester have pedestrians following literally in the footsteps of the Romans, even though the buildings of Turin reflect mainly the grand designs of Piedmontese kings and of Mussolini, and those of Chester the smaller perceptions of the medieval English and modern aldermen. In the same way buildings are among our more plastic creations, surviving changes in geography and style that transform Diocletian's palace at Split into slums and the mews of Victorian coachmen into the flats of Bentley-driving gentry in today's London.

Function and Form in Morphogenesis

The architectural revolution of the International Style, signaling the birth of a "modern architecture," represented itself—with the overdramatization so much a part of cultural warfare—as an utter break with the past. To press that point, dicta of all sorts were made up and adopted as the creed for a new religion. The one that most concerns us is the dictum "form follows function." Such a dictum could have seemed new or radical only in a nation as besotted with romanticism as was Germany in the nineteenth century. When we look at the house in classical Athens, the buildings in the medieval bastides, or the farmhouses of eighteenth- and early nineteenth-century New England, the pretentiousness of the Bauhaus and its theorists is most evident. Yet we must accept that their conditioning has been effective, leaving many intelligent people with the view that Baltic culture just after World War I first discovered that a building is beautiful by being appropriate to its function. We must put the lie to this antihistorical nonsense; quite demonstrably, in vast periods of human history, building has been predicated entirely on fulfilling a particular function in terms of the best technology then available. Perhaps the house of the medieval town had less light than one in Dessau in the 1920s, but not by design. As long as timber or masonry construction had to be used and glass was costly and poor, little else in lighting could be accomplished, however much one wished for better conditions. We know that the wish was for light: far more work was carried on out-of-doors and the working days were of variable length, as were the working hours, according to the season and the length of daylight. Structural necessity, not lack of awareness of the functional needs, led to most of the characteristic forms of the medieval city. In fact, most medieval solutions were far more functional than were those of Baltic design, given the technology available to their use. Even in the nineteenth century, the Boston and Salem rockers of Massachusetts were more comfortable than any chair designed by Mies or his Scandinavian disciples; according to their own dictum, those rockers must be more beautiful than their own chairs.

Throughout most of urban experience in Western civilization, distinction must be made between the validity of the "form follows function" doctrine in the earliest stage of an area within a city and its bearing on subsequent reuses of that same area. The question is not one of the age of the city but rather the stage of the area within the city, because most cities grow by accretion of parts. A city such as Paris has quarters that derive part of their form from the acts of the Romans and others from the doctrines of Le Corbusier, a range of thought with vast differences of philosophy and aesthetics and a range of time of two thousand years. In normal circumstance the oldest creations lie at the center and the newest at the edge, yet in some cases the pattern is reversed, as in Paris with Baron Haussmann's rebuilding in the nineteenth century, or in Boston with Edward Logue's destruction and reconstruction of much of the Federalist town in the years since World War II. Then we must use morphological staging as our measure rather than time of first urbanization.

Function has always been a difficult thing to understand, and most builders have dealt more successfully with forms than with the purposes of their constructions. Thus, reading function from form is a hazardous occupation, perhaps particularly so in the works of the greatest architects, who tend to be those with both the freest hand and the most dogmatic viewpoint. The extravagant buildings of the Renaissance were no more functional than the glass-box office buildings constructed today in the blazing sun of Dallas. In each case the internal use of the building is subjugated to the pompous image produced by its exterior, and neither is ideal for the conduct of productive work. In contrast, similar features may represent sharply differing adaptations of form to function. Today, the low doorways of our ancestors and their scaled-down furniture are constraining, but no more so than the buildings and the furniture of a dainty Frank Lloyd Wright, who built dogmatically small after men and women had grown taller. Given those conflicting relationships of form and function, we must be very careful how we read from one to the other. And we must watch for the transformation of older buildings. The cutting of windows in medieval buildings as they were transformed in the seventeenth and eighteenth centuries for handloom textile production tells us as much about changing urban function as does the cutting of a New Road or a Commercial Road through surviving medieval cities such as London.

Morphological Adaptation

One of the commoner structural processes is that of adaptation of city forms from one stage to another and from one form-and-functional relationship to another. We shall see repeated instances of such transformations. The agora in the Greek town became a religious place transformed to a

multitude of other uses, from schoolroom to political hustings. The basilica began as a place of public and private business among the Romans but came after Rome was Christianized to be the holiest of religious places. And the public building forms of an autocratic Rome served both as the model for a most democratic Washington when Arthur Brown, Jr., was seeking the proper symbol for his Federal Triangle, and as the birthplace of the United Nations when that institution was founded in Brown's Roman Opera House in San Francisco in 1945.

Who can truly believe that form follows function so much as adaptation follows change? And even in more modern, or at least unselfconscious building, the practice remains. America is blossoming with transformed mills in New England, markets in Omaha, railroad stations in Savannah and Spokane. Their architects and landscape architects follow the lead of William Wurster and Lawrence Halprin, who revamped a disused chocolate factory in San Francisco. But even Ghirardelli Square was not the first such reuse in recent America. A New York specialty store developed its first branch in Boston in the 1950s in the only recently abandoned building of the Museum of Natural History, which itself was a successor tenant to a land-grant college that, in a declining agricultural state, had become the Massachusetts Institute of Technology. How wonderfully flexible the urban fabric is! Once we reject the canon of modern architecture, which decrees generational shift and destruction with change, we find that instead of this rather rootless nature for cities we have a real continuity with support in human cravings. Such continuity refuses to suffer the oversimplification of modern design into a "law" that form follows function.

Critics often look upon the adaptation of buildings from the past, and parts of towns that survive as entities, as a dull-witted escape into nostalgia

Urban
Morphogenesis

or romanticism. Their argument is that innovation rather than adaptation is the measure of art, to be a rootless pioneer is to have the greatest freedom. We see a certain wisdom in what they say when we compare the showy "modernistic" qualities of Toronto's somewhat effeminate City Hall with Boston's innovative, rather brutish but powerful contemporary civic head-quarters. But the truth is that at no period in urban history has a city been simply a matter of contemporary practices, and thus free of either the past or the future. The Washington of the early nineteenth century reflected little of the past but left great holes for the future, as is the case with Brasilia today. And in Rome, London, or Boston the past is everywhere. Almost without question Boston's City Hall is so impressive because it is framed by Faneuil Hall from the eighteenth century and the Quincy Market and the Sear's Crescent from the nineteenth. Its framing on the north by the new Kennedy Government Center adds no luster to the concepts of modern architecture, and no argument for destruction of the buildings of the past.

Preconception and Organic Growth

Pioneering has always captured our imaginations. It is not strange that the process of city making is commonly brought to mind as the act of one great builder, whether a Roman consul planting Mediolanum, Milan's roots, or L'Enfant envisioning Washington. Yet such total preconception of a city is fortunately rare—fortunate because few builders have done the job well, and rare because such overall plans have required a degree of power and control uncommon in history. What, then, are the alternatives? We find in broad terms that cities fall into two classes. The *preconceived city* is laid out by an emperor, bishop, or other authority possessed of the power to start a settlement from scratch, still believing strongly that his work is that of city founding, and thus needful of an elaborate and inclusive plan. The *organic city* includes those settlements established at a geographical point but left to evolve in physical patterns as functions and fates determine.

The creation of a single building or even of a preplanned city is fairly easy to comprehend, but to see all of the processes that go into the creation and evolution of a city without a plan is difficult. We know from observation that most places grow by these organic processes, so they must exist and their nature needs to be better understood.

The concept that form follows function works fairly well in dealing with the initial stage in the shaping of the organic city, but where do we go from there? Physical adaptation comes about when the functional demands out-reach the tolerance of the form to deal with that change. This insufficiency comes in two ways: space may be insufficient to deal with the new demands, or needs may arise that cannot be met in any way by existing structures. If we take as an example the Industrial Revolution of the textile industry in the eighteenth century, we find both insufficiencies. The original hand-production of textiles, starting with the spinning of yarn, had been a domes-tic activity and was easily carried on in the home. But to improve the standard of quality and, incidentally, to speed up production, exercise of greater supervision over the weavers, in particular, became desirable. They were collected together, but no longer could the cottage contain them;

instead, "factories" were built where the hand operations could be carried on under the direct supervision of factors. Thus, a scalar change without any transformation of actual function carried on within the structure brought a new form of building.

Later in the Industrial Revolution the need for yarn to feed the looms of greater productivity brought on the need for the other kind of structural change, that in fundamental form. As first machines and then waterpower were put to use in spinning yarn, locational and formal change became necessary. The watermill, with its riverside setting and vertical compaction, permitted the mechanical transfer of the rotative power of the mill wheel to machines nearby. At that juncture suddenly the siting of the factory became significant. Initially, the site had simply been a spot where a potential factor could effectively bring together a potential workforce of the needed scale and ability. With the coming of mechanical power, the location of the availability of that power determined the site of the factory.

This analysis may serve to introduce the notion of the adaptive process in urban morphology. Through it we may learn a great deal from a Janus-like analysis wherein we build a bridge of probable relationship between the two stages of city form. Commonly, evidence remains both as to the earlier as well as the subsequent form of the city; what is missing is the transition process. By contrasting the two forms, we may often establish what new demands are cared for in the new form. Thus, we can make deductions as to that change of function in the city, which frequently goes unrecorded in historical records.

Connectivity in the City

Whereas states tend toward revolution and radical transformation, cities tend toward tenacious endurance and evolution.

The most notable absence in the study of city forms has been the notion of evolution, a grievous omission when we are dealing with entities that are, under most circumstances, nearly the most long-lived of all human physical creations. While any idea of a greater Greece is patent imagining today, the cities of Magna Graecia remain; the Greek Patriarch lives in Istanbul as a tolerated and exotic Christian in a Muslim city whose mosques copy the architecture of early Christendom if they do not use those ancient building themselves. The nation-state, which seems so powerful and fundamental today, is a late and transitory successor to the enduring city. The notion of eternal Rome rings true, but who would believe in an enduring Italy? In little over a hundred years of "national"existence, the fundamental form of the Italian government has seen revolutionary changes several times, as well as almost endless instability and tinkering. But Rome endures and evolves as do Istanbul (Constantinople), New York (New Amsterdam), Bombay, Singapore, and a number of other great cities for which the founding state has shriveled or disappeared.

Time bears far less on the city than it does on individuals, political systems, or states. Napoleon captured most of Europe and swept away the Holy Roman Empire, an institution that had endured for thirteen centuries, yet he did not fundamentally change any city, even Paris. But he cocked a snook at Christendom and history when he destroyed the Roman church's greatest political creation—begun when the pope crowned Charlemagne emperor in the year 800—and the line of dynastic legitimacy for a millennium of history. After Waterloo no attempt was made to undo the emperor's work of demolishing such European institutions, but had he destroyed a city, such indifference would have been rather improbable. Witness the rebuilding of Washington after the British burned it, the medieval rebuilding of Milan after its savaging by the Holy Roman Emperor, and the rebuilding of London, Rotterdam, Warsaw, and a number of German cities since 1945.

It becomes evident that within urban evolution there are several basic processes at work:

1. Stages in urban experience are related to the functional life of the town more than to the chronological time of history.
2. Although stages change with the passage of time, physical traits of the city tend to persist, once established, and no city ever absolutely denies its past.
3. What change in cities are particularly the functions undertaken and carried on at various stages in the course of urban evolution.
4. With those changes in function comes a need to adapt the physical form of the town, so the process of adaptation is a notable feature of cities and one that tends to set the city apart from the nation-state.
5. Not only does adaptation work on the physical structure of cities, but also endless compromise is made between form and function, to the point that the process is more one of mutual transformation than a free rein for function over form. In this fundamental persistence of mutual adaptation, we find the basis for urban evolution and continuity.
6. Throughout history the city has proved particularly susceptible to enlargement, and catastrophe is the main interruption in the course of scalar growth, as in the fall of the Roman state or the plagues of the Middle Ages. Otherwise, the city has grown even when states are contracting (as they have recently been, with the notable exceptions of the surviving imperialist powers—the Soviet Union, India, and China—each of which has grown significantly since 1945).
7. That tendency toward continuing growth has made morphological and functional dynamism a notable features of cities. In cities we find particularly active experimentation with physical forms (planning and design of buildings and public spaces) and social and economic systems (capitalism in the Middle Ages and socialism in the nineteenth century).
8. Dynamism has been expressed through the operation of two related processes, that of congregation of forms and activities and that of segregation between forms and activities.
9. This physical growth and increasing complexity of structure within the city has made necessary an ever-enlarging concern with the connectivity among the various congregations of buildings, public spaces, and activities.
10. The evolutionary nature of the city attaches not merely to forms and functions but also to the third of the major components of urban physical structure, connectivity.

On this tripod—*form*, *function*, and *connection* among forms for functions—we must base our analytical procedures, and within it we must shape our methodology.

Some periods are dominated by the creation of new forms, functions, or connections, and in some periods maintenance of existing patterns seems dominant. Because of the fundamental interaction among these three aspects of physical structure, change in one is likely to induce rather marked change in the others. Sometimes the form changes, as in the case of steel-cage construction, which after its introduction in Chicago in the 1880s and 1890s worked a major transformation in functions. From its use came in considerable measure the apartment house, the large department store, and the office building; in connection with its use arose the need for subways and elevated railways, and the division between commercial and residential parts of the city with the need for mass transit. At other times a major transformation in function leads directly to great changes in building form and city layout (multistory construction to tap mechanical power during the Industrial Revolution, single-story construction to make use of pallets, fork-lift trucks, and computers in the mechanical handling of goods). Connection is also affected (single-story plants must be located toward the edge of the city to gain adequate space at a reasonable cost, which requires the substitu-

The Home Insurance Building (1884–85), by William Le Baron Jenney, was the first skyscraper in that it had a skeleton of iron and steel and merely a skin of brick and stone. The top two floors were added in 1891, something possible with iron construction.

Urban
Morphogenesis

25

tion of automotive transport of goods and people for the former movement of each by public and common carriers). And the introduction of a new technology of movement, such as came with the internal combustion engine, radically shifts the conditional balance that existed before its utilization in both form and function.

Periods of Adaptation

The cities we are concerned with have a collective history of more than two thousand years; we may look at them only at rather infrequent moments during their evolution to modern times. The search of the urban scene is most rewarding in times of morphological adaptation, which tend to come when the main action of political or economic change is focused on cities. By concentrating our attention on periods of adaptation, we may begin to establish the dynamics of urban form.

THE GREEK CITY-STATE

Cities existed before the time of the Greeks, but "the Greeks do not appear to have been inspired initially either to develop cities or devise for them a new form of urban government by any direct impulse from the older civilizations of the Middle and Near East."[2] Earlier cities—those in the Indus and Nile valleys and in Mesopotamia—had been the creations of absolute monarchs, though perhaps Sidon and Tyre had been the earliest beginnings of *the city of people* as opposed to the palace of the king extended; at best they were transitional forms. Only in the archaic period in Greece, beginning around 900 B.C., was the city of people formed. Then, in contrast to earlier "urban" places, a morphology that could hope to be continuous throughout subsequent history without reference to dynastic whim or succession was shaped by structural processes, as distinct from royal fiat. "During the seventh and sixth centuries, therefore, the Greeks through their own talent and in response to particular local circumstances evolved the city-state."[3] This era becomes our first period of adaptation, truly one of initiation when a fundamentally rural and pastoral land was first urbanized.

The city-states grew in size and expanded in numbers by new colonization until the Persian Wars, which ended in 479 B.C. In those wars many cities were destroyed, so a new era of urbanization began when peace returned. From 479 (or perhaps 404 B.C. with the close of the Peloponnesian War) until the capture of Greece by Philip of Macedon (338 B.C.), the Classical Age of the Hellenes witnessed the adaptation of the earlier organically evolving city into a more preconceived, planned place. The rebuilding after the Persian destruction made that morphological transformation both possible and likely in a culture gripped by a new rationalism.

2. Mason Hammond, *The City in the Ancient World* (Cambridge, Mass.: Harvard Studies in Urban History, 1972), p. 152.

3. Ibid., p. 174.

The next period of adaptation that concerns us was fairly contemporaneous with the reconstruction of cities under Greek rationalism, though it operated in a quite different geographical situation. In Italy, beginning around the year 800 B.C., a group of pastoral aristocrats, the Etrusci to the Romans, began to establish "cities," of which at least twelve were built. These places seem to have been established to serve, perhaps mostly as religious centers, the surrounding countryside, as evidenced by the absence of popular participation in government and the heavy dependence on slavery in nearby agriculture. These Etruscan towns were the first indigenous congregated settlements in Italy, and the direct ancestors of the Roman city. In establishing their towns the Etruscans observed elaborate religious practices and, in turn, made of them the city as a temple; the process of initiation, the process of land assignment, and the physical form of the city were greatly influenced.

DISINTEGRATION AND DECLINE IN ROMAN URBANISM

The course of Roman urbanization is detailed in the next chapter. That halcyon period closed as surely as it began, as a consequence of the fortunes of the state. The Romans, using Etruscan practices and forms, had projected urbanization over the whole Western world, using cities to exact tribute and taxes from a subject realm. But Rome both as a state and as a system of cities began to shrink rapidly once military power was no longer sufficient to perpetuate that tribute. In the fifth and sixth centuries of our era, Rome as a vital state disintegrated, leaving many parts denuded of urban populations, though not of the physical relicts of a great system of cities. Those remains passed into oblivion more slowly, by the removal of a bit each year through the agency of weathering and human quarrying.

Two sections of the once-continuous Roman Empire maintained some functioning urbanization for many centuries—Byzantium centering on Constantinople in the east, and Septimania preserving the urban culture of the west in Provence and Languedoc in southern France. Byzantium withered slowly, finally disappearing with the conquest of Constantinople by the Turks in 1453. Septimania was lost in the evil Albigensian Crusade of Pope Innocent III and Philip-Augustus of France begun in 1207. But Byzantium and Septimania can be given only minor notice in a book with as long a story as this. Each played a crucial supporting role in the story and must be considered, but neither was the ultimate hero. That role came unexpectedly as the scion of the semibarbaric West, where the urbanity of Rome survived just long enough that it might, in the hands of a vigorous society, restore cities to their essential place in human life.

THE MERCHANTS' TOWN AND MEDIEVAL URBANIZATION

The same crusading spirit that was so corrupted by Innocent III did enter importantly into the return of cities to the West. Even before the expeditions to the Holy Land, the rise of distant trading had begun in Italy, Germany,

Urban
Morphogenesis

Flanders, France, and England; the Crusades, however, demonstrated beyond doubt the tie between economic overlordship and political expansion. The Venetians and citizens of other Italian city-republics had played a critical role in financing and outfitting the expeditions, and they gained in return what we today would term trading concessions in the Levant.

The brawn of the expeditions was provided most notably by the Normans of western France and England. On their return from the Holy Land they brought two invaluable experiences as trophies of the Crusades: a much clearer notion of the ultimate riches to be gained from expanding the trade of a duchy or a kingdom, and a considerable technical knowledge of the arts of castellation and urban fortification. Those trophies, combined with the general mercantile inclinations at home, soon produced the great merchants' towns of Europe north of the Alps, which within the course of several centuries came to equal those of Italy and ultimately totally eclipsed them. The shadow was cast on Italy by the better-developed role for common people in the communes of Flanders and Germany and in the tendency toward open-minded appraisal of thought and condition more true of Europe north of the Alps. The collegial form of civic government was the institution most responsible for the advance of the West. But the concentration of interest in Western cities on the matter of commerce and the avoidance of the cruel political factionalism internal to the Italian city led the way to the ultimate supremacy of the city of northwestern Europe from medieval times until the beginning of this century.

THE ADAPTATION TO COLLEGIALITY IN THE BASTIDE

The great periods mentioned to this point are widely known and accepted. The same cannot be said for the next transformation of which we take note—the founding in the High Middle Ages of the new settlements that have come to be known collectively as bastides. The word derives from the great development of these places in Languedoc and Aquitaine in southern France, the same Septimania that the Albigensian Crusaders sought so viciously to destroy. In so doing they created such an urban wasteland that new beginnings could be made. The adaptation was to a nondynastic and nonecclesiastical role for settlements, particularly one rather separated from the geographical servitude and social deficiency comprehended by the then current rural system of feudalism. The bastides were not fully nonfeudal; feudal landholders set them up, but the settlements were without the serfdom, geographical bondage, homage, and fealty characteristic of feudal society. In these towns where collegiality ruled, the purpose was so strongly that of economic development of wastelands that the distinction to the earlier town founding of the Middle Ages was most marked. The bastide was a philosophical as well as a morphological ancestor of the American city.

The bastide building was a classic instance of adaptation of the functions of the town to a new purpose—the occupation of underdeveloped regions by a free pioneering population, something not too frequently undertaken since the time of the Greek colonist. Between 1150 and 1350 more than a thousand bastides were established. An examination of their location, layout, and social and political organization provides us with useful insight into

what cities might look like when democratic institutions came to rule more widely in Western civilization.

THE ABSOLUTIST'S CITY: THE RENAISSANCE

The faint beginnings of the popular city in the bastide failed to accomplish much of a hold on Western urbanization for centuries. Instead, the age was one of political and religious absolutism. A Byzantine visitor to Innocent III's Rome noted that he was "the successor not of Peter but of Constantine." The desire to recapture the "grandeur" of Rome in a great Renaissance swept over a Europe of kings by divine right and popes by apostolic succession. Whoever the god, the morphological contrivance to his glory tended to have shared characteristics, most notably disregard for functions other than grand display and procession. These are functions, whatever we may think about their justice, so the Renaissance city was functional in these terms. Fortunately, the popular city began to gain ground over that of the autocrat, so the Renaissance as a model for use today is of most limited interest.

THE EMERGENCE OF THE MERCANTILE CITY

The age of mercantilism commenced only in odd ways, as most ages begin, but by the sixteenth century it was a coherent and articulated system that could guide the politics of a state. For the practice of mercantilism, cities were a critical feature. From them the ships set sail for distant ports with goods to sell and returns to be collected. To them from the surrounding countryside came the flow of staples to sustain such a distant trade, and

Urban
Morphogenesis

29

within them tended to grow up the crafts that transformed either the national staple or the imported one into goods that moved ultimately either landward or seaward in search for customers. A true circularity was found between the mercantile economic philosophy and the urban settlement form. Cities needed trade to grow, and trade needed cities to have goods to handle.

With mercantilism came a potent force for the establishment of cities in distant lands, notably in North America. The first American cities were mercantile places, set out under the operation of a mercantile system of urbanization. They were highly receptive to a socially and economically liberal form, such as that pioneered in the bastide first laid out in France in 1144, but more widespread in the thirteenth and fourteenth centuries. Thus, the mercantile expansion elevated the economic purpose of the city to the summit and brought to America the society, economy, and, to a considerable degree, religion of the bastide.

THE INDUSTRIAL CITY

The evolved form of the mercantile system was a fundamental base on which rose the great surge of industrialization that swept Western civilization during the eighteenth and nineteenth centuries. The expansion of the demand for goods was a necessary precondition for the growth in production of those goods. Furthermore, the mercantile city played a role in encouraging an Industrial Revolution, by providing the necessary risk capital for nascent industry, the business practices and systems of organization that would allow distant and future dealings to take place, and, in many cases, the simple plots of ground and work forces for early attempts at organized manufacture.

The early development of industrial cities came in England and Belgium for quite predictable reasons. England and Belgium had great amounts of coal, a long history of textile manufacture, and a generally numerous rural population whose labor was not fully engaged. There were areas of wool production in most British counties and in Belgium's episcopal County of Liège. England was the premier mercantile nation and therefore the most likely to sell large amounts of goods. It was the first nation to mine coal in vast amounts but, as a land of large landowners and rural tenancy, had potentially many surplus people resident in the countryside. England was unlike France, where a traditional peasantry had vested rights in the small plots they tilled. When industrialization came, it took courses that influenced urbanization in sharply different ways. In Britain the quick turn to coal for powering machines went along with the landlessness of the rural working class to encourage industrialization within existing cities, and the cities' consequent growth to great size during the early years of the Industrial Revolution. In America, where waterpower remained the force for mechanization for fifty years after industrialization came and where the rural population in New England tended to be underemployed but landowning, factories were set up in the country bringing urban growth to the site and creating new cities in the nineteenth century. Few cities in England began as industrial places—not Birmingham, Manchester, Nottingham, or Cardiff, which simply saw industry grow into existing towns. In the United States many cities that began as factory towns changed over the years into more broadly based urban centers.

We shall consider the industrial city under each of these adaptive processes—enlargement of the existing settlement in Britain and initiation of new urbanization in America. In each case the three aspects of the physical city (form, function, and connection) as well as the human systems at work there (the journey-to-work, the provision of housing apart from ties of employment, and the expanding role of the nuclear family) are considered.

THE MODERN CITY

The commonly used term *postindustrial city* contains such a misapprehension of the past that I shall not use it. It suggests several partially or completely wrong assumptions: (1) that in a clearly defined period of the "industrial city," industry had been the main cause of urbanization, (2) that there was a clearly defined "preindustrial time" with demonstrably "preindustrial cities," and (3) that the post– World War II trend toward the substitution of high energy consumption for high labor input will persist. The basis for the term is particularly Gideon Sjoberg's title *The Preindustrial City*, which in a world of assumed symmetry seems to many to require a "postindustrial time."[4] Sjoberg tells us that "our principal hypothesis is that in their structure, or form, preindustrial cities—whether in medieval Europe, traditional China, India, or elsewhere—resemble one another closely and in turn differ markedly from modern industrial-urban centers." By *form* Sjoberg means "numerous patterns in the realms of ecology, class, and family, as well as in their economic, political, religious, and educational structures, arrangements that diverge sharply from their counterparts in mature industrial society." If the word *form* is used in its more normal sense of the physical characteristics of cities, then the resemblances between the medieval and the Roman city are too slight to justify such lumping together. And even in many institutional characteristics, such as the national economic system, a rather fundamental difference is apparent between the preindustrial Roman city, the preindustrial medieval German town, and the early industrial English port of the seventeenth century.

Many objections may be raised to Sjoberg's work; for instance, his dichotomy of human experience into a "feudal" time and an "industrial-urban" society is too gross. The Middle Ages were far from entirely feudal and more recent centuries even more so. And much of the industrialization in the past and even now is not so very urban.[5] If Sjoberg's "preindustrial

4. Gideon Sjoberg, *The Preindustrial City: Past and Present* (Glencoe, Ill.: Free Press, 1960). Quotations are from pp. 4–6.

5. This is not the place to pursue a full critique of Sjoberg's work, and I am not the man for the job. John Langton compared Sjoberg's and my ideas on the "preindustrial city" and, though finding us both wanting, decided that my "stress upon the importance of economic power and relationships as ecological determinants within the city undoubtedly gets nearer to the truth of the matter than Sjoberg's feudal social order, in which the dominance of an elite group was derived from non-economic and extra-urban sources." John Langton, "Residential Patterns in Pre-Industrial Cities: Some Case Studies from Seventeenth Century Britain," Institute of British Geographers, *Transactions*, no. 65 (July 1975), pp. 1–27. The note is to p. 22.

city" was not really preindustrial, then the modern city doubtless cannot be labeled "postindustrial." It is simply modern in the sense that it is the city of our own experiences.

To date the beginning of the modern city is difficult. As I wish to look in detail at the modern city of the United States, I have adopted the close of the Civil War, basically 125 years ago, as the beginning of modern urbanization. At the close of the war, the United States had nearly overtaken Britain as the premier industrial nation, was incontestably the greatest agricultural producer, and incidentally was a military power with which Europe had to contend. When after Appomattox we frowned southward, the emperor Napoleon III quickly withdrew to Europe, leaving the unfortunate Maximilian to a usurper's justice before a firing squad in 1867. And when we expressed our just indignation at the unneutral support of the rebel cause by the English ruling classes, the response was a rapid setting up of a quasi-independent government for Canada, shed of the more obvious features of British imperialism, under the British North American Act, also of 1867. If the United States could without firing a shot face down the two imperial giants of the world, little question remains that this immediately post–Civil War period was the beginning of the American century of urban dominance, and the beginning of the modern city, for our purposes.

Periods of Initiation and Adaptation

The times of initiation of urban development must of necessity be infrequent. When the archaic Greeks began city building early in the first millennium before Christ, they could do so in a situation of considerable freedom, a situation that did not come again in history. Instead, there arose times of only relative freedom: at the onset of town formation soon after A.D. 1000 when the medieval city was shaped in opposition to the land in which it must stand; again in the twelfth century when a number of wastelands of Europe—those in southern France, in Germany east of the Elbe, and somewhat later in the areas of Spain recaptured from the Moors—were the scene of active town founding in the form of bastides; and most strikingly in the North American New World where, after 1600, more towns were formed within the course of three centuries than had ever been founded in such a short period of time. Because we can learn most about urban morphogenesis by observing the process of urban initiation, we will concentrate on these particular scenes of what was a continuous urban experience.

Contrasted to the times of real urban initiation were times of adaptation to changing demands on cities, or responses to more limited catastrophes visiting particular cities. Times of significant adaptation, of great concern in a study of urban morphogenesis, include the Persian Wars that destroyed so many Greek towns just after 500 B.C.; the conquest of Greece by Rome, and the supercession of Greek practices by those of the more directly religious Romans; the shift from the more narrowly bounded medieval to the more commercially extensive mercantile city; and the onset of industrialization at the turn of the nineteenth century.

Finally, we may define times of urban decline or stagnation: the course of urban history following on the decline of Rome; the demographic crisis in urban history resulting from the plagues of the late Middle Ages; and the more narrowly regionalized experiences of Italy and Germany in the seventeenth, eighteenth, and early nineteenth centuries. In a search for process such times hold only minor interest.

The General Processes of Urban Morphogenesis

Before looking at actual evidence of how cities are shaped and transformed over time, we may usefully ask what the general processes of urban morphogenesis are.

LAND ASSIGNMENT

The first dynamic of city form applies as readily to the adapted city as to the newly initiated one. In each case some basis must be established for the assignment of land within the city to its several possible uses. If we deal with the initial stage of urban development, no great problems arise in resolving land assignment, with few if any competitors for the often single function that brings a town into being. Once the town grows and evolves, however, problems of land assignment are likely to be knotty. It is far from automatically the case that the first use in time has the primary choice in internal space. Quite possibly, that first use may be shunted aside in favor of a later but more economically aggressive function.[6] For this reason the process of land assignment is essentially the first dynamic at work in the city. It operates in two ways, serving as the major determinant of the design of the place during the period of initiation and as the major determinant of the processes of adaptation during the period of transformation.

CONNECTION

The second process to bear upon the morphogenesis of cities is that of connection. Once a settlement grows beyond the level of a village or a small town, the matter of connection must be taken into account for its own innate qualities. The qualities have two expressions: internalized and interfunctional connections. Ties exist between such functional areas as come into existence within the city; there are even connections internal to such a functional cluster of activity, which John Rannells called linkages (in a study establishing the various expressions of connective relationships).[7] Thus, we may adopt his term to refer to internalized connections.

For the ties external to the functioning cluster we may easily adopt the common descriptive English term *journeys*, which fall into several obvious classes—journeys-to-work, to shop, to sell goods, to attend to social needs, and a number of others. These connections are interfunctional.

---

6. For a presentation of the major questions with respect to land assignment and the practices that have grown up under different economic systems, see Vance, "Land Assignment," pp. 101–20.

7. John Rannells, *The Core of the City*, Publications for the Institute for Urban Land Use and Housing Studies, Columbia University (New York: Columbia University Press, 1956).

Urban
Morphogenesis

Quite a bit has been written about these journeys, most commonly about those to work or to shop. Heightened concern for social welfare in cities has recently turned the attention of geographers to such questions as the delivery of medical service, access to employment, and the availability of cultural institutions. Although these many different journeys are strong shaping forces in the physical build of cities, apparently little writing on the journey-to-work has dealt specifically with the morphogenetic contribution of repeating movements internal to the city.[8] The medium of transportation can be shown to play a critical role in determining the form of the city shaped by the journey-to-work,[9] a statement that must be construed in both physical and financial terms. Thus, the impact of transportation innovation will be differentiated by class of income and type of employment.

The connection between workplace and residence throughout human history before the early nineteenth century, and before the generalization of housing, required few journeys-to-work. But with the development of massive factories employing hundreds or thousands, this journey rose to great importance, and its dynamic impact on city form was great indeed.

INITIATION AND TRANSFORMATION THROUGH ADAPTATION

Constantly in attendance on these processes are those already mentioned—initiation of form and its transformation—which need no further elaboration in this simple catalogue of forces at work in cities.

CAPITAL ACCUMULATION AND TRANSFER

The next process to be considered is that of capital accumulation and investment (transfer) for the construction of the physical forms of the city. In the simplest terms, we must be aware that at the stage of initiation few resources of labor or capital will be available for the creation of large buildings or vast built-up areas. The exception to this rule shows its validity: when a city is created from outside in response to the desires of economic or political interests elsewhere, the general truth that the beginnings of urbanization are likely to be small and tentative, and organic in form, is not always applicable. The Romans could build elaborate towns on the Dalmatian coast through transfer payments from elsewhere, just as Washington and Brasilia were built. But if a town is to grow on its own, it must do so by accumulation of resources to support that increased size. In part, the repeated reconstruction of towns results from a sort of economic ratchet, which makes do with existing physical provision until the resources are available for enlargement, modernization, and a greater show of prosperity and probity. This ratchet had already become a part of the dynamics of cities in Greek times when it

---

8. My elucidation of morphogenetic processes related to the internal journeys, still the main writing on the subject, is contained in three articles: "Labor-Shed, Employment Field, and Dynamic Analysis in Urban Geography," *Economic Geography* 36 (1960): 189–220; "Housing the Worker: The Employment Linkage as a Force in Urban Structure," *Economic Geography* 42 (1966): 294–325; and "Housing the Worker: Determinative and Contingent Ties in Nineteenth Century Birmingham," *Economic Geography* 43 (1967): 95–127.

9. See Vance, "Labor-Shed."

was expected that successful leaders would endow Athens with new monuments, to celebrate themselves and to gain the approval that was Athens' to give.

In the Renaissance the ratchet was so fast-moving that cities could hardly stand the strain. Popes and princes had to assert their power and culture by rebuilding, not so much to improve the functioning of the city as to magnify its grandeur. The popes did have fountains built in Rome, but many things closer to the needs of the people could have been built if the worldly glorification of the papal reputation had been pushed farther into the background.

In modern America, the hand of business has turned the ratchet, leading to the construction of office buildings of great boasting and inhuman sheltering. The glass-curtain-walled structure in a hot, sunny climate cannot be seen as functional, but rather as showing the corporation administration to be *au fait* with style, if not with the desirable conditions of labor. When energy becomes more costly, as assuredly it will, the folly of much modern skyscraper architecture will be emphasized and a new ratchet for reconstruction will take hold.

SPECULATION

Even before the seventeenth century, speculation in land in cities had begun, but by then two necessary preconditions had come into being: (1) the creation of a system of capitalism needed if individuals were to engage in this activity and profit from the sale of land, and (2) the understanding, rough as it might be, of the patterning and transformation of the physical structure of cities, which was required if investors were to anticipate change in use value, and profit from it speculatively.

A process had transpired in medieval times that we might justly term proto-speculation. Individuals and institutions, particularly church foundations, had commonly let out for an annual rent lands and buildings in their possession. Kings and great ecclesiastics who held lands commonly joined (in *paréage*) with bastidors to seek to found a town and gain, again in parity with the settlers, a greater profit on the success of the place than they would have gained from the simple agricultural, or even pastoral, use of their lands. In any event, the landowners earned their *cens* (quitrent) from the settlers in a fashion far more stable than was true of their portion of the changeable manorial production. But under *paréages*, capital—in the sense of land—was tied up for long periods of time. True speculative profits were not so readily obtained as under later practices of fully developed capitalism. Nonetheless, the act of bastide formation was an excellent training ground for the later practices of capital formation.

PLANNING AND THE MARKET

Planning has been a process at work in cities from the very earliest times. When cities were the creation of the king's whim, they were most assuredly as planned as facets of New York City built to the whim of Robert Moses. To a very considerable degree, any preconceived town pattern is an

Urban
Morphogenesis

35

act of planning; it always contains assumptions as to the desirable gross form of the place, its probable size and function, and a number of other culturally derived "goods." Only since the development of the capitalist city in the sixteenth century has planning become a separate concern, one viewed by its proponents as a white-hatted defense of the interests of society against the black-hatted interests of capitalism and speculation. The critical point is that the capitalist city was the city of the individual, dominant in a way that the medieval and earlier towns were not. Then, the gild or the monarch, or both, were equally in control of city development and presumably so vested with authority because they held the common good paramount. With the introduction of capitalism, no such presumption of the care for the common good could be made. An urban dualism was introduced: development, speculation, and individual desire were seen as the work of a god of darkness; restraint, public action, and authoritarian control were seen as the work of enlightenment. In this dualism the rub comes in the creation of city forms. Under absolutist governments there was usually established a view of appropriate culture and design, as well as proper purposes and undertakings. The rich could be allowed to move to London by royal exception, but not the poor. In imperial Rome, in the Paris of Napoleon III, and in the London of Victoria, taste was arbitrary, but all-powerful, as the Albert Memorial so sadly confirms.

For all the castigation of "private" development as the work of a god of darkness, it did possess a mechanism of popular control and adjustment lacking under either royal fiat or much of latter-day planning. The mechanism of the market determined the form and extent of development and periodically adjusted those qualities to the shifting demands of the people. The main trouble with the market until recently has been that it reflected the interests of only a part of the populace: a large part in the United States because of the higher standard of living and the lesser role of established privilege, but a much smaller part in Britain. In this contrast is to be found much of the difference between the two nations in appraisal of the efficacy of the market and, in turn, of the need for land planning, management, and design.

In a very specific way, planning and the market mechanism are necessary components of a single overall process shaping urban form. As the market is reduced in contribution, planning must be increased; if one is in complete control, serious deficiencies in morphogenesis result. The experience with the industrial city of the nineteenth century, which we will see through Engels's eyes, confirmed how insufficient was total capitalist, market, control; experience in Eastern Europe with the total municipalization of land and control of development by planning has shown how equally rigid and disregardful of the individual an antimarket system can be.

SEGREGATION, CONGREGATION, AND JUNCTION

The activities that grow up in cities show a strong tendency to come together in limited areas of specialization drawn into a congregation by the internalizing linkages among them. Whether it be the use of shared sources of materials, the selling to a common body of customers, the practice of a specific religion, or the speaking of a particular language, the institutional practice shapes the process of *congregation*, which is internally induced and highly responsive to matters of scale. A few persons doing a particular thing normally congregate, but not in an obvious congregation. When numbers are increased to the point that they present an areally extensive pattern, then a geographical congregation is to be seen.

In contrast to a congregation is a similarly extensive grouping of ostensibly similar individuals induced by external forces. Instead of being drawn together, they are forced together by segregation. The process of *segregation* is more widely attributed than is justified by facts. To show the difference between congregation and segregation, we may examine the case of orthodox Jewish settlement in American cities. One of the provisions of orthodox Judaism is that the members of a congregation may not drive between sundown on Friday and sundown on Saturday. Thus, attendance at a synagogue, which is essential to the practice of the cult, must be on foot. Clearly, a very strong force is at work among orthodox Jews to live near the synagogue. At times allegations have been made that Jews are discriminated against and segregated in housing. To the extent that they seek to maintain such a congregation as I have described, this assertion is invalid. On the other hand, those American blacks who are of vastly varying religious attachment, often of quite diverse birthplaces, and frequently of different education and income levels who similarly live together in a black district are obvious victims of segregation unless they live there through personal choice, shunning the socially upward and geographically extensive mobility of the American suburb. Finally, in American cities the blacks are mostly segregated, whereas the Jews, Italians, Poles, Germans, and Swedes are largely congregated.

The operation of congregation and segregation reaches beyond the housing of particular social groups into the assignment of land to commercial, industrial, and institutional activities. Recently, we have seen a strong tendency for medical facilities to congregate just as medieval teaching functions congregated into student quarters such as the Left Bank in Paris, which was already a student quarter with extraterritorial administration during the Middle Ages. In the commercial aspects of city life, congregation works mainly along institutional lines. In the classical city, the government often set up specific quarters for merchants and required their congregation there, particularly if they were foreigners complying with extraterritorial laws and social practices. In later centuries the institutional basis changed: commonly, the need to grant a charter of rights to a collegial body, a synthetic person or corporation, required congregation. The gild and the occupation congregation were the result. In this way the corporation could supervise and in turn be easily supervised.

Junction is a subprocess that seeks neither to collect together by internal desire nor to exclude through external pressure. Its purpose is simply to keep things together for mutual benefit. In junction all institutions divided are in basic agreement as to the wisdom of the process. It is meant to apply

Urban
Morphogenesis

specifically to the matter of providing connectivity among various congregations, if you will, to afford a pattern of use and form common to all congregations.

The street is a concrete example of forms introduced by the process of junction to gain universal interconnection. Commonly within the medieval city, quarters were so self-contained as to be forbidden and largely unknown to outsiders. These areas are often called residential mazes with the idea that they were deliberately made so arcane that the outsider could not pass easily about the quarter. In a sense this practice would be a negative process, one of disjunction. In a rather striking example of the conflict between congregational concerns and those of junction, we may observe that the present argument as to freeway building within American cities resolves itself in these terms. Many city congregations view the freeway as an intrusion on their "rights" to the unrestricted use of their land, yet they expect when they wish to go elsewhere to have junction—a freeway—that gets them there with expedition and ease. San Francisco began this disjunction movement in the early 1960s when it refused more urban freeways, yet the flood of San Franciscans heading for resorts on weekends makes necessary driving in the surrounding areas dangerous and unpleasant. More recently in the city of Berkeley, where local social congregation in neighborhood turfs is carried to an extreme, a street-closing program has been undertaken that fundamentally returns a modern city to the conditions of the medieval Italian city-republic with its clan quarters forbidden to outsiders.

Morphogenesis as Synthesis

Although these processes have been dealt with individually, obviously they work in conjunction to shape the city. This overall effect of processes is what I have called urban morphogenesis—the creation and subsequent transformation of city form. Morphogenesis, like most processes, operates more radically at some times than others, with intervening periods of conditional equilibrium. The medieval city could persist as long as the occupational household combined the residence and workplace of most employed hands. But with the onset of the Industrial Revolution this correspondence was no longer true; the journey-to-work was introduced, and the conditional equilibrium of the city was so disrupted that a new era of massive morphogenetic change was induced, leading in the end to a new form of the city with residential separation and strong class congregation. Other disruptions of equilibrium can be introduced by new productive processes (the suburban factory or warehouse), new transportation (the automobile suburb and outlying shopping centers), or new social conditions (the flood of rural poor into central cities). Social and morphogenetic processes interact constantly and intimately, but social process does not subsume all of the explanation of city form. We must look at morphogenesis itself to find a full answer to how the city got its shape.

In the end all is change, though it may come at differing rates. When we ask how the city got its shape, we may think back to Kipling's elephant's child who was "full of satiable curiosity, and that means asked ever so many questions" during "High and Far-Off Times." For us the first of those times is perhaps more Far-Off than High. We must turn next to archaic Greece to observe the first usable example of the interacting forces and processes that create urban morphogenesis. So we must now set off "a little warm, but not at all astonished" to seek an answer to the way the city got its shape. In so doing we must try to share with Kipling's Mariner the practice of "infinite-resource-and-sagacity."[10]

10. Rudyard Kipling, "The Elephant's Child," in *Just So Stories* (New York: Doubleday Page, 1917). The second quotation is from "How the Whale Got His Throat."

The Gods Look Down

The Classical City

2

For several millennia before our scientific age, not much thought was given to why cities existed or why they stood where they did. They were thought to be part of the organized world given to human beings by gods or God, who decided on their form and placement. Even in the more recent Christian era, though the divine generosity was less formal, people continued to thank God for His providence and to seek His support in a preservationist instinct. These thoughts represented faith, not scientific curiosity; as long as they persisted, little thought was given to the actual origin of cities, the provenance of their morphology, or their placement in the world's space. Acts of God were not necessarily intelligible to human beings so, in essence, why ask about them? The worm of curiosity condemned in Genesis peeped out again only in the last century, when post-Darwinian students looked at the origin of man, and those interested in cities began in similar fashion to question the neatly divine origin of those places.

Although Darwinian thought may have made a shambles of Eden and other divine contributions, such as monarchies, paradoxically the evidence grew that gods really had created the earlier cities—not in reality, but certainly as humans conceived the truth. Paul Wheatley and others have looked at the origins of early cities,[1] but without considering the morphological process at work in them, which I shall now summarize.

The Classical City of Divine Architecture

The dominant feature of pre-Christian urban history was the belief that the gods played a central role in both foundation and organization. Almost all towns were felt to be protected and occupied either by individual gods or by gods in pantheon, but not all towns were physically structured in accordance with assumed divine logic. In times of slow growth, there was a much stronger force toward locally based and determined structure with practical considerations paramount, or *organic growth*, than toward the application of a divine architecture. *Preconceived growth* is town planning, and for its full unfolding two conditions are needed. The age must be one in which, whether through growth or through movements of population, towns are being freely founded or freely enlarged, and almost as a matter of course attention is drawn to methods of arranging and laying out such towns. And second, the builders of these towns must have wit enough to care for the well-being of common people and the due arrangement of ordinary dwellings.[2] The real problem was to sustain a plan. Slow expansion allowed for forgetfulness or changed concepts, whereas an initially complete layout of the city, or its rebuilding after a catastrophe, permitted a single integrated concept to be applied.

1. Paul Wheatley, *The Pivot of the Four Quarters: A Preliminary Enquiry into the Origins and Character of the Ancient Chinese City* (Chicago: Aldine, 1971).

2. F. Haverfield, *Ancient Town-Planning* (Oxford: Clarendon Press, 1913), p. 11.

The most ancient world held relatively few states large enough to require a number of cities, so even preconceived plans applied to a single city or a small system of cities. As states expanded geographically, the urge toward replication of design was strong, notably so in states of reasonably central administration. Two conditions had to be met: (1) the city must have rational expectations of survival and prosperity—not always the case in a time when destruction by a conqueror could be so complete that a place eluded efforts to rediscover its nature or even its specific location, and (2) the central authority had to desire to create an urban orthodoxy that would help to maintain the widespread state. Consistent views have always tended to produce similar morphologies.

In seeking a standard solution to the physical form of cities, city founders would most probably turn to the gods for justification, if not for guidance. The main public expression of urban life was religious, and some argue that cities first came into existence for religious purposes. The temple anchored the city at the close of a history of nomadic wandering about the land without fixed abode. Around that temple, residence was spread; in the wake of residence came the trading and handworking activities that ultimately supported the city. The main public buildings of the Greek city were temples of one sort or another. This narrow inheritance made the American attempt in 1783 to use the Greek republics as a model for the restoration of republican government so peculiar in architectural terms. Temples make dark and drafty houses and bad places of assembly. Yet the Greeks seem to have had no other building that anyone would find worthy of emulation in a cold or wet climate. The Greek theater was even less appropriate to American climatic conditions than the temple, and the acropolis, a fortified hilltop, was not needed.[3] Seeking to copy Greek buildings, we could find only the temple.

3. For a discussion of the impact of Greek and Roman thought and urban morphology on nineteenth-century America, see James E. Vance, Jr., "The Classical Revival and Urban-Rural Conflict in Nineteenth Century North America," *Canadian Review of American Studies* 4, no. 2 (1973): 149–68.

The
Classical City

It is difficult to make any generalization about the internal structure of Greek cities, because only fragmentary evidence survives, and because the city-state political organization worked somewhat against the shaping of a standard *city*. Arthur Evans[4] tells us that Knossos in Crete possessed a three-element structure with (1) a labyrinth at the center that served as the palace of the king-priest, housing his retainers and the various ceremonial courtyards, reception rooms, and storehouses of a powerful ruler. (2) Around the palace were ranged a series of freestanding "burgher" houses occupied by the leading townspeople, separated from one another by narrow lanes that were little more than drains. The palace and town houses were so continuous that a close-packed town was created. (3) Farther from the religious-political heart of the city was a broader band of lowly abodes, built of rubble, seemingly leaning on each other in groups of two- and three-story buildings that formed a street block delimited by narrow lanes.

Several important facts emerge from this description. As early as about 1550 B.C., class stratification of the town was demonstrated by both geographical and architectural distinction. Whatever the class of dwelling, the building, either freestanding or as part of a street block, possessed a fundamental *locational identity*. The lines of access to the houses, lanes, alleys, and narrow ways—which can hardly be called streets—followed upon the placing of buildings instead of the building site coming into existence from the street plan, as today. A certain modular quality to houses is suggested; note the very clear distinction between the burghers' and the laborers' dwellings, but the absence of distinction among the derivative streets.

If we advance the notion that most cities have some sort of *normative component*, the house at the base and the quarter or district at the summit, then the size of the normative component is an observable and ready measure of the degree of "planning" or preconception to be found in the place. To add a single house is probably the most basic manner of growth for a town, requiring, in the simplest instances, only the decision of the builder and owner. To add a distinct or a virtually incremental city is the most elaborate form, and needs either a vast centralized power or a broad agreement among citizens. In any event, the ultimate design and size of the town must be perceived. Using this proposed scalar measure of the normative component, we may say that the simplest or most dubious places add only buildings, with those increments serving to recount for us unrecorded contemporary thoughts on the likelihood of the city's growth. Cities basically expand organically, with a house added when the need is felt and, in all probability, in a rather unstructured fashion. Growth merely takes place at the edge— the most central site still open for development. When wider knowledge of the probable future of the city or a grand design for its enhancement is available, the increments are likely to come in a more structured fashion and over a geographical area not necessarily limited to the physical edge of the city. If a massive quarter is conceived of, the houses can with reason be built over the entire area of the addition.

4. Arthur Evans, *The Palace of Minos* (London: Macmillan, 1921–36).

The Role of the Colony and Plantation

The division between organic and preconceived growth appears most clear when we consider the early instances of full-town planning, which came when population pressures forced an exodus from a prior place, most likely built along organic lines. When a city in the Hellenistic world reached a size that created a demand for food equal to that produced in the area that could supply the city, a self-evident pressure arose for some relief mechanism. Long-distance trade ties might have been established, with goods flowing in from a greater area, or the now too great population could have been spread over a large producing area. Both solutions were used in classical times, with the Greeks inclining toward migration and the Romans toward trade. Paradoxically, the political difference between the two states was greater than the morphological contrast between the cities they produced. Out of trade and tribute expansion, as well as other motives, came the Roman Empire and its pattern of urbanization. Out of the migration of people to some distance from the mother city came the confederations of Greek city-states.[5]

Roman provincial cities were truly colonial settlements in the modern sense; a large group of inhabitants, normally of indigenous origin, was held in political domination by outside conquerors. As with the Greek plantation city, the layout of the Roman provincial city was almost exclusively preconceived. If we reflect on the prerequisites for such planning, we realize that some notion of the ultimate size and function of the place was required, as well as both the authority and precept to create and execute an overall design. Whether a Greek plantation city or a Roman colonial city was to be built, its founders had these requisites. Other ancient societies as well possessed them, particularly when the religious nature of the place was clear. As distant in space and society as were ancient China and pre-Columbian Yucatan, each produced preconceived towns, seemingly because each viewed the town as a critical part of religion. But our search is for the emergence of the city in a Western society only quite recently become knowledgeable about either ancient China or the Mayan settlements. Similarity may have existed among the classical, Chinese, and Mayan notions of urban conception, but we may reasonably view these as separate, independent origins rather than as any diffusion of a single creation. Thus, we may leave to others a concern for the non-Western creations.

5. Unfortunately, the term *colony* seems not to connote the control of an indigenous population by a ruling group introduced from outside. When the endless debates on "colonialism" take place in the United Nations, we hear as much confused terminology as piteous self-excuse. The Greek colonies were for the most part made up of Greeks or slaves they captured elsewhere; in the same way, the thirteen American colonies were settlements of Britons. The Providence Plantations at the head of Narragansett Bay provide us with an alternative term. It originally meant planting of men and women at some distance from their homeland, precisely the situation we deal with in classical times, so, seeking to avoid the imprecise, polemic, and derogatory qualities of the term *colonial* today, let us call the creations of human migrations "plantation cities."

The Role of Catastrophe

Faced with the need to create a town, settlers or conquerors must have been forced to improve on experience. It is hard to imagine that any leader faced with the problem of laying out a town would merely build his abode, leaving all else to chance. Athens might have grown in that way, but it is unlikely that fully supported Athenians' plantations would. We do know that for a time plantations were rather inchoate in morphology, possessing the temple and the meeting place—the agora—but beyond that conforming to the socially structured but unplanned qualities of Knossos described above. Once the planting of settlements became common, rationality seems to have entered. The first recorded instance is slightly different from the simple plantation, but it serves to bring out a second historical process in the shaping of cities, that of a physical catastrophe and its aftermath.

Map of Miletus as laid out by Hippo-damus, ca. 450 B.C. From Armin von Gerken, Milet *(Berlin: Verlag Walter de Gruyter, 1935).*

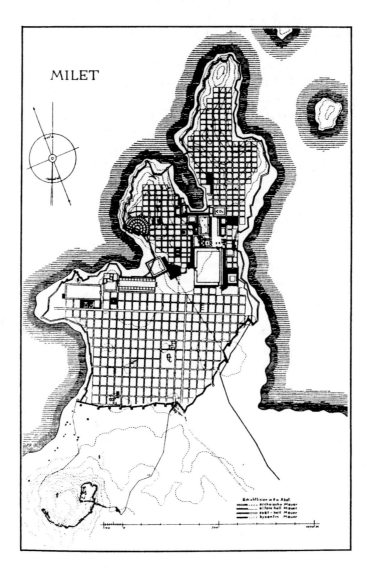

In 494 B.C., the Persians sacked and destroyed Miletus, the greatest of the Ionian plantations in Asia Minor. For fifteen years the city, or more exactly its remnants, was held by the conquerors, but after its liberation in 479 or 466 B.C. it was rebuilt on a preconceived, regular pattern. Again, the necessary prior conditions were met: Miletus had been the greatest of Greek mercantile cities before 500 B.C., dominating the Black Sea trade and establishing some fifty trading entrepôts on the Hellespont, Propontis, and the Black Sea. Although the city never recovered that status after the Persian Sack, its rebuilders could reasonably impute to it a future deserving a true morphology. Yet in distinction to its earlier slow advance to supremacy in a mercantile settlement system, Miletus was now born both anew and nearly full-grown. Both the site and the probable scale of the new Miletus were determined; only the layout of the town seems to have been at issue.

The Modular Division of Land

Records are almost nonexistent, though Aristotle tells us that "Hippodamus, the son of Euryphon, a native of Miletus, [was] the same one who invented the art of planning cities, and who also laid out the Piraeus [the port of Athens]."[6] The invention he made was certainly not unknown before his time, but his role seems to have been to bring it first into a body of morphological practice, formalized and probably stated as a principle of town formation in an era of active town plantation, and to push its adoption. In Aristotle's words, Hippodamus was "a strange man, whose fondness of distinction led him into a general eccentricity of life." From the hands of this eccentric came the rectilinear street grid, which has been endlessly criticized by recent generations of planners for being both too mundane and too monotonous, a strange fate indeed for Hippodamus's ideas.

The street grid is fundamentally a land-division practice and is not necessarily conceived of as a particular circulation system. It does afford routes to get about the town; any public way will do that. But little evidence suggests that the grid was advanced for that purpose. Again, Aristotle furnishes us the clue, in an instance where almost no others are to be had, when he tells us, "The city of Hippodamus [Miletus] was composed of 10,000 citizens divided into three parts—one of artisans, one of husbandmen, and a third of armed defenders of the state. He also divided the land into three parts, one sacred, one public, the third private: the first was set apart to maintain the customary worship of the gods, the second was to support the warriors, the third was the property of the husbandmen." The grid facilitated the creation, *de novo*, of a land-use and occupational separation when the design size was fairly apparent. Although laid out on the grid, Miletus contained empty street blocks well into Roman times, and the streets of the grid so disregarded terrain as to make it obvious that their function was cadastral more than circulatory. Haverfield holds that the introduction of the grid came when

6. Aristotle, *Politics*, II, IV (Jowett's translation).

in the Macedonian period the individual cities came to be parts of a large whole, items in a dominant state, subjects of military monarchies. The use of public buildings, the splendour of public festivals in individual cities, declined. Instead, the claims of the individual citizen, neglected too much by the City-states, but noted by the newer philosophy, found consideration even in town-planning. A more definite, more symmetrical, often more rigidly "chess-board" pattern was introduced for the towns which now began to be founded in many countries round and east of the Aegean. Ornamental edifices and broad streets were still indeed included, but in the house-blocks round them due space and place were left for the dwellings of common men. For a while the Greeks turned their minds to those details of daily life which in their greater age they had somewhat ignored.[7]

Difficult as it is to assert a simple causative tie between the grid-pattern town and the existence of a responsible citizenry, some sort of interaction seems likely. Once the ordinary citizen—a member of the burghal class, the bourgeoisie, a body of freemen, or even the proletariat—enters into consideration in laying out a town, a quite natural force seeks the creation of a basically *modular division of land*. Looking again to Knossos, we may recall the *evolved division of land*, starting with, and centering on, the king-priest's palace, surrounded by the residential area for his retainers, and filled in at the edge by a band of mean housing casually thrown together by what we would call the working class. Knossos' structure can hardly have been planned; at best, we can say that it must have emerged in response to what today we would think of as a land-rent principle—that is, the group with the better ability to pay for space is located closer to the city center or political seat than that with the lesser ability. Probably no actual "rent" or tax was paid, but great differentials must have existed in the authority of the command of different classes for the use of specific sites. Clearly, strong class division must have existed from the beginning and militated against a cadastral regularity, though it seems quite logically not to have repressed a certain consistency in building type within the specific class area.

An odd element of support for this notion of the classlessness of the grid pattern comes from ancient Athens in the laudatory comment of Demosthenes: "The great men of old built splendid edifices for the use of the State, and set up noble works of art which later ages can never match. But in private life they were severe and simple, and the dwellings of an Aristides or a Miltiades was [*sic*] not more sumptuous than that of an ordinary Athenian citizen."[8] We must assume that class distinctions existed, but their puritanical repression seems to have produced a rather uniform, if distinctly mean, city. Athens seems to epitomize the city of organic growth, as inchoate as Knossos but not class-divided by reason of the denial of personal ostentation it honored. Public display was its glory; when we think of Athens our vision is of the Acropolis and its temples—its public buildings, if you will—not of

7. Haverfield, *Ancient Town-Planning*, 16–17.
8. Demosthenes, *Third Olynthiac*, 25.

its houses. As noted before, when Federalist America sought to mold itself after Athens, it was forced to live in clapboard temples because no one wished to live in the Athenian house.

Miletus: The System in the City

Reflection upon the creation of Miletus by Hippodamus brings forth one fact as central to the morphogenesis of cities as the more clearly perceived matter of regularity and the grid: the role of total conception. Perhaps Hippodamus's greatest contribution was in seeing the city as a total system and providing for the complexity of elements it needed. His three parts, though a bit crankish to our thinking, still assert an integration of reality to include all the elements of an actual system. Even after several centuries, not all the street blocks enclosed by the grid were occupied. At first this fact might suggest that the conception and the need were greatly out of phase, but it could as well suggest that, in a conception of a total system, room must be left for growth and evolution. We can draw an analogy to the periodic table of elements. That table was devised before all the elements occupying places within it were known, and some still elude our search, but the overall system could be erected because the basic relationships are understood. In the same way, Hippodamus understood, however oddly, the system of the city and devised a physical form in which it could grow. The great contribution of such an appraisal is that it creates a form sufficiently adaptable to handle growth and change over a very long time. Instead of castigating the preconceived town with its modular components as dull-witted, unaesthetic, and somehow speaking of a lower use of human intellect, we might better view it as one of the great inventions of the human mind. It raised proportion, adaptability, and a certain equality to the central place in the constitution of cities. We may then question the assumption, so common in European aesthetic thinking, that such a rare creation was mechanical and uninspired.

The Common Morphological Elements

We have no checklist of common elements in Greek cities. Nevertheless, certain consistencies may be cited to convey a general picture, even if it does not accurately portray any single place.

Every place, however chaotic or ephemeral, must have a ground plan, as even the medieval fair had a pattern for the duration of its meeting. The two versions of the ground plan were the evolved organic layout and the modular preconceived design. Common sense tells us that the organic was the easier of the two. The older Greek cities appear to have had a point of location— often a rocky hill guarded by cliffs—on which the religious and defensive structures of the place were set. An acropolis may ultimately have been endowed with sacred significance, but its precise location seems surely to have been a result more of geomorphology than of hagiography. Once its site was determined, the acropolis fostered the town, furnishing the religious justification for the place and protecting its inhabitants in case of attack. When the gods smiled upon it and the walls preserved it, a town could grow,

The
Classical City

soon clothing the hill slopes with other public buildings and housing.

To serve the acropolis itself, what may well have been the first type of urban open space was shaped. We might term it a circulation area, implying a moderately equal proportion between length and breadth. The typical pattern would be a series of public buildings scattered about an area, as in Athens' Acropolis, or ranged around one, as became more typical of the wall of buildings enclosing the Greek agora in the planted cities.

The residential areas would logically cluster around the point of location for the city. At first they might exist in some form of cellular accretion, with the house being the unit of growth, located as close to the outermost existing house as building techniques and the most primitive form of circulation would permit. Interstitial space would be private, or at least excessively parochial, and certainly spatially minimal. Narrow paths between buildings would suffice, and their direction could be determined by the needs of the immediately adjacent residents. The result was the residential maze we read of in the sociological and defensive justification. The ancients themselves seem to have perceived the defensive qualities of the maze. According to Lavedan, Aristotle tells us that the narrow and tortuous streets of Athens were an enigma deceiving to strangers and a labyrinth dangerous to enemies.[9] No doubt the maze produced these effects, but were they the reason the city grew in such a way? Cellular accretion would produce such effects even among most outward-looking people living in total peace with the world.

The problem with the residential maze is that, as a complete ring around the acropolis, it would serve effectively to immure the place against external contact. Thus, we may easily explain the next contrast we perceive, that between the paths of the maze and the preexisting pattern of roads that must have been present at the time the would-be inhabitants selected their point of location. These roads would have given access to the fields that fed the city, to battle sites, and to the sea that was Greece's national highway. As housing clustered about the acropolis, it would tend to group into mazes whose extent would be determined by the width of a sector interstitial between two roads to the outside and as deep as the peripheral growth of the city required.

The roads to the outside would easily allow greater visual depth than the paths of the maze, so we should not be surprised that newly endowed public buildings would be built where a road afforded a distant prospect of the structures. The wish to endow the city with a new building would be joined with the desire to make such a building impressive to the beholder, an objective impossible within the residential maze. Self-conscious architecture withers without public adulation, so only the vernacular form can live in the crowded area of organic growth. For that reason the Greek cities, even when basically organic in their growth, appear to have evolved at least a limited use of preconception in the location of public buildings and the opening of vistas along which to admire them. It is a short step, intellec-

9. Pierre Lavedan, *Histoire de l'urbanisme: Antiquité–moyen age* (Paris: Henri Laurens, 1926), 1:114–15.

tually, from such a limited use of forethought in morphology to its common practice. The need to use even short stretches of straight street to gain a perspective of a building becomes clear when we appreciate that in Athens, outside the agora, the only open space was an area of twenty by forty meters in front of the principal fountain. [10]

Once the concept of the straight street as an adjunct of monumental public architecture had been established, several amplifications were possible. The street might be made straight over a greater distance, permitting an even more impressive view, or it might be made wider, to gain a similar end. Given the relatively undeveloped state of Greek engineering, only the second course was of much importance. Greek building depended almost wholly on post-and-lintel construction, which limited the clear span that could be accomplished and placed a rather low height limit on building. These building strictures seem to be the reasons for widening the street along which a prospect was to be gained. We learn from Aristotle that Hippodamus first urged both wide and straight streets. We can only infer that he may have been among the first to realize that to view public buildings properly it was more important that the street be wide than that it be excessively straight.

Hippodamus is generally credited with inventing the grid pattern or at the least the orthogonal town, much as that claim is unfounded. What he did do was to institutionalize it as the way a proper city should be laid down. It is doubtful that his streets would today be thought very wide, but for their time they seemed so. In the absence of accounts as to why he surveyed as he did, we can only guess that it was to permit the distant prospect and to gain modular land division rather than to encourage an improvement in the exterior architecture of private dwellings. There can be little doubt that no real desire could be felt for the embellishment of the private house when its exterior could be seen from no more than five to ten feet away. Thus we have little reason to question the plainness of the exterior walls of buildings in the housing maze, though we know their interior courts were often quite elaborately decorated. We may more easily imagine the extreme narrowness of these alleyways in the ancient Greek cities when we note Plutarch's observation that in those places the custom was to knock on the inside of a door before opening it (in the normal fashion outward) to avoid striking and injuring passersby. Consequently, the Greeks had a word for knocking from the inside as well as the outside. [11] When the straight, widened street was introduced, the revelation of the exterior of the house must have been even more startling than had been the exposure of the public buildings. From this we might expect a great flowering of domestic architecture, yet the evidence from Greek times is not very clear.

We must take note of the paucity of record that has come down to us with respect to everyday building in this first time period we have considered. We can reconstruct the ground plan of a number of Greek houses, since excavation of ruins normally tells us where both the internal and exterior walls of

10. Ibid., p. 114.
11. Plutarch, "Pyrrhus," 34, quoted in Lavedan, *Histoire de l'urbanisme*, 1:115.

the house were to be found. Seldom do we learn much about the superstructure. To use what little evidence we have, we must first set the frame in which the urban morphology evolved.

Internal Structure of the Greek City

The Greeks were, in our lexicon, an ancient people; thus, they viewed the establishment of a city as a religious act. Auguries were employed, orientation to celestial bodies was common, and the nexus of the city always remained in its temples. The Greek temple was not a meeting place, but a building dedicated to a god in the hope of gaining protection, into which individuals entered to pay the god homage. If the populace or a selection from its numbers were to meet, that meeting normally took place outdoors. For that purpose the Greeks created a public open space, called the agora, which was first merely circulating space with buildings spread about it, as exemplified by Athens' Agora of the Potters.[12] Apparently the role of the agora did not change as the years passed, but its shape became stylized; fairly clear evidence suggests that Hippodamus was the first to give regular form to the open space. His was a regular design for the agora to be laid out in the reconstruction of Priene, when that city of Asia Minor was moved away from the flood plain of the Meander River in the fourth century B.C. As far as we can tell, Hippodamus advanced this notion of regularity more for religious and metaphysical reasons than for practicality. He was a Milesian, and in Miletus Thales and Pythagoras had introduced the primitive Egyptian geometry to the Greek world, and vastly improved upon it. Hippodamus worshipped order and possessed a mystical view of numbers, to the extent that he found three social groups in Greek society, three districts for their residence in the city, and even three divisions of law. It was quite to be expected that in his hands the formless circulating space of the early agora should be transformed into the rectilinear, ultimately enclosed, space of the agora as it was built in new plantation cities laid out during the two centuries before Christ.

Initially, the agora was an area with symbolic buildings surrounded by potential meeting places, but in Hippodamus's hands a ternary system was applied. The agora became a sheltering portico for the merchants in distant trade, a political forum with the creation of the Bouleuterion, and a marketplace for the sale of all sorts of perishable goods.[13] And it was given an ordered outline. His subsequent design for the south agora of Miletus was that of a public square so architectural in its details as to have been at home in the rational design of the Renaissance, nearly two millennia later. Surrounding these squares that were coming even in themselves to stand as monuments, with their porticoes of columns often several ranks deep, were cubicles that seem to have been intended as shops for artisans and merchants. As the squares were repeated in the design of a single city, it seems

12. See Lavedan's discussion of the shape of the agora, ibid., pp. 169–76.

13. Ibid., p. 171. Lavedan says, "The perishable food market had special provision, notably tables for the sale of fish, some pipes for washing, water in abundance, and cool cellars underground."

The
Continuing City

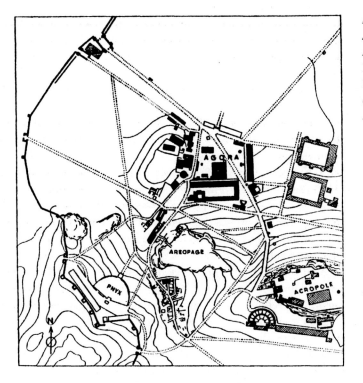

Plan of Athenian Agora. From Roland Martin, L'Urbanisme dans la Grèce Antique *(Paris: A. and J. Picard, 1956).*

to have become true that one or several would take on the commercial functions, leaving others to religious and political uses. Even within a single agora, specialization of activity would lead to clusters in parts of the vast open courtyard. On the west side of Priene's agora the sellers of food gathered; in the courtyard itself were numerous, ultimately a clutter of, monuments; and on the north side lay the offices of the magistrates.[14] In a real sense the agora was a primordial central business district, locationally unspecialized in its early days but ultimately possessed of distinct functional parts, sufficiently adjacent to each other to permit a single visit to accomplish several goals.

At first, in the stage when the agora was merely a place for buildings, those structures appear to have been specialized enclosures for religious or governmental purposes without the capacity to shelter crowds that such activities might today imply. Popular assemblies were held in the circulating space around the temples and rooms of the magistrates. As the central area evolved, two growth processes took hold. The first led to specialization of a building to the particular process it served, and the second to some vertical differentiation within the building. These *segregating processes* seem to have existed in cities from their inception, and in ancient Greece we can begin to trace their consequences.

The formal organization of the agora area, dating from the fourth century

14. Anthony Kriesis, *Greek Town Building* (Athens: National Technical University of Athens, 1965), pp. 75–86.

B.C., merely established a conscious design to care for the segregation that was taking place. Perhaps the first separation came when what have been called the theatrical activities of urban life came to be cared for in an open amphitheater in a form we still term a Greek theater. These theatrical undertakings were not merely drama as we know it but included all manner of public spectacles and activities that could be observed by large crowds; by *thea* the Greeks meant "the act of seeing." Thus, formal observation of a locationally fixed activity by a large group required a specialized building with an amphitheater shape.

The agora evolved into a formal area mainly in the use of its open space. The establishment of a theater was one separation; another was the creation of arcades. The Greeks termed them porticoes because they did not know how to build the arches that made a true arcade, but we may use that later term as more suggestive to us of the ground plan and enclosure of the place, if less correct as to its method of roof spanning. These arcades were in truth specialization of open space, and intended for the ternary functions that Hippodamus observed in his analysis of the activities carried on in the agora. For religious activities, a long, perhaps more enclosed, portico was shaped, to which the name *stoa* was given. In these stoae, one of the walls parallel with the long axis was commonly solid, while the other was colonnaded. Not all stoae were for religious purposes, but when a covered spot for quiet meditation was sought, it normally became stoa-like in form.

The second of the ternary functions, commerce, was apparently provided for in two ways. In some agorae, trading took place in an open corner of the space; in others, a covered colonnade came into use. This portico produced a "public market" open on all sides but in which the wares were sheltered more from the ever-present Aegean sun than from the erratic rainfall. Such open porticoes of the merchants must have suffered from security problems, tolerable when merchants came to the market for a single day, but ever more onerous as they became perpetual sellers on that site. Although no records tell us why the change came, we may infer that the appearance of enclosed shops ranged along the sides of such a colonnade, leaving at least one side open, served to allow merchants to be "in the market" without having to remove their wares each day at nightfall. From the fourth century B.C. onward, this alignment of shops has been a characteristic feature of marketplaces, and seemingly its evolutionary history had to be repeated in the Middle Ages and again in more recent times.

How much locational specialization was there in the agora market and in other areas of shops? The evidence exists that ultimately the agora became too small to contain all the merchants' premises. Athens, in addition to the potters' agora already mentioned, had quarters for marble workers—observed by archaeologists through the vast accumulation of marble chips—armorers, and other artisans, as well as sellers of wine, oil, and other commodities brought into the city. We cannot establish a detailed picture of the commercial geography of Athens or other classical cities, but we can reasonably accept the idea that one did exist. The segregation was horizontal, into the quarters already mentioned; it seems also to have been vertical to a small degree. Foundations remain that suggest the existence of upper-story storage of goods, as well as "living over the shop." We know there were two-story porticoes and can only hazard the guess that some might have been similar in layout to the multistory shop arcades of the nineteenth-century American city. The geographical anchor of all this internal structuring of commercial areas was an agora. Traders first congregated there; from there, they came to occupy more differentiated craft and traders' districts.

Not only was the agora the anchor of the commercial geography, but also it served to fix the pattern of housing, which grew either organically or in a preconceived pattern around it. Both history and logic tell us that the first residential development came in the mazes of rather plain houses reached by narrow alleyways, and in a city of true antiquity such as Athens this pattern persisted even well after the time of Hippodamus. Housing blocks are not clearly discernible in these cities, despite the fact that the Greek house became rather consistent in its room components, focusing on the courtyard of an inward-looking house. Unfortunately, our knowledge comes from the more lustrous houses of the wealthy. The vernacular house of the urban masses remains in shadow.

For the rich, the house was a succession of often stately rooms, starting behind the plain façade with a columned peristyle and succeeding to the megaron, a vast classical equivalent of the Victorian drawing room. Like it, this room was often divided into two parts by door piers that afforded a wide-open connection when desired. Beyond or sometimes before the megaron lay the courtyard, off which were placed a lavatory, bedrooms, and entrances to a cellar or upper story, if these existed. The cellars may have been religious—related to the cult of the underworld more than the storage of amphorae. We know little of possible upper floors because their evidence has been totally carried away by time. What emerged for the wealthy is a low house pierced by courtyards to let in light, walled against the outer world, and probably including ostentatious rooms for social purposes and mean quarters for slaves and retainers. We are interested less in the variation and elaboration of these houses, for they must have been numerically exceptional, than in the enclosure, their low height, and their individuality. They might be assembled slowly and in an evolving pattern, as in the older cities, or they might be grouped into street blocks after the fourth-century urban revolution, but they remained cloistered, flat, and personal.

Today we wish to know how the masses lived, but the answers are sparse. Their houses were probably as enclosed and low as those of the aristocratic citizens, but perhaps less individual. Priene, for example, had some four hundred dwelling houses and an inferred population of around four thousand, yielding an average per dwelling population that was unlikely to have been approached by a poor family.[15] As well there must have been decay of the house fabric on a major scale, as in Pergamon the Astynomi were enjoined to enforce housing repair upon owners and to fine them if necessary as a compulsion.[16] The poor probably lived in one- or two-room houses having party walls shared with adjacent houses, small provision for sanita-

15. Haverfield, *Ancient Town-Planning*, p. 43.
16. Ibid., p. 54.

tion, little specialization of rooms, and probably even less concern for the public impression created by the house. They had no room for entertaining, certainly little decoration, and probably no formal architecture. These buildings were built of rubble and perhaps easily prey to collapse; the surviving laws repeatedly call for the repair of houses. They were without water and sewerage provision, and almost certainly they classed as the most basic accommodation that could be envisaged. Because of their rickety quality, it seems unlikely that they were multistoried. They did shelter the poor population, but more against the sun than the rains. The ancient commentators began a clamor against the mild Mediterranean winter that can only be understood in the context of badly designed and poorly constructed housing, in the time either of Pericles or of the Grand Tour of the eighteenth century. In classical times when regular planning was introduced, calls were made for the east-west alignment of the important streets, with narrow crossing streets and an emphasis on the south-facing façade of the block.[17] These plans turned the backs of the houses to the cold north wind in wintertime and allowed the sun to flood the street. In a very early awareness of public hygiene, it was argued that the prevailing westerly winds would also clear the air in the compact housing quarters as they swept along the wider streets extending parallel to an east-west axis. Some Greek theoreticians even advocated houses taller on the south frontage, to gather winter heat, with low northern sides to protect against the bora blowing in winter from the north, and possessed of deep eaves to give protection in the summer from high rays of the implacable sun.

The cramped site of many Greek cities, on cliffed spots gaining natural protection or on narrow colluvial slopes between such rocky hills and the sea, meant that the suburb as we know it was missing. In a few instances Greek colonies already scattered around an estuary or on an extensive plain might grow together to form a polynucleated city. Yet this joining of formerly separate villages tended to leave them as discrete units, each possessing an agora and the other physical attributes of a city. The explanation of such continuing identity may lie in the traditional balance to be maintained between the supporting countryside and the city that produced it, particularly in the planted cities. So commonly does the history of a city show it to be a planted settlement with its hinterland growing about it in a seemingly indivisible symbiosis that we may question whether a higher level of association ever seemed fitting. We do know that despite the paucity of surviving evidence, the main segregation of groups within Greek cities shows up not so much racially or by class as by geographical origin. Attica, before Pericles called its residents into Athens (431 B.C.), consisted of demes—large villages strangely anticipatory of the New England town in location, function, and government—whose residents on arrival in Athens seem to have continued their geographical loyalties. As other peoples came to live in Athens or the Piraeus, they settled in quarters grouped by place of origin. With such associations strong in the Greek mind, we may fairly say that Hellenic urban geography revealed little of a hierarchical quality. Instead, the process of

17. See Lavedan, *Histoire de l'urbanisme*, 1: 142–46.

collecting people periodically into the city—synoecism—forged an intimate tie between city and countryside.

When we ask what the limits were of classical Greek cities, notably Athens, we must begin to appreciate the evolutionary quality of the towns that ultimately gained ascendancy. Athens began as a fortification of the Acropolis within which all of the urban functions were clustered. Slowly the hilltop became the sanctuary of the gods and the citadel of the government, with housing pushed outward down the slopes of the hill. We know that these residential areas must have been enclosed by a wall, and that the focus of the commercial life of the city came to rest in the agora in a hollow between the Acropolis and another hill, the Pnyx. We may reasonably assume that in the sixth century B.C. that the *process of land-use separation* was already at work. The original area that was the whole town, the Acropolis in this case, had been transformed into a specialized area by the external clustering of those activities that could gain through migration. This shift was itself a process, as observable in archaic Athens as in twentieth-century New York, that led within a city district to *functional simplification*, wherein one use gains ascendancy and the others formerly intermixed with it depart to an area that they, in turn, may dominate.

The wall would continue to be pushed outward as this spread of the urban fabric took place. This constant juxtaposition of forces—growth pressing against circumvallation—would tend toward rachet-like expansion. As pressure built up within a particular wall, crowding would increase, leading in turn to a leap over the wall into what were unprotected sites. Those exposed sites would eventually call for a new wall for their protection, and the city would reach a temporary adjustment of the forces of growth and circumvallation, only to start the rachet movement again if expansion continued.

Let us look specifically at Athens. In 480 B.C. the Persians invaded Greece, captured Athens, and destroyed the buildings both on the Acropolis and in the city. We may be convinced of an organic growth process in the morphology of cities, but we cannot exclude extinction from it. But unlike a single organism, a city can survive as a vital force either by the flight of a component of its population, which returns to begin again, or by the transplanting of a new vital force from outside. In Athens' case the indigenous vital force continued the city's history. Themistocles led the Athenians back into the cycle of organic growth, an enlightened replication of past history. The first efforts were those of rebuilding the city's walls, but experience survived and the functional simplification undertaken before the onslaught of the Persians was introduced at the beginning of the reconstruction of that city we now think of as classical Athens.

The reconstruction of Athens took place in the century in which Hippodamus proposed the application of preconception to city structure. In fact, the port of the city, the Piraeus, was rebuilt on his plan and ultimately connected by the Long Walls to Athens itself. As the city recovered its fabric, a pattern emerged that combined organic with designed growth. The agora was more regular than previously, and certainly much more massive, having several instances of a two-story stoa of shops, but it was not rectangular as in the truly new towns. The housing, what little we know of it, was improved and probably better served by streets, yet in no way did it match the beauty and order of the public buildings and public areas of the city. Only when the Romans came, initially in the second century B.C., does domestic architecture seem to have received much attention.

In the second century A.D. Hadrian endowed Athens with many monuments, not least among them Hadrianopolis, a newly walled area of villas, gardens, and baths on generous sites. By the Roman period Athens had become rather an urban museum, repeatedly the recipient of benefactions from kings and magnates beyond its boundaries but exercising no function beyond the perpetuation of increasingly archaic morphological solutions. The Greek city was the model for antiquity and Hellenic architecture was its paradigm until the Romans faced the problem of designing and constructing a thousand towns and of engineering buildings on a scale previously unimagined. The ironic finis to the Greek urban epoch came in 15 B.C., when the Roman magnate Vipsanius Aggripa presented Athens with an odeum, to seat a thousand persons, built along the lines of Greek architecture with a roof span of some twenty-five meters. But the enclosure collapsed and had to be reduced to two halls seating only five hundred.

Catching the Attention of the Gods

In the words of Pierre Lavedan, "The Etruscan cities occupy a critical position in the history of urbanization. . . . All the structure (*l'amenagement*) of the Roman city was derived from them and, by Rome, that influence was passed on to many people."[18] The contribution of the Etruscans was a ritual to be used in the setting up of cities to focus the attention, and thereby presumably the protection, of the gods on that particular place. Further, given a ritual of location and orientation, it would follow that the shape of the city would be predetermined. With a linear base and a specific size, probability would call forth the grid-pattern town, as apparently it did. Only when ritual is standardized for a fairly large group of people can it be looked upon as a shaping force for cities; otherwise, it is only an idiographic explanation of the outline of a particular place. In Greece as long as no metaphysical quality attached to the laying out of towns, only the temples and agora were the common feature of the cities, but, when the Hippodamian proposal was advanced, Greek cities became patterned, admittedly formed in response to rationalism rather than ritual of a simple religious sort. But among the Etruscans, the *libri rituales* governed their conduct in the founding of cities, the placing of gates, and the prosecution of daily life.

The city was seemingly the basic governmental unit with a League of Twelve Cities, comprised of a group whose membership list has not survived, standing as Etruria. When the Etruscans expanded, sometime before the

18. Ibid., p. 98. Some recent writers disagree with Lavedan, finding Etruscan cities not so regular as he supposed and arguing instead that Roman towns were more shaped by the Greek than the Etruscan precedent. Thus, the view is advanced that the plowing of the sacred furrow was more a religious than a morphological control, with the orthogonal shape coming from Greece rather than the structuring within the *pomerium*.

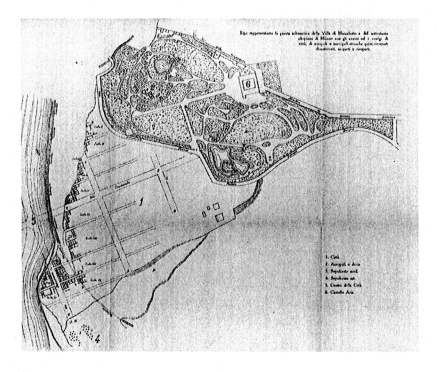

sixth century B.C., from their hearth in present-day Tuscany both north to
the shaded slopes of the Apennines and south into Latium and Campania,
they shaped a "state" composed of two such duodecimal leagues. From their
obscured origins through a considerable domination of a younger Rome by
the Etruscan Tarquin kings down to the battle of the Vedemonian Lake (309
B.C.), Etruria was independent, wealthy, civilized, and emulated by the
Romans. So, as Lavedan suggests, we must seek in its history the foundation
of Western urbanization as a morphological system.

The foundation of the Etruscan city followed a precise course, only the
initial element of which is unknown to us. We cannot determine on what
basis the Etruscans chose the precise locations of the places, but evidence
suggests that a combination of defensive position and productive tributary
area would account for most choices. Certainly, the Etruscans were not
simple farmers shaping central-places in their midst; they dominated the
Tyrrhenian Sea, controlled Corsica, and carried on an extensive long-
distance trade that must have made them more wealthy than Rome almost
until the advent of the Christian Era, as we have material evidence they
were.

Once the site was chosen, the Etruscan ritual intervened and recourse
was taken to consult the auspices, the tools of augurs. Auguries did not
locate cities, but they might lead to the rejection of a proposed site. If those
auspices favored the site, then the Etruscans created a *mundus*, by dividing
the place from the undifferentiated mass of land about it. The *mundus* came
to be symbolized by a collection of monuments and temples, often located in
the inner *pomerium*. To define a *mundus*, an enclosing furrow must be
plowed with a bronze share drawn by a white ox and a white cow harnessed

The
Classical City

59

The Etruscan Gateway of Perugia furnishes evidence of the size and importance of cities in the Etruscan league. The loggia at the top of the left buttress is not part of the original gate.

together. At the proposed location of gates in the city wall, the share must be lifted to leave a connection to the outer world. The sod cut by the plow must be thrown inward, apparently as a symbolic beginning of the wall that ultimately would defend the city. That defense had ritualistic expression in the *pomerium*, which for the Etruscans was a band of ground on both sides of the wall left clear of obstruction. Such an enfilading band, shorn of its mystical qualities, remained common in European cities until the late nineteenth century. It existed simply so attackers could be shot at along the length of the wall as well as before and behind it. For the Etruscans it was undoubtedly both a practical necessity and a symbol of the edge of the realm of the gods' support, the *mundus*. The Romans lost much of the practical need for walls when they conquered their known world, but they continued the practice of building light walls for their religious virtues. With the Roman acceptance of Christianity under Constantine in the fourth century A.D., those virtues seemed to disappear, but rather soon the practical need for circumvallation returned, to persist until long-range guns finally made walls obsolete in the late nineteenth century.

The world within the sacred furrow seems to have had no regular shape, posing a problem if we seek to derive any consistent pattern for cities. Some authors have tended to discount the Etruscans as the originators of the regular Roman town because the furrow did vary, but Lavedan supplies a plausible explanation. He argues that, though the furrow was irregular in shape, it was bordered on the inside by the band of open land, the *pomerium*, which could serve as a transition to a regular street pattern. But how do we account for the creation of a regular grid in an irregularly enclosed area?

The explanation lies in a second operation that attended the layout of the town, that of giving it its orientation. Urban creation required a baseline on which division would be based, and it took no exaggeration of practice or mysticism to propose the rising sun in the *east* as the basis for *orientation*. Projecting a line thence to the point of the setting sun created such a baseline.

Before looking at how this base produced the full cadastral structure of the city, let us compare the Greek and the Etruscan city, with their contrasting solutions to the same problem at very much the same time in history. The Greeks created the domain of the gods in the acropolis; the Etruscans defined the gods' domain as the full area within the *pomerium*, though religious activities came to be centered in the collection of monuments and temples in the *mundus*. For the Greeks the city grew around the temple (acropolis), whereas for the Etruscans the temple was merely a specialized corner of the god's domain. In Greece the city spread around a sacred point by organic growth processes, whereas the Etruscan city was preconceived, with a fixed area and structure from the beginning. The Greek city was ever an "open system" in which only the morphology of the small initial core was determined in the beginning. The Etruscan city was largely a closed system at the start, with most morphological processes already fixed. Thus, the nature of the religious precinct in the city may be most important just for this determination of the way the city will grow. Even a partial adoption of the religious *mundus* of the Etruscans involved the Romans in dividing up an area in the beginning rather than building it up as needed, as among the Hellenes.

The *Cardo* and *Decumanus*, and What Followed

The east-west line already mentioned may not have been precisely oriented—"east" depends upon the day of the year involved—but still it was the basal coordinate. The *Gromatici*, based considerably on Etruscan practice, describes the *decumanus* as a line connecting east and west *ab oriente ad occasum*.[19] From the *decumanus* was projected perpendicularly a line that was basically north-south, called the *cardo*. That line furnished the other axis necessary to define a system of regular divisions of land, which was surveyed by sighting the sun with a groma. As early as the laying out of Marzabotto in the fifth century B.C. we see the Etruscans shaping a rectilinear town, exactly as one would expect with a coordinate system extending from a *cardo* and *decumanus* intersecting at a right angle. In primitive Marzabotto, located fifteen miles south of Bologna, the street blocks formed are not identical with one another, but they are regularly rectangular. No doubt the surveying practices inherited by the Romans from the neighboring Etruscans were those of grid-pattern towns.

Our problem is not how to account for the regular Roman provincial cities, but rather how to explain the irregularity of Rome itself.

By common agreement Rome is believed to have grown by synoecism, with a village on the Palatine hill serving as the core. The neighboring hills are by tradition thought to have been the site of villages housing other ethnic

19. Frontin, *Gromatici*, I, pp. 15 and 27, quoted in ibid., p. 102.

The
Classical City

groups,which came to join the Palatine in founding a city. The groups involved were probably not very different in level of urbanity from the early residents of Attica who combined a rural with an urban residence, returning to the countryside at times of harvest, during the hot months, and when food was scarce.

Legend tells us that Romulus plowed a furrow with an ox and cow to define Rome, and Plutarch held that that furrow was circular in outline. The streets and buildings within the *pomerium* on the Palatine hill probably had no very regular layout, but when the Palatine joined with its neighbors to form Rome, some order was introduced; a great sewer, the Cloaca Maxima, was built through an intervening valley to drain it, providing a site for the great central meeting place, the Forum Romanum. The fundamental expression of this synoecism was the creation of the forum, which came to be the Greek agora writ large, a place where citizens met and political and commercial life centered. To provide access to the forum, the cliffed sides of the original hills were cut down and regraded to make possible the building of streets up the sides of the hills, a process continued into our times. The forum became as well a point of beginning for a *cardo* and a *decumanus*, leading, in turn, to a somewhat irregular rectangular street system. In Rome not all was preconceived; the original villages had grown organically, so the pattern could not be simple. Much of the wealth and effort of imperial Rome was turned toward making the city appear more preconceived than it really was, laying out the later fora of the emperors, Forum Julium, Forum Augustum, Forum Pacis, Forum Nerva, and Forum Trajiani.[20]

Rome seems to have proved intractable in this search for order and grandeur largely because of its excessive vitality in a republic and empire that focused prosperity and regard so heavily on the capital. The greatest honor open to the provincial worthy was citizenship in Rome, which should clarify for us the distinction that existed between the metropolis and all other places. As a consequence, two morphological patterns seem to have arisen: that growing at Rome, and that planted elsewhere. Population size accounts for much of the contrast; Rome probably had a population of at least one million and possibly as much as a million and two-thirds under the empire.[21] The physical history of Rome must also be considered; the city emerged and grew by the interplay of such diverse forces as to make a consistently grained morphology most unlikely. Rome might more easily decree the pattern of Mediolanum (Milan), whose size and purpose were rationally assigned in the

20. Pierre Grimal, *Les Villes romaines*, Que Sais-Je? no. 657 (Paris: Presses Universitaires de France, 1971), p. 40. The *pomerium* of the original Palatine city, Roma Quadrata, lay along the foot of the artificially steepened slope of the Palatine to an angle point at the Ara Maxima in the Forum Boarium (the cattle market mentioned, which must have lain just outside the original Roman walls), the Ara Consi in the Circus Maximus, the Curia Veteres (near the Arch of Constantine), and the *Sacellum Larum* (as the north angle). Pliny tells us there were three gates: the Scalae Caci on a roadway built sloping upward toward the heights of the Palatine, the Porta Romanula, and the Porta Mugonia, with some relics remaining of the last two. The first expansion of Roma Quadrata came when the Esquiline and Caelian hills were joined with the Palatine, and the intervening valleys were drained and used for the Forum Romanum. Later another six or seven hills and the valleys among them were joined into a great city and surrounded by a wall built by the emperor Aurelian.

21. Jérôme Carcopino, *Daily Life in Ancient Rome* (1940; rpt. New York: Bantam Books 1971), p. 24.

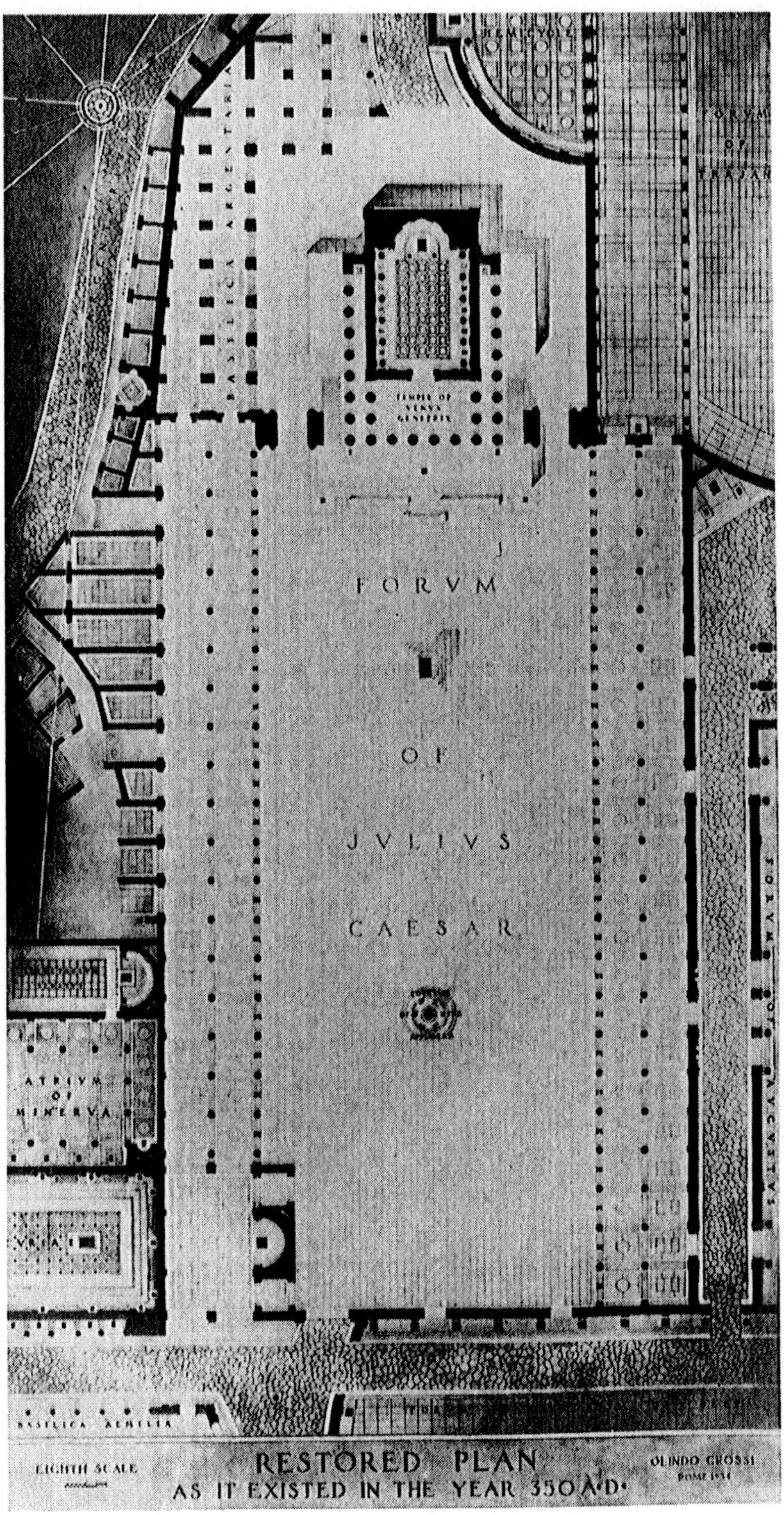

TEMPLE OF
VENVS
GENETRIX

FORVM

OF

JVLIVS

CAESAR

ATRIVM
OF
MINERVA

EIGHTH SCALE

RESTORED PLAN
AS IT EXISTED IN THE YEAR 350 A·D·

OLINDO GROSSI
ROME 1934

Romanization of Cisalpine Gaul, than gain enough ground on the almost continual growth crisis within the capital to hope for more than alleviation of the urgent problems found there. Efforts were made to give Rome the trappings of a properly ordered urban design, but they won little against the yeasty organic growth of the place.

Rome and the City House

We know that Athens and other Greek cities grew apace in the Hellenic period, but little has survived of their domestic architecture, either in writings or in archaeological remains. Athens itself had shrunk to a city of five thousand people when liberated from the Turks in 1833, so the lesser buildings had been little used and badly preserved. These were probably largely constructed of rubble masonry with a poor or absent mortar bond, so over at least a millennium of declining use they largely disintegrated. The stones of Athens remained, but as a heap they tell us little.

Rome and its empire instead furnish us a wealth of detail. Because some cities continued to be used, the buildings were kept up or incorporated into other structures (as in the church of St. John and St. Paul on the Caelian hill); other towns might be virtually abandoned without a major relict population (as in northern Gaul or in Rome's port of Ostia). The Romans were so very much more skilled as builders as truly "to build for the ages." Starting in the second century B.C., concrete infilling was used as the core of the walls and cement mortar in places. Both materials were strong and remained as a cast of the idea the architect had in mind, unlike the situation experienced when the stone blocks of Athens fell into a heap. The Romans may not have invented the city, but doubtless they developed the fundamental module of most subsequent cities, the apartmented house.

The bucolic ancestors of the Romans probably lived in timber huts of post-and-lintel construction roofed and walled by mats of reeds or withes. Like most rural habitations, these would be expanded by adding another unit of similar form until a new module—the courtyard enclosed by single-story rooms—was shaped. In masonry construction this became the basal Roman house built with two courtyards, the atrium and peristyle, inward-looking, with blank walls to the street, and light and ventilation provided by the opening of the court. In Pompeii rich and poor lived in these atrium houses, though the poor had a single room opening off a court rather than the whole building. Because Pompeii was the best-preserved Roman town, and the first to be studied when archaeology was begun as a serious study in the nineteenth century, the notion grew up that the courtyard house was the Roman norm, a notion that appealed to our grandparents because it showed the continuity of history from the Greek to the Roman house. Unfortunately, Pompeii was far from typical, in much the way that Newport (Rhode Island) or Carmel (California) would afford future excavators an odd vision of contemporary American housing.

As small settlements, Roman cities might be composed of such atrium houses, but once growth became brisk these houses would tend quickly to yield to larger multistory structures, just as the brownstone has yielded to the tall apartment house in Manhattan or Chicago's North Side. Certainly, only the very well-to-do could preserve a flat house in the face of vastly increasing land prices such as those already experienced in Rome by the time of the late republic. At first, the courtyard house was transformed by the addition of casual extenders—penthouses built on parts of its roof to add an attic or a bedroom or two, infillings of the courtyards, or possibly cellars dug in the relatively soft tuff of Rome. The courtyard house was initially conterminous with its lot, leaving no peripheral open space for subsequent enlargement. The sort of casual extension possible under such conditions was rather small; to add penthouses would soon cut off the light in the atrium as well as disrupt the collection of rainwater in the *compluvium* of the roof for storage in the *impluvium* in the court itself. And despite all the aqueducts that survive as the glory of Rome, those conduits more often led to public fountains than to domestic faucets, or their ancient equivalent, so the system of roof collection was important. Added to the pressure of increased land rents was the real possibility of destruction by fire of the older buildings, which were built somewhat more of timber and of stone tufa, which did not stand up to fire.

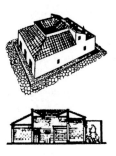

Plan and cross-section of a typical domus *or atrium house, fourth to third century* B.C.

The conditions in the city of Rome encouraged innovation that led in two directions. For the wealthy a larger house requiring less land had to be devised, whereas for the ordinary people some less land-consuming house must be found. Initially, the mass of people had crowded into older buildings that had experienced rather piecemeal transformation—families occupying parts of previously individual houses, and casual extensions to the structure itself—but subsequently new forms were shaped. The wealthy began to occupy multistory buildings, still inward-looking with rooms opening on several levels around a courtyard. Thus was devised the house of the magnate, which in succeeding centuries changed little other than coming to be called a *palazzo* by the people of the Middle Ages. The Romans termed this a *domus*, a somewhat wry antecedent for our generic term for everyday life. When, in the fourth century A.D., the Romans collected statistics on the parts of the city summed into the *Regionaries*, 1,782 *domus* were found. Thus, the *domus* was hardly the standard type of dwelling in a city of certainly a million souls, particularly since a *domus* was a single-family residence, though that family in all likelihood had numerous retainers and slaves.

These were "city mansions," to give them a closely approximate modern name; "palace" is a bit grand for the class, though not for individual examples. Originally, they stood as building units, but as land rents rose, even the rich felt the pinch and, to borrow Lucius Beebe's phrase, only the Big Spenders continued to occupy independent houses. At that point the analogy with the medieval *palazzo* becomes precise, though not signaled by a distinction in Latin; the *domus* could be either a freestanding palace or a rich apartment located almost invariably on the first floor of a larger building. Much as these apartments were part of an apartment building otherwise listed, the *domus* was tallied in the *Regionaries* as such, meaning that of the eighteen hundred such dwellings only some were true palaces, though the proportion cannot be determined.

The more common abode was furnished in those massive buildings that

must by some measure have been the building module of the Roman city, the *insulae.* We may assume that these structures were from four to six stories high, as Augustus decreed that *insulae* could be no more than seventy feet in height—Nero reduced it to sixty feet—which would allow at most five or six stories as we count them.[22] Such a uniform height is a joint result of housing pressure and civil restraint. Rome was greatly crowded, which increased its land rents, though the crowding itself is a sufficient explanation for housing pressure. Yet it could not be allowed to grow too tall, so the Augustan and Neronian limits were set. It appears that the Insula of Felicula next to the Pantheon stood much taller, how tall we do not know, causing both wonder and condemnation.[23] In general, the height limit was established because the buildings were in danger of both fire and structural failure. Accounts have it that it was a daily occurrence for *insulae* to collapse, killing occupants and pedestrians alike. Though built of masonry, these structures were both thin-walled and wooden-floored; they burned rapidly and failed spectacularly, leaving the poorest tenants in the attics no escape from being roasted alive. The emperor's hope was that escape down four flights of stairs might be possible when a greater run would not. Like many imperial expectations this seems to have been somewhat chimerical, but like many imperial decrees it persisted despite that fact.

The apartmented *insula* seems to have had a fairly consistent structure, though it varied widely in design. It was normally a rectangular building with relatively smooth sides rising perhaps four to six stories in height, with a sloping roof, though some appear to have had merely a terrace on top. The body of the building commonly held an opening—sometimes little more than the nineteenth-century air well, but in the better buildings a true courtyard surrounded by balconies that gave access to the separate apartments, termed *cenacula.* Perhaps the most distinguishing feature of the *insula* was that it opened by windows and balconies to the outside of the building, unlike the atrium house and, to a lesser degree, the self-contained

22. Russell Meiggs, *Roman Ostia* (Oxford: Oxford University Press, 1960), p. 236.
23. Carcopino, *Daily Life,* p. 29.

domus. The *insula* had rows of fairly large windows facing outward on the city streets as well as windows and doorways opening onto the interior galleries. In this way the thickness of the building could be increased without abandoning the natural light, which was all that Rome had save for poor and smoky oil lamps. Glass seems to have been uncommon, so windows were closed either by solid shutters or by selonite, a crystalline form of gypsum, which gave some light, though less than was needed.[24] These apartments had no effective heating; at least no chimneys or other flues survive, and the possibility of an open brazier burning charcoal, the rural and palatial form of heating in central Italy, seems small.

Reconstruction of a Roman cenaculum or apartment house based on evidence at Ostia Antica.

Much as we are taught that the Romans solved the problems of public sanitation, some question remains as to the effectiveness of the solutions. No doubt exists that the Romans were the first to devise an adequate system for bringing water into the city; after all, they were the first to make daring and effective use of the arch—a prime requisite in any system where the distribution of water depended on straight gravity flow. The aqueducts were true monuments, named for the emperor or magnate who built them as a gift to the city. When they reached the city, they did continue on to particular quarters in what we would term distributaries, but for most people the flow stopped at a public tap or conduit. The public fountain, in classical times and until very recently, was not merely an element of Roman display; it was the public tap as well. A modest number of *insulae* seem to have had water connections, but because of the open, gravity-driven flow of the water, these could not normally be led to the upper stories. Such conditions created a fairly inverse relationship between height in the building and social quality of the occupants. Let it be recalled that the *domus* of the wealthy tended to occupy the

24. Meiggs, *Ostia*, p. 239. Meiggs apparently incorrectly identifies it as "selinite," but neither Merriam-Webster nor the Oxford English Dictionary identifies such a substance.

*Excavation of a
public latrine at
Vaison-la-Romaine
(Vaucluse).*

ground floor of these apartmented buildings. In the attics, the poor found shelter, but usually neither water nor sewage service.

Jérôme Carcopino has given us a detailed analysis of the municipal services of Rome. He concludes that, as with water, the city was well served by the main sewage system—so well that the main sewer, Cloaca Maxima, is in use up to the present.[25] What the Romans did superbly was to build vast engineering works; they did not provide for the universal use of those services. In Rome it seems that the upper stories were perhaps most commonly not provided with sewage collection, though in Ostia drainpipes seem somewhat more common[26] with privies provided on most floors. Massive public latrines have been excavated in Rome, which served both their obvious purpose and that of social gathering, as attested by their decoration and lack of interior privacy.

Later-day delicacy toward corporal needs seems largely absent in Roman cities, where urinals might stand exposed at the entrance to impressive public buildings and brothels could operate freely "after the ninth hour."[27] At the same time, in decoration and furnishing the Romans carried delicacy almost to the extreme; their houses had little furniture but rather collections of small *objets d'art* that served to show the wealth of the owner and were displayed ostentatiously on a pole stand that must class as the original for the Victorian whatnot. Similarly, in public buildings detailing could be carried to great extremes of lavishness, suggesting an aesthetic sensitivity strangely paired with the blood sports in the Colosseum. Perhaps violent contrast was one of the more significant features of Romans' lives. Thus, it is not surprising to find the Romans displaying the first really modern approach to housing urban masses and, in their engineering, the initial awareness of what a large city needs in municipal services. But alongside their dwellings and aque-

25. Carcopino, *Daily Life*, pp. 43–50.
26. Meiggs, *Ostia*, p. 240.
27. Carcopino, *Daily Life*, p. 289.

ducts, we find the continual collapse of *insulae*, night soil flung from top stories into the narrow streets, and dirt and bugs in *cenacula* whose windows opened onto squares with plashing fountains.

Without question the *insulae* became the pattern of Rome as time passed. In the fourth century A.D., 46,602 *insulae* were recorded, but we do not know into how many further parts, the *cenacula*, these buildings were split. Certainly, we are dealing with a total of apartments that must have numbered in the hundreds of thousands. To contain this number even within the walls of the imperial city required teeming quarters of tall buildings separated from each other only by narrow access streets, *vici*, which seem to have become the main open space outside of the spectacular fora and buildings at the center. It has been argued that the passion for ostentatious public buildings was so great, and so well backstayed by money from senators and emperors, that part of the city's crowding came from displacement of people for these great architectural and planning works. We do know that Rome experienced a continual rebuilding process under which land rents continued to rise, leading in turn to reconstruction of existing buildings to make them more capacious to house a growing mass of people. The economic returns seem to have been high for the landowner, and possibly his lessee, the occupant of the ground-floor *domus*, who in turn might let out the upper stories to increasingly large numbers of tenants. The rents were often high: "We know in Caesar's day Caelius paid for his annual rent . . . 30,000 sesterces ($1,200.00)."[28]

Commerce in the Roman City

So few detailed records survive that we cannot answer two fascinating questions about the Roman city: (1) in what way did this primitive land-rent system work to sort out activities in space, and (2) what was the functional geography of these cities? Some broad facts do, however, survive and they help us to reconstruct the land-use pattern as it existed in the time of the empire.

We may safely conclude that the ground floors of the *insulae* tended increasingly to be occupied by shops; numerous surviving wall footings in Timgad and elsewhere show the door openings of such shops ranged in long ranks along the frontage of more important streets. In some cases, these shops seem to have been both workplace and residence, as evidenced by such survivals as the lofts or mezzanines of Roman Ostia. These were the premises of producers more than traders. Despite its lesser stature as a town, in Ostia "the import of ready-made articles was, however, exceptional. A very large proportion of the goods that were sold in the shops were made on the premises. A terracotta relief from a tomb in the Isola Sacra cemetery shows a shopkeeper with a wide range of tools for sale: on the same relief a craftsman is shown making tools. This is a fair illustration of typical Roman practice, for production and distribution were normally in the same

28. Ibid., p. 30.

hands."[29] And apparently most streets were lined with these shops, suggesting a classical origin for the geographically integrated daily activity pattern of common people.

Meiggs provides us a general picture of these shops-with-residences:

> The commonest form of shop resembles the Pompeiian type and can still be seen in many Italian towns today [1960]. On the street is a large room in which the goods are stacked and sold; behind it there is a smaller room which can be used for production or for extra accommodation. In the corner a wooden staircase leads up to a small mezzanine floor where the family live. The shop front during the day is completely open; at night wooden shutters are run across. Some shops have no back room and were perhaps confined to retail trade; others have a back room as large as the shop, suggesting larger-scale production. Not all shops have living quarters above them.[30]

The shops were commonly in ranked frontages along the streets, but "occasionally they are grouped together in independent architectural units," or bazaars. When Trajan constructed his vastly monumental forum in Rome at the opening of the second century A.D., it was provided with arcades of many shops apparently clustered to some degree by the type of goods fabricated and sold. To argue that complex distinctions existed between shopping areas may be too bold, though likely at least a two-part division was made between local shopping facilities and those of a more specialized, comparative quality in the arcades surrounding the fora of Roman cities.

The Economic Colony

Ostia, the original port for Rome, furnishes us clear evidence of the existence of a long-distance trade carried on by various types of wholesalers, *mercatores*. Their premises can be distinguished from the local shops by their size and the succession of modular spaces logically viewed as storage rooms, as they lack the wide open façade necessary to provide light and observation for selling. The collection of these *horrea* into courtyards was evidently common and their siting shows us whether they were intended for local provisioning or as stages on a longer trading linkage. Those central to a town can be inferred to serve that place, but those with a riverbank location seem to have been intended as transfer points; we know that Ostian warehouses supplied riverboats on the Tiber with grain for Rome that had been brought in turn from North Africa or the Crimea in seagoing barges.[31]

As already noted, the continuing growth of the city's population made grain a crucial commodity and one with great political significance. In attempting to unseat existing dynasties of dictators and emperors, pre-

29. Meiggs, *Ostia*, p. 271.
30. Ibid., pp. 272–73.
31. Cf. ibid., pp. 270–98.

tenders often sought to use the scarcity of grain for the populace to raise a mob. With the practice of free distribution of breadstuffs to an urban proletariat, numbering ultimately in the hundreds of thousands, the supply line for this politically motivated benefaction became a central concern of the Roman emperor. In part the conquests of distant lands, notably Egypt, were motivated by the desire to increase the supply of grain for the city of Rome. But to make use of that greater provision, a system of long-distance trade had to be worked out and the physical facilities for its conduct constructed. We can examine briefly the effect of the imperial trade of Rome on the urban structure of the capital.

Ostia had been the initial port of Rome located, as the name tells us, at the mouth of the Tiber. Even this outlying port was not the initial provisioning point for the city; while the environs of Rome, Latium, fed the city, grain could be collected in that plain and dispatched to granaries in the city. From those granaries the populace secured wheat for their bread. But with the success of wars against other tribes in Italy and against the Carthaginians, a class of magnates arose in Rome for whom increases in wealth were related most closely to what we would term land speculation. The economic aristocracy began buying lots in Rome and, as Latin peasants tended to abandon the land in response to the seemingly greater attraction of the burgeoning city, farming land outside the city.[32] As the magnates took over the Roman countryside, they found it more profitable, and I suspect more attractive visually, to transform a grain-producing area into a grazing area. The result was a decline in the local provision of grain and an increase in the demand projected to distant producing areas. At that juncture, Ostia was transformed from a naval port into an integral part of the economic geography of the city of Rome. This period seems to have witnessed the beginning of the urban use of the countryside that came when the city's wealth and culture were projected outward to transform Latium.

As Gaul and Egypt began sending grain as a tithe to Rome, Ostia became Rome's first developed port, after having been its first planted colony—for naval defense—in the fourth century B.C. Because the imperial city lay some miles inland from the mouth of the Tiber, the river's mouth became a site of economic settlement only when Rome needed a point of attachment to a maritime supply route bringing goods by merchantmen from an initially thalassic empire. The port that emerged was a river-mouth port built with quays on the bank backed by warehouses (*horrea*); access to the sea was impeded by a typical river-mouth bar, and river navigation to the landward city was subject to great fluctuations in water level. As the demands on the port increased, alleviation of the impedances became a national concern. To correct the river-mouth bar, the emperor Claudius in A.D. 42 began construction of an artificial harbor at Portus, located several miles north of the mouth of the Tiber. The harbor was presumably protected from the silting problem that ultimately added the problem of shallow water at the quays of Ostia to the constant difficulty of its bar. Yet that solution was only good for a time. Then an additional port, Portus Augusti, had to be added to the one

The
Classical City

32. Ibid., p. 27.

begun by Claudius (which was named for Trajan, Portus Traiani). Finally, silt from the Tiber was carried northward in sufficient quantity to grade the shore so heavily that all three ports now lie some distance inland. Rome in modern times depends instead on Livorno or Naples some distance away.

The Distant Trade of Rome

Although no other part of the empire had such a specialized pattern of places engaged dominantly in long-distance (wholesale) trade, doubtless the extensive and economically integrated nature of the Roman Empire led to the existence of what we would term wholesalers and foreign traders, or merchants, in most Roman cities. And, as in the case of Rome itself or Ostia, those merchants would tend to locate peripheral to the city rather than central to it, as did the retail traders clustered around the various fora. In fact, in Rome a special district outside the city's walls and along the bank of the Tiber became the workplace of the merchants. This emporium extended for hundreds of feet along the Tiber (487 meters) and back from it for some distance (90 meters), and was enclosed by a wall and paved.[33] After 193 B.C., goods could be set down there from river boats and held for later distribution to city traders. The next year a specialized lumber dock was added, where timbers from upriver or brought from the west coast of Italy or Sardinia could be discharged and held for use in the rapid expansion of the physical build of Rome that came by both intensification of land use and expansion of the city area. Additional emporia have been found by excavation in Ostia and other places, suggesting a clear distinction in both the Roman economy and the Roman mind between wholesale and retail trade. The emporia were the workplace of wholesale merchants, whereas the *insulae* and *cenacula* served to house the premises of retail shopkeepers. The *horrea*, storing grain, oil, and other staples, were yet another distinct component of an extensive trading system that tended to be located at the edge of a city or port accessible to a strongly ordered and organized flow of goods from established and specialized sources. Within both the *horrea* and the emporia must have been found merchants whose jobs were to anticipate the needs of the city and express those needs in forward orders to distant sources, without ever dealing directly with the ultimate consumer.

A test of the direct tie between the extensive trading system and the size of the city is furnished by the decline and deterioration of the entrepôts with the shrinking of Rome. Because of both barbarian invasions and the visitation of the plague, the city's population declined in the third century A.D., and that drop was reflected in the fast disintegration of Ostia. With smaller needs the imperial ports to the north of the Tiber could suffice, leaving the original colony to stagnate. Ultimately, with the collapse of the Roman Empire and the shrinking of Rome to a small city with mainly local importance, Ostia died, persisting only as a quarry for local builders. Its mercantile system collapsed and with it the city, which had housed at least fifty thousand people in the second century A.D. No longer was it a social and

33. Ibid., p. 30.

The entrance to one of the great warehouses at Ostia, the Horrea Epagathiana.

economic reality but despite the destructive forces of nature and man, much remained. "If we wish to clothe the bare bones of the (surviving) marble plan of Rome with the flesh of buildings a visit to Ostia is an essential complement to a visit to Rome. . . . The streets of Ostia as rebuilt in the second century are the best illustration we can find of the *nova urbs* created by Nero after the great fire (of Rome) of A.D. 64."[34]

The City beyond the Walls: Dioecism

From the Roman experience we can first perceive a persistent expression of city life undervalued for nearly two millennia: the existence of a city life outside the city walls. To set the stage, we should recall that in the Greek pattern of urban settlement the force of synoecism was at work, seeking to join dispersed rural settlements into an urban entity. A duality of residence emerged; most city dwellers considered their roots to be planted in the countryside they had come from initially. In the summer heat or in times of adversity and famine, these city dwellers returned "home"; perhaps even more important, the residential structure within the city reflected these origins with quarters occupied by descendants of people who came from fairly definite rural locales. Under this synoecism the city and the country were one, and citizenship could be held by those few who remained continuously in the countryside as much as by those who returned there only periodically from a normal residence within the urban walls. The relationship was clearly expressed in the Greek political unit, the city-state, which comprised a city and the region around it that had the most direct and continuing synoectic association.

34. Ibid., pp. 13–14.

The
Classical City

Whether we accept the mythological account of Rome's founding as historical fact or not, it seems reasonable to draw a distinction with Greek experience: Rome was the hearth and from it Roman power and culture spread outward to overrun Latium, Etruria, Italy, and ultimately the Western world. There was a single Rome, and citizenship in the republic and empire implied a man's rights while in Rome, and more than his rights when he might be at home in the provinces. The concept was one of the city as the *fons et origo* of civilization, power, and culture—exactly the inverse of the Greek notion. Thus, we find the substitution for the Greek synoecism of a new force that we might, in the absence of a Greek term, make parallel by calling it dioecism, the periodic dispersion of an initially urban population into the countryside.

This dispersion differs totally from the Hellenic example; there danger and crisis depopulated the city, whereas in the Roman instance adversity drew citizens within the walls and closed the gates. Only in prosperity and peace was the countryside part of city life, and the reality of Pax Romana brought forward the urban occupation of rustic areas. When the peace declined, the first signs of change appeared in the disruption and abandonment of the rural part of this geographically complex pattern of dual residence.

The fundamental unit of the rustic part of the Roman duality was the villa, a suburban or rural residence of a person of means. The word derives from *vicus*, a row of houses in the city, implying both the urban origin of the settlers and affluence sufficient to permit them accommodation adequate for a fair retinue of minions. The ultimate in villas was probably that of the emperor Hadrian at Tivoli near Rome. In a park setting he shaped a mélange of extravagant buildings suiting his indulgent fancy, and supplying us with a generic term for a more democratic frivolity in our day—such as Copenhagen's Tivoli Gardens. As wealth accumulated in the hands of Roman senators and other aristocrats and among the administrators and proconsuls in the provinces, the villa became a necessary symbol of middle- and upper-class standing. Perhaps because even the magnates of Rome could occupy only fairly cramped sites within its walls, when they went out to their country villas they sought a sense of openness as expressed in landscaped and organized gardens; the almost inevitable chaos of the crowded city was left behind, and nature was made to conform to human design in the countryside. The Alban Hills and the coast south of Ostia both became dotted with villas, giving evidence that even in the time of the empire the bucolic landscape and marine relief were considered proper contrasts to urban life. In the Alban Hills, however, Rome was nearby and the association was nearly a suburban one, but the journey to the Ostian coast was twenty to twenty-five kilometers (twelve to fifteen miles), so the degree of rustication was greater.

Throughout the empire, villas served as evidence of the attainment of Roman civilization. Numbers of these villas have been excavated; we know them as large and urbane structures decorated with mosaics, fountains, statuary, and murals, more reflective of the city in the countryside than the other way around. The creation of these country estates worked a transfor-

The exurban spread of aristocratic residence reached its epitome in Hadrian's Villa Adriana at Tivoli.

mation of the rural economy and landscape that cannot be overlooked in any analysis of the physical structure of the city, even though that structure was definitely extramural.

As Roman civilization was assailed by barbarian invasions, this component of settlement withered first under the chill of violence and disorder. In 455 the Vandals attacked the Ostian coast, and it is likely that the marine relief to city life held less appeal after that. Certainly within a century or so, most of the countryside of the decaying empire became unsafe and brutal, a quality it retained throughout the Dark Ages. City people gave up dioecism as a practice and spent five hundred years seeking the doubtful protection of walled cities increasingly too commodious to be defended by the shrinking urban populations. Ultimately, many places shed much of the physical city of the Romans, huddling instead in a corner protected from a decaying ruin as much as from the countryside by new walls enclosing the most defensible fragment of the once large imperial city. But it should not be lost on us that Roman civilization sought refuge in the city, maintained its existence there, and ultimately blossomed forth from that seedbed.

City and Countryside

The existence of the two processes, synoecism and dioecism, suggests that the relationship between city and country cannot be assumed to repeat forever throughout history. Doubtless people lived in small, probably wandering bands before they became settled, and their first settlements would seem rural to us. But once cities came into being, did they similarly evolve from a rural to an urban state in all instances? This question is not an idle one but is fundamental to most of the theoretical proposals about cities, as we shall see when we consider the Middle Ages and the two theories historically rooted then. Both von Thünen's "isolated state" and Christaller's "central-place" revolve at least in part around the question of synoecism versus dioecism, though neither phrased his argument in those terms.

Historically, either process seems to find support; the coming together of rural people to found and use a city while continuing an attachment to the countryside was strongly the Greek way, whereas the dispersion of city dwellers into the adjacent open spaces and their shaping of an urban extension better describes what the Romans did. Interestingly, many of the words

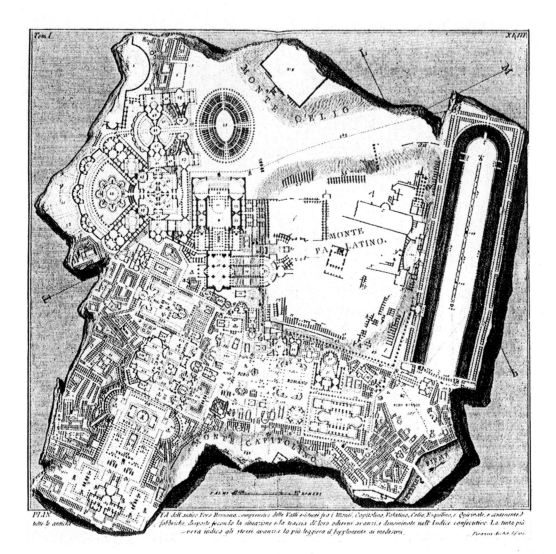

Map of Rome in classical times as reconstructed by Piranesi.

we use to compliment the countryside (idyllic, Arcadian) we inherit from the Greeks, but when we intend to insult that area we turn to Latin derivatives (rustic, villainous, sylvatic, savage, bucolic, rural). Only the Latin word *pastoral* conveys any feelings of appreciation for the countryside, and most of the societies derived from Roman culture most directly tend to employ words of rural reference derogatorily (heathen, pagan, yokel, peasant) while viewing urban reference as complimentary in tone (courtly, courteous, urbane, civilized, citizen).

The contrast between the Greek and the Roman dynamics of settlement ostensibly offered to later times a choice of practice. Presumably cities could grow out of the land, serving as the locale for the exchange of goods among agriculturalists and the site for collection of potential exports and distribution of goods imported from outside the local system. The walls of the cities served to protect these specific economic functions, leaving unsolved

The Continuing City

76

the problem of rural security. Protection could be afforded only very close to the town; more distant areas must depend on local strongpoints, fortified villages or, later, castles. Operating under such a rurally based system, the Greeks shaped first the city-state with an intimate admixture of rural and urban residence and then the planted city as a means of dealing with growing population and expanded political interest. In essence, these communities repeated the scale of the mother state but, unlike the situation found in the older Greek settlements, the new fields of settlement offered no base for synoecism. Even if an aboriginal population remained, and often it was nearly decimated before the planting, the city founded was not a bringing together of its members. This circumstance was likely to set up a cultural and political contrast between the city and the countryside, with the power and decision to effect the settlement pattern remaining largely with the walls.

We may conclude that synoecism is a practical possibility only in a two-stage settlement history, starting with a rural base of an indigenous population and leading to urbanization only as that rural population reaches a level of productive surplus necessitating the establishment of interfamily exchange. If instead the city becomes the instrument of planting population and political power in a different area, its tie to the countryside must be by dioecism. The existence of a prior settled population does not change the conditions; if they come into the city it will be in a dependent, if not actually enslaved, relationship. The planted city, whether a demographic expansion (as were some of the Greek city-states) or a colonial settlement seeking outright the domination of a native population, spreads its culture and influence outward, whereas an emergent central-place witnesses the inward collection of rural attitudes and institutions. Rome itself was an example of a city that, as it became more powerful, spread out to dominate its environs in Latium. And as the empire based on Latium spread, it used the city as the fundamental instrument of cultural, political, and economic integration of the vast state. If Greece was a case of rural implosion to form a city, Rome was a case of urban explosion to shape an empire.

The truth that planted cities spread outward to dominate the region in which they are sited was the prime tool of Roman conquest. By devising a network of settlements and planting its cities, Rome came to dominate the West politically. And because each of those cities was a germinal point for the outward spread of culture, economy, and political power, the area of the Western world came under Roman sway. This point must be understood to comprehend the decline and fall of Rome. If the system had been produced by synoecism, then its destruction would have been slow and mainly biological. Because the system was from the beginning geographically integrated and areally comprehensive, once the core network was disrupted, the collapse was rapid. The populations remained but the basis of urbanization disappeared and the settlement pattern of the western Roman empire rapidly disintegrated into a series of small rural strongpoints, moated keeps and, later, castles, with a battlefield strewn with the dead and decaying bodies of previously vital cities. In the eastern Roman empire the network continued in history and had a stronger base of places that had been originally Greek city-states. So in Byzantium the classical city persisted but ultimately died.

The Disintegration
into Feudalism and
the Dawn of Freedom

3

After the open coun-
try within the Limes
of the Roman Em-
pire, the need in
feudal times was for
walls to protect even
quite small places.

On Christmas morning in the year 800 the Roman pope, Leo III, placed a golden crown on the head of Charles the Great, Charlemagne, as he rose from prayer at services in St. Peter's basilica in Rome. Charles affected surprise; his contemporary biographer, Einhard, tells us that Charlemagne would not have entered the building that morning had he known this event would take place. This tale may have sufficed in the age of romantic chivalry, but in our cynical times doubt does intrude. Nevertheless, the act of Charlemagne's crowning serves well to divide classical from medieval times. Although Charlemagne was proclaimed emperor and *augustus*, those offices could function only in the West. Yet his sway there finally signaled the end of the orthodox succession from the Caesars, and the establishment, first, of a rival to Byzantium and, second, of what we have come to call Western civilization. We are most concerned with that tradition, for within its diverse components the city we wish to look at arose, and the present-day concept of the city in almost all cultures was founded.

The medieval city, as a physical entity and an economic and social institution, established the basic conditions for the domination of modern history both by the political control of the West and by its form of urbanization. Even now, when that political domination has largely disappeared, the urban power shows little sign of decline. Just as the Roman city lasted for a thousand years after the Roman Empire, so the Western city carries on after the end of Western suzerainty.

The Survival of the Roman City in the West

We may profit from a few rather summary conclusions about the history of Rome's decline to help us visualize the experience of cities during the four centuries between 400, when Alaric led his Visigoths southward across the Alps for the first barbarian invasion of Italy, and 800, when a coequal but separate western Holy Roman Empire was created by Leo III and Charlemagne. Those four centuries held numerous barbarian invasions, attempts to control Italy by Byzantium, betrayals, murders, assassinations, and other evidences of destruction of the political and economic order. The city as the central institution of Roman life suffered early in this anarchy and came to be its most obvious victim.

To understand why, we must consider the role the city played in Roman life. First, it was the organic base on which the Roman state grew; largely by replication of the organic unit did Rome take over the Mediterranean and West European world. Just as the republican Romans had spread outward from Rome into Latium, coming to be the political overlords of the countryside in the process of dioecism, so the imperial Romans by dioecism took over their empire, effectively controlling and organizing it through a system of cities.

The Roman Empire was a system of cities interconnected but singly focused, reaching from Mesopotamia to Hadrian's Wall in northern England,

Aachen Cathedral was begun during Charlemagne's reign, and the octagonal section to the left was completed at that time in Romanesque style. The Gothic choir, to the right, was completed in the early fifteenth century.

as a political and economic unit, though the fundamental structure was that of a vast area tributary to Rome itself. In the view of the empire the Eternal City should also be the center of life, culture, political power, and luxury. To fulfill that role, the empire must produce for Rome and, to a lesser degree, for the cities planted by Roman dioecism in Gaul, or Spain, or Mesopotamia. To support their roles as the provincial expression of the imperial state and civilization, these Roman cities of the empire had to harvest a greater return from their hinterlands than their own efforts had produced. As Robert Latouche has noted of all Roman cities, "They were centres not of production, but of expenditure. They constituted for the Empire sources, not of wealth, but of impoverishment."[1]

In such a political situation the economic system must be heavily centered on the support of cities, with every effort made to cause more goods to flow to the center—either Rome itself or its provincial progeny. If the flow of slaves and goods could be maintained, so might the political system, but once the flow decreased, the central city was likely to suffer badly. The denizens of late imperial Rome lacked the patriotism of their republican forebears, showing a tendency to betray the city for material rewards. In Gaul, the chaos of the third century arose when the Alamanni and the Franks broke through the Danubian *limes*, the border defenses, leading to a successful Gallic Empire under Postumus that lasted for a decade (259–69). Only the restoration of those border defenses by a strong central authority

1. Robert Latouche, *The Birth of Western Economy* (New York: Harper and Row, 1966), p. 5.

Feudalism
and the Dawn
of Freedom

81

Even quite small settlements required strong and costly walls to provide reasonable security for towns during the Middle Ages.

under the emperor Diocletian destroyed the Gallic separatism and that of the princes of Palmyra in the east. These events foretold the ultimate experience of Rome and its cities.

At the close of the third century the pattern of Roman defense began to change from one based on frontier protection (and within those *limes* the maintenance of the Pax Romana), which had allowed open cities. Traditionally, walled cities had been necessary only toward the edge of the empire, but as the whole imperial structure began to show cracks, even Rome in 271 had to be walled by the emperor Aurelian. Previously, the imperial city and the larger provincial towns of Gaul and Italy had grown unhindered by walls. "Spacious and airy, possessing many fine, handsome public buildings, they were often completed by residential suburbs much favoured by the wealthiest inhabitants, as for instance those of Trinquetaille at Arles and of Sainte-Colombe at Vienne, separated by the Rhône from the main block of town buildings."[2] But the threat that came with the failure of the *limes* caused walls to be thrown up rapidly in the third and fourth centuries, and certainly the "open city" began to shrink and disappear within the walls.

In part this contraction was probably urged on by the beginning of a secular demographic decline. Slave trading fell with the extinction of Roman conquests. A fairly virulent onset of plagues and epidemics appears to have

The
Continuing City

2. Ibid., p. 7.

flared up in the second century, continuing until the mid-sixteenth century.[3] With circumvallation went population decline, so little need arose to reconstruct the city cores now surrounded by walls. In fact, the urban history of the late empire and succeeding centuries appears to have been one of contraction. The city became both a refuge and a quarry—even in Rome, where Aurelian's Wall was made up of "ramparts hastily thrown together, the masons using indiscriminately altars, inscriptions, columns, whatever material came to hand."[4] The first wall at Autun in Burgundy, built in the early empire, extended for 5,922 meters, whereas the second, constructed in the late empire, was only 1,300 meters.[5] The city did not die, but without question its survival was largely one of hibernation, though some active summers interrupted the aging process.

Understanding the rapidity of the contraction of the Roman city depends in part on an awareness of the basic support of these places. The view is fairly widespread that the barbarian invasions "destroyed" these cities, leaving us with some notion that the hordes sought to shatter a higher civilization. But the "barbarians" were more foreign than vicious, more desirous of participating in the Roman luxury than of destroying it, and not at all numerous. They were vigorous and uninhibited, qualities that did not jibe too well with the fragility of Roman civilization in its later stages. The foreigners wanted to be Romanized, and were to a considerable degree, so the destruction of the Roman urban geography was not their intent. The collapse came because the conditions that allowed the barbarians to enter the empire also tended toward the dismemberment of its integrated network of cities.

The truth of this assertion is shown by the restoration of the Pax Romana in the fourth century when, under Diocletian and Constantine in particular, the *limes* were restored and the empire was ostensibly reintegrated. But the restoration was illusory. Diocletian never succeeded in making Rome whole. He himself established his capital at Nicomedia (fifty miles east of Istanbul) but subsequently added three capitals in an attempt to control a disintegrating empire. They were at Mediolanum (Milan), August Trevivorum (Trier), and Sirmium (in northeast Yugoslavia). In each he placed a member of the imperial quadrumvirate of two emperors, *augusti*, and two heirs apparent, *caesari*. This system rapidly deteriorated into a factionalism tied to geographical partitioning. Even while the quadrumvirate lasted, the emperor Honorius in 402 shifted the dominant capital to Ravenna from Mediolanum, where it had been for a century. Constantine had already moved the eastern capital fifty miles westward to the Golden Horn, founding Constantinople in 330. By the end of the fifth century the division between east and west was becoming decisive, and after that century there were no emperors of the west. Instead, the Gothic invaders established themselves in the Po Basin, raising Mediolanum to a higher political position than Rome, creating the Lombard Kingdom with its crown of iron, and causing the eastern empire to set up a rival capital at Ravenna on the remnants of the land it held in Italy.

3. Robert S. Lopez, *The Commercial Revolution of the Middle Ages, 950–1350* (Englewood Cliffs, N.J.: Prentice-Hall, 1971), p. 12.

4. Latouche, *Western Economy*, p. 7.

5. Ibid., p. 8.

Feudalism and the Dawn of Freedom

We need not follow all of the peregrinations of the seats of government or the varying fates of Rome under the early Roman popes, but we will note the clear destruction of Rome as the primate city of the empire.

The consequence of this destruction was the parceling out of the area that had previously been tributary to Rome and the near destruction of the integrated network that focused trade and administration on the Eternal City. In this dismembered state the provincial cities did not gain at Rome's expense: they all lost, and the "total urbanization" was not as great as it had been.

To understand this absolute decline of city life, we must be aware that the city was economically a parasite on the countryside—but we must beware of generalizing this relationship as the one found throughout time between cities and the countryside. The Romans were architects and engineers, but they were not merchants who could occupy and use effectively the structures they knew so well how to build. To cite several instances of their failure: the Romans had a superbly integrated system of very expensive military roads extending from Armenia to the lowlands of Scotland, but these roads were too narrow to carry the carts that would have been necessary for effective long-distance trade; the city of Rome was the largest ever built up to its time, but it seems to have experienced no economies of scale in the production of goods and to have engaged in no considerable export of manufactures that might have repaid the empire for the vast incoming flow of raw materials and food; and the Romans viewed trade as so lowly an occupation that even the possibly higher economic return from it could not persuade Roman patricians to take it up in place of the less rewarding practice of agricultural capitalism. The basis of Roman wealth remained extractive. Taxes were drawn in ever harsher sums from an empire that was declining in wealth. The Romans captured slaves whose sweated labor would allow the poor manufacturing technology of the times to creak onward for a couple of additional centuries. The accumulated wealth of their neighbors was plundered to add capital to the Roman pot, but that wealth was consumed to maintain the decadent grandeur of Rome.

When taxation dried up, when enslavement was reversed, allowing the enemies to capture and sell Romans, and when plunder was beyond the reach of the legions, the Roman urban system collapsed—not all at once, but with irreversible certainty. In this sequence we find the basis of the *process of contraction* that was the Roman dynamic from around the year 300 to the time of Charlemagne. The failure of the Roman system, its parasitism on the distant countryside, and its critical dependence on the network of urbanization brought the functional structure down. Let it be emphasized that the barbarians did not do it; they sought with all their might to preserve Rome, but they lacked the numbers or the skill to do so, as the Romans lacked the energy or the will. We tend to look upon the Romans as superb city builders, which they were only in the precise sense. They were great engineers, but as breadwinners who could maintain the life of the cities they designed, they were incompetent. Not insignificantly, the political successor of the Roman emperors, the Roman pope, is still denominated the leading engineer—*pontifex maximus*.

Contradiction Almost to Extinction

The search for the roots of the modern city in the Western world must begin in the Dark Ages, whose obscurity unquestionably hides a revolution of urban life similar to that of the seventeenth to nineteenth centuries. To borrow a modern term, the Dark Ages are perhaps more a black box than a time of collapse of civilization, as they once were thought: at the onset of the ninth century the classical Roman city still existed, whereas at the close of that period a new form of city emerged. The process of transformation may not be fully chronicled, but its outcome is reasonably clear and well known.

Charlemagne's Holy Roman Empire was ostensibly shaped from a Roman inheritance, but it was markedly different from its predecessor. It contained most of present-day East and West Germany, the Netherlands, Austria, and Czechoslovakia, which had not lain within the older *limes*, whereas it omitted Spain, southern Italy, the Balkans, the Near East, and North Africa, which had. The Holy Roman Empire was basically German rather than Roman. Charlemagne may have been crowned in Rome but he lived, when he was at home, in Aix-la-Chapelle, Aachen, at the juncture of modern Belgium, Holland, and West Germany. Much of the time he was wandering about his empire, pushing its limits outward in warfare, enjoying its pleasures in hunting, or seeking its governance by periodic residence in Frankfurt or some other provincial city. The cities of the Holy Roman Empire either stood as contractions of formerly more extensive classical towns, or were newly founded by the Franks in that part of Charlemagne's empire added by those warriors to what they had taken over from the Romans. In either case the towns were small and weak. Seemingly, the Franks inherited an almost dead institution, and they possessed too little personal understanding of its form to rejuvenate it.

The Franks had been barbarians with a history of movement rather than strongly fixed settlement. For many years they were thought to have been practitioners of a primitive collectivism, *Markgenossenschaft*, but that view has been rejected by recent historians who think instead that the Franks ultimately became at best a village people:

> The hamlet appears to have been, in many instances, their primitive unity, for though the Germans (Franks) had little liking for town life they seem from early times to have been loath to live in isolation. Families willingly joined together in small settlements (*Weiler*) consisting of several homesteads detached from each other, wooden huts covered with thatch, or even underground shelters roofed with turf, examples of which can still be seen (among the people of Germanic origin) in Iceland. Huts and shelters were dotted here and there without any preconceived plan and the same lack of order was evident also in the villages, groups of dwellings believed to represent a more recent stage of settlement. To these villages which have no set plan, German scholars have given the name of *Haufendorfer* ("thrown-together villages").[6]

6. From August Meitzen, *Siedelung*, 1:47, in ibid., p. 33.

Feudalism
and the Dawn
of Freedom

Around these *Haufendorfer* the land was organized in private holdings cultivated by the residents. The Frankish invaders brought this pattern with them into Gaul when they crossed the *limes*, which extended basically along the Rhine from Lake Constance to the North Sea.

When the Salian Franks gained control of this area in the fourth and fifth centuries, they brought with them a form of settlement different from the one the Romans had developed in Gaul and a contrasting viewpoint on property. The Franks had shaped a society dependent on small landholding and, in simplest terms, the sanctity of private property. Of the Salian Franks, Latouche concludes, "What a study of the Salic Law does bring out . . . is the strong preference of the Franks for individual ownership. . . . This makes it clear that the Frankish occupation strengthened the small peasant and family holding in those areas in which the Franks settled."[7]

The Franks introduced to Gaul, and to its border zone with Germany, private small holdings that contrasted sharply with the landed estates that the Romans had developed there. Those Roman villas were the domain of a group of aristocrats, *potentes*, who shunned trade as ungentlemanly and who had come to look upon country living as the proper state of those possessed of power. At the same time that the Franks were bringing in the peasant holding for the masses, their leaders were taking over the notion of the villa and transforming it into what we now term the medieval manor. In doing so, however, they were introducing a potential conflict with their own followers of lesser status, who held strongly the Frankish view of a free peasantry. This view was protected by a Salic Law that came to be recorded, and thus less subject to tampering, when the art of writing was learned from the Romans.

A second conflict grew up in a rather complicated way when the Franks invaded this frontier zone just west of the Rhine. As a barbarian group they had lacked any understanding of speculation on capital and lending money at interest, as noted by Tacitus,[8] yet they held to private ownership of property. When they moved into the frontier of Gaul, the migration was in part a peaceful fusing of peoples, so the Franks took over some of the practices of the Romans. One practice often frowned on but engaged in of necessity was trade for profit and the use of capital for interest. Mingling all of these practices, the Franks brought forth a powerful potential for important advances in the world of trade. But as their skills were ripening, Christianity overtook them, and they were confronted with the attitude enunciated by the Fathers of the Church, who looked upon profit and money interest as *turpe lucrum*, sinful gain.

The Processes of Contraction and Parochialization

Historians extensively discuss the reasons for the Dark Ages of urbanization that came in the ninth and tenth centuries. The great Belgian economic historian, Henri Pirenne, argued that the breaking of the Mediterra-

7. Latouche, *Western Economy*, p. 80.

8. Tacitus, *Germania*, 26, trans. by H. Mattingly (West Drayton, Middlesex: Penguin Books, 1948), p. 122.

nean trade link, due to the coming of the Muslims, brought on economic stagnation and decline in Europe. That Mediterranean link had for Rome been "the bulwark of both its political and economic unity."[9] Pirenne held that the barbarian invasions had not led to urban decline, because the "supposed dislike of the barbarians for towns is an admitted fable to which reality has given the lie." On the frontiers barbarians may have pillaged and burned Roman towns, but "it is none the less true that the immense majority survived the invasions." Most of the larger cities of that part of Europe held by the Romans are even today those founded by that empire.[10] "It is also well established that these cities were centers of an economic activity which itself was a survival of the preceding [Roman] civilization." All cities were markets for the surrounding countryside, "the winter homes of great landed proprietors of the neighborhood and, if favorably situated, the center of a commerce the more highly developed in proportion to its nearness to the shores of the Mediterranean."[11] This last condition reveals the critical nature of the link across the Mediterranean, broken by the radical transformation of the urban geography of Europe.

The barbarians did not seek to destroy cities; nevertheless, they experienced their decline. The change came in an odd way, as trade contracted under the barbarians from the general exchange of bulk commodities—grain, oil, wine, and the like—as under the Romans, to the trading in small quantities of high luxuries. Two processes were at work: contraction of all trade into a much smaller compass than before, and parochialization of the provision of most staples into local production and consumption. This change in trade created two new institutions that became archetypal of the Dark Ages: first, contracted trade, and its handover to a group of foreign merchants able to deal internationally in a new multinational and multi-religious Western civilization; second, the creation of a new rural economy to care for what were now localized productions and demands—feudalism, with its economic backstay, the manor. The international traders came to be known as Orientals, which translates today to Jews and Levantines or Syrians. As non-Christians they could trade with Islam more successfully; as international men they could pass through a newly fragmented Europe serving, strangely, as the agents of the papacy, collecting the massive tithes that beggared Europe outside Rome and kept the Roman curia in luxury and hauteur. As papal agents, these Orientals could cross the multitude of frontiers yet remain exempt from the exactions that made trade almost impossible to the Frenchman or the German. Thus, they conducted what little distant trading was done, in lines where the price could be vastly inflated to reflect the difficulty encountered. Only luxury items moved any distance.

The parochialization of staple provision shaped the feudal economy, causing a strong push toward autarky—local self-sufficiency—so that each area could produce only the most essential of products. Necessity became

9. Henri Pirenne, *Medieval Cities: Their Origins and the Revival of Trade* (Princeton: Princeton University Press, 1925), pp. 1–2.
   10. Ibid., p. 11.
   11. Ibid., p. 13.

institutionalized to the extent that manors of petty feudal holdings sought self-sufficiency and rigid control of trade. On the one hand, they were assured a continuing sufficient supply of those things produced locally before feudalism by keeping the items at home; on the other, this rigid control sought to protect infant local activities against periodic disruption through more distant trade. And finally, the absence of much long-distance trade necessitated a system of financial support for the manor or barony through excises on goods locally exchanged. Market tolls, murrage tolls to cover the assumed cost of providing walls for protection, pontage at local bridges, and other tithes, assizes, and excise taxes assured that the protected local economy furnished the feudal lord the support that had come previously from exactions on more distant trade. In the end, the desire to defend those local excises was crucial in seeking a clearly defined parochial trading area.

The processes of contraction and parochialization in the Dark Ages had a rather distinct expression even within the low level of urban development characteristic of the time. The dependence on the foreign trader led to the need to create areas of tolerance within the small towns where alien religious and social practices would be permitted under the notion of extraterritoriality. Quarters were defined for Syrians or Jews distinct from the rest of the orthodox, Catholic town. As agents of the Roman curia, these unbelievers were protected and given great power. In part, a strong rejection of this ultramontane meddling caused the main Western nations to evict the Jews in the later Middle Ages, as they did the Jesuits in the nineteenth-century period of anticlericalism.

The parochialization of the staple economy to that of the manor or barony had two effects on cities. First, it greatly reduced the need for, and support of, cities. Roman towns shrank in size as well as in numbers, because distant trading no longer amounted to more than a periodic peddling of luxury goods by foreign traders. In their place came the local central-places for the feudal economy, little more than marketplaces to which the country people came in order to swap with one another the goods produced in the local natural economy, as it is sometimes called. These central-place villages were the outgrowth of feudalism and were new on the urban scene, literally unknown among the Romans and little developed wherever the distant-trading economy could be preserved. Thus, Walter Christaller's central-place theory, which we shall subsequently examine, was an outgrowth of the two contractive forces of the Dark Ages.

The constraints placed on the Oriental merchants circulating through the Europe of the early Middle Ages reflected their moral ambiguity, which Pirenne cites. "The Oriental merchants of the Frankish Empire were virtually engaged in wholesale trade. Their boats, after being discharged on the quays of Marseilles, certainly carried back, on leaving the shore of Provence, not only passengers but return freight." Among the most important of those freights was "human chattels—that is to say slaves."[12] This was a trade of slaves for luxuries; Western Europe provided the unfortunates and

12. Ibid., pp. 19–20.

the Levant the luxuries. Providentially, the disruption and chaos of post-Charlemagne Europe substantially cut off the supply of slaves. In their absence, the Syrians and Jews no longer very actively sought to trade. With wholesale trade in the hands of foreigners, town life began to suffer an eclipse. In the fifth century industrial production in Europe was declining and trade was so precarious that export over any distance became nearly impossible. In that situation the occupation of merchant fell "into the hands of Orientals, chiefly Syrians. . . . These men engaged in trade fully alive to the risks it entailed in an unsettled age, and determined to reap enormous profits, drawing upon themselves universal execration in the process." In such a climate of trade it is little wonder that "it was probably at this time that lack of merchants resident in towns which were becoming ever more depopulated gave rise to the practice of entrusting to specially commissioned agents the task of buying articles and provisions in the local market."[13]

The process of contraction led, oddly, to more markets than existed with distant trading. But Pirenne holds,

> The great number of markets (*mercatus*), which were to be found in the ninth century, in no way contradicts [the notion of the decline of trade]. They were, as a matter of fact, only small market-places, instituted for the weekly provisioning of the populace by means of retail sale of foodstuffs from the country. . . .
>
> For an economy of exchange was substituted an economy of consumption. Each demesnes, in place of continuing to deal with the outside, constituted from this time on a little world of its own. It lived by itself and for itself, in the traditional immobility of the patriarchal form of government. The ninth century is the golden age of what we have called the closed domestic economy and which we might call, with more exactitude, the economy of no markets.[14]

In that economy the central-place was born. Local people traded among themselves and only specially constituted agents—either Oriental peddlers or servants of the monasteries and great manors sent to buy at a distance—had any trading function independent of actual production and consumption. It was a world of no markets, which saw the rise of the chapman, or peddler. It had no true cities, in Pirenne's view. If by *city* is "meant a locality the population of which, instead of living by working the soil, devotes itself to commercial activity, the answer [to whether there were cities in the Dark Ages] will have to be 'No.' The answer will also be in the negative if we understand by 'city' a community endowed with legal personality and possessing laws and institutions peculiar to itself." But if by *city* is meant a place of administration and fortification, then the Dark Ages had nearly as many cities as the later Middle Ages. "That is merely another way of saying that the cities which were then to be found were without two of the fundamen-

13. Latouche, *Western Economy*, pp. 27–28.
14. Pirenne, *Medieval Cities*, pp. 34–35, 46.

tal attributes of the cities of the Middle Ages and of modern times—a middle-class population and a communal organization."[15]

The Church Preserves the City

The Roman city became a fossil shell, beginning in the fifth century but most notably at the end of the ninth century in late Carolingian times. What, then, became of cities? Who could benefit from possession of such a fossil shell? The answer is obvious: the medieval church. Despite the humility and simplicity on which Christianity was founded, the formal church, which viewed itself as the instrument of ecclesiastical continuity, quickly eschewed such gentle poverty. When Constantine was won over to the new faith, he was not gripped by any will to abandon either his power or its physical expression. In the New Rome that was Constantinople, grandeur was decreed. Soon the greatest church in Christendom—the church of the Holy Thought, Hagia Sophia—was built and opened with Constantine's boast, "O, Solomon, Thou art Vanquished." Though the eastern and western churches ultimately separated, neither sought austerity or simplicity of structure. The Roman church deliberately attempted to become the successor to Constantine as much as or more than to Peter. In this attempt, the geographical system of cities that the imperial Romans had shaped was most appealing to the powerful clerics.

Not only were the cities themselves useful, but also the system of tribute on which they were founded seemed directly applicable to the new religious empire. We have already seen the significance of the collection of tithes from all parts of Roman Christendom; it was important enough to make allies of the curia and the Orientals. While Catholics were told by Ambrose and other Church Fathers that profit itself was dubious, interest on money was sinful, and trade suspect, the pope did not inveigh against the traders from the East whose transport of tithes supported the power and pomp of the church.

Because the cities so symbolized established authority yet stood so useless in early feudal times, the church was probably the only institution giving them much thought. Tours, Lyon, Narbonne, Cologne, Trier, and a number of Roman towns became the seats of powerful bishops, who wielded influence within the church but also served on occasion, or commonly, as lay lords of the cities themselves. The bishops of Trier were among the great magnates of medieval times, and even as late as the beginning of the Industrial Revolution, the prince bishop of Liège was a ruler of great significance. As the most universal institution of its time, the church maintained considerable trade. Even more, its practices of relic worship and pilgrimage encouraged travel. Several of the bastides that we will consider in chapter 5 began as way stations on the great pilgrimage to Santiago de Compostela. Thus, it was the church that first saw the glimmerings of an economic purpose for towns greater than their rather rustic base of serving as tiny central-places.

15. Ibid., p. 56.

Society Diffuses in the Countryside: Feudalism

At the same time the church came to dominate cities, in the countryside a new order, which reflected in part changes begun in Roman times, was coming into existence. While the empire was growing, interregional commerce had been "more lively, but dwindled as the entire Roman world became more and more uniform. Differences in latitude, and hence in climate, are not exceedingly great between one Mediterranean region and another; wherever they went, the Romans planted the vegetables and trees which they liked, and shunned both the far North, where grapes would not ripen, and the far South, where olive trees would not grow."[16] And artisans in Roman towns learned to reproduce the products of Greece and Italy. The real change came, however, when the Carolingian Empire shifted the basis of power to those rural estates that had evolved from the Roman villas. For a while after Charlemagne the integrated imperial state could be maintained, but the vote of the knife led to assassination of so many of the Frankish kings that the coherence of the rural aristocracy nearly disappeared. In its place came the concentration of real political power and economic concern on the rural manor operated under a system of feudalism.

The late French historian Marc Bloch remains the most respected scholar of feudalism; we may usefully adopt his definition of that system. The age was an interregnum of great length between the highly centralized organization of the Roman Empire and a return to that integrated state at the hands of the fifteenth- and sixteenth-century French and English monarchs who pi-

16. Lopez, *Commercial Revolution*, p. 7.

The cathedral in Trier, to the left, was begun as a Roman building before the inhabitants were Christianized, and transformed into a church for the powerful Prince Bishop of Trier.

**Feudalism
and the Dawn
of Freedom**

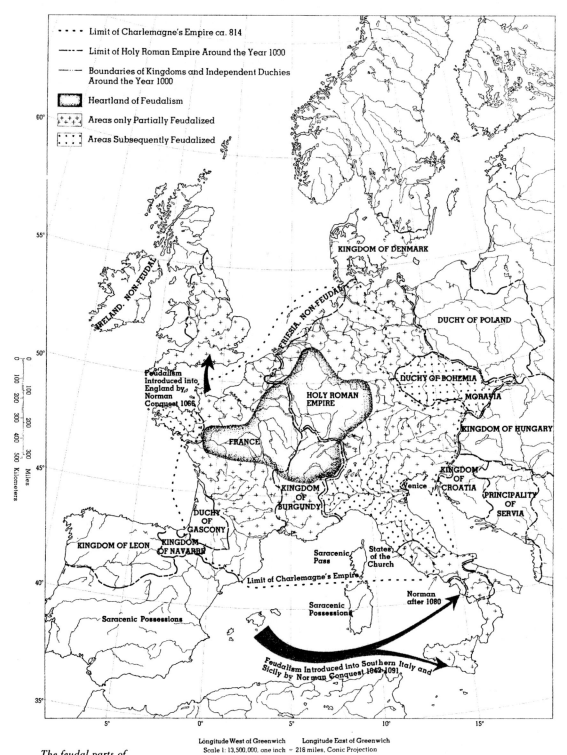

Legend:

- **· · · ·** Limit of Charlemagne's Empire ca. 814
- **—·—·—** Limit of Holy Roman Empire Around the Year 1000
- **—··—··—** Boundaries of Kingdoms and Independent Duchies Around the Year 1000
- Heartland of Feudalism
- Areas only Partially Feudalized
- Areas Subsequently Feudalized

IRELAND, NON-FEUDAL

KINGDOM OF DENMARK

FRIESLA, NON-FEUDAL

DUCHY OF POLAND

Feudalism
Introduced into
England by
Norman
Conquest 1066

HOLY ROMAN
EMPIRE

DUCHY OF BOHEMIA

MORAVIA

FRANCE

KINGDOM OF HUNGARY

KINGDOM
OF
BURGUNDY

Venice

KINGDOM
OF
CROATIA

PRINCIPALITY
OF
SERVIA

DUCHY
OF
GASCONY

KINGDOM OF LEON

KINGDOM
OF NAVARRE

Saracenic
Pass

States
of the
Church

Limit of Charlemagne's Empire

Saracenic Possessions

Saracenic
Possessions

Norman
after 1080

Feudalism Introduced into Southern Italy and
Sicily by Norman Conquest 1042–1091

Longitude West of Greenwich   Longitude East of Greenwich
Scale 1: 13,500,000, one inch = 216 miles, Conic Projection

0 100 200 300 400 500 Kilometers
0 100 200 300 Miles

The feudal parts of
Europe.

oneered the nation-state. European feudalism was "the outcome of the violent dissolution of older societies," unintelligible outside the context of the Frankish invasions of Gaul at the time of the collapse of the Roman Empire. Those invasions "by forcibly uniting two societies originally at very different stages of development disrupted both of them and brought to the surface a great many modes of thought and social practices of an extremely primitive character." The primitive qualities were shown by "a far-reaching restriction of social intercourse, a circulation of money too sluggish to admit of a salaried officialdom, and a mentality attached to things tangible and local." But the transitional quality of the custom of the period was clearly shown by the fact that when "these conditions began to change, feudalism began to wane."[17] In this broad context, cities shrank until feudalism came into bloom; as it withered, cities grew anew. The system of feudalism and the structure of cities appear historically to be reciprocal.

Most significantly the cause of this period of urban eclipse was the concept of wealth innate to feudalism. Historically, the system had grown up to provide fighting men to sovereigns of one sort or another who were engaged in endless bloody bickering. Unlike the Romans, these kings and princes had no real source of money after the era of plunder and tribute passed. So in return for the dual grants of "homage" and "fealty," passed upward from their feudal vassals, the sovereign made to them a retributive grant of a "benefice," almost invariably a source of income. In an agricultural economy, this practice meant that the sovereign gave to a knight an estate of some sort from which that vassal could hope for economic support. The scale of the estate was normally proportional to the importance of the vassal, because the benefice was a substitute for any salary he might expect for his services. Principal feudatories, the major servants of a king—dukes, margraves, and counts in the lay establishment and important bishops and abbots in the ecclesiastical one—could expect large domains, which they in turn divided into smaller benefices for their subfeudatories. This system of support for the monarch and for his principal feudatories required geographical division of the economy, because the area a man might dominate was in direct proportion to the scale of his wealth.

In the West and in feudal times, the equation of areal dominion and possible wealth is striking:

The feudal system meant the rigourous economic subjection of a host of humble folk to a few powerful men. Having received from earlier ages the Roman *villa* [which in some respects anticipated the manor] and the German village chiefdom, it extended and consolidated these methods whereby men exploited men, and combined inextricably the right to the revenues from the land with the right to exercise authority; it fashioned from all this the true manor of medieval times. And this it did partly for the benefit of an oligarchy of priests and monks whose task it was to propitiate Heaven, but chiefly for the benefit of an oligarchy of warriors.[18]

17. Marc Bloch, *Feudal Society*, vol . 2, *Social Classes and Political Organization* (Chicago: University of Chicago Press, 1954), p. 443.
18. Ibid.

The Manor: The Anticity

The manor was truly an economic institution, though it had legal, customary, and social attributes. Its purpose was to maximize sufficiency of local provision by undertaking to grow as many necessary crops as possible, to fashion its own tools, to weave and make its own clothing, and otherwise to create a closed economic system. Did this system come from desire or resignation? Did the manor seek autarky, or merely accept it in a world where trade had become very difficult? Without question, the lords of manors appreciated the value of trade; they used most jealously any market privileges they could garner, as well as rights of pontage, murrage, tollage, and other levies on goods moving in trade through their domains.

Much as lords might accept the desirability of increasing the geographical system of trade, geographical and political conditions made enlargement unlikely. As in the Roman Empire, a strong force must have existed under feudalism and within the system of manors leading to the creation of identity. If one seeks self-sufficiency to cut down money flows in a time when money is rare, then one tends to try to do everything that the climate and resources allow. Thus, if one member of the oligarchy produces certain commodities, every member is likely to produce them; there being no other basis of both wealth and power than land, monopoly of its produce and the local market would be most natural. One can then ask how much extra-manorial trade is likely. The manorial market is valuable mainly because the lord can control the economic lives of his vassals, use the satisfaction of their needs to gain wealth—either through market tolls or through purchase or barter of goods produced on the manor, in which he has the landlord's share of interest—and exact the largest possible share from the overall produce of the manor. In essence, the manorial system offered a great incentive for the lord of the manor to deny economic access to his tenants to any but himself. No better system could be devised to damp down tendencies toward urbanization.

The conflict arose between the lord of a potential trade center and his peer in the countryside. Since the return to be earned from the manor and the wealth of the master stood in direct equation, two courses were open to the lord seeking to maximize his economic position: (1) he might seek to produce an item for sale through a possible city market in open trading, thus earning money that he could in turn employ to buy goods to compensate his feudal minions for their efforts oriented to this money economy, or (2) he might seek to contain the economic activities of his manor to reduce the outflow of money; that is, he might seek a localized autarky. Clearly, neither system would be absolute even in feudal times, but one or the other course would probably dominate.

The key to which form of economic endeavor—autarky or specialization for external trading—would take over on the manor lies not in the manor itself but in the successful survival of a nonmanorial urban market. This argument contradicts much of the established thinking on the trade base of urbanization, but logic requires the introduction of such a caveat. The central-place theory holds that cities grow out of rurally based "support" of

The manoir in the French department of Lot et Garonne still shows some of the characteristics of medieval manors that gave it its name. Outbuildings and barns were used for manorial artisans and stores, and the house itself sheltered a large biological and occupational family.

customers seeking to converge on a town market to secure satisfaction of their physical wants and demands for service. Yet if we examine the feudal economy, which has at least implicitly been assumed to have created this central-place pattern, we find that the process does not work out as the theory assumes. Trade among self-sufficient economic units does not bring towns into being. We may assume that within any geographical region sufficiently interconnected to permit trade in feudal times, uniformity of productive opportunities was sufficient to make intermanorial trade idle. The productivity of the manor was shaped to create as closed an economic system as the local resources would permit. Natural disaster might project the manor into outside purchasing, but normally such trade would exist only for those items of desire that could not be produced on the manor. For the most part the local failure would be in luxury items that only the lord or his most intimate retainers would purchase. The basis of trade existed, but on nothing like the scale assumed in central-place theory.

In a geographical situation where cities are interspersed throughout a rural manorial economy, we may reasonably assume trade in basic commodities. Townspeople could not and would not practice the sort of autarky typical of the feudal countryside; for them, trade would be absolutely essential to survival. Much of the accepted thought would have it that towns grow out of the countryside to care for its demands rather than that they have a separate and independent existence. Yet the separate existence must be the case, for there was no large basis for trade among manors.

Among the Romans the city came from a system independent of the countryside; to the extent that it survived, we may assume that feudalism and urbanism are two distinct systems, each with a striking historical base and possibly of simultaneous occurrence. We may question the relative power of the two systems; the Romans and their eastern successors in Byzantium managed to maintain an extensive-urban system whereas, following Marc Bloch's argument, the grafting on of the Germanic notion of localized chiefdoms first disrupted and then replaced the Roman system in the West by one we call feudalism. This substitution was no doubt slow but could not have been stopped once the concept of the manor was shaped as the basic component of power, protection, and trade. Every withdrawal of land from

Feudalism
and the Dawn
of Freedom

95

the Roman extensive-urban system weakened it, but the system could continue as long as any remnant remained of its original purpose—interconnecting distant places and providing an externalized system.

A Germanic Theory of City Formation and Support

In 1933 the German geographer Walter Christaller published what has come to be a classic proposal in which he sought "the causes of towns being large or small, because we believe that there is some ordering principle heretofore unrecognized that concerns their distribution."[19] That ordering process is, in its most fundamental form, a "crystallization of mass around a nucleus" according to a "centralistic principle" that produces a "central organ," whether it be a medieval town or a modern town, a village or a vast metropolis.

Quoting Robert Gradmann, Christaller states that the "*chief profession* of a town [is] namely, 'to be center of its rural surroundings and mediator of local commerce with the outside world.'"[20] The framework of Christaller's thought is regional, and "the chief profession—or characteristic—of a town is to be the center of a region." The only alternative comes in "dispersed places, i.e., all those places which are not centers." Such dispersed places may be "areally bound ones—those settlements the inhabitants of which make their living from resources found at specific locations," such as mining settlements or towns "bound at absolute points (not relative ones as in the case of central-places)—for instance, bridges and fords, border or custom places, and especially harbors." Christaller finds a major exception to this dichotomy between areally bound and point-bound places in those "settlements which are not bound to a central point, an area, or an absolute point. Monastery settlements (but not shrines, which are usually bound by the place of miracle) are examples," as are "settlements of workers who perform work in the home, and *large industrial settlements*, the locations of which are seldom determined according to any economic advantages such as transportation facilities or the labour supply."[21]

We may emphasize the strong areal and rural base that Christaller uses. He constantly reiterates his notion that towns grow out of the countryside, that the flow of country people to and from the town accounts for its location and functions. He does not accept a long-distance, systemic, base for cities, or the notion that the town may preexist the rural hinterland and, in fact, bring that agricultural development into being. Looking back at the history of the classical city, both Gradmann and Christaller accept the possibility of a Greek-style synoecism but overlook entirely the possibility of a geographically extensive dioecism such as Rome brought into being. In their minds, evolution can come only from the gathering together of small, local, agricultural support in the erection of central-places.

19. Walter Christaller, *Central Places in Southern Germany (Die zentralen Orte in Süddeutschland)*, trans. Carlisle W. Baskin (Englewood Cliffs, N.J.: Prentice-Hall, 1966), p. 2.

20. Robert Gradmann, "Schwäbische Städte," in *Zeitschrift der Gesellschaft für Erdkunde* (1916), p. 427, quoted in ibid., p. 16.

21. Christaller, *Central Places*, p. 17. Emphasis supplied.

Christaller next defines the method of this collection of small increments of support. He introduces the notion that people seeking to secure a good or service will establish a limit on the distance they are willing to travel to obtain that good. This property of local trade has been rendered in English as the "range of a good"; it is measured in radial distance from a center when that place still serves as the origin of goods or services for the "dispersed population" living outside the town. Related to this property of convergence is the notion that in creating and maintaining that central-place, a minimum total of activity would support a retailer or service worker there. Christaller called this activity the "inner range of a good," because it referred to the minimum radial distance from the center that would be large enough to enclose a population sufficient in number to support one unit of retail trade or service. Because of this marginal quality of the inner range, American geographers have tended to substitute the term *threshold,* leaving *range* to designate the maximum travel distance of potential customers. Thus, *threshold* refers to the minimum total of support that will bring a retail trade into being, and *range* to a maximum distance people are willing to travel to secure that particular good.

It is assumed that if the population density increases, a threshold population can be secured from a less extensive area. Equally, if the threshold can be tightened up, a considerable economic advantage would fall to potential customers if they could secure a good by traveling less distance. The Christallerian argument is that alternative central-places would spring up somewhere outside the original town, cutting a new tributary area out of its original hinterland. In this way, the argument holds, successive basic central-places will be carved out of potential-customer regions, and in this process we can find the explanation for a dense distribution of towns across an agricultural region.

The other dynamic quality that Christaller seeks is found in the erection of a superstructure of larger towns on this basic central-place base. If the range of a commonly sought good is limited, that of a rarely purchased good can be assumed to be much greater. Thus, the trading town in which it is purchased may be far more distant from the customer. Related to this quality is the lesser frequency of purchase, which implies that a larger threshold population will be needed to support one establishment providing that particular good or service. Thus, the basic central-places will stand in relationship to a smaller number of more specialized places—with higher threshold populations and greater ranges of goods. If this second step is possible, so are further increases in threshold and range, leading to ever-smaller numbers of central-places of increasingly higher "order." The result is a hierarchical place pyramid, broad on the bottom to include all the basic trading towns, with the one dominant city of a country at the top.

Failings of Central-Place Theory

Let us examine critically the basic tenets of central-place theory in light of the historical geography of Western European urbanism up to the time of the classical-medieval transition.

Although it is not formally stated, central-place theory has woven within it an assumption rooted deep in the German attitude toward settlement and cities. The Germanic notion of the local chiefdom was the contribution the Franks brought to their forcible embrace of Roman civilization. Charlemagne, though a great warrior and a quintessential Christian ruler, was a barbarian Frank in his understanding of cities. When he died, the Frankish practices inherited from a spacious rural past took bloody effect. His empire was divided, as every schoolchild knows, among his three sons, and Europe has never been the same again. That dynastic history does not concern us, but rather the practice of viewing land as personal holdings unrelated to a broader geographical system of regional or economic integration. The Romans would never have split their empire into bits; instead, they created four jointly ruling emperors in an effort to maintain its geographical integrity. But the Germanic Franks did split Charlemagne's empire among his three sons, and their heirs in turn split it much more complexly.

This concept of land as the personal possession of the sovereign or the major feudatory fostered the peculiar economic-geographical pattern of the Middle Ages. Land was used selfishly and defensively, kept apart from its neighbors in the interest of increasing the landowner's return to maximum possession. As powerful families, and the dynasties that followed their founders, married, gave birth to sons, and witnessed the death of the successive generations, the view of land as personal property was enhanced. A powerful duke or count might hold manors in a dozen different areas; his possession was most important in determining the economic practices employed there. Given the commonly discontinuous nature of feudal family holdings, it is not the least surprising that economic separation usually dominated over economic integration.

In this basically Germanic context of settlement, Walter Christaller shaped his theory. A man may write unaware of the parochial quality of the geographical environment in which he operates. The notion that towns grow out of their adjacent countryside would not sound questionable to Christaller, raised in Bavaria where the last vestiges of feudalism had been given up less than a century before his birth. Only in 1808 was the practice of serfdom abolished there. And "on the whole serfdom appears as a characteristic corollary of feudalism. It grew up as a consequence of customary subjection and natural husbandry; it melted away with the coming of the industrial and commercial age."[22] No one would question Christaller's wide knowledge of commerce, but we have on the evidence of his own major work the justification for doubting that his system had much applicability to the location of industrial activity. His was a late feudal picture and pertinent as such to the Germany of his time. But this picture was a poor design for discussion of the industrial world without a feudal past in which all Americans, and many other people, live.

Central-place theory is a classical expression of economic design based on excise taxation—the imposition of levies on the transport, import, export, storage, and sale of goods in clearly defined geographical markets.

22. Paul Vinogradoff, "Serfdom," *Encyclopaedia Britannica*, 11th ed. (1910).

Related to excise levies was the requirement of charters of right to engage in trade, again a way to "tax" entry to and participation in trade. To give a charter value, local monopolies on entry and participation are essential. Thus, by splitting landholdings into manors or defined fiefdoms, lords could gain more repayments for charters than otherwise, a fact that would have encouraged the minute parceling out of medieval holdings, as history tells us happened. Within the Holy Roman Empire, this minute geographical division was carried to the extreme. In an area of that empire, at Berneck in Bavaria, Walter Christaller was born in 1893 and made the early observations in support of his theory.

After the creation of the notion of the nation-state, other forms of taxation came to substitute for excise levies. Edward IV of England in the mid-fifteenth century was the first king to turn away from land grabbing as a source of revenue and begin investment as a road to personal wealth. In this he followed on the model of the Renaissance magnates of Italy. But as late as 1785 the Bavarian king, Charles Theodore, had so little attachment to his kingdom that he plotted tiresomely with the Hapsburgs in an attempt to swap that south German realm to Austria in exchange for the Austrian Netherlands and the title of king of Burgundy. It is inconceivable that the French or English king would have so lacked national patriotism in the eighteenth century, but such was the case in still semifeudal south Germany, where central-place theory was first worked out.

If we accept the proposal that Walter Christaller was operating in a historical-geographical context that carried feudal notions as near to the present as is to be found anywhere in Western civilization, then we can relate this theoretical proposal, central-place theory, to the rural-urban structure of feudal times to some useful effect. Feudalism in its essential form was basically a rural system. What towns grew out of feudalism, rather than surviving from earlier times in the inhospitable medium of feudal rural structure, would of necessity be based on agricultural support. Additionally, they would tend to have as their tributary areas—within the composite upper range of their collective goods—that amount of country over which the lord of their domain held sway. Because his wealth was the wealth of his domain, he would try hard to prevent trading beyond his bounds. Thus, in trying to account for the size of tributary areas we are to a reasonable degree accounting for what has been historically the possible domain of the basic subfeudatory. To phrase it another way, we are answering the question of how much countryside a baron could defend as his own in a time of political fragmentation and conflict when the desire for increased wealth led almost inexorably to the coveting of another man's domain.

A further component in this shaping of the basic trading place to emerge from the originally rural-agricultural medium of feudalism is to be found in serfdom itself. One of the fundamental concepts of the institution exists when "serfdom is very often conceived as a perpetual adherence to the soil of an estate owned by a lord" on the part of the laborers in those fields, so "serfdom became the prevailing condition of the lower orders during the middle ages."[23] The serf possessed a half-freedom, which Paul Vinogradoff

23. Ibid.

saw as an outgrowth of a dual background that brought into a single medieval serving class the descendants of Frankish and Roman slaves (for whom feudalism decreed the loss of half their enslavement) and the descendants of the overrun Roman *coloni* (for whom feudalism meant the loss of half their freedom). A particular consequence of that half-freedom was the loss of the freedom of movement while keeping, by custom, a fair part of the freedom of person. What resulted was a praedial attachment, which decreed that the serf must not leave the immediate confines of the domain to whose soil he stood in "perpetual adherence." Given this loss of the freedom of movement, it is not surprising that rural people went only to the lowest-order trading place, normally within the lord's domain, to satisfy their wants. This tradition began as early as the seventh century in Bavaria[24] and lasted there for a thousand years, to within one lifetime of Christaller's birth.

The *Heerschildordnung*

Accepting the low order of mobility under feudalism, we still must deal with the superstructure of trading places that Christaller erects on this settlement base. One of the key characteristics of German feudalism may furnish us at least a partial explanation not fully dependent on the normative economic geometry that the author of central-place theory employs. Under German feudalism an ordering of feudatories grew up called the *Heerschildordnung*, which depended on an assumption that some gradation of rank related to the size of the holding. The practice was never very neat. "Actually not even in the most regular of feudal countries, like England or Germany, was there any fixed gradation of rank, title or size. A knight might hold directly of the king, a count of a viscount, a bishop of an abbot, or the king himself of one of his own vassals, or even of a vassal's vassal, and in return his vassal's vassal might hold another fief directly of him."[25] Much as the individual organization was disordered, the notion of the geographical order did exist. Baronies were the most basic component, just as the barons were the building blocks of the political system and came ultimately to be the basic element in the judicial system. Larger in size were the domains of counts and, in increasing scale, those of viscounts, margraves, and dukes. One man might—through conquest, inheritance, or marriage dowry—be a duke and a baron, or hold any other combination of titles, but an integrity of the geographical units remained, sometimes recognized in the bestowal of lesser titles on the heir to the greater title or even on the cadet line of the family.

The existence of a geographical ranking of feudal fiefs meant that a basis for larger trading places always existed even within the closure of the feudal economy. The Holy Roman Empire, a strange conglomerate that left Germany both the largest "state" and the most divided one, encouraged this sort of compartmentalization of land even in an era when the nation-state was elsewhere long established. We should not forget that Germany's first effective customs union, the famous *Zollverein*, dates only from 1834. The free

24. Ibid., p. 665.
25. George Burton Adams, "Feudalism," *Encyclopædia Britannica*, 11th ed.

flow of customers and goods could only begin to develop in that area in the hundred years before Christaller formed his theory, whereas it had been possible for up to five hundred years in England and for only a slightly shorter time in France. Areas such as those in Germany and Italy characterized by feudal survivals, where feudalism was given up only in the nineteenth century, could accomplish long-distance trading only during the last century and a half. But what success they had in overcoming the geographical compartmentalization during the Middle Ages came not in the rurally based feudal area but rather in the exceptions to its uniformity found in the nonfeudal free cities. The Venetian *empire da mar* or the Hanseatic League were exceptions, but they were exceptions as well to Christaller's theory; they were not central-places serving as the focus of a region but were instead what he largely disregarded as either "point-bound" places or industrial places with home production.

I wish to propose that Walter Christaller's central-place theory represents a very special case rather than a universal prescription. It is both culturally and geographically relative to the Germanic feudal institution and its realm. And perhaps most important, it is basically a rural rather than an urban system, depending on the evolution of an agricultural system and culture into an urban one. But central-place theory does not prove able to explain some considerable number of situations where feudalism was more short-lived (as in England), less complete as a system (as in Byzantium), or actually absent (as in most of the New Lands). Additionally, our survey of the transformation of the classical world into the medieval world has shown that cities did persist, admittedly small and weak but still present. To deal with that situation Christaller is inadequate, as he is to handle either Byzantium or the New World. We need not reject central-place theory but rather must restrict it to that area where historical geography justifies its application—to the groundmass of feudal land in Western civilization. Even there we must maintain the exception of the germinal Roman towns that limped through the Dark Ages, and probably the development of towns in Britain, France, the Low Countries, and Italy after the close of the general feudal era in the

Feudalism
and the Dawn
of Freedom

thirteenth century. Central-place theory may serve to explain some German urbanism well up to the nineteenth century and some events in Western civilization in general between the ninth and thirteenth centuries, but it should not be viewed as an explanation of urbanization, either universally or throughout time.

What will replace central-place theory? When we consider the mercantile city of the fifteenth through seventeenth centuries, I will propose the mercantile model of settlement in a historical-geographical context. Its contrast with central-place thinking comes in the role to be played by a geographically extensive trading, administrative, and protective system. We have already seen that such an extensive system existed in Roman times; the germ of its rebirth remained even during the shadowed time when feudalism emerged to dominate Western civilization. The non–rurally based city was that germ. But before we follow its course through the period of rural domination, we shall look at the physical expression of the geographical parochialism of the feudal era.

A World of Parts: Manor and *Bourg*

The geographical partitioning that feudalism brought into being is expressed in three dominant ways: as the baronial unit of administration and justice, as the closed economy of the manor, and as the protective unit of the castle with the attendant settlement. Despite all the elaborate upward ties of homage and fealty represented by the feudal system, effective sovereignty really lay in the barony. The baron possessed almost absolute powers over his serfs and tenants. The manorial economy concerns us directly; its nature helps to explain why the town was not a significant component of feudal settlement. The word used was *town*, not *village* or *nucleation*. Villages were perhaps the most common form of settlement in Frankish Europe, though Neustria in the west had a greater number of dispersed farm settlements than Austrasia in the east. Villages were a form of rural settlement brought about at least in part by the need for defense at a time when the Pax Romana no longer stretched across the land. These clusters of dwellings had nothing directly to do with the execution of urban functions, and the traditional concept of classical geography that the village grows to the town and the town in turn to the city is little supported by either history or logic. Villages remain villages, for the most part, and towns begin as towns. The manorial economy needed villages to carry on its attempt at autarky as well as to gain some physical protection. But manorial autarky ruled out the true urbanism of town life.

This point is made more clearly when we introduce the notion of the military strongpoint, the fortified town, known in French as the *bourg*, in German as the *burg*, and in Erse as the *burgh*. To understand these towns, we may draw some contrast with the manor. The manor was a social and economic organization because it was the basic unit of landownership. The most common benefice from a major feudatory to his vassal was the bestowal of the occupance of such a unit of agricultural land, presumably large and diverse enough to permit the reasonable expectation of self-sufficiency. To it were

Laroque Ste. Marguerite (Aveyron) shows, in a small town of the present, the relationship between the bourg *and the* faubourg *in the Middle Ages.*

attached the basic administrative rights—the manorial court with its additional judicial functions. The only institutionally required outflows from such a manor were those of feudal tribute to the liege lord, often a thin trickle indeed, and the tithe due the church. Even the tithe was often diverted to the local lay lord rather than flowing in the channels of the universal church. In light of these facts, the manor can be looked upon as so fundamentally parochial in its economy as to be only the weakest encouragement to urban foundation. The small local stream of tithes might continue the germ of the Roman city, if the church dominated it, but otherwise the manor brought about village rather than town support.

Quite in contrast stood the *bourg*: it gained significance by increases in scale in a way that the manor did not. If a baron sought truly to dominate an area, he would seek to build such a fearsome castle that he could stand immune to conquest, with a homage and fealty that would rest lightly on him. In such immunity lay true power and freedom, as well as possible domination of others if they lacked similar protection. Feudal Europe is full of examples of political power brought about and backstayed by the possession of a fearsome castle, depending on nature's gift of an easily defensible site or on walls of exceptional strength.

In the castle we encounter the most notable morphological contribution of feudal times. The manor was the villa carried forward with relatively little change. The town was so vestigial as to lack any new components other than the Christian churches, and often, as in Syracuse or Rome, even these were renovations of Greek or Roman temples. The basilica, which stood as the great church of early Christendom, was an architectural form taken slavishly from the Romans, who had used both the term and the form to describe law courts and other places of public resort. Only in Byzantium was the church given a form all its own, the domed place of assembly fully developed in Hagia Sophia.

The state was doubly perplexed: new walls and fortresses were constructed to deal with the threat and invasion of brigands and pirates from Scandinavia who sailed up the rivers destroying Carolingian civilization and exacting tribute, yet the walls gave power and protection to dissidents among the king's nobles. In the end they fostered true geographical feudalism,

Feudalism
and the Dawn
of Freedom

103

destroying the effectively extensive state, and became the instrument of the creation of a new form of extensive state when, in the hands of a partially civilized Norman horde, the practice of personal colonization was devised.

This practice grew out of the social organization of this second wave of barbarians who attacked the realm of Western civilization. Just as the Germanic invasions had changed the Roman Empire, shaping an amalgam of centralized Roman state and Frankish chiefdom domain, the second wave transformed the feudal order of the late Carolingians into the instrument of a new but much more divided colonization.

La Sylvestrie, a fortified manor near Villeneuve-sur-Lot in Aquitaine, shows the form and strength of medieval walls.

The first castle is lost in the incompleteness of history. Likely it may have emerged either in the Touraine, Maine, or Anjou. The disintegration of the Frankish empire of the west, first into Neustria, led finally to the creation of a group of important domains possessed by counts (Anjou, Rennes, Nevers, Vendôme, Tours, Vexin, as well as others) who came to covet their neighbors' possessions—always their lands, and often their wives and daughters as a means to gain those lands. Taking one example, we see Count Fulk Nerra of Anjou, who was born around 970, succeeding to his father as count at the age of seventeen and having to repel an attack by the count of Rennes on Nantes soon thereafter. Little more than a boy, he set about making marriage alliances that eventually brought to his family the countship of Vendôme and Touraine, and by arms he secured the countship of Maine. His heirs came ultimately to rule first as dukes of Normandy and then as kings of England beginning with Henry II. All of this activity had to be based on the ability to defend lands gained by conquest or inheritance, either of which was likely to be challenged.

Although these castles were not devised by the Normans—in fact, they were built for defense against them—those medieval bullies took up the form most effectively. As usurpers in a foreign land they found themselves in need of personal protection against both the populace they were seeking to dominate as serfs and the remnants of the imperial power they sought to reject. Theirs became a game of overawing the people and snubbing the kings, in which the castle was a major instrument.

More than any other group, the Normans used the castle to dominate an alien and often hostile population. In France they built castles with the same objective the Roman builders had. One "has only to open his Caesar to see how familiar wooden towers and wooden palisades were to the Romans" in their conquest of Gaul,[26] and we must turn to the Normans to see how the stone tower and its rubble-filled *enceinte* became the instrument of a new economic empire. The Norse conquered Normandy for economic advantage; as Normans, they went on subsequently to conquer England for greater gain. In each case they constructed motte castles, keeps surrounded by an embankment or an actual wall, to dominate the conquered land. "M. Viollet le Duc says that the Normans were the first people in Western Europe to build castles not as isolated fortresses, but as part of a scheme of general defence in which the individual castle became subservient to a political idea, which affected the geographical distribution of the fortresses, and even their individual planning and arrangement."[27] That political idea was the conquest of an extensive area and the subjugation of its people to a ruling group of foreign origin determined, at least initially, to maintain cultural distance. When the Norse invaded France, they seem not to have fully understood that idea; they were transient raiders receptive to their subjects' culture. When the Normans expanded from France in 1066 they entered England with the notion of permanent conquest, possessed of a system of colonial occupation made up of the castle and the feudal order. They fully desired to maintain their recently adopted French way of life rather than their more historical native culture of the Anglo-Saxon and Danish institutions of England. They were to become lords and strangers, and the castle was essential to that purpose.

William could hardly avoid building castles in England. The Normans could not have occupied the country without them; the natives rebelled against the occupiers through William's lifetime. He essentially exterminated the native barons and even the more important freemen in putting down the resistance, so the peace he gained was restive and resentful, requiring the Normans to guard themselves constantly. Further, William had, in mounting the conquest, depended dominantly on mercenary soldiers drawn from Flanders, Catalonia, and Germany, whom he had to pay off with lands in England since he lacked any easy access to money. Those mercenaries could be expected to use conquest themselves, if the opportunity were offered, so William found himself defending the newly stolen crown against

26. Ella S. Armitage, *The Early Norman Castles of the British Isles* (New York: Dutton, 1912), p. 78.

27. Alfred Harvey, *The Castles and Walled Towns of England* (London: Methuen, 1911), pp. 1–2.

many of his "supporters" as well as his "people." The Norman keep of the Tower of London was a structure outside the City of London guarding William's front against the frustrated anger of the English; it also was secure above all other fortifications to guard his rear against the disloyalty of his recent hirelings.

> Geographically, too, the castles were not isolated fortresses, but were arranged on a definite scientific plan. Strong castles were placed at almost all the large towns, not so much to provide homes for their lords as to overawe their turbulent inhabitants; Derby alone among county towns probably did not substitute a masonry castle for its early (defensive) mound; many of the lesser towns were similarly threatened or protected; the river valleys, the main channels of traffic, had castles posted at every coign of vantage, the important fords and bridges being especially guarded; on the coast, particularly in the southeast, the part most obnoxious to invasion, all convenient landing-places were similarly protected; other castles kept open the main lines of communication across country, and in dangerous districts each large estate possessed its agrarian castle, which though primarily built for the protection of the tenant (lord) and his dependents, their flocks and their herds, performed its part in the general defence of the neighbourhood. Such castles were particularly numerous on the Scottish border and in the Welsh Marches, where they stretched tentacle-like into the valleys of Wales, and especially along the fat and fertile belt of land between the south Welsh mountains and the sea, reaching to the great fortresses of Pembroke and Haverfordwest, and keeping open the main road to Ireland.[28]

Yet with this truly national system of castles built over a relatively short time and shaped in what we can see to be a fully conceived plan, William sought to avoid furnishing the geographical backing for any partition of effective sovereignty. No counties palatine would arise in the conqueror's England save under his direct control, and he planned against them by spreading the manors granted to any one lord over the whole kingdom, making sure none too many of them were in one place.

This defense of central authority by dispersal of private estates created in the higher peerage of England an interest in the royal realm as an entity, and in the maintenance of a national economy, missing in much of Western Europe. Although an earl might be given defensive responsibility for a county, he was not given the legitimate possession of its wealth and the submission of its barons, as would have been the case in France. No palatine dukes were created such as those in Aquitaine or Burgundy, nor powerful counts to match those in Toulouse or Flanders. If the regional nobility presumed toward independence by building unauthorized castles that seemed to question the royal writ, those adulterine structures were ordered

28. Ibid., p. 3.

The Château-Gaillard, the first important siege castle in the West, was built on a pattern brought back by the Crusaders from Palestine. This fortress guarded the boundary between the English and French possessions on the Seine and was built by Richard the Lionhearted.

demolished. The king ruled in the whole of England, and he intended to maintain a country of central authority based on the incontestable and undivided right of conquest.

When William, king of England and duke of Normandy, attempted to keep his original domain in Normandy together, he called upon his vassal, the seigneur of Perche, Robert II of Belleme, to hold the duchy's eastern frontier in Vexin against Philippe I of France. Henry I and II of England continued the building of a defensive line of castles, and Richard the Lionhearted gave it a primary citadel in the Château-Gaillard, perhaps the greatest of the medieval fortresses in France. These castles were built not in relation to a system of internal governance as before, but rather to deal with the almost ceaseless warfare of the first Hundred Years' War.[29] Geographically, this shift was even more fundamental, representing the creation of a physical form, perhaps more appropriately termed a fortress than a castle, whose purpose was to guard a frontier rather than assure royal sway within the kingdom.

The fortress was anticipated in the castles built to guard landing places on the Channel coast, passes in the Alps, and other such gaps in a naturally adequate frontier. Yet this beginning use hardly predicted the ultimate nature of the form, which came to stand as totally distinct from the feudal castle as that structure had from the fenced agricultural villa. The fortress was an element in independence of sovereignty, which pitted one powerful ruler against another, be it the king of England against his French cousin or

29. J. F. Finó, *Fortresses de la France médiévale* (Paris: Editions Picard, 1967), pp. 117–18.

Feudalism
and the Dawn
of Freedom

the independent city in Germany or Italy against the pretentious Holy Roman Emperor. The Château-Gaillard of 1196–98 was merely the initial form of fortress to be followed by many others—Ghent, Gisors, Freteval, and the Crusader fortress Krak in Syria—as the rulers sought to advance national purposes in an international context. Fortresses guarded the frontier at Château-Gaillard, defended a suzeraine against more powerful neighbors at Ghent, and served as a base for invasion and occupation of a foreign land at Krak and Palermo. The critical difference between castle and fortress came in the scale of possible conflict. The castle had been threatened with possible civil disturbance, but the fortress had to survive the more drawn-out siege within the capability of a sovereign ruler such as the king of France, the count of Flanders, or the Norman king of Jerusalem.

In a historical geography of cities, this shift of the castle's role to poliorcetic defense from the earlier purpose—a king's attempt to overawe his urban subjects—meant a new morphology. In place of the moated keep at the edge of the town came the citadel and greatly strengthened city walls joined together and overlooking the enemy's approach from without. Where external threats were slight, as in England, fortification never progressed much beyond the administrative castle of the Normans, but where fears of invasion remained, the fortified citadel was built on the national frontier or at major interior cities.

The Colonial City in Europe and the Mediterranean

The Normans played a central role in the Crusades of the twelfth and thirteenth centuries. Going to the Holy Land as soldiers of the cross, many Normans stayed on to found feudal holdings in the Levant, in the islands and peninsulas of southern Greece, in Sicily, and in Calabria and Apulia in southern Italy. In this activity the Normans were following on practices they had learned in their conquest of England. The same warriors were not always involved, but in that relatively simple society and time, the word of the English colonial experience must have been widespread among this still relatively small group.

The great authority on the Normans, Edward Augustus Freeman, held that "these two conquests, wrought in the great island of the Ocean and the great island of the Mediterranean [Sicily], were the main works of the Normans after they fully put on the character of a Christian and a French-speaking people." He notes that a contemporary historian, Geoffrey Malaterra, had long ago set "the Normans before us as a race specially marked by cunning, despising their own [Scandinavian] inheritance in the hope of winning a greater, eager after both gain and dominion, given to imitation of all kinds" and "holding a certain mean between lavishness and greediness." In England the Normans became Englishmen "because there was an English nation into which they could be absorbed. The Normans in Sicily could hardly be said to become Sicilians, for there was assuredly no Sicilian nation for them to be absorbed into."[30]

30. Freeman wrote some fifteen volumes on the Normans and an unfinished *History of Sicily*, but his most succinct statement is contained in "Normans," *Encyclopaedia Britannica*, 11th ed.

What the Normans learned about colonizing in these pre-Crusade endeavors they combined with a knowledge of fortification much advanced by the campaigns to the Holy Land and their administration of that area after its conquest. In that operation the Normans had partners drawn from their Italian "bankers"—those from Venice, Genoa, and Pisa who furnished the supplies and ships for the seaborne Crusades—who learned as well from this early religious-colonial episode. The Normans returned from the Levant as masters of the siege castle, the Italians as masters of the trading port dotted along the shores of a foreign but trade-bound land. The Normans used their knowledge to complete their conquest of England, adding Wales and parts of Ireland to their realm, and to hold the line against French encroachment in Normandy, Anjou, and Aquitaine. The Italians, particularly the Venetians, used their equally specialized knowledge to shape an *empire da mar* spread by a hundred trading harbors along the east shore of the Adriatic, into the Greek islands, and even as a foreign colony across the Golden Horn from Constantinople in Galata. The Norman towns were all-of-a-piece colonial cities. Not surprisingly, then, the French and the English, successors to the Normans, knew best how to shape medieval bastides, built in considerable numbers during the period of the Crusades. They knew too how to build the colonial cities of the continents beyond Europe that shaped both the New World of European plantations and the Imperial World of European political conquest.

The City's Emergence in the High Middle Ages

During the second part of the Middle Ages, beginning in the twelfth century with the emancipation of the city from much of the repression of feudalism, the traditional function of urban places as the cradle of change was restored. The result was the birth of a conflict that still persists. The conservative, often hierarchically ordered countryside, where wealth came in tangible and geographically accountable property, fell into conflict with the evolving and socially mobile city, where wealth came in transferable capital whose return disappeared unless it was put to work, most effectively in geographically extensive trade. Throughout this period the conservative, hierarchically organized Roman church, medieval Europe's greatest landowner, made a moral question of a clearly economic argument, attempting to contain or even stamp out the substitution of the city economy for a feudal one, to avoid any questioning of the Western Catholic order. This repression ultimately destroyed the universality of that church, though it did not destroy the castigated cities or the economic, social, and religious liberalism that grew up in them.

The Expression
of Liberalism

====================

The Face of the Medieval City

4

The fully developed medieval city emerged sometime in the thirteenth century, a time of fundamental reorientation of human activity. It had completely original qualities, both socially and morphologically. Our inheritance of those qualities is great indeed; modern cities draw more from the Middle Ages than from the Classical Era, however much the Founding Fathers of the American Republic wished and thought otherwise. Urban evolution in Western civilization has been essentially continuous since that birth of the medieval city.

The most notable feature of the medieval city was its effective separation from the countryside. It was not an "up-to-date" instance of classical synoecism; during the Middle Ages, once people had left the land they were reluctant to return to it and submit again to the restriction of geographical and personal freedom. Similarly, the medieval city was not a modernized Roman one; in place of the great military and administrative roles assigned to towns under the empire, urbanization under medieval controls had a strongly economic quality. That quality has remained the most central to urbanization in the eight hundred years of Western life since the medieval city was devised.

It is sometimes assumed that the city in the Middle Ages was always the seat of a king or powerful lord or bishop, yet the truly important towns frequently were not. When the count of Paris, Hugh Capet, became king of France in A.D. 987, he began a split between his interests as local lord and as sovereign that widened over the years, causing the king to depart Paris more and more frequently, to have on occasion to besiege the city to return, and finally to abandon it completely—in the seventeenth century, with Louis XIV's permanent move to Versailles. In England conditions were not so different. Westminster became the royal seat, and the kings of England were allowed in London only by special permission. The monarchy became the fountainhead of the traditional, rurally based order, whereas the city was the font of innovation and the urban-based efforts toward transformation and liberalization.

The medieval cities were in other ways functionally separated from the countryside, especially in their economic life, which was their most novel feature when they rose to importance. Like the castles, they might challenge the king's authority, but unlike those feudal strongholds that had been the summit of morphological ingenuity and creation during the Dark Ages, they did it with a system of support fully outside the medieval order.

As the French historian Boissonade expressed it a half-century ago, "Feudal government was designed rather to hamper than to assist commercial activity. Moreover, the public opinion of all classes misunderstood the role of trade, and continued to look upon the trader as a parasite, a speculator, a usurer, and movable wealth as the fruit of fraud and rapine, but not of labour. Moreover, the conditions of economy on the great domain left only a limited field of action in commerce."[1] Thus, "during the first two centuries of

1. P. Boissonade, *Life and Work in Medieval Europe: The Evolution of Medieval Economy from the Fifth to the Fifteenth Centuries*, trans. Eileen Power (French ed., 1921; English trans., 1927; rpt.

the feudal age, a movable or money economy, which has its source in commerce, possessed only an infinitesimal importance." In geographical terms, "economic life had become, as it were, stationary in this purely agricultural society, enclosed in a rigid framework of the landed aristocracy." In the only markets to function within the feudal order, "a man would trade a horse for a sack of [grain], a piece of cloth for a measure of salt, a pound of pepper for a pair of boots." In truth, "the only markets known were local, held in the gateway of a castle or monastery, or on the outskirts of a neighbouring town. Insecurity, anarchy, the multiplicity of seigneurial monopolies and tolls, the scarcity and difficulty of means of transport, the chaotic diversity of weights and measures and moneys, the scarcity of currency, and the imperfection of instruments of credit were all obstacles to the circulation of merchandise."[2]

If we look at this succinct description of the nature of trade in the feudal centuries—the ninth and tenth—in terms of the arguments for and against central-place theory, we find substantial contravention in historical and geographical terms of its basic assumptions: the city's location is determined by a geometry of access from potential customers to a central-place at which they may secure, with the least geographical effort, the satisfaction of their demands for goods and services, and thus cities grow out of the countryside. As Boissonade and virtually all historians of the Middle Ages would have it, (1) the location of the market was due to historical forces of privilege held by a lord, agglomeration of dynastic landholdings, the natural occurrence of a strongpoint, or the somewhat adventitious bequeathal of lands to the church, rather than any historically determined and discernible normative geography; and (2) this trading in local markets was not geographically free; it converged on the market held by the lord, not always the closest possible market. Virtually no evidence points to a hierarchy—a nesting, as the central-place theorist would have it, of such places. Boissonade's "natural trade" was parochial or highly periodic, with those goods not found naturally in the vicinity being furnished by itinerant traders, peddlers, distinguished most in a legally sedentary medieval population by their possession of no fixed abode. In law their property was viewed as *waif*—implying goods washed up on shore by an act of God—hardly the status that would be accorded to a denizen of a closed, ordered central-place, or feudal, system.

The Two Classes of Medieval Settlement

We might recognize two basic forms of nucleated settlement in the later Middle Ages. *Natural settlements*, to borrow and reshape the economic historian's phrase, emerged inside a closed political-economic domain, whose extent was due to historical rather than geometrically determinative forces and whose market would be sited because of those same human rather than mechanical forces. *Systemic settlements* were based on long-distance

---

New York: Harper and Row, 1964), p. 159. Professor Power characterized this work as one of popularization, but she thought enough of it to undertake its translation and "popularization" among the English economic historians of whom she was the doyenne.

2. Ibid.

trade but, of necessity, possessed an independence from the constraining feudal order that produced the more repetitive natural settlements. In essence, towns were patterned in two ways, and the two were to a fair degree in conflict, or at least in competition.

The natural settlement of the lord's domain emerged within an area whose size and shape would be determined not by the convergence of customers, but because it could stand as a defensible and administrable unit. "Geographical base" was not geographically determined; rather, it was geographically described. Its modal size was more likely to come from realities of demography than geography. If a grant were given to support a subfeudatory in reasonable fashion, then the areal scale of that grant would depend on the productivity of the land, rather than the outer limit of practicable access to the lord's market. True, most individual medieval grants were small enough to permit this access by customers, but it is extremely doubtful that the overlord used this attribute to determine how much land he would grant as a benefice to his feudatory. The common usage of the term *tributary area* for the collecting area of a market is historically more accurate than those who use it might suspect. Because of the modal scale of such domains, they tended to be relatively evenly spaced about the countryside. But because they were based on closed domains and a natural economy, these small places were ranked in a single order without any hierarchical superstructure. What nonlocal trade existed was almost certainly carried on not by distant trading centers but by peddlers bringing wares within the closed-economy area and taking from it, most frequently, goods obtained in barter.

Standing in sharp contrast to this constrained pattern were the systemic settlements, those that participated in a geographically extensive system. The systemic town would of necessity stand outside the local closed economies, and hold a status far more independent of feudalism than the local market town. Systemic places might be divided into "feudal towns" and "nonfeudal towns," but such a dichotomy would not be historically accurate. Most systemic towns at least ostensibly still existed within a feudal system; their distinction was that they had managed to break the conservative, order-maintaining quality of that political and social order. Tribute, if it was paid, was likely to be determined by contractual relations, which limited its scale and gained in return some "liberties" and "freedoms" from the endless, stultifying regulations of feudalism. The greater the economic power a city possessed, the larger its body of freedoms was likely to be, because the wielding of that economic power gained for the urban settlement its degree of departure from the rigid traditional feudal order.

Because cities had different degrees of economic power as well as differences in history, they had contrasting freedoms. These distinctions allowed differences in the role that a town might play in an extensive trading system. Some towns were free, as in upper Italy. Others were nearly free, as were the imperial free cities of Germany. Some were still integrated to varying degrees within the feudal order, as in France, south Germany, and the Holy Land, and some were under fairly direct control of the crown, as in England. Given this diversity of status, the probability of classes of towns was strong. This tendency toward differentiation would be enhanced further by the fairly direct relationship between freedom and economic power. Those places already possessing a high level of freedom would tend to gain thereby a greater access to trade; consequently, they would extend even further their lead over places of lesser freedom.

All of these general truths lead to the realization that if a hierarchy of towns did develop, it was likely to do so within the systemic settlements rather than within the natural ones. But within the systemic settlements the differentiation would be more functional than hierarchical, because the trade they practiced was proto-wholesaling rather than retailing. In retailing the customer remains an indivisible unit, having to go in turn to a diversity of geographical locations. In wholesaling, on the other hand, the powerful tendency was toward specialization in trade, with one man serving as the agent to facilitate trade in wool while another facilitated the trade in a different staple, such as fish. The first man might be a resident of Calais, while the second lived in Bristol, leading not so much to a hierarchy of places as to a system of places specific to each staple of trade. Thus, even in systemic settlements staple-specific systems were more likely than general ones, and a greater ability to maintain a historical lead was enjoyed by an early center independent of "status" within a hierarchy.

To recapitulate, the systemic settlement grew first out of a separation from the feudal order that allowed the town to push out trading linkages beyond its own "natural" domain, which in most cases would be very limited in a geographical sense. Exceptions to this rule included the *empire da mar* that Venice shaped, which was geographically extensive and clearly a case of the flag following trade. Most peoples, however, substituted a pattern of trading alliance for political control; more common than the Venetian type of empire was the Hanse of trade, an alliance among fairly independent cities that sought mutual gain through a facilitation of long-distance trade. Unlike the Venetian system, the Hanseatic system might be viewed as one of special-purpose association; the basic sovereignty of the city remained unchanged while special arrangements were made with respect to trade. The result was the growth of the notion of extraterritoriality as a fundamental concept operating within the important towns of the medieval trading networks.

The Hearths of Medieval Urbanism

Two areas of medieval Europe were particularly significant in the ultimate spread of urbanization: Flanders, and the Po Basin and Tuscany. In each, large and important towns were kept busy and prosperous by manufacture at the hands of skilled artisans and the trade of the goods carried out by quick-witted traders traveling all over Europe. These areas might be called *trade-originating Europe*. From these hearths, city filling spread widely to turn small towns into truly great cities. In particular, growth came in towns where the staples needed in an industry could be collected from their rural producing areas: Norwich, Colchester, and Boston in the east of England; Bristol in the west; Liège in eastern Belgium, which collected fleeces from the Ardennes; and the Spanish ports that collected them from the vast

The Face of the
Medieval City

115

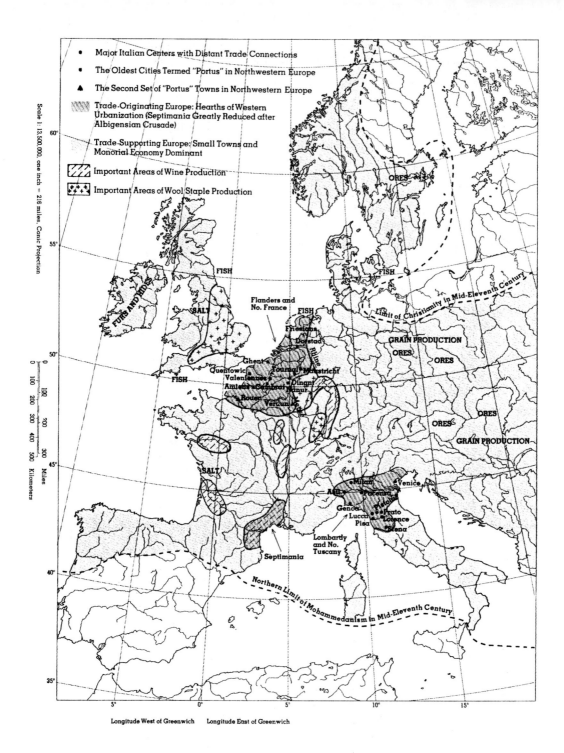

Legend:

• Major Italian Centers with Distant Trade Connections

• The Oldest Cities Termed "Portus" in Northwestern Europe

▲ The Second Set of "Portus" Towns in Northwestern Europe

Trade-Originating Europe: Hearths of Western Urbanization (Septimania Greatly Reduced after Albigensian Crusade)

Trade-Supporting Europe: Small Towns and Monorial Economy Dominant

Important Areas of Wine Production

Important Areas of Wool Staple Production

Scale 1: 13,500,000, one inch = 216 miles; Conic Projection

0 100 200 300 400 500 Kilometers
0 100 200 300 Miles

Longitude West of Greenwich   Longitude East of Greenwich

Map of trade originating in Europe.

pastures of Iberia. In contrast to the hearths, these areas where cities were fewer but often of considerable size and importance became *trade-supporting Europe*. This trade-supporting Europe felt much of the initial change of the Industrial Revolution of the eighteenth century. Finally, in a third realm almost outside trade where neither staples nor manufactures were to be found—as in thinly settled parts of distant kingdoms—*feudal Europe* with its antipathy to cities remained for centuries longer.

Historical Events, Chartered Rights, Potential Locations

Charters provide us with most of the written evidence we possess for when, where, and how cities were established during the Middle Ages. Unfortunately, they seldom tell us why the place was given the distinctive and valuable privileges they enumerate. In seeking an explanation we should realize that "great lords, however, were quick to see the economic and financial advantages which might accrue to themselves and their territories from the advancement of 'their' towns, and consciously set about their promotion." But this viewpoint was far from universal in medieval Europe. "Pioneers of this policy were the counts of Flanders and the Capetian kings, who took care both to keep for themselves the two most important cities of their kingdom, Paris and Orleans, and to strengthen their power by taking towns in the lands of the great feudatories under their special protection. In the Angevin Empire [within France], the English kings, as Dukes of Normandy and vassals of the French crown, promoted the towns of Rouen, La Rochelle, Bayonne and Bordeaux, in keen competition with their suzerain in Paris."[3] Thus, the potential town gained a certain weight in its struggle with a great lord; it might succeed in convincing him that his prosperity could be enhanced by a greater degree of economic, and incidentally personal, freedom for the burgesses of his town. Perhaps more important, once the great lords—basically kings, regional dukes, and palatine counts such as those of Toulouse—had envisaged the potential wealth to be gained from serving as the lords of trading towns, they had the geographical raw materials to aid such prosperity. The course of a baron with a localized manor was limited to guarding the local trade jealously by enclosing it within the dominial economy. But being great lords, the kings, dukes, and palatine counts could favor "their" town by giving it privileges denied to others, mainly that of engaging in long-distance trade. We have seen how shrewdly the Capetian kings held Paris and Orleans. The Burgundian, Spanish, and Austrian lords of Flanders were equally shrewd, elevating Brussels at the expense of Mons or Louvain, largely because that city fell in the lands directly held by the counts of Flanders and their Hapsburg heirs.

Not all towns made it, however hard their lords and commonalty tried. Some never transformed a potential for growth into actual construction, and others faltered after making a serious beginning. "Cities which had been wealthy and flourishing were laid low by more successful rivals, as for instance in Italy: Amalfi, Siena, and dozens of smaller towns failed to hold

The Face of the
Medieval City

their own against Venice, Milan, Florence and Genoa. New foundations often turned out to be unsuccessful speculations. *They attracted insufficient trade and traffic*, and after a few generations, as the grass grew again, the town reverted to its former agricultural status, or the port silted up."[4]

Social Urbanization

Once a city had been founded in a place that possessed the potential for trade, the first process that began to fill its walls might be termed social urbanization. That social movement responded to the classical dynamics of migration; the serfdom of the countryside and the inability to own property there created a push-factor that encouraged people to leave the feudal domain, often by stealth, while the greater hope of personal freedom and prosperity in the city formed a pull-factor to draw refugees from the country within the city walls. This migration was first a physical translocation, but its continuing impact was cultural, as settlers from a rural background must necessarily make massive adaptations to city life. Adaptation must have dominated medieval society in the twelfth century in much the same way it dominated American city life in the nineteenth, simply because the urban demographic base had been small and the migration influx had been relatively as great. The impact of urban culture on the simple rural migrant must have been greatest in the "communes" of Flanders and parts of northern France and in the towns of the county of Toulouse in the south, where city life was more free and the government of the towns fell more directly into the hands of the citizen-burghers.

The rural implosion on the town seems to have focused on two distinct modes of settlement, as Professor Friedrich Keutgen noted long ago:

> There is evidence that in the *quondam Roman towns* (in the north) the German newcomers settled much as in a village, i.e. each full member of the community had a certain portion of arable land (some of which might lie within the commodious Roman walls) allotted to him and a share in the common. Their pursuits would at first be mainly agricultural. The *new towns*, on the other hand, general economic conditions having meanwhile begun to undergo a marked change, were founded with intention of establishing centres of trade. Periodical markets, weekly or annual, had preceded them, which already enjoyed the special protection of the king's ban, acts of violence against traders visiting them or on their way toward them being subject to special punishment. The settlers invited (to the New Towns) were merchants (*mercatores personati*) and handicraftsmen. The land now allotted to each member of the community was just large enough for a house and yard, stabling and perhaps a small garden (50 by 100 feet at Bern). These building plots were given as free property or, more frequently, at a

4. Ibid., p. 70. Emphasis supplied.

nominal rent (*Wurtzins*) with the right of free disposal, the only obligation being that of building a house.[5]

Keutgen's picture is basically typical of the medieval German realm: Germany itself, present-day Austria, the Netherlands, Flanders (both Belgian and French), German Switzerland, and Alsace. In contrast stood the world of the Italian urban communes with their more continuing link to Roman urbanization, which resulted in a more "political" component in city life and in the control of urban government on the peninsula. Throughout the barbarian invasions of the fifth and sixth centuries, the northern Italian towns had tenuously hung on to their identity and some freedom, though they tended to be dominated by bishops whose yokes had to be thrown off to gain the enhanced freedom that came in the twelfth century. This persistence of Roman foundation, save in Venice, which was founded only during the barbarian invasions, maintained a particular relationship of town and country. In upper Italy, and to a lesser degree in Languedoc, which until the Albigensian Crusade of the thirteenth century was more Mediterranean than French, the town dominated the countryside with either the city republican government, as in Italy, or the counts palatine, as in Toulouse and Narbonne, effectively controlling the countryside. In these city-dominated landscapes, most nobles with estates in the surrounding countryside (the *contado* in Italy) were expected to maintain city houses and to reside in them for at least part of the year so that they might be watched over by the urban authority.[6] The pattern of these cities around the northern shore of the Mediterranean became domination of an area outside their walls until the boundary with the area tributary to another city was reached. Thus, there was never the loss of urban experience on the part of all classes of society or the need for a new period of acculturation of country people as was necessary in the Germanic, French, and English lands.

This considerable migration of country dwellers to the city presented difficulties that necessitated the creation of institutions to acculturate the migrants, or else to contain their rebellion against the new demands of employment found there. Urban Holmes has noted that "there was something in the air of the medieval community such as London which we moderns are apt to forget. This thing was authority. There was unquestionably much mob violence and considerable injustice on all sides practiced everywhere daily. But even the outraged person felt awed by authority, whatever form it took." The potential always existed for changing allegiance, but not for lawlessness. "Rebellion in twelfth-century England and France meant attachment to another overlord; it did not mean becoming a law unto oneself, unless the rebel chanced to be placed very high." The city rabble, the *ribauz*, could rise and men-at-arms could waver. But authority—that of the

5. Friedrich W. E. Keutgen, "Medieval Commune," *Encyclopaedia Britannica*, 11th ed., 6: 785. Emphasis supplied.

6. In Zoë Oldenbourg's *Cities of the Flesh*, much of the activity takes place in cities, Toulouse and Narbonne, despite the story's concern for the lives of knights with feudal domains. In those towns, the alliance between the free-thinking Cathari merchants, Jews, and the nobility was formed quite in contrast to conditions in most of northern Europe.

bailiffs over the *ribauz*, and that of the feudal oaths and villeinage over the men-at-arms—normally kept matters in hand when competent authorities were in control.[7]

These negative forces had to be applied. There were as well positive institutions, whose purpose was to use the productivity and skill of the recently settled city people while constraining too exuberant outbreaks of personal liberation—the gilds that so widely controlled city life. Their job was made far easier than that of their modern equivalent by the fact that rural landowners had no great wish to lose potential workers, even fairly poor ones. The burden of welfare was not shifted from the country to the city as at present, and little urban unemployment occurred; a certain vigor was found among the migrants to the city, who had often fled the serfdom of the countryside with an ingenuity and determination not characteristic of human castoffs.

A sharp distinction arose between the towns north of the Alps and those in the Mediterranean. To the north the towns were new social creations founded strongly on economic purposes, with power held by the more economically important men. In the south the towns were of great antiquity, having been founded by Greeks, Romans, or Etruscans for purposes long since lost, for the most part. These towns had survived into the Middle Ages mainly because of their Roman walls and because they had been taken up by the church. The domination by a single, coherent, evolutionary body such as the burgesses of northern towns was missing, and the Mediterranean towns remained more bound up in social contest than in the advancement of trade. Because these Mediterranean towns were immured for so long during the barbarian invasions, manufacturing rather than trade dominated urban life. The contrast had great historical-geographical significance: artisans tended toward parochialism and protectionism, merchants toward worldliness and freedom of exchange. Do not forget that the Hanse was a league of merchant towns, something unthinkable among artisans. Even in trade, the north exercised less parochialism and suspicion, as is demonstrated by the outcome of the decline of the Hanseatic League and the collapse of the Venetian *empire da mar*. When the league disintegrated, it left many great cities— London, Antwerp, Frankfurt, Bremen, Hamburg, and a lesser string about the Baltic and in Russia; when the Venetian Empire collapsed, it left mostly a string of beautiful fossils—Ragusa (Dubrovnik), Trogir, Rhodes, and Corfu among them—but only one real city, Venice.

Only in the invention of banking did Italy show the vigor of the commercial north. But because banking lay so near the edge of medieval ethics, being easily condemned as usury, and because it proved so sensitive an institution when the national economy was being hammered out in the fourteenth and fifteenth centuries, the first act of powerful kings was to evict the Italian bankers. Not having shaped a political empire to match their economic power, the Lombard bankers were forced to return to Italy, adding stagnation in banking to the earlier stagnation of manufacturing and urban

7. Urban Tigner Holmes, Jr., *Daily Life in the Twelfth Century* (Madison: University of Wisconsin Press, 1952), pp. 36–38. Paperback ed., 1962.

factionalism. This illness crippled the Italian city-republics of the late Middle Ages.

Both north and south, the city had been the seedbed of religious dissent and striving for freedom. The first strong expression of that dissent came with the emergence of the dualists, the Cathari, who in the twelfth century questioned the luxury and corruption of the Roman church from their centers in several cities in the Po Basin, most importantly Milan, and Narbonne, Beziers, and Toulouse in southern France. The barbaric crusade organized against them by the pope and the king of France destroyed this and most subsequent questioning in the south, so the flower of cities that had remained in Languedoc since Roman time withered. Subsequently, cities continued their dissenting role but mainly north of the Alps, where John Wycliffe and John Huss preached within the walls of receptive towns.

Much of the great Cluny Abbey was destroyed during the French Revolution, but until that time it was the largest church in France and one of its more powerful monastic establishments.

Religion and the Medieval City: Cluny and Nonretributive Trade

A fundamental dichotomy has been drawn between the organic and the preconceived city. When we apply that distinction to medieval towns, we find that many things had changed since the Classical Era. Thus, when towns began to be founded anew after the Dark Ages, they were at first outside the established order of feudalism, and they became, quite naturally, the locale for experimentation and change. Unlike the experience in Roman Gaul, that in medieval France called forth the individual, atomic qualities of towns. No standard was applied and no rule had to be followed. Religion had become transmuted. It no longer found physical expression in the city as holy territory, bounded by a *pomerium* and protected from evil

The Face of the Medieval City

spirits by the plowing of the sacred furrow. Individuals now protected their salvation through repeating acts of their own, executed within the walls of a special part of the city, the early Christian basilica. No line now divided sacred from profane territory; thus, the protected world had no extent and, ultimately, no limit. Necessity required two forms of defense against evil: the sacrament for the soul, and the wall for the safety of the person. Two institutions evolved from the one that had been the Roman city—the city corporation for the physical defense of the person and the church for the soul's salvation.

To characterize the cities as anticlerical and potentially heretical would certainly present a false picture. For the most part the burghers were devout in their Catholicism and generous to the church, particularly in its local expression. Gilds were the patrons of particular churches; they built almshouses and hospitals and endowed educational and religious foundations. But the tendency of the medieval Roman church to support what today we would characterize as reactionary governments and institutions always placed the merchant community slightly apart from the church and made it potentially divisionist in its thinking. During the High Middle Ages the church and the merchants maintained Western orthodoxy, but the seeds of ultimate dissent were present. The successful development of the city, which necessitated first a conflict with feudalism and its natural economy, and ultimately the destruction of that medieval order and its replacement by the state and its national economy, became possible when the local commercial community came to have a power greater than the parochial clerical one. The rural society continued its traditional ultramontane slant, while cities came to be Gallicist in viewpoint.

To understand the nature of the conflict between burgher and cleric, we must perceive that the Roman church encouraged and demanded the maintenance of an established order, as had feudalism. Possessing too much business initiative was thought to be a misplacement of zeal, which should focus on the church rather than the counting house; to seek to transform local natural economies into components of larger trading systems gained no grace for the geographical pioneer. The church was so suspicious of profit, so dubious of change, that it wished to maintain surveillance of business; it could do this best by localization. The somewhat oversimplified notion remains that the church sheltered long-distance trade during the Dark Ages, thus showing its regard for that activity.

The organic nature of the medieval city was real, while that of the church must be questioned. As laity began to seek out the frontiers of trade and urbanization, they pioneered routes of commodity flow and founded or filled towns built on profit. If trade was healthy, the city and its partner places prospered and grew; if not, then towns shrank, even to extinction, in a way not common in the church. The Normans sought to encourage trading towns both in Normandy itself and in England after the conquest. Their efforts in the homeland were largely frustrated by their loss of long-distance connections in northern France due to the resurgence of the French monarchy. As a consequence, their Norman towns for the most part failed, withering into villages, whereas their English places burgeoned.

Organic Growth and Freedom

The burghers' town, with its organic growth shaped by practicality, represented a historical break that began an emancipation of common people that had never previously existed. Cities did not become democratic overnight, though important advances were made in the twelfth and thirteenth centuries—and subsequently lost in the urban contraction of the fourteenth and fifteenth centuries. Instead of instant democracy, this medieval urbanization produced a physical form for the city that could become the backstay for a relatively democratic life.

The first contribution of the organic form to the improvement of the lot of the common people came in the creation of *an expansible city*. Within it, changes in function and in overall demand could be more easily comprehended and satisfied. It is a sobering truth, even today, that a constraint of city growth almost inexorably favors the elite at the expense of the common people. Beauty, order, administration, and other goals may be advanced to justify "control," but the actual quality of life for the common people will not necessarily be enhanced. So when burghers devised a process for urban growth that became highly responsive to demand, they probably unconsciously shaped a way of caring for the average resident that was a great advance on the past.

The second contribution of the organic form came in its encouragement of what we would today call *functional architecture* through the shaping of the medieval house. This remarkably adept structure was socially democratic in its inclusiveness, permitting the city of the time to expand its support functions, both in trade and in manufacture. For a working populace this adaptability to the demands of occupations was a real benefit.

Yet another contribution of the organic growth of cities came in its hospitality to *functional separation* on the ground. If we reason that the clustering of workers in the same trade produces benefits for both workers and society through increase in technical skills, greater likelihood of invention, and more effective structuring of the market, the practical dynamics of the medieval city were finely wrought to accomplish those ends. As new trades emerged, space was made available to them, and as old trades were transformed, their new demands could be met. Since the broader distribution of material benefits was one of the great social advances of the medieval city, economic advance may to a real degree be equated to social advance. The creation of capital wealth was at first an emancipation of common people from slavery to landed wealth under feudalism. Capital wealth is less emancipating today, but we do not need to know the present to understand the Middle Ages. We may, however, better understand the present by knowing those times in their turn.

The Point of Origin

Certain general practices attached to urban places in Western medieval civilization. Perhaps the most obvious was the reuse of the quiescent if not abandoned Roman towns when a new purpose for cities arose. Throughout

Gaul, Cisalpine in the Po Basin and Transalpine in France, Roman towns virtually in ruins awoke to a rattle of new activity, fleetingly in the time of Charlemagne but more permanently during the tenth and eleventh centuries. In Germany, Spain, and England the rebirth was less striking, perhaps as much because the Roman past was less sure and extensive as because of any weakness of the urbanization trend during the Middle Ages.

When trade integration returned during the High Middle Ages, a location the Romans had pioneered might well regain its appeal. The roads built by the Romans could still be used in places; their spatial judgment had normally been astute, so their town locations were likely to return to importance with the resurgence of distant trade. Their crumbling town could be refurbished or used as a quarry adjacent to a desired site. Few places returned rapidly to their classical magnificence. Boissonade tells us that the average size of the rebounding medieval town may have been little above one thousand to fifteen hundred souls.[8] These towns cannot have been totally mundane, as the Roman amphitheaters, arenas, and other public works must have been generally in evidence. Trier on the Moselle had its great Roman gate, the Porta Negra, Arles its arena, Nîmes its temple and arena, and Vienne its Pyramide and the largest theater in Gaul.

Sometimes the Roman inheritance was lacking, either because the Romans had failed to site a town at a spot where one now seemed needed, as at Pavia or Venice, or had failed to conquer the territory and plant any towns, as north of the Danube and east of the Rhine in Germany. Other general practices attached to the siting of towns in those places. In much of France, Germany, and England, the fortified castle became the urban germ. In some places these castles were located where the Romans had had a villa but nothing larger; in others, at sites whose defensibility was so striking as to gain more significance in the chaotic times of feudalism than in the more stable ones of the Pax Romana. The requirement of the feudal era for many strongpoint fortresses provided a much denser net of possible town locations than did the Roman system of fortified towns within relatively secure provinces. One might argue that feudalism built so many castles that only with difficulty could any town be founded at a distance great enough from a castle as to seem independent of it. Correspondence in geographical location does not always demonstrate causal succession of forms.

However, evidence suggests that the strongpoint was the common locating force for the town, other than the Roman settlement, begun in the Middle Ages. Traditionally, the strongpoint on its rock is envisaged as the *bourg*, the term of settlement drawn from the feudal order, charged with the self-defense of the small enclosed domain; nestled below it, the settlement of merchants and workers seeks the protection of the fortress by living in a *faubourg* or *portus*. Such a model of settlement equates lordly protection with town founding—which was often the case, yet often the town and the knight were engaged from the beginning in a conflict that seems ill represented by the *bourg-faubourg* theory.

A third possible site for a town, apart from a Roman resurrection or a

8. Boissonade, *Life and Work in Medieval Europe*, p. 114.

feudal *portus*, was the geographically distinguished site as yet unoccupied. These places were relatively few in number. Venice is the most obvious instance—a place well protected from the barbarian invasions of northern Italy, where in the fifth century a settlement arose. From that beginning grew a town that by 1002 had subjected the whole Adriatic shore to its sway, by 1082 had gained a hundred-year access to free trade in the Byzantine Empire, and by 1204, during the Fourth Crusade, had led the religious warriors first to the Golden Horn to capture Constantinople for Venetian trade. Notable among other sites first occupied in the Middle Ages were those places that early gained trading significance—as resting places on new routes, the sites of fairs, ports on seas only recently opened to trade, or entrepôts in new trading territories. As new foundations, they might exist to all intents outside the system of inherited hierarchy that often subjected the resurrected Roman town to the power of a bishop and the *portus* to that of a feudal baron.

Shaping Processes

The medieval townspeople shaped a physical structure that grew mainly by adaptive incrementation. As places that had begun as fishing ports— Great Yarmouth, Amsterdam, and even Venice—grew to great cities, they had to change both the land-assignment and land-division practices and the actual structures built in the city. Thus, unlike the situation in Roman towns, a constant evolution of forms was active to the extent that the medieval city reflected a functionalism unknown in the Classical Era. There were no "orders" of building, no inviolate or immutable forms; a town could change in form as much as in function. Thus, each increment to town growth serves as a tangible record of the functions then conducted there, because its form, which tends to be preserved, was functionally determined when first laid out and developed.

The Face of the Medieval City

125

The Origin of the Medieval House

Given its functional architecture, the medieval house reveals its origin in its initial purposes—the housing, nearly always, of both workers and their work. Medieval towns were founded, or refounded, mainly to engage in productive activities of either trade or manufacture, in contrast to Roman towns, which were at first basically administrative and military places. Rather than the center of administrative and military power, the medieval city was usually a near pariah within the feudal order that commanded and controlled those activities. Only in the absence of a strong feudalism, as when a bishop controlled a town and its environs, was a town north of the Alps likely to engage in administration over rural areas. Only in Italy, where the city had vanquished the countryside early in the post-Roman period, did cities tend to be the centers of military power and the garrison of large numbers of soldiers. The medieval purpose of towns was heavily economic, and where bishops or urban communes were absent, the alloy of administration and military power was largely absent.

In cities, in places where space is at a premium because of the constraint imposed either by circumvallation or by pedestrian access to a focal point, does the house decide the size of the plot, or the plot determine the ultimate outer dimensions of the house? This question can be answered historically; we can learn whether a plot map came first, fixing divisions on the land to which subsequent building must conform, or whether the plots were made to conform to the normal house of a certain size in the region. Yet such a resolution may be illusory. Perhaps a considerable circularity lends to the process: the space needs of the total urban activities are projected into the practicable walled area, thus largely determining the amount of land available to become resolved into a plot, creating the practical size that best compromises between individual and community needs. Perhaps in some cases the individual building is determinative of the plot; in others the reverse is true. And in the greatest number of instances, the two forces may compromise.

During the Middle Ages certain truths helped to determine the size of houses, and thereby the plot sizes that could be used efficiently. First, a particular type of construction was used within a region. Eclecticism in architecture came with a greater availability of architectural design information and with the easing of the problems of assembling building materials at a particular site. Information tended to be parochial and materials to be difficult to gather even from the neighborhood. Exceptions to both those generalizations included Caen stone from France, used fairly widely by the Normans when they conquered England, and the architectural forms seen in the East employed by returning Crusaders. But those exceptions tended to come mostly in public, monumental, and basically religious buildings for which distinction was sought. The initial house of the burgher was unlikely to be built either of imported stone or in any exotic manner.

The basic component of the burgher's house was wood in the form of structural timbers of some size. Though it is now hard to believe, medieval Europe was more a land of forests than any other landscape, so lumber was relatively plentiful and reasonably cheap, because it came from close by and did not have to carry much cost of transport. Oak seems to have been the favored wood, though beech must have been used, as well as some other hardwoods. Softwoods were scarcer in that band of broadleaf forest native to Europe from England eastward to the Russian plains. Scandinavia was softwood country, but not a land of towns for the most part. In the Mediterranean, wood had become scarce even by medieval times, and stone was cheaper. In the central band from England to Poland, lumber was least expensive.

A certain modular unit for construction applied to hardwoods. A beam of some sixteen to twenty feet was the modal product of the greater number of forests. Trees did grow taller than the norm, though to gather them meant careful searching in the forest and, most likely, a longer haul, both of which would make unusual timbers expensive. Modal size was not the single controlling factor; the sag that affects any beam suspended between two upright posts must as well have borne on the question of beam size. Sag is a function of beam cross section as well as span, so the answer is hard to resolve at this late date without access to cost and availability figures. For whatever reason, the modular beam seems to have ranged between sixteen and twenty feet.

The other modular value of the house comes from the height at which this beam would be supported above the floor. This is not a question of material but rather one of people, for the purpose of the house was to enclose their activities. Again, an average gains control; too high ceilings would be wasteful, even if a few men and women in the Middle Ages were tall. We may assume, then, that the height of posts used to hold up the beams would be enough to clear most people's heads but not enough to clear them all. With little furniture in houses and not very much machinery in workshops, the scale of people fixed the height of posts, which ranged on the average between perhaps six and seven feet.

To utilize these two modular values, we need to understand the basic structure of the medieval house. Both stone and timber houses would be influenced to some degree by the size of timbers available; even stone buildings normally used a fair amount of wood in flooring and upper stories. The all-timber house of central Europe was a simple derivative of the material available. As long as fair-size trees were to be had, the cost of producing timber components of a house was the cost of felling the tree and shaping it into a beam or post. In a two-variable equation, cost of material (wood) and cost of labor (shaping into a beam or post) were worked out to the least-cost compromise. In general, to overuse wood was cheaper than to economize on it and then have to pay large sums for the laborious work of hand-sawing it in a pit. Heavy timbers were the basic components of construction—just as they were in colonial America, where similar conditions obtained—and they tended to be assembled into that very simple structure produced by heavy, relatively rigid and unsagging beams and posts.

This post-and-lintel construction produces a building composed of bays six to eight feet high and sixteen to twenty feet wide and deep, with a horizontal plan sixteen feet square, and a story height of seven or eight feet depending on the rigidity of the timbers and bracing at the corners, where they commonly were mortised into each other. Given good beams and posts, one modular unit can be built on another to a height of as many as six to eight modules, producing a building fifty or so feet high at the façade. Total height may be considerably greater than that when a steeply pitched roof is added. In post-and-lintel construction the actual wall is merely sheathing to keep out the elements and provide privacy for the occupants. If we were to strip a typical medieval building of its walls, we would be left with a series of beams, lintels, plates, rafters, and flooring. The structure would look very much like a newly erected steel-cage skyscraper, before windows, mullions, and other sheathing are added, except that the structural components would be shaped from wood and would possess its strengths and weaknesses.

The use of post-and-lintel construction had two important influences on the physiognomy of the city: it gave a basic module on which the shaping of plots could be based (the bay of sixteen to twenty feet, or its simple divisions into four or eight feet), and it determined that differentiation among buildings would be largely surficial and flat or, at most, in low relief. The second condition arose because of the constraints of the construction style. Finally, the plastic quality in post-and-lintel structure was found in the infilling of the rectangles delimited by the sixteen-foot beams, at the floor and ceiling of a story, and the posts at their ends. This infilling was constructed sometimes of withes woven into a hurdle and plastered with clay mud, sometimes with bricks with smaller timbers inserted to give stiffness to the wall (half-timbering), and sometimes with studs on which laths and plaster were fixed.

The flat, often basically smooth surfaces must at first have stood untreated, but soon they became the main medium for decoration in the medieval city. In some places, notably in the Alpine lands, the flat plaster surfaces were decorated with mural paintings, often in strong colors. Innsbruck and Augsburg still display such wall paintings. In other places, more commonly it seems in the north of France and in England, the plaster surfaces were scored with true graffiti in regular patterns often produced by a comb, giving them the common English name of combwork. Elsewhere the infilled surfaces were of brick, as commonly found in the Low Countries and Baltic cities such as Lübeck; the decoration came from placement of the surface bricks to form observable patterns. Medieval architecture, though highly functional, tended toward a certain uniformity of construction technique, which meant that the urge for differentiation and expression had to be concentrated in surface detailing. The result was that the medieval town of Europe north of the Alps had the textural uniformity of primitively modular construction but the surficial variety of distinct regional cultures seeking to relieve the innate sameness of the townscape.

The Burgage Plot

Although we cannot answer categorically the question of whether the nature of house construction determined the scale of the lot, seemingly the modules of construction tended to determine the frontal dimension. How deep in proportion to the frontage did lots tend to be? Common description holds that in laying out the medieval city, the objective was to furnish each citizen, or burgher, with frontage on the important street where he might carry on those economic activities that supported his family and his associated workers. In this view the street frontage was the critical commodity, and the size of the lot was an outgrowth of family and household needs. Implicit is the thesis that the city grows out of the countryside, with the burgher representing a transitional form of half-farmer, half-craftsman raising much of his own provender in conjunction with the pursuit of his trade. Thus, the lot would have to be rather large, to allow the family to maintain a cow, chickens, perhaps a pig, and to plant fruit trees and a kitchen garden. Given the high value attaching to street frontage, such a large lot could be provided only by shaping the burgage plots as long and narrow, extending to a considerable depth from the street frontage.

Downward Division and Upward Assembly

The totality of the classical city was established from the beginning, though it might be added to in later years by similar large-scale increments. Thus, the finer aspects of urban morphology were conferred by downward division. In the medieval city those finer aspects came in the beginning and tended to produce a city by the upward assembly of the modular parts. In the classical city, the monuments and deliberately impressive streets were established within a previously thought-out whole where the vista was important and where location within the city of these morphological features assumed considerable significance. But in the medieval city, the intimate individuality of each town assailed the visitor, and the internalized qualities of buildings and space gained significance. The Middle Ages were the time of the cloister, the courtyard, and the market square. Even in the great cathedrals of the time, those marvelously light and architectonic Gothic structures, the interior counted. The outside was often hidden by a close crowding of city houses, with only the west front of the building treated to exterior adornment. A few cathedrals stood on open ground with a full exterior sculpturally treated, but they were the exception.

The Marketplace

The widespread textural consistency in the street fabric that characterized these medieval cities was interrupted in one important way, by the street market. Some commentators on the medieval town feel its retail-trading origin can be read clearly from the central location of the street market and its use as the site for the important civic buildings, even the dominating church or cathedral. Such an argument tends to hide truth in circularity: the marketplace would be the site for large, ostentatious buildings for the obvious visual endowments of the place. The cathedral in particular was often not in the marketplace and is today so placed as much by nineteenth-century "restoration" and razing as by original siting. Town halls were normally on the square, but those monuments of civic boasting were almost universally built long after the city was founded, and thus tended to be placed on an open

The Piazzo del Campo in Siena is a striking example of the piazza in an Italian medieval city, a place for sports, meetings, and, on occasion, conflicts.

space where ostentation gained the highest reward. Brussels' Grand Place contains the city's strutted pride from the late Middle Ages, the fifteenth-century city hall, but the thirteenth-century cathedral is elsewhere.

The specialization of streets was not limited to a division between market and common way. A good-size town had many markets: markets for perishable produce, grain for baking or feed for domestic animals, hay and, near the coast, fish. Sometimes these markets were square-like widenings of the street, such as in London's fish market in Billingsgate, with its notorious verbal contest; or they were in a building, as Venice's fish market still remains. Beyond these street markets were numerous specialized uses of the street made possible by increased width or special configuration. One of the more striking examples of street adjustment to specialized need is found in the old city of Syracusa in Sicily.

The Syracusa of Greek foundation seems the last place to find the complexity of organic growth represented by the specialized street. But the fabric of the place was destroyed in the earthquake of 1693; when the town rebuilt itself, it expressed in the naming and layout of individual streets the diversity of functions that had come to be carried on in the street of a town in a warm, dry climate. During the Middle Ages it is doubtful that the streets would have been physically so differentiated; thus, the seventeenth-century reconstruction probably preserves distinctions more of function than of design. In Syracusa, we find *piazzi*, wide open spaces intended for symbolic and social purposes; the *piazza maggiore* of the Renaissance Italian city; *fora* carried over from the Roman use of a Greek town; a wide *corso* for strolling; *viali* to afford access within the old tightly built quarter of the town; a *lungomare* along the shore where boats could unload; and the other market layouts specific to a particular need.

Evidence supports the notion that markets may initially have been held in ordinary streets with the somewhat variable street lines common in the Middle Ages. Choosing a wide stretch of street in which to display goods brought in for the day, traders at first departed with the waning of the daylight. But those engaged in full-time commerce would seek to store their goods nearby; in that way, the houses fronting on the market street would gain value. Given the rise in significance of a street, or more particularly its frontage, it would be a short step to the creation of a market quarter in which retail trade would be clustered.

Departing from the Roman practice of providing a building, the early basilica, for the conduct of trade heavily controlled by the state, medieval town authorities yielded control and provision for selling to the merchants and the impact of organic processes. When the town was small, a single wide street or a field at the edge of the tiny town would suffice. But with the economic success of the town, the marketplace became incorporated into the fabric of the settlement as housing grew to surround it. The existence of that marketplace as a focus of urban interest separate from the church is demonstrated by the great number of cathedrals that are not built on the square, or that lie even today at the edge of the city. Bourges and Chartres in France and Salisbury and most other English cathedrals show this peripheral location. Only in Italy, where the Renaissance *piazza maggiore* came to be built, is the big church usually on the main square. In Flanders and Germany, the center of affairs and the locale of the church are clearly separated.

The Separation of Functions

The classical city exhibited two types of functional separation: social classes were separated from one another, and most types of economic activity were apart from residence. This separation was horizontal within the city and was a matter of institutional forces. The Romans sought to care for industry and trade in established places with special physical provision. Only in the smallest shops were workplace and residence combined. And among the imposing buildings, private as well as public, careful separation of the mundane from the exalted was maintained.

In considering conditions of land-use separation in the Middle Ages, we must distinguish between the two basic urban realms of Western civilization: in the Mediterranean world *social division* seems to have remained an important component of urban morphogenesis, whereas in the lands across the Alps economic forces largely controlled urban structure. The south had considerable social segregation, but to the north *functional segregation* was the controlling force. To add another contrast, the Mediterranean city, particularly as expressed in northern Italy, was a place of discrete and very definite social quarters, whereas the northern city, particularly as it developed in the lands around the North Sea, was a place of well-perceived occupational quarters. This contrast led in the south to a city of factions and in the north to one of gilds. The tower palace became the architectural expression of the Mediterranean urban power structure; the differently towered gildhall became the focal building in the north.

We cannot summarize internal separation simply for the Middle Ages, and perhaps its simplicity in the Classical Era comes mainly from the paucity of information on which we must build our analysis. We shall look first at the medieval city of the Mediterranean, more transitional in form than the northern city and, in real terms, the first expression of the modern city.

The Mediterranean city of the Middle Ages inherited most of its ground plan from classical times. The grid of streets of relatively equal importance, the fairly equidimensional street blocks, the squarish houses of stone construction, and the tendency—enhanced during the Renaissance—for there to be a single civic forum—the *piazza maggiore* of medieval Italy—can all be traced directly to Roman practice. But a ground plan does not automatically control all aspects of the functional organization of the town, and the medieval Italian city developed important modifications of the Roman social and political organization of urban space. Perhaps the most striking modification came in the introduction of factional society, growing out of the conflict between the loyalty to one overlord or another.

Along with this almost classical urge to faction, immortalized in *Romeo and Juliet*, went a further disruptive force that might be termed the urbanization of feudalism. In Italy as elsewhere, the feudal order was based mainly on the division of the countryside among barons demanding fealty from their villeins. But the survivals of Roman cities were powerful enough both to encroach through territorial political expansion on the countryside and, ultimately, to force the nobles to take up city residence so they might be watched and kept in some sort of subservience to the city authority. But taking up residence in towns did not end the nobles' search for henchmen, and many candidates stood ready for the job. Fritz Rörig clearly portrays the role of factionalism in shaping medieval Europe, contrasting Germany and Italy:

> It is a fact of profound significance that both these countries which provided an immediate stage for the universal policies of the Emperor—Germany and Italy—differed in the formation of their national state and ended in extreme political disunion and internal strife. But in the territorial formation of states on the old imperial soil in Italy the towns had a far more important role to play than they did in Germany. In Germany the political future belonged to the emergent states bearing the stamp of territorial feudalism. The formation of territories by the imperial towns did not produce zones of power of any significant size, even in their greatest manifestations, as for example the territory of Nuremberg; and the country towns, until the fifteenth century, were only able to assert their independence when the circumstances were favorable. Not so in Italy. Here the towns did not develop, as in Germany, within the power system of the countryside, but grew at the expense of feudal power areas until finally city-state bordered on city-state. The rural nobility was forced into the municipal sphere of interests. But in the process the leading classes of the individual towns—with the sole exception of Venice—lost their internal solidarity. In all the larger towns families of different political outlook—even the old opposition of Guelphs and Ghibellines was still going strong— regarded each other with hate or mistrust; at the same time the

lower classes, organized into guilds, were striving for political power.[9]

Little wonder that the faction became the social unit, because it was at first the more critical political unit, shaping a town of quarters ready for riot and infinitely suspicious of others equally enclosed by the city wall.

City of Factions

What, then, is the morphology of a city of factions? Its beginning lay in a fact observed by the eleventh-century chroniclers of Milan who realized that citizens of that powerful but representative town "when they lack external adversaries . . . turn their hatred against each other."[10] The need was for a city form that might afford protection for groups, against the threat posed by their neighborly enemies, when all lived within the enclosing city wall. It was not possible in times of peace to surround the faction with walls and an empty glacis in which the evil intentions of a neighborly enemy might be perceived and dealt with forcefully. The city had to continue as a governmental and economic entity, usually as a commune in Italy, which required daily association. Yet each political or social faction in the place had to live and operate from an internal strongpoint in which it could gather to defend its factional interest and from which it could sally in an attack on those outside the faction.

The state of bristling accommodation that obtained in the Italian towns made them clusters of self-seeking minorities only occasionally, and then only in response to great external danger, able to join in a majority action. Though the medieval city communes of Italy are often viewed as great cohesive bodies possessed of liberty and a common will to resist the enslavement of rural feudalism or urban capitalism, they were none of that in collective action and all of that in individual thinking. The city residence of knights, first invested with nobility for their power in the countryside, brought within the walls all the personal animosities and practices of revenge typical of the half-civilization of the Italian feudal order. Equally, the striving of merchants for wealth and power domesticated within the city class conflict between them and the nobles, on the one hand, and the mass of workers on the other.

The factional geography was composed of two morphological components: the tower and the quarter for henchmen. The tower determined location; once built, it tended to be surrounded by the residences of the supporters of the faction—the henchmen. The towers both were defensive and, to quote a contemporary contract, might "be necessary for doing harm to their enemy or enemies."[11] Most cities in upper Italy bristled with towers; in 1160 the Jewish traveler Benjamin of Tudela described Pisa as "a very great city,

9. Fritz Rörig, *The Medieval Town* (Berkeley: University of California Press, 1967), p. 56.
10. Quoted in Daniel Waley, *The Italian City-Republics* (New York: McGraw-Hill, 1969), p. 164.
11. Ibid., p. 175.

with about 10,000 turreted houses for battles at times of strife."[12] Attempts were made to limit that strife by controlling the height of towers, but most agreements seem to have been an invitation to even further conflict. Daniel Waley sees these structures as an outgrowth of the close social and political ties between countryside and city, with the city's victory in forcing the rural nobility to reside within its walls standing as Pyrrhic indeed:

> But this vertical quasi-military domestic architecture demands rather more explanation. It represents the import into the city of a form of watch-tower which was very common in the countryside. Moreover, the institution which made the tower a necessity was itself familiar in rural areas: this was the blood feud or vendetta, a tradition both of violence in settling (and prolonging) private disputes and of unwillingness to settle such matters in the courts. Essentially the purpose of the tower was defensive; its owner's home was his castle, to which he could retreat if under attack and where he might hope to conduct a prolonged defense. It became conventional for those who could afford it to inhabit a "house tower". Many did so because they had inherited one from ancestors and this was the accepted form of residential architecture, rather than because an aristocratic way of life dictated an unending series of vendettas for all. It has been suggested that the high cost of land within the cities encouraged vertical building: there is probably some truth in this but most cities normally had unused building space and in the main the towers should be seen as the product of fear, fashion and a taste for display, rather than an economic necessity. Some towers were set very close to each other, as may still be seen for example, at San Gimignano and Bologna. In these circumstances fighting from tower to tower, as described by Benjamin Tudela, may have taken place and some advantage could be derived from building higher than one's neighbour, but normally ostentation must have been the main motive for building very high.[13]

The component of ostentation in the building of towers came to be an integral element in Italian urban morphology, gaining ascendancy as the military requirements declined. Such ostentation in the Mediterranean was more than skin deep, more than detailing on the façade and painted murals; ostentation was first having a taller tower and ultimately a larger and more pompous palace.

The most fundamental factions allied families of similar political views, usually in an effort to dominate the city government partly by their own power and partly by borrowing the power of the Roman pope and his henchmen (the Guelphs) or the German emperor and his supporters (the Ghibellines). Such accumulations of power were made most effective by massing residence in a particular part of the city, isolating a particular quarter to the use of that group. In this creation of factional districts we find a peculiar urban manifestation of the very rural notion of territorial conflict.

12. *Itinerary of Benjamin of Tudela*, p. 5, quoted in ibid.
13. Ibid., pp. 176–77.

The establishment of the family compound as one of the modules of urban structure, probably first in a tower house and later in a *palazzo* of Renaissance design, demonstrates the socially stratified nature of urban morphogenesis in Italy. For magnates, this compound, somewhat consistent in form but variable in capacity, was the clay from which a city was to be shaped. The number of members of powerful families and the nearly feudal retainers who surrounded them determined the commodiousness of the form. We might assume great luxury and vast personal space in a tower house, but those that survive suggest more that a large group of people were forced to live together. Thus, when physical protection declined somewhat as a critical need, the tower was redesigned to become a bit more livable and somewhat more opulent, yet retained its frowning sense of menace to those who might wish to do harm to the family and its supporters. At that stage the Renaissance palace was born, preserving the large modular size of the family compound with its residence for numerous retainers, but becoming more gracious in its apartments and more carefully conceived as an architectural creation. The *palazzi* of Florence clearly demonstrate this transformation, combining a rather formidable grace with the reminder of ancient and arbitrary power present in the tall tower. (Strangely, such personal palaces gained great popularity in North America at the beginning of the twentieth century for use as city halls and railroad stations. The almost anarchic history of the form and the disdain for democracy possessed by its developers was completely overlooked, creating for the historically minded observer totally garbled symbolism.)

Houses in Italy

In upper Italy, the city house for the common people was taller than that on the fringes of Iberia, southern Spain, and the Balkans. Seemingly the ground floor was taken up with the shops of both artisans and merchants while the upper stories housed workers and masters. One common charac-

The Face of the
Medieval City

teristic of these tall Mediterranean houses was their use of arches to support the heavy weight of the masonry walls of upper stories while affording an increasing opening of the wall at its base. Perhaps to make up for the constraints imposed on merchants and artisans in the factious Italian city, the public market and market hall gained greater importance, not for whole-sale trade, as in the impressive cloth markets of Ypres, Bruges, and Cracow, but for the daily trading in consumer goods, as in the food market halls at Orvieto and Venice. The two somewhat conflicting needs of an especially secure house and an open selling place could be met by the tightly shuttered Mediterranean house for residence and the market hall for selling.

Little documentary evidence survives to help us reconstruct the full pattern of life in the northern Italian city during the Middle Ages—the way ordinary people lived and how they were housed. It would be valuable to know with more certainty the role played by occupation and employment in providing workers' housing. Were most ordinary people housed in buildings owned and provided by their employers, or did a generalized rental market make shelter available to workers? As the Italian cities were the largest in the Western world, we might logically anticipate that the provision of rental housing would appear first there. We do know of the widespread practice of "putting-out" yarn for weaving into textiles, with merchants serving as the organizers. In addition, we know that the system of "truck," wherein these factors of production issued scrip or credits for the purchase of food and staples, rather than money, was already developed in northern Italy. Members of the working class were clearly becoming more impoverished as a result of the competition with the capitalist magnates over the rewards to various elements of production. Looms were increasingly mortgaged, sug-gesting that it is highly unlikely that many weavers would have been able to pay for their housing.[14] Housing must have been provided by the factors organizing production by "putting-out," or the rental market in houses must have been sizable. But the details are missing.

Little evidence remains as to the nature of housing for common people, but certain logical assumptions help us to fill the gaps. Once a rental market for housing is established, constant pressures urge reduction in the size of individual units. If capital is cheap, then new competitive housing might be provided; if it is dear, then the only way to keep it in housing is to increase the return on a particular investment. Usually, such an effort not only reduces the size of units available to workers and their families but also often leads to sharp increases in rent, even for the diminished units. Another way to increase the return on capital is to diminish the actual investment by allowing the deterioration of the property. All of these influences came into play when the rental market for housing replaced the provision of shelter by masters of a craft, as during the High Middle Ages. As that era waned, the quality of housing declined in most cities; we must conclude that the tene-ments of the working class in Italian cities probably became smaller, more crowded, and more expensive, further worsening the condition of that class.

One of the most common responses as people crowded into the medieval cities was the enlargement of structures by all sorts of often jerry-built

14. Rörig, *Medieval Town*, pp. 84–89.

extensions. Houses were pushed backward to fill the entire burgage plot; extensions encroached on the street in the form of bay windows and shed-like lean-tos, or more commonly as overhanging extensions of upper stories—sometimes, as in the "covered streets" in Cahors and Perigeux, as a full bridge across the street.[15] Such crowding was normally unpleasant and proved in the long run to be even dangerous.

This wooden model of Siena in the fourteenth century was based on Ambrogia Lorenzetti, The City of Good Government *(ca. 1337–40) and suggests the nature of housing at that time, particularly the tower structures.*

Housing Pressure and the Plague

Beginning in the eleventh century, housing pressure built up but was repeatedly relieved by inadvertent but positively draconian reductions in urban population. These were brought about by "massacres provoked by the great wars which were then bleeding Christendom white," by the ravaging of the countryside by bands of brigands, and by "excesses of religious fanaticism" such as the brutal Albigensian Crusade we shall note in the next chapter. Famines were frequent, sweeping Austria in 1343 and France in 1351, 1359, and 1418. "The last carried off over 100,000 persons in Paris, where groups of twenty or thirty poor wretches at a time died of starvation on the dung-heaps, and where wolves came to devour the corpses." Earthquakes destroyed other areas such as Villach in Carinthia, and the sea battered a number of towns on the slowly subsiding coast of Holland. "But worst of all were the ravages of epidemic maladies, leprosy, and typhus, which raged among the masses, who were already weak from want and wretchedness."[16]

Given the epidemic quality of these diseases and the deteriorated state of much of the housing, doubtless the ravages were most severe in cities. In a generally grim situation, the Black Death of 1348 to 1350 savaged Europe to such a degree that the population did not recover for several centuries. Estimates hold that central Italy lost two-thirds of its population, while between one-third and two-thirds of the population died in the Po Basin, northern Spain, France, England, and the Low Countries. "The towns were

15. Pierre Lavedan, *Histoire de l'urbanisme: Antiquité–moyen age* (Paris: Henri Laurens, 1926), 1: 409.

16. Boissonade, *Life and Work in Medieval Europe*, p. 284.

The Face of the Medieval City

attacked with special severity. Venice lost two-thirds of its population; Bologna, four-fifths; Florence, 80,000 to 100,000 souls; Majorca, 30,000; Narbonne, 30,000; Paris, over 50,000; Strassburg and Bâle, 14,000 each; Vienna, 40,000. . . . As far as can be calculated [the Black Death over a period of repeating epidemics between 1350 and 1450] cost from twenty-four to twenty-five million human lives."[17]

Florence as an Example of a Mediterranean City

Not only in urban-rural relations but also in morphology, a sharp contrast can be drawn between the physical form of the Mediterranean city and that north of the Alps. We have viewed the differences in platting and street layout. But let us look in detail at Florence, which serves as an archetype of the south at least symbolically, if not in all details.

Since the general outlines of the southern house and the factional quarter have been established, we can easily understand the specific qualities of the city on the Arno. A difficulty faces us from the very beginning because although adequate "evidence from documents and buildings survives to describe the aristocratic mode of living in Renaissance Florence, [the] information on lower-class housing is scantier and more fragmentary. The dwellings inhabited by the urban poor were primitive and unsubstantial; they have not survived the ravages of time."[18]

Gene Brucker turned to tax records, which offered some glimpse of how the working class lived. "Most artisans and laborers lived in small houses of two or three stories (one room per story) or single-room cottages. . . . Tax records contain a few references to buildings in which rooms or stories were rented out to several individuals or families, but the apartment house was a rare phenomenon in fifteenth-century Florence."[19] But the notion of reducing the quality of residence for speculative gain in rent, if not of property value itself, had seemingly entered the minds of those who had capital to invest. One Alessandro Borromei, a wealthy Pisan émigré with large real estate holdings in Florence, was reported in 1427 to have bought the palace of the noble Amieri family. "He converted this structure into a multiple-unit tenement, renting shops on the ground floor to merchants and artisans, and single rooms in the upper stories as living quarters."[20] Clearly, fifteenth-century Florence must have been entering a stage when the prototypes for worker housing were beginning to shift from the country cottage to the townsman's house, necessarily transforming its interior arrangement. We witness this shift all over Western Europe; the scale of city activity increased as the reach of the resident traders was pushed outward and the calls they placed on indigenous manufacture were enlarged. The technology of cottage industry continued but, when located in the city, the physical provision to shelter it changed.

The role of the factional quarter persisted, though its expression seemed

17. Ibid., p. 285
18. Gene A. Brucker, *Renaissance Florence* (New York: Wiley, 1969), p. 22
19. Ibid.
20. Ibid., p. 23.

The Palazzo Ricardi Medici in Florence is still suggestive of the secure home (Fondago) of the leader of a political faction in an Italian city. No longer a simple tower, it still remained a frowningly powerful structure.

to hide its origins. As Brucker notes, the distinctive feature of Renaissance Florence was the heterogeneity, in social and economic terms, of neighborhoods and quarters. The rich had no quarter of their own, as had been true in imperial Rome, and there were no districts solely occupied by the poor. Cottages and *palazzi* were intermixed, as were woolen factories and retail shops, churches and religious foundations. As in Roman times, shops occupied the ground floor of sometimes palatial buildings, and the rich merchant and shoemaker might live side by side. Brucker tells us that this great mixing of classes and occupations resulted from Florence's method of growth (organic, in our terms) and a social practice wherein each important family was associated with a particular neighborhood. There the founder of the family had first resided and subsequent generations had remained clustered for protection in a city of factionalism. Even after 1400, when the threat was much less, there was still great social pressure to remain in the "family neighborhood" to enhance the political role of one of the main elements of the urban patriciate.[21]

Only in a city ruled by authoritarian patriarchs and divided by factionalism would such a social geography be shaped; we do not see this pattern north of the Alps. Its persistence to the south even into modern times may help to explain the differences in the location of higher income in lands of northern European colonization and lands of Mediterranean settlement. Throughout Latin America, the rich and powerful seem to favor central-city residence to a degree unknown in North America above the Rio Grande. Possibly the role of social and political leadership enjoyed by the powerful

21. Ibid., p. 23.

The Face of the Medieval City

patriciates in Mediterranean cities may in some way be thus expressed in overseas areas.

We have given sufficient notice to the tower house and its cluster, but we should look briefly at the compound of the merchant and the street of the manufacturing *fattor*. The turn of the fifteenth century gives us a picture of the trader's compound:

> The centre of their life, as for every merchant in foreign trading settlements, was their own *fondaco*—the group of buildings which was at once shop and office, warehouse and dwelling. If at home [at Florence] in Calimala or Por S. Maria, a *fondaco* was often merely a merchant's counting-house and shop (above which, perhaps, he lived), in settlements abroad it still kept much of the character of the Arab *funduk* from which it took its name. Originally built, no doubt, to shelter merchants and their wares from the assaults of wild desert tribes, these *fondachi* still had something of the aspect of fortified castles. In their great inner courtyards the long trains of pack-animals were watered and stabled, the slaves assembled for inspection and sale, and the bales of merchandise unpacked and stored, while the buildings served as offices, warehouses, and dwellings. Here under the jurisdiction of their own consul . . . the merchants could safely transact their business according to their own laws, and pray to their own God. Here . . . they tried to teach their Moorish slaves the rudiments of Tuscan cooking.[22]

This picture of the *fondaco* does not distinguish quite so clearly as we might wish the trading compound of the native from that of the foreigner. Each would tend to have a cluster of buildings surrounding a courtyard in which goods were loaded, unloaded, sorted, and inspected. If located in a foreign land, its gate and walls might be sturdier and the functions of the consul and accompanying chaplain were introduced. In such a situation the merchant would be a foreigner to the culture and the polity, tolerated for the time being but not fully admitted to its life because of his insistence on maintaining ties to an alien state, culture, and possibly religion. Just as the Jew might live in a ghetto to maintain his identity, the foreign merchant must live and operate in an enclosure with a similar degree of extraterritoriality. Among Mediterraneans this enclosure was the *fondaco*; for Germans it remained a *stahlyard*, which the English corrupted into the "steelyard," as in London. The domestic trader still favored the cluster of buildings about a courtyard since pilferage and theft were ever-present problems.

For a picture of the establishment of a wealthy and powerful merchant, we may turn to a striking survival, the palace of the great French merchant Jacques Coeur, in Bourges in Berry. Probably the most splendid building built by a commoner in France during the Middle Ages, this magnificent palace still combined the counting house with the château. A great doorway opens from the street into a courtyard where goods as well as noble guests

22. Iris Origo, *The Merchant of Prato* (New York: Knopf, 1957), p. 120.

were received and dispatched. Stair towers led from an arcaded ground floor, where goods could be stored and trade and inspection carried out in rainy weather, to the upper floors. A second level was given over to elegant rooms for Coeur and his family; the attics were used for storage and the counters at which less bulky goods were traded. Jacques Coeur did not have to defend himself against a foreign populace or as yet against a suspicious monarch—he was the king's treasurer until his fall from favor in 1451. Yet he felt it necessary to have an enclosure in which to trade, and his attics for storage were remarkably proof against pilferage, not only by virtue of being at the top of his palace but, further, because the building was erected atop the walls of the Gallo-Roman city of *Avaricum.*

The Rise of Industrial Quarters

Much as Florence was a great combination of hundreds of family neighborhoods, such as the cluster of the Albizzi along the Borgo degli Albizzi or the palaces of the Peruzzi around the Piazza dei Peruzzi, there was some concentration of workers in particular trades in certain streets. These suggest the partial existence of occupational quarters so typical of cities north of the Alps. Even more, they herald the initial stages of the creation of true industrial quarters in cities. Brucker tells us that cloth manufactories were widely spread in Florence, but some of the most demanding and mechanized of the stages of production were beginning to show concentration. Dyeing, washing, and soap making clustered on the banks of the Arno. Forges were concentrated in areas devoted to other trades such as arms making, and it was decreed that certain pariah industries must locate at the edge of the city.[23]

Areas of Customer Access and the Rise of Land Rent

Among the merchants who sought to deal directly with the public, perhaps for only a part of their total sales but still for a component of sufficient worth to influence the choice of premises to be occupied, location was based not on occupational association but on customer access. "Rents for both houses and shops were naturally higher in the center, and they tended to diminish as one moved toward the periphery. Commanding very high prices were shops located near the Piazza della Signoria (Palazzo Vecchio) and the Piazza del Duomo (cathedral), or along the street connecting these squares."[24] Brucker shows that a retail clothing shop near the center rented for 118 florins per year in 1427 and a barber shop on the Piazza della Signoria went for 27 florins. Houses near the center rented for about 25 florins annually, but at the edge such houses could be had normally for less than 10 florins' annual rent. As might therefore be anticipated, the poorer workers—cloth workers, servants, and casual laborers—lived at the city's edge. In those areas with the worst-paid workers—wool carders, beaters, and combers—the rents for truly slum dwellings were one or two florins a year.[25]

In the fifteenth century, provision of housing for workers was already strongly based on rent and rent-paying ability. Some of the self-contained establishments, where master and workers occupied the same quarters, were quite ample in scale. In Datini's great house at Prato we find such an example. "It will be observed that, though there were many servants [in Datini's house], there were no servants' rooms—the explanation being that they slept wherever was most convenient—in the kitchen, on the landing or on truckle beds in the room of their master and mistress."[26] Normally one or several of the employees in the counting house also slept there. Independent workers, at least in the sense that no one cared much for their wealth, health, or soul, were cast out into the rental market for housing, to fare badly for the most part. No doubt to a considerable degree the uncertainty of the market for rental housing caused its provision to be halting and inadequate and its pricing often unreasonable in terms of current wage levels.

23. Brucker, *Renaissance Florence*, pp. 23, 24.
24. Ibid., p. 24.
25. Ibid.
26. Origo, *Merchant of Prato*, p. 248.

The Medieval Structure in Cities North of the Alps

The fascination of the Middle Ages is greatest when we turn north of the Alps. In the youthful cities in the north and west of Europe, the rootstock of the Roman city was still vigorous enough to allow the successful grafting of vital and functional morphologies characteristic of the economic reactions of medieval commerce. The Romans had built cities all the way from the Welsh and Scottish marches to the Rhine and Danube. Something of that heritage had survived into the eleventh and twelfth centuries even after five hundred years of quarrying by Frankish and Anglo-Saxon farmers living nearby. The quality of the site remained, leading fairly promptly to the renewal of city growth once the long-distance connections were reestablished with the end of the Dark Ages. The frequently wooden buildings of Roman urbanization in these distant reaches of the empire had been swept away, but the street grid and other elements of the urban support structure often survived. And in a few places Roman monuments remained, battered but not demolished—the gates of Autun and the great Porta Negra of Trier, the amphitheaters at St. Albans, Moudon, and Autun. Finally, the site of the Roman settlement and the often considerable remains of the Roman road system stood as the significant bequest of the empire.

Whatever the form of the modular plots found in the medieval cities of the north, the buildings placed on them grew out of a fairly consistent need and a basic technology common to most of the lands in the north and west of Europe. The need was to house a population directly engaged in commercial and craft activities, who were in many instances the political and social leaders of the town. This combination of economic activity and political control distinguished the north from the Mediterranean. Although in the north conflict might arise between the burghers and their lord, as for example between the leading men of Ghent and the counts of Flanders, there was no herd of petty nobility steeped in notions of feudal vassalage, such as disintegrated society in the typical Italian town.

In the north the city powers in conflict or cooperation with the suzerain did not lead to endless blood feuding and retaliation, as in Italy, but to one of two normal relationships. If burghers were powerful in comparison with the overlord, the urban commune emerged, as in Flanders during the High Middle Ages; on the other hand, when the suzerain came to dominate, as did the Spanish overlords in later centuries, a cruel and despotic repression of civil liberties took place. But there was not the malady of internal conflict that became the wasting disease of the Mediterranean city. When the evil of Austrian and Spanish control was overthrown, the north still had a firm basis for civic cooperation and development that did not exist in Italy at the end of the Middle Ages.

In considerable measure the eclipse of the Italian city as the urban leader in Europe stemmed from this contrast between its internalized conflict and the conflict with a basically outside force found in the north. The contrast was like one between a pain coming from external pressures that, when relieved, leaves the body able to recover its health and an internal cancer that saps the body's basic vitality. As we shall see, the efforts of the

The Face of the Medieval City

despotic popes could "beautify" Rome in the sixteenth and seventeenth centuries, but their highly undemocratic practices left it a pathetic shell of a city until after Pius IX, Pio Nono, was deprived of control in 1870.

The absence of unremitting internal political conflict did not mean that all was harmonious in the north. Competition was active, with occasional outright conflict, but it generally stemmed from efforts by various groups to gain similar objectives, though with different apportionments of the ultimate benefit. Workers and masters argued over wages and powers, and various gilds sought to monopolize particular activities to the exclusion of others. Contest was not missing, but dogma; basic agreements existed as to the needs for civic liberties, and common efforts were made to expand the economic sphere of the city. Just as the conflict between city and suzerain was fundamentally an externalized fight, so the objective of the northern city tended to be scoring off against another city rather than one's closest neighbor. Some cities lost their external support and thus shrank as economic organisms, but the towns that prevailed grew rapidly. The urban glory of Europe had moved north of the Alps by the close of the late Middle Ages. The architectural grandeur of the Renaissance cities in the south confuses the truth. These fast became the glittering façades of nearly empty purpose surrounding a decadent aristocracy of feudalism and the church with a pomp it had not earned and could not maintain. When the vital forces of the Enlightenment, economic liberalism, and increasing personal liberty emerged in the seventeenth and eighteenth centuries, the rot behind the façades of Rome, Naples, Milan, and Florence began to show through.

Competition and Its Restraint Shape the Northern City: The Gild

Just as the factional conflict of the Mediterranean city helped to shape its urban morphology, the occupational competition in the north helped to determine the shape of the city there. To understand the role of occupation, we must look at the institutions that came to represent collective economic interests. Evidence suggests that early in the course of urbanization of the north, the city's economic life was conducted on a rather individual basis. Some men, and occasionally women, proved better merchants or artisans than others; that is, they were more successful economically, not necessarily more skillful workers. The medieval notions of profit, just price, and excessive ambition in the material world were greatly challenged by too obvious an individual success. The church, utterly dependent on a traditional order for survival in the face of obvious corruption, was strongly urged to a course of resisting change, institutionalizing balance and order, and rejecting the notion of individual decision in matters of ethics, freedom, and conscience. Demonstrably, collegiality was far to be preferred to individuality, save in the instances of divine ordination thought to be the foundation of the decrees of monarchs, temporal and spiritual.

To maintain order and balance became the central purpose of medieval economic institutions, though breaks in the smooth flow of that tradition did take place and were often the events of which history takes the greatest

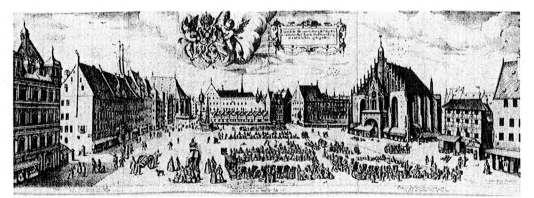

Market square in Nuremberg. Etching by Lorenz Stauch, 1599.

notice. Still, in seeking to understand the normal development of northern cities and their morphogenesis, we must be concerned with the institutions as generally conceived.

Fritz Rörig visualized the origin of the gild, which became the institution of order and control, as first rooted in the conflict between the workers in newly established towns and the ecclesiastical authorities and lay overlords who tended to dominate those places. Conflict had been present even when the town's residents were mostly independent workers at a craft. When the long-distance traders settled in the proto-towns, the situation of conflict was enhanced because they brought their own law with them, the law merchant that they had developed on long "trading journeys which at the time were still conducted in the cooperative manner of a caravan. Nor did the traders who settled in the new towns wish to abandon this spirit" when they settled down. "The guilds were an inevitable consequence. This was where they met together [and] where they celebrated their festivals, which occasions were liable to be rather more sumptuous than the spirit of ecclesiastical decorum considered appropriate." Gilds combined men of common economic and social interest and formed a strong force against the bishops' efforts to force more production from reluctant workers through the powerful threat of excommunication. The gild was "an organization in which the small man in the town—the artisans and small shopkeepers—saw a remedy for his complaints against the bishop and his officials."[27]

Boissonade finds a different origin for the grouping of small men for fraternal purposes in these "secret associations, brotherhoods, gilds, *stellungen*, prohibited by the authorities, wherein were organized seditious movements, and those peasant revolts which broke out on all sides in Italy, Gaul, Fresia (Holland), Flanders, Saxony, at irregular intervals during the eighth and ninth centuries." Those original uprisings of "bands of serfs and their womenfolk, who were more cruel even than the men, attacked seignorial domains, pillaged, burned, tortured, massacred without discernment or pity until a cruel repression brought them back for a while to obedience."[28] The return to "obedience" came with the acceptance of an estab-

27. Rörig, *Medieval Town*, pp. 19–20.
28. Boissonade, *Life and Work in Medieval Europe*, p. 101.

lished order repressive of human freedom and the concerns of common people and was, as a consequence, restive indeed. The reestablishment of that order strengthened the loss of geographical freedom that became serfdom, tying the more common folk to the lands they tilled and making escape from the countryside the only possible emancipation. Because the church was the largest landowner of medieval times, it made common cause with the powerful nobles in enforcing this geographical bondage, adding the weapon even more awful in medieval times, denial of indulgence and solace to serfs who broke their enforced contract to remain in the country.

Henri Pirenne looked for the basis of urban liberty in the functional contrast between urban and rural institutions. "In no civilization is city life evolved independently of commerce and industry." Pirenne goes on to argue specifically of the medieval city, "At no era in history is there so marked a contrast as that which their social and economic organization presented to the social and economic organization of the country." And the contrast was greatest in human qualities: "Never before had there existed, it seems, a class of men so specifically and strictly urban as was the medieval bourgeoisie."[29] In Greek city-states, synoecism tied the country and town together from a rural beginning; in Roman times, the tie was as strong but knotted in the reverse direction. But during the Middle Ages, the country and the town were in constant confrontation with one another.

That opposition was probably of little worry to the rural magnates— barons and great ecclesiastics—until "the organization of commerce in the Middle Ages . . . obliged the peripatetic . . . 'merchant venturers' . . . to settle at fixed points." That obligation came because "in the interval between their trips and especially during the bad season which made the sea, the rivers and the roads impassable, they necessarily had to gather in certain places in the region."[30] With this powerful economic group possessed of good organization and a virile will resident periodically in towns, those places took a firmer stand against the repressive policies of baron and churchman. We have inherited a partisan view of this period, as Pirenne explains, because what records and accounts survive were prepared by churchmen who presented their view of the time and their obsession with the religious purpose. "They could not neglect the recital of the wars and political conflicts which reacted on the Church, but there was no reason for them to have taken pains to note the beginnings of city life, for which they were lacking in comprehension no less than sympathy. . . . As for first-hand sources—that is to say, written and compiled by townsmen—there are none in existence earlier than the end of the twelfth century. . . . [Then, a few] maps and records supplement this poverty to a certain extent."[31] In light of this poverty of sources, Pirenne calls for a recourse "to inference and hypothesis in this study of origins." Accepting that *modus operandi*, in the study of morphogenesis the existence of maps assumes greater importance to

29. Henri Pirenne, *Medieval Cities: Their Origin and the Revival of Trade* (Princeton: Princeton University Press, 1925), pp. 135, 136–37.

30. Ibid., pp. 139–40.

31. Ibid., pp. 145–46.

us and the survival of some physical pattern within the city can serve as an invaluable crutch to steady inference and as a tool to focus hypothesis.

Which of possible sites for towns will be taken up and developed? Central-place theory supplies an answer, but history shows it unresponsive save in the most dominantly feudal of areas. As Pirenne points out, rich areas "in the agricultural and desminial civilization of the Middle Ages [places such as Stavelot and Malmedy] . . . were notable for their wealth and influence. But situated too far from the great highways of communication, they were not affected by the economic revival nor, so to speak fecundated thereby. In the midst of the flowering which it inspired, they remained sterile, like seed fallen upon stony ground. *None of them rose above the rank of mere half-rural market-towns*." Clearly two systems of settlement existed in the Middle Ages: one we might call "central-place" in deference to Christaller, and the other "mercantile" to reflect both purpose and origin. One explanation, one model, cannot serve for both these systems of settlement location and support. As Pirenne noted, these central-places, as we have called them, "had on the whole only an auxiliary function. Adapted to a social order very different from that which witnessed the birth of cities, they could not have been able to give birth to the latter by their own forces. [Cities] were, so to speak, the crystallization points of commercial activity. It did not arise from them—it came to them from without [in long-distance trade]."[32]

Looking at the economic institutions within the cities that were growing on distant trade, Pirenne notes in a different study, *Economic and Social History of Medieval Europe*, "It is a familiar fact that the clergy were a foreign element in the medieval town, their privileges excluded them from sharing in those of the city." In this status they were allied to the great rural landowners, and with them it was true that "amidst the commercial and industrial population [of the city] their economic role was simply that of consumers." Noting the residence of nobles in Italian towns, and their involvement in trading and merchant navigation in some of them, he contrasts the lands north of the Alps. "In Northern Europe, on the other hand, almost all the nobles left the [Roman] towns to settle in the castles in the country [and they were not forced by the towns to return, as in Italy]. It is only in exceptional circumstances that a knightly family is to be found, here and there, isolated and, as it were, astray in the midst of bourgeois society. It was not until the end of the Middle Ages that the aristocracy, by that time less quarrelsome and more eager for comfort, began to build themselves luxurious town houses."[33] For the rural aristocracy, those town houses were to remain a secondary residence occupied only periodically during a "social season" shaped by their peers in the countryside, not by the bourgeoisie.

Thus, in the northern city the ground was left clear, uncluttered by inherited power, for the shaping of the first truly urban society, of which we have the great good fortune to be the heirs. When the formerly wandering merchants settled on that ground, they could begin to organize social,

32. Ibid., pp. 151–52. Emphasis supplied.
33. Henri Pirenne, *Economic and Social History of Medieval Europe* (French ed., 1933; English trans., New York: Harcourt, Brace, 1937), pp. 168–69.

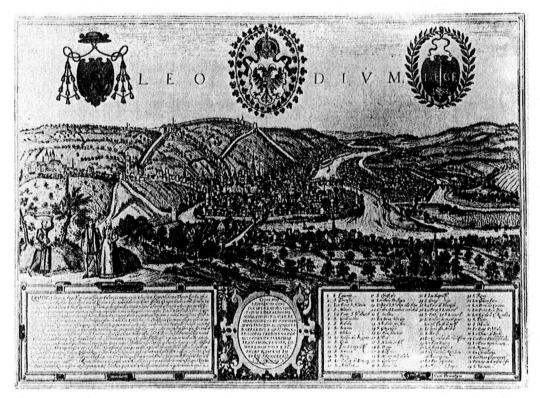

Liège as a market town.

political, economic, and even religious institutions to meet the needs of the two supporting activities of a town—commerce and industry. Though industry was less widespread than commerce, it tended to follow in the path of commerce for supply of the trading goods on which it relied. The first urban institution tended, therefore, to be the gild merchant, which had existed even while the merchant venturers were peripatetic and came to be domesticated when they took up city residence.

The functions of the gild were several: to assure the quality of production or the ethics of trade; to serve as a representative element in the creation of a collegial form of city government; to care for the social and personal security of its members; to limit the entrance to a trade in the guise of assuring the applicant's mastery thereof; and, less consciously, to shape an organization whose power would be sufficient to defend the rights of merchants, artisans, and the city against the repression by the established order of aristocracy and church. For each of those groups the dislike of merchants was deep.

The *Portus*: The Place Where the Merchants' Town Began

The wandering merchants often settled first at the gates of the town, the *portus*, which initially was a small specialized settlement set up in timid fashion at the foot of a *bourg* or at the gate of a tiny walled village. These may have been the most common form for the settlement of merchants, but we cannot be sure. Preexisting towns included those of ecclesiastical and palatine origin as well as fortified villages:

> Details are lacking concerning the gradual peopling of towns. It is not known how the first traders, who came to locate there, settled in the midst of the preexisting population. The towns, whose precincts frequently included empty spaces occupied by fields and gardens, must have furnished them at the start with a place which soon became too restricted. It is certain that in many of them, from the tenth century on, they were forced to locate outside the walls. At Verdun they built a fortified enclosure (*negotiatorum claustrum*), joined to the city by two bridges. At Ratisbonne the "city of merchants" (*urbs mercatorum*) arose beside the episcopal city, and the same thing is to be seen at Strasbourg and elsewhere.[34]

Thus, the general practice, either in the classical model of the castle (*bourg*) and its merchants' camp below the walls (*faubourg*) or in the *urbs mercatorum* outside the bishop's town, was that of a separate, self-contained area in which merchants practiced their art. Such a place was called in medieval terms a *portus* or *bourg*.

> Between a *portus* and a market or a fair the distinction is very clear. While the latter were periodic meeting places of buyers and sellers, the former was a permanent place of trade, a center of uninterrupted traffic. After the seventh century Dinant, Huy, Valenciennes and Cambrai were places with a *portus*, and in consequence transfer points. The economic slump of the eighth century and the Norseman invasions naturally ruined their business. It was not until the tenth century that the old *porti* took on new life or new ones were established, as at Bruges, Ghent, Ypres, St. Omer, and elsewhere. At the same date there appears in Anglo-Saxon texts the word "port" employed as a synonym for the Latin words *urbs* and *civitas*, and even at the present day the term "port" is commonly met with in the names of cities of every land of English speech.[35]

The *portus* became the first place where mercantile government could be envisaged and a law distinct in its practice worked out. In the market town itself, the regulations were those of baronial or clerical overlord aimed at restricting sharp trading practices, gaining a proper assize of goods and a tax return for the privilege of the market. This form was essentially domestic law of a particular sort. For the fair something else was needed, as the merchants found operation impossible in a context that viewed them as aliens. The special code for the fair, *pied poudre* or piepowder law, was created and

---

34. Pirenne, *Medieval Cities*, pp. 146–47.
35. Ibid., p. 149.

restricted to its geographical locale. Under it, alien and denizen were equal, but only within the fair's confines, for interests directly associated with it, and for its term.

The *portus* when it grew up was both continuous in occupation and geographically determinate, to the extent that it had to seek its own law to survive socially and economically. Market regulations applied to retail trade alone, piepowder law to the special temporal and geographical conditions of the fair, and feudal law to a serfdom unable to move or to engage in the realities of trade. As Pirenne saw it, "The bourgeois themselves were far from taking up a revolutionary attitude towards this society. They took for granted the authority of the territorial princes, the privileges of the nobility and, above all, those of the Church. . . . They merely desired a place in the sun, and their demands were confined to their most indispensible needs." Those needs attached to the residents of a particular area, so, given the strongly territorial quality of medieval law, special laws could be adopted to gratify needs:

> Of the latter the most indispensible was personal liberty; without liberty, that is to say, without the power to come and go, to do business, to sell goods, a power not enjoyed by serfdom, trade would be impossible. Thus they claimed it, simply for the advantages it conferred, and nothing was further from the mind of the bourgeoisie than any idea of freedom as a natural right; in their eyes it was merely a useful one. Besides, many of them possessed it *de facto*; they were immigrants, who had come from too far off for their lord to be traced and who, since their serfdom could not be presumed, necessarily passed for free, although born of unfree parents. But the fact had to be transformed into a right. It was essential that the villeins, who came to settle in the towns to seek a new livelihood, should feel safe and should not have to fear being taken back by force from the manors from which they had escaped. They must be delivered from labour services and from all the hated dues by which the servile population was burdened, such as the obligation to marry only a woman of their own class and to leave the lord part of their inheritance. Willy-nilly, in the course of the twelfth century these claims, backed up as they often were by dangerous revolts, had to be granted.[36]

To understand the growth of towns, we must keep clearly in mind the attachment of liberty to place; to understand the growth of capitalism, we must keep in mind as well the extinction of the duty of heriot, which had until the late Middle Ages diminished the individual's possession on death.

The geographical concept of the merchant's *portus* furnished the legal basis for the peopling of cities through the transformation of serfs into cityfolk. "Freedom became the legal status of the bourgeoisie, so much so that it was no longer a personal privilege only, but a *territorial* one, inherent

36. Ibid., p. 50.

in urban soil just as serfdom was in manorial soil. In order to obtain it, it was enough to have resided for a year and a day within the walls of the town. City air makes man free, says the German proverb."[37] Admittedly the lord could recapture his errant serf if he caught him within the year, but the natural antipathy between burgesses and barons made the search of even a nearby city difficult, and of a distant one impossible. We cannot measure the impact this feudal law had in setting up migration over a fair distance; we can logically assume that it encouraged it.

With a legal mechanism making rural implosion on the city possible, the growth of the town was assured if economic demand materialized, as we know it did, particularly in the twelfth century. "Thus the medieval town was essentially the home of the burgesses; it existed only for them and because of them. It was in their own interest, and in their own interest alone, that they created its institutions and organized its economy."[38] The institution most universally adopted was the confraternity of workers in a particular trade. Since these gilds were not everywhere the same, no concise picture of them will apply in all aspects to any particular city, or in any specific aspect to all cities. Yet we must examine the gild to understand the internal physical and social structure of the town during the Middle Ages.

The Occupation Quarter in Europe North of the Alps

The discontinuity of urban institutions in Europe north of the Alps led to a sharply contrasting social foundation for cities there as opposed to the Mediterranean. The gild took the place of the political faction, and the occupation quarter replaced the factional district. These gilds, preexisting the city residence of merchants, became the basis for the collegial government of towns when these powerful and energetic people came to settle there. The expressions of the gild—its hall, and the shops and houses of its members—met the eye of the visitor in the north, rather than the tower houses and the restive collection of people centering on them typical of Italy. In many places the gilds assumed the support of particular parish churches, so religion in turn took on this occupational division, to such an extent that the medieval city of the north became a physical collection of occupation quarters and a political college of gild representatives.

The gild fitted particularly well into the ordering of medieval society. Individuals were seldom thought of outside their class, and overlords and monarchs desired to deal with corporate entities rather than individuals. The tendency toward syndicalist combination was further strengthened by the nature of medieval taxation; excises on sales, transactions, and other activities might with some assurance be anticipated and commuted into an annual value. Thus, if a king found himself short of money—a regal fault to this very day—he might anticipate taxes ultimately due him by trading important privileges to a gild, or to the collection of gilds that formed the town, in return for early "payment" of the expected return from the excise.

37. Ibid., p. 51. Emphasis supplied.
38. Ibid., p. 169

Given their power and increasing wealth, the gilds often managed to commute many small payments into one large one, buying for the future freedom not yet enjoyed by that group. So the fondness that governments have ever had for dealing with a corporation joined with the search for increasing social, economic, and even religious freedom by the townspeople to strike a bargain unapproachable in the faction-divided city of the south.

The gildhall became the locus of the basic component of the collegial organization and the repository of its charter. Charters were of such value in holding the monarch to his past bargains, as the Massachusetts Puritans learned five hundred years later, that they were guarded with great care and displayed with equal pride. The gildhall was the center of the life of people in trade because trade was at the core of their existence. As the economic community in a town gained control over its own activities, the gild came to represent the basic unit of government. It controlled access to the status of freeman by requiring mastery of a trade and admission to the "mystery"; it sent representatives to serve on a board of aldermen who ran the town. In controlling a trade, the gild was a mechanism for quality and maintenance as well as economic balance. To be admitted to a gild, a boy normally had first to be apprenticed to a working master. Although apprenticeships could vary, they were normally for seven years, during which the apprentice lived in the household of the master under a legal contract, an indenture. Special conditions might be made—the boy might be provided with a feather bed or given a certain endowment on completion—but he could neither reside elsewhere nor work for another, save on forfeit of a considerable sum. Often the apprentice had no blood relatives in the town, so he also needed protection; the master also wished to protect both his considerable fee, in a number of cases, and the labor of the apprentice.

These workers trained in the mystery of a trade, but not yet admitted to the gild as freemen and masters, were called journeymen. They engaged to work for another, but not under an indenture, as did the apprentices. In the absence of an active rental market for housing in the medieval cities, journeymen often had to be sheltered at night as well as during the day. They came to form the third component of the occupation household, which was both the social unit of medieval life in cities of the north and the structure that formed their morphological module.

The Functional Development of the Northern House

We may now understand how the basic building structure of the medieval town of the north came into being. The construction of the time, as we have noted, was made up of bays shaped by posts and lintels of relatively small dead weight. Depending on the infilling, this structure could be remarkably light in relation to the space it enclosed, so relatively great heights could be attained. We cannot determine the tallest timber structure from the Middle Ages, but certainly it must have been of seven, eight, or even nine stories. Such heights would have been tall for private buildings even a hundred years ago, so due respect must be paid the medieval timber builders. Height alone did not faze these carpenters and masons, as their church towers show.

Salisbury rose to 404 feet, Strasbourg to 466 feet, and Cologne and Ulm were designed to 515 feet and 528 feet respectively, though they remained uncompleted until the nineteenth century. We may reason that medieval builders did carry timber construction to the limit of their technology, or at least to the extent necessary to provide the space required by the sometimes large occupational households of the time.

The result was the tall, narrow house normally elongated away from the street and buttressed by its neighbors. The use to be made of the house was reflected in its structure. The master, his family, and his apprentices and journeymen formed not merely an economic but a social unit. Thus, the medieval burgher's house would have had to contain (1) production space, if he was an artisan, (2) selling space, whether he was a merchant or an artisan, (3) storage space for the staple of his production or the goods of his sale, (4) housing for him and his biological family, and (5) housing for an apprentice or two, and quite possibly for a journeyman, and even his biological family. To contain such an occupational household a large building was needed, which has misled some into thinking that the quarters of the medieval merchant were quite spacious. In fact even a quite prosperous merchant had few physical possessions and little privacy or space. He and his family probably occupied only one or two rooms, sharing a single bed in many cases and using only a few chairs and benches, a simple table, and some armoires

The Face of the Medieval City

153

and storage cupboards. People at ease tended, as did monarchs, to recline in bed, both for its comfort and for the warmth its covering afforded in the bone-chilling winters of northern Europe. What heat there was came from fire-places, which also served as the cooking place of the simple and unrefined food of the time.

So simple was the design of houses that merchants of substance had little more than a "hall"—a large room that served most of their needs. "Their hall took up the full height of their house from floor to rafters, and in the two-storied back portion of the house, they used the ground floor room as a store [storage room], and the upper floor, which had to be reached by outside stone or wooden stairs, as the solar or private room in which members of the family slept. Kitchen, brewhouse, and dairy were banished into separate outhouses as a precaution against fire." These were outstanding merchants, though "not rich enough to build on a baronial scale, but they aped the aristocracy as sedulously as they could."[39]

In England, internal peace and the minor constraint of town walls meant that houses tended to be lower and more elongated on the ground than on the Continent, where greater danger from external attack required the walls to be maintained until the nineteenth century; houses thus tended to be made

39. J. J. Bagley, *Life in Medieval England* (New York: G. P. Putnam's Sons, 1960), pp. 60–61.

high to contain the large occupational household. But in both places, most of the functional separation of the city took place within the house.

The typical pattern gave over the first floor to selling by merchant or artisan; the front of the house normally opened through fairly wide, shuttered windows and doors to the street. Goods were displayed for sale; the artisan might also use this area as a workshop. If more space was needed for manufacture, that might be secured on the second floor, or even at the top of the houses, where the improved daylighting made weaving or other fine handworking more practicable. This society worked from dawn to dusk, with workdays longer in summer than in winter, and in those places where light was best.

Generally, the second story was used to house the master and his family and their simple possessions. Apprentices and journeymen occupied a third or even possibly a fourth story. The attics stored staples away from dampness and rats, and whatever food the occupational household might lay up for winter or times of shortage. Thus, the high pitched roofs of medieval houses had a distinctly functional quality, affording a large amount of dry, covered space for such storage in an economic situation where transport was commonly interrupted and unreliable. To reach these attics, doors were let into the gable, if these overlooked the street, or dormers closed by doors were let into the gable roof and extended to reach the front wall of the house. Pulleys, though apparently not blocks, were used to raise heavy bundles directly from the street to these openings. Given the impedance of movement in vehicles along the bad roads of the Middle Ages, it was much more efficient to handle goods vertically with a pulley than horizontally in a cart.

Morphological Differences within the City

Though the primary division of land use within the medieval city came in the vertical separation of functions, specialized buildings and land uses existed on the ground as well. Commonly these specialized uses—including the castle, the church, abbey, monastery, gildhall, later on the city hall, and quite commonly the covered market hall—lay within a great areal mass of modular buildings given over to the sheltering of occupational households. What was the original morphological feature around which these occupation houses and quarters were ranged? In the *bourg-faubourg* model of medieval city origin, the castle clearly served as the nucleus around which the concretion of the city grew, though as Lavedan noted, "It is not always very easy to designate precisely the element of attraction, in particular to choose between the church, the castle, and the square, when they are found united at the same place. In all these cases one finds a square and one can maintain that there was no other origin for the '*radio-concentrique*' plan of the city."[40] This *radio-concentrique* town has a fairly simple but definite morphogenesis, beginning with the point of urban initiation—be it church, castle, or trader's mart—and growing outward along roads originally converging on that point. Because the area within a particular radius increases geometrically with

40. Pierre Lavedan, *Histoire de l'urbanisme*, 1: 261.

Antwerp was the greatest entrepôt of trade north of the Alps, a fact reflected in its great public buildings and solid bourgeois houses.

movement away from a point, a conservative force works to limit the outward extension of the town and encourage a compact form.

The circular form of the medieval town has commonly been asserted to be the result of circumvallation. But, in fact, we often find considerable areas of open land within walls, as well as cities of circular form that were never walled, or ineffectively so. The geometrical increase in spatial increments to the city with outward growth, as much as anything, shapes a circular form for the city. Extension comes in a web of radiating roads converging on a small central point. Growth is not by preconception, though it may be by periodic incrementation, with annular rings brought into possible use but not fully built on for many years. This case would exist particularly with the periodic enlargement of the city area contained within walls, but it is also true in American cities, where walls were almost unknown. Finally, the conservation of radial effort within a city decrees circular outline regardless of any possible circumvallation.

Let us assume the clustering of common specialized institutions at the convergence of the roads leading to a potential town site; merchants would be likely to settle near those institutions in their *portus*. To serve those coming in from outside to buy their wares, the merchants would find it advantageous to be at the edge of the small settlement, though not too far to the side if access by all the converging roads is desired. Thus, as the city grows, the quarter selling at retail would tend to cluster and remain near the convergence of the external routes, favoring none over another. In wholesale trade the customers would be fewer and more likely to be professional peddlers and chapmen aimed toward a trading partner well known to them rather than to the general public. Thus, warehouses could be toward the edge of the city on one side—as they were at St. Denis, Winchester, Stourbridge, and Lübeck. We should therefore distinguish the marketplace from the fairground as we do the market from the fair as institutions.

The marketplace was originally an open space, not necessarily given over only to selling. The medieval town square had a number of other purposes. It might be a *place d'armes* where the burghal militia gathered in times of danger to be dispatched along radial streets to the part of the wall in greatest danger.[41] Or it might be the site of civic procession and pageant, when illumination was afforded almost entirely by the sun. Or it might be a buffer between two *bourgs*. Only as the town's population grew and occupational specialization became possible would the retail market really be needed. Initially, the burgher raised much of his own food; his time was not fully occupied by the exercise of his trade, and he lived in a town where space for gardening and pasturage of animals was not yet scarce. But with urban growth we may logically reason that his specialized skill came into increasing demand, as did the urban land that served as his garden plot, and thus increased in value. This conjunction of demands would tend to make the purchase rather than the production of food a common practice.

Given a potential market for the sale of food and other simple daily needs that might earlier have been met by household efforts, retail trade could be established. But in the beginning it would be somewhat experimental and, in all likelihood, periodic. During the Middle Ages,

> the diet of the masses was mainly vegetarian and frugal, two meals being usual. There is a medieval saying that angels need to feed but once a day, mankind twice, and beasts thrice or more. The impression we have of colossal meals washed down with great quantities of wine, mead, and beer derives from occasions in the lives of royalty and aristocracy which chroniclers have recorded for special reasons. Such feastings were the exception, even for the rich. The many feast-days of the calendar were counterbalanced by even more fast-days, when the morning and evening meals were limited by strict rules.
>
> Except that they feasted more frequently, many of the richer classes shared the diet of the artisans and townspeople, which consisted of some kind of soup in the morning and of porridge or soup, fish and vegetables in the evening. Apart from bread and cakes, cereals in the form of pastry were still a luxury because of the cost of fats. Meals of fish—fresh, dried, or salted—were much more frequent than nowadays, for meat was still expensive and was taken

41. Ibid.

hardly more than once a week. Water and milk were drunk, as were beer and wine by those who could afford them. The choice was largely regional; thus beer was more common in the northern districts of Germany, wine in the south.

Medieval cities took great pains to obtain regular and cheap food supplies for their artisans. The rise of agriculture and husbandry in Flanders was a leading factor in the independence of the Flemish towns and their successful resistance to the encroachment of royal power.[42]

Under these circumstances, we could hardly expect a very elaborate physical provision for retail trade. Instead, the most primitive provision was made to do. The open space in the town, for whatever purpose established, was occupied one day a week, or perhaps two, by carts brought in from the surrounding countryside, from which the farmers would sell their fresh vegetables, a bit of meat, or other local agricultural produce. Barrows might contain fresh fish from local rivers or the nearby coast, or salted and dried fish sent in barrels.

The almost universal practice in Western Europe was the strict control of these markets by both church and state. State controls arose because the markets occupied public space and exercised a privilege for which the lord wished recompense. The church was concerned with severe limitation of profit and control of weights and measures. Because the public space had other uses, the privilege of occupying was commonly granted for one or, at most, two days. In a few sizable places, such as medieval Cambridge, a "perpetual market" was granted that might be open on all workdays; Sunday was not yet the day of pause in human industry it became at the hands of religious reformers in the sixteenth and seventeenth centuries.

These first patterns of retailing found in the medieval city were of the most elemental provision. Throughout history the unhoused, periodic, and commodity-specialized trader has served as the pioneer, as much in medieval French or German towns as in towns of the non-Western world or in today's Berkeley. When either demand or supply is problematic, street hawking in towns or peddling through the countryside becomes the standard practice.

As support for retail trade became assured, and as the essentially market-gardening production of food was shaped around the cities of Flanders, the Rhine valley, and northern and eastern France, local selling could take on a more settled abode, both in towns, as opposed to the hawker's circuit, and within the settlement in the marketplace. At first, the retailers were likely to substitute a modest covered stall in the open square for the barrow or wagon that had previously sufficed. As trade grew, the chance increased for the transformation of the single-day market to one of longer term, requiring, if carried to full-time selling, the separation of the square's market functions from its other civic and religious uses. Thus, we find that as

42. Charles Singer et al., *A History of Technology* (Oxford: Oxford University Press, 1950), 2: 123.

cities grow they tend to have several open spaces, one or two of which become institutionalized as markets—often called the old and the new markets—while other spaces become true public squares free of the impediments of trade. With such segregation, the marketplace itself can begin to be filled with light, flimsy, but unmovable structures.

A frequent argument has been that increasing trade at this point further encouraged the urge to permanency, causing retailers to move indoors into shops on the first floor of the houses surrounding the marketplace. Doubtless, partial historical and geographical truth stands behind this view, but it is too simplistic to represent accurately all of the processes at work. The fundamental fault of such a model is that it ignores the fact that from the very beginning there were, in fact, three kinds of trade: (1) selling local goods to the local populace, which was likely to be a fairly small-scale activity, probably conducted by the principals involved; (2) selling imported goods to that same populace, an even smaller activity in most cases and thus not usually a sufficient support for an entrepreneur; and (3) selling local or imported goods to customers located at some distance from the town, the scale of that activity depending on the extent of the territory dominated by the town in that trade.

We have so far been concerned only with the first of these types of trade. When the peasant came to town to sell his domestic surplus, "he supplied a tiny market usually held periodically, where he sold perhaps three eggs, a chicken, several pounds of wool, and sometimes even a little cloth woven in the household."[43] The supply of goods was small, and we may reason that such a provision could serve only a relatively modest demand focused on that place. The temporary barrow in the public square would serve both participants well. But as the population grew, the need arose to assure a larger and

43. Georges Lefranc, *Histoire du commerce*, Que Sais-Je? no. 55 (Paris: Presses Universitaires de France, 1965), p. 27.

more predictable supply of goods. To do so would require forethought and a geographical search for goods, activities likely to be undertaken only by professional traders. Their livelihood came not from production—as did that of the peasant with his three eggs, one chicken, bag of wool, and cloth—but from an exercise of the agency of trade.[44] However, these professional merchants would have little interest in trading only in a small local surplus or in selling only to a modest local market. If the city were large, local custom would suffice, or if the locally produced surplus were massive, then the traders might be content with its sale, though obviously such a sale would have to be to a larger market than that furnished by the customers flocking to the town's marketplace. Thus, the professional trader would of necessity, and of personal interest, seek to expand the field of endeavor beyond the parochial interests of the town itself, becoming in the process what the medieval chroniclers term a merchant—a long-distance, basically wholesale trader. In these accounts, "sellers" served the local market and "merchants" encountered a geographical search in their efforts to obtain a source or sale.

Large-scale trading, then, fell largely into the hands of merchants, and they were most often confronted with the problem of storing large quantities of goods. A considerable part of their activity was taken up with anticipating future demands and placing orders, often in distant places, so as to have goods on hand ultimately to meet those demands. In such an activity the storehouse became a needed structure in the city. We may recall that in the Roman Empire, the anticipation of demand and its fulfillment fell to the lot of the state, which maintained emporia at Ostia or on the banks of the Tiber in Rome itself. During the Middle Ages, neither the demand nor the concentration of agency of trade was such that these vast buildings might be constructed, filled, and emptied by sale. But a beginning of a return to forethought and search in trade was made, and the merchant became the leading commercial figure of the medieval town by using such talents.

In that role as leader, the merchant tended to occupy a particular physical position as well as a social and political one. The merchant's house would have had to be relatively easy for strangers to locate, and accessible for goods coming into or being dispatched from the town. And the scale of the premises must be great enough to permit the storage necessary to support considerable selling activity. Given these needs, merchants tended to locate their houses on one of the squares or riverbanks within the town, often on the square in which the market was held. From this fact arises the confusion as to morphogenesis within the market. Because a merchant's house might look out on the marketplace, it is easy to assume that it essentially grew out of that institution. Yet when we examine the evolution of the functional role and physical provision for merchants, we see it had only a partial relation to the marketplace itself. Doubtless, merchants would sell the goods they dealt in to local people, but few merchants would have possessed the power they did

44. For a detailed discussion of the role of the agency of trade in the support of towns, see James E. Vance, Jr., *The Merchant's World: The Geography of Wholesaling* (Englewood Cliffs, N.J.: Prentice-Hall, 1970).

had they been totally dependent, or perhaps even fundamentally dependent, on the local trade. Functional efficiency of a different sort and ostentation within a wider world brought the merchant-burgher's house to the square. The fact that he traded with his neighbors in a ground-floor counting house or shop should not be allowed to confuse our understanding of his activities.

The test of this reasoning comes in those places where the merchants' houses lie at some distance from the marketplace, as they do in Venice, Augsburg, Antwerp, and a number of other superlatively important emporia of the Middle Ages.

A medieval house in Ypres, Belgium, is characteristic of worker housing in textile towns, where light was needed and crowding was not extreme.

When the scale of local demand rose, the merchant became interested in supplying its needs. The specialization of labor, so much the foundation of development theory in economic thought, could also take place. In a town with a demonstrated market for a particular class of goods, the artisan could take up residence; in fact, the trade itself might there be begun with the slow evolution of the skill and technology that came ultimately to attach to the "mystery." In the shaping of the physical structure of the city, this meant that with increase in urban size, and market, the occupations could begin to emerge as coherent local activities where the union of practitioners into gilds might take place. We have already seen that the nature and functions of the gild make clustered residence desirable. Thus, just as the gild merchant

The Face of the Medieval City

tended to cluster around squares where large, obvious, and ostentatious buildings could be built, the other gilds shaped their own quarters.

A tie existed between these two evolutions. With the existence of a strong gild in a particular type of manufacture, we might expect a considerable as well as a highly competent production of goods. Fairly probably, such a production might overreach the demands of the town itself, leaving a surplus for possible export. In that case the members of the gild merchant would be versed in geographical search—as much for markets as for sources of goods. They would have the associations with traders elsewhere, as well as the geographical knowledge of possible markets, to aid the artisans of the gild in selling their products at a distance. Such a symbiosis is the product of an urban life and production, not of the agricultural hinterland that might have grown up around the town to supply its needs.

If we carry this evolution of city functions and forms to a logical conclusion, we end with a town divided among trades—both in long-distance selling and in craft manufacture—whose interests encourage clustering in the urban space. From this end comes the occupation district as the second-level modular unit in the morphology of the medieval city, where the first-level module was the house-shop structure with vertical segregation leaving the first floor to be used in a nearly identical way throughout the quarter. In the city of the Middle Ages, we find a different kind of segregation, into occupation quarters. Still, the first floor would remain in commercial usage even if in differing trades.

The Quarter of Tolerance

The main exception to this broad picture of two related modules is the district of extraterritoriality or ethnic identity. We have seen that the traders coming in from outside were often permitted, sometimes required, to live and work in a defined quarter where they might be subject to their own laws and practices rather than those of the denizens. Similarly, certain minorities with different culture, religion, and ethnicity might be tolerated within an orthodox native body when confined to a distinct, definable, and delimited quarter where their heterodoxy might exist without infecting the natives. No clear exception is made to the general model of dual separation represented in these two types of outsiders living within the city. Normally, the tolerated outsiders were engaged mainly in one or a small range of trades. The Jews and Italians were moneylenders, bankers, and, in earlier times, long-distance merchants. The Germans of the Hanse took over these trades in the late Middle Ages. The main justification in the medieval mind for the toleration of outsiders, disbelievers, and those of external loyalty was that they performed a service to the natives that warranted toleration of qualities automatically suspect, feared, and even reviled. Once the functional role disappeared, no justification remained for permitting heterodoxy.

We should avoid the pitfall of applying present-day dogma to past acts and events. No German, Italian, or Jew possessed a whit more basic tolerance than did the Frenchman or Englishman who held him to living in his quarter of tolerance. Need could make foreigners living within the city far more adaptable than the natives, but that fact does not represent a fundamental philosophical difference. The diaries of Lombards resident in the north, the assiduous defense of Hebrew practices of law and customs by Jews living in medieval Europe, and the creation of German compounds in cities around the Baltic by and for Hanse traders all speak to the same dogged attachment to particular external views and practices despite free residence in the the country. Those living in quarters of tolerance were not slaves, so their frequent cries of enslavement ring rather hollow; normally, they were slaves to their own property, refusing to yield it as a price to leave the country, rather than being actually held personally in bond. We must appreciate the medieval view that national strength and wealth came only by striving to hold as much specie and staple within the country as humanly possible. This view may be economically unsound, as Adam Smith showed, but his writing was five hundred years in the future.

The quarter of tolerance was the morphological expression of the needs of a particular kind of long-distance trader. These traders were foreigners living for a time within the society of a country, tolerated as other foreigners would not have been for the critical needs of that long-distance trade to the national economy. The quid pro quo was fairly obvious in the case of the Italians and the Germans, though as the Middle Ages advanced the balance between the benefits came more into question. But for the Jews the situation was far more obscure; they had no homeland whence they came and to which they returned on retirement from trade. Additionally, they had no national staple sought in other lands, unless it was gold, and that commodity was of particular sensitivity in medieval times, as much for its scarcity as for its symbolic role in national wealth. So in a number of cities the quarter of tolerance of the Jews had to be larger than that for the Lombards or the Hanse because it became a homeland in miniature.

Today it is hard to see the problem, because tolerance is considered a right of the individual or the group; in no sense was it such in the Middle Ages. As a result, to permit such a quarter to exist meant both to delimit it geographically and to constrain its residents to particular occupations. This second consequence arose from the equation in the medieval mind of the ideas of residence and occupation. You could not have workers in a particular trade wandering about the city with no effective supervision and, through the absence of a gild, no provision of social welfare. Jews could join gilds, but only very select ones, those that could undertake to deal with their highly ambiguous status. The Germans and the Italians had little reason to join gilds; their trading organizations were as powerful as the local gilds and fully as able to care for the trade and its practitioners.

From House to Quarter to City

The modular components of the medieval town build up to a single entity—the city, as we know it. Yet the forces that actually shaped it cannot be fully revealed to us. They were unremarked at the time of operation, and no medieval town of sufficient size has come down to us enough unchanged to permit our "reading of the rocks." If we are to answer questions about process, we must rely on a fair component of conjecture. Fortunately, we are not without a script, even if a modest one. In 1603 the English topographer John Stow published his *Survey of London*, to which he appended a relic from the twelfth century, *Libellum de situ et nobilitate Londini* in which William Fitzstephen set out to present the London of that time.[45] Fitzstephen's description is the oldest detailed account of a city that remains in Western European literature. From examining it we may sense, if not read directly, certain morphological forces at work.

Fitzstephen begins by noting the glories of London, citing its "abundant wealth" and "extensive commerce." The implication comes through that these result from its situation on the Thames. In essence we have the merchants' town, a fact made more evident when he notes farther on that the king's palace lies "situated in a populous suburb, at a distance of two miles from the city." Thus, two points of initiation occur in what became a great city even in the twelfth century, and the notion of the *bourg*, with its *faubourg* hovering in its shelter, is far from the universal situation that some historians would have it.

The sense that the city is for merchants is enhanced by Fitzstephen's comment, "Adjoining to the houses on all sides lie the gardens of those citizens that dwell in the suburbs, which are well furnished with trees, spacious and beautiful." From other evidence we know that these houses were commonly occupied by powerful noblemen and bishops who had to be resident near the court but wished not to be under the control of the merchants' town with its collegial government by gildsmen. Thus, the settlement really had three components: the merchants' town, the king's court, and the residential area for the country magnates, of the sword or the mitre, who maintained an astute spatial independence from either of the other powers.

In that suburban area were mills "whose clack is very pleasing to the ear" (suggesting those powered by water, as windmills were thought to screech), the tillage of crops yielding "Ceres' plenteous sheaf," and "an immense forest, in which are densely wooded thickets, the coverts of game, stags, fallow-deer, boars, and wild bulls." The image comes through of a countryside reduced to the control of the city rather than one exercising domination over the settlement, as Christaller would have it. And the suburb, a band of residential land use related directly to the city, can be seen even in the twelfth century, which should put the lie to the notion that the automobile began the spreading out of the housing fabric of cities. That fundamental process was seemingly an outgrowth of rural security: once security could reasonably be assured, those with economic independence from city toil could and sometimes did seek to live outside the bustle and constraint of the town.

Within the town, "the artisans of the several crafts, the vendors of the various commodities, and the labourers of every kind, have each their separate station which they take every morning." There were as well "wine-

45. John Stow, *The Survey of London* (London: Everyman's Library Edition, 1912; rpt. 1960), pp. 501–9.

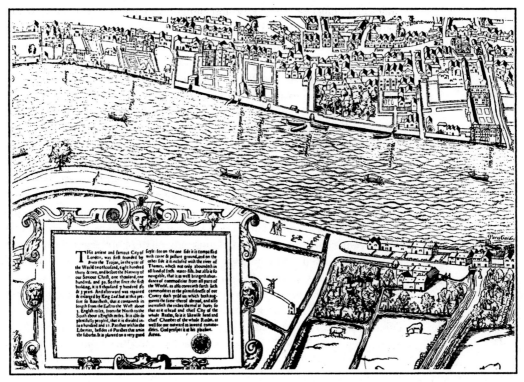

The text within the map cartouche reads:

This antient and famous City of London, was first founded by Brute the Trojan, in the yeer of the World twothousand, eight hundred thirty & two, and before the Nativity of our Saviour Christ, one thousand, one hundred, and 30. So that since the first building, it is 3 thousand 7 hundred 60 & 3 yeers. And afterward was repaired & enlarged by King Lud but at this present so Banesbeth, that it containeth in length from the East to the West about 3 English miles, from the North to the South about 2 English miles. It is also so plentifully peopled, that it is divided into a hundred and 51 Parishes within the Liberties, besides 16 Parishes that arise the suburbs. It is planted on a very good Ayres.

Soyle: for on the one side it is compassed with corne & pasture ground, and on the other side it is inclosed with the river of Thames, which not only aboundeth in all kind of fresh water-fish, but also is so navigable, that it is as well bringeth abundance of commodities from all parts of the World, as also conveieth forth such commodities as the plenifidnesse of our Contry doth yeild us; which both augments the fame thereof abroad, and also increaseth the riches thereof at home, so that as it is head and chief City of the whole Realm, so is it likewise head and chief Chamber of the whole Realm, as well for our outward as inward commodities. God prosper it at his pleasure. Amen.

Ralph Agas's map of London (ca. 1560–70) shows the large houses that lined the Thames, often with gardens, along the Strand west of the gate of the City of London at Temple-barre.

shops which are kept in ships and cellars, [and] a public eating-house." During the Middle Ages, wine was drunk fresh from the harvest and pressing, so the first ships to arrive from Gascony would be sought after to replace the fast-declining vintage of the previous year. On Fridays at a horse fair outside the gate at "Smooth Field," agricultural implements and beasts were also sold.

In the twelfth century we can already see the notion of periodic residence at work in the case of the process of class assembly. For the elite of society and power—the nobility and the bishops—rural residence of necessity enforced isolation. That select group gained its power through administration of rural territory: the bishop had his see and the baron his manor, the earl his county, and the duke his principality. But in seeking to consort with his peers, each was required to remain in the city. For that reason, "moreover, almost all the bishops, abbots, and great men of England, are in a manner, citizens and freemen of London; as they have magnificent houses there, to which they resort, spending large sums of money, whenever they are summoned thither to councils and assemblies by the king or their metropolitan [the archbishop, originally resident in London, was subsequently removed in titular residence to Canterbury, though maintaining a London palace at Lambeth at least as early as Fitzstephen's time] or are compelled to go there by their own business."

Class assembly became a strong force in shaping cities, adding to their

The Face of the
Medieval City

165

fabric buildings of a magnificence unmatched in medieval times in the buildings of merchants. Class assembly, like the city residence of Italian nobles, in the end proved highly inimical to the political and social health of cities. The presence of the aristocracy tended to corrupt the original collegial government by burghers, with its reasonable representation of the social and economic mass of the city, into one of privilege and selfishness. The rotting of the English boroughs came not merely through loss of population, as the term is usually used, but was influenced by the increasing limitation of the franchise to a small group, as the most powerful city men joined with the leaders of the gentry seeking periodic residence in the city.

Fitzstephen concludes his account in the common English fashion by expatiating at immoderate length on the sports of London and the citizens' use of the fields around for jousting, wrestling, stone throwing, and a full range of other purposeless heavings. The presence of dramatic presentations in the twelfth century foretold Britain's magnificent obsession with drama, but also suggested the tendency for a national culture to depend on a center from which such reasonably popular activities could be spread outward. Formal education, as at Cambridge and Oxford, could be isolated into the countryside, but not such popular education as the morality plays of the Middle Ages. London had drama at least eight hundred years before it gained a university, which came only first in a most timid way, and then not before 1826.

The Medieval Land Market

Evidence concerning the value given to land in various sections of the medieval city is scant indeed, yet differences seemingly occurred from place to place. The enclosure of land by the wall may not alone have made urban land scarce; the legal availability of land may have tended as well to create a scarcity value. Feudal landowners hoarded land; many of them were so struck with terror as they approached death that bequests to the church, in craven search of salvation, were very common. By the later Middle Ages the church was a powerful, sometimes almost monopolistic landowner, to the extent that those seeking land within the city may have had difficulty obtaining it, particularly by freehold occupation. As the most certain source of wealth and security, land was more endowing than speculative.

In her classic study of the merchant class in medieval London, Sylvia Thrupp states that "one of a merchant's chief motives in acquiring real property and rents was to provide for the future of his wife and children in event of his early death. As has been shown [from a study of marriage contracts], many purchases were made under the pressure of marriage settlements; another urgent incentive was the desire to leave a source of income out of which chantry priests could be hired to sing for the family souls. *Under favorable conditions the returns were probably not much below average trading profits*."[46] These land-investment purposes were not likely to encourage

46. Sylvia L. Thrupp, *The Merchant Class of Medieval London* (Ann Arbor: University of Michigan Press, 1948; paperback ed., 1962), p. 122.

dangerous practices of speculation, particularly as more and more land fell into the hands of the church—one of whose firmly held beliefs was that undue profit, *turpe lucrum*, was the work of the god of darkness.

We should not discount the influences of the land market merely because it was likely less fluid and volatile than it was to become in the seventeenth century. No doubt in the earlier years of medieval urbanization a high degree of parity held between ownership of land and buildings and practical use thereof, but as time passed reasons for ownership divorced from occupational use increased. We have already seen the rise of class assembly; we must now look at it from an economic viewpoint. In doing so, we find perhaps the first evidence to support the notion that the countryside determined the size and significance of cities. But the grave question remains whether the existence of the city forced upon those living in the country some periodic assembly of the aristocratic classes in the city.

Thrupp furnishes us a valuable picture of how very great indeed were the ties between the merchants of London and the manors, but the ties were those of ownership from the center rather than complete domination by barons and bishops. It was a two-way street—the "great men" of England's countryside did collect in London for part of the year, but more commonly the powerful merchants began to buy manors in the rural areas to furnish themselves with food, peace and quiet, and ultimately the trappings of gentility.

Thrupp believed that about 15 percent of the London merchants owned country land at the beginning of the fifteenth century; including town holdings, "the number of citizen households that were backed by landed property, then, must have been between 900 and 1,000" in a total merchant class numbering no more than 3,400 households. "The merchant who was both successful and socially ambitious might by the time of his death have a third to half of his fortune or more in the form of lands."[47] A considerable part of this property was probably acquired as a result of the foreclosure of mortgages merchants had taken in security for loans made to previous owners. Perhaps more by this means than by outright speculative increases in land values were fortunes from land collected.

Perhaps fully as strong a force in projecting the city merchant's interests in land outward was his desire to shift his role from prosperous tradesman to prideful gentleman. Since lands with feudal history equated gentility with service to the king, particularly with raising men-at-arms in time of war and administering justice and charity in time of peace, one could far more easily become a gentleman outside the city than within. The wealthy merchant could live as a gentleman in the country while earning the support for that unproductive life by labor on some days in the city:

> It may be granted, at least, that the possession of a country house
> could set a city merchant on the way to changing his class status.
> If, as many of the wealthier men are known to have done, he then
> assumed the social role of a gentleman in his county, serving on
> public commissions, acquiring private hunting rights, modernizing

47. Ibid., pp. 125, 127.

his manor house, making arrangements to marry his daughters into gentle families, and preparing at least one of his sons for one of the careers that were associated with gentility, the degree of change was certainly significant. In so far as can be judged from office-holding and marriage into older families, assimilation to the landed gentry was still further advanced in the second generation after such a move, and in the counties more distant from London there might be a severance of all formal ties with citizen life.[48]

In such fashion, class assembly in the countryside worked to draw out of the city those wealthy citizens who saw their future in gentle rather than productive roles. But like the country magnates coming to the city for periodic residence, the wealthy merchants tended very much to cluster together in the pastoral environment around the city. "Two of the citizens' favorite counties, where their purchases of land were most frequent, were Middlesex and Surrey."[49] These areas then became the "Home Counties" of urban gentry, much as Bloomsbury and Mayfair became "in town" in later centuries for rural gentry resident for a time in the city.

Processes of Assemblage in the Medieval City

The Middle Ages were a time of slow, almost cellular, shaping of the town. Its parts were brought together in no conscious design, save possibly one determined by the demands of fortification. But this time was not one of elaborate, often theoretical, defensive structures; these came with the use of gunpowder and the creation of the structurally theoretical world of the Renaissance. We may, however, cite a few of the forces dominant in medieval city growth.

The first process serving to shape the medieval city we might justly call concretion—the deposition from a fluid state of a body of different composition that lies within and surrounded by a groundmass of contrasting form and function.[50] The groundmass was the feudal countryside, and the fluid that collected and concreted in its midst was trade, wandering and periodic at first, but ultimately settled and of characteristic physical presence. This concretion of long-distance trade was the nucleus for the main medieval cities. In a study wherein he set out to find a central-place system for the Middle Ages, Josiah Cox Russell found instead that the great and lesser entrepôts of distant trade and the connections among them comprised the skeleton of medieval urbanization.[51]

48. Ibid., p. 280.

49. Ibid., p. 284.

50. This geological term seems particularly appropriate as an expression of what was going on in medieval cities. Merriam-Webster defines it as "a mass of mineral matter found generally in rock of a composition different from its own and produced by deposition from aqueous solution in the rock." These concretions stand rather like the medieval merchants' town, filling a space carved out of the groundmass—the feudal economy of the countryside—but filled with a different substance, city form, brought by the slow accumulation of that material from a fluid state.

51. Josiah Cox Russell, *Medieval Regions and Their Cities* (Bloomington: Indiana University Press, 1972). For a critical analysis of Russell's study, see my review in the *Journal of Urban History* 1 (1975): 484–88.

As long as the medieval city was being produced by concretion of fluid elements from outside, its size would be enlarged directly by accretion, the slow and simple growth of a single form. We must distinguish *concretion*, the collection from outside inward, from *accretion*, the physical expansion of the city by adding layers to its form. Cities have always grown fundamentally by accretion, simply because when new needs expand the necessary size of the city, the easiest place to increase its physical extent is around its edge, where "redevelopment" is of countryside rather than of existing city. The city form accretes on land taken from the country. As long as a single concretion of activity is taking place, the accretions may not differ in structure from the earlier germ. But if several different kinds of fluid are concreted inward, we are likely to get knobs or bands of differing composition, still in physical association but not in simple chemical bond. The same process has been at work in the city: we know that as long as merchants built their town *tout simple*, the place might grow but would be unlikely to separate into distinct physical entities. Individuals might shift from one place in the city to another, but the physical form they would occupy would remain unchanged and highly consistent in form. With several concretions from the outside, the chances of necessary physical distinctions would rise rapidly. Just as bands occur in nodules within rock, physical knobs—multiple nucleations—occur within the city. We have seen how class assembly for the "season" within the city ultimately created distinct residential quarters for the magnates coming to consort with their peers. Equally, the merchants of the town seeking to rise above simple citizenship left for the clearly exurban Home Counties, where they hoped through the dusting of a different geography to gain gentility.

Obviously, congregation is a social process, but its direct physical expression occurs in socially specialized areas. To take one case, the extraterritorial quarters of medieval cities—the Hanseatic steelyards or the Jewish ghetto—emerged not because their residents were doing things very different from the natives, but because they had contrasting social and legal practices in the pursuit of what might be a common occupation. The result is a social separation, based either on the function to be carried out, which led to the occupation quarters so typical of the time, or on the social class and caste of the residents which led to aristocratic suburbs, merchants' manor belts, Jewish ghettos, and Hanseatic steelyards, as the case might be. These various separations came, with the passage of time, to take on distinctive physical forms to match their increasing social and functional separation. And once those physical forms had been developed along specialized lines, they themselves tended to reinforce the process of separation.

We may distinguish two forms of separation: the active choice to divide, and externally enforced division. *Congregation* implies deliberate coming together; *segregation* connotes forced division, leading in turn to a clustering that may be voluntary only after the acceptance of a *fait accompli*. Medieval cities usually had directly outside their walls shanty settlements where all manner of rejected civic activities lodged, even if very badly. Some activities were merely noxious, such as slaughtering; others were illegal, though tolerated. Still others were legal under specific circumstances, as in the case of fairs with their own commercial law administered by a piepowder court.

The medieval city held a large array of geographically specific law and practice, resulting in the intimate use of areas to partake in one legal practice, or instead to avoid it. Ecclesiastical foundations might well seek to reside outside the city so as more fully to control their property and practices; thus, we find a range of activities that were voluntarily or necessarily extramural. Legal accommodation was given to this idea in that some structures and areas within cities could be given a conferred extramural quality—as in Ely Cathedral or the embassies of foreign states—without being outside the city. In England today, county buildings may lie on a city's High Street but in law reside outside its bounds.

Paris during the Middle Ages faced a significant application of this concern for extramural status in its university quarter on the Left Bank. The problem arose from the fact that students came from all over Europe to study there and wished to return home on completion of their labors. Thus, while in Paris they found themselves in a legal quandary produced by medieval ideas as to the three classes that belonged to a city; citizens, who had been born there or formally accepted into citizenship; "foreigners," who were merely subjects of the king born elsewhere and not given local citizenship; and aliens. Medieval practice assumed that only citizens could reside for any time in the city—often inns had to lie outside the gates to avoid the question of whether the wayfarer was residing overnight in the town. So the vast group of "foreigners" and aliens flocking to a university posed a legal problem to the medieval mind. Paris got around it by restricting the university to the Left Bank, establishing a special law there that permitted outsiders to remain without legal contest. In Britain this problem did not arise; the universities were outside London, and were more expressly ecclesiastical foundations, which normally possessed this quality of legal extramurality to shelter strangers.

These relations had the full complexity that medieval legal practice could summon up; a geography of law existed unlike anything that has followed. The ghetto was part of a vast array of such quarters and districts. The rule of law in the Middle Ages was indeed a powerful force in shaping cities.

Finally, we must mention the process of reconstruction, which we have already seen in the special application of the accretion of rural land into the city. Reconstruction occurred within the city, but not so much in the manner we know today. Our level of rebuilding is very much tied to the operation of land economics; during the Middle Ages, functional change rather than shifting values created most reconstruction. A merchant might need more space, or his interests might evolve from some level of production to a concentration on trade alone. In response to those shifts, he would seek to gain more appropriate accommodation, most likely where his property stood. As a result, we find the medieval house a marvelously evolving structure given to all sorts of physical additions and adjustments. The haut pas, the penthouse, the ell, and a dozen other additions were sufficiently common as to have specific names. Because medieval structures were transformed rather than replaced, few indeed stand as built. Inference from physical evidence is thus difficult, but it suggests that reconstruction was a factor in the conservation of overall patterns in the city—and, by the way, in the employment of materials; even though a city grew in size and importance, it might be expected to reflect conditions from earlier times.

The medieval city had great rigidities of institutions and laws but remarkable flexibility in the use of its physical structure. Only when the institutions became creakingly conservative did the structure become rather frozen. And as the late-medieval city found a new form, for a time a new society allowed medieval people to jump over the walls and begin the journey to the modern era.

A Town for Everyman

===

The Late-Medieval Bastide

Puymirol. Photo:
Ray Delvert,
Villeneuve-sur-Lot.

The ease with which we can assemble a vivid and encompassing picture of the medieval city attests strongly to its vitality and active role in the life of the times. Many democratic traditions cited today in support of civil liberty and economic justice began in those times. Similarly, the contribution of towns to the material prosperity of citizens, both lowly and exalted, first became apparent then. Social structures based on ethnic identification and residential division by cultural attachment gained greater sway in the complex trading towns of the late Middle Ages than had been possible in the less far-ranging commercial towns earlier in that era. The half-millennium that has intervened since the close of the Middle Ages may have shown a secular decline in universal ethnic identification. But recent trends toward greater social complexity—"cultural pluralism"—reversed the course and made medieval experience of more direct relevance to our understanding of cities today. A particularly sharp contrast between the medieval town and the current one is the vastly enhanced role of economic class in modern cities.

Two periods of morphogenetic experimentation and transformation come clearly into focus as times in which to seek an explanation of the emergence of economic class as a force in the shaping of cities. The first period came when people could begin to conceive of the city as a physical and functional entity, subject to a preconception of design that differed greatly from the slow organic evolution that had occurred during the Middle Ages. From this conscious design came the bastide. The other period centers on the radical transformation of the scale of economic activity in cities, which grew into the Industrial Revolution of the seventeenth, eighteenth, and nineteenth centuries. During this period, the space within cities was so radically expanded that the question of distance as a factor internal to the city gained economic significance, with land rent emerging as the mechanism for measurement of "value" and the assignment of location. The outcome was the modern metropolis.

Even in the organic towns of the High Middle Ages, economic distinction was made among people, but without the locational association and interclass separation that have existed for the last several centuries. Rich merchants lived above their counting houses and prosperous artisans above their workrooms. But as some people gained great wealth, they also began to grab great political power. Possession of that power seems to have made them desire physical demonstration of their distinction. Unlike the Pearly King and Queen, medieval magnates could not wear their wealth incontestably blazoned on their coats; they sought to show it in the build of their houses. That search for morphological distinction allied the powerful merchant-politician with the bishops and nobles who lived in the town in increasing numbers as the fourteenth and fifteenth centuries advanced. This alliance elevated design of houses and housing quarters to the central concern of the elite and, as a result, of the decreasingly democratic city governments. The city of the Renaissance was shaped and became the habitat of princes possessed, by the late fifteenth century, of absolute power.

While the Renaissance city was being shaped to the desires of the leisured group possessed of great and arbitrary authority, wastelands of one sort or another had grown up in odd crannies of Europe. These had arisen from the religious conflicts, the Hundred Years' War between France and England, and the great folk battles between Spaniard and Saracen, German and Slav, and the Balkan peoples and the Turks. A set of new settlements had been established first to reoccupy these wastelands but even more to make them flower economically. These bastides became the closest thing to a classless society the Middle Ages produced, and served as a laboratory for social, economic, and religious innovation that was to bring forth many institutions and attitudes. They shaped the beginnings of the modern world, and the tradition of relatively egalitarian economic settlements that became the basis for the urban structuring of the European plantations overseas, most notably in North America. Before considering the nature of the bastide, we must see how class division came generally to medieval cities.

The Rise of the Class-Bound City

The lever the townsman used to raise himself and his family above the level of the mass was his pile of capital. It brought him a country house with the potential for social elevation; it could also mean that his sons might inherit position without the hard labor of learning a trade and gaining admission to the status of freeman. A "gentleman" might always be given civic freedom without mastery of a trade. Unlike the feudal lord of the manor, whose path to power was the traditional deference given his family by the serfs with backs bent in his service—his exalted status was birthright knowledge to all living in his neighborhood—the city merchant often needed obtrusive assertion by visible and understandable physical symbols. The city house, first perhaps only a roomy example of the modular form in most towns, soon became a mansion reflective of growing capital. To show the façade of the house became of critical importance, because that was the only part the masses would ever be invited to observe. In the fifteenth century, prominent, observable sites for the location of a private house became important for the first time since the fall of Rome.

The early organic growth of medieval towns made the creation of impressive building sites extremely difficult. Few had any clear view of what the ultimate form of the city would be. Only as experience indicated the way a city would grow and the processes involved did it become practical to think about city design to accomplish specific aesthetic, architectural, and social ends. By the thirteenth century the form had become organized, if not really standardized, and a town could be thought about as an entity. Once a reason arose to perceive future forms and uses, as it did when people sought to build impressive structures, the process to accomplish that goal was now understood.

Cities offered reasonable security of person, of land, of goods, and of equitable judicial procedures, up to a point. To defend those rights the city had a distinct territoriality, separated from the different laws and practices of the countryside, a set of punishments visited on those living within its boundaries if they broke its rather severe restraints, and a system of taxation to pay for the building of strong walls to defend it against outsiders. As Pirenne has said, "The city of the Middle Ages was simultaneously a legal district and a commune."[1] The legal administration was in the hands of the magistrates, whereas the general administration was in the hands of a council, each group drawn from the citizenry by majority will.

The medieval city that emerged with a communal government was a fully developed system to provide for economic and social health and security for its citizens. The system that was worked out so thoroughly and so successfully within the city walls disappeared at the gates. Only in the later Middle Ages did people begin to have some hazy idea of the city as part of a larger interdependency, which might equally profit its corporators as had the medieval commune. For such a larger system to function, an economic system had to come into being fully emancipated from the narrow regionalism, the gross greed, and the central trading-town ideas of the earlier communes:

> The civic spirit which animated them was singularly egotistic. They jealously reserved to themselves the liberties they enjoyed within their walls. The peasants who dwelt round about them did not seem to them to be compatriots at all. They thought only of profitably exploiting them. With all their might they stood on guard to prevent the peasants from freeing themselves from the industrial system of which the cities had a monopoly. The task of provisioning these cities was likewise imposed upon the peasants, who were subjected to a tyrannical protectorate whenever it was possible to do so, as in Tuscany, for example, where Florence subjected to its yoke all the surrounding countryside. [In sum,] the city of the Middle Ages, as it existed in the twelfth century, was a commercial and industrial commune living in the shelter of a fortified enceinte and enjoying a law, an administration and a jurisprudence of exception which made of it a collective, privileged personality.[2]

Bourgs, Faubourgs, and Bastides

Let us recall the model of urban morphogenesis that Henri Pirenne brought to our attention in his *Medieval Cities*. In studying the emergence of the commune in Flanders, Pirenne tells us, "All these cities show, first, the characteristic feature of having been organized around a central burg which was, so to speak, their nucleus. At the foot of this burg was grouped a *portus*, or 'new burg,' populated by merchants to whose numbers were soon added artisans, either free or serf, and where, after the eleventh century, the textile

1. Henri Pirenne, *Medieval Cities: Their Origin and the Revival of Trade* (Princeton: Princeton University Press, 1925), p. 203.
2. Ibid., pp. 219–20.

industry came to be concentrated. Over the burg as over the *portus* extended the authority of the castellan."[3] From this description, this model is commonly referred to as that of the *bourg* and *faubourg*, using the French form to create a more felicitous pairing.

Fundamental to the *bourg-faubourg* model is the notion of prior authority and, as the legal form and social practices of the commune evolved, a certain element of class conflict. The tension between the local lord and the town populace was a commonplace of the era. In the *bourg* both the morphology of the place and the legal standing of the townspeople partook of several somewhat conflicting systems. To cite one example: when the merchants first took up residence in the *portus*, they undoubtedly did so at the legal sufferance of the lord of the *bourg*, if not in outright commendation to him, which made them liable for labor and military service to that lord. The land they held in possession was under a form of leasehold, which preserved to the landlord considerable power to affect the lives of the merchants.

But as the merchants gained economic power, they tended as well to secure more personal freedom. "With freedom of person there went on equal footing, in the city, the freedom of land. In a merchant community, land, in fact, could not remain immobile and be kept out of commerce by unwieldy and diverse laws that prevented its free conveyance and kept it from serving as a means of credit and acquiring capital value." In explaining the reason for this shift in the view of land and the strong effort that merchants made to transform its legal status when held by them, Henri Pirenne saw evolution of rights to property as certain. "This was the more inevitable in that land, within the city, changed its nature—it became ground for building. It was rapidly covered with houses, crowded one against the other, and increased in value in proportion as they multiplied. Thus it automatically came about that the owner of a house acquired in the course of time the ownership, or at least the possession, of the soil upon which it was built." At that point the continuing conflict with the ancient landlord was likely to be resolved in a final, legal form. "Everywhere the old desmesnial land was transformed into 'censal estate,' or 'censal allodium.' City hold thus became free hold." In contrast, in the countryside, occupation and utilization of land were likely to be feudal or at best leasehold tenure until the nineteenth century.[4]

The Planted Town in Europe: Colonization at Home

Traditionally, history is divided into European and "colonial" phases and stages, yet I wish to suggest that before colonization spread across the broad western ocean, it already existed within Europe. It was particularly tied to the attempt to expand local economies into national economies, both by substituting national for local initiative and by creating a form of colonial settlement, the bastide, that might be used to develop the wastelands or incompletely developed regions of the kingdom. No wonder that the most active of the European bastidors, those shaping these settlements, were a couple of centuries later the great colonizers of the New World. Although the

3. Ibid., p. 191.
4. Ibid., p. 202.

Germans and the Spaniards did build many bastides, they did so for political conquest rather than economic development. Throughout the most active times of overseas colonization, they lacked the national economy at home to make the most of the form as an economic development device. In the end the Spaniards in the New World shaped not a true bastide but instead a Roman *castrum*, an armed camp to exact tribute from a subject people.

The Bastide

The instrument of colonial settlement may have been fairly clear in the sixteenth century, when the call to the New Lands was voiced, but that settlement form—the bastide—had evolved over a period of nearly five hundred years. During that same epoch, the trading "counters" of the Germans and Italians were to have their greatest spread and be most effective in repressing full-fledged economic development in northwestern Europe. The very term *bastide* recalls a set of specific circumstances that brought the new town into existence and gave it the particular qualities that would be of such importance in settling the New Lands of the New World.

No doubt the notion of a planned, preconceived town was not what brought about the founding of new settlements, but rather the great need that existed for towns in an area deficient of them. The townless waste might be small—part of a forest, a bogland only currently being cleared, or an estate as yet not fully developed. It might, on the other hand, be vast by the standards of the time, such as the area devastated by the savage Albigensian Crusade of the thirteenth century. In either case, the actual, planted town would be much the same but in the vaster areas, the systemic ties among towns might be quite different, since they were products of the times rather than inheritances of cloudy provenance. Thus, it serves our purposes better to look at the situation in southwestern France, where geographical scope existed both for many new towns and for a reasonably extensive network of economic interaction among them. As an experiment for New World settlement, this was the best Europe had to offer.

The most commonly understood derivative of the word *bastide* today is *bastille*, which was once widely used in northern France to designate a fortress. T. F. Tout in *Medieval Town Planning*, certainly the seminal work on bastides in English, drew the comparison between the bastille and the bastide and left the suggestion that the defensive quality of these places gave them their name.[5] Yet in looking at them we find that sometimes the bastide was unwalled, suggesting that a distinction must be drawn between the use of the new foundations as a defensive place, a strongpoint, and their use to plant settlements and to utilize economically deserted lands.

The key to the question of whether these were defensive places, with normal fortification, or simply towns that might or might not be walled is to be found in the relations between the town and the populace of the surrounding countryside. Where a hostile subjugated population was held in rural serfdom (as in the German conquest east of the Elbe) or in continuing

5. T. F. Tout, *Medieval Town Planning: A Lecture* (London: The University Press, 1917).

International boundary

Departement boundary

Approximate boundary
of English Gascony

■ Bastide

Elevation over 200 meters

0   50 km

Map of Aquitaine showing representative bastides.

resistance but at bay in marchlands (as in the investing of Wales by the English kings, particularly Edward I, of the twelfth and thirteenth centuries), the bastide would of necessity have to be defensive in every instance.

The Economic Role of the Bastide

The bastide has been dealt with almost exclusively as a rigid, geometric creation in the literature of urban design and city form. Given an interest in design rather than morphogenesis, such a misrepresentation is likely to take place; in most instances, the eye sees what it seeks, and architectural and urban historians have sought regularity and self-conscious design. If we turn the quest to the forces at work in shaping the city rather than to the acts of individual designers, richer evidence confronts us than a crisply correct Monpazier or Aigues Mortes; we see instead towns of human quality, only vaguely correct and, in fact, adapted to accidents of nature and human thought.

The fundamental dynamic of these places was preconception, not regularity. Most founders—and a number of their names and purposes are well recorded in Maurice Beresford's study[6]—wanted to build a town *de novo* and rather quickly. We cannot reconstruct their thoughts, yet logic suggests that they did not at the outset say, "It shall be foursquare, meticulously ordered, and of pleasing overall design!" We must be skeptical that the shape of the place's plan was thought very important. Maps were little known, and isometric or perspective drawings virtually unknown; the human eye would not be able to see the town as a totality save in a few exceptional sites that might be viewed both at a distance and from above. Villefranche de Rouergue might have been so seen, but certainly neither Monpazier nor Aigues Mortes on its dead-flat plain was so conceived. Thus, regularity must have been the result of forces other than self-conscious design, at least in the beginning. As experience with bastides became more rich, we might expect the individuals invested with the job of establishing the town to think in terms of overall design. Even then, the use of certain fundamental dynamics of design rather than copies of existing plans seems to have created regularity.

The establishment of a bastide was a determined act supported by a lord, either temporal or ecclesiastical, into whose purse the quitrent, *cens* in French, would fall. Normally, possession of land determined both who the founder would be and where the town would be placed. If the king held lands in his own name, he was likely to seek their development by placing a new town upon them. If he wished to found such a new town in a particular place, he commonly sought by thinly veiled confiscation or by exchange to gain possession of the title to the site he wanted. Commonly, joint ventures were undertaken through the institution of *paréage* between king and vassal or bishop and petty nobility. Among the lesser lords and the magnates of the Roman church, possession of a domain was determinative. The numerous inheritances by the church from penitents were often geographically scattered, so we find bishops and other ecclesiastical leaders developing bastides in places well away from their sees. The bishop of Winchester in southern England created bastides in six different places, only four of which were within the rather wide limits of his own county.[7] The town-founding efforts of temporal lords were often equally wide-ranging, as their possessions were commonly made up of inheritances and dowries gained in a very direct effort to expand the family holdings.

Once a landowner had decided to found a town, he would most likely consider geographical location, with two questions in mind. Where was there a deserted or underused tract of land within his domains? And where within that general tract was there a precise site conducive to the building of

6. Maurice Beresford, *New Towns of the Middle Ages* (New York: Praeger, 1967).
7. Ibid., p. 441.

a town that might return the largest total *cens* to its lord? As we shall see, these questions have entered the minds of land speculators throughout the ages. To a very considerable degree, the bastide founders of the Middle Ages were among the forebears of the speculator who has done so much to shape the urban geography of the Industrial Age.

The tract within a broad domain that the landowner would choose to develop by the building of a new town was likely to lie at the frontier of existing settlement, if such a margin existed. In general, to the north of the Alps the lighter soils were among those first cleared for agriculture, so the bastides were set up on the heavier lands, particularly in copses and woodlands. Even within existing farmland, potential might remain for a planted settlement. "The planted towns were particularly likely to increase the demand for food, since many of them had no agricultural land beyond their walls. The land immediately surrounding them already belonged to the fields or commons of an older settlement and the burgesses [of the bastide] could claim no part of them." This new place detached from agricultural pursuits was less common in Gascony and the Perigord than in England; in those provinces, the unsettled sections were far more extensive, and organically evolving towns were absent from wide areas, having failed to develop or having been destroyed in the Albigensian Crusade or the Hundred Years' War. In England, however, the "organic towns, being promoted villages, already had their fields and were not so dependent on food grown elsewhere."[8] Thus, the landowner who planted a new town might well add to the market for the produce of his existing estates.

Beresford summarizes graphically the role of the new town in increasing the wealth of the great landlords whose grip on the countryside was so selfish but so strong:

> Yet there was an important difference between the increase in a lord's income that came from the sale of more demesne produce and an increase that came from the successful plantation of yet another town. In order to obtain any extra demesne produce, the lord (or his stewards) had to jerk into faster action the whole apparatus of villein services (for in the period of greatest urban expansion, after 1150, production by conscripted villein labour was normal in the manors of the English lowlands). When village populations were small it had been possible to increase the demesne (and its product) by taking in assorted land, but as the thirteenth century progressed, the ploughs came nearer and nearer to the margins of cultivation and England began to look like a fair field over-full of folk. Attempts to wrench a greater product from the soil came up against the dumb resistance of the peasantry and the harsh fact of diminishing marginal returns. Compared with these wrestling matches, how effortless it must have seemed to be able to increase one's income by using seigneurial authority to say, "Let there be a town."[9]

8. Ibid., p. 75.
9. Ibid., pp. 75–76.

In Gascony the picture was different and more interesting. The margins of settlement had not been reached and the bastidors were true pioneers in a forested land. The English examples leave us with the sour taste of grubbing for profit in a milieu of repression of basic human liberties, whereas the French cases show a much more palatable social situation, matching the clean pleasantness of the wines whose grapes were grown on the newly cleared fields. The forceful extension of a mercantile frontier was leading to the planting of bastides in the Perigord and Agenais; that situation cannot help but suggest a strong parallel with later and more distant extensions of such mercantile frontiers.

Bastides and Staple Production

Given the fundamentally economic motive for the creation of bastides, we need not amplify the discussion of the functions initial and fundamental to their support. We know from records of the anxious desire that early settlers include a goodly number of merchants as well as the necessary artisans; special inducements were offered such people to settle in a bastide. To make these towns prosperous, and thus most rewarding to the landowner creating them, the merchants would best engage in distant trade rather than the sort of local retailing that took place among the denizens in the marketplace. Distant trading was made possible only by creating a local agriculture productive of trade goods, those staples that would stand the heavy cost of transportation in the Middle Ages. In that interest, we find bastides tending to be located on the major rivers of southwestern France—or at least to be only a short distance from their banks, possibly served by another bastidal port located directly on the bank, as Villeneuve-sur-Lot, one of the important bastidal creations. But something must be transported, so crops and products were chosen in reference to distant markets. Thus, the greatest distinction in the bastidal settlement and its economy would be between the farmer producing only for local consumption—food, wool, and wood—and his brother producing staples for export from the locality. The important distinction was not, as might be assumed on the evidence of the earlier split between mercantile town and feudal countryside, the divide of the city walls.

The tying together of bastide and countryside seems to have had great social importance. We know that most settlers in the town also owned two kinds of land outside its walls, or confines, if walls were absent. They held what might be called allotment gardens, in a *bari* just outside the walls, where vegetables and herbs for home consumption could be grown. Farther away, many, though not all, townspeople had true agricultural holdings where they could grow crops in sufficient volume to produce a surplus for export out of the community. Grain growing (wheat and barley) and grazing were almost universal undertakings. But in the Aquitainian Basin of south-western France, grapes were grown for wine production. That production of wine makes this area useful in the study of medieval distant trading. The English, who held the main part of the area, were so unfortunate as to live north of the line where grapes for drinkable wine might be grown. Thus, they had to import wine from their French possessions, and it moved in strikingly

large quantities for the Middle Ages. All the conditions were present for the shaping of a system of trading towns, backstayed by staple-producing agriculture, such as became the design for the world that Europe developed overseas after the onset of the Commercial Revolution.

This system of trading towns was settled by a large body of what were essentially yeoman farmers, *censitaires*, who paid a quitrent annually to the lord. They were otherwise free to pursue their own course without feudal duties or the geographical restrictions associated with feudalism. The destructive class divisions that still plague Britain were largely missing, and a new society could be formed to match the new morphology of these towns. In that relatively liberal milieu, many economic, social, and religious advances could be attempted and perfected. From this overall concept of the town, a model for later use in the New World was fashioned.

Blandishing Settlers

Because these new towns lay away from existing cities and outside the established feudal order, they had to recruit settlers; to do so required the creation of pull factors that would encourage a basically conservative, even timorous, people to pull up stakes and move into the danger of the unknown. To gain that level of adventurousness, the initiating landowners had to offer truly novel advantages, the more important of which were the chance to

Villeneuve-sur-Lot was an important bastide founded in 1253 by Alphonse de Poitiers. This town, with its rectangular layout and square of arcades, is located on the north bank of the Lot, where it served as an anchor for a string of such fortified towns in the Guyenne. Photo: Ray Delvert, Villeneuve-sur-Lot.

The Late-
Medieval Bastide

make a real economic advance and the opportunity to gain personal and social freedom not previously available. In a way the Turnerian thesis of the impact of the frontier in national life applies as much to the thirteenth-century bastides as to the trans-Appalachian settlements of nineteenth-century America. Thus, most charters, and the other evidence that survives from the time, indicate a greater level of freedom for the residents of the bastides than was common elsewhere. Taxes were often remitted for a time after settlement, settlers were normally made freemen—absolved of any prior feudal duties—on taking up residence in the new town, and certain rights of local self-government were granted. And, the tenure of land in bastides was considerably more free than that of peasant farmers in the countryside.

A Practical Place of Real Equality

In searching out the morphogenetic processes that shaped the bastide, we shall first consider how the economic purpose and the social equality of the places were expressed concretely in urban forms. For such a complex economic creation to work, it had to come into full operation as quickly as possible. A single basically self-sufficient agricultural estate could operate independent of those around it. But a town such as the bastide with its occupational specialization could not stand so easily, if only one of a very small number of families was occupied with a particular activity. The failure rate—which was moderately great among these new towns, if Beresford's research is as complete as it seems—tells us that where the critical number and mix of settlers were not to be found, the town withered almost on initial sprouting.

To develop a town as quickly as possible, yet with the necessary initial complement of people and activities, required at least some broad conception of the town's layout on the ground. One hesitates to use the term *plan* because it suggests determination of the look of the place—that the aesthetic image and ordered and balanced fundament were the objects the founders had in mind. No doubt, with the range of bastide initiators, some founders may have envisioned such a self-conscious design, but in most cases likely all they sought was rapid and relatively complete development. They formed a concept of what a town *de novo* would contain and how, with the least impediment to normal growth, that end could be accomplished. Thus, the regularity among bastides comes probably not so much from an effort at design as from an effort to remove conditions impeding growth. These impediments might be introduced by large or inconveniently located private landholdings, by interruptions in street patterns making local circulation difficult or inefficient, or by the absence of certain fundamental functional components of a town—its market, its church, its occupation quarters—requiring subsequent spatial additions or serious replatting of the town. Let us use *pattern* to indicate the ground layout of the town to avoid suggesting that someone prior to its establishment drew a formal *plan*.

The most probable pattern was the regular grid of streets. Such a pattern avoided many resistances to rapid, orderly growth by providing a continuous, integrated, and fairly fine-grained circulation network within the town. Quite in contrast to the organic layout of the earlier medieval town, the grid pattern of streets would show less tendency toward distinction; it had no High Street and, in turn, fewer narrow cul-de-sacs. Further, pedestrians might follow alternative courses to pass from the edge to the center of the town, offering potential shopkeepers a greater number of reasonable sites for their shops than the organic place had. No doubt some sorting out of these pedestrian flows took place, as not all streets could lead from gates in the wall to the central marketplace. The level of distinction, however, would have been less ruthless than in the older organic towns with their few streets radiating from the marketplace to the gates.

Another virtue of the grid pattern in a new but preconceived town would be its assurance of reasonably proportionate plots for building. In the older towns, the High Streets, with often unimportant streets leading out of them, had made the lot rather like the tourmaline crystal—red with the fire of activity at one end and often a lustrous but quiet green at the other end. The economic consequence of what M. R. G. Conzen termed the "High Street layout"[10] was a sharp division in the utility of urban land, leaving open to question whether such a pattern was really very efficient or productive. Any rational economic appraisal of the utility of land within a wall might have suggested to an intelligent initiator—and they were often both bright and shrewd—that a rectangular lot of fairly equal dimensions would be the most productive way to use a scarce land resource. Such a reasonably equidimensional lot would make more likely the use of all or the better part of the plot for activities directly associated with city functions, leaving the raising of kitchen produce to allotments or gardens outside the walls. The grid pattern itself would as well make for relatively better and more consistent circulation within the walls or confines of the town.

We need not prove that the knowledge of the street grid had survived from Roman times; we may logically infer that the form would have been reinvented if the need were felt. The high development of cities in Gallia Narbonensis, one of seventeen provinces into which the Roman Empire was divided, is well recorded; we know of the existence there of Nîmes, Narbonne, Béziers, and Toulouse. The cities were not only large and prospering but cosmopolitan as well; the council of Narbonne in A.D. 589 noted the residence of five races—Visigoths, Romans, and Jews in large numbers, and Greeks and Syrians less numerous in the population. Soon the Arabs became a force in Septimania—the land of the seven cities: Agde, Béziers, Carcassonne, Elne, Lodève, Maguelonne, and Narbonne—adding their urban tradition to those already present. The resulting culture was the most urban to be found in the West, rich in poetry and drama, courtly in the extreme. If any area across the Alps managed to preserve Roman civilization with its urban and urbane practices, it was Septimania, and Aquitaine farther to the west. Doubtless, Roman city-designing practices would have been fully appreciated in such an area until the culture was shattered in the

10. M. R. G. Conzen, *Alnwick, Northumberland: A Study in Town-Plan Analysis,* publication no. 17 (Institute of British Geographers, 1960), p. 28.

The Late-Medieval Bastide

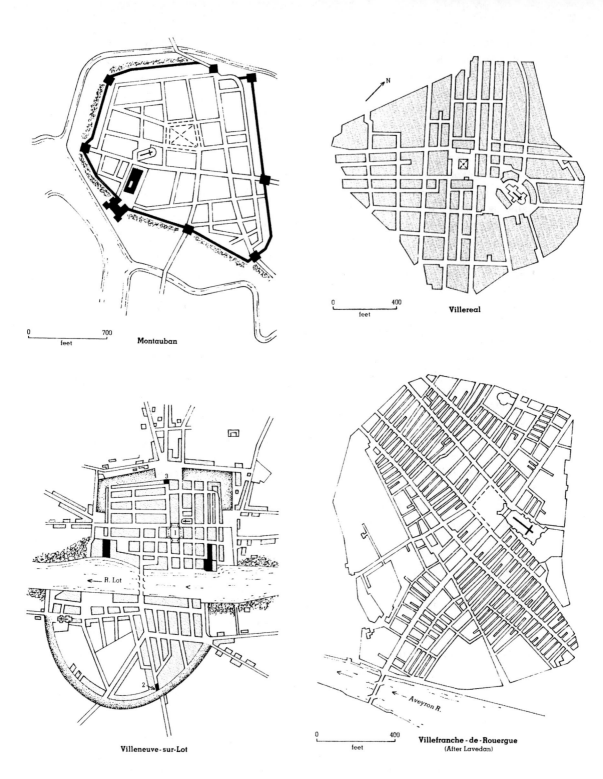

Montauban

Villereal

Villeneuve-sur-Lot

R. Lot

Villefranche-de-Rouergue
(After Lavedan)

Aveyron R.

N

0   700
feet

0   400
feet

0   400
feet

The
Continuing City

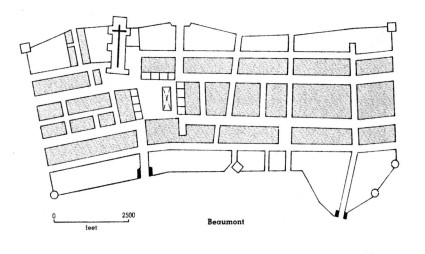

0   2500
feet   **Beaumont**

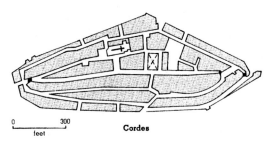

0   300
feet   **Cordes**

Albigensian Crusade. Appalling as that campaign of ecclesiastical sadism was, fortunately it was not complete. Despite the best efforts of the inquisitors, some educated and worldly people were left to carry forward the traditions of a higher culture—among them, the look of imperial Roman towns. But having abandoned the religion of ancient Rome, which used the city as temple in a particular design to serve that purpose, the survivors in Septimania would likely have recalled the efficiencies of the orderly Roman system without seeking to restore the rigid, orthodox application that the primitive religion of Latium carried with it.

The bastides reveal an almost infinite variation in actual pattern; yet most have elements of a system of thought that can be analyzed as a whole. They are orderly and seemingly logical, possessed of a functionally effective interconnectivity of streets that avoids the perhaps intentionally confusing maze-like quality so characteristic of the Middle Ages. In addition to interconnectivity, the bastides show a rectilinearity of plots. This form suggests that the house intended for these building sites possessed a fairly consistent module and an architecture that had the efficiency of the roughly equidimensional box, whatever that shape lacked in grandeur and visual impressiveness.

The Late-
Medieval Bastide

187

Interaccessibility and Popular Provision

The shaping of the bastide also reflected the emergence of the average citizen to a position of concern. We may question whether democracy, either as an operating system of government or as a humanist viewpoint on social justice, was consciously understood or sought at that time. But the practices necessary to gain settlers for the bastides with the speed needed for their economic survival and prosperity led to an outcome that would have been consistent with a democratic intent. Whether the cause was philosophical or practical matters not. Henri Pirenne said, "Democracy in the Middle Ages, as in modern times, got its start under the guidance of the select few who foisted their programme upon the confused aspiration of the people."[11] The "few" must have been those needed to initiate the settlement of the new bastidal creation. Since it seems that most bastidors were townspeople led to migrate elsewhere, they must have required inducements to move from an existing town. The carrot held before them was an economic and social liberalism denied them in the older towns. Through moving they could hope for more freedom, greater control of their property, and some relief from the class- and church-ridden qualities of an increasingly conservative medieval urban society. The design of freedom appears in the physical build of the bastides.

The grid pattern of streets was the beginning of such a more equal treatment. Although many bastides were rigidly rectilinear, this layout was primarily an expression of the desire for interconnectivity and proportion. Puylaroque in Bas Quercy and Domme in Perigord in southwestern France are examples of bastides without rigid plans; their locations on the top of steep hills seem to have dictated the use of subparallel streets; even, in the case of Puylaroque, streets radiating somewhat from a center near the impressive fortified church. The use of straight streets and the division of the land into rather consistent plots show up in these grid patterns. These qualities are more indicative of the bastide than is the checkerboard so often thought the key. If anything supports the argument that these were not preconceived *designs* but rather preconceived *towns*, it is this consistent interconnectivity and proportion in the face of a fair range of specific patterns on the ground.

The street pattern of the bastide can be thought of as logically consistent and initially complete, sufficient for the laying out and development of an economically viable place with a considerable diversity of activity. In these proprietorial creations, the layout of the streets determined the ultimate grain of the town, not, as in the organic towns of earlier centuries, the nature of the individual holding, the burgage plot in many cases. The whole town was not an abstract creation of some designer's mind. Instead, the creation of an orderly framework furnished interaccessibility among the lots and proportion within which the longstanding organic processes could be allowed to work.

The way these processes worked emerged in the buildings that came to fill in the spaces bounded by the streets of the bastide's pattern, whether the

11. Pirenne, *Medieval Cities*, pp. 184–85.

typical grid or a more specific layout for a particular terrain. We cannot describe the infilling for all bastides. Beresford lists 184 undoubted bastides in England, around 8 for Wales, and about 125 for Gascony; he omits any lists for Languedoc. [12] In addition he does not mention a number of bastides even in southwestern France—for example, Puylaroque, Villefranche de Rouergue, and Sauveterre de Rouergue. When the bastides created in Languedoc, the most obvious of which is Aigues Mortes, are added, [13] we must deal with as many as three hundred in southern France alone. Adding the Savoyard examples and those in the German marches across the Elbe, as well as those of Britain, there must have been at least a thousand such creations in the later Middle Ages merely in the lands of Western and Central Europe. The bastides of southern Spain built by Their Most Catholic Majesties on lands recaptured from the Moors swell an already sufficiently impressive total. No catalogue of these new creations of the late Middle Ages exists, but we cannot doubt their real importance in any study of urban morphogenesis.

The New Bastidor's Plot

If the burgage plot was the basic module of the organic medieval city, the bastidor's plot was the basic component of the laid-out town—but not its module. Instead, the street blocks served in the later town to establish the pattern, though the plots had a proportionate quality. The plots seem to have been conceived of as the space necessary to an individual or family economic unit for the conduct of the activity that would support it, and at the same time not waste space within the bastide. Since trade and artisan manufacture were the two activities for which the towns were established, though walled bastides might stand as strongpoints on the frontier of the realm in times of warfare, the marketplace and the artisan's streets must be given fundamental attention. The bastide plan in its archetypal form was the physical expression of such attention. Always located near the center of the grid layout was a market square, one of the modular street blocks left free of buildings and used for the sale of agricultural produce. Typically, this marketplace was apportioned periodically into sites for small barrows and stands on which farmers sold produce. At night and when the market was closed, the square would be swept clean of commercial activity to become a place of social contact among town residents. This nonpermanent quality of the market barrow, and its clustering in the square, tells us much about the specific role of the activity carried on there. This market was essential to sustaining the town, but was not the reason the town existed. In most places the barrows occupied the square not every weekday but only at certain specified times. Such a periodic effort seems hardly to have been the reason for the founding of a new town.

12. These lists refer to the gazeteers of England, Wales, and Gascony given in Beresford, *New Towns*.

13. Charles Higounet's article "La Frange oriental des bastides," *Annals du Midi* 61 (1949), shows just over fifty on a map of Languedoc and its immediate borders in the Vivarois, Rouergue, and Toulousain.

This market square in Beaumont-en-Perigord shows many of the distinctive features characteristic of bastides: the church—in this case a fine example of a fortified structure—located just off the square, the square itself, and the arcade beneath which merchants operated. Photo: Ray Delvert, Villeneuve-sur-Lot.

Around the square the more fundamental activities of the town—those affairs that kept the citizens busy every day save Sunday—began to show up. Immediately adjacent to the square in the bastides of southern France, and sometimes in Savoy, Switzerland, and other Germanic lands, the houses tended to reflect the selling and buying function carried on there through the construction of a covered arcade in which activities could continue even in wet weather. Sometimes such a shelter stood even in the square itself, now usually termed a market hall, in which certain activities that must transpire whatever the weather could continue. In Villeréal in Perigord, such a structure stands in the center of the square, though there are some arcades at the side of the open space. Certainly market halls were not limited to bastides, but they seem to have been common there; unfortunately, most have disappeared in the last couple of centuries, because of their wooden construction.

The real trading life of the towns was located in the arcades at the side. The more important merchants normally resided in the houses fronting on the square. In those towns where an arcade, called in the bastides a *cornière*, had been built, those traders seem to have spread their wares brought from distant places under the shelter they afforded. These *cornières* seem to have been rather consistently possessed of arched openings, both toward the front, giving onto the square, and to each side, leading to the *cornières* of adjacent houses to create a continuous arcade along the sides of the square. To call these features arcades may be imprecise, as they were probably not actually arched over, save at the openings in the house walls. Under the house itself, the ceiling of the *cornière* was usually flat, carried by wooden rafters and closed by floorings. In other words, this *cornière* was essentially a room in the house left open for entrance from the square or movement along its sides.

Few very specific records of the structures built in these new towns of the

Middle Ages survive, and virtually no accounts of life therein; we must infer from what facts we do have and the physical forms of the town just how life was carried on in the bastides. We have already noted their greater freedom. In France, bastidors seem to have been allowed to select from their own numbers a group of "consuls" who were given the right and the responsibility of governing the town. Similarly, the citizen of a bastide was permitted to select his daughter's husband; the lord had done so in the true practice of feudalism. The infamous *droit de seigneur* was apparently undemanded within the bastides. The sense we gain of the places is one much closer to the powerful towns of several centuries later than to the feudal countryside in ⬛ they were planted. Perhaps this fact as much as any puts in question any assertion of a central-place origin for these bastides.

The general practice of permitting the emancipation from feudal duties of a refugee villein from the country, after he had been resident in a city for a year and a day, seems as well to have adhered to the bastides. But Beresford states strongly, though in a different analytical frame, the argument against thinking of these places as having grown directly out of their native soil:

> Useful as refugee villeins might be in providing an unskilled labour-force in a new town, its success depended upon a very different sort of immigrant: the man already possessing some knowledge of a craft or trade. If the project [for a bastide] was to succeed, the number of such immigrants would have to be substantial and their recruitment rapid. A numerous influx in the first months was not only a good advertisement to induce waverers, it provided the essentials of urbanism: sufficient specialists to be able to meet each other's needs; sufficient numbers to engender purchasing power that would attract sellers to their markets; and sufficient products to turn aside buyers from their accustomed routes to

The Late-
Medieval Bastide

venture in new market places. Hence the insistence of many towns that burgage plots must be taken up within stated periods or else fall forfeit.

To recruit new townsmen with experience of crafts and trades it was necessary to draw on existing skills, and to lure men from other places where they were already practising them. Who could such men be? where were they to be found? and what liberties, privileges and franchises did the founders of the new town offer them?[14]

As Beresford admits, it is easier to answer the last of these three questions than the first and second. We know from surviving charters that wide privileges were given and most adult males were enfranchised in municipal elections. The morphological impact of such basic liberty and essential equality was considerable, as we shall see presently. We might first summarize the slight evidence that exists to explain who the immigrants were and whence they came, for in that explanation we can begin to see both the existence of a long-distance trading network and the early trials toward an urban economy to replace the feudal one.

Beresford suggests, "A likely source of recruits to the new towns—although there is no direct evidence—would be from among the younger sons of burgesses in the older towns. From at least the mid-twelfth century, and possibly earlier, general demographic conditions were favourable to migration from older centres, and it was possible for new towns to develop without destroying older towns by the loss of skilled and semi-skilled townsmen."[15] Numbers were sufficient as the population of the existing towns expanded, and the younger sons must have been well aware of the practices of trade and craft. By moving they might expect to engage in their occupation less fettered by their fathers or other members of the gild. A number of historians, notably Bernard Bailyn,[16] have shown persuasively that migrations hold the possibility of establishing long-distance ties of family and friendship that might serve to connect merchants in distant towns within a trading network.

We may reason that the more successful merchants would tend to take up locations around the squares of bastides employing the *cornière* both to display the trade goods they used as tender and to collect the staple they might gain in return. Gold and silver were not in common circulation until the Age of Discovery opened the rich mines of the New World. Instead, the exchange of goods facilitated the trade of medieval times. Merchants exercised their function both as distributors and as collectors, and their premises had to be sufficient to comprehend both activities.

If the leading merchants might be expected to take up plots on the frontage of the square, either when the town was being laid out or later, the

14. Beresford, *New Towns*, p. 192.

15. Ibid., p. 197.

16. Bernard Bailyn, *The New England Merchants in the Seventeenth Century* (1955; rpt. New York: Harper Torchbooks, 1964).

lesser merchants might be assumed to come to occupy an intermediate economic and morphological position. How many merchants engaged in distant trade would there be in any one bastide? We must fall back on probability to venture that there were never more than could be accommodated in the houses with *cornières* surrounding the square. Lesser tradespeople, more in the class of artisans than of merchants, came to occupy sites within the town that would best accommodate what was clearly a compromise demand.

On the basis of this logical breakdown of locations within a bastide, we may envisage some characteristic divisions of the land use within the town. Since virtually all these towns had squares, we may designate the first of these land-use divisions as that related to the market square. Within the square itself would be found a periodic market.

More to the point in explaining the origin of the bastide is the second half of the marketplace land-use component—the ring of merchants' shops fronting on the square and often giving on it by means of the *cornières*. Even in England where the *cornière* was little used, save in a very specialized form such as the second-story galleries found in medieval Chester, the symbiosis between merchant housing and open marketplace appears to have held. In Bristol's Old Market, the building that served as the piepowder court still stands to attest to this tie, and in many towns the more impressive burghers' houses survive or are recorded as having fronted on the marketplace.

Land Assignment in the Bastides

In the bastide we are able to assert with fair confidence the initial importance of merchants based on their location around the square. In encouraging rapid and economically successful settlement, proprietors must have employed a reasonable strategy of "land assignment,"[17] the evidence of which should suggest the relative ranking of various urban activities when weighted by town founders. Reasoning that the sites around the square or at the gates would be most prized, the unassailable presence of merchant housing—evidenced by morphological remnants—on the frontage of the marketplace must be taken as support for the highest ranks being accorded to that group. Neither the agriculturalist nor the artisan stood in first place, but rather the merchant most likely to engage in long-distance trade for at least a fair part of the time.

Unlike the situation in the *bourg* and *faubourg*, in the bastide the terrain is less likely to confuse the evidence or cause a misinterpretation of development stages. When a town, even one largely supported by distant mercantile activities, evolved over a long period, the writing of the past is not always so easy to read, because location of various activities within the town might stem from several different stages in past conditions and constraints. Not so in the bastide: "The planted town was not the architectural prisoner of its past, for it had no past. If the best was to be made out of the limited space

17. James E. Vance, Jr., "Land Assignment in the Pre-Capitalist, Capitalist, and Post-Capitalist City," *Economic Geography* 47 (1971): 101–20.

available it was natural to be orderly and have a planned town"[18] and, we might add, to assign land on some ranking of economic importance.

How, then, was land assigned within the bastide? Broadly, it was done in terms of the rough model already sketched: at the town center stood the marketplace with the surrounding shops-houses of the leading merchants, often extended by *cornières*; farther away from the square but probably ringing it on all sides, save where a church might intervene, would be ordinary, rather simple, rectangular houses, sheltering the workshops of artisans producing for the local market or fabricating products for shipment to more distant buyers; finally, toward the edges of these towns, which were not very large even when they were quite successful, would be the housing for people dealing directly with the agricultural hinterland, wherever one existed, who went out to the fields to supervise or themselves to labor. Probably no extensive, wage-employed, urban proletariat existed for whom a separate housing provision had to be made.

The relatively small number of casual laborers who might have been found in the bastides were probably housed in odd spaces by chance left free in the broad structure of occupation districts that accounted for the shape of the social geography of the town. Thus, we may look at that occupation geography to gain a reasonable view of the nature of these places.

Occupations in the bastides were those of active workers, rather than of capitalists and magnates. The gentry, who might have encouraged a bastide on their land for the wealth it would return, still lived outside it, either in the older organic cities, where their *bourg* might have brought to their vicinity the first merchants, or more probably in the country castle, whose power symbolized and sustained their class distinction. The bishop was almost certainly to be found elsewhere; his see was normally in a town of antiquity, whatever other qualities it might lack. In a few places other ecclesiastical personages—priors or abbots and abbesses—might take up residence in the new towns, but usually only at the edge, as in the rather separate monastic institution at Beaumont. For the most part, the bastide presented a remarkable base for trying out relatively egalitarian land-assignment practices. The society was one in which great scalar differences were ruled out by the simple fact that people prospered finally from their own labor, not from inherited or bestowed wealth and distinction. The bastide became the nursery and laboratory for experimentation with a more egalitarian society, which depended on hard work to break the power of inheritance, and which came to take over the town in the Mercantile Revolution of the fifteenth and sixteenth centuries. From such forebears came the early settlers of America. Here at last we begin to see the conditions that fairly directly shaped our own heritage.

The basic land-assignment unit of the bastide was the actual plot held by a single bastidor. The tenure on which citizens of these towns held their land was characteristic of towns rather than the surrounding countryside, with its duties of furnishing labor in the fields. Instead, in the towns a quitrent (*cens*) was charged—in England commonly a shilling a year—which discharged

18. Beresford, *New Towns*, p. 142.

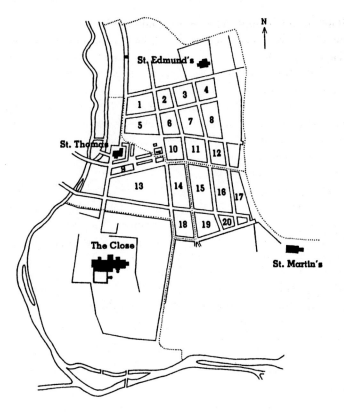

100 0   500 feet

the landholder of any further responsibilities to the landowner. The socage, which had begun as a return for labor in the countryside, was transformed into a return for money in the town. The freedom given the bastidor by such a shift must be fully appreciated. Although the actual land, whose early unrestricted use he enjoyed, was minute even by comparison with the small agricultural holdings of the time, his freedom in using it more than made up for its geographical restriction. He was a member of that group of outsiders called in the charters *hôtes*, guests or visitors who had been invited to the developing town to seek its prosperity and their own fortunes under a set of conditions contained in the *contrat d'hostice*.[19]

Though no precise dimensions can possibly serve for all bastides to show plot size, we can employ average ranges of dimensions to suggest the basic scale with which we are dealing. Beresford gives the common street frontage as "20 to 27 feet and a depth of about twice these dimensions. . . . Documentary references to the actual operation of laying out and assigning the building plots of a new town are few, but in compensation there is the dumb witness of the sites in England, Wales and Gascony that have the simply rectilinear grid of streets."[20] For the observer of urban morphogenesis, the

19. Pierre Lavedan, *Histoire de l'urbanisme: Antiquité–moyen age* (Paris: Henri Laurens, 1926), 1: 286.

20. Beresford, *New Towns*, pp. 146–47. Dimensions are cited on p. 330.

**The Late-
Medieval Bastide**

Monpazier is the classic bastide in plan but distinctive in actual construction (compare with figure on page 14). Photo: Ray Delvert, Villeneuve-sur-Lot.

term *dumb* appears neither precisely nor symbolically more valid with respect to the evidence furnished by the urban landscape than to that furnished by the urban document. Either reveals its record and the truth to be found there to the insightful reader. Following the practice of the Romans in their towns, the scribes of the bastide commonly referred to the street blocks as *insulae* or *îlots* (islands), though in the new bastidal town of Salisbury in Wiltshire they were called chequers, apparently from the overall pattern they formed. Within each *insula* the individual parcels were termed the *placeae*, themselves "also rectangular since it could most easily be marked out by lines drawn parallel to the sides of the Island. There was, however, no standard size of *placea*, and even in the most regular towns such as Monpazier there is more than one size apparent. In the most crowded quarters of the town [closer to the marketplace] the house frontages were short, but in the more open, residential areas the better off might take a whole Island. One whole Island was commonly assigned for the church and another for the market-place."[21] On occasion the individual houses were separated one from another by narrow passageways, *androynes*, hardly wider than a man's shoulders.

Within the bastides the *hôtes* were given proportional lands, generally easily measured. As Lavedan noted, "To be easy to calculate an area, one needs a simple geometric figure: the simplest of all is the rectangle. The

21. Ibid., p. 147.

villages of the *hôtes* seem then to show us a layout of rectangular blocks more or less cleverly constructed. . . . The form of the *îlot* is only one element in the plan, a stone in the edifice. How will these rectangular blocks be arranged? One can put them in a checker-board; one can also arrange them in a circle around a church or a central square. The material is so flexible it can take a thousand combinations.[22]

If we take perhaps the most representative of these new towns, Villefranche de Rouergue, as an example of how these lands were distributed, we find a significant pattern:

> The plan of the bastide of Villefranche was worked out in advance (the usual procedure for bastides). The territory consisted of three zones: the zone of the *bastide* proper subdivided into equal lots; the zone immediately surrounding the circumvallation, the *bari*, for gardens and vineyards, with the number of allotments corresponding to the number of families in the town; and finally, further afield, the rest of the acquired land for cultivation, since it was assumed that agriculture would remain for a long time the basis of existence for the majority of citizens.[23]

Again, the idea was that of proportion among the *hôtes*. Each *hôte* was given (1) a town lot within an *îlot*, where he might carry on his trade, be it in a craft or in commerce itself, (2) a garden-vineyard holding in the *bari*, where he might raise much of his own food as well as the wine that came to be of ever-increasing importance to the functioning of the long-distance trading system of the region, and (3) a more extensive agricultural holding on which he might expand his vineyard or perhaps engage in grazing or field cultivation. In such a division none was favored, and none was disadvantaged, much as in the similar ternary division of lands in the early Puritan villages of Massachusetts.

The role of agriculture in the bastides is a debated point. E. A. Gutkind clearly thought it substantial to the point of domination; others have viewed it differently, restricting agriculture to the status of a specialized trade whence came the staple of long-distance trade.

Beresford makes the point that sharp division existed between townsmen and countrymen in terms of cultivation: "What inhibited the efficient exercise of a craft and the pursuit of trade was not the possession of land but the obligations that went with a [feudal] tenement if it were held by unfree tenure." If a man held land that required of him labor service, he was severely handicapped in the pursuit of his interests in trade:

> That was irksome enough for a peasant, but for a would-be craftsman and trader it was crippling. The place where bargains and sales offered themselves was the marketplace and not the selions of the lord's demesnes. The time when strangers might pass by, or for the market-bell to ring, might be just when the lord's reeve was

22. Lavedan, *Histoire de l'urbanisme*, 1: 293–95.
23. E. A. Gutkind, *International History of City Development*, Vol. 5, *Urban Development in Western Europe: France and Belgium*, (New York: Free Press, 1970), p. 63.

calling for work on the demesne. Ships made port, commercial news arrived, and hungry travellers drew near according to a timetable that took no account of whether villeins were free that day from the demesne works. A craft might demand continuous application to a task or a manufacture might need continuous supervision of a process; a demand for carting services and harvest work would then be a fatal interruption. Of these demands the generality of burgesses were free.[24]

We should not assume that either distant traders or the lesser entrepreneurs among the bastidors shunned land absolutely; they fled feudal service and their escape was made sure by moving from an older town to the new foundation established in freedom—the Villefranche, Sauveterre, Villeneuve, La Bastide, La Salvetat, or Castelfranc. Thus, on the burned ground of southern France, where the internecine Crusade had struck as heavily against the nobles as the common people, and where forest still remained to be cleared, the chance of a combination of commercial agriculture and the pursuit of an urban trade was probably greater than in England, about which more has been written.

This combination of agriculture and trade has a direct bearing both on the shape of the bastide and on its role in the emergence of the modern city. In essence, these planted towns became the instrument both of the occupation of undeveloped land and of its attachment to a geographically extensive trading system. In the case of the bastide, there is no question that in many instances, perhaps most, these towns formed in economic terms the germ around which the countryside developed. This use of the town as a developmental tool was an important contribution. The Romans had used towns as instruments of conquest and political domination, as the Spaniards soon would do in the New World. But the bastides of France—in England they had less geographical scope—showed how towns might attach to one another in an initial economic bond that would strengthen into a firm political attachment.

The Bastide, the Wine Trade, and Mercantilism

Though bastides themselves are fascinating, their role as a school for larger things introduces them to our attention. My basic thesis is that the French and the English experimented in the bastides with plantation settlement; through the bastides, the ministers in both kingdoms learned how profitable economic settlement could be; through the working of the bastides, the rudiments of a national economic policy of planted settlement emerged. In its developed form, that mercantilist policy of the sixteenth and seventeenth centuries was the force that projected European settlement into the New World; and in the form of the bastide, both social and morphological, towns were introduced into North America.

The bastides were planted towns where it was necessary to offer the planters some very strong inducement to give up in one place and begin

24. Beresford, *New Towns*, p. 210.

again in another. For some, failure would be a sufficient push to migrate; for the more critical members of a planter group, those with particular skills or necessary trading connections, a pull more than a push factor was required to bring about the shift. That pull had in general to be a breaking out from the society and economy of the Middle Ages, with an advance toward the modern era of social, political, and economic liberalism. Obviously, the present liberal state was not reached in one move or a single generation, but the strategy commenced when young merchants or artisans passed through the gate of their birthplace on the road to the bastide, later to the colonial town and, in the nineteenth century, to the interior of the United States, where Frederick Jackson Turner clearly understood the way such pioneering on the frontier affected individuals and society. The role of the frontier in American settlement began with the founding of the bastides starting with the first, Montauban, in the year 1144. The signs were faint, but they can be seen if carefully sought.

The inducement that the bastides used was remarkably simple. It was essentially equality: equal ownership of land within the town and in the *bari* and forests around it; equal participation in the economic life of the place, with no established monopolies to narrow its scope; equal entrée to the political life of the place through the *contrats d'hostice et d'accensement*, which gave the settler a voice in government and a contractual responsibility for the tax to carry on that government.[25] Though movement to the bastide

25. See Lavedan, *Histoire de l'urbanisme*, 1: 293. These contracts might be translated as those of occupation and assessment, of the right to run the town and of the responsibility to pay the costs thereof.

The Late-Medieval Bastide

did not lead directly to religious freedom—the term was rather meaningless in the theological state of the time—it perhaps began to open the door. Certainly the Huguenot movement was remarkably successful several centuries later in the bastidal towns. It had its heroic last stand in a bastide, La Rochelle, that the Norman kings of England founded between 1130 and 1150 as a port to tap their southern domains. There we find the northernmost occurrence of the characteristic *cornières*. These towns grew up in the land devastated by early medieval religious wars and were absolutely central to the Wars of Religion of the sixteenth and seventeenth centuries that followed their foundation. If they did not give religious liberty, they at least were scattered about the battlefield where its cause was fought and finally lost at the bloody hands of Richelieu.

The form devised for the bastide was as "liberal" as its social, economic, and political practices. That form was centrally concerned with offering equality to citizens. Lots were modest and proportional; streets were rather neutrally "equal" without the great disproportions so typical of the older medieval towns; the houses were highly functional and largely lacked the ostentation that was creeping into the burghers' and bishops' towns. Even the "mansions" that Lucien Testut so lovingly sketched and studied in Beaumont-en-Perigord finally were the homes and workplaces of productive citizens, containing bakeries, dairies, and other relatively humble quarters.[26] These citizens earned a prosperity that was reflected in the reconstruction of their houses, but they seem always to have been democratic in the same high sense that Paul Revere, of a Huguenot family himself, was in eighteenth-century Boston.

The central morphological truth learned in the bastides was that interaccessible and proportionate layout of the town is one of the more concrete expressions of a functional equality, and a strong bulwark in its defense.

The social and morphological egalitarianism of the bastide was only one part of its contribution to the shaping of a model for New World settlement, though the most commonly understood. Equally significant was the proof the bastide offered of the ultimate national and personal enrichment to be had from shaping an interacting system of long-distance trade. Again, as with the inducement to settlers, the real need was to break away from the strictures of the traditional medieval economy. The bastides were particularly towns in a national framework. The English foundations in France, of which La Rochelle was only one of the larger, were encouraged both with the idea of defending English possessions against the French and with making those lands valuable to the crown and to its supporters and agents. Although these lands were the personal possessions of the English king rather than of his people, they were to be used for the collective prosperity, which in the end was indissoluble.

To test the strength of the argument that these bastides were particularly

---

26. The great French anatomist Lucien Testut was born at Beaumont-en-Perigord, one of the most unspoiled of the bastides. The second volume of his study of Beaumont presents detailed pictures of the house of the bastide. As a famous anatomist, Testut drew surpassingly well and more than most other observers was clearly aware of the role of morphogenesis. Lucien Testut, *La Bastide-en-Perigord*, 2 vols. (Bordeaux, 1920).

merchant towns for a distant trade, we may contrast the bastidal settlements that the Germans placed in the Slavic lands they were overrunning at this same time with those in the Aquitainian Basin. We must distinguish between the defensible settlement planted by the German conquerors east of the Oder and the bastides of France. The differentiation extends beyond the relations between the town and the countryside surrounding it to the actual layout of the place. To understand the forms, we must look back at the traditional village morphologies of the Germans and the Slavs.

The villages that evolved in the German lands, those areas between the Rhine and the Elbe-Saale frontiers that remained outside the Roman *limes*, were of a particularly loosely agglomerate sort, the *Haufendorf*, in which the houses were in truth farmsteads collected into an open village. The buildings were physically separate, adjoined by gardens and barnyards, and little distinguishable from an isolated farmstead, save by being brought into loose proximity with other, similarly individual barn-house complexes. Farther to the west in what is now the Rhineland, the arrangement was slightly different. The assembly was made up of the same barn-house units, but they tended to cluster in a line, along a street, rather than more compact morphologies. The *Strassendorf* of the Rhineland was what the French term a *village de route*, which in New England becomes a "string village." The *Haufendorf* was the French *village agglomeré*, and seems to be the rather imprecise equivalent of our village.

The difficulty of finding French or American equivalents for these Germanic forms is that in France and America the dispersed farmstead was a more common unit of rural settlement, so the parallels are not too exact. In the French Midi, the characteristic rural settlement form is the *mas*, a Provencal word meaning "an isolated farmstead," derived directly from the Latin, apparently from *mansio* (dwelling), though the etymology is not fully agreed upon. In France south of the Massif Centrale, and in Armorica as well, the village is not apparently the original rural settlement form, quite in contrast to the rest of Europe beyond the Alps. This fact helps to justify the view advanced that the bastide in the French Midi was fundamentally an urban form, not a rural one. As Robert Dickinson notes, a difference arises between northern France with its rather open "market" villages and the Midi where "the compact, congested settlement is much more characteristic."[27] These towns show a strong preference for hilltop sites; Pierre Deffontaines found at least two-thirds of the towns in Aquitaine were so located.[28]

The contrast may as well show a different role for many of these southern towns, not that of a local market center but rather that of a collecting and distributing point in a much more geographically extensive trading system than found in the rural north. In the Midi the production of wine for distant shipment was important not merely economically but politically as well. As André Simon wrote in his unfortunately never completed history of the wine trade of England, this trade was critical:

27. Robert E. Dickinson, *The West European City: A Geographical Interpretation* (London: Routledge and Kegan Paul, 1951), pp. 358–59.

28. Pierre Deffontaines, *Les Hommes et leurs travaux dans le pays de la moyenne Garonne* (Lille: S.I.L.I.C., 1932), quoted in ibid., p. 359.

The Late-
Medieval Bastide

Abroad, the English monarch's continental possessions were more considerable than at any other time in this country's history. Henry [II] was at the same time master in the right of his father of Anjou, Touraine, and Maine; in that of his mother, of Normandy; in that of his wife, of Guienne, Poitou, Saintonge, Auvergne, Perigord, Angoumois, and Limousin: these provinces which were amongst the most opulent of the French monarchy, were nearly all wine-producing and owed their wealth entirely to agriculture and commerce. The surest way for the Plantagenets to retain under their allegiance the subjects of these distant provinces was to attach them to their dynasty by bonds of interest, assuring them of a ready market, in England, for the sale of their wines, and granting them special privileges which might be termed, in modern phraseology, preferential tariffs. The result of this policy may be easily detected in the remarkable faithfulness of Bordeaux to the English Crown during the three following centuries, and the rapid decay of the Metropolis of Aquitaine after it was lost to England. Although Rouen was reunited to the French monarchy long before Bordeaux, the loyalty of its inhabitants to their English lord was very staunch; they offered a long and gallant resistance to his enemy and became French very much against their will.[29]

Because glass bottles were "then unknown, and the proper treatment of wine in casks only very imperfectly comprehended, wines were mostly drunk new, and custom had engendered a taste for their natural harshness. The stronger the wine the better it would keep, although the longer it would remain on tap the worse it would become, so that either light or old wines were always considered the worst by medieval consumers."[30] Speed in reaching the market was so important that a distinction was made between "wines of the vintage," which left Gascony for England in the fall of the year pressed, and "wines of the rack," which had been stored in Bordeaux for the winter, racked in the spring to remove their lees, and then sent off to England. The wines of the rack were charged less freight because for them time was not so critical. We have already seen how in the London of Fitzstephen's time—just when the bastides were being settled—wine was often drunk directly on ships tied up at the Thames wharves so it would travel no farther than absolutely necessary and be drunk as soon as possible in the vintage year.

The combination of the longer political ties between Gascony and England, which were not fully broken until 1453, and the speed with which wine had to reach the market in those centuries certainly encouraged the creation of an elaborate trading system in the southwest of France. Even the wines of the rack could not tarry for more than a few months. The trade had a clear geographical structure; the vineyard areas closest to Bordeaux and Bayonne were the more important sellers in the London market, though wine

29. André L. Simon, *The History of the Wine Trade in England* (London: Wyman, 1906), vol. 1 (all published), pp. 58–59.

30. Ibid., p. 261.

was shipped from as far east in Aquitaine as Albi, Agen, Cahors, Cordes, Rabastens, Villeneuve-sur-Lot (Ste. Livrade), and Toulouse; thus, most of the area wherein the bastide had become an important settlement form was included in this tributary region that produced wine needing to be sent, with great speed for the Middle Ages, on to a distant market.[31]

The great appeal of the Gascon wines in the English market, a greater appeal than existed for more northerly French wines, was the strong color and flavor they possessed and their abundance and relative cheapness. "The other French wines which were well known in England during the Middle Ages were those of Auxerre and La Rochelle,"[32] though they were consumed in far smaller quantities. The citizens of La Rochelle fought against the effort of King John of England to forfeit his title to the town to the French king but without avail, so their trade declined greatly. Given all of the attendant conditions in the medieval wine trade, the ties between Gascony and England were assured by the strength and cheapness of the wine, its relative ease of shipment, the organization of the supply, and the adequacy of the commercial agriculture of the Midi to produce sufficiently and consistently.

The system of towns in Aquitaine and Languedoc—included because Montpellier and other areas of the province exported to England—must

31. Ibid., pp. 270–71.
32. Ibid., p. 273.

have reflected this large and particular trade. From the trade they may well have gained the support for the distinctive type of towns being planted anew in those parts, towns quite different from those emerging from the rural countryside of northern France.

André Simon's description of the Gascon wine trade of England in the twelfth century makes clear why the bastides could be different from small urban settlements elsewhere. To a degree uncommon to the time, the wine trade meant a long-distance movement, unique because it required careful organization and efficiency. Wool staple must be handled efficiently but not necessarily with dispatch. Other items, such as woad, might move as far and as quickly as wine, but not in the same volumes. In the three centuries during which England held major possessions in Gascony, from 1152 to 1453, this region produced one of the premier export products of the time and shipped it in quantities vast for the Middle Ages. A bit later, in the mid-fifteenth century, wine was imported into England at a rate of over three million gallons a year.[33] Although the traditional towns of Gascony were important in the trade, Bordeaux standing at the head as the port from which all wine must be sent on to England, the bastides seem to have played a vital role. Simon in his catalogue of towns from which wine was sent to medieval England lists many bastides—Libourne (the only port other than Bordeaux and Bayonne that might export directly), Castel Sargat, Castel Sarrazin, Cordes, Marmande, Mirabel, Montauban, Montclar, Rabastens, Ste. Livrade, Villeneuve d'Agen, and others—to the extent that perhaps a third of the exporting towns were bastides. Thus, the wine trade seems to have been a critical element of support in many of these places, judging from the records that have survived.

The nature of agriculture around these towns no doubt aided in their attachment to long-distance trade. Because the townspeople held plots in the *bari* and beyond, they could and did raise grapes for the making of wine. In this way the prospective merchants could also be vintners to assure their supplies, avoiding as well the rather rigid controls on winemaking in other areas where large estates and the church might well dominate production. During the English ownership of Gascony, the area of the bastides was the area of the great expansion of wine production. If, as Henri Pirenne suggested in 1933 should be done, this wine trade were studied in full, likely we would see the first tentative steps toward a mercantile system tying one region with a distant region"overseas" and fostering in both the growth of cities. Bordeaux grew vastly in English hands, Libourne was founded along with the other bastides and waxed fat, Bristol in England began its great rise, and all told there seems most evidently to have been a major trading system at work causing this urban expansion. The bastide was a novel element in this system. The urban plantation served to develop the countryside and to handle the staple it was producing in a rapid and efficient onward shipment to the large metropolitan market—which was then, as later, England. Without the bastides I doubt that the vast increase in production, the rapid

33. E. M. Carus Wilson, *Medieval Merchant Venturers*, 2d ed. (London: Methuen, 1967), p. 271.

handling necessary, and the simple enterprise to make it all work would have been possible.

The social, political, and economic experimentation that the bastide represented had a strong morphological base. The town of proportion and interaccessibility was not simply a coincidental associate with the social and economic liberalism; it was a fundamental part of it. In this role, the bastidal form became a model for later mercantile expansiveness, perhaps unconsciously but certainly powerfully. As we shall see in the next chapter, the mercantile city in England became a thing apart and the hearth from which New World urbanism spread. England would not so clearly have been the fountainhead of change without the historical accident of Henry's marriage to Eleanor of Aquitaine in 1152, and the experiments his subjects subsequently undertook to use her dowry in developing the national wealth. In the period that followed, an Age of Discovery may simply have been a historical accident, but the urbanization practices perfected in Gascony and the form of the bastide served even more handsomely to shape a New World once the English lost their French possessions and were forced to turn instead to trade pioneering across the western ocean.

The Prince's Capital and the Merchants' Town

The close of the Middle Ages" sounds final and determinate, yet this epochal event was unperceived at the time, and the probable direction of change once the door was closed was uncertain. We need not be concerned just when the Middle Ages came to an end and what led to their demise; by the beginning of the seventeenth century a new world was at hand. The previous century had witnessed such a vast expansion of the horizon of Western civilization that the new geographical scale alone would have made a new society necessary.

In the hundred years between the 1490s and the 1590s, such shifts of geographical perspective and political weighting had taken place that the European world of the Middle Ages was already "historical" and unreal. Germany and Italy became civilized backwaters, where increasing intellectual and artistic refinement was harnessed to a local political treadmill that revolved incessantly but gained no perceptible ground. The English and Dutch during this century changed from medieval Europeans to modern world citizens, much to the surprise and ultimate dismay of the other members of what had been an intimately interacting society and generally coherent culture in the Middle Ages. France was racked with religious ferment, which caused its economic shots to ricochet sometimes rather wildly; France entered this transition period along the same open and novel path as its Atlantic neighbors—the path to overseas colonization and conquest—and ended it treading the same grand road to nowhere followed by its overly æsthetic neighbors. Spain stood determined and medieval throughout, using its vastly expanded geographical horizon to show that the old order was the best, that the economic system of tribute and dynastic possession—devised by the Romans and perfected by the Normans and Angevins—could be made to work anywhere the Most Catholic King's flag could be flown.

Almost all the countries of Western civilization set about expanding their geographical knowledge. The Norse and possibly the Irish began exploration even during the Middle Ages. Certainly the Norse were voyaging to Iceland and Greenland in the tenth and eleventh centuries. No doubt they visited North America, but their visit made little difference to history; they had no system for utilizing such a distant land and no desire to become lost in its vastness.

Only in the fifteenth century did the European economic frontier begin to expand. Until then, the East had been experienced only indirectly through a trade confined by Muslim middlemen to the eastern margin of the Mediterranean. But at the hands of the Portuguese navigators, following in Prince Henry's wake, the economic frontier moved quickly to the East, passing around the end of the Muslim barrier and making all of Europe deeply envious of Lisbon. As dynastic siblings of the Portuguese, the Dutch participated in that expansion, while the Spaniards, French, and English sought to join in the outward thrust of the European economic boundary. The English followed up on their early-sixteenth-century success in driving the mercantile frontier with the Italians from London to Livorno (Leghorn) and with the Germans from Southampton to Hamburg; they set out to project their trading realm across the North Atlantic. In this effort they were joined by the Protestant merchants of Rouen, St. Malo, La Rochelle, and other fishing and trading towns on the French Atlantic coast.

The Portuguese experience in reaching the Spice Islands of the East was a most inappropriate model for most of this economic expansion. In the East Indies, as slightly later in India and China, a highly developed land rich in products for trade was able to begin exchange almost the moment the Portuguese navigators reached its ports. In contrast, when the other Atlantic Europeans reached the New World they found an economic wilderness with few commodities they had experienced before and, in virtually all cases, little production of what was to be had. At first, nearly all that could be traded were wild pelts of deer in the south and of beaver in the north. Years of developmental activity and the education of European taste to a marvelous array of new products were required before trade could blossom. Even then, the native population of America was small and its economic organization ill-suited to the fiercely mercantilist society making a landfall on its shores.

To make the New World a second East meant far more diligent labor by the Europeans than had been required in the Far East, and the planting of towns and European populations to draw from the virgin soil the riches that might be had but were not directly at hand. In the West Indies, gold was thin in the rivers and the native agriculture still produced products not craved by Europeans. Instead, the Spaniards carried to the New World a crop from the old—sugar. They had come to know it well in the preceding several centuries as its cultivation spread from the Near East through the Spanish possessions in Sicily and Andalusia to Moorish Morocco and newly discovered Madeira, which the cane reached in 1420. Only three-quarters of a century later (1494) sugar arrived in the Antilles, giving the Europeans their first realistic hope for profit from the strange New World. In the sugar boom that followed, all the Atlantic states of Europe planted colonies in tropical and subtropical America to gain a foothold in the trade. In those colonies, the first European towns appeared in the New World, towns of a peculiar and unfortunate sort. These towns of a caste-bound society came shortly to be characterized by the legal enslavement of large numbers of people. That most vicious of rank stratifications is the tie that connected these places more with the Renaissance towns of Italy and the Hapsburg lands than with the merchants' towns of the European Atlantic shores.

The Two Cities of Europe and America

Europe in the sixteenth century was fast developing two patterns of city: the capitals of powerful princes desirous of creating great visual expressions of their absolute authority in a manner as close as practicable to the model of classical Rome; and the merchants' towns that grew from the economic replacement of medieval practices by mercantilism. Both the *capital* and the *merchants' emporium* were shaped along lines that emerged only in Elizabethan times to replace the order and balance so much the measure of medieval life. In matters political, absolutism came to substitute for the detailed definition of duty and privilege, which tied in mutual responsibility the sovereign and vassals of the Middle Ages. In matters economic, the broad and expanding horizon of mercantilism quickly replaced the bounded and rank-ordered "natural economy" of feudal Europe. Each shaped its own city and, like the *bourg* and *faubourg* in medieval times, those places tended to be separated from one other.

In the New World, the division was more than a local phenomenon. The realm of tropical agricultural development, with servitude of the masses, was the home of the Renaissance capital city transported to America, whereas the realm of colonization by the free merchant class led to the implantation of the merchants' town in temperate America. The European nations where mercantilism made greatest progress (France before Louis XIV, England, and Holland) were the planters of merchants' towns, while the countries where liberalism (economic, social, and religious) was fought to a stop in the Counter-Reformation were the planters of capitals with rigid social caste.

Europe during the Counter-Reformation came to be dominated by the administrative-political city. These cities were ordered and ranked by their administrative standing and assigned politically dependent territories, which have always shown a greater tendency for fixed geographical integrity than have the tributary regions of merchants' towns. Trading territories overlap, but political territories do so only by design and normally with fixed hierarchical relations. Significantly, in that part of Europe where the Counter-Reformation was strongest and liberalism was least advanced, the administrative-political order and its central-places were best developed. In such a region, the kingdom of Bavaria, Walter Christaller devised his central-place system; on closer examination, it stands more as a political-place system than one of trading places free to compete with each other.

Expansion in the Context of Trade

We must distinguish between the drive to advance a nation's economic frontier and the conditions under which advance was carried out. During the seventeenth and eighteenth centuries, most European countries—England, Holland, France, Denmark, Scotland, Spain, Austria, and Sweden—chartered "East India companies" not all of which showed much mercantile initiative; the best were more monopolistic in design than the free development of trade would have required. All were considered sufficiently risky to be vested with a geographical monopoly of trade thought sufficient to gain the necessary investment in their undertakings. The instrument chosen by the East India companies for engaging in trade was almost universally the planted "factory" where traders became resident in the distant land in order to facilitate ties with European trading partners. Under such a system, the factory took on a function of long standing in Europe, serving rather as the medieval "steelyards" served the Hanse or the "English nation" in Antwerp. But Europeans in the East quickly began to exercise greater force than had been practical in the Middle Ages, and to seek an exclusivity of trade that came to mind only with the onset of mercantilist economic thinking. The trading wars of Holland and England in India and of France and England in the Ohio Country of North America were a direct outgrowth of competitive factory establishment undertaken by a mercantilist society.

This historical and economic context led rapidly to a conquest of trade through the use of planted towns, but often with a genuine reluctance to seek political domination of the area where the factory was sited. England placed factories in India just after the East India Company was founded (on December 31, 1600) but resisted asserting sovereignty for a hundred and fifty years. Similarly, the first English voyages to North America came in 1497, but nearly a full century intervened before any political claim was advanced—Newfoundland was claimed by Sir Humphrey Gilbert only in 1583—and a century and a quarter before any very effective settlement was achieved. At first, mercantile Europe around the North Sea sought not conquest but trade. Its towns were long in coming; when they arrived, they were simple merchants' settlements of distinctly isonomic structure.

Expansion in the Context of Conquest

The Spaniards were conquerors and administrators from the very beginning. Columbus sailed in 1492; before the year was out, old style, Spain's first colony had been set up at La Navidad on Hispaniola. By 1498, the year of his third voyage, outright political domination of Hispaniola had been accomplished and a capital established at Santo Domingo. From then on, the history of Hispanic America was for four centuries—until the last colonies, Cuba and Puerto Rico, were liberated by the United States in 1898— one of political domination of subject peoples in the New World by a still partially medieval Spanish kingdom. From that political conquest, the world inherited a string of capital cities located to serve Spanish needs, and little urbanization that might advance the interests of the lands held subject to the monarch of the peninsular kingdom.

Crucial to the subjugation of the New World to the Spanish kingdom was the extension thereto of an administrative system typical of Catholic Europe, the same that has been memorialized in Christaller's central-place theory in the guise of its Bavarian expression. The town was a critical feature of this administrative-political system, but one to be viewed only in an ordered, dependent role given by devolution of authority from above, in what the Middle Ages called the *Heerschildordnung*. The citizen of the Roman Empire had known it as imperial administration a thousand years before; the Spaniards termed it the Laws of the Indies in the late sixteenth century. Authority remained at the top with downward grants for the carrying on of particular activities (Christaller's central functions): the decree of city form and function from afar, the creation of a caste-divided society to reside in the colony (with the town serving as the citadel and ultimate refuge for the overlord caste that would make up a minority of the total population), and the strong practice of symbolic and eunomic land assignment within the city.

All of these things strongly suggested the Roman conquest of Europe with subjugation of all to the imperial will, and its later modification to meet the more localized social and administrative structure of feudal Europe in the Middle Ages. As under feudalism, the economic base of Hispanic American development was rural and caste-based, with the town seen as the impressive capital and severe restrictions placed on occupational and geographical mobility for the indentured or enslaved "vassals" of the rural activities of plantation agriculture and mining.

The Roman Empire Reaches the Western Shore

Occasionally history's evidence is so clear that we must suspect our conclusions, questioning whether we have been too easily persuaded by neat lines of evolution and descent. These lines may be so powerful because something of great importance that might controvert them has been misplaced with time's passage. Such is the case with the Spanish planting of towns and cities in the New World. This settlement seems so clearly the onward projection of the Roman colonization of ancient Iberia, modernized to the fifteenth century through the Spanish resettlement of the areas considerably devastated in the campaigns against the Moors, and then carried clean and powerful to the Antilles as the accepted practice for Charles V's conquerors of the New World.

So the planting of Roman *castra* during the second Punic War had brought the western peninsula into the Latin world through city founding. The Romans perfected a rather standardized town model to pacify and control a conquered area, whether won through peaceful acceptance of inevitable domination by the powerful Roman armies or by actual fierce warfare with the native peoples. The *castra* were foursquare, regular, laid out all of a piece, with a land-use pattern determined as much by the symbolic activities the Romans assigned to cities as by defensive concerns, and generally lightly walled and alert to the need for vigilance as the strongest protection.

What we know about those Roman camp-towns comes from many sources, but the most detail is furnished by the *Ten Books of Architecture* of Vitruvius, rediscovered in the early fifteenth century. This work became the greatest literary guide to the Renaissance recreation of the Roman world. At the onset of the Spanish conquest of the New World, the great force sweeping Catholic Europe and motivating the elaborate construction by its princes was the wish to recreate concretely the grandeur of Rome. To that end, the rediscovery of Vitruvius in manuscripts surviving from the tenth century was rapidly influential on the Roman pope and the Holy Roman Emperor. Whether either had read Vitruvius is not important; we know that their architectural advisers had.

The parallelism between the Vitruvian manuscript[1] and the Laws of the Indies—the proposals made in 1573 in the name of the king of Spain, the violent and cruel Philip II—is sufficient to suggest a conscious emulation at

1. The standard translation is that of Morris Hicky Morgan, *Vitruvius: The Ten Books of Architecture* (Cambridge, Mass.: Harvard University Press, 1914, rpt. Dover, 1960). Citations are to the Harvard edition.

work.[2] Vitruvius begins (in chapter 4, book 1) his prescription for the founding of a town with a note on its site: "For fortified towns the following general principles are to be observed. First comes the choice of a very healthy site. Such a site will be high, neither misty nor frosty . . . further without marshes in the neighborhood. . . . Again, if the town is on the coast with a southern or western exposure, it will not be healthy, because in summer the southern sky grows hot at sunrise and is fiery at noon, while a western exposure grows warm after sunrise, is hot at noon, and at evening all aglow." In the words imputed to Philip II, writing at San Lorenzo on July 3, 1573, "The chosen site shall be on an elevation; healthful; with means of fortification. . . . It shall be open to the north wind. If on a coast care is to be taken that the sea does not lie to the south or west of the harbor. If possible the port is not to be near lagoons or marshes in which poisonous animals and corruption of air and water breed" (Law 111, the second one dealing with cities).

In chapter 6, book 1, Vitruvius goes on to deal with the question of the physical layout of the town:

> 1. The town being fortified, the next step is the appointment of house lots within the wall and the laying out of streets and alleys with regard to climatic conditions. They will be properly laid out if foresight is employed to exclude the winds from the alleys. Cold winds are disagreeable, hot winds enervating, moist winds unhealthy. . . .
>
> 3. By shutting out the winds from our dwellings, therefore, we shall not only make the place healthful for people who are well but also . . . diseases due perhaps to unfavourable situations elsewhere . . . will here be more quickly cured by the mildness that comes from the shutting out of winds.

To protect dwellings and other buildings from the effect of the wind, the Vitruvian town is to be oriented with respect to the winds, most ideally through the shaping of an eight-sided plan:

> 8. On this principle of arrangement the disagreeable force of the winds will be shut out from dwellings and lines of houses. For if the streets run full in the face of the winds, their constant blasts rushing in from the open country, and then confined by narrow alleys, will sweep through them with great violence. The lines of houses must therefore be directed away from the quarters [cardinal points of the compass] from which the winds blow, so that as they

2. A translation of those parts of the so-called Laws of the Indies (*Bulas y Cedulas para el Gobierno de las Indias*) dealing with the laying out of towns is furnished by Zelia Nuttall, "Royal Ordinances Concerning the Laying out of New Towns," *Hispanic American Historical Review* 5 (1922): 249–54. A more recent translation—contained in Dora P. Crouch, Daniel J. Garr, and Axel I. Mundigo, *Spanish City Planning in North America* (Cambridge, Mass.: M.I.T. Press, 1982)— varies in phrasing and minor detail from that of Zelia Nuttall. As a discussion of the detail of Spanish city planning in the New World, it adds much to our understanding. But as a text for comparing the provisions of Vitruvius and Philip II none of the conclusions presented in the original edition of this work is significantly altered.

come in they may strike against the angles of the blocks and their force thus be broken and dispersed.

In the Laws of the Indies the same principle is advanced, though far more succinctly than in the Roman's rather wordy tract:

> 114. From the plaza the four principal streets are to diverge, one from the middle of each of its sides and two streets are to meet at each of its corners. The four corners of the plaza are to face the four [cardinal] points of the compass, because thus the streets diverging from the plaza will not be directly exposed to the four principal winds, which would cause much inconvenience.

The town plat having been decided upon, Vitruvius urges in chapter 7:

> 1. Having laid out the alleys and determined the streets, we have next to treat of the choice of building sites for temples, the forum, and all other public places, with a view to general convenience and utility. If the city is on the sea, we should choose ground close to the harbour as the place where the forum is to be built; but if inland, in the middle of the town.

Philip II followed suit:

> 112. In the case of a sea-coast town the main plaza which is to be the starting point of the building of the town, is to be situated near the landing place of the port. In inland towns the main plaza should be in the centre of the town and of an oblong shape, its length being equal to at least one and a half times its width, as this proportion is the best for festivals in which horses are used and any other celebrations which have to be held.

In the Roman town, many public shrines and temples were ranged round the forum, but the multiplicity of gods required that others be built in the emporium (those for Mercury, Isis, and Serapis), near the theater (Apollo and Bacchus), at the circus (Hercules), on the training ground (Mars), and at the harbor (Venus). Somewhat similarly, the Spaniards decreed that the cathedral should usually be on the plaza, but elsewhere in an inland town, and that other foci of interest be placed elsewhere in the town:

> 118. At certain distances in the town smaller, well proportioned plazas are to be laid out on which the main church, the parish church or monastery shall be built so that the teaching of religious doctrine may be evenly distributed.

For the Romans, a similar spread was called for, though with rather different justifications (chapter 7, book 1):

> It is moreover shown by the Etruscan diviners in treatises on their science that the fanes of Venus, Vulcan, and Mars should be situated outside the walls, in order that the young men and married women may not become habituated in the city to the temptations

incident to the worship of Venus, and that buildings may be free from the terror of fires through the religious rites and sacrifices which call the power of Vulcan beyond the walls. As for Mars, when that divinity is enshrined outside the walls, the citizens will never take up arms against each other, and he will defend the city from its enemies and save it from danger in war.

We might find further parallels between Vitruvius and the Laws of the Indies, but these suffice to show that the Roman prescript was updated for Christianity and adapted to the needs of a more clearly maritime conquest. Yet the fundamental practices are remarkably similar. The ordinances in both Rome and Spain were set out to secure the planting of towns to dominate a subject population. Thus, walling of sorts and protection internal to the town gained much greater attention than in the English and French colonies farther to the north. In both Mediterranean examples existed an ordering of land use, reserving the forum or plaza for public buildings, and suggesting or decreeing the increasing exclusion of activities not thought appropriate to the town center, a remove established in order of their pariah status.

In each model, a clear statement set out physical design proper to all sites. For the Romans, it was the *castrum*—Vitruvius's octagon seems entirely to have been a utopian scheme—built on its rectangular grid with the street block standing as the basic module for city development. In Spanish America, a nearly identical grid was evolved. The very first law (110) dealing with city founding decreed that "the plan of the place, with its squares, streets and building lots, is to be outlined by means of measuring by cord and ruler, beginning with the main square from which streets are to turn to the gates and principal roads and leaving sufficient open space so that even if the town grows it can always spread in a symmetrical manner." Perhaps borrowing from the bastides of southern France more than the Roman *castra*, the plaza was to be surrounded by an arcade, "for these are a great convenience for those who resort thither for trade" (Law 115). That plaza was to be the beginning of the town, just as the meeting of the *cardo* and *decumanus* was the base point of laying out the *castrum*. The morphological result was the same even if the Roman town evolved inward from its encircling *pomerium*, whereas the town described in the Laws of the Indies grew outward from its plaza:

> 117. [Beyond the arcades] the other streets laid out consecutively around the plaza are to be so planned that even if the town should increase considerably in size it would meet with no obstruction which might disfigure what had already been built or be a detriment to the defense or convenience of the town.

The Laws say nothing more about the street plan, yet in virtually all cases a grid-pattern town grew up.

The strong parallel between Vitruvian notions of town planning and those of the Spanish king must have been apparent to the conquerors of America. They would have at least realized that the Romans colonized with the *castrum*, of which sufficient examples survived in Spain to serve as guide. Thus, though the Laws did not decree a grid-pattern town—merely

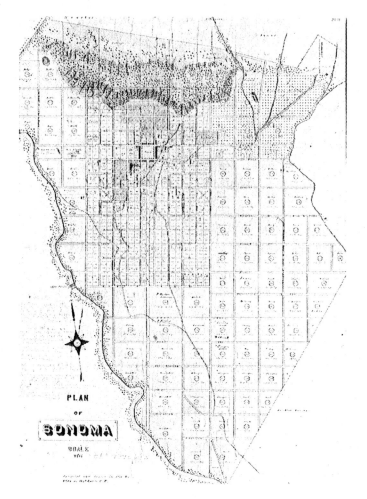

Sonoma, California, was the last of the California missions founded, and the civil pueblo adjacent to it was laid out by General Vallejo in 1835 under the Laws of the Indies. The distinction from the speculator's town in the Middle West seems rather slight beyond the existence of the forty-acre small holders' lots to be found surrounding the town plat in this irrigated valley.

an orderly, symmetrical, and convenient one—the concrete visualization of those town qualities would logically have reverted back to a Roman model; not among the conquistadors to the utopian octagon of Vitruvius, but rather to the workmanlike grids of the Roman legionnaires. This theory is conjecture. After all, no law among either Romans or Spaniards required the grid-pattern town, but observation of actual towns shows how universally they adopted it. The Spanish colonial towns were detailed under the several Laws already quoted and in a manner strongly suggestive of Vitruvian principles of town planning. But they did not follow the octagonal scheme of his writings any more than did the Roman camps in Iberia. Instead, both the Romans and the Spaniards seemingly had two classes of prescription for town founding: that guiding the location, land assignment, and composition of the land use of a town, and that for the overall platting of the town.

The Vitruvian principles and those of the Laws of the Indies detailed where the town should be sited, what it should contain, and, within that settlement, how the rank order of location should be carried out. From these Latin practices we derive three basic morphological processes: *settlement initiation* based on the specific purpose of the town, *land assignment* within the town on some order of merit that reserves the more desirable or impressive sites to the more pompous uses, and *use exclusion* that places beyond the limits of the town certain activities, mostly those of a pariah nature, but not only those. Thus, the two texts follow almost identical lines of reasoning as to settlement initiation: these places are to overawe and command a subject people tied to a distant suzerain first by the sea (the seacoast towns) and then by land (the inland towns). With nearly identical imperial designs, the Romans and the Spaniards came forth with nearly identical principles of initiation. Similarly, each practiced a basically *noncommercial land assignment,* turning instead to a highly elaborated political and social ordering to be reflected in the assignment of space within the town. Unfortunately, beyond the prescription with respect to temples, little comes down to us from Vitruvius on the Roman ordering, though we appreciate from observation of the relics that such a conscious placement was at work. However, the actual prescription of the Laws of the Indies has survived. It begins (in Law 120) with the plaza:

> After the plaza and streets have been laid out building lots are to be designated, in the first place, for the erection of the main church, the parish church or monastery and these are to occupy respectively an entire block so that no other structure can be built next to them excepting such as contribute to their commodiousness or beauty. (Law 121) Immediately afterwards the place and site are to be assigned for the Royal and Town Council House, and the Custom-House and Arsenal which is to be close to the church and port so that in case of necessity one can protect the other. The hospital for the poor and sick of noncontagious diseases shall be built next to the church forming its cloister.

Only after such institutional provisions were carried out did assignment turn to individuals (Law 126):

> No building lots surrounding the main plaza are to be given to private individuals for these are to be reserved for the church, Royal and Town House, also shops and dwellings for the merchants, which are to be the first erected. . . . (Law 127) The remaining building lots shall be distributed by lottery to those of the settlers who are entitled to build around the main plaza. Those left over are to be held for us to grant to settlers who may come later or to dispose of at our pleasure. In order that entries of these assignments be better made a plan of the town is always to be made in advance.

The rank-order assignment of space within the city became a distinctive feature of Roman towns, Mediterranean towns that came as successors, and, finally, those towns in Hispanic America that followed in direct succession from Roman imperialism. In this method we find a great contrast with land-assignment practices in the North Sea realm and the colonies planted by its merchants. No free land-rent market was intended in the Hispanic towns. These towns were to be administered to make certain that rank rather than

The Prince's
Capital and the
Merchants' Town

ability to pay determined where activities were located. In this way it became characteristic of Hispanic American towns that rank precedence was indicated by central location, with the reverse also the case. In the merchants' towns of the English and Dutch a merchant might pay a high land rent for a central site, not to elevate his social image but to increase his income. Thus, we find in these contrasting land-assignment practices—the Latin one socially derived and the northern one commercially based—much of the explanation of the contrast between the frenetic core and grim edges of the Latin American city and the decaying heart and prosperous suburbs of the Anglo-American one.

This contrast seems to have a strong and traditional base in the notion of land-use exclusion; the Laws clearly prescribed (in Law 122) that "the lots and sites for slaughter houses, fisheries, tanneries, and such like productive of garbage shall be so situated that the latter can be easily disposed of." This sensible provision seems to have been construed as placing these uses outside the town, thereby encouraging a further downgrading of the status of the area beyond the walls. No such wise provision was decreed in the northern colonization; neither did the low esteem for the edge of the city grow up so vigorously.

Within the Hispanic American towns a residential morphology distinctly different from that of the medieval bastides grew up. "All town homes are to be so planned that they can serve as a defense or fortress against those who might attempt to create disturbances or occupy the town. Each house is to be so constructed that horses and household animals can be kept therein, the courtyards and stockyards being as large as possible to insure health and cleanliness" (Law 133). Again, a clear division is made between the desirable qualities of the town center and the threats existing beyond its walls. The last law dealing with the layout of towns (137) decreed that the Indians should be kept outside the place while it was being built, and generally be distinguished from the town residents so that "they will consequently fear the Spaniards so much that they will not dare to offend them and will respect and desire their friendship." In this way the town became the instrument of colonial domination in the same fashion it had for the Romans fifteen hundred years before. Only as a "Spanish peace" was enforced could the townspeople look upon the countryside with other than distrust and fear. Even then, they moved into the rural area largely as foreign overlords of a subject people, normally required by this lonely role to keep one foot within the city where during certain seasons they maintained ties with their Hispanic peers. In this context the town was a very different thing socially and economically from that in Anglo-America; as a result, land assignment within the place followed quite different practices.

The Emergence of Mercantilism and the Mercantile City

While the past was conquering the lands that became Hispanic America, Europe itself was experiencing great changes that portended a new form of city in a new form of society. The general ferment that accompanied the questioning of religious orthodoxy tended to open lines of enquiry long closed by the strong barricades of established truth. The almost unrecorded shifts began with the planting of bastides in the Middle Ages, with the elevation of economic over dynastic concerns and timid steps toward a more democratic society. For those most questioning of nations, the ones infected by Luther's and then Calvin's doubts, enquiry could not be restricted only to religious questions. Soon both the social ranking of individuals and the constraint of their economic efforts to the narrow "natural" realm of feudalism were brought into question.

In place of the "natural economy" of feudalism came the "limitless economy" of mercantilism. Francis Bacon believed of his time that "the jealousy of trade" among nations was the economic rule; in that he was expressing an idea that came formally to be advanced by Jean Baptiste Colbert somewhat later. Inheriting economic chaos from Richelieu and Mazarin, the two cardinal-ministers who had preceded him, Colbert proposed a system of protection for French industry and trade, but active expansion of its economic frontiers. His real problem lay in establishing an economic basis for the state at a time when several policies seemed possible. To understand the quandary faced by ministers of finance or the others concerned with the king's purse during the sixteenth and seventeenth centuries, we must briefly recount the sharp change that was taking place. George Clark in his study of the seventeenth century summarizes the conditions with clarity when he defines mercantilism:

> It was a system of political economy, that is to say it was a system
> for the regulation of economic matters by the state. It was, in
> Adam Smith's words, a system for "enriching the people," and its
> essence is that it was to do so by means of commerce. It starts from
> the assumption that a people is a community with a common
> wealth—the wealth of the nation—and that by proper measures
> this wealth can be increased. It is in fact the direct continuation for
> the larger unit called a "people" of the system of regulation by
> which in the Middle Ages the government of each separate town
> controlled the enrichment of the town as a whole. The aim of the
> multifarious ordinances of the medieval guilds and towns was, first
> of all, to ensure the provision of necessaries for the life and labour
> of its inhabitants. There must be a sufficiency of corn for consump-
> tion; there must be a sufficiency of raw materials for industry. A
> sufficiency meant not only an adequate total for all those who
> demanded it taken together, but also for each separate consumer
> or user an adequate quantity at a possible price. . . . These two
> elements of protection and regimentation remained throughout
> the mercantile epoch the fundamental principles of economic
> organization, but with this great difference, that now it was the
> state, no longer the town or its organ, the guild, which granted the
> privilege and protected against the unprivileged and the foreigner.
> That the state should have superseded the authority of the town in
> this matter requires no longer explanation: it was a consequence
> of the whole development of the power of the state which marks

the essential difference between medieval and modern political history.[3]

The system was already developing before it came into full form and expression in England in the seventeenth century.

Another of Francis Bacon's aphorisms may serve to draw the contrast. He held that "the French are wiser than they seem, and the Spaniards seem wiser than they are" (*Of Seeming Wise*). Statesmen of the late sixteenth century were beset by how to guide the course of their nations in a world wherein the Iberians, particularly the Spaniards, had gained great wealth and impressive power. The way to advance the wealth of the nation seemed to be to tread in the footsteps of the conquistadors. For a time, expeditions were sent out to search for other cities of gold, but few were found. By the time of Henri IV the king's minister, the Duc de Sully, showed his understanding of modern economics and more liberal politics—he was one of the Protestants who, then as now, show up unusually frequently as French finance ministers. Sully argued, *Paturge et labourage son les deux mamelles dont la France est alimentée, les vraies mines et tresors de Perou* (Grazing and arable farming are the two breasts by which France is sustained, her true Peruvian mines and treasures).[4] The vast increases in French wealth and power in the succeeding two centuries, accompanied by the commensurate and never reversed decline of Spanish power, show us that the agriculture and labor of the French were indeed what nourished France and gave it a never failing Peruvian gold mine.

The mercantilist system had several theorists, of whom Colbert is usually considered the first and Adam Smith the most important. But we see that at the turn of the seventeenth century Sully was already phrasing the ideas, but the Dutch and the English were proving better at practicing them. The monopolistic trading companies were one of the major instruments of such an economic policy, and they had come into existence sixty years before Colbert became a minister.

The canons of mercantilism were several:

First there was protectionism, by which a state restricted certain economic opportunities to its own subjects. . . . Its typical instrument is the tariff. . . . [Second,] seventeenth century economists regarded some branches of trade as advantageous and others as detrimental. They favoured most highly those which brought in such goods as they could not supply for themselves, especially the precious metals in exchange for manufactured articles which employed their labour at home. The colonial trades fulfilled these requirements, while much of the trade within Europe did not. Each country therefore tried to draw up its tariff, and its other protective arrangements such as navigation laws, in such a way as to reserve

3. George Clark, *The Seventeenth Century* (New York: Oxford University Press, 1929; Galaxy ed., 1961), pp. 22–23.

4. Quoted in John Lough, *An Introduction to Seventeenth Century France* (New York: David McKay, 1969), pp. 111–12.

colonial trade and other paying trades for its own people, and to confine its own people to these selected channels.[5]

The Split between the Merchants' Town and the Court Settlement

The motivating force in the shaping of the mercantile city was the opportunity that the Age of Discovery afforded to Europeans to expand their trading frontiers. That spatial spreading of trade brought the Middle Ages to a close with a sharp change in the scale of activity and a rapid transformation of the morphogenesis of cities.

The expansion of the trade frontier reshaped urban form in two ways. First, it created an increase in trade that made necessary the enlargement of trading facilities—shops, warehouses, and counting houses. The medieval structure could not comprehend this change, and as a result gave way in the creation of new, postmedieval urban forms. Second, the transportation facilities were elevated to a dominant position as the acknowledged lifeline of urban existence. When we read Fitzstephen's account of London life toward the end of the twelfth century, the port on the bank of the Thames is portrayed with none of the bustle and urgency it gained with mercantilism. By 1550 the port functions dominated London life. Toward the end of the century, when Elizabeth sought to contain London's growth, she specifically exempted the port from further constraint.

The rupture of the medieval order came in the elevation of commerce to a position of absolute supremacy over the formerly more powerful artisan activities. Commerce needed a concentrated quarter in which to operate, where enlarged "business administration" could be carried on and where the information of trade was readily at hand. With distant trading, commercial intelligence was essential.

The mechanism of adjustment to needed changes in the physical structure of the mercantile town was a land-rent system wherein bidding for particular parcels of land took place in a market, with the highest bidder likely to gain possession of the site. At first the bidding must have been mainly for the choice site, with the building already standing on it taken as a matter of course. We know that in the sixteenth and seventeenth centuries most urban buildings were merely transformations of the medieval house— tall and narrow if the city were walled, but somewhat less so if the place were either effectively open or little developed with space relatively freely available. The mercantile city tended to reuse these properties in a variety of ways, with great ingenuity.

Most of the splendor that comes down to us in descriptions from the sixteenth and seventeenth centuries was nonurban, if not outright and consciously a rejection of the city. Kings became a suburban class well before the commonality, and the nobility trotted along in their enslaved fashion. London's Whitehall and Paris's Versailles may have differed in grandeur but

5. George Clark, *Early Modern Europe, from about 1450 to 1720* (New York: Oxford University Press, 1954; (Galaxy ed., 1960), pp. 196–201.

This view of London in 1749 is taken from the easternmost of the three panels of the Buck Brothers' Panorama of London. It suggests a closely built merchants' town even though it shows almost entirely a London rebuilt since 1666.

not in fundamental location within the city pattern; they lay outside the merchants' town.

In the seventeenth century, some medieval houses were torn down to be replaced by the town houses of the powerful, as Antonio Canaletto's drawings of London in the early eighteenth century show us. In general, the housing for the aristocracy lay beyond the edge of the merchants' town,[6] as further confirmed in a panorama of London drawn by the Buck Brothers and published in 1749.[7] Again the city represented is a bit later than the time we are considering, but it furnishes us with a summary useful in weighting the physical components of the city that resulted from mercantile conquest. The picture is of a town medieval in grain in the east, in the City of London, becoming increasingly Renaissance and ostentatious with westward movement to Whitehall and Westminster. Few actual medieval buildings remain within the medieval town; most were destroyed in the Great Fire of 1666. But the scale and form of the reconstructions conformed reasonably well with what was there before, though rebuilt in more fire-resistant materials.

Paris and London had become, by the year 1600, the two largest cities of Western society. Each was in the full sense a merchants' town, London more so than the French capital. In each, the court's presence served to stimulate a large-scale construction of town "houses" for the nobility, who were required, either by self-interest or by the king's will, to reside at court for part of the year. In London the requirement was less direct and the number of

6. Adrian Ecles, *Canaletto* (London: Paul Hamlyn, 1967). Although painting in the 1740s, Canaletto was depicting the city as it stood just before the great changes that came to the British economy with the Industrial Revolution then beginning.

7. *Panorama of London, 1749*, drawn by Buck Brothers (London: Sidgwick and Jackson, 1972), with notes by John Wellsman.

houses smaller; nonetheless, the area west of Temple Bar became a region quite distinct from that to the east within the workaday city. In the Strand, "houses" were being built in even greater numbers than had been the case among the powerful bishops and dukes of the Middle Ages. Thus, residential relocation of the wealthy was occurring in the late sixteenth and early seventeenth centuries.

Paris was the largest city of the West when Henri IV entered it in 1594, and certainly one of the more perplexed. The Wars of Religion had battered it about, particularly the suburbs outside the walls where many houses had been razed. But from around 1600 for another half-century, Paris grew rapidly, expanding a third in size and prospering greatly, to such an extent that urgent calls arose for new building. King Henri IV played some role in that construction when he sought to have a silk factory set up near Le Marais, the marsh to the east of the city, and to bring Italian weavers there to complete their products. This plan was carried out on the unsold lots of a royal land speculation at the razed site of the former Les Tournelles Palace.

The scheme failed, but from it grew the Place Royale,[8] the first defined aristocratic development Paris was to experience. Around that square the important nobility just below the top rank took up residence. These lesser lights were seeking a compromise solution to a problem of aristocratic residence that had already been solved somewhat differently by the most powerful nobles and the *princes du sang*. Those proud courtiers had begun to build town residences of a distinctive sort—large, elaborately decorated

8. The Place Royale suffered a number of changes of name. During the Revolution it became the Place des Fédérés, in 1793 the Place de l'Indivisibilité, and under Napoleon the Place des Vosges, when Lucien Bonaparte, in order to speed up the collection of taxes, conducted a contest, naming the square for the first *département* to pay its taxes.

buildings, often located on open lots but sometimes merely the largest building in a continuous street façade. These *hôtels* (perhaps best rendered in English as "great mansions") followed an aristocratic pattern fashionable at least since the fifteenth century. They comprised a central block flanked by lower pavillions at either side enclosing a courtyard closed from the street by an impressive gateway. At first these *hôtels* were not notably concentrated in any particular quarter of Paris, if we may believe the maps of their location presented by Pierre Couperie for the reigns of Henri IV, Louis XIII, and Louis XIV.[9]

But particularly in the time of Louis XIV—when attendance at court was required and the city of Paris remained as crowded and riotous as ever—the pattern began to change. The monarch had abandoned his several palaces within the city; Les Tournelles had been razed in favor of the Tuileries located outside the city wall in the west. As a result the districts of St. Germain and nearby St. Honoré were taken up by the aristocracy, a trend strengthened by the increasing rage for carriage driving. Within the old city, these vehicles were virtually stranded by the narrow streets and the press of pedestrians. But west of the Louvre, a carriage circuit—Cours-la-Reine—was set up for this folly of mobility without any geographical purpose. When an aristocratic quarter had been firmly fixed in the west, the former symmetry in the location of *hôtels* began to disappear, destroying along with it the social cachet of the Place Royale (des Vosges) and Le Marais in general. Only in the last few years has this area returned to fashionable approval.

The flocking of the aristocrats to be near the king became even more evident in 1680 when Louis XIV moved his government and ministries along with his retinue to Versailles. The clarion call of the court and fashion could not be overlooked; seventeenth-century Paris firmly adopted a practice that has been one of the prime dynamics of city growth ever since: the backstaying of aristocratic status by residence in the currently fashionable quarter of the city. This practice would have been incomprehensible to the medieval mind. In previous times, most certainly in the Middle Ages, no clear evidence suggests that where one lived in the city was viewed as a cachet of social distinction. Housing choice was based on avoidance of unhealthy areas, clustering together of political factions, occupational association, and the search for the extraterritoriality of the steelyard or ghetto.

The Form of the Merchants' Town

The towns that prospered during the Middle Ages were those of the merchants, so these seventeenth-century cities were in effect their direct descendants. Water had been the main practicable method of transport in the earlier period and remained so until the eighteenth century; thus, no fundamental shift was made in the desirable location for such mercantile places. As its port grew, a city tended to divide between a working area of quays, warehouses, and shops and an area for upper-class housing. Behind

9. Pierre Couperie, *Paris through the Ages* (New York: George Braziller, 1974), plates XIb, XIc, XId, and XIIc.

this segregation lay a general principle that still holds true: the wealthy normally favor investing their money in structures, which show their wealth, rather than in excessively costly central land, which does not present its price to the naked eye. The wealthy, particularly the attenders at court, also became greatly concerned with style, adopting new fashions of architecture and new designs for housing to such an extent that the relict of medieval building remaining in the city held no appeal for them. But the merchants found these rather functional buildings readily usable for their purposes. The older sections in the heart of the city tended to convert to mercantile uses, broadly defined, which further encouraged the aristocracy to move out to their own "quarter" with its physical evidence of the leisured and wealthy life. Soon the notion grew up of neighborhood reinforcement, wherein the social standing of the individuals living near one assumed importance lacking in earlier centuries.

The mechanism for change within the merchants' town was the relative utility of the site, measured by the bid rent that potential occupants were willing to pay for its use. A separate bid-rent scale for residential locations, based on social esteem, did not grow up for some time. Within the mercantile component of the town, residence was based on the utility it offered for quick and easy access to the place of employment. Because of the scalar increase in commercial undertaking, no longer could the occupational household furnish lodgings for all workers. Some must seek rental housing; their search brought the introduction of a new bid-rent scale for worker housing based on utility of access.

By the late seventeenth century, at least three different rent scales operated in the city: (1) that for commercial premises predicated primarily on the quality of the site in the matter of access to transportation and exterior connections to customers, (2) that of the working people based on the ease of daily access to the workplace from the residence, and (3) that of the leisured class based on the levels of social cachet associated with various residential streets and neighborhoods. This classification, although neater than fact, serves to clarify the forces of separation at work in the city with the onset of major growth in commerce and population in the seventeenth century.

Some measure of the need for city enlargement is furnished by the growth in shipping use of the port of Bristol during the seventeenth and eighteenth centuries. "In 1687, 240 ships cleared from Bristol, thirty years later in 1717 the number had increased to 375 and in 1787, 448 vessels left Bristol in the year." The number of ships entering shows a similar growth. "But those totals understate the growth of trade since the size of vessels rose during the century. In 1701 the average tonnage of ships owned by Bristol merchants was 105 tons, by the end of the century it was 144 tons." In 1700 Bristol received 19,878 tons inbound shipping, while in 1790 it received 76,000 tons. This eighteenth-century growth was merely following a trend begun with the Commercial Revolution two centuries earlier, which meant that the medieval urban structure came less and less to suffice.[10] The ports

10. Walter Minchinton, "The Port of Bristol in the Eighteenth Century," in *Bristol in the Eighteenth Century*, ed. Patrick McGrath (North Pomfret, Vt.: David and Charles, 1972), p. 129.

The Prince's
Capital and the
Merchants' Town

of the Atlantic fringes were the scene of the urban revolution of the Mercantile Era. Some places had already been large because of medieval trade; Antwerp, for example, had stood as the greatest trading city of Europe in 1560. Antwerp had taken the trading crown from the Mediterranean and Venice, and it remained on the Western Ocean shore never again to leave, though Antwerp was eclipsed for over two hundred years when the Dutch choked off its access to the sea by denying its navigation on the lower Scheldt, a sorry state that ended only in 1863.

The list of European ports becoming great cities between 1500 and 1800 is considerable. Antwerp was the first, but was soon followed by Amsterdam, Rotterdam, Rouen, and the north German ports. Even more spectacular was the rise of the marine cities of Britain and America. So many towns rose to large size and great economic activity that we can look in detail at only one representative example—Amsterdam.

Amsterdam as a Mercantile City

Amsterdam had been a medieval port of modest importance greatly exceeded in influence by Antwerp and even Bruges. Through its opening via the Zuider Zee to the North Sea, Amsterdam entered into the Baltic trade in herring and grain; with the swift decline of the Hanse in the sixteenth century, that Baltic trade increased. The city's rise was furthered after the cruel reconquest of the southern Hapsburg Netherlands by the Spaniards when a number of skilled workers—Protestants and Jews, for the most part—came to Amsterdam, bringing trades and skills essential to the growth of a great merchants' town. Still, for much of the seventeenth century, Amsterdam's real financial prosperity came from the traditional grain trade. Local merchants bought grain in the Baltic, brought it to the port on the Amstel for storage in great high warehouses until the market price rose, then sold it to make a speculator's profit. Such activities fitted far better in a Protestant city than they would have under the economic teachings of the medieval Catholic church, with its concern for just price and its abhorrence of regrating—which this storage in anticipation of a price rise really was. Once free of Spain and the Hanse, Amsterdam entered earnestly into the carrying trade, building larger ships. These *fluiten* came by the end of the sixteenth century to be the leaders in merchant marine activities. The dangers of navigation led to the creation of insurance, and the city on the Amstel became a great insurance center, even insuring Holland's enemies in time of war. Refugees from the final reconquest of Antwerp by the Spaniards brought the glass, diamond-cutting, jewelry, and damask-weaving trades to Amsterdam, adding further to its wealth.

The Form of the Dutch City

What sort of town grew from the rapid expansion of the Dutch trading horizon? In an interesting study of Holland at the time of Rembrandt, the seventeenth century, Paul Zumthor tells us:

For the most part Dutch cities were constructed according to one or the other of three typical plans: rounded, with more or less circular

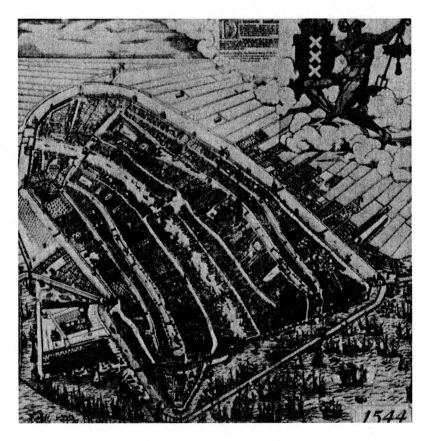

streets, as in Leiden, Haarlem, and Gouda; or nearly quadrangular, with rectilinear streets, as in Delft and Alkmar; or finally a point, often of unequal sides, between two arms of water, as at Dordrecht or Medemblik. Along the principal canal, which forms an axis, irregular façades are aligned with stalls [for selling] sheltered by penthouses; there is then a bridge like the back of donkey, another canal, here a long marketplace dominated by the building of the Public Weigh House; a market of meat, the city hall, itself the testimony of a municipal charter; and higgledy-piggledy around all this are ranged the steep gables, and the spire of a tall Gothic church, as at Gouda. This marketplace is the center around which the daily life is organized.[11]

At the beginning of the seventeenth century, the streets of the marketplace were first being paved to overcome the nuisance of mud and grit tracked in from the sand and clay plains on which these Dutch cities were built. (Sir William Temple, British ambassador of this time, brought back the tale of a man who visited the mistress of a Dutch house whose sturdy maid hoisted him to her shoulders and carried him to the staircase within to

11. Paul Zumthor, *La Vie quotidienne en Hollande au temps de Rembrandt* (Paris: Librairie Hachette, 1959), p. 18.

The Prince's Capital and the Merchants' Town

avoid the scuffing of polished floors. [12]) Streets were paved as much to make commerce easier as to limit the grime, for in the Dutch pantheon trade and cleanliness already stood equal. By 1650 most public streets had been paved, to such an extent that the Calvinist ministers viewed this as a most questionable luxury. [13] On the alignment of many streets flowed a canal, sometimes bordered by paved ways on either bank; the more elegant streets were lined with trees. These conditions held in the newer or more wealthy districts.

In the poorer quarters life was different, as were the physical conditions under which it was lived. Streets were unpaved, with sewers running down their centers; houses were built of wood, following the architecture of the Middle Ages. Upper stories hung successively farther over the street until, when no canal separated the houses, the occupants of the attics could shake hands across the way. Zumthor tells us, "A heterogeneous population swarmed in these quarters, at least in the larger cities. The housing problem, continuous during the seventeenth century as a result of demographic growth and the speculation in rents, had made virtual barracks of these medieval hovels. Traffickers in rent bought such houses to cut them up only to let them in turn at usurious rents." [14]

Dutch houses came to be built from brick with stone trim, and were low if space were available. But normally they were fairly narrow, though not exceptionally high. An unusual feature was that they normally stood separate, even if the gap between them might be little more than an inch or two. Structures in areas outside the slums were usually occupied by single families, and when more housing was needed it came in the outward spread of the city rather than in pushing upward within existing quarters. No doubt a large part of this spread resulted from the difficulty of securing good foundations in a city such as Amsterdam, which had of necessity to be built on piles driven into the argillaceous muck of the polder belt. Three or four stories became the norm, though in Amsterdam some houses reached as high as five to eight. [15] But even so, height in housing came to be associated with wealthy bourgeois residents rather than with crowding in the poorer quarters.

Four or five windows sufficed for lighting the interiors of most houses, which were often quite deep. The façade frequently bowed out to protect a lower part from the rain. Below the street level was a cellar, reached through an areaway closed by a grating. Raised a few steps up was the first floor. Along its front just above the tops of the windows ran a *luifel*, or awning, of painted wood under which an artisan might work or the family might take the air in warm weather. When the building was used for selling, the single large window of the first floor would give way to a large door opening to a shop.

At the top front of the house, the basically triangular gable was likely to be handled decoratively, with an attic window and rather fancy outline sometimes effectively masking the actual roof line. Four or five distinctive façades characteristic of mercantile Amsterdam still define the skyline of the

12. Geoffrey Cotterell, *Amsterdam, the Life of a City* (Boston: Little, Brown, 1972), p. 190.
13. Zumthor, *Vie quotidienne*, p. 19.
14. Ibid.
15. Ibid., p. 20.

heart of the city. Some have sinuous curves typical of the baroque, others are stepped in clear sharp angles, others are slanted or scroll-like. These faces have been the distinguishing feature of Amsterdam from "the golden century," the seventeenth, when simplicity was still a virtue but wealth was flooding in from the Baltic, the merchant marine, and the Indies trade.

Amsterdam houses differed greatly. The façades of the houses of the wealthy were decorated with insets of marble or faience, pilasters and deep window embrasures, and shutters rather than the covered *luifel*. Among the most modest class the houses were of a single story, and the only luxury was the careful varnishing of wooden surfaces. In a climate as damp as Holland's, this feature was not simple vanity.[16]

In the seventeenth century, the occupational districting of Dutch cities was still very clear. Trades lived together in specific streets. As Zumthor notes, "The concentration of similar activities in the same place makes simple and most effective the right of supervision which rests in the different 'corporations' [gilds]. . . . A city is thus a conglomeration of small worlds each of which has its own complexion, its gossip, and its odors. From house to house one spies, keeps watch, and maintains an order based on tradition. The masters of a trade give their name to a street, or a square: the canal of Glazers, the port for Wine, Cheese Street, Flower Street, that for Spices, and the Blacksmith's Brook; Amsterdam has its Canal of the Lords."[17]

With their prosperity the Dutch began to beautify their cities, particularly by laying out some of the earliest public parks (called *mails*), in the form of promenades. Utrecht's *mail*, established in 1637, was nearly half a mile long.

The true nature of the seventeenth-century Mercantile Revolution emerged in Amsterdam, which remained in the center of the Dutch trading empire. One of the largest cities of the West, it was undoubtedly the most wealthy and orderly of its time. It ranged along concentric canals by which the city had expanded outward from the medieval dam where it began. A great wall of brick surrounded the place, beyond which the poor lived in hovels that suggested even at this time the vast contrast found in our day between Paris and its *bidonvilles*. Wealth and squalor have always cohabited in great cities.

Amsterdam became a cosmopolitan city, perhaps the first since Constantinople, and grew apace. By 1600 the city was so crowded that new building space was badly needed. Within a few years, its area was increased threefold, to 726 hectares, which still proved insufficient. A ring of new suburbs was added, with wider streets radiating out from the old city center along which new shops were opened. Growth continued, finally far distant from the medieval core, which had been largely transformed by replacement structures. In these outlying quarters, rectangular street patterns were introduced in the Plantage, which formed the city extension of the late seventeenth century.

While the city grew, another change became visible that was to have great effect on the building of civic monuments and churches—the increas-

16. Ibid., p. 21.
17. Ibid., p. 22.

The Prince's
Capital and the
Merchants' Town

ing democratization of urban society, which showed up in both secular and ecclesiastical structures. To take two examples: the great City Hall in Amsterdam, built between 1648 and 1656, startled contemporary observers both by its vast size and by its lack of monumental and ceremonial entrances. Seven equal and small arches flanked its front on Dam Square. Within the building all sorts of municipal services were carried on, ranging from the Bank of Amsterdam to the arsenal, the courts, and the jail. This City Hall was no longer a ceremonial gildhall, but rather a municipal service building, however grand its frescoes and reliefs. Similarly, with the Reformation, Protestant churches became houses of preaching to a far greater degree than even the preaching barns of the twelfth century that brought on the marvelous innovation of Gothic architecture. The Dutch Reform church rejected Gothic architecture and the church of nave, crossing, and choir in favor of a much more austere neoclassicism and a basically circular preaching hall. As Zumthor has it, "It was no longer important to turn the eyes of the faithful toward the East but rather their ears toward the center, toward the pulpit."[18] For this goal, the linearity of the Gothic church was a nuisance fast overcome in so pragmatic a place and time as seventeenth-century Holland.

Holland in the seventeenth century possessed a peculiar blending of power and parsimony, of display and thrift. Italian architecture with elaborate or even excessively extravagant ornamentation was rapidly introduced. But still Amsterdam was a merchants' town with housing plots to match. Even wealthy merchants' houses seldom gained great width—Amsterdam's average at the time was twenty to twenty-five feet with a depth of no more than two hundred feet, sometimes even including fairly extensive gardens. All large houses must still have access to the canal, as attested even today by the pulleys affixed to their gable ends over which ropes may be thrown to raise large items to storage in the attics. In a city that grew from one hundred thousand population in 1600 to some one hundred and fifty thousand at midcentury, the combination of a more widespread distribution of wealth, or at least fairly general sufficiency, with a desire for material comfort meant that housing was to be solid and even ostentatious but rather democratically modular in scale.

The Renaissance City: The World of Inequality

While the merchants' world of the fifteenth and sixteenth centuries was fairly rapidly transforming itself into the Industrial Age in which we live, a corresponding movement occurred among those possessed of traditional distinction. They sought to crown their world of privilege and aristocracy with surpassing monuments only newly available through enhanced technical competence. The discovery of the aesthetics of visual perspective, probably first in the West and in early-fifteenth-century Italy, combined with improved technology to encourage great and ostentatious building. Filippo Brunelleschi (1377–1446) and Leon Battista Alberti (1404–72) are gener-

18. Ibid., p. 29.

ally credited with the first effective use of the concept of visual perspective, in their efforts to record on flat paper the carefully proportioned image of the Roman ruins that were entering anew into the concern of Western civilization.[19] The logical followup to the discovery of how to represent a three-dimensional building on a flat surface was to design buildings to be seen as a totality, presenting a designed, three-dimensional impression.

During the Middle Ages, three-dimensionality of design of building space was in terms of the interior of the building, not of its exterior. Space in the medieval building was functionally intended, while the outside of the structure was left to evolve as it would, generally as a flat and functional plane on which existing decoration would be in mural form, or at most low relief. Even the great works of the Middle Ages, the cathedrals, tended on occasion to have fairly uninspiring exteriors, saved usually by the superb qualities of the building structure, which in Gothic architecture could not fail to be in evidence. But the surfaces were often "exceeding plain" (as at Albi in southern France, where a fortress church looks almost modern in its functionalism), or were treated as two-dimensional, to be decorated with basically painterly designs rather than architectural ones (as at Orvieto in Tuscany, where the mosaic "façade" of the cathedral is a superb picture but a rather unimpressive building exterior).

Only with the introduction of visual perspective did the exterior of buildings begin to take on a designed visual quality, often, in fact, rather divorced from the handling of the interior space. One may look at the façade of St. Peter's basilica in Rome and learn little indeed about the nature of the enclosed space, something that never happens when you look at the exterior of Chartres, Salisbury, or Albi.

The emergence of the cult of the exterior plays an important role in the morphogenetic analysis. For the first time since Roman days, and in large measure because of the great concern that Alberti and his contemporaries had for a "rebirth" of the Classical Era, buildings were designed from the outside in, or at least with the two concerns given equal weight. The result

19. Bates Lowry, *Renaissance Architecture* (New York: George Braziller, 1971), pp. 13–14.

The Prince's
Capital and the
Merchants' Town

231

was an attention to exterior spaces unknown since classical times. The Middle Ages had witnessed market squares and other working open spaces, but little that existed simply for the visual impression it presented. With the Renaissance, as the high-art world of Western civilization beginning in the fourteenth and fifteenth centuries came during the last century to be called by historians, open space became a design necessity. If perspective were to be used, space outside buildings must be introduced so that the visual qualities of that perspective design could be appreciated. Cathedrals did not change greatly; even in the Middle Ages, they commonly fronted on market squares, since the medieval church served as the watchdog of consumer concerns. But for private houses, even rather large ones, the Renaissance was truly revolutionary.

As the concern for the visual surface of the building increased, the appeal of sites outside the city grew. The creation of villas outside Italian cities, the beginning of the châteaux in the environs of Paris and in the Loire valley, the creation of the great houses of rural England—all stem from the full expression of the cult of the exterior. It is a short step from designing the outside within the city to doing so in a carefully worked out landscape outside the city. The final exterior design arrived in the seventeenth century when the palaces in great parks came to every monarchy seeking to borrow the ultimate grandeur of Louis XIV, who at Versailles had combined the greatest house ever built with the most impressive gardens.

A morphological concern pulled the aristocracy out of the city and made their life increasingly distinct from the life of the rich merchant or artisan. During the Middle Ages, those rich city people had sought social distinction through civic benefactions. During the Renaissance, they had of necessity to take up country residence, building a great house that could furnish both the reason and the title for the barony to which each aspired. Only in the last decade or so has any Englishman shown the affront to tradition of adopting a title based on a city neighborhood.

The Renaissance as a historical period has been characterized by rather consistent exaggeration, particularly as to the role played by high art and architecture. In an era so heavily turned toward the rebirth of a classical model of the city, with the new component of employment of visual perspective, self-conscious design had to take precedence over any other morphogenetic process. In concentrating on the designer's city, scholars have dealt with the essence of the place. They have not, however, dealt very effectively with these cities as the homes of ordinary people. The basic problem is that of institutionalized inequality: to allow a small group to design and create the city of their own elite conception, other interests must be subjected to that narrow goal. The Renaissance would be most fully developed, and least interrupted by features jarring to the self-conscious design, in cities with the weakest and most subservient economics. The merchants' town and the absolute ruler's would be polar extremes. The Rome of the Renaissance popes was a feeble place economically, living on the tribute of a vast ecclesiastical empire, but was constantly growing as a grand urban design. In contrast, London became the capital of a vast empire long before it gained much that was imperial in design.

My purpose is not to denigrate high art or architecture, but to put it in human perspective. Because the Renaissance was so strongly concerned with a formal city, only those persons in society who could predetermine formal components had much bearing on design. The church could play a vastly important role in the rebirth of the classically ordered city, as could the increasingly absolute rulers. One of the clearest expressions of the Renaissance came when Brunelleschi set about redesigning the quarter south of the Arno in Florence to serve as the proper setting for his newly designed church of S. Spirito.[20] In this action he was following in the footsteps of the Roman emperors, who in presenting a new basilica to imperial Rome had it placed in a new forum adequate for its setting. Bates Lowry tells us of Alberti, who must stand as the true exemplar of the Renaissance in architecture and design:

> Shortly after Brunelleschi's death in 1446, Alberti began to put his ideal of architecture into material form by following closely the model provided both by the Roman ruins and by the writings of Vitruvius, the only existing classical treatise on architecture. His approach to the creation of a work of architecture was a natural extension of the general concept Alberti held about the nature of a work of art. Any work of art was envisaged by Alberti principally as an object to be judged in terms of its relationship to a model taken either from the world of Nature or from the work of her most accomplished interpreters—the artists of the classical era.[21]

In this work, "Alberti sought the creation of an image—painted, sculptural, or architectural—that would be as 'lifelike' or perfect a rendition of the model as possible."

Renaissance design requires a model, preferably one harking back to a precedent of appropriate antiquity and grandeur. The fact that the social connotation might be narrowly authoritarian carried no negative weight in the decision of an all-powerful church or civil administration. "Immediately upon becoming Pope in 1503, Julius II began the most grandiose building program undertaken in Rome since the time of the Emperors. These architectural works were intended to help create the image of a Papacy equal in grandeur to Imperial Rome."[22] His architect, d'Angelo Bramante, devised an "oriented space as a means of controlling the observer's experience of the building" that clearly led to the creation of vast and complex spatial designs in the Renaissance city, which dealt arbitrarily with that place as workshop or emporium. The "common man" entered not at all into the scheme of things save to experience the building within an oriented space. Crowds were needed as evidence of power, but having served to exalt the ruler, they must disperse into a city where their physical comfort or economic productivity were of most minor concern. This was a city of vast inequality.

In our present world, despite massive problems, equality is nearer real-

20. Ibid., p. 18.
21. Ibid., p. 21.
22. Ibid., p. 36.

The Prince's
Capital and the
Merchants' Town

233

ization than ever before. The precedent of the Renaissance has relatively little application, and consequently rather little interest. The Renaissance was a time utterly weighted down with a concern for precedent—every building, whatever its ostensible purpose, must offer a clear physical expression drawn from a classical or natural precedent. In rejecting the era of classical rebirth as of much concern to us, we merely accept the standards the time itself set. If our purpose were the study of the designed city, we could not dispatch the Renaissance so briefly.

The Georgian City: A Scene for People

How did the modern world come about? What produced a society wherein equality and democracy have taken on overriding importance? If we look at the past through elite eyes, the change to popular control breaks largely unheralded and quite unexpectedly some time in the middle of the nineteenth century. Yet the abruptness of that change is due more to suppression of knowledge of its origins than to the rapidity of its successes. Change was a long time in coming, but was far less revolutionary and restricted to the nineteenth century than it might seem.

During the late Middle Ages, in the bastides, the roots of equality, popular sovereignty, and the whole context of liberal thought were already to be found. In the merchants' town of the seventeenth century, the sapling was healthy. In the successor mercantilist city of Restoration and Georgian times, the tree grew large enough to produce the seeds of the great change, which came quickly with industrialization and the nineteenth century. The notion of the Georgian city is itself partially elite in form and origin; still, if we project that Georgian image so as to encompass all urban people, the emerging pattern far more clearly explains present urban life than it projects the life of the Renaissance city then slowly withering away on the Continent. The Georgian city held a functional competence lacking in the Renaissance; it was designed as the home of a productive society. The Renaissance city stood as an intellectualized setting for a dogmatically unproductive society founded on a thousand-year history of traditional order and complex social, economic, and even geographical immobility.

We are fortunate in having a classic study of the Georgian town in John Summerson's *Georgian London*. He summarizes that city's morphogenesis:

Another conclusion to be drawn from our bird's-eye view [of Georgian London] is the rather obvious one that London has never been planned. Beside other 18th century capitals, London is remarkable for the freedom with which it developed. It is a city raised by private, not by public, wealth; the least authoritarian city in Europe. Whenever attempts have been made to overrule the individual in the public interest, they have failed. Elizabeth and her Stuart successors tried bluntly to stop any expansion whatever. They failed. Charles II and his pet intellectuals tried to impose a plan after the Great Fire. They failed. Nearly every monarch in turn projected a great Royal Palace to dominate at least part of his capital. All failed until George IV conspired with [the architect] Nash to cheat Parliament into rebuilding Buckingham House. The reasons for all this are embedded deep in England's social and political history. London is one of the few capitals where church property and church interests have not been an over-riding factor; where Royal prestige and prerogative in building matters have been set at naught; where defense has never, since the Middle Ages, dictated a permanent circumvallation to control the limits of development. London is above all a *metropolis of mercantilism*. The basis of its building history is the trade cycle rather than the changing ambitions and policies of rulers and administrators. The land speculator and the adventuring builder have contributed more to the character of the Georgian city than the minister with a flair for artistic propaganda, or the monarch with a mission of dynastic assertion.[23]

Thus, a contrast in morphogenetic process existed between the mercantile towns developing in England—and by extension in the English colonies in North America—and the towns of autocratic rulers and their courts on the Continent. Summerson has merely suggested the contrast in process; we shall concentrate on that difference. The fundamental distinction to be drawn is between a city shaped by land speculation and land and housing-market forces in the English world, and a city far more clearly the product of design decisions taken for purposes of "taste" and ostentation on the Continent. Because speculation has such a black name in the modern world, this battle might at first seem to be one of darkness with light. Though that may in part be true, I suggest that the forces of light were those supporting speculation and those of darkness were the proponents of authoritarian practices within the city.

Beginning as a rather typical medieval town based heavily on its port and governmental functions, by the year 1600 London had begun to show the signs of giving birth to a wholly new existence, particularly in the City itself. A rapidly increasing role was being played by a morphogenetic process long present but until then merely one of a number of forces at work. That process, which seems most appropriately called congregation, led to the concentration of activities and social groupings in particular places within the City. Instead of the medieval occupational clustering, a specialized form of congregation according to the work carried on, the merchants' town that London so strikingly represented tended to develop an economic-class structure associated with particular places in the urban fabric. This clustering had long existed as an exceptional force—as in the Savoy suburb of magnates' houses found even in medieval times—but in London after 1600, the exception became the rule. The social complexity that had characterized the medieval town tended to disappear in favor of two separate postmedieval "towns," each partaking to some degree in the Middle Ages as well as anticipating modern times. The inheritance from the past was the extended

23. John Summerson, *Georgian London* (New York: Charles Scribner's Sons, 1946) (more readily available in a Penguin paperback). This quotation is from pp. 9–10. Emphasis supplied.

The Prince's Capital and the Merchants' Town

occupational household; the anticipation of the future came in the more clearly emerging economic-class districts that were earlier largely unknown.

The occupational households of London in Stuart and early Georgian times were of two main sorts: those still carrying on the medieval tradition of the master, with his apprentices and journeymen living together under one roof in a house he held, and a new form of occupational household based fundamentally on what Thorstein Veblen characterized much later as a "leisure class." In this upper-middle-class or aristocratic household lived the blood relations of the family head, as well as a sometimes surprisingly numerous corps of servants. Characteristically, these households were not headed by someone directly and constantly employed. Instead, the head might most likely be the holder of capital, either in the form of rents and shares or in rural estates that might have been highly prosperous before the expansion in the New Lands in the nineteenth century. These men might hold offices under the crown or Parliament, but the day-to-day orderliness of the true businessman was not required of them; thus, they could live in places more removed from their work than was possible for the real worker. In contrast:

> The substantial merchant who lived about Cornhill, Throgmorton Street, Lombard Street, and the close purlieus surrounding the Royal Exchange, or, having shipping interests, resided in Thames Street, had the apartments devoted to his counting house on the street level, and his warehouse very likely built in the rear or at the side; he dwelt with his household in the rooms above. The mercer of Paternoster Row, and, indeed, the shopkeeper everywhere, traded indoors. Sometimes he built out a pent-house to the street, but he did not make his great display in front, nor did he expect his goods to be seen from outside. . . .
>
> It was not a pleasant place to live in, this City which was more than full of people. Where a man had business, there his life was spent, and with him were his wife and often a large family of children, and his assistants and apprentices, all in one household. This made every street populous. Stuart London was, too, excessively noisy. London's vibrating note, which Lowell likened to "The roaring loom of time," has been attuned to many keys, but never has this been a silent city.[24]

Alongside this teeming, solid, and traditional working population was an even more numerous class of urban poor, which had grown up as the mercantile city expanded and had become badly housed in "meaner dwellings, built back to back," commonly "a mere casing of weather boards fastened to their shaking frames." "A smear of black pitch made the only water-proofing. These were the homes of thousands of London's toiling populace—two rooms or at most three, dark, stuffy, and horribly insanitary. Narrow and filthy alleys, without pretence of paving and often ankle-deep in mud, gave

24. Walter G. Bell, *The Great Fire of London, 1666* (London: Bodley Head, 1920; rev. ed., 1923), pp. 11–12.

the only access. Wanting even such accommodation as this other thousands were forced to find refuge in underground rooms. Others, again, were herded into tenements, falling rapidly into ruin by willful destruction and want of repair."[25]

The Great Fire of 1666

Is it any wonder that even before the Great Fire of 1666, which physically swept most of this structure away, the leisured classes were moving out of the City? As Summerson tells us:

> In Tudor times, when Britain's mercantile strength was in the making, the City of London became the main fortress of mercantilism; and as the merchants increased their riches and influence the aristocracy shifted westwards towards Westminster. By the end of the Civil War, the sturdy wealth and coarse puritanism of the merchants had won every inch of the ground. The old mansions were demolished or split up, their gardens covered with tenements. The gentry, the luxury traders and the upper layers of the professional classes followed the aristocracy westwards. The City became a mercantile stronghold, inhabited by its freemen, the manufacturers and merchants, and ruled by livery companies, in the persons of their elected representatives—aldermen, sheriffs and Lord Mayor.[26]

So, when that most misbegotten Stuart monarchy was restored in 1660, London was already actively pursuing a clearly separated congregation of merchants in the City and of the leisured class in the until then open "liberties" of the City along the Strand and in the royal city of Westminster. The great plague was first visited upon this two-part city in 1665, removing by death over 55,000 souls from the jurisdiction of the Lord Mayor; the Great Fire burned in September 1666, removing some 13,200 houses, about 80 percent of the City within the walls and a considerable district that had grown up in its liberties to the northwest and west. In all, 373 acres within the walls were divested of their buildings.[27] Relatively little aristocratic property was destroyed beyond that held for rents within the City or that occupied by lawyers in one of the Inns of Court. As a result, the Great Fire was a harrowing experience for the working City of London, leaving a nearly vacant slate on which to build a new, truly mercantile City; in contrast, the world of the gentry was little affected. The act of rebuilding London perhaps did more to create a "modern" class within the increasingly out-of-date social class structure in England than any other event before World War I. Walter Bell in his classic study of the fire shows how the split between the landowners, firmly ensconced in the countryside, and the merchants, the true city people, was increased by the catastrophe: "Wealth was restricted to

25. Ibid., p. 14.
26. Summerson, *Georgian London*, p. 36.
27. Bell, *Great Fire*, p. 266.

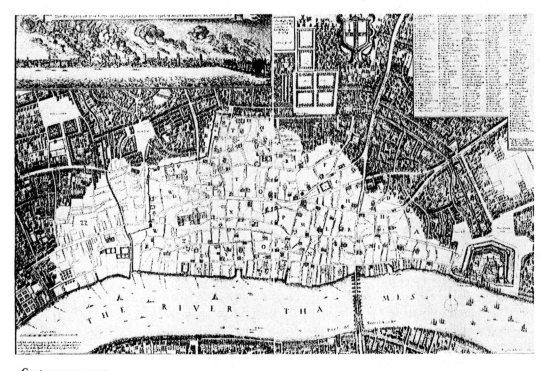

Contemporary map showing the extent of the Great Fire of London in 1666. The medieval wall is clearly visible, so we can see that in the northeastern part of the city some buildings survived, and that west of the wall there was destruction in the Liberties. Reprinted by permission of London Topographic Society.

two classes, the landowners and the merchants, between whom the cleavage was sharp; where the landowner spent his money in ostentatious display, the merchant saved. Time and again, as the long experience of City loans has shown, the merchants' hoard bore the national burdens, and now it came out to restore the burnt city."[28] For the merchants, the fire was a crushing financial blow, matched by the chance to shape a City more suited to the needs of an economy expanding rapidly with the overseas spread of the mercantile realm. In addition, the building experience it necessitated was in the end of great use to the freemen of the City, whose numbers expanded rapidly with the final abolition of the severe gild restraints on entrance to a trade. As an emergency measure, Parliament removed the constraint of trade, the fundamental basis of medieval gild law, by enacting the following:

> All carpenters, bricklayers, masons, plasterers, miners; and other artificers, workmen and labourers to be employed in the said buildings [in the reconstruction of the City after the Great Fire] shall for the space of seven years next ensuing, and for so long time after as until the said buildings shall be fully finished, have and enjoy such and the same liberty of working, and being set to work in the said building, as the freemen of the City of the same trades and professions have and ought to enjoy; Any usage or custom of the City to the contrary notwithstanding. And that such artificers as aforesaid, which for the space of seven years shall have wrought in the rebuilding of the City [of London] in their respective arts, shall from

The Continuing City

28. Ibid., p. 284.

and after the said seven years have and enjoy the same liberty to
work as freemen of the said City for and during their natural lives.[29]

After the Fire

Conditions for rapid economic growth could hardly have been better
once the blow of the Great Fire itself was met. A new fabric was introduced
that provided somewhat better streets for the City; along those ways ranged
buildings far sturdier and more suited to the growing trade of London than
those swept away in the first four days of September 1666. Along with this
physical improvement came a considerable social change that at first did not
seem too radical; in the end, it proved as transforming as the actual physical
reconstruction of the City. Trades were opened to outsiders and in considerable numbers as never before. The sharp losses of population experienced
during the plague the year before were considerably made up, and the City
was on the whole somewhat more healthful as a place to live than when it was
still a creaking relict of medieval times. Finally, the experience of large and
active works and the more productive employment of capital in the development of lands and buildings gave to the City's inhabitants skills found
nowhere else in the kingdom.

Strangely, the physical separation of the aristocratic from the merchants'
City came at a time when the differences in wealth between landowners and
merchants were probably less than they had been previously, or were to
become when coal mining and speculation in lands on estates near London
and the provincial cities gave noble landlords incomes beyond the expectations of all but the most eminently successful merchant. But the separation
had come, and for more than a hundred years the City was the fortress of
mercantilism that Summerson has described so fully. Thus, we may look at
postfire London—London Rebuilt—as perhaps the first modern city. It was
a really large town, approaching a population of half a million people,
increasingly organized for productive and expansible economic activities, in
sharp contrast to the rigidly constrained economy of medieval times.

The Origin and Form of the Expansible City

We now must note the efforts of Elizabeth and the early Stuarts to stop
London's growth. Significantly, the one activity not constrained—the functions and occupations associated with the port—led most directly to the
growth they sought to obviate. The great expansion of the mercantile frontier
of England directly produced the growth of the port of London, in the specific
guise of the various monopoly trading companies resident there, and made
new docks essential and storage of goods from distant lands a necessity.
A backward glance clearly shows Elizabeth's policy to have been ill-
conceived, whether or not one agrees with her goal of limiting growth.

We can understand the fatal flaws in crown policy toward London as a

29. This clause is from the Rebuilding Act enacted by the House of Commons in 1667. *Ibid.*,
p. 254.

natural outgrowth of normal political processes. Two main alignments of power were emerging within London—the court and its minions, and the merchant class of the City. Each had an increasingly characteristic purlieu: the "West End" of Mayfair and Westminster for the gentry, the City and its environs for the merchants. Each group argued the absolutely essential nature of expansion of the city in its own interests. Elizabeth's Proclamation of 1580 bears quotation:

> The Queen's Majestie perceiving the state of the city of London (being anciently termed her chamber) and the suburbs and confines thereof to increase daily, by access of people to inhabit the same, in such ample sort, as thereby many inconveniences are seen already, but many greater of necessity like to follow, being such as her majesty cannot neglect to remedy. [As] . . . where there are such great multitudes of people brought to inhabit in small rooms, whereof a great part are seen very poor, yea, such as must live of begging, or by worse means, and they heaped up together, and in a sort smothered with many families of children and servants in one house or small tenement . . . if any plague or popular sickness . . . enter amongst those multitudes . . . a great mortality would ensue . . . [and] the infection would be also dispersed through all parts of the realm. . . . [Thus] her maj. . . . doth charge and strictly command all manner of persons, of what quality soever they be, to desist and forbear from any new buildings of any house or tenement within three miles of any of the gates of the said city of London, to serve for habitation or lodging for any person, where no former house hath been known to have been in the memory of such as are now living: and also to forbear from letting or setting, or suffering any more families than one only to be placed, or to inhabit from henceforth in any house that heretofore had been inhabited.[30]

Two functioning exceptions to this embargo on building were permitted: (1) housing for port workers was allowed in the Act of 1592 that implemented Elizabeth's proclamation, and (2) housing for the middle and upper classes might be built through special permissions granted specifically by the crown, as in the case of Bedford's development of Covent Garden beginning in 1630. The merchants' interests were guarded through permitting an expanding port function; the gentry's needs were cared for through the tolerance, under exceptions, of the aristocratic housing development growing up north and west of the City and in the environs of the government quarter in Whitehall.

The Georgian Residential Estate: Covent Garden

Henry VIII in the exercise of his absolute power confiscated the properties of the church that were no longer needed for the practice of religion after

30. Steen Eiler Rasmussen, in *London: The Unique City* (New York: Macmillan, 1937), discusses at length in chapter 4 the attempts to contain the growth of London. The quotation is from Rasmussen, pp. 67–70.

his split with Rome in 1534. Among these were most of the monastic and conventual establishments in the kingdom, many of which were forthwith granted to powerful minions of the crown. John Russell was such a man. In 1552 he was given a leasehold of seven acres of the convent garden located on the Strand. On this site he built a great mansion—Bedford House, named for the earldom he was given in 1550, comprising many rural estates as well as several in the liberties of the City of London. In the gardens behind Bedford House, the fourth earl decided to lay out a grandiose housing estate that Summerson viewed, in what seems an oddly myopic frame, as "the first great contribution of English urbanism."[31]

Perhaps at the insistence of the king—on granting a license to build in a time when growth was legally disallowed—Bedford had Inigo Jones lay out an Italian piazza with houses on the west and north side, a church to the south, and the Bedford gardens to the east. Development was slow; evidently the land was not quite ripe, or else the Italianate row houses of considerable size were ahead of their time. Eventually the land was built upon. The houses were of fairly uniform style, certainly with fixed elements of the façade—notably the roof line and the arcades that came to be called piazzas—thus contributing a splendid Americanism to New England speech, which democratically gives this title to even the ordinary person's front porch—and suggested a general level of upper-class accommodation.

One of the major elements in the ripening of land for speculative profit was the creation of a fashionable quality in these districts. Covent Garden was probably slightly too early; the City had not yet fully lost its social image, and the country gentry had not yet fully accepted the need to occupy a town mansion for a part of the year. But by the time of the Restoration of 1660, the world of London was divided. Steen Eiler Rasmussen tells us how it came about:

> When the [country] magnates purchased houses near London it was not town-houses in narrow streets but country-houses with a service of different buildings and vast gardens. The arrival of each noble family increased the population not only by the family itself and its many servants with their relatives but also by merchants, artisans, and others who lived on the aristocracy. Besides London, the town of producers, the capital of the world-trade and industry, there arose another London, the town of consumers, the town of the Court, of the nobility, of retired capitalists. Where a little room was left between the big mansions the middle classes settled in groups of smaller houses which sprung up as best they could. But very soon the proprietors discovered the chance of using the areas for considerable housing enterprises which would provide suitable quarters for people of quality. In the long run the development of the town made it impossible to leave large areas as private gardens. On the other hand, when an earl or a duke *did* turn his property to account he wanted to determine what neighbours he got. The great

31. Summerson, *Georgian London*, p. 13.

The Prince's
Capital and the
Merchants' Town

landlord and the speculative builder found each other and together they created the London square with its character of unity as it is by dignified houses, all alike.[32]

The City was firmly in the hands of the businessmen. The West End had become the world of "quality" and "fashion" to the extent that to live too far east was a social solecism. With respect to a later development of the (then) dukes of Bedford, "the Right Honourable John Wilson Croker once solemnly propounded the question in the House of Commons: 'Where is Russell Square?'" in a classic put-down of London's second largest residential square. It became the silly fashion of the Quality "to affect a superior ignorance of localities not actually within the purlieus of Mayfair."[33]

The two worlds of the City and Mayfair operated under quite different morphogenetic processes, contrasting in the nature of speculation, in the style and form of buildings and the way they would be assembled into "contributions to English urbanism," in the lifestyles they engendered, and, finally, in their transferral to other cities and other lands. The speculation practiced in the West End was geared to a very concerted effort, expressed over considerable areas, to shape a social definition of land use. One use of land was obvious: the housing of the ever-growing city population. But beyond that, the selection among potential tenants came largely by design. A fair number of great landowners were seeking to develop their estates—the Russells, the Grosvenors, the Cavendish-Harley alliance (dukes of Portland), Lord Burlington, Lord Southampton, the crown on its own account, the Rugby School as well as Harrow and Eton and Westminster colleges, Marquis Camden, and a number of others.[34] Each sought to shape a particular social image within a minutely class-bound society in order to ripen the land, not merely in time but as well by social class.

The square became the device by which the speculator sought to gain the highest "quality" of patronage to follow the lead of one or several aristocratic families who might be encouraged to take up residence "in the square." The dukes of Bedford, as experienced speculators in land values and properly accustomed to the ermine, shaped such a social grouping at the Bloomsbury Square around Bedford House.

The prototype came from Paris, where Henri IV sought to develop land in Le Marais, the former swamp that lay inside the extended walls of the city. In 1607, the area was designed as a great square—the Place Royale (later des Vosges)—321 feet on a side, surrounded by thirty-eight "pavilions" (that we would term row houses) intended for occupation by upper classes. The fourth earl of Bedford's piazza at Covent Garden was a pale image of this design. But when William, Lord Russell, married the daughter of the earl of Southampton and came into possession of his landholding northwest of the

32. Rasmussen, *London*, pp. 165–166.

33. E. Berresford Chancellor, *The History of the Squares of London* (Philadelphia: Lippincott, 1907), p. 211.

34. Summerson gives a map of the earlier estates to develop (*Georgian London*, fig. 22, p. 149); while J. T. Coppock and Hugh C. Prince, eds., *Greater London* (London: Faber and Faber, 1964), give a map of the nineteenth-century estates (fig. 20, p. 96).

Dean & Chapter of Westminster

Dean & Chapter of Westminster

Eton College

880 yards
800 metres

John Powell

Highgate +

Sir Thomas M. Wilson

Earl of Mansfield

Lord Southampton

Duke of St. Albans

+ Hampstead

Thomas Rhodes

Sir Thomas Maryon Wilson

Edgeware Road

John Powell

+ Kilburn

Westminster College

Manor of Cantelows

Bishop of London

Harrow School

Henry Samuel Eyre

Eton College

Chalk Farm +

Lord Southampton

St. Bartholomews Hospital

Duke of Portland

Marquis Camden

The Crown Regents Park

Edward

Lord Southampton

Duke of Bedford

Bishop of London

St. Bartholomews Hospital

Grand Junction Canal

Marylebone

Bishop of London

Berkeley

Marylebone

Lord Somers

Brewers Company

Portman

Duke of Portland

Road

Skinners Company

New River Company

Lucas

The Crown Hyde Park

Park Row

(Cavendish-Harley)

Lord Southampton

Harrison

Lloyd Baker

Oxford Street

C of L

Duke of Bedford

Southampton Row

Foundling Hospital

Calthorpe

Grosvenor

Regent Street

Berners

Rugby School

New Oxford St. opened 1847

Bedford Charity

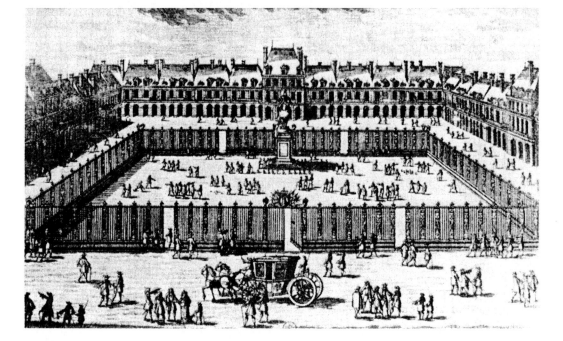

The Place Royale (present Place des Vosges) was completed in 1615 at the instigation of Henri IV, becoming the first great public square in Paris and the model for residential designs in London and other Western cities.

City, the development of a square such as was to be found in Paris could begin in earnest in the fields about Southampton (later Bedford) House.

Henry Jermyn, first earl of St. Alban's, had several years before laid out St. James's Square in Mayfair, probably on the model of the Place Royale, which he would have known as a wealthy royalist refugee living in Paris during the Commonwealth. At first this speculation faltered, as Jermyn held only a lease from the crown. When subsequently he talked the king into a freehold title to the property, he managed slowly to develop it into the square with the highest social cachet of the time.[35] These aristocratic landowners and speculators no doubt gained the pick of the social roster in those class congregations they managed to draw to their squares.

The Concept of Class Congregation

The general concept of class congregation was of far wider application and of more enduring force in shaping the City than just these land speculations in Restoration London. The massive growth of the City of London's business activity had caused the congregation of merchants and manufacturers, of dockworkers, hawkers, clerks, and a hundred other tradespeople. The City was crowded and increasingly alien to the traditional country-based aristocracy. Not surprisingly, when the Restoration came in 1660 the gentry had literally disappeared from the City. The process was one of separation rather than segregation; enough wealth had fallen into the hands of the great

35. These developments are detailed in Summerson, *Georgian London*, in the section on Bloomsbury Square, as the development around Bedford House came to be known.

merchants that they could command their own district within the city, and, as well, sufficient power and privilege attached to nobility to assure that their purlieus would be those of their choice rather than eviction. Two groups may show strong separation without the one-sided push of segregation.

This separation by class into two distinct social and economic congregations created distinctions in lifestyle and the practices of speculation that were to have great bearing on the settlement of America. Let us summarize the contrasts in land-development practices and city forms that grew out of them.

London Rebuilt

In the City an increasing domination of development by business requirements and the reconstruction made necessary by the Great Fire meant the creation of a new physical form. The medieval pattern was swept away by the fire, but also by the City's changing needs. After all, the town could have been rebuilt in a medieval form. Instead, the great merchants, those with the money and power to do the job and thus the group who decided how it would be done, settled on a moderate reshaping of the medieval morphology. A numerous body of commentators bemoan the failure of London to adopt one of the grandiose and highly Renaissance plans for the rebuilding proposed by Dr. Christopher Wren, John Evelyn, and Robert Hooke. They argue that London would have been so much more impressive a city, and a fitting physical skeleton on which to place examples of great architecture, if one such overall design had been adopted.

The critics overlook the fact that after 1666 the City was the epitome of a merchants' town; a quite different set of demands took precedence over those of national image and refined taste. As Summerson tells us, "Taste in architecture reached London about 1615: taste that is, in the exclusive, snobbish sense of recognition of certain fixed values by certain people. Taste was a luxury import from Italy, received and cherished by a small group of noblemen and artists whose setting was the not very polished Court of James I. [Thus,] architecture was a late comer to this little circle of intelligence in a still half-medieval England."[36] The City retained more of the medieval than did the West End, but not in any pejorative sense; rather, in the City, the concept of form follows function in urban design and house architecture was carried over from the Middle Ages to the modern world. In the West End, the tyranny of visual design arose and began its increasingly arid course.

The rebuilding of the City came in two basic programs. The first tried to improve the conditions of circulation about the place; the second attempted to devise houses both more fire-resistant and more structurally appropriate to the times than the old and frequently tinkered-with medieval gable houses the fire had swept away. The street-improvement program had few grand accomplishments but many quietly significant ones. For the first time, wheeled vehicles could move rather generally about the town as most streets, other than cul-de-sacs and simple alleyways, were made broad enough for

36. Ibid., p. 11.

wagons and carts. Carriages were less maneuverable than carts, and the tale remained that the City was closed to wheels; in truth, it was opened to the worker's wheels if not the noble's. Other changes came in widening and improving the alignment of a few arterial streets—those leading to London Bridge and the more important gates—such that the commerce of the place could grow and continue to function.

The fire meant the beginning of building specialized with respect to both location and function. The commissioners entrusted with guiding the rebuilding established the use of four types of houses, the choice among them depending on the width and importance of the street on which each fronted:

The first and least sort were to be built in bylanes, two storeys high, irrespective (as in all cases) of cellars and garrets;

The second sort in streets and lanes of note, to be three storeys high;

The third, fronting high and principal streets, of four storeys; and

The fourth type, the merchant's mansion houses "of the greatest bigness," not built to the street front also not to exceed four storeys.

For each type of house the thickness of brick walls, heights from floor to ceiling, depth of cellars and sufficiency of party walls, scantlings of timber and much other detail were set out in scheduled tables, to which the builders were required to conform.[37]

Unspecified in law but still the outcome of the rebuilding process was the increasing rationalization of land use within the City. Thames Street, along the river, was enlarged, straightened, and given a fully constructed quay between it and the river—perhaps Dr. Wren's greatest contribution in the reconstruction other than his wealth of churches and the reconstructed St. Paul's Cathedral. For the first time, ships could tie up at a dock and gain access to cranes for lifting cargo and to warehouses just across the quay.

Such improvements of economic activities are hard to demonstrate at this late date, but seemingly the general form of the postfire house was more conducive to efficient manufacture and commerce than its medieval predecessor had been. These square, small but essentially modular buildings tended to present a common roof line on the street frontage and a common height for stories; these aspects would have made opening one house into the other more straightforward. Also, although the housing of the poor was hardly a priority concern, probably some improvement was made over the worst conditions of the prefire town, if only because the terribly modest new housing for the poor was probably more healthful than that it replaced.

In the absence of a full study of the workaday world of London at the end of the seventeenth century, we must depend largely on quite indirect evidence. That evidence suggests that the City as rebuilt after the fire was fully a commercial town, dominated by economic activities and with economic

37. Bell, *Great Fire*, p. 251.

tests of spatial allocation. Although it was not designed for specific trades—save in the docks and the areas where the noxious trades were finally driven outside the City walls—for the time, the best physical conditions for economic activity were to be had there. Thus, within a few decades of the crushing fire, the City of London became the world's emporium. Because of that, the metropolis that grew around it became the greatest city on Earth until the beginning of this century.

The World of the West End

The world of the West End was very different. There, rule was by privilege and social congregation. The squares were merely the diamonds of clearest privilege in a setting that was everywhere class-bound. The aristocratic developers came to realize that theirs was a socially complex society dependent for order on the top but for comfort on the bottom. This society required shops for trading, housing for servant classes, mews in which carriages, horses, and their attendants could be housed, and other expressions of the social pyramid. The upper middle class, gripped by the notion that social mobility meant occupational inactivity, sought doggedly to take up residence near the gentry, and to be equally unproductive. Thus, the squares were adjoined by streets in which the uniform façades hid housing of lesser ostentation, but still commodious beyond basic necessity. Those in the side streets had few servants, though many by present-day standards. The rise of this extensive and increasingly leisured middle class shaped the extensive housing areas in Bloomsbury, Mayfair, and Kensington.

A recurrently separative process was at work in both the City and the West End. As merchants gained increasing wealth, they could afford to ape the aristocracy; in a class-bound society, their doing so was almost inevitable. As generations succeeded to commercial wealth, their ties with the City became less burdensome and more periodic, if not in actual fact abstract. In such a situation, the commercial middle class began to take up residence in nearby Bloomsbury—no doubt explaining the unawareness of the haughty members of Parliament as to that district's whereabouts. Lawyers from the Inns of Court to the south also moved into this area, when they married and left the bachelor quarters the Inns afforded.

The result was the creation of an extensive class possessed of considerable capital but, at least in the first generation, engaged in productive labor. For them, a social rise meant a shift in residence out of the City. The line was fuzzy between the leisured middle class and the gainfully occupied component of that same economic stratum. Likely a careful study would show that, as the broad class grew in size, internal congregations evolved within the middle class, based on such distinctions as work or leisure.

The West End Model

The physical complex that became the basic morphological component of the Georgian city was inextricably related to the social desires of the middle and upper classes at that time. To assure the desired surroundings

when the lands about a previously suburban great house—such as Bedford (Southampton) House—were developed for the income that could be secured from urban housing, it was essential to try to give a specific quality to that project. Much of the land in London's West End was entailed, forbidding sale of the freehold. Thus, the practice became to develop "estates" wherein title to the land remained with the landowners, who offered leaseholds, originally of fairly short duration but ultimately commonly around sixty or ninety-nine years in term. At the end of the lease period, the land and all improvements on it would revert to the landowner. No more effective device could have been found to control the long-term use of land in an era when the concept of zoning was unimagined.

Because these developments were often adjacent to aristocratic mansions—though as time passed most of the mansions were torn down to be replaced by more intensive urban housing—great effort was made to maintain an elevated tone for the neighborhood. Forced construction of housing of sufficient size and cost guarded against the encroachment of "other classes." But the tone of a housing estate was conferred even more by the architectural style decreed for its construction. In these attached row houses, a common façade presented to the street was essential. First, the frontage of each house was predetermined. These houses were usually fairly narrow in width and normally limited to three construction bays—perhaps sixteen to forty feet at the outer limits.

As a matter of fact there arose only a few types of buildings, which with their characteristic features were repeated over and over again in long rows of streets and they only varied in scale and in interior decoration. Facing the parks—St. James's Park and Hyde Park— houses were built as very narrow and very deep buildings. . . . In the squares and places of Bloomsbury where the street front is the best the houses were less deep. The largest room on the first floor was a broad room facing the street, and facing the yard there were two deep rooms side by side. . . . This Bloomsbury house with its three bays we find in large scale in Bedford Square. Here each room is as large as a ballroom, but in streets near by the same type of house is also to be found in smaller scale, down to quite small dimensions, as for instance the houses in Doughty Street where Charles Dickens lived in No. 48 (1837–39). Houses smaller than these have become two-bay buildings, but little by little the composition of façades as systems of bays was abandoned and one large window for each room was considered sufficient.[38]

Rasmussen's description speaks of the London house in the mid-nineteenth century when Londoners had a bit more social range in their occupation, but it serves well to present the type of house and the standardization that came quite early to the housing of the moneyed classes. The façades along a single street-block frontage were made uniform with roof lines, and the height of individual stories was kept consistent. Normally, the three bays were revealed by three large windows in the upper stories, and two windows and a doorway on the first floor. Cellars were increasingly used as builders sought to enlarge the accommodation of the houses without making them visually too tall. The main cellar—a subcellar below it might be used mainly for storage of coal and other household needs—was built at ground level, affording windows to the back; at the front, the street was raised on a causeway-like feature, bordered on each side by areaways that allowed some light to reach the fronts of the cellar, and access to the first floor was more or less on a level. Most commonly, these were really four-story houses with the true ground floor (cellar) hidden at the front by raising the street one level upward to give entry directly into the public entertaining rooms of the first floor.

This feature of city row houses in England was not widely copied when the form was brought to the large cities of America. Perhaps London's poor drainage conditions, brought on by the underlying layer of clay, encouraged what was really an above-ground cellar, a feature unnecessary with the commonly superior drainage found in American cities, where cellars could be occupied even when dug well below the natural surface of the land.

The range of class variation within Georgian housing was kept fairly narrowly bounded. The squares were the most desirable spots, sporting the largest houses and the wealthiest occupants. Wider streets leading out of the square came next in order of precedence and would be occupied by the firmly established middle class. Their houses were less commodious than those fronting on the square but were still impressive in their architectural presentation to the street. In lesser streets or near the small cluster of shops commonly built into these developments to save servants' shopping time, the housing would be relatively modest. In these lower-middle-class infillings, working authors such as Dickens might find lodging.

The Georgian world was all "front"; when one turns to the rear elevations

38. Rasmussen, *London*, pp. 233–34.

The Prince's
Capital and the
Merchants' Town

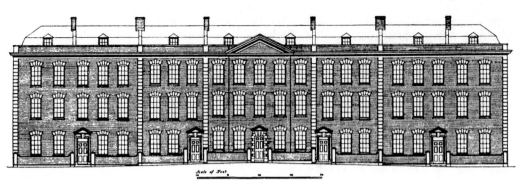

Clifton in Bristol still preserves some of the finest Georgian buildings of England. This South Row in Brunswick Square was constructed on leaseholds by the house carpenter Edmund Workman, who let them out in 1771. Of the seven houses in this row, only the middle one is double-fronted, though the end houses have their entrances on the intersecting streets (thus the entrances are not shown in the drawing). From Walter Ison, The Georgian Buildings of Bristol *(London: Faber & Faber, 1952).*

of these buildings, the disappointment is extreme. Their rear walls are grubby and cluttered beyond common practice, even in the most architecturally condemned of American housing tracts today. Mews for the housing of horses and the storage of carriages were sometimes accommodated at the back. There too were frequently found somewhat haphazard outbuildings for the overflow of household storage.

The small open space behind the main building seems to have been provided entirely for sanitary purposes, to admit light and air at the rear and to contain cesspits used by the household "closets." The kitchen garden of the medieval burgage plot was gone, and the landscaped yard of the American house had not yet been discovered. The aristocracy required landscape gardening to be formal and a bit bleak, certainly space-consuming and stylized. It was associated with the sort of landscaping found in big country houses; for that, one needed lawns, sheep, carefully placed clusters of ancient trees, and all sorts of things impossible in the city courtyard. Apparently the middle class drew the gauze curtains on the backyard and gave up. A family was known by what street or square it house was "in," so the rear was yet another of those Victorian unmentionables. As Rasmussen had it, house fronts were Georgian; their rears were Gothic.

Two Models of Urbanism for Transport to America

Clearly, two forms of urban development were available to the persons who crossed the Atlantic during the Great Migration of the seventeenth century. The first was that associated with the aristocratic districts in London and a few other cities. The other model that must have been known well was that of London Rebuilt, the commercial town risen from the ashes to become the most important economic place on earth, and the previous home of Boston and Philadelphia settlers. Because of the social class of those migrants and their purposes for going to America, this London Rebuilt model was the more important. It was a working place of relatively moderate reforms in society, politics, and religion and, above all, it was a city. The holds of the small ships in the Great Migration contained far more townspeople than would a representative sample of the English population; their first act on reaching the western shore was to attempt to reproduce the town life of

The Continuing City

the England they had left in search of a more perfect world. Part of that quest for perfection was the improvement of the city; they did not abandon it, as so commonly modern reformers do.

The Planting of the American City

We are fortunate indeed that Carl Bridenbaugh a generation ago set out to dispel the myth that the European settlers in America were coming as countrypeople and agricultural pioneers. In his two classic volumes on colonial urbanism—*Cities in the Wilderness* and *Cities in Revolt*—he covers the American city experience up to the time of the American Revolution.[39] That experience was rather different in contemporary view from what it seems to have become in retrospect today, rather reversing the notion that hindsight is the more perceptive. Bridenbaugh states at the very beginning of his first book:

> Cities rise and flourish in proportion as their natural advantages correspond with the demands of a particular age. This correspondence may be either accidental or the result of preconceived purpose, but history provides many instances of towns which, lacking this harmony between the physical and economic environment, have despite artificial efforts of founders or promoters remained condemned to comparative unimportance, outdistanced by more fortunate rivals. In the seventeenth century material greatness was commercial, not industrial. Those towns prospered, therefore, whose sites commanded certain vital trading advantages—the possession of good natural harbors, the control of avenues of trade and communication, or the dominion of a productive countryside. When in this period the Old World began to plant its colonial settlements on the North American continent, commercial considerations as such largely dictated their locations. Design rather than accident endowed the principal offspring of seventeenth century colonizing impulses with situations favoring the pursuit of trade and navigation.[40]

In the minds of the promoters of North American colonies, the advance of the trading, mercantile frontier shaped their actions; otherwise, their efforts would have borne little economic return. Many merchants, and perhaps more settlers, were of dissenting religious view or of unhappy social or economic status. Still, those who put up the money for the voyaging, and held out some hope for a continuing economic support of the plantations once established, saw this venture as one of economic trade.

This classic problem is part of most migration movements. Push factors must propel settlers against the resistance that distance always interposes,

39. Carl Bridenbaugh, *Cities in the Wilderness (1625–1742)* (1938; rpt. New York: Knopf, 1955); and *Cities in Revolt (1743–1776)* (New York: Knopf, 1955). Republished jointly in 1955 as *Urban Life in America*.

40. Bridenbaugh, *Cities in the Wilderness*, p. 3.

The Prince's Capital and the Merchants' Town

but attractions must draw them out as well. For religious and social outcasts, the gain might be personal satisfaction and a sense of a better psychic existence. But the merchant paying their way must have some reasonable anticipation of economic return. He would back their venture, or even originate it and subsequently recruit their association with it, basically to extend the economic system in which he was functioning. In seventeenth-century England and Holland, this system of mercantile endeavor was fairly simple and certainly most effective. In France the same economic motives were involved. But a resolution of the Wars of Religion in favor of the Roman church had meant an unbridgeable gap between the court and government on the one hand, and the most effective merchant group and potential population for recruitment to migration on the other. The less than impressive history of French colonization in Canada owes as much to that schism as to all other causes combined.

If we accept a commercial motive for all colonies, and that only some as an additional concern were religious commonwealths, then we can see that the trading entrepôt must be the logical model for the developing towns. Plantation of settlers came first in just such towns with "the dominion of a productive countryside." The European peopling of America came from the initial coastal towns outward rather than, as frequently imagined, from the growth of the towns serving the needs of an earlier developed countryside. History in America utterly contradicts the assumptions of central-place theory, whose role on the American stage must wait for the third act, when the nation had become as densely settled and politically and administratively complex as the medieval Germany in whose relics this special system was conceived.

The wave of European plantation came as a town-founding effort with great similarity to the conscious spread of economic towns—bastides—into the wasteland parts of Europe in the twelfth, thirteenth, and fourteenth centuries. The purpose was closely similar and the *dramatis personae* nearly the same, given a few elements of changed costuming. As during the Middle Ages, the notion existed of a sovereign capable of asserting a claim based on assumed divine support. The Spaniards and the Portuguese drew straight from the past when they secured a papal decree dividing the unknown world into two spheres wherein each of the Iberian kingdoms separately might explore and claim lands. Other Catholic powers bridled at this act, though only the French did so effectively. The Protestant kingdoms treated the matter with the reverence it deserved, ranging the seas and claiming land not actively defended by another European power. But once an area was claimed, whether by the Protestant English and Dutch or the Catholic French, Spaniards, and Portuguese, the notion of national sovereignty was in operation. Subsequent development within the claimed area was controlled by royal grant, much as it had been during the Middle Ages.

French Colonization in North America

When Champlain established his *Habitation* at Québec in 1608, his purpose was seemingly rather complex—imperial in politics, proselyting in

religion, and mercantile in economics. That rather bureaucratic quality remained throughout the French sovereignty of Canada, until 1763. In seeking colonists for the Laurentian settlements, the French reverted directly to feudalism rather than to the more evolved social and economic system of their own bastides. The king granted basically feudal estates to a group of *seigneurs* (persons and ecclesiastical foundations) whose jobs it became to secure settlers for the colony of Canada. In return, the *seigneur* was allowed to collect a feudal quitrent such as we have already seen in the bastides, a *cens*, from the residents on the holding, thus termed *censitaires*, as well as other forms of excise taxation characteristic of the feudal economy. The result was the creation of a rural society and an agricultural economy quite distinctly different from that emerging across the Appalachians in New England, New York, the Jerseys, and Pennsylvania.

Seemingly because the Huguenots were forbidden entry to Canada by a militantly Counter-Reformation government in France, the colony that resulted was economically stunted and productive of a feeble and somewhat artificially maintained urbanization. Québec was a proper town, though unbelievably priest-ridden, even when compared with the rather grim religiosity of Boston. The combination of bishops as the religious rulers and the rural feudalism of the seigneurial system produced a limping economy, while the economy of the English colonies dashed forward under the aegis of the merchant class working from London and the West Country ports as well as resident in the New World. To change matters, the French government began, in 1663, the operation of a royal government for Canada, guided by another viceregal figure alongside the bishops of Québec, the intendants of the crown. The crown monopolized the pelteries of the forest, the one trade that showed much hope of producing profits, setting back the course of city building by further committing Canada to a peculiarly rural economic base. The commercial agriculture then developing in Maryland and Virginia, or the resident mercantilism growing up in New England, was obviated by Canadian dependence on the production of products gathered from the

The Prince's Capital and the Merchants' Town

forest, fish that might be caught by fishermen coming seasonally from France, or the subsistence farming practiced on semifeudal holdings by a basically peasant agriculture. What towns might grow in this barren soil were those of administrators and viceroys—ecclesiastical or royal—more than merchants. Québec, Three Rivers, and Montréal became the only towns, but were towns of control more than commerce. Their glory was found in their seminaries rather than their depôts of trade.

To complete the picture, we find the one North American instance of the siege castle being built by the royal administration of Canada to defend the colony against the depredations of the merchants of Britain and British America. At Louisbourg on Cape Breton Island, a great fortress was built between 1720 and 1740 to defend the frontiers of the colony, as the Norman siege castles such as Château-Gaillard had done in the Middle Ages. Like them, Louisbourg proved less than invincible, falling after siege to a body of New England merchants and their henchmen in 1745. As a frontier fortress it was a failure. A certain allegorical quality attaches to the siege of Louisbourg in 1745; then, perhaps more clearly than at any other time, the supremacy of the mercantile era over the feudal era was signaled. The expedition that captured the fortress was almost entirely American, made up of men whose families had lived for several generations free of the yoke of Europe's traditional social order. And the anger felt in New England over the return of the place to the French at war's end was an attitude that a people long used to the peculiarities of dynastic warfare—as were all Europeans—would have been unlikely to entertain.

If Canada represented the effort to project an incompletely evolved mercantile Europe into North America, as I believe it did, then the failure of France's policies there can be read not merely as the early warning of the collapse of the dying monarchical system, which came in France itself not more than twenty-five years after the loss of Canada. France's failure may also serve as evidence of the disastrous policy of "ruralization" practiced in royal Canada. The conquest of Canada by the British in 1763 led to two events that tell us much about the role that cities have played in the broad history of North America.

Once sovereignty shifted to the British, northward migration of city people from the English colonies lying to the south was considerable, to the extent that Montréal was a predominantly English city throughout much of the nineteenth century, and Québec had a considerable English minority population at the same time. The English in Canada became the denizens of the towns and the French tended to retreat into social, political, cultural, and religious isolation in the protective realms of the countryside. The "habitant" became the French Canadian, rural, parochial, devout, politically and socially conservative, and economically stagnant.

In the meantime the English were acting like their merchant forebears, building and dominating towns, expanding their economic interests over the vast realm Canada became, and generally acting like the hated Americans south of the border. Only since World War II have the French Canadians turned to the cities in great numbers, taking control of those urban clusters within their own province, gaining stature as businessmen, and becoming increasingly typical North Americans. But the rustication of the French Canadian for almost two hundred years after the conquest has placed a grim economic inheritance on Jean Baptiste's shoulders. We might well interpret the Québec nationalism of the present generation as an effort to recapture from *les Anglais* the cities of the province of Québec for the use of the dominant population group that had never given up the countryside around them.

The City in the English Colonies

In the thirteen English colonies south and east of the Appalachians—which for simplicity we may call the American colonies—a very different situation was found. Perhaps at the very beginning, the distinction between the English and French colonies was not so striking, but it evolved into a fundamental contrast. Again we may best turn to Bridenbaugh's characterization:

> Pursuit of trade and commerce was the all-embracing activity of the early colonial villages—the very basis for their existence. These little seaports served as the focal points at which immigrants and manufactured articles from the Mother County converged for redistribution in the New World, while through them the produce of rural and frontier settlements found its way to distant markets. The colonial town was primarily a commercial community with its daily exchange of goods—a community of market places, warehouses, wharves and shops.[41]

These towns were dominated by a merchant group whose ties were not with the bureaucracy of England, as those of Québec were with the church and state in France, but rather with the merchant class in London and the West Country port towns. As Bernard Bailyn has clearly shown, ties were constantly reinforced between the merchant groups in the English towns on both sides of the Atlantic; the motivations of the economic life of London or Bristol were immediately reflected in Boston or Philadelphia. Cities on the Charles or the Delaware constantly resisted any high-handed assertion of a hierarchical subjugation of New World activities to rural production alone, or even in the main.[42] If the employment of mercantile economic practices for the production of wealth was the right of the English, it was so in each geographical world they might reside in. The result was that the towns were the key to the use of the American colonies as a settlement for English migrants. Those people came to the New World mainly as freemen, seeking greater personal liberty—as much economic as religious. Thus, the analogy with the medieval bastides was most direct. *Stadtluft macht frei* ("City air makes one free") was not the motto of these pilgrims only because they did

41. Ibid., p. 26.
42. Bernard Bailyn, *The New England Merchants in the Seventeenth Century* (New York: Harper Torchbooks, 1964).

not think in German, not because the concept was foreign to them. The perpetuation of feudal servitude as found in the Laurentian colonies of France would have destroyed whatever pull the New World offered to English settlers. Where assisted passage was necessary, it was accomplished through indentured servitude for a fixed period of years rather than by the direct transfer of continuing feudal practice to America, as in Canada. In Maryland, for example, the Calverts' attempt to recreate the manorial system with feudal duties came to nought.

The Planted Town in New England

Provincialism is a term that has lost virtually all of its meaning in modern America; every region has its distinctive qualities but none is enclosed, distinct, and sufficient unto itself as were the English counties and colonies in the seventeenth century. Additionally, today we do not find the sharp contrasts in degree of development that once existed. Few now would think Boston the cultural hub or New York the fulcrum for commercial concerns, as they were in the eighteenth and nineteenth centuries, and the rest of the land a provincial backwater. Yet in the early years of American settlement, the province was far more real than was "America" as a concept of spatial integration. "The conditions of settlement and of development within each colony meant that each evolved its individual social and political system. Geographical isolation, the date and character of the several settlements, the degree of absence of outside supervision or control—all had their effect in ultimately developing thirteen separate legal systems."[43] The contrast in urbanization among the thirteen colonies was so sharp that the more earnest efforts of the middle colonies to copy English law could also be related to like efforts of the Chesapeake colony to reestablish the feudal social basis on which that English law was originally founded—the concept of the landed estate, the landed elite, and the geographically bound working class.

In England, as in Europe in the Middle Ages, attachment of a labor force—and thereby a potential military levy—to a rural area was written into law, broadly as serfdom but with local variants almost without end. In the Chesapeake and Carolina colonies a similar attachment was eagerly sought, first through the indenture of agricultural servants brought to America from England, Scotland, Ireland, or the Continental possessions of the monarch, but ultimately by actual enslavement of forcibly transported Africans. Certainly the ability to enforce continued rural residence and legal attachment to a local commercial-agricultural estate made slavery too attractive for any moral resistance among the economic and social traditionalists of the South. In such a context it is not surprising that Southerners, with a semimanorial economy, resisted the building of towns, took on most energetically the manorial system of England, with its particular law and courts for

43. George L. Haskins, *Law and Authority in Early Massachusetts* (1960), quoted in Lawrence M. Friedman, *A History of American Law* (New York: Simon and Schuster, 1973), pp. 30–31.

its enforcement, and shaped a fundamentally anti-urban society.[44] Whether or not they knew the phrase *Stadtluft macht frei*, they certainly knew the concept of a city's providing freedom, and resisted the creation of cities for that reason.

In New England the law reflects a very different practice. Two interesting innovations took place. Instead of depending on an English common law drawn from a kingdom run with paramount concern for the landed economy and its aristocracy, "Massachusetts law was not common law at all, but a new-made system of law based on the Bible."[45] The biblical commonwealth was envisioned as actually operating there, starting in 1629 when the Puritans established their settlement, more than a decade before that biblical polity became a reality in England.

The other innovation was that Massachusetts came well ahead of England in incorporating commercial law into its judicial concern. "When the colonies were first settled, the *law merchant*—the rules and practices of commercial law—had not been fully 'received' into common law, that is, by the royal courts of England." Yet as early as 1647 Massachusetts began to enforce that law merchant as it was not enforced in England.[46] Thus, Massachusetts and by emulation its neighbors—New Hampshire, Rhode Island, and Connecticut—became biblical commonwealths of a merchant class. For them geographical attachment of labor was anathema, for its irrationality in an entrepreneurial society. Only indolence and sloth need be condemned. As a result laws were quickly adopted against idleness,[47] leading to the "warning off" of uninvited migrants from afar,[48] and generally against the powers of wealthy leisure as contrasted with earnest labor and productivity.

The Form of the New England Town: The Bastidal Model

Although the settlers on the wild western shore of the Atlantic had experienced both the bastidal form (Salisbury, Hull, and the London-towns in northern Ireland) and the organic town, they tended to make their choice on the basis of terrain. Because the Shawmut peninsula, where Boston was placed, was outlined by coves and possessed of sharp rises up the side of

44. For a discussion of the manorial law and courts of Maryland see ibid., p. 40, which notes that even a truly medieval piepowder court was organized at St. Mary's, the first provincial capital.

45. Ibid., p. 30.

46. Ibid., p. 69.

47. The *Laws and Liberties of Massachusetts* of 1648 required that no person shall "spend his time idlely or unprofitably under pain of such punishment as the Court of Assistants or County Court shall think meet to inflict." Quoted in Friedman, *History of American Law*, p. 70.

48. The resistance to newcomers was in part a fear for the welfare responsibility they might ultimately pose. After a residence of three months they had created an "establishment" entitling them to poor relief. To avoid this the newcomer might, if of questionable estate, be "warned out," thus removing the local responsibility. (Josiah H. Benton, *Warning Out in New England* [1911], cited in ibid.) Much as this was a concern under the poor law, we may reasonably infer that if labor were much desired the concern for labor would greatly outweigh the unease with respect to the poor law. After all, in such a grim frontier society as Worcester County, Massachusetts, 6,764 persons were "warned out" between 1737 and 1788 (Benton, *Warning Out*, p. 59), when the numbers of those physically unfit for labor must have been small indeed.

drumlins, an irregular siting of houses grew up along easily traversed paths. Thus, Boston's essential design was set as organic. At the same time, in Newtown (Cambridge) a short distance away, the bastidal form was adopted on a flat site.

In New England, particularly in Massachusetts, we must distinguish between the universally used basic modular component of town founding— the house of essentially late-medieval form constructed of wood—and the way those units were collected together into a town. That act of collection could conform to terrain and to readily apparent functional assemblies—as in Boston—leading to the truly organic layout so much the norm for the merchant towns of Europe in the Middle Ages.

These places were not formless or shapeless, and they most assuredly were not laid out by cows, as is so inaccurately asserted. Rather, they were places where the functional needs of the time were given free rein and where the guiding concern must have been to furnish for the greatest number of settlers the closest and most equal access to the one essential part of the town—the waterfront. If we reflect on the Boston pattern at its beginning in 1630 and immediately thereafter, the point of initiation was one of a series of coves where land-sea connection was made first on the beach, and soon at the sides of wharves extended out to adequately deep water. From that cove, houses stretched back along a path of collective will, rising up the sides of the drumlins that surrounded the landing place.

A test of this concept of morphogenesis is fortunately ready to hand in the towns of the Avalon peninsula of Newfoundland—Calvert's first colony. The same ethnic stock is involved with fairly similar economic concerns and the same freedom to evolve a pattern to meet specific contemporary needs. The persistence of squatting tenure down to the present, the practice of fishing and trading connection with the West Country of England until World War II, and the drawing of a major part of the population from English stock all contribute to a good reproduction of Boston's conditions in the seventeenth century.

From these Newfoundland towns on the Southern Shore below St. John's and around Conception Bay, a beach-oriented pattern of town layout is obvious, wherein the control feature is the beach, or a series of beaches, along which houses are ranged in close proximity. Their rather free siting disregards front lines and absolute parallelism of structures; often basically rural house forms are used in a physical fabric still more urban than rural. Not insignificantly, the only remaining seventeenth-century residence in Boston—Paul Revere's House—is actually such a rural form, with the roof slope parallel with the street and the number of windows thus somewhat restricted. The house in the Newfoundland fishing towns is rural by way of its physical separation, but strangely urban in form. Thus, the street layout is seemingly the distinctive feature of these beach-controlled towns, more than any particular house type.

If we look at Salem and Cambridge, the first of the Massachusetts Bay towns—Plymouth was settled by a different group with contrasting background and interests—we find an important element not to be observed in Boston, "established" more than laid out formally in 1630. When Salem was

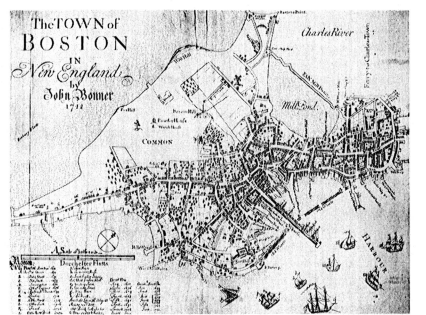

The beach layout of Boston is clearly shown in John Bonner's map of 1722, nearly a century after the town was founded in 1630.

laid out a year earlier in 1629, a proportional quality in the assignment of lands became even more clearly evident when a "Newtown" was set out on the Charles River upstream from Charlestown in 1631.

This new town was soon called Cambridge; it combined proportional land assignment with a street patterning that would encourage functional equality. "The average home lot measured about 100 by 80 feet. Most of the streets were 30 feet wide. The market square in the northwestern part of the village was approximately 150 feet by 200. Midway along the principal northwest-southeast street stood the meetinghouse on a plot only slightly larger than those allotted for houses. Virtually the entire village with its little grid-iron of streets occupied a site hardly more than 1,000 feet square. In its scale and the clear distinction between village and countryside the Cambridge plan resembles the tiny *bastide* towns of southern France or the similar settlements in Britain like Winchelsea, Flint, Salisbury, or Hull."[49] Cambridge was not a port; later, Cambridgeport developed to the east to fulfill that function, and the site was fairly level, so the bastidal form was consciously or unconsciously adopted.

Even where the bastidal layout was missing, as in Salem and other places that came to reflect the elongated (linear) town pattern first established there, fairly narrow limits to lot size were found, with none of the obvious class distinctions present in the Renaissance town. Furthermore, whichever of the two "community forms" common to New England—the bastidal or the linear—was undertaken, the layout was predicated exclusively on practical needs, with open space restricted to usefully employed units.

49. John W. Reps, *The Making of Urban America* (Princeton: Princeton University Press, 1965), p. 126.

New England saw the town common elevated to the role of a standard component, but the space was distinguished by common use rather than by abstract visual design. Thus, it was normally termed in New England a common, not a green, as outsiders consistently misname it. It existed to provide for grazing "in common," for the drilling of a militia drafted by universal conscription, and for the multitude of uses that a functioning community makes of adaptable open space. That latter-day churches came occasionally to be built on the common says merely that with the sapping of their original austere role as meeting houses for civil and religious purposes, and their consequent adoption of a modified English Renaissance architecture, churches began to have visual pretensions that could not be served by location on a house lot as they were when Cambridge was a "Newtown."

To reiterate a critical point, the layout of these New England towns differed from English precedent, save in the odd instances of the bastidal forms that existed in odd places in Britain. The towns of New England had no Big Houses, no churches on imposing sites, no designs of dominance or subordination. When Boston became the capital of the Massachusetts Bay Colony, little thought was given to constructing pompous buildings. Even when a "state house" was built in 1658, it was placed in functional, not visual, perspective. It stood in the middle of King Street and consisted of no more than the upper floor above a covered market used for daily and mundane needs. It is historically fitting indeed that Boston's Old State House, which stands even today, has in its basement a subway station for the use of Everyman. No Williamsburg Capitol this, in landscaped grounds that create isolation from the people.

Colonial New England buildings were those of the very end of the Middle Ages transferred across the ocean in the form being built just before the Great Fire of London. But the street layout of the small merchant towns being placed on the harbors of New England was different from that in the mother country. These towns were orderly in one of two ways, neither of which would have been particularly at ease in the English countryside. The structure of the linear town was usually given by some elongated natural feature—a strand line on the shore, a river front inland, the alignment on a river terrace (as in the Connecticut Valley towns), or a deeply incised valley site (as in Worcester or Fitchburg). The second layout was the simple and usually small rectangular grid reminiscent of the bastide. Linear towns sought constantly to adopt the basic features of the grid layout and more common arrangement of streets, the fundamentally bastidal form that became the American grid-pattern town. Most linear towns had thin and elongated grids aligned along with the initial strand or valley-strike street. Constraint of the physical site usually limited the expansion of the grid, rather than any turning away from that pattern. Towns such as Worcester or Providence are gridded where and to the extent possible.

The only real exception to this classification into two types of towns by street plan came where a simple road intersection in the countryside was subsequently struck with urbanization, causing the town to grow, logically, out along the roads intersecting there at acute angles. Even when the resulting pattern was one of a star-like branching of main streets, gridded infilling usually occurred between those major arterials. American towns constantly turned toward the egalitarian, economically productive bastidal layout wherever possible, even when the major skeleton of the town began as strand- or star-like.

The real character of the New England town was to be found in its vernacular architecture. This was shaped by culture and terrain, rather than by overall design of the city as in the Renaissance and Georgian "quarters." The house forms developed in Salem and Providence were essentially rural frame houses, made fashionable by a bit of Renaissance decoration, placed within small gardens sufficient to allow this urbanization of basically bucolic architecture. A rough bastidal grid, as on Federal Hill in Providence or west of the Derby Wharf in Salem, was adequate for the placement of these structures in small yards that would permit the opening of all sides to the admission of light and air and the maintenance of a basically rural architecture.

In Boston, because of the expectation of greater growth on a small peninsular site, the architecture soon began to adapt a closed-in building style. The Paul Revere House of 1676 was a country house, showing some adaptation to the city with its blind side walls; the brick row houses soon emerged to make better use of a confined site. In the 1630s we find the General Court of Massachusetts already adopting legislation permitting the building of party walls, a necessity of this sort of construction. The house in Boston evolved over the early history of the town, becoming truly urban in form. But the street system retained permanently its initial strand-line quality, however urbane the houses might become. In the same way the bastidal towns, much the more common sort in colonial times, still might maintain a rural-seeming style in the houses that lined their regularly gridded streets. A continuing interaction between houses and streets, in towns like Salem, Providence, and Newport, shaped a distinctive, organically evolving merchants' town as the model for New England.

The Emerging American Grid-Pattern Town

The bastidal form that rose in New England, when nature permitted, must be understood in cultural terms. Although the Roman towns will not serve as the most basic prototype—little military and political domination characterized colonial Anglo-America as it had Rome's and Spain's empires—we still may cite the bastide as a form akin in purpose and layout to the planted towns of colonial America. The absence of open space for visual—as opposed to practical—purposes, the modular division of town lots, the relatively egalitarian urban society and government, and the heavy economic dominance by trade all support the role of the bastide as the prototype for American town building. Particularly in New England, the historical similarities were heightened by a great tendency toward Protestantism and what Max Weber called the Protestant ethic in business practices, and the wish to advance the commonwealth. These were religious congregations in the guise of New England "towns" but they were above all else economic places. Only a relatively small fraction of the population

New Haven as it was laid out in 1638 was an American bastide with a distinctly egalitarian land assignment and an orthogonal plan. The map shows the modest development in 1748.

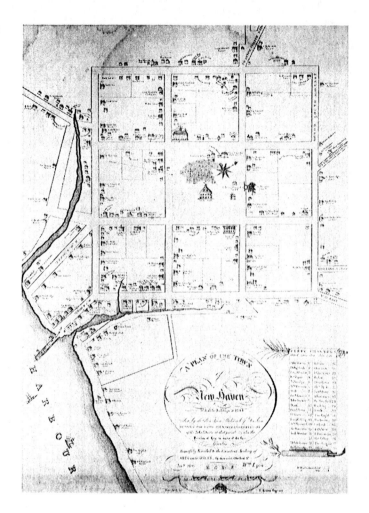

actually belonged to the Puritan consociated churches of visible saints, but all residents seem to have shared the belief in the Protestant ethic of hard work, honest dealing, and personal enrichment as a sign of God's grace.

The role of the port was so strongly the urbanizing force in New England that the strand-line alignment of streets was perhaps most common in the coastal towns. Boston, Newport, the earlier parts of Providence, and Strawberry Banke (Portsmouth, New Hampshire) display this pattern. The dockside was the point of initiation of the town; by 1645 Boston had fifteen wharves for its trade,[50] and had become the largest town in all the English colonies. New England was rich in organically patterned towns (Boston, Worcester, Fitchburg, Portsmouth, and Portland) or sections of towns (the older parts of Salem, Hartford, Providence, and Newport). The bastidal layout was even more common, particularly away from the coast (in Cambridge and Springfield) or as later increments to ports (in Salem, Providence, Newport, and even Boston). New Haven had stood a splendid example of the bastidal layout from its beginning in 1638.

Which pattern was to be adopted seems to have depended largely on (1) the presence or absence of a strand-line point of initiation, and (2) for an inland place, the availability of a relatively level site. The houses dotted along these streets, of whatever pattern, were initially late-medieval in form and wooden in construction. But as the material prosperity of the New England colonies advanced and London was rebuilt into what became a Georgian city, the architecture of that reconstruction was adapted in wood for many port towns, notably Newburyport, Salem, and Providence.

The Development of Philadelphia

By the time William Penn and his neighbors in the Jerseys and recently captured New York were setting about town founding, the models had changed from those employed two generations before in New England. Because the pattern they adopted became so dominantly the one that was spread across a continent as the American frontier advanced, the London Rebuilt model is worth describing in some detail.

Philadelphia was surveyed in 1682 and laid out as a town along the Delaware River, only to be expanded almost immediately, at Penn's order, to reach to the Schuylkill River to the west. Between the "Front streets" at either river, a rank of 22 blocks was set out spreading for eight tiers north-south, or a total of 176 street blocks in an area measuring one mile by two. One main street of one-hundred-foot width, then labeled High Street, though subsequently called Market, extended from river to river. Eleven blocks west of the Delaware and eleven east of the Schuylkill, a north-south street of the same width, Broad Street—then as now—was run. The center of the town was at the crossing of these hundred-foot streets, which were twice as broad as the ordinary ways. "In the Center of the City is a Square of ten Acres; at each Angle [of that square] are to be Houses for Publick Affairs, as a Meeting-House, Assembly or State-House, Market-House, School-House, and several other Buildings for Publick Concerns. There are also in each Quarter of the City a Square of eight Acres, to be for the like Uses, as the Moore-fields in London; and eight Streets (besides the High-street), that run from Front to Front, and twenty Streets, (besides the Broad-street) that run across the City, from side to side; all these Streets are of Fifty Foot breadth."[51]

At first glance this layout might seem to be the adoption of a Renaissance visual city as the "American standard," but such an impression would be highly deceptive. Philadelphia was regular and proportional, and offered sites for public buildings. But from the number of "Houses for Publick Affairs" listed for siting around the main square, clearly they could be only fairly modest individually. The four other squares were specifically intended for public use, rather than restricted to access by householders living around them, as were the residential squares of London.

51. *A Short Advertisement upon the Situation and extent of the City of Philadelphia and the Ensuing Plat-form thereof, by the Surveyor General* (London, 1683), quoted in Reps, *Urban America*, p. 161.

Moorfields had originally been a swampy area beyond the walls of the City of London where refuse was dumped throughout much of the late Middle Ages. When its surface rose to the point that the land drained reasonably, the "moor-field" came to be used for bow shooting and other sports engaged in by the city populace. "The citizens [of London] acquired the right of prescription to the fields, although they were not by any means the property of the City." Yet by 1592 Parliament determined "that it shall not be lawful to any person or persons to inclose or to take in any parte of the Common or Waste Groundes scituate lienge or beinge within thre[e] Myles of any of the Gates of the saide Cittie of London" ("An Acte againste newe buyldings," 1592).[52]

So the squares of Philadelphia were for a purpose no different from that of the Boston Common. That area had been set aside at the settlement of the town and guaranteed against further diminution in size four years later when the Town Meeting decided on March 30, 1640, that no further encroachment by gardens or buildings could be cut out of "the open ground of Common field."[53] The squares of Quaker Philadelphia were more regular, but their purpose was the one that had kept open ground available around medieval London and had brought it to the heart of Boston a generation before. To read a great Renaissance "design" purpose into the squares of Philadelphia seems hardly justified by contemporary intentions.

Philadelphia's orderliness was that of a merchant seeking to rationalize units of sale and make them of sufficiently standard form that purchases could be made sight unseen. Penn was anxious to sell lots to Englishmen who never departed the island's shores, as well as to those migrating. His desire was greatly aided by the standardization of house lots in the new town, whose plat he had largely decreed if not surveyed. In this concern for distant disposal of land, Penn was truly the father of the American speculative town, and the originator of a lineage of development quite distinct from that of the medieval bastide and the New England town. In those places, strong pressure was exerted or it was outright required that the landowner be a resident of the town where his land stood. Penn importuned his absentee landowners: "The Improvement of the place is best measur'd by the advance of Value upon every man's Lot. . . . And though it seems unequal that the Absent should be thus benefited by the Improvements of those that are upon the place, especially when they have serv'd no Office, run no hazard, nor as yet defray'd any Public charge, yet this advantage does certainly redound to them, and whoever they are they are the great Debtors to the Country."[54] Thus, the order and system of Philadelphia's layout was that of the merchant class addressing at a distance an investing class of capitalists, rather than, as in Boston, a merchant class seeking to found a New World mercantile system such as was carried by those coming across the ocean to set up in Massachusetts Bay. Such a difference most likely explains the contrast between the morphogenesis of the New England town—be it linear or bastidal—with its resident commonwealth, and that of Pennsylvania with its

52. Rasmussen, *London*, pp. 81–82.
53. Bridenbaugh, *Cities in the Wilderness*, p. 21.
54. William Penn, *A Further Account of the Province of Pennsylvania* (London, 1685), quoted in Reps, *The Making of Urban America*, p. 167.

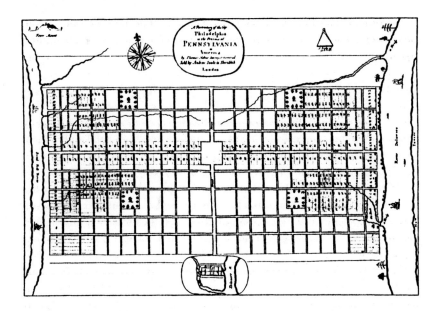

strong admixture of Quaker theology and Quaker capitalism. Theology was present in New England, but capitalism was somewhat muted in a society of more economic land assignment, which clearly assumed that land was bestowed for and at the time of use, not as a speculative commodity, as in the Quaker town.

William Penn seems at first to have envisaged an open place when he decreed, "Let every house be pitched in the middle of its plot so that there may be ground on each side for gardens or orchards or fields, that it may be a green countrie towne that will never be burnt and always be wholesome."[55] But Philadelphia did not grow that way. As laid out, the blocks in the Quaker City measured usually 425 feet wide east-west and between 500 and 675 feet north-south, with the shorter blocks located adjacent to High Street.[56] The lots seem to have been fairly small; those in the second block back from the Delaware River averaged around 48 feet in frontage, while those on the waterfront—which were to be used for warehouses—were similarly around 100 feet in frontage. Along High Street, original frontages seem somewhat more ample, perhaps between 140 and 150 feet. Everywhere the sense given by the 1682 map of Philadelphia is that of a town with fairly small lots and a great degree of standardization. At first the lots were the site of such modest structures that crowding was not great. But soon, "in older sections large three-storied brick houses and other buildings began to replace the 'mean and low' frame or brick structures of earlier years. A sign of overcrowding in these areas was the gradual appearance of tenement houses; in 1772 four of them were erected on Front Street and two on Second." The evidence is not extensive but subdivision of lots must have taken place, and certainly before long the row house was introduced, filling the street frontage with a continu-

55. Quoted in Struthers Burt, *Philadelphia: Holy Experiment* (Garden City, N.Y.: Doubleday, Doran, 1945), p. 37.

56. Reps, *The Making of Urban America*, p. 163 and fig. 97.

The Prince's
Capital and the
Merchants' Town

ous façade of buildings. Land was increasing in value and Christopher Saur told in 1724, "House rent is high because the houses are all built of bricks."[57]

The Nature and Intent of the Philadelphia Model

All the faults of speculative town development in America during the three succeeding centuries cannot be blamed on William Penn and the plan he so earnestly fostered for Philadelphia. His plan had virtues, and many others have contributed less well-intentioned changes to the Philadelphia model of urbanization. Nonetheless, the fairly hardheaded developmental notions first advanced in the Quaker City were adopted enthusiastically and applied widely. Penn's writings do not omit even the notion of profiting from the development of a religious haven. He castigated Pennsylvania for what it had cost him, tending to disregard the fact that the sales of land there even in his lifetime were very considerable—over $100,000 alone for lands outside the city on a grant he secured in recompense for a debt of £16,000, a debt hardly likely to have fetched a full return if sought in money. This proprietorial colony was run from England, and was characterized by both the practice of leasehold and the assessment of quitrents. Whatever his philanthropic purposes, Penn also sought to enlarge his competence; in doing so, he devised a system of town founding that could be widely used by others who might have interests purely for gain. Again, the contrast with New England is sharp. Philadelphia became a town of small lots with continuous ranks of houses, rather than the open, far greener towns of New England Puritanism.

What, then, were the elements of the Philadelphia model? First, it permitted the rapid, simple, and determinate division of larger landholdings into small parcels that might be verbally described and sold to others. In New England, *land utilization* seems to have been the main test of the forms of land division; in Philadelphia, *land sale* probably determined the form. Furthermore, land was raised to the status of a commodity, which might be standardized, precisely described, and reasonably appraised as to value from afar. That factor dominated the design. Quite unlike the situation in the medieval bastides or their successors in Cambridge and elsewhere in New England, Philadelphia was a promoter's town, of a size completely different from the milieu in which it was set. When Boston and New York were tiny places half a mile across, Philadelphia was laid out two miles deep and a mile wide, a size not the least inferior to that of large European cities, and twice that of the City of London. It is usually said that Philadelphia had its extensive form with the purpose of providing an open, healthy, and green town over an extensive area. Yet the scale of lots even in 1682, and more apparently a few years later, suggests that the conservative consumption of economically valuable land was intended, as if land were the main commodity on which investments might be recouped and fortunes enhanced.

The basic layout of Philadelphia, and thereby the model based on that town's founding, had reasonably but not excessively wide streets. London

57. Quoted in Bridenbaugh, *Cities in the Wilderness*, pp. 305–6.

reconstructed after the Great Fire had streets nearly as wide as those of Philadelphia. We must infer that William Penn's father, who was engaged in a speculation to bring wooden deals from Scotland to London to be sold in supply of the reconstruction,[58] knew all about that reconstruction. The committee established to determine the regulations for the rebuilding of London settled upon a series of street widths between sixteen feet for alleys and a hundred feet for the "high and principal streets," figures similar to the fifty- and hundred-foot widths in Philadelphia.[59] Although we cannot argue that Penn foresaw the continuous façades with uniform front lines that became typical of Philadelphia, he would have known what the reconstruction of England's metropolis had produced: "Houses rose singly, as landowners or tradesmen were able to find money [for rebuilding]. With here a finished building standing alone and next to it uncovered sites, the town for some years wore the appearance of a crazy patchwork; but the work was good. The houses keyed correctly one to another in continuous streets, precaution having been taken that all breast-summers should range of an equal height house to house, breaking only where ordered by the Surveyors. Roofs in the same way were made uniform."[60] Certainly the scale of the lots in the New World metropolis seems more appropriate to this continuous band of houses than the detached house found in New World towns, where the lots were generally wider. As has been shown by the architectural historian William Murtagh, "The regularized face which resulted [from the reconstruction of London] is startling close to the type of domestic architecture associated with colonial Philadelphia." Murtagh notes that both pre and postfire types of buildings were employed by settlers in Pennsylvania, but row housing emerged less than a decade after foundation when, around 1691, Budd's Long Row was constructed on Front Street between Walnut and Dock streets. Murtagh quotes John F. Watson's 1830 description: "The houses of Budd's row, were all two stories, were first framed in heavy timber and filled with bricks. The wood was, however, concealed and only showed the lintels or plate pieces over the windows and doors, which were covered with mouldings; the uprights for windows and doors were grooved into that cross timber, and looked like ordinary door and window frames."[61] These houses were essentially medieval in style, but their assembly into blocks was a harbinger of the modern city, quite likely founded on practices begun in earnest in London after the fire. Workers constructing these row houses would probably have been trained in the construction of the past, but the landowners and surveyor were cognizant of the way the rebuilt City of London was being shaped. The key to Philadelphia's morphogenesis was not so much building technique as the plot and block assemblages that came to be the "American norm" founded on a "Philadelphia model," which was in truth the London Rebuilt model.

Penn had laid out a city of vast extent broken into superblocks of long frontages. Soon those blocks were subdivided by cutting additional streets

58. Bell, *Great Fire*, p. 279

59. Rasmussen, *London*, p. 119.

60. Bell, *Great Fire*, p. 292.

61. William John Murtagh, "The Philadelphia Row House," *Journal of the Society of Architectural Historians* 16, no. 4 (1957): 8.

and narrowing the individual frontages. From the early colonial period, evidence survives of a merging of construction style and land division; we know what was done but not exactly why it came about. The colonial houses of Philadelphia were "seldom more than sixteen feet on any dimension," and they might be assembled two to the initial lot, the one lying behind approached by an alleyway. "With the rapid growth of the city, the large blocks of Holmes' original plan were subdivided into smaller portions by secondary streets. The urban lot which resulted from further subdivision of these smaller blocks was the same narrow lot which also existed in England [sic] after the Fire." The lots were not merely narrow, but also quite deep. Murtagh found them four to five times as deep as wide in a random sample.[62] If we accept the value of around sixteen feet as the construction module in these colonial houses, it is easy to understand why the sixteen-foot frontage became the modal figure for towns laid out on the Philadelphia model.

The tight packing of houses along street frontages came early in Philadelphia history, and stood quite in contrast to New England practices. Save for Boston, the Puritan towns still were characterized by houses of broader base, almost certainly detached and standing in a fairly ample garden, and constructed of wood. The medieval technology of heavy corner posts with mortised beams let into them, with weatherboard covering ("clapboards" in New England), was used in the northern colony well into the nineteenth century. Thus, it seems hard to believe that in the even better-timbered Delaware Valley, brick building was required by the shortage of readily available and relatively cheap lumber. Instead, the speculative recourse to narrow lots seemingly made brick building necessary in order to avoid recurrent fires.

Once such brick row housing had evolved, the standard construction and layout of the city in the Middle Atlantic colonies, and subsequent states, were fixed. Ranging from New Brunswick and Trenton on the north to Philadelphia, Chester, Wilmington, Baltimore, and Georgetown on the south, the row-house towns were developed. Similar assemblages of houses on lots and street frontages were to be found in the Hudson Valley, along with some inheritance from Dutch city building, which was, as we saw in Amsterdam, equally dependent on narrow lots built up in brick row housing. But in the New Netherlands, brick building was probably carried on more from habit brought from Holland than from the absolute needs of fire protection and the utilization of narrow frontages introduced by land speculation. In time, however, the speculative urge must have arrived, encouraging the use even on Manhattan of the Philadelphia (London Rebuilt) model of town layout for maximum land capitalization.

The English Renaissance in America: The Third Model

We have already noted the great problem Southern proprietors experienced in creating towns within their colonies. The first real town built south of the Mason-Dixon line was located at the confluence of the Ashley and

62. Ibid., p. 9.

Cooper rivers in South Carolina where, in the reign of the second King Charles, a town was precisely laid out in his honor. Around the year 1672, Lord Anthony Ashley-Cooper, for the Carolina proprietors, instructed the governor of the colony to lay out a town on the peninsula between the two rivers. As in Philadelphia a few years later, this instruction was issued from afar by a land developer rather than by a group of planted settlers. The intention was to create a port through which goods could pass to and from the large landed estates being set out on the Carolina coastal plain. On those plantations the proprietors were attempting to establish a direct and highly self-conscious extension of feudal England under a plan whose social and political organization came from the reactionary pen of John Locke. Attempts were made to create a neofeudal class of "landgraves" and "caciques" supervising a serfdom of "leet-men" who would plow the fields and raise the crops that were to support a new rural aristocracy in leisure.

Fortunately, much of this plan failed to come into being, but on its malign foundation grew the slavery for which South Carolina became the most ardent champion, and, as well, the political and social domination of the colony by a small rural oligarchy, which made true democracy unknown in this part of the South until the last few years. With such a rural domination, towns might never have emerged in the South without the need for import of luxuries for an increasingly wealthy rural aristocracy and export of the commercial crops of rice, indigo, and, later, cotton, which paid for such refinement to be brought from England. Charleston was little needed at first, when "prior to 1710 the produce of the [South Carolina] colony was considerably diversified, the principal exports being deerskins to England, and pork, corn, a few naval stores and lumber to Barbados."[63] But the provisioning trade for the West Indies could prove very profitable even in the early years. And the deerskin trade was of utmost importance until interrupted by the Yamassee War in 1715, which not only cut off the peltery but also threw many outlying settlers back upon the protection of Charleston. Despite these problems and fluctuations, the Carolinians were wealthy enough to import £150,000 worth of goods, largely from England, in 1718. And when the rice trade between the Carolinas and the West Indies began in earnest soon thereafter, the base was created for a port concerned with the shipment of a staple and the return of manufactures—usually in fair quantities for a basic material such as cloth, or in tiny lots for the luxuries of the planter class.[64]

Given the Lockean grand design for Carolina society and the proprietorial quest for return on investment and privilege, a town must be built. On Ashley-Cooper's orders, Charleston was laid out:

> The Town is run out into four large streets. The Court house which
> we are now building is to be erected in the middle of it, in a
> Square of two ackers of land upon which the four great streets of 60
> foot wide doe center, and to the water side there is laid out 60 foot
> for a publick wharfe as also for other conveniences as a Church

63. Bridenbaugh, *Cities in the Wilderness*, p. 32.
64. Ibid., p. 177–78.

yard, Artillery ground, etc., and without there is care taken that the front lines be preserved whereby wee shall avoid the undecent and incommodius irregularities which other Inglish colonies are fallen unto for want of ane early care in laying out the Townes.[65]

Certainly this early Charleston was the germ of the "designed" city then gripping the aristocratic mind of England. But it was not the true speculator's town, such as Penn laid out a couple of years later, wherein a vast area out of all proportion to any demand yet experienced in the New World was set out and made ready for sale. The Carolina proprietors seem to have had in mind a "Grand Modell" for the town but were never willing to make the investment it would require. Instead, they urged orderly design upon the residents and kept their own purses firmly closed. Only when the Carolina plantation economy began to burgeon could the exhortation be taken up in earnest and effected, by a native aristocracy who anxiously sought the approbation of the class in England from which the proprietors were drawn. Like that English oligarchy, they were forced into the city during a "Season," a periodic migration for which a new "Grand Modell" had grown up in London's West End.

Why did the Carolina planters repair to the the city during a Season? The expansion of field cultivation in that province came first in dramatic terms through the production of rice to supply staple food to the sugar islands of the English and Dutch in the West Indies, and to Surinam. Given the hot, very humid summer climate of the Carolina coastal plain, malaria and other fevers were encouraged even further by the waterlogged cultivation of rice; those of wealth and leisure who could sought to leave the plantation during the fever season, shaping a periodic social congregation at the better-ventilated and somewhat drier town near the coast. The Charleston merchants, already trying to create a local-aristocrat caste, were aided by this seasonal influx of the planting aristocracy, the class most revered in the neofeudal society of South Carolina. The impact on city design is obvious: they sought to create a subtropical "West End" fronting on the Cooper River, with large houses built in a consistent pattern on sites that could clearly be ranked, as to precedence, by those carefully erecting the social pyramid Charleston society became. As so rarely occurs, the merchants' town lost out to the aristocrats, but only because the merchants wished to be included in that class.[66]

The shaping of the aristocratic quarter in London, Bristol, and other English county towns had created the layout and house design that architectural historians call the English Renaissance in its earlier phases and Georgian in its later. These quarters were quite consciously "designed," with careful determination of the accepted architecture, lot and street-frontage assembly, and overall form of the quarter. These morphological elements were impressed upon the city from above, rather than evolving through the actual functioning of the place. In this way the classic division between the merchants' town and that of the leisured class had to come about before the

65. Maurice Mathews in 1680, quoted in Reps, *London*, p. 177.
66. Bridenbaugh, *Cities in the Wilderness*, p. 417.

Renaissance design could be erected into a social necessity, which could be used as a measure of the worthiness for admission to status, class, and culture of a particular group. In London's West End, the system reached its most evolved form, taking on subdivisions probably found nowhere else. But as the American South developed, with its all too conscious effort to borrow distinction through emulation of the English gentry, the morphology of social acceptance was ready to hand. The transformation of Charleston, particularly in the one hundred and fifty years between the Yamassee War (1715) and the Civil War, demonstrates how social striving could shape a city. The number of examples that we might find in England—Brighton, Bath, Buxton, Eastbourne, Harrowgate, and Cheltenham, to name only the more obvious—is great but, to America's more egalitarian good fortune, the number here was far smaller.

The English Renaissance town in colonial times was probably the only form taken by these towns of emulation; later in our history, others arose such as the "shingle style" house of Newport, Narrangansett Pier, Bar Harbor, and Pasadena, which created a new architectural expression of the social striving. But we shall examine the English Renaissance town of the colonial South. In that era and region, four towns must be noted as conforming most strongly with the English Renaissance model—the two Chesapeake Bay capitals, Annapolis and Williamsburg, and the two South Atlantic neofeudal "towns," Charleston and Savannah.

In the history of Virginia and Maryland, many efforts were made to found towns during the first half-century or so of settlement, most of which proved stillborn and all of which were stunted. Jamestown, the oldest English settlement in the thirteen colonies, was certainly one of the feeblest. In 1662 orders from England sought to make the town more presentable as the capital of a colony already half a century under development. An "Act for building a towne" was passed and Jamestown was ordered to be so recast:

> That the towne to be built shall consist of thirty two houses, each
> house to be built with brick, forty feet long, twenty foot wide, with-
> in the walls, to be eighteen foote high above the ground, the walls
> to be two brick thick to the water table, and a brick and a halfe
> thick above the water table to the roofe, the roofe to be fifteen foote
> pitch and to be covered with slate or tile.
> That the houses shall be all regularly placed one by another in
> a square or such other forme as the honorable Sir William Berkeley
> [the governor] shall appoint most convenient.[67]

The individual Virginia counties were each expected to build one of the Jamestown houses, and all sorts of subventions and exertions were envisaged to accomplish the creation of a proper provincial capital. But in 1676 the embittered small holders of Bacon's Rebellion burned Jamestown to the ground, putting an end to a notoriously unsuccessful experiment at town founding. When Bacon's forces were defeated after their captain's untimely

67. William Henning, *The Statutes at Large . . . of Virginia* (New York, 1832), 2: 172, quoted in Reps, *The Making of Urban America* p. 93.

The Prince's
Capital and the
Merchants' Town

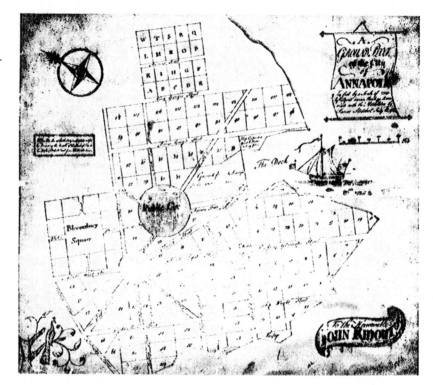

death, Governor Berkeley viciously hanged thirty-seven of their leaders, causing that none-too-timid monarch Charles II to comment, "That old fool has hanged more men in that naked country than I have done for the murder [*sic*] of my father."[68]

This grim farce had only one fortunate consequence—the final destruction of Jamestown, which, in its seventy years of trying to be a town, had been uncomfortable, unhealthy, and notoriously ungrowing. In its place, a new capital would have to be laid out: that job was done by Berkeley's more astute and intelligent successor, Francis Nicholson, who had just completed a similar job for Maryland where previously he had served as governor.

When Nicholson became governor of Maryland in 1694, he had behind him a considerable knowledge of the fashionable quarters of London (he is believed to have been the natural son of the duke of Bolton) and of Paris (where he went frequently as a diplomatic courier). Arriving in Maryland, he secured passage of legislation establishing two new towns, one of which was named originally for Lord Baltimore's wife, Ann Arundel, but was subsequently named instead for Princess Anne, soon to reign in her own right. Annapolis, the new town, became the provincial seat, and Nicholson assured that its design would befit the capital of an aristocratic province of landed manors.

The plan of the town may well have been Nicholson's; we do know that he

**The
Continuing City**

68. S. E. Morison and H. S. Commager, *The Growth of the American Republic* (New York: Oxford University Press, 1942), 1: 80.

superintended the construction of a town with two massive "circles" and a "Bloomsbury Square" of 350 feet on a side. The "Public Circle" was over five hundred feet in diameter and soon became the site of the provincial capitol, while the "Church Circle" was one of about three hundred feet. Streets radiated from these circles, though Reps points out that they did not always line up with the center of the circle, assuring the visually impressive focus so desired by Renaissance planners. Nonetheless, the town of Annapolis was an obviously visual construction, set out to impress with its plan and to assert a haughty dominance of those entering from the countryside. The place was small compared with Philadelphia, about 25 rather than 176 blocks within the initial design; some blocks were quite small in contrast to the superblocks of the Quaker City. The town plat was about three thousand feet by twenty-five hundred feet, little more than a quarter of a square mile, in the face of the two square miles of Penn's capital. The lots were large in Annapolis—outside the 9 unnumbered lots ranged around Bloomsbury Square, only 108 numbered lots were included in the original layout.[69]

Clearly Lord Baltimore's capital was more a town for the gentry than one to meet the vast expectations of the merchant class. A Maryland law of 1695 had specified "that when any baker, brewer, tailor, dyer, or any such tradesmen, that, by their practice of their trade, may any ways annoy, or disquiet the neighbors or inhabitants of the town, it shall and may be lawful for the commissioners and trustees . . . to allot and appoint such tradesmen such part or parcel of land, out of the present town pasture, as . . . shall seem meet and convenient for the exercise of such trade, a sufficient distance from the said town as may not be annoyance thereto."[70] The adoption of such a provision would have been most unlikely in Massachusetts, and its implementation unthinkable. But the Maryland capital, as a town of social collection and emulation, must be, as was Georgian London's West End, sheltered from the merchant's world. The plan, the background of the designer, and the early history of Annapolis all support the view that the town was set out in the English Renaissance style for the housing of the socially elevated.

Before the layout of Annapolis was completed, Francis Nicholson was appointed governor of Virginia. With Jamestown—or what had not already rotted away from neglect of an initially misplaced town—largely destroyed by the firebrands of the rebelling farmers, he could plan a second capital, at Williamsburg, near the college he had earlier aided in founding. Nicholson persuaded the legislature to place its new capital at Middle Plantation between the James and the York rivers on a site with a design on which he almost certainly exerted the dominant influence. Two impressive buildings—the Capitol and the Governor's Palace—were set at the end of open vistas, the first at the eastern closing of Duke of Gloucester Street, ninety-nine feet wide, and the second at the north end of the Palace Green, two hundred feet wide and about a thousand feet long. Houses fronting on

69. These computations are taken from the "Plan of Annapolis, Maryland: 1718" given in Reps, *The Making of Urban America*, as fig. 62.

70. "An Act for Keeping Good Rules and Orders in the Port of Annapolis," quoted in ibid., p. 106.

To the Hon.ble the Trustees for establishing the Colony of Georgia in America' This View of the Town of Savanah is humbly dedicated by their Honours Obliged and most Obedient Servant. Peter Gordon.

Duke of Gloucester Street were to be uniform in face and impressive in design.

Throughout the description of the town—in the specifications of the act creating the capital and in contemporary accounts—runs the desire to make this as strutting a place as its small number of inhabitants would permit. It was to be a government town, laid out to serve that purpose, and intended only for the social class that had much voice in the running of a proprietorial province before the American Revolution. Thus, not insignificantly, in 1779 while the war was still going on the Commonwealth of Virginia deliberately abandoned Williamsburg in favor of Richmond. In part, this move was the result of the shift of the economic heart of Virginia westward into the Piedmont, but it was as well a turning away from the town so ostentatiously the seat of an arrogant king's haughty lieutenant. Richmond grew rapidly and in much more characteristic clothing for an American city—in the working attire of the merchants' town, where the government met only occasionally and not for too long.

The final English Renaissance town in the South was Savannah, which grew up to support the cotton kingdom that emerged after Eli Whitney's invention, in that city, of the cotton gin. Savannah did not begin in the form of a trader's town but rather as an English Renaissance place to serve a social experiment. James Oglethorpe sought to salvage the debtor class from the barbaric practices of eighteenth-century England by combining humanity with defense of the realm and expansion of the settlement frontier. Resettling debtors would take them out of English prisons, provide a market for English goods and a source of staples for English manufacture, and defend rich Carolina from the Spaniards of Florida. "In June 1732, King George II, convinced that the new colony would be good politics as well as good works, granted the vacant lands south of Carolina to twenty-one trustees for twenty-one years and modestly gave it the benefit of his name, Georgia."[71]

An enthusiastic effort was made to shape a new society through the imposition of a utopian morphology: six "wards" of the town were confidently expected to be needed as the colony grew. Savannah's wards were an intellectual creation distinctly different from the design of the speculator's Philadelphia. The ward as adopted was some six hundred feet on a side, little larger than Penn's original superblocks, and divided sensibly into four residential blocks of three hundred-foot length, called "tythings," whose depth of slightly more than two hundred feet was, in turn, divided by an alleyway of twenty-two and a half feet. Between the two ranks of two blocks bounding the ward, a square was delimited at its ends by four small blocks ultimately intended as the sites for public buildings. This assemblage of the ward was square in outer form, with straight streets; great care was given to the creation of vistas. This was the first expression of an effort that became common in nineteenth-century America—the use of a physically deterministic model to "improve" the social condition of citizens. Clearly, Georgia was the first American instance of "social refuge and reform," as opposed to religious congregation.

The houses of Savannah were small clapboard affairs not appreciably different from the simpler houses of the West Indies. The great planters' houses of those islands, which had been copied in the impressive mansions on Charleston's Battery, were originally absent from Savannah. Savannah was characterized as "an agglomeration of rural hamlets" as originally laid out, but when the rise of this town as the premier cotton port brought wealth, similar mansions were built and Savannah in turn became a place of summer refuge and social congregation for the inland planters. As such, the port remained an island of the English Renaissance in an otherwise mercantile America until it began to decline in the years following the Civil War. When mercantile activity came strongly to Georgia, it grew along the rail lines, notably in Atlanta, which was set up at the terminus of the Western and Atlantic and was clothed in the garments of a proper speculator's town, copying Philadelphia rather than London's West End.

A Useful Model for American Cities

Three broad models were used for the creation of towns in the thirteen colonies. The earliest used was the late-medieval, prefire London and

71. Ships of the Sea Museum, Savannah, *Savannah Revisited: A Pictorial History* (Athens: University of Georgia Press, 1969), p. 6.

provincial-English-town model adopted in New England. These places were economic towns but free of most of the trappings of class to be found in England. In physical form they owed a great deal to the bastide, having on reasonably level sites a forthright rectangularity, or on more broken locations greater linearity in alignment with the terrain. Like the bastides, these were cities of workers at work rather than plattings of open land in search of urbanization and speculative profit.

In social terms, the bastidal nature of the New England town became the useful, and employed, model for American urbanization. But as a physical form, the New England town was laid aside beyond the Connecticut Valley, even by those migrants to Upstate New York, the Western Reserve of Ohio, and the Upper Lakes states who took in their emigrants' wagons the concept of the biblical commonwealth represented by Massachusetts.

The physical pattern for the American city had to be found among the other two models brought from England: the English Renaissance model used in the few large towns that grew up in the South, and the London Rebuilt model used in the mercantile quarters after the fire of 1666. In the New World, the form of London Rebuilt could be made regular and expressed in a true grid pattern, looking more like the "perfect" bastides than did Cambridge, New Haven, and the other New England towns shaped in their image. The form was true in Philadelphia, but not the social structuring. As a speculator's town the Quaker City lacked the fundamental land assignment that had characterized the bastide and that became the backstay of the New England biblical commonwealth.

The great mass of urbanization took place in America west of the Appalachians. The first trans-Appalachian towns were Lexington and Louisville (1779), Pittsburgh (1784), Marietta (1788), and Cincinnati (1790), and in them a particular pattern became fixed, that of Philadelphia, or London Rebuilt. In Pittsburgh, the Penn heirs copied William's speculator's town laid down first in Philadelphia. This town at the forks of the Ohio was rectilinear with relatively small blocks, narrow and equal-size lots, and only a single public square. Its form was regular despite a constrained site within a deeply incised valley at the confluence of the Allegheny and Monongahela rivers, where the Ohio begins. The original plat[72] had ninety-four blocks, but only one open space was left; even the spectacular riverbanks were given no visual design. So much for the Penns' alleged passion for baroque design. Just as Philadelphia, its several squares notwithstanding, had less open space than "late-medieval" Boston, Pittsburgh had less open space than Louisville.

Louisville was laid out by settlers rather than speculators and, like the bastides, showed a craving for isonomic order and proportion. The first meeting of the prospective residents, held in April 1779, ordered

> that a number of lots, not exceeding 200 for the present, be laid off, to contain half an acre each, 35 yards by 70 where the ground will admit of it, with some public lots and streets.

72. Fig. 121, in Reps, *The Making of Urban America*, reproduces a plan of Pittsburgh for 1787, which is the one determined some three years earlier by the Penns.

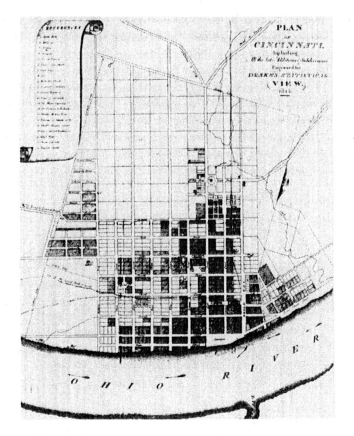

Cincinnati, as sketched in Drake's Statistical View *of 1815, was a recently established speculator's town with the rigid and fine-grained orthogonal qualities that role assumed in the American Middle West.*

That each adventurer draw for only one lot by chance. That every such person be obliged to clear off the undergrowth and begin to cultivate part thereof by the 10th of June [1779], and build thereon a good covered house, 16 feet by 20, by the 25th of December. That no person sell his lot unless to some person without one, but that it be given up to the Trustees to dispose of to some new adventurer on pain of forfeiture thereof.[73]

Unlike the Penns' towns, Louisville was not a speculator's town, yet its design was nearly the same. The Kentucky town showed strikingly the two components that were coming to make up the American model of urbanization: (1) a regular grid of small lots and moderate-size blocks, easily described, occupied, and transferred (useful to speculator and occupant alike), and (2) an urban society given to democratic land assignment and the generally liberal social, economic, and political practices characteristic of the medieval bastide.

Louisville's physical form is contained in a plan drawn in 1779, showing twenty-one blocks of house lots and twenty-one parcels of fairly equivalent size, noted as public. Seemingly the settler's bastide could be more liberal in

73. Quoted from the original minutes of the meeting in Reuben T. Durrett, *The Centenary of Louisville,* Filson Club Publication no. 8 (Louisville, 1893), p. 34.

The Prince's Capital and the Merchants' Town

its provisions for the future than was the land speculator's, however grand his stated or imputed motives. The emerging town of Louisville tended toward the lesser standards of the marketplace, but let us not confuse the relative initial generosity of popular and proprietorial intentions on this matter.

Cincinnati serves to clinch the argument for an American norm—the amalgam of bastide, London Rebuilt, and speculator's town. Dr. Daniel Drake, frequently called the "Benjamin Franklin of the West," set out in 1815 to present a *Natural and Statistical View, or Picture of Cincinnati and the Miami Country.* In the forthright manner of his mentors, Franklin and Dr. Benjamin Rush, Drake establishes the tie:

> Philadelphia seems to have been the model after which the portion of this town first laid out, was planned. Between Broadway and Western Row there are six streets, each 66 feet wide, running from the river north 16° west and lying 396 feet asunder. These are intersected at right angles by others of the same width, and at the same distance from each other; except Water and Front streets, the former of which are nearer, and the latter, on account of the brow of the *Hill,* more distant. Not a single alley, court, or diagonal street, and but one common, was laid out. The blocks or squares were each divided into eight lots, 99 by 198 feet, except those lying between Second and Third streets which were made ten lots each.[74]

Although these lots originally sold for $100 each, by 1814 "the lots in Main, from Front to Third streets, have sold at $200 per [front] foot." On a ninety-nine-foot lot, such a speculator's gain would indeed serve to increase the capital of the original owners and argue for the virtues, in a capital-deficient nation, of town speculation as a national economic endeavor.[75]

The role of such speculations in city life is well shown by Cincinnati's history as an administrative town. First bruited in 1789, the town began its existence during the 1790s. It gained the palm of a true "city" by being constituted a county seat and the site of a courthouse, built on the waterfront Common in 1802. When the courthouse burned in 1814, the county commissioners decided to move the building site nearer to the heart of the emerging town and, in turn, "sold out on perpetual lease, the whole of the public ground." The little public space included in the original plan was thereby lost.[76] The town, like most in the Middle Atlantic states, was possessed of market houses—"the two older are supported by a double, the newer by a triple, row of brick pillars"—which somewhat made up for the absence of public space. They showed as well how much the growth of

74. Daniel Drake, *National and Statistical View, or Picture of Cincinnati and the Miami Country . . . Illustrated by Maps. With an Appendix Containing Observations on the Late [New Madrid] Earthquake, The Aurora Borealis, and Southwest Wind* (Cincinnati: Looker and Wallace, 1815). Extensive portions of this rare book are reprinted in Henry D. Shapiro and Zane L. Miller, eds., *Physician to the West: Selected Writings of Daniel Drake on Science and Society* (Lexington: University Press of Kentucky, 1970), pp. 66–129. Quotation is from p. 80.

75. Ibid., pp. 81–82

76. Ibid., p. 84.

the surrounding countryside sprang from the existence of the town. Cincinnati prospered as a distant-trading town, as was clearly shown by its most impressive building in 1815:

> The most capacious, elevated and permanent building in this place, is the *Steam Mill,* erected in the years 1812, '13, and '14, under the direction of William Green, an ingenious mason and stone cutter, on a plan furnished by George Evans, one of the proprietors [of this rental property]. . . . Its height is 110 feet, and the number of stories is nine, including two above the eaves. . . . Through the building there is a wall dividing each story into two unequal apartments—the one designed for manufacturing flour; the other for receiving wool and cotton machinery, a flax seed oil mill, fulling mill, and several other machines.[77]

As the agricultural economy of southern Ohio quickly matured from clearing the forest to exporting its field products, the need for processing before shipment was obvious in a nation where transportation was primitive and costly. Cincinnati fulfilled that processing role, and took on a form that was to be repeated westward to the edge of the vast Middle West agricultural realm and in favored economic spots all the way to the Pacific. Lest there be any question as to which came first, the town of Cincinnati or the countryside that supplied its raw materials, we may wisely return directly to Daniel Drake, who had observed the truth at the time the town began: "As this town is older than the surrounding country, it has at no time had a surplus of laboring population or of capital. The former have been required to assist in clearing and improving the wilderness; the latter has been invested in lands, which from their low price and certain rise, have held out for the capitalists a powerful inducement. The conditions which are said to constitute the basis of manufacturing establishments, have not, therefore, existed in the same degree as if the town had been younger than the adjoining country."[78]

Thus, we see in Cincinnati the true nature of the town as it became a general form in the growth of the American republic. After a colonial period when three main urbanization models were adopted—along with a fourth, if we accept as a model the absence of towns found for so long in the Chesapeake Bay area before government efforts finally bore a sickly but showy fruit in Annapolis and Williamsburg—the pioneers knew what the appropriate model for settlement should be. Many of them, such as Daniel Drake's father Isaac, were crossing the Appalachians just before the Constitutional Convention to settle in Kentucky in 1788, thus entering the first "West."

That model was the speculator's town drawn largely in morphogenesis from Penn's Philadelphia but fortunately shorn of the late-medieval trappings of rural feudal tenure that never quite disappeared in the Keystone State. The role of speculation so castigated today was perhaps the most

77. Ibid., p. 86.
78. Ibid., p. 88.

hopeful tool they carried in their wagons, or on the riverboats such as Isaac Drake used to reach the West. The rise out of frontier poverty was made more rapid by the hoped-for increment of pioneering, which was the speculator's profit. But in this American model the actual settlers most commonly gained, as Louisville's first town ordinances sought to assure, rather than the distant and leisured landowners who had emerged as the social elite at the end of the Middle Ages. Their efforts to shape America as a New World extension of that rural class system of Britain and France were largely failures. Québec struggled to little avail; the Middle Colonies leaned too heavily on the land and the undesirable social stratification found to be required in the pioneer plantations; and the towns of the South sought to reproduce an economic-social system truly foreign to the emerging society and economy of the Great Republic.

In the end, a combination of New England social and economic institutions and the speculative practices initiated in the wealthy proprietors' towns of New Jersey, Pennsylvania, and Maryland was carried westward. Daniel Drake did not comment on that social and economic synthesis, probably because his father was moving westward to get away from just such an area developed for speculators from the English gentry. Isaac Drake left Plainfield, New Jersey, because as Daniel said, "My father and his brothers were not contended [sic] with their position,"[79] which was that of landless younger sons. The father sought improvement in the countryside but his son, Daniel, could see how much more hopeful was the future in the town. As he tells it,

> I was in a stage of transition from one state to another; from the rural to the civic, from the rude to the refined, from obscurity to notoriety! . . . The conception of this change was less my own than my father's. . . . His poverty he regretted; his ignorance he deplored. . . . In consulting the traditions of the family he found no higher condition than his own as their lot in past times; but he had formed a conception of something *more* elevated, and resolved on its attainment; not for himself and [my] mother, not for *all* his children—either would have been impossible—but for some member of the family. He would make a beginning; he would set his face toward the land of promise, although, like Moses, he should never enter it.[80]

To gain his end, Isaac Drake, "on a cold, damp and dreary day of December 1800 [took] fifteen year old Daniel Drake, a timid, home-loving country boy from Kentucky . . . to the home of the leading physician in Cincinnati, Ohio," to be apprenticed to a trade and to come to enjoy the fruits for which his father had fought during the Revolution and which had drawn him to the frontier, but not to his hoped-for security that would permit a reasonable standard of life and learning.[81] Only in the city could true

79. Daniel Drake, *Pioneer Life in Kentucky, A Series of Reminiscential Letters*, Ohio Valley Historical Series no. 6 (Cincinnati: Robert Clarke, 1870), p. 6. Reprinted with extensive comments by E. F. Horine (New York: Henry Schuman, 1948).

80. Ibid. (Horine edition), p. 110.

81. Ibid., p. xiii.

social mobility, with its premium of education and the broader view, be secured in this time on the frontier. Thus, we may close our consideration of the planting of the city in the American lands on this note of hopefulness that the city engendered in the minds of our ancestors, in this case in the person of my own distant grandfather, Isaac Drake. For them, the accomplishment of the general promise betokened by the physical generosity of the New World came in the social and intellectual advance to be had only in the cities of the Great Republic in the years before they became industrial metropolises.

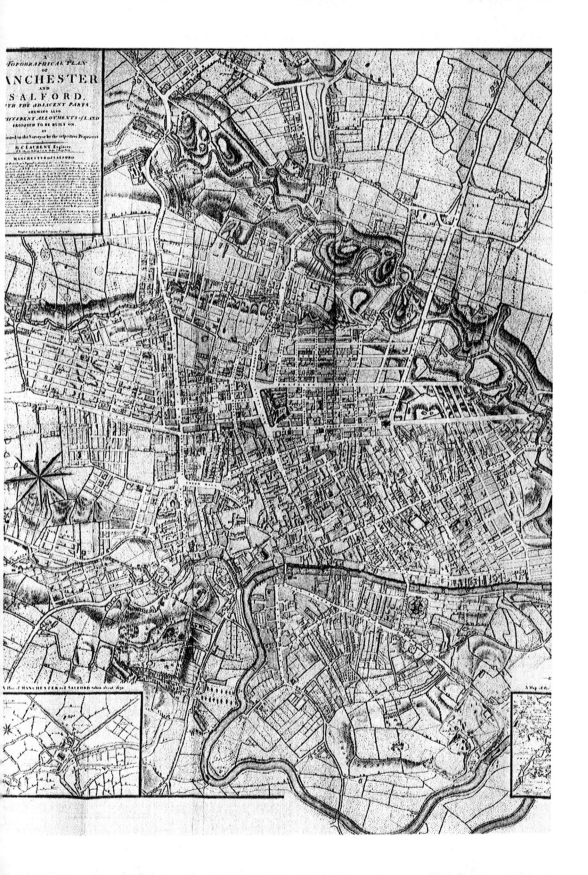

A TOPOGRAPHICAL PLAN
OF
MANCHESTER
AND
SALFORD,
WITH THE ADJACENT PARTS,
SHEWING ALSO
DIFFERENT ALLOTMENTS of LAND
PROPOSED TO BE BUILT ON.

By C LAURENT Engineer

MANCHESTER and SALFORD

The Revolution of Economy and Evolution of the City

================================

Urban Morphogenesis in the Industrial Age

7

England: Industry Comes into the City

One of the more surprising myths about the Industrial Revolution is that
this wrenching change in economic practice took place in England
outside the traditional manufacturing areas. To the extent that industrialization collected the domestic labor of country cottars into cities, this myth
might be true, but the flow of work and workers to the city was so slow as to
take at least a century to complete. Even as late as the 1860s, nails, pins,
and other traditional domestic products were still being forged in sheds
behind farmhouses in Worcestershire and Lancashire. Eventually, machine
production took over completely, but hardly by storm. Instead, the quantitative economy placed such demands on traditional trades that they could not
cope, and increments to production had to come in factories. Because
incremental labor was more readily available in cities than in the English
countryside, those new factories tended to be urban once Mathew Boulton
and James Watt's steam engines made that a possibility.

Nor were the great industrial towns of Britain all, or even dominantly, the
creation of the Industrial Revolution. Birmingham was the second town of
Warwickshire in the thirteenth century, exceeded in size only by Warwick,
the administrative center, with its castle. Similarly, Nottingham was a county and a city in medieval times, as the tale of Robin Hood shows us; he
tangled with the sheriff of Nottingham, not of Nottinghamshire. Manchester,
we know from its name, owes its origin to the Romans, and certainly Bristol,
another county-city, was well known before the Industrial Revolution.

There is some truth in the view that the Industrial Revolution shaped the
urban geography of Britain outside of London. A few new cities rose to
extreme importance under industrialization, but to a considerable degree
they were less true factory metropolises than additions brought on by the
expanding system of long-distance trade and transportation. Liverpool is an
undoubted child of the Industrial Revolution, starting as a small port on the
west coast in 1700 and outdistancing Bristol as the port of the West by 1800.
After the formal union of Scotland with England in 1707, and the grudging
and dilatory implementation of commercial equality for Scots in the English
realms, Glasgow grew greatly as a port. We should not, however, forget that
the city on the Clyde had been important even in the late Middle Ages for its
university and cathedral.

The First English Industrial "City": A Countryside of Segmental Labor

The greatest problem confronting us in viewing the urbanization of
England as a result of industrialization comes from the narrow, excessively
"historical" view of the city entertained by British observers. To them, a city
must be an important medieval creation, even though it might also have
Roman roots (as Manchester did), be possessed of a royal charter (as Manchester was not), be normally the site of a cathedral and a surrounding wall,
and serve as part of an administrative-military system intended to maintain

the king's peace and sovereignty. Yet even before the real onset of the Industrial Revolution, Manchester was larger than all but London and Bristol among the traditional British "cities." Perhaps we should examine anew the notion that Manchester, Birmingham, Leeds, and the other "factory towns" had no historical underpinnings and grew only with the development of machines and steam engines.

We must first recognize that the Industrial Revolution had several stages, extended over some two centuries. The first stage was an outward turning from the city at the end of the Middle Ages. It has been thought of as an escape from the constraints of the gild and other civic regulations, but may also have been the initial effort to create a quantitative economy. The emphasis under the gild system in medieval cities was to maintain quality and, not incidentally, prices. By projecting manufacture into the surrounding countryside, both increase in production and, to a considerable degree, reduction in the cost of the finished product could be accomplished.

Sweating labor was very real, but not necessarily the central force in reducing production cost. That reduction came as well from tapping the unused labor of the agricultural population, potential productive effort that remained after the necessary farm work had been done. The first stages of "industrialization" in the Cotswolds and other areas active under the "putting-out" system took on this pattern.

A further encouragement for this rural domestic manufacture was the survival of manor practices under which an earnest effort was made to create localized self-sufficiency on the estate. Country people determined the products they consumed mainly by what they themselves might produce. Existing "trade" tended to be between rural neighbors. Thus, the notion of manufacture had always existed in the countryside; the emerging quantitative economy in the sixteenth and seventeenth centuries could turn to supplying long-distance trading demands, once a system of trade organization and improvements in internal transportation could be shaped. Particularly in the seventeenth century, the explosive spread of Britain's trading empire shaped a mass market, while the turnpike and river navigation improvements substantially bettered internal communications. For light items or modest volumes of goods, these initial improvements, the first in transportation since Roman times, could suffice.

This incremental work, a part-time employment that went along with basic agricultural work, may be called segmental labor. We need anticipate the time of full city industrialization and distinguish *time*-segmental labor such as this in the country from *family*-segmental labor, which came when families were housed within the city and under conditions where only the father or the male members of the family might be employed in a particular industry. With time-segmental labor, the whole family likely worked on the land for a period of the year and in the nail-shed or weaving-shed at other times. If, however, the trades were specific to a particular age and sex, family-segmental labor was the practice. The occupation of spinster was so characteristically family-segmental as to supply us the term reserved for unmarried adult women, a state which the Scots seemingly consider irremediable when women reach their majority unmarried.

Urban
Morphogenesis
in the
Industrial Age

During the first stage of industrialization, the demands for goods in a quantitative economy were projected from the cities, where that new economy was understood and implemented, into the countryside surrounding them. In the countryside, the existence of vast amounts of time-segmental labor combined with the vestiges of the manorial economy made for easy expansion of hand-production of goods into a full rural domestic industrialization.

The next stage of industrialization began when the quantitative economy expanded beyond the competence of rural domestic industry, into a situation where some application of powered machinery was needed. We cannot easily select a date for that event. Fulling mills were already at work in the twelfth century. The first waterpowered fulling mill, in 1185, became for England the first known application of waterpower to a process other than grinding grain. [1] So the use of power even in textile manufacture had medieval roots.

The application of power to the making of yarns ushered in what we think of as the Industrial Revolution. We must look at the textile trade of the early eighteenth century to see what made the application of power a necessity; in doing so, we see the critical difference in system and form between medieval industrialization and that under a quantitative economy. During the Middle Ages, most manufacturers (we have called them artisans to this point) took raw staples—furs, fibers, leathers, and the like—and completed from them a finished product. If they used a partially processed staple, it was, like their own work, a product of hand labor. Thus, the scale of handworking was universal and the chance for great discrepancies in the rate of production among the various processes was somewhat held down. But with the development of a mass market, such as the one the Mercantile Revolution of the sixteenth and seventeenth centuries saw, the pressure to produce in quantity encouraged innovation. The efforts were diverse, affecting a number of trades. By looking at the most historically important, the textile industry, we may see how innovation in one aspect of production forced change in another.

The Evolution of the English Woolen Industry

Before the middle of the eighteenth century, woolen and worsted manufacture was Britain's most important industry, as well as perhaps the most dispersed. Three major areas were heavily involved in producing woolens: the West Country in the Cotswolds and Somerset, centering on Bristol; East Anglia with the greatest focus on Norwich; and the West Riding of Yorkshire, where Leeds and Bradford had been centers of the trade for several hundred years.

In the West Country and East Anglia, "the organisation and the capital were provided by wealthy merchant clothiers. They bought the raw wool from the farmers, they passed it on to the spinners, they sent the yarn to the

1. Kenneth Hudson, *Industrial Archaeology: An Introduction* (London: John Baker, 1963), p. 90.

This factory in Ashton-under-Lyne in Lancashire was located on a stream to obtain process water for washing but was operated by hand, as shown by the absence of a mill dam or a mill race. From John Aikin, A Description of the Country from Thirty to Forty Miles Round Manchester *(London: Stockdale, 1795).*

weavers. Once the cloth was woven the merchants either had it taken to other specialists for finishing or else undertook the bleaching and dyeing themselves on their own premises." Production was organized, but manufacture was not collected in a single village or even a single premises. "The spinning and weaving were easily done in the workers' own houses, without the need for expensive equipment. The finishing processes, even before the introduction of power-driven machinery, were more efficiently and cheaply carried out in larger units, because a good supply of water and more elaborate buildings were essential."[2] The geographical pattern produced by this industry was one of rural domestic production, with spinning at the cottage door and weaving in a shed built on behind. Interspersed within this industrial countryside were mill sites and places where process water could be secured, at which a fulling mill or a bleachery would be found in a small "mill building" that might be little larger than a house. Clearly, two different location systems were at work: the segmental labor of the agricultural areas determined the location of spinning and weaving activities, whereas the sources of water for power and processing served to locate the "mills."

"The system in the West Riding was different. There, in the earlier part of the eighteenth century, the workshops were 'embryo factories without steampower'. The industry was in the hands of master-craftsmen, who bought their own wool, spun it, wove it, dyed it and eventually sold it." This manufacture was not at all located by the availability of segmental labor; instead, it was a self-contained production depending on hand labor. And we know that the availability of process water and small wagon pits for coal—to be used for heating the workshop and the water used, not initially

2. Ibid., p. 53.

Urban
Morphogenesis
in the
Industrial Age

for power—served, along with available village or country housing, to locate the "manufacture." Because the workplace was determined by the traditional location of the master and the processing was under his direct control, masters "employed assistants, [and] they were in direct contact with the market and they controlled all the capital needed to convey raw wool into finished cloth." Even before the creation of steam-powered factories the geographical pattern of the woolen industry of the West Riding was clustered and rather specialized as to the particular woolen cloth produced.[3]

A Bottleneck in Weaving

The strongest force at work in bringing the locational shift from domestic to factory industry was the invention of the flying shuttle. Weaving was perhaps the most constraining process in the traditional textile manufacture. The weavers' need for daylight in which to work limited their productive hours, but as well they could only weave at the rate their hands could throw the shuttle across the loom. Light was hard to improve, but John Kay, in 1733, accomplished a great advance in throwing by his invention of the flying shuttle, which speeded up weaving remarkably. The device was comparatively simple, but it halved the labor input in weaving, allowing the same labor force to produce twice as much cloth. Before the flying shuttle, two men were required to operate a loom—they stood on either side to throw the shuttle back and forth across the warp—but now one could do the job. Kay developed the process at Colchester in Essex, but met with such resistance from the local weavers that he was driven from the town, which led him to the West Riding.[4] In the north, where the primordial "embryo factories without steampower" existed, the invention was rapidly taken up by the masters who were themselves workers. And the flying shuttle forced upon textile production a new shortage.

The Spinning Engine

During the Middle Ages, when England began to attempt to staunch the outward flow of wool staple and force its processing and weaving in England, a disproportion had already shown up between the productivity of spinners and weavers. The ancient distaff spinning was so slow that several spinsters were required to keep up with the consumption of a single weaver. To aid in this difficulty, the English in the fourteenth century imported the spinning wheel from Italy, where to a considerable degree English wool was then being woven into cloth at Prato and Florence. More yarn could be spun and the industry could grow without a vast enlargement of the labor force. In the mid-eighteenth century, a new disproportion arose, requiring a further improvement in spinning. The authorship of that improvement has been argued ever since that time.

In 1738, Lewis Paul took out a patent for a roller-spinning device, and

3. Ibid.
4. F. George Kay, *Pioneers of British Industry* (London: Rockliff, 1952), p. 97.

the basic shift in technology was begun. Paul's machine was not ultimately successful, but its principle was. In the hands of Richard Arkwright, Paul's principle—whether stolen outright or simply "developed" further— became a successful machine for automatic spinning devised and patented in 1769. If any date deserves to be counted as the first year of the Industrial Revolution, it was 1774, when a mill was set up to use this machine. Because Kay and others had encountered so much opposition in the introduction of their machines, Arkwright and his partner, Jedediah Strutt, established their mill in rural Derbyshire, at Cromford, where a small waterpower was available from the outfall of the drainage of the nearby lead mines. Fortunately, that first Cromford mill still stands so we can learn directly from its physical evidence.

The improvement in spinning came rapidly thereafter, particularly as Arkwright's patent was soon thrown out for several irregularities and by the simple greed of potential manufacturers who fought its remaining in force. James Hargreaves, a weaver at Standhill near Blackburn in Lancashire, found that his wife could not spin fast enough to keep up with his loom, so he invented a machine named in her honor. On it, he could simultaneously spin at first 8, but ultimately 120 threads. The "spinning jenny" became a successful machine, to be shortly improved by Samuel Crompton into the "spinning mule," which combined features from Arkwright's and Hargreaves's machines.

Too Much Yarn Leads to Machine Weaving

The increased ability to spin yarn by machine produced such a flood of yarn that it could not be woven into cloth. A Lancashire minister, Edmund Cartwright, went in 1784 for a summer holiday to Matlock Bath, only a short walk from Arkwright's second and then most successful mill. There, in conversation with some Manchester millowners, he learned of this overtaxing of the hand-loom weavers. In the innocence of the open-minded, he remarked, "Then Mr. Arkwright must set his wits to work to invent a weaving machine." Their assurances that it could not be done further induced a curious man to make the attempt, which was successful. Thus, Cartwright established the notion that technical improvement was generally possible, and that disproportions that arose in a continuous process must be dealt with by technological experimentation and improvement.

The Coming of Steam Power

In such a context, the problem of power came up for solution. The notion of powered machines was neither new nor unsuccessful. Obviously, the quickening pace of the quantitative economy had first introduced traditional forms of power to the manufacturing process. We have already seen that waterpower was introduced to fulling during the Middle Ages. Strutt and Arkwright used horses for power at Nottingham during their experiments there, turning to waterpower only at Cromford in 1774. Since England is not well supplied by waterpower, the use of steam for power had been toyed with

Urban
Morphogenesis
in the
Industrial Age

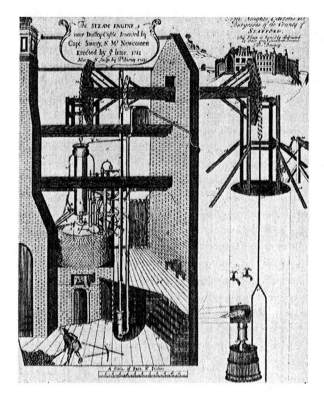

for more than a century when the need within the textile trade became urgent. The Greeks had appreciated the power inherent within the expansion of steam, and had used it, as had the medieval Chinese, for rather frivolous purposes (opening temple doors and producing "magic" effects). But only in the seventeenth century was a purpose equal to steam's power given to the medium in the pumping of water from coal mines. Initially, the steam was used directly to create a vacuum into which the water was drawn. Thomas Savery in 1698 patented an engine "for raising of water and occasioning motion to all sorts of mill works by the impellent force of fire."[5] Through this device for the first time in human history water was raised more than the twenty-four feet at sea level that natural law determines.

A French refugee, Denis Pepin, was the first to employ the piston, which was to prove the central element in the generation of steam power. But only the pressure-cooker, which he also invented, proved a success, as he demonstrated in a dinner tendered to the Royal Society in 1680. Final success in devising a steam engine came when Thomas Newcomen built a practical "atmospheric engine," possibly in 1705 but certainly by 1712. From that time on, many improvements were made, but the steam engine was a practical device in increasingly wider use. James Watt's great advance come not in "inventing" the steam engine, as is so commonly supposed, but rather in making it a generally economic engine that could be used to create power independent in location from the winds and falling water.

5. Ibid., p. 28.

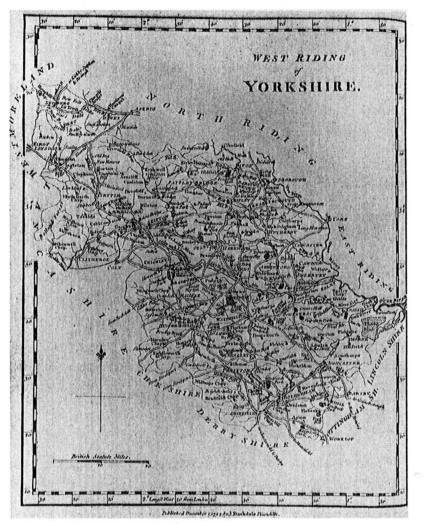

Map of Yorkshire. From Aikin, Country Round Manchester.

The West Riding of Yorkshire: An Industrial Landscape

In the West Riding of Yorkshire, we may see in what fashion the steam engine shaped the geography of the Industrial Revolution. Given the local integration of all processes that go into the production of finished textiles, it is not surprising that steam power was to play a larger role in the West Riding than in the other traditional textile areas—the West Country or East Anglia. "When steam power became available, the Yorkshire clothiers were able to convert their workshops into factories with little difficulty and to push their Southern competitors out of the market. This, rather than 'Because they were closer to the coalfields', seems to be the answer to the classic question, 'why did the woolen textile industry transfer its headquarters to the West Riding?'"[6] The West Riding manufacturers had found it greatly to their benefit to invest in machinery. Now they found it both within their financial

6. Hudson, *Industrial Archaeology*, p. 53.

Urban
Morphogenesis
in the
Industrial Age

resources and greatly to their profit to apply steam power to their works. In this way the Industrial Revolution could take what were small process integrations located in villages or small towns and allow them to become great factory cities.

Manchester: The Spreading Village of Manufacture

The growth of the woolen trade of the West Riding came in a sense before the onset of what we normally recognize as the Industrial Revolution. The scale of production was already rising rapidly in the 1720s—strong proof that the use of steam power was the result of an upswing in demand rather than the other way around. But how could demand first be demonstrated and then focused on a restricted geographical area such as the West Riding or Lancashire? After all, during the Middle Ages, much of England's land and labor was being used to produce the golden staple and work it up into cloth. There emerges a picture of a twofold separation of textile manufacture: that between woolens and cotton goods, which transpired during the eighteenth century, and that of various functions within the making and selling of textiles. This functional separation within the sphere of business operation had considerable geographical implications beyond the simple one of the location of the market for sales. What emerged was the division between the making of cotton textiles, which was carried out in the country towns around Manchester, and the organization of the trade and the selling of its products, which continued in Manchester, in the end becoming Manchester's main function. Meanwhile, manufacture grew in size in Oldham, Bolton, Ashton-under-Lyne, and the other towns-become-cities that lay up to twenty miles away.

To understand the evolution of Manchester's city form, we must consider the mid-seventeenth century when, as a result of the creation of the East India Company monopoly, trade with India was being encouraged. Part of that trade centered on the import of cotton textiles from the East, uncommon indeed in the Middle Ages. Cottons—lighter, brighter, and more fashionable than woolens—were taken up by the increasingly fashion-conscious upper classes of England. That shift worried the woolen manufacturers. So they began what proved a long but futile campaign against the import of cotton products.

First they gained Parliament's support in forbidding printed cotton calicoes, restricting the trade to "gray cloths" to be printed in Lancashire and the Clyde Valley where the finishing trade grew up, replacing to a considerable degree the older but not too vigorous woolen manufacture. Then the woolen manufacturers succeeded in gaining the embargo of gray cloths and further limiting the import to cotton yarn. At last in 1721, Parliament even forbade the import of cotton yarn. But at that juncture, two realities turned aside the impact of that partisan legislation. The first was the increasing production of cotton in the West Indian and American colonies, outside the monopoly of the East India Company with its sensitivity to legislation; the other was the established interest of the calico printers of Lancashire and the Clyde Valley. Cotton fiber could continue to be imported, so the real problem was getting it spun into yarn. To do so required two things not in great supply: a segmental labor force, and the greater skill needed to spin cotton as opposed to wool.

Woolen yarn was normally rather coarse and weak, gaining its strength through the greater thickness of woolen fabrics and their frequent "finishing" by felting and fulling. Cotton yarns were normally finer and the fabrics were seldom as radically "finished," so the spinning problem became acute after the Indian yarns were forbidden. In this context, the efforts to develop a spinning machine took place. And when Richard Arkwright patented the water-frame spinner in 1769, the campaign was well started. In 1774, Arkwright's mill at Cromford opened, producing a great quantity of yarn superior in strength and fineness to anything that could be made by English hands, and he made it with a small and untapped segmental labor force— the orphans who were wards of the county of Derby.[7] The timing was critical, as it was in 1758 that the flying shuttle, originally invented for woolen weaving, was introduced to the production of cottons, thus greatly increasing the demand for cotton yarns.[8] The conjunction of these two developments expanded the production of cotton textiles very rapidly, encouraging still further technological development—most notably the introduction of machine weaving, of which the first example in Lancashire was only in 1790. The complex history of the textile industry is a tale of interacting technological advance leading in the end to the first unquestionable quantitative economy. To serve that vast industry, with its hundreds of thousands of employees, the new geographical settlement, the industrial metropolis, first evolved in and about Manchester.

The nature of the transition from the Middle Ages to modern times in England helps explain the morphogenesis of that new settlement. In their classic study of the Industrial Revolution, J. L. and Barbara Hammond present a surpassing summary of the events of the time. "The disappearance of the medieval economy was the essential stage in the Industrial Revolution. It came earlier in England than elsewhere; it led to great technical improvement and a rapid increase in production; it took a different course and its ultimate consequences were different."[9] For these reasons the English Industrial Revolution is of great importance and interest, but hardly serves as a universal model for industrialization. For that we must eventually establish other distinct models that are as valid as the English but rule elsewhere.

Landowning and the Industrial Revolution

The Hammonds find the critical difference between England and the Continent in the manner of the destruction of the peasant villages, where the

7. For a discussion in greater detail of this industrial emergence of cotton spinning, see James E. Vance, Jr., "Housing the Worker: The Employment Linkage as a Force in Urban Structure," *Economic Geography* 42 (1966): 294–325.

8. Arthur Louis Dunham, *The Industrial Revolution in France: 1815–1848* (New York: Exposition Press, 1955), p. 269.

9. J. L. and Barbara Hammond, *The Rise of Modern Industry* (London: Methuen, 1925), p. 90.

death throes of the Middle Ages were felt. "On the Continent the peasant as a rule survived. The commercial motives that gave such encouragement in England to headlong enclosure [of previously common lands] had less play elsewhere: reasons of State that had once made all Governments wish to keep a peasant population still counted in countries with a land frontier: [and] the enclosing class nowhere else made the laws [as they did through their control of the English Parliament]." They argue that on the Continent the absolute monarchies tended to check the power of the aristocracy. In England, however, the aristocracy was supreme, managing to establish its pattern of landownership as the most powerful one. "Consequently England alone emerged from this revolution as an agrarian society without peasants or the obstacles a peasant economy presents to an industrial system based on concentration of power and specialization of tasks. In other countries the capitalist system was confined for the most part to industry; in England it began by over-spreading the village as well as the town."[10]

The most striking contrasts existed between France and England. In France the demise of the medieval economy came through political revolution, and in England, through the usurpation of common rights by a tiny and arrogant minority. "Thus when the medieval village disappeared in France the peasant became an owner, whereas when it disappeared in England he became a labourer. This happened because the relationship between lord and peasant was abolished in France in a revolution that made the peasant more powerful than the lord, whereas in England it was abolished when the lord was supreme."[11]

The aristocracy's fierce drive for control of the land had several stages, all leading to a common goal: the capitalization of farming. The Hammonds cite the rise of the merchant class to wealth and its display as forcing upon the traditional aristocracy the practice of capitalism. "In the sixteenth century the chief motive for enclosure was the stimulus given to farming for the market by the rise in prices and the expansion of the cloth industry. When commerce increased its profits and the classes engaged in it stepped into a more lavish style of living, the landlord found himself in a world in which he had to make drastic changes if he wished to maintain his social prestige. [This was a change from] feudal times [when] the lord's pomp and state depended on the number and condition of his tenants." To more democratic observers, simple social arrogance seems as likely an explanation of the narrowing of English landownership. Even the Hammonds admit, "As domestic order became more secure, the command of men counted for less and less; as wealth grew and all classes [sic] acquired more expensive habits, the command of money counted for more and more."[12]

As landowners sought to increase their incomes, they began a systematic theft of the rights of the common people to common lands, and introduced the practice of the farmer's holding land under a lease rather than common rights. In the end the landowner succeeded in capturing the use value of

10. Ibid.
11. Ibid., p. 89.
12. Ibid., p. 84.

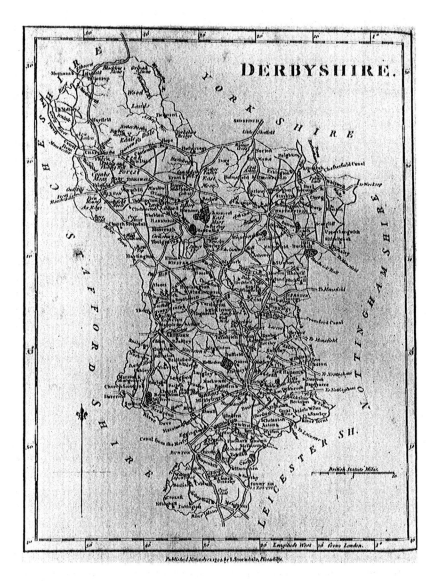

*Map of Derbyshire.
Note the location of
Matlock, Cromford,
and Belper on the
River Derwent at the
center of the county,
with the duke of De-
vonshire's estate at
Chatsworth just to
the north. From
Aikin,* Country
Round Manchester.

most land, and created a situation in which "he believed that the best work
was done by labourers who depended on their wages and had nothing to
distract them from their duty to their employer. This relationship he considered the best for production, and production was everything."[13] The
result was the capitalization of farming, and the creation of a rural proletariat
that might remain in the country only as long as it served the financial
interests of the aristocratic landowners; it could hardly become a major
source for securing segmental labor.

This rather harsh indictment of the landed gentry has not been the
common view; instead, it has been argued that "public spirit and private
interest seemed to draw the landlord to the same conclusion. The population

13. Ibid.

was growing faster than its resources; the Industrial Revolution was throwing up towns where food was consumed and not produced. . . . [Grain] growing was immensely profitable to the landlord and urgently necessary for the State."[14] One might as well argue that making cotton textiles was "urgently necessary" for England, but it produced no more than grinding poverty for its laborers. And those laborers had not even the slight protection that access to land furnished to the working class in other lands—as in the peasant holdings of France and Germany and the homesteading of the United States.

Landownership proves a somewhat disregarded aspect of the Industrial Revolution. In the West Riding, it produced a distinctly different geographical cast to industrialization from that found in Lancashire, where the small holding was less common and the proto-factory was not the normal business organization before the introduction of machinery and waterpower or steam. Yet our standard view of the coming of the Industrial Revolution tends to be projected from the conditions in and about Manchester—a fascinating and important instance of the industrialization process, but not the only form or indeed the universal model.

The Industrial Revolution rapidly came to be widespread, and affected other nations—Belgium, France, the United States—in its earlier stages, particularly within the general textiles trade. We will here look first at the pattern as it evolved in Lancashire, and then at the distinctly different pattern that emerged in New England.

The Arrival of the Cotton Manufacture through Long-Distance Trade

In cotton, a long-distance trade was essential, extending initially to Syria and Cyprus but subsequently to the West Indies, Brazil, and the American colonies. To organize such trade required the skills and offices of the wholesaler, so we find nineteenth-century Manchester becoming the center of organization of what came to be both a massive industry and a world marketing system. The cotton trade differed greatly from the traditional woolen industry of the West Riding, with its internalization of staple and production. Even when the Yorkshire woolen industry had to turn outward for wool, which it did not do for a long time, it still conducted trade on a far less massive scale.

In the end the handling of cotton was further split with Manchester serving more as the trader in cloth while Liverpool, the port that grew from the trade, dealt in cotton fiber. In a study of the Liverpool merchants and the cotton trade from 1820 to 1850, D. M. Williams shows that "if the entire period . . . is examined, certain trends are plainly visible. Most outstanding is the fact that in the twenty years from 1820 to 1839, a period of very rapid expansion, the cotton trade became more and more concentrated into the hands of a small group of merchants. Thus up to 1839 the increase in imports was not met by a greater number of importers but by an expansion in the leading merchants' scale of operation. . . . Clearly, after 1820 the cotton

14. Ibid.

trade became the preserve of large operators dealing in United States' cotton."[15]

That group of large merchant firms dealing in raw cotton included several from the United States—Nicholas Biddle in his guise as a speculator in cotton among them—and from Scotland. In any trade needing long-distance connections, the need for temporal and geographical intelligence is such that a few specialized dealers will come to the fore, and they are as likely to come from the areas supplying the staple as from those consuming it. Like all such operations based on commercial intelligence, a strong force operates within such a trade to congregate its practitioners in one or at most a few cities.[16] The Lancashire cotton trade came in the end to have two types of distinct intelligence—that with respect to the supply of the cotton staple, and that with respect to the selling in a world market of the cotton textiles produced around Manchester. The trading center for cotton staple rapidly became Liverpool, whereas that in textiles came to be Manchester, which drew to itself the selling functions of a complex producing region whose manufacturing soon departed the metropolitan core.

The External Evolution of the Industrial Metropolis

This external evolution of the manufacturing phase of industrialization was present in most of the early factory districts. Manchester was followed in turn by Boston in Massachusetts, Rouen, and Verviers in Belgium as centers of commercial intelligence around which factory towns would be ranged. Over time the links have been further lengthened, as when cotton textile production was shifted from New England to the American South, in a movement ending during the 1920s. Boston and more particularly New York remained the centers of commercial intelligence from which textile factors worked to finance production and whence the market for textiles could be appraised and production and sales efforts initiated. More recently, the same linkage has been further extended, as so-called multinational corporations push production even farther away—to Korea, Taiwan, Hong Kong, or Singapore—while maintaining the factoring, organizing, and selling functions in the commercial heart of the industrial system of cities. The system began in Manchester in the early years of the Industrial Revolution, changing not in basic relationship but simply in the geographical extent of its external evolution and the length of the linkages.

Towns Become the Support of the Countryside

The Industrial Revolution is seldom considered from the perspective of the countryside; in fact, we tend to think of industrialization as almost a

15. D. M. Williams, "Liverpool Merchants and the Cotton Trade, 1820–1850," in *Liverpool and Merseyside: Essays in the Economic and Social History of the Port and Its Hinterland*, ed. J. R. Harris (London: Frank Cass, 1969), pp. 189–91.

16. For a more detailed and processional view of this creation of wholesaling towns, see James E. Vance, Jr., *The Merchant's World: The Geography of Wholesaling* (Englewood Cliffs, N.J.: Prentice-Hall, 1970).

destructive element sapping the strength of the rural areas and seeking to encroach upon their long-established purlieus. Yet such could hardly be further from the truth, in either Britain or America, though the two countries experienced sharply different settlement consequences of industrialization.

In Britain, a new practice of farming could come into existence only as a result of industrialization and urbanization. The chance for rural landowners to rationalize economically their land-use and cropping practices came as a result, on the one hand, of the ability to encourage surplus rural population to migrate to the rising industrial cities and, on the other, of the establishment in those metropolises of a large and protected market for English agricultural produce. Enclosure of common land into privately held pasturage, expansion of the land given over to wheat production for an enlarging urban proletariat, and agricultural reform of a sort impossible if the traditional rural economy had persisted all made farming far more profitable as a result of industrial urbanization than it would have been without those cities and their factories and workers. If it had ever been true, as some believe, that towns can only grow out of the countryside, it certainly became untrue once the Industrial Revolution was in full effect. Not without significance, von Thünen's study of the "isolated city," written in 1826,[17] was a city-centered study of the economics of agricultural land use, a system of land assignment based on the city as the originator of farming practices. Von Thünen was writing in the decades of the early nineteenth century, when industrialization was in full sweep, even if not directly so in the area near Tellow, his estate, in what is today East Germany. He leaves no doubt that the town shapes the economic life of the country in the modern world of industry.

The rise of the industrial city restored economic vitality to rural England, and the landowning classes became wealthy as a result, though they showed no gratitude toward the cities that made them so. Instead, political lines were drawn between Tories, raised to great power by rural wealth gained within a rejuvenated farming system, and Whigs, first made wealthy and powerful with the rise of commerce and industry in the eighteenth and nineteenth centuries. The split came to be one between the country and the town, because the first attempts at powered industrialization, which came in the country, tended in Britain to be short-lived and succeeded by a massive development of factories in cities.

In a study of Ashton-under-Lyne, the manor lying directly east of Manchester, Winifred Bowman showed that in the fifteenth century that manor already had the privilege to hold two annual fairs at which wool fleeces and cloths might be traded. As the manufacturing component of the metropolitan industrialization began to concentrate outside Manchester, Ashton rose to great importance as a manufacturing place, and rather soon after cotton came to dominate in southeast Lancashire. The first cotton mill was established in Manchester in 1781 and the first in Ashton-under-Lyne in 1785.[18]

17. Published as Jonathan Heinrich von Thünen, *Der Isolierte Staat*, introd. Heinrich Waentig (Jena: Gustave Fisher, 1910).

18. Winifred M. Bowman, *England in Ashton-under-Lyne* (Altrincham, Cheshire: John Sheratt for the Ashton-under-Lyne [City] Corporation, 1960), p. 425.

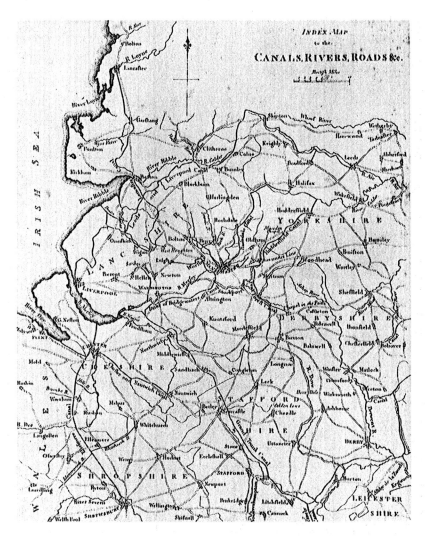

Map of canals, rivers, and roads in the region where the English Industrial Revolution began. From Aikin, Country Round Manchester.

Initially, these mills were powered by water. When the endowment of waterpower was soon taken up, attention had to turn to Boulton and Watt's steam engines.

The ease with which power was adapted to spinning was probably a result of the critical need for more yarn to support the expansion of the textile industry along basically traditional lines of domestic production within a quantitative economy. The technical improvement in one process was not necessarily directly or rapidly followed by a change in another, as the case of the power-loom shows beyond question. First developed in the 1790s, the power-loom was violently opposed by the weavers of Lancashire. Ashton was so in the forefront of that group that the town of Manchester had established the precaution of ringing its church bells to warn that potentially riotous Ashton weavers were marching on the organization at the hub of the metropolis. [19] In face of that opposition, for many years power was not brought to the

19. Ibid., p. 439.

Map of Lancashire. From Aikin, Country Round Manchester.

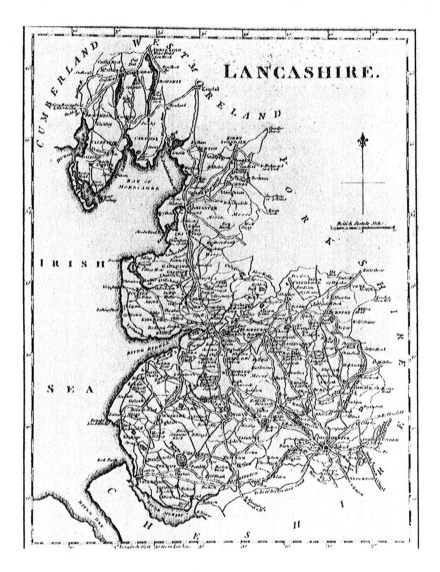

weaving of even fairly cheap textiles, with the result that Lancashire displayed a mixture of hand- and machine-weaving even as late as the middle of the nineteenth century. Thus, the great early application of steam power as a supplement to the fully utilized waterpower came in the carding and spinning phase of textile production, which led to a much greater concentration of yarn production than of cloth making. Again, this fact was a force creating the complex metropolitan area with distinct industrial satellites surrounding a dominant center of organization and commercial intelligence.

Weavers tended to continue to operate in outlying industrial towns but to secure the yarns to be woven in their looms through Mancunian manufacturers' "putting-out." This organization required more workers than might have been called for in a fully mechanized operation. At Ashton and a dozen other places lying just beyond Manchester's boundaries, great tracts of very cheap houses were laid out, often by aristocratic landowners such as the

The Continuing City

earls of Stanford and Warrington, who owned much of Ashton. In those tracts, hand-loom weavers operated a little-appreciated form of what might be called "collected domestic production." Unfortunately, this domestic production was shorn of the backstay of the "weaver's plot" of earlier Lancashire or the small holding of the Yorkshire woolen manufacturer.[20]

In addition, these tracts of small row houses served as the homes for families—often further crowded by boarders—employed in the spinning mills and the machine-weaving establishments that came into being after about 1825. In essence, this housing supply was made available by private investment to allow the concentration of workers coming from the surrounding countryside or, in the case of southeast Lancashire, from the south of England where the economy after the Napoleonic War was none too healthy. The flow of in-migrants also included a number of Irish who were fleeing that verdant land of hunger in the 1830s and 1840s. All these groups crowded into Ashton, and Lancashire in general, and the landlords provided tiny houses for them. The Royal Commission Studying the State of the Large Towns and Populous Places in the 1840s brought out evidence that these houses were so modest, if not outright mean, that they could be built for as little as £50, perhaps $250 in American money of the time. But in this collection of domestic manufacture into a new industrial metropolis, we have a peculiar and rather unappreciated stage in the industrialization of cities.

Friedrich Engels on the Morphogenesis of Manchester

Though hardly the sole example of industrialization, Manchester is a fascinating and critical pillar in a more encompassing edifice. Such a wealth of material has come down to us about the Industrial Revolution in the city that we cannot turn away from it, yet we must take Manchester as a prime example, hardly a universal one. A case in point is furnished by the detailed and perceptive analysis of the society and form of Manchester made by Friedrich Engels after twenty months' residence there in 1842–44, just at the onset of full factory development. On his return to Barmen in the Rhineland, Engels wrote *The Condition of the Working Class in England*, publishing it in 1845 and thereby establishing his credentials as one of the fathers of socialism and communism. Because his picture of England was painted in such dark hues, for more than a century his book tended to be viewed as a political tract, which it was. But the accuracy of its description of those conditions, which seems incontestable from a wealth of less doctrinaire writing that has subsequently been made public, was disregarded.

No one, it seems to me, looked upon Manchester as an Industrial Age city with the perceptive morphogenetic eye that Engels seems to have possessed. The great criticism lodged against Engels is that in this first applica-

---

20. This view of Ashton is based on a careful appraisal of the manuscript 1851 census of England for Ashton-under-Lyne that I undertook some time ago. Unfortunately, too many of the enumerator's books have been lost to make a detailed study possible. But on the basis of the evidence available to me, I became convinced that this notion of the "collective domestic production," even as late as 1851, is valid.

tion of dialectical materialism, well before Marx used the term of analysis, he romanticized the quality of rural life in the preindustrial era while painting the Industrial Age even blacker than it was. I would incline toward the view that the hues of his Manchester in 1843 are those of a careful realist, while the colors with which he paints the domestic production before the development of factories are far brighter and more cheerful than reality would have required. As the editors of the recent retranslation of the book point up, the lot of earlier nail workers in Willenhall in the Black Country and the sewing girls of London's East End was certainly no better than that of Manchester's "little piecers," the most depressed workers in the cotton mills.[21] The apprentices in the Willenhall lock trade are graphically described by Benjamin Disraeli in his *Sybil, or: The Two Nations* (1845) wherein a basically "domestic trade" is presented in colors as dark as those employed by Engels.[22]

Engels begins with a description of "the face of the country [which] has been completely changed as a result of the Industrial Revolution." Painting perhaps too strong a contrast with the past, he finds southeast Lancashire "an obscure, poorly cultivated bog" before industrialization, which had "increased ten-fold in 80 years" with many large towns growing up there. "Liverpool, and Manchester, for example, have together 700,000 inhabitants. Near [Manchester] are Bolton (50,000 inhabitants), Rochdale (75,000), Oldham (50,000), . . . Ashton and Stalybridge (40,000)."[23] The vast expansion of numbers in the industrial cities came as a result of the initial need for workers when industry was mechanized. To gain that labor, wages were increased over those to be earned in domestic production in the countryside, drawing to the emerging cities hordes of workers, under- or unemployed in the country, as well as those simply seeking financial improvement. Signaling a proclivity of the Irish population that we may recognize, but mixing up its cause, Engels tells us, "Meanwhile, in Ireland, where law and order had only been fully established at the beginning of the eighteenth century, the population—formerly decimated by English barbarity—was expanding quickly. With the expansion of English industry many Irishmen migrated to England to seek work there. These [together] are the reasons for the expansion of the great factory towns and commercial centers in the United Kingdom, in which at least three-quarters of the inhabitants are members of the working classes."[24]

It was essential to establish the rapid growth of population in the cities through massive in-migration from the country, because the conditions Engels describes were so grim that the expansion in numbers in the working classes could never have been accounted for by localized biological growth. Those rapid increases in population also serve to explain why, after an initial

21. Friedrich Engels, *The Condition of the Working Class in England*, trans. and ed. W. O. Henderson and W. H. Chaloner (Stanford, Calif.: Stanford University Press, 1968; original English ed., London: Basil Blackwell, 1958), p. xii.

22. Benjamin Disraeli, *Sybil, or: The Two Nations*, (Harmondsworth, Middlesex: Penguin Books, 1954).

23. Engels, *Working Class*, p. 16.

24. Ibid., p. 24.

inflation of wages through migration to the city, the working classes experienced a rapid decline in those same wages, to the point that former handworkers might very well be earning less than they had earned in rural domestic industry. Essentially, though Engels never states the case, the oversupply of the labor force answering the call to the city created, at least in considerable measure, the deterioration of social and economic conditions there. Thus, to blame the entire decline on the process of industrialization and the "middle classes," as he repeatedly does, is to whitewash the evidence. Fully as guilty—perhaps more so, depending upon your point of view—was the rural landownership system, which forced the rural unemployed into cities as rural land was concentrated outright into a few, generally aristocratic, hands.

I think this tendency to internalize the Industrial Revolution to the city alone—finding there both its victims and its oppressors—is rather a case of partisan pleading and bad historical geography, particularly when we attempt to analyze and understand the effect of the industrialization process on the common people. In justice, we cannot deny the very considerable mistreatment of the working class by the manufacturers, but to think that the malign intent of a single small, though powerful, group produced such misery is too simple. Instead, responsibility lies both in the events taking place within the city and the forces outside the city that were causing people to move into them and further contributing to their hunger. The rural landowning class must bear as much responsibility for the evils of the Industrial Revolution as do the actual final agents of oppression—the factory managers.

The Morphogenesis of an Industrial City: Manchester in 1843

What, then, was Manchester like when Engels went there in 1842? In the classic mold of travelers to the north, he begins by descending upon the city from the crest, the Blackstone Edge of the Pennines, noting "a beautiful hilly countryside . . . intersected by the charming green valleys of the Ribble, the Irwell, the Mersey and their tributaries" on the lower courses of which is to be found "the most densely-populated part of England. In Lancashire—particularly in Manchester—is to be found not only the origin but the heart of the industry of the United Kingdom." Engels held that with good endowment of the "three factors that are the essence of modern industry"—the application of water and steam power, the use of self-acting machines, and the division of labor—"the evolution of the modern system of manufacture has reached its climax in Manchester." Because of this climax position and his intimate knowledge of the place, Engels proposed to look at Manchester. "In the circumstances it is to be expected that it is in this region that the inevitable consequences of industrialization in so far as they affect the working classes are most strikingly evident."[25]

In this sober fashion we learn that in the mind of this young German visitor, Manchester was to be erected as a model of the "inevitable conse-

25. Ibid., p. 50

quences of industrialization" in changing for the worse "a beautiful hilly countryside" and a reputedly humane domestic industry—romanticized in works like Peter Gaskell's *The Manufacturing Population of England* (1830)—which Engels seems to have taken as his Eden before the industrial fall.[26]

With these cautions in mind, we may still gain a useful picture of the classic industrial town just after its time of greatest growth. "Manchester proper lies on the left of the Irwell, between this river and two smaller streams, the Irk and the Medlock, which flow into the Irwell at this point. Salford lies on the right bank of the Irwell in a sharp bend of the river." Round about are a number of places that have merged with the city during its rapid development. Slightly farther away, but generally continuous with Manchester, are the satellitic towns—Ashton, Oldham, Stalybridge, Stockport, Bolton, Rochdale, and several others. "In the centre of Manchester there is a fairly large commercial district, which is about half a mile long and half a mile broad. This district is almost entirely given over to offices and warehouses." Quite in contrast to the medieval city, the Manchester of Engels's time anticipated modern conditions: "Nearly the whole of this district has no permanent residents and is deserted at night, when only policemen patrol its dark narrow thoroughfare with their bull's eye lanterns." This quarter, which today we would call a central business district, lay near the medieval core of the town and was "intersected by certain main streets which carry an enormous volume of traffic. The lower floors of the buildings are occupied by shops of dazzling splendour. A few of the upper stories on these premises are used as dwellings and the streets present a relatively busy appearance until late in the evening."

"Around the commercial quarter there is a belt of built up areas on the average one and a half miles in width, which is occupied entirely by working-class dwellings. This area of workers' houses includes all Manchester proper, except the centre, all Salford and Hulme, an important part of Pendleton and Chorlton, two-thirds of Ardwick and certain small areas of Cheetham Hill and Broughton [all of these former outlying villages now continuous with Manchester]. Beyond this belt of working-class houses or dwellings lie the districts inhabited by the middle classes and the upper classes." Thus, even in the early 1840s the notion of a social class stratification outward from the center, with a rise in status accompanying the outward shift, had become characteristic of the English city. This point is important to appreciate when we come to the modern city, as it has direct bearing on the question of so-called white flight.

The middle-class districts "are to be found in regularly laid out streets near the working-class districts—in Chorlton [in-Medlock] and in the re-

26. A number of observers, including the translators and editors of the edition of Engels being cited, have pointed out the German's uncritical acceptance of Gaskell, leading through its overly sanguine view of England's past to a fundamental exaggeration of the "inevitable consequences of industrialization." To accept Engels's view of the future, one must first overlook the real conditions in the past, accept dialectical materialism, and rule out any possible improvement within the capitalist system. Because Engels—perhaps unwittingly, but still rather doctrinally—mistakes the degree of change wrought by capitalism, one may question the singleness of solution he perceived for this situation.

moter parts of Cheetham Hill." Obviously, these housing "estates" were built by speculative builders who were laying down monotonous carpets—perhaps doormats is a better image in the case of Manchester's modest-size middle class—of uniform and eminently "respectable" row houses along carefully identical streets of stultifying "order" and "correctness." Engels elsewhere speaks critically of the absence of plan in the working-class areas, but, a true son of a class-ordered society, he smiles on the neat dullness of the middle-class terraces.

Beyond these regimented accommodations lay the suburban landscapes of the well-to-do. "The villas [detached houses] of the upper classes are surrounded by gardens and lie in the higher and remoter parts of Chorlton and Ardwick or on the breezy heights of Cheetham Hill, Broughton and Pendleton." Apparently, this outward movement from the city was fairly recent, as it was observed by L. M. Hayes, "In Manchester about the year 1840 and onwards, the middle classes began to realize that town life was not very desirable, and families began migrating and settling in the various suburbs."[27] The nature of the undesirability of the central area was apparently largely a matter of public health, not one of personal safety or chance association. The slow emergence of the idea of contagious disease had done much to condition persons with money to move out in "duty" to their family, shielding the family from possible contagion. This notion was strengthened when cholera struck Britain yet again in the 1830s.

In a tantalizing reference to the use of public transportation, which he simply does not amplify, Engels continues his discussion of the villa areas. "The upper classes enjoy healthy country air and live in luxurious and comfortable dwellings which are linked to the centre of Manchester by omnibuses which run every fifteen or thirty minutes. To such an extent has the convenience of the rich been considered in the planning of Manchester that these plutocrats can travel from their houses to their places of business in the centre of town by the shortest routes, which run entirely through working-class districts, without even realizing how close they are to the misery and filth which lie on both sides of the road." One wonders whether this arrangement was planning or land-and-transportation economics. Only the well-to-do could use horse-drawn omnibuses; many recent studies have confirmed fairly conclusively that until the coming of the electric trolley, *mass transit* was a rather ironic term. This transit was shared among the relatively small and well-washed numbers of the fortunate classes. But it may have been the result of little conscious planning. A capitalist society need not plan that way; the market brought the situation about. Perhaps this quibble is academic, though I think assertion of cause and proof of cause are equally essential elements in a simple act of support; to assign the cause wrongly does put in doubt statements of the process at work.

This argument is further developed when Engels holds that "even the less pretentious shops adequately serve their purpose of hiding from the eyes of the wealthy ladies and gentlemen with strong stomachs and weak nerves

27. L. M. Hayes, *Reminiscences of Manchester and Some of Its Local Surroundings from the Year 1840* (1905), p. 51, quoted in Henderson and Chaloner's translation of Engels. Quotations from Engels are from pp. 54–55.

the misery and squalor which are part and parcel of their own riches and luxury." Interestingly, Engels observed 140 years ago the same façade of shops that develops today in more humane expressions of capitalism and in socialist societies. "These shops have naturally been greatly influenced by the character of the population in the area which lies behind them. Those shops which are situated in the vicinity of commercial or middle class residential districts are more elegant than those which serve as a facade for the workers' grimy cottages. . . . [One of Manchester's main arteries] Deansgate, for example, changes in character as one goes due south from the Old Church. At first there are warehouses and factories. Next come shops of a somewhat inferior character and the street becomes dirtier, while taverns and gin palaces become increasingly frequent. When he reaches the end of the street the appearance of the shops can leave no doubt in his mind that no one but the workers would dream of patronizing them."

Engels does not support his original contention very effectively when he looks at another artery, which we would tend to call a radiating business street. Market Street ran southeasterly from the Manchester Exchange, "the thermometer which records all the fluctuations of industrial and commercial activity" in the metropolis and in England; it ran first into Manchester's Piccadilly "with its huge hotels and warehouses," in an association we will see become particularly related to railroad stations, but its further continuation, as London Road, "which lies near the river Medlock, has a very different appearance. Here are to be found factories, public houses and shops which cater for the needs of the lower middle classes and the workers.

By the time Ardwick Green is reached, the street has changed its character yet again, and is flanked by residences occupied by the upper and middle classes."[28]

The pattern emerging in Manchester by 1840 was very strikingly that of the modern city, with separation of one function from another and the separation of one social class from all others. Following the Anglo-Saxon model of housing that we saw in chapter 6, the city showed an increasing elevation of social status as one moved out from the center, with the Old City in Manchester standing as a slum even in 1840. Scattered around that Old City, intermixed with poor housing, and spreading out along the valleys of the Irk, the Medlock, and the Irwell, were the industrial quarters—grimy, noisy, plagued by smoke and stench, but finally the source of employment for most of the population, a group without the earnings to pay for any transportation to and from work. The streets that ran through Manchester came to be lined with shops, as they have remained to this day despite a socialist social revolution and the introduction of automobiles.

One item—working-class housing—has changed most strikingly; with that change, we must believe both in the improbability of society and in the tempering of the worst features of capitalism. To understand that change we must turn to Engels's most perceptive and valuable description of Manchester. His descriptions of the working-class housing areas are so graphic and so detailed that it is hard to find the best summation of his writing. His account covers the several working-class quarters, which, though much the same in character, were diverse when described individually.

Taking as perhaps the worst extreme "the district near the 'Old Church' . . . one sees immediately on the right hand side a row of antiquated houses where not a single front wall is standing upright. This is a remnant of the old Manchester of the days before the town became industrialized. The old inhabitants and their children have left for better houses in other districts, while the houses in Long Millgate, which no longer satisfied them, were left to a tribe of workers containing a strong Irish element." Engels noted that even the shopkeepers and publicans in this district "make no effort to give their establishments a semblance of cleanliness . . . [as it] is quite obviously given over entirely to the working classes." Not only were the old houses deteriorating, but they were also being crowded by the filling in what little open space they had had by the building of additional houses on the tiny lots. "The condition of this street may be deplorable, but it is by no means as bad as the alleys and courts which lie behind it, and which can be approached only by covered passages so narrow that two people cannot pass. Anyone who has not visited these courts and alleys can have no idea of the fantastic way in which the houses have been packed together. . . . And the fault lies not merely in the survival of old property . . . [for] only in quite modern times has the policy of cramming as many houses as possible on to such space as was not utilised in earlier periods reached its climax." What was no doubt the case for Manchester certainly was not true for London, where even before the Great Fire such crowding could have been found

28. Ibid., pp. 55–56.

Urban
Morphogenesis
in the
Industrial Age

Diagram from Engels, Condition of the Working Class in England. *By permission of Stanford University Press.*

without any recourse to industry, or for some Italian medieval cities, without any reference to capitalism.

This sketch will be sufficient to illustrate the crazy layout of the whole district near the River Irk. There is a very sharp drop of some 15 to 30 feet down to the south bank of the Irk at this point. As many as three rows of houses have generally been squeezed on to this precipitous slope. The lowest row of houses stands directly on the bank of the river while the front walls of the highest row stand on the crest of the ridge in Long Millgate. Moreover, factory buildings are also to be found on the banks of the river. . . . To the right and left a number of covered passages from Long Millgate give access to several courts. On reaching them one meets with a degree of dirt and revolting filth, the like of which is not to be found elsewhere. The worst courts are those leading down to the Irk, which contain unquestionably the most dreadful dwellings I have ever seen. In one of these courts, just at the entrance where the covered passage ends there is a privy without a door. The privy is so dirty that the inhabitants of the court can only enter or leave the court if they are prepared to wade through puddles of stale urine and excrement. . . . Several tanneries are situated on the bank of the river and they fill the neighbourhood with the stench of animal putrefaction. . . . The first court below Ducie Bridge is called Allen's Court. At the same time of the cholera [1832] this court was in such a disgraceful state that the sanitary inspector evacuated the inhabitants. The court was then swept and fumigated with chlorine. . . . If one looks at the heaps of garbage below Ducie Bridge one can gauge the extent to which the accumulated dirt, filth and decay permeates the courts on the steep left bank of the river.[29]

Engels's view of the slums of Manchester is undoubtedly correct: we must judge whether this phenomenon was geographically restricted or was the general pattern of working-class life in an industrial city. Engels himself, as well as other observers, suggests that we should divide the question: What were the general qualities of housing and life for the working class in Britain as a whole? Was variation to be found within the housing of this working class in industrial cities? Crowding within the worker's cottage was considerable even in the countryside. Families tended to be fairly large—they had numerous children, and households were commonly composed of several generations living together—with the result that the accommodations of most working-class households, whether of agricultural or of factory workers, must have been reasonably crowded. No doubt the operation of urban land economics assured that workers' houses in the city were more certain to be small and cramped than those in the country. But since most of those in the working class, in country as well as city, were renters rather than freehold owners, small scale in housing provision was seemingly their common lot.

The Continuing City

29. Ibid., pp. 58–60.

Building on observations elsewhere and later in history, we may argue that part of the problem was one of acculturation. Rural people, used to living in open country, were collected into cities and failed to adjust to that new environment. To take one example: the common practice of reutilizing broken items, which are stored for repair and reuse in the country, becomes intolerable in cities. With no open space for storage, the broken items that may look to be "thrifty storage" in the farmyard become "garbage and junk" in the city. Similarly, the privy and pigsty that stood for sanitation in the farmyard could, with the tightly packed numbers of the city, become absolutely intolerable. But is the presence of filth and poor health conditions the result of capitalism rather than the simple necessity in certain economic activities to cluster people together? The urban landowners and factory operators do not bear all of the blame. The habits of the rural proletariat when transferred to the city and collected into working-class neighborhoods can produce hair-raising conditions without the help of capitalism or industrialization. Both classical and papal Rome faced these problems in the absence of both of these economic institutions; the difference came rather in the existence of an absolutely powerful government that could command the resources, and the use of urban land to bring water to the city and remove the wastes so easily dealt with in the open country and so nearly intractable in the city. Yet biologically and socially, the people are pretty much the same in both areas. The simple Irish peasant remained relatively little changed between Galway and Manchester or Boston, but practices that remained unremarked in the peasant cottage were quite valid housing and health problems in the city.

The Concept of the Generalization of Housing

This picture of slums raises a second question: Did the working-class areas of these industrial cities differ? The answer begins to emerge as we introduce a new concept, the generalization of housing—a simple but useful idea. Throughout most of economic history before the Industrial Revolution, the basic unit of housing in both the country and the city was the occupational household. On a farm, the farmer and his biological family were joined by hired hands—either single men or men and their families. In the city, the medieval master of craft brought together in his house not merely his own family but the production and sale of the goods of trade and the housing of the apprentices and journeymen most commonly producing them. We know that some renting of housing occurred in the medieval city. Though the evidence as to the proportion is not readily available, probably little outright rental housing existed apart from the occupational household of the master. Until the Industrial Revolution, one normally gained housing through gaining employment. This pattern of housing provision was probably traditional from the very beginning of permanent residence in cities.

One of the fundamental changes wrought by the Industrial Revolution was the shaping of a substitute for the occupational household. This change was not at first apparent when Richard Arkwright set up a factory to utilize his water-frame for spinning yarn. He turned to several waterpower sites on the river Derwent in the Peak District of Derbyshire where, in partnership with Jedediah Strutt, he established a mill at Cromford in 1771 and downstream at Belper in 1776. In 1783, a year after the partnership was ended, Arkwright built his own mill at Cromford, just upstream from the original mill of 1771.[30] In each situation, the occupational household was used in one of two ways. The original Cromford mill depended heavily on segmental labor drawn from the adjacent villages and farms, mostly the children of lead miners at nearby Wirksworth, farm children, or orphans who were wards of the county of Derby. In the case of the orphans, Strutt and Arkwright accepted the responsibility for housing their workers. This same responsibility was increased when they built the Belper mill in 1776; at that site they took over an existing waterpower facility, previously used to drive the hammer of a forge, which had a mill village adjacent to it. That village was enlarged to house Strutt and Arkwright's workers. Thus, in a specialized sense the "occupational household" can be considered to have survived the first stage of the Industrial Revolution.[31]

When the mills began to move into larger cities, to be powered by steam engines, the change came. Those larger towns already had an urban labor force, a proletariat if you will, which could be secured without having to provide housing. Particularly as the Industrial Revolution began to pick up speed with the introduction of steam power, more machinery, and a larger scale of production, the manufacturers found this abdication of responsibility for housing provision highly desirable. Instead of having to invest part of their never-sufficient capital in workers' housing, they might concentrate it all in building factories and in financing the purchase of staple raw material and the various stages of manufacture. But by abdicating responsibility for housing, the capitalists fundamentally transformed the conditions of employment. Essentially, they threw their workers onto the general market for housing in a change I have called the generalization of housing. With that generalization, subvention from the manufacturing process to the housing, as had probably occurred throughout much of economic history, came to an end. Instead, workers had to buy housing with their wages. Even if those wages remained unchanged, which they did not in the early nineteenth century, workers would probably have experienced an actual cut in their disposable income as the housing provisions shifted to a market transaction between a worker and an independent and distinct investor in housing.

No doubt the expectations of investors rose with the Industrial Revolution. They could see Arkwright and other manufacturers, as well as aristocratic landowners whose estates were underlain by coal measures, becoming extremely wealthy. It must have seemed the normal course for investors in housing properties to gain equally. Certainly in many cases those investors were the great landowners, who had shown no compunction at sweating the coal miners or evicting the rural working class, so we could hardly expect otherwise with regard to housing. Even when the landowners did not them-

30. The dates of these several mills are from Nikolaus Pevsner, *The Buildings of Derbyshire* (London: Penguin Books, 1953).

31. For a detailed discussion of Cromford, Belper, and the whole matter of segmental labor and housing generalization, see Vance, "Housing the Worker."

selves engage in building, their leasing practices frequently contributed to the deterioration of housing. In what was perhaps his most deadly accurate shot at English legal and social practice, Engels showed the tie between leasehold and shoddy construction and rapidly declining upkeep on rental housing:

> The English practice is to lease building land for twenty, thirty, forty, fifty, or ninety-nine years. When the lease falls in, possession of the land and the buildings on it reverts to the ground landlord [commonly a member of the aristocracy], who does not have to pay for unexhausted improvement. The builder, therefore, constructs the cottages of a type unlikely to survive beyond the period of the lease. Since some of the leases are as short as twenty or thirty years it is easy to understand that builders are not likely to sink much capital into cottages built on such land. Moreover, the owners of the houses who are bricklayers, joiners and carpenters or factory owners are generally not prepared to spend very much money on repairing or maintaining their property.[32]

An often disregarded problem is that this shift from the occupational household to the generalized provision of housing shifted housing cost from beyond a worker's discretion and put it within his control. Thus, when wages proved insufficient, as they commonly did then as now, the worker had to choose between various ways of disposing an inadequate income. How did the worker spend the money, and was this a factor in the deterioration in the quality of housing? Table 7.1 summarizes testimony (quoted by Winifred Bowman) given before the royal commission of 1843 with respect to the

32. Engels, *Working Class*, p. 69.

Urban Morphogenesis in the Industrial Age

311

Table 7.1 Expenditures of Cotton Operatives in Ashton-under-Lyne in 1843

Item	Expenditure (pounds sterling)	Percentage of Total
Food	185,720	64.32
Clothing	26,410	9.15
Fuel	9,350	3.24
House rent	33,870	11.73
Sundries	8,180	2.83
Education	2,220	0.77
Ale and spirits	14,430	4.99
Medicine and medical aid	6,160	2.13
Savings Bank	2,410	0.83
	288,750	99.9

expenditures of "cotton operatives" in Ashton-under-Lyne.[33] No doubt the most startling budget feature is the large part taken up by the cost of food. This testimony was given at the very time Engels was resident in Manchester observing the conditions of working-class life. We can see that the cost of food truly impoverished that working class. Once housing became discretionary, it would probably rank in almost any person's mind as second to food, as it does in these figures, and clothing would follow in order, as here. The exactions of the high cost of food become clear in their bearing on the amount of money available for housing. The high cost of food was very much the outgrowth of policies adopted by Parliament for the benefit not of the industrial capitalist but of the landowning aristocracy.

In the interest of maintaining and increasing the income of rural landowners, no doubt in a political response to the growing wealth and power of the commercial and industrial interests, severe restrictions were determinedly maintained on the import of grain from overseas. The resulting high price for basic food consumed nearly two-thirds of the income of the working class, if the figures from Ashton were at all representative, and they seem to have been. In response to this large exaction for food, other expenditures, particularly those for housing, which now fell within the category of discretionary assignment, tended to be of necessity reduced. Out of this came the practice of spending on average only around 15 percent of income on housing. At first, workers had no alternative; food was so costly that all else had to yield to its demands. But after 1846, when the repeal of the Corn Laws rapidly brought down the cost of some foods by permitting the import of cheaper American and Argentinian products, the practice of assigning no more than 10 to 15 percent of working-class income to housing persisted. Right up to the present, the notion has been firmly held that such a part of the family budget was sufficient for housing. The result has been that British workers' houses have been much more modest than those of Americans of the

33. Bowman, *Ashton-under-Lyne*, p. 433.

same class. The poor quality, though certainly better than the state described by Engels, continued up to the time of World War I when, at the close of hostilities, it became obvious that the government must adopt a comprehensive program of public housing to improve on the quality that workers could, or would, buy for themselves.

The Row House Terrace and Back-to-Backs

In the satellitic industrial towns surrounding Manchester, the basic pattern of working-class housing that was to serve Britain until the 1920s was nearly evolved by Engels's time. This pattern was the row house, in England usually called a terrace of houses, with party walls between adjacent houses and small backyards behind, which were held separately and fenced one from another. As the years passed, certain improvements were made. A small front yard might be added, a few square feet tacked on to the rear as sheds or later as a closet off the garden in which a flush toilet was placed—the water closet—but in general the pattern of the row houses was highly consistent. The frontage might vary, but it generally ranged between about fifteen and twenty feet, with sixteen feet probably the most common width of the façade. That width would contain a front hall, normally quite narrow, with a front room beside it that would be used for daily living. Behind these, a kitchen opened onto the backyard, where the coal shed and privy (or later the water closet) could be found. A narrow set of stairs led from the front hall to two or three "chambers," as chill and damp as the mind may imagine, where the family slept. This example would have been good working-class housing where land was not too expensive, wages were reasonable, and the family could and would spend perhaps a full 15 percent of its income for housing. Where any of those factors was less favorable—land too expensive, wages low, or discretionary expenditure for housing less, all quite likely occurrences—the housing might be far more austere.

The most typical form of housing austerity was the so-called back-to-back house. These structures had only one wall open to the outside; two houses on adjacent streets would share a rear party wall, leaving neither with any backyard. The savings on land costs were such that these houses could be built, and as a result rented, for less. The Royal Commission Studying the State of the Large Towns and Populous Places found that these houses might, in the 1840s, be built for as little as £50 each. As a result literally hundreds of thousands of back-to-back houses were built, and they became the basic component of the housing stock in most of the larger industrial cities. In 1919, the city of Birmingham had some one hundred and fifty thousand working-class houses[34] of which more than half must have been back-to-backs, for in 1939 some seventy-five thousand back-to-backs still stood, even after the city had built fifty thousand working-class houses in the interwar years.

Whether back-to-back or the more ample single-depth terraces, these

34. Herbert J. Manzoni, *The Production of Fifty Thousand Municipal Houses* (Birmingham: City of Birmingham, 1939), p. 17.

row houses were assembled in similar fashion along fairly narrow streets with sidewalks on each side and in street grids that were either truly rectangular—as they were most likely to be in back-to-backs—or slightly curving but with streets basically parallel to one another. The density of land coverage was very high, perhaps because almost universally the houses were of two stories without either cellar or attic. In the back-to-back areas, the streets had, of necessity, to serve as the existing open space. Until flush toilets were introduced, a line of shared privies stood down the middle of the street. One day a week, the street was closed to vehicles so that washing lines could be strung across it for housewives on both sides to use for their laundry. After cars were introduced and were beginning to be owned by the working class in the years after World War II, the usual system was for alternate streets to be so obstructed. Before then, seemingly all washed on Monday, as was the longstanding British tradition.

The 1843 budget figures of the Ashton cotton operatives suggest several other components of the industrial housing area as it emerged by the middle of the last century. Very basic food needs could be met at the small shops that tended to be scattered about the working-class housing areas. Opinions differ greatly as to the merits of the various types. One of the worst in virtually all minds was the "truck" or "tommy" shop run by the factory owners. Trading was in exchange for a scrip given instead of currency by the mills in the workers' pay envelopes. This system is generally believed to have further victimized the workers both by forcing them to trade only in the truck shop—the only place accepting the scrip—and by so monopolizing their trade that excessive prices could be charged for the goods exchanged for scrip. When a neighborhood housed workers from a single plant, the chances for the successful operation of the truck shops were great, particularly as they often offered small advance credit that firmly tied the necessitous or improvident worker to the truck shop, seemingly forevermore.

Even in those areas where truck shops were not present, or after legislation had caused them to be removed, the small shops that served the workers were probably not on the whole the cheapest places for them to shop. But the small shopkeeper's role is not as yet finally determined; I shall leave that argument to others. The use of such small shops carrying a very limited range of goods fitted well physically into these working-class neighborhoods. A shop could be slipped into a row house or a back-to-back—commonly at the end of a block—without any special morphological provision. Within the neighborhood, another form of retail trade, that of the street hawker, assumed considerable importance. Vegetables and fruits, fish, meat, and other fairly common and often perishable commodities were sold from barrows. Markets beyond the neighborhood—in ancient marketplaces in all parts of England, in market halls in the more carefully planned towns, or in street markets in Lancashire and some other highly industrialized areas—served special needs or particularly the demand for perishable products. These markets would be the most likely places to seek clothing and very basic household items such as dishes, pots and pans, and bed coverings.

Pubs and Public Conveniences

The 1843 figures for Ashton suggest yet a different need that was met within each neighborhood, that for ale and "spirits," normally gin. In that era, the production of ale was most likely to be within an inn or the farmstead, with a brewhouse in the yard. Thus, in the pattern of production and consumption at the beginning of the Industrial Age, brewing was domestic. As industrialization spread and factory towns became larger, the opportunity arose for a brewery in the town to supply a number of possible drinking places. Inns might continue to produce their own ale, but working-class areas held few traditional inns, though a normal Briton's thirst remained. Town breweries solved the problem of supply by establishing "public houses" where their product was sold to the general populace living in the vicinity. These pubs came to serve relatively small neighborhoods, particularly when several breweries in a city each sought a set of "tied houses" that sold only their own ale and, later, beer. Thus, the frequency of pubs was in part a function of working-class thirst, itself related to the general drabness of industrial life, but also a function of the pattern of intense competition among breweries. The early nineteenth century had seen much drinking of gin, when a dram could be had for a penny; the gin shop was often little more than a room in a house within a working-class district. The effort to reform the habits of the poor led to the imposition of ever-higher taxes on gin. By midcentury, gin and other hard liquors had become much more the downfall of the prosperous than of the poor; beer and ale had become the nearly universal drink of the working class, save on special occasions. And the brewing and handling of unpasteurized beer—all that was available at the time, and much the English preference until recently—required some basic level of organization that the small publican could not easily provide. Thus, the city brewer interjected himself into the picture; he set up a large brewery, the products of which were consistently and rationally distributed in his own wagons to his own public houses within the metropolitan area. The English came to drink almost exclusively in public and at the neighborhood pub, which became a critical component of the social geography of working-class areas.

This practice led quickly to the provision of public conveniences to make socially acceptable and sanitary the homeward journey on chilly, damp evenings of those who had congregated in the pub until it closed. These "public conveniences" are a striking feature of British urban morphology, which is understandable mainly in terms of the concentration of drinking in working-class areas to men and in public houses, one of the odd social outgrowths of the Industrial Revolution still reflected frequently in the comic strip *Andy Capp*.

Districts within the City

The fundamental assemblage of buildings and uses in the English industrial city was the working-class district composed of row housing ranged around one or several factories and served by quite local shops and pubs.

The locating factor was the factory, because the hours of labor were long and the virtually universal way of going to work was on foot. The result was the creation of a city, or even a metropolis, of small, very definite neighborhoods, which contained the life of most people save for weekly or less frequent visits to the market square, the market hall, or the street market for the buying of items of clothing, house furnishings, or perishable food. This parochial existence was enforced by conditions of work and housing and the economic unavailability of access to mechanical transportation. Only later in the nineteenth century, when the bicycle, the trolley, and finally the cheap excursion to the seaside by train began to come into the life of the working class, did any appreciable breaking out of this narrow geographical frame of life occur.

The factories built in English cities were for the most part rather tall and compact structures, requiring relatively little land and occupying sites quite comprehensible within the standard street grid of the city. The height came from the use of mechanical distribution of power, largely by gears and shafts, from the rotative motion of the steam engine, which forced the general compaction of the plant. Only where specific processes, such as glass making, brass founding, or chemical manufacture, required specialized sorts of buildings were particular sites required. Even then, the chances were good that the plant would be located well within the built-up fabric of the city where the firm would have begun at an earlier time, with worker housing growing up around it.

The central area of cities in industrial England tended to be the province of the middle and upper classes, as Engels saw it. There were clustered the offices of bankers, solicitors, and other persons dealing specifically with financial interests; stores for the more well-to-do—jewelers, tailors, dressmakers, and other lines of trade beyond the reach of the working class; and governmental and ecclesiastical offices. Shops were on the ground floor and offices in the stories above, though only to a height of two or three floors. Interspersed amid these newer undertakings would probably be a few old inns, a railway hotel or two, the stations of the separate railroad companies serving the place, and some remnants of the preindustrial town. In back courts, small alleys, and hidden spots were quite commonly found "stews," where tiny deteriorated buildings housed the very poor who served as the casual or most menial labor in the central activities. In few industrial places had any overall design guided the growth of the towns, so buildings tended to stand as individual conceptions of what a city should look like, showing stages of fashionable architecture, a landlord's parsimony or generosity, and a generational mixture of structure—some virtually medieval, others essentially modern. Because of such a mixture of things, and the absence of the orderly plan made fashionable by the Georgian city, a constant craving arose to promote "development schemes." These schemes sought first to sweep away the stews and the corners occupied by the interests of the poor, replacing them with grand streets with proper façades and "appropriate" uses. Joseph Chamberlain began his political career in masterminding the Corporation Street Scheme in Birmingham, which in 1876 provided that ancient place, but rather recently incorporated city, a new "main street." In other

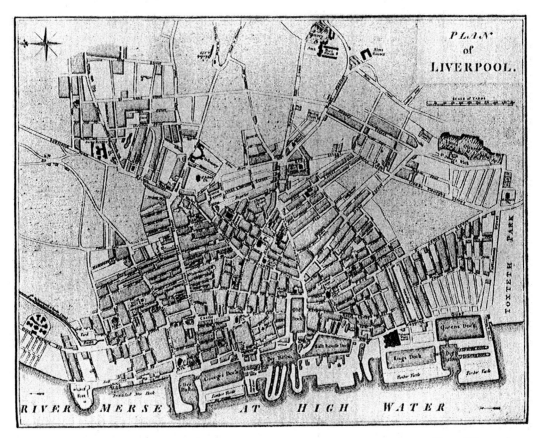

growing industrial towns, improvement likewise was heavily equated with physical reconstruction into genteel uses of the former purlieus of the poor. A strong strain of physical determinism argued that bad houses made bad people, so razing the slums would raise the people.

Railroads and the City: The Right to Mobility

This notion was so confidently held that an avid welcome was often extended to railroad companies when they sought to build into or through the center of the city. They were asked merely to pass through the neighborhoods of the poor, for the dual purpose of razing the worst of that property and shielding the middle- and upper-class quarters from the smoke and noise of the trains. The force that railroads exerted on urban land use, removing from other uses large areas and destroying working-class neighborhoods without a general practice of replacement elsewhere, has been well covered in John Kellett's *The Impact of Railways on Victorian Cities*.[35] As Kellet points out, the railroad companies were given two unusual privileges—that of being a corporation allowed to raise capital from more than six persons, a privilege

35. John Kellett, *The Impact of Railways on Victorian Cities* (London: Routledge and Kegan Paul, 1969).

industry did not possess until the 1860s, and that of being allowed to exercise the right of eminent domain (compulsory purchase). In return for these vastly important privileges, social responsibility was not as well developed as one might have hoped.

Giving evidence before a royal commission on the Metropolitan Railway Termini, the great social commentator Charles Pearson (solicitor to the Corporation of London) stated the problem succinctly: "A poor man is chained to the spot; he has not the leisure to walk, and he has not the money to ride." And the intrusion of rail lines in the dense working-class neighborhoods of inner London aggravated that situation. "They are crowded together still more, they are pressed together more densely in a similar description of houses to those which they formerly inhabited."[36]

Quite simply, little was done to care for those evicted. Instead, they were forced upon an already overcrowded working-class housing supply, aggravating its existing plights. In such a way does the destruction of bad housing, without other actions, lead to even worse people, to the extent that increased crowding leads to increased crime and social disintegration. But the royal commission study buried action on the problem, if not the truth of its existence.

Voices were raised in objection to the snobbish and condescending policies of the railroad companies and their parliamentary spokesmen. Those gentlemen argued that lowering the price of travel was against the best interests of the companies. Those able to pay first- and second-class fare might travel a class lower just to save money. James Smithells, traffic manager of the Lancashire and Yorkshire Railway, testified in 1866 in answer to the question, "Would it not be an advantage to the public to attach third-class carriages to all trains?": "I should scarcely call it an advantage. Our district is full of men who have risen by their own industry and energy, but their economy is such, although they occupy a respectable position in life that if third-class carriages were put on with every train they would avail themselves of them. I think that many persons who take advantage of third-class trains ought not to do it."[37] Similarly, some held that, though third-class travel paid its way, it took a much larger increase in numbers in that class than in higher classes to enlarge the profit of the company. Daniel Gooch of the Great Western Railway argued that the working class had not the time to travel. William Cawkell held that offering low fares to the working class was "an inducement for a great many people to take advantage of them and take long journeys which they can badly afford to do." That exemplar of the established order, the duke of Wellington, believed that railroads might become "a premium to the lower orders to go uselessly wandering about the country."[38]

None among the upper classes believed that the poor should have mobility, daily or periodically. Best they stay in their quarters in the central city, even if those places came to be yet more crowded by the increasing influx of

36. Quoted in ibid., p. 37.
37. Quoted in ibid., pp. 89–90.
38. Quoted in ibid., p. 91.

migrants to the city and by the absolute reduction in the supply of working-class housing as it was destroyed to provide routes and stations for rail lines entering the city. In 1844, William Gladstone had sponsored an act that finally held "that each company be required to run over their line on each weekday at least one train conveying third-class passengers in carriages provided with seats and protected from the weather, at a speed of not less than twelve miles an hour, including stoppages, and at a fare not exceeding one penny a mile for adults, children under twelve half price, and under three free, 56lb. of luggage to be allowed without charge."[39] Thus, for the first time the notion was accepted that the laboring class had the right to mobility along with the more fortunate members of society. After 1871, when the Bank Holidays Act finally made a few days a year available to workers for recreation, these third-class fares could take on greater importance. The railroads even found it both possible and financially profitable to offer excursions to the seaside from Manchester, Birmingham, London, and the other large industrial towns on Bank Holiday Mondays.[40] The business view was far from favorable in many cases. Jack Simmons quotes the general manager of one company: "The London & North Western company have hitherto held the belief that society in this country, for all purposes, naturally divided itself into three classes, and that the wants and tasks of the community are best served by their present practice of sticking to a truly subservient third-class, tolerated mainly by government order."[41]

Within cities we can hardly expect that the views of such managers would be at all favorable to providing cheap transportation to workers commuting to work. Only in 1854, when the Great Eastern Railway sought to extend its lines into the northeastern part of the City of London to Liverpool Street Station, was the working class given any regard in the matter of intraurban transportation, and then only because that extension would have destroyed so much working-class housing that Parliament would not authorize it unless the company provided "workingmen's trains" early in the morning and after five or six in the evening. The destruction in Shoreditch and Bethnal Green in East London was to be compensated for by providing access by train, for a fare of a penny for working men, to the newly emerging working-class suburbs of Edmonton and Walthamstow. For the distance of eight miles these trains were truly cheap, but for twenty years they had no reflection in the practices of other London rail lines. As the pressure on central-city housing grew, and the quality of those areas deteriorated, an Artisans' and Labourers' Dwellings Act of 1868 required that "the obligation placed upon the Eastern Counties (Great Eastern Railway) system of railways out of London to provide trains for artisans at the rate of a penny for each passenger per course of seven or eight miles should be extended to other suburban railways as opportunity may offer."[42]

39. Quoted in Hamilton Ellis, *British Railway History: 1830–1876* (London: George Allen and Unwin, 1954), 2: 129.
40. Jack Simmons, *The Railways of Britain* (London: Routledge and Kegan Paul, 1961), p. 26.
41. Ibid., p. 26.
42. Ellis, *British Railway History,* 1: 319–20.

Only as these cheap workers' trains became more available was there much impact of the railroad on the life of the industrial class, and even then mainly in London. In the provincial cities, train commuting was much less common, and apparently of particularly little significance among what we would today call blue-collar workers. Seemingly, their wages were sufficiently low that the cost of transport, by whatever medium, was too great to be borne save for the odd excursion to the seaside during Bank Holidays or the later "wakes weeks" of industrial Lancashire and other areas in the North. These vacation periods apparently represented the modern version of the medieval "wake" of the local parish when a festival was held in honor of its patron saint. In northern industrial towns, as wages and working conditions improved, the local mills would close for a summer week, and all workers would be free to go to Blackpool or other seaside resorts during the specific wakes week for Bolton, or Rochdale, or the other parishes.

Abandonment and Succession

The effect of the train on the middle- and upper-class housing pattern was very different indeed. These were the two of the three orders envisaged by the manager of the London and North Western Railway (LNWR) for whom the railroad was a true emancipator. As cities grew, formerly desirable housing felt the pressure for change through crowding and the possibilities of the wealthier classes realizing large returns on capital by abandoning those premises in favor of new ones more distant from the city center. Doubtless it was not the social pressure from below that caused the middle and upper classes to move; rather, their desire to move came to be paired with the chance to sell leaseholds or freeholds closer to the center—with no great loss or even a considerable gain—bringing about the creation of the suburb. As early as the 1820s omnibuses had been introduced into London and other cities; we have seen them by Engels's time in Manchester. These original mass-transportation vehicles came to be used by middle-class men in commuting back and forth to central offices and warehouses. The "villa" or detached house began to be the ideal of the upper social strata, who had the money necessary to cover the increased cost of commuting. When the London and Birmingham Railway (later the LNWR) was finished in late 1838, "halts" near London became possible, around which villa communities might be laid out.

A rather unsuspected, and certainly unplanned for, growth of suburban commuting traffic began to emerge on the other rail lines built out of London. Generally, the development of this traffic depended on the social status of the housing areas along the line. The LNWR, already frosty toward workers on its own account, was further dissuaded from encouraging working-class commuters by the elevated status of the suburbs in the northwestern quadrant of London's growth through which it passed. There, for several reasons that Hugh Prince has identified, the housing was middle and upper class, particularly to the west of the London and North Western lines.[43] The

43. Hugh C. Prince, "North-West London 1814–1863" and "North-West London 1864–1914," in *Greater London*, ed. J. T. Coppock and Hugh C. Prince (London: Faber and Faber, 1964).

railroad tended to fix in all too firm masonry, and nearly as rigid social practice, the division of London into "two cities." The working-class city lay mainly to the east of the LNWR, and the city of the "quality" lay west of George Stephenson's overbuilt line. The LNWR reached London from the provinces; some would question how long it would have taken the metropolis to make use of railroads had not the greater "drive" of industrial Britain to the north projected lines to and into a rather reluctant London to the south. The London and Birmingham and the later lines to the north continued to have poor connections to the workplaces of the metropolis, which lay in the East End.

Intra-Urban Railroads

To remedy the problem of connecting London's mainline railroad stations with the City and, as a result, affording use of the railroads for the suburban commuting of City men, two schemes were developed that ultimately made London a city of vast commuting flows. The first proposal grew out of the LNWR's initial failure to profit from its ostensible connection of Birmingham with London's docks for the export of the vast array of goods produced in the West Midland metropolis. As originally planned, the London and Birmingham reached Camden Town just beyond the built-up limits of London, where the railroad established a junction with the Regent's Canal to be used for carrying export products to the docks on the Thames in London's East End. The service was slow and difficult, thus failing to develop as foreseen. To improve on this situation two things were done: the London and Birmingham was carried to Euston Square at the edge of the built-up heart of the City of London, and a rail line was built to the docks and, at a slightly later time, into the edge of the City at Broad Street Station, which was opened as the North London Railway in 1865.[44] This line to the docks and the City, which came to be known as the North London Railway, provided after 1865 an easy and efficient access from the business heart of the City to the potential suburban areas located along the LNWR, and subsequently along the Great Northern Railway (whose mainline station was King's Cross). This easterly line of both railroads made the mainlines and metropolitan branches a great system for well-to-do commuting back and forth to emerging suburban areas. When the London and Birmingham was built, London's northwest was already the socially elect area: the North London with its mainline connections made certain the survival of the pattern already shaping in this quadrant—the rise of probably the largest suburban district of any city in the world. The great suburban band made Broad Street Station, despite its obscurity, almost the busiest station in London; more people passed through there daily than through Isambard Brunel's Paddington and Stephenson's Euston combined.

The other solution to the problem of making the railroads useful for suburban commuting was the creation, under the aegis of Charles Pearson,

44. A detailed account of the reason for, and the construction of, all the London stations is given in Alan A. Jackson, *London's Termini* (Newton Abbot, Devonshire: David and Charles, 1969). Also in paperback, Pan Editions, London, 1972.

of the Metropolitan Railway, an underground line beginning at Paddington on the west to provide a City connection for the Great Western Railway. It passed near the other mainline stations (Marylebone, Euston, St. Pancras, and King's Cross) to the City at Farringdon Street, where the authorities had recently cleared the site of the offensive meat market. It was assumed, as was the practice for many years, that mainline steam trains would pass through Paddington and King's Cross to go on to Farringdon Street, where they would gain better access to the City.

When the line opened in 1864 it proved highly successful, but along with the North London line to Broad Street, its patronage was largely that of the middle class. "Until 1875 indeed, the North London Railway was exempt from the obligation to carry third-class passengers; the stockbrokers and merchants travelled first-class, and the clerks a respectable second."[45] Again, the improvement of the travel of the middle class showed little benefit filtering downward to the working class. Only after 1900, when the American notion of true mass transit was brought to London by Charles Tyson Yerkes with the Central London Railway, did the working class gain much thought or benefit. Then the two-penny tube brought a transformation of the lower-class housing areas that was a radical, and a frightening, vision to the proper classes west of the LNWR.

What sort of suburbs did the railroad bring to London and other English cities? In Engels's words we have already seen the broad outlines. Strong class division existed among the residential areas, based fundamentally on the ability to pay for suburban rail service. London and the industrial metropolises that grew rapidly in the nineteenth century tended to be surrounded by rolling countryside, sometimes, as in the case of the land on the London clay, rather gentle in slope. On these lands surrounding most cities grew up a belt of large houses and market-gardens where wealth was able to maintain or secure convenient access to the city. As pressure for intensification of land use grew, the high productivity of the fields planted to crops of a perishable nature could ward off for one further generation the expansion of housing areas. But as the economic return to be gained by "urbanizing" the estate or the vegetable field grew large enough, as it usually did once convenient and direct rail service was locally available in the journey-to-work to the central area, then the breaking up of the large parcels into "housing estates" became so common as to be almost the universal practice. These estates could range over a fair social spectrum, but they did not reach very close to the bottom of the social heap. Instead, the poorer members of society either had to depend on deteriorated housing of the middle and upper classes or had to seek housing in the cramped and mean workers' housing developments close to mills or the casual employment found largely in the city center. Those working-class housing developments were dense in population and truly constrained in form—tiny in the ground area given to each house and limited to generally undesirable sites where no one but the most socially disadvantaged could be expected to live.

This social stratification was the most significant feature of the Victorian

45. Ellis, *British Railway History*, p. 318.

Map of Sultan Street, Camberwell, in 1871. From H. J. Dyos, Victorian Suburb *(Leicester, England: Leicester University Press, 1966).*

suburbs. The society housed was unbelievably concerned with image and address, to the point that the dreary conventionality of these areas can hardly be imagined if unexperienced. Streets were classified in an urban social taxonomy clearly perceived by the Victorians of the upper two classes. "It is worth noting, incidentally, that since the right suburban address was to the resident primarily a social requirement, it was nearly as much a matter of nomenclature to him as it was of the site or of architecture, and sophisticated builders knew this. The monotonous but purposeful recital of Debrett['s *Peerage*-]—Burlington, Montague, Addington, Melbourne, Devonshire, Bedford, and so on—was, therefore, a special characteristic of the pre-Victorian and early Victorian suburban address."[46] As each large

46. H. J. Dyos, *Victorian Suburb* (Leicester, England: Leicester University Press, 1966), pp. 170–71.

Urban
Morphogenesis
in the
Industrial Age

parcel was committed to development, the builders operating there tried to appraise the market and determine the most profitable use to be made of the land in terms of total return. Surprisingly, construction for the lower middle class or even the upper working class might prove more profitable than that for the more elevated. H. J. Dyos in his classic study of Camberwell, a mixed suburb in south London that housed elements ranging from the upper working class to the upper middle class, adduced evidence that, size for size, working-class housing paid considerably higher rents than did that for the middle class.[47]

The houses built in these suburban areas were of two sorts—detached villas on rather sizable lots, and row houses ranged continuously along a street frontage. The terraces of row houses were much the more common. The villas were often the remnant of an essentially semirural pattern when they housed within the limits of an outlying village persons of urban culture but independent income not needing a daily journey-to-work in the city. They were within easy periodic reach of the city but not truly a morphological part of that place. Only as rail transportation was extended to the villages of the surrounding country would daily commuters of considerable wealth take up these villas, and as the city grew the villas would form merely an enclave within the generally expanding carpet of terrace housing.

Those terraces were structurally rather similar, though scale and architectural detailing might vary somewhat. The most expensive row houses would be of three stories and a cellar and of reasonable width, perhaps twenty or even twenty-five feet. Such a household would hold public rooms on the first floor, with the kitchen and other servants' quarters in the basement. Family bedrooms would occupy the second floor, and servants rooms the third. Normally, the house had the front door and the stairway to one side, with the rest of the space given over for use in entertainment as well as family life. Beyond a reasonable number of villas, the upper middle class depended most heavily on the row houses: "The two-storeyed brick terrace was the almost standard component, even for fairly substantial houses, which might signify their superiority by an extra storey (if only an attic with a dormer window) or by a wider frontage."

Class showed not in the basic plan, but rather in the architectural detailing. Normally, a shallow door-surround produced a basic porch, which might be pushed outward from the front wall to convey a greater sense of elegance. Pilasters and columns, more elaborate surrounds for windows and doors, and the introduction of a one- or two-story bay window gave higher class to the house in a clear and visible fashion, something that along with the proper address became a matter of intense concern to the socially imprisoned Victorians. "The principal roofing material was blue Welsh slate, sometimes cut in a petal shape or surmounted by a fretwork of ornamental red ridge tiles, and terminated at the gable ends by narrow wooden or even leaden barge boards; on the larger houses the barge board almost became a piece of architectural millinery, an elaborate frippery which was intended 'to do something' for the whole appearance."

47. Ibid., p. 185.

These houses, (a) on Trafalgar Avenue, built in 1852, (b) in Vicarage Grove, built between 1866 and 1868, and (c) on Ivydale Road, built in 1900, show the changes in style as well as the diversity of classes found in the South London suburb of Camberwell.

Brick was so universally the building material that only its color remained in question. Color depended mainly on the geographical source of the clays used, and ranged from gray through blue to yellow and red. Sometimes the red was rather fierce, as in the University of Birmingham. There the immoderate intensity of the color gave the whole class of provincial universities the sobriquet of Red Brick as their most instantly apparent quality, and one intimately tied up with Victorian building—not so dominant at Cambridge or Oxford as in Birmingham or Leeds. Those areas with blue brick—particularly favored, it seems, for small city halls and public conveniences but not unknown in rather unhappy residential areas—stand as the epitome of Industrial Revolution building, commonly holding up the rafters of Methodist chapels or giving security and strength to police stations in working-class areas.

The fronts of houses were adorned by "distinctive embellishments" in the better order of construction, normally in "the form of plaster mouldings to make sham balustrades to unusable balconies above the bay-windows, or to form tooled columns which were often of absurdly bulky or slender dimensions. It was no rare thing for each of the capitals to these—usually composed of fossilized fruit and unidentifiable foliage—to be quite different from each of its fellows on the same house, but to be repeated (in a different permutation) a few doors away."[48]

Uniformity in substance was matched by novelty in completion in a harness fairly typical of Victorian material life. Identical houses were more common in the cheapest streets and the "geometry of the ground plan tended to settle some of the social issues from the outset, for the longer and straighter and flatter the street the fewer the pretensions it normally had." Most cultures seemingly make some qualitative association with regularity and irregularity. During the Renaissance the orderly and straight was most respected, but though the romantic Victorians thought highly of conformity in social behavior, slight irregularity in civic design gained a certain desirable cachet. "The choice of trees, too, had its social overtones: planes and horse-chestnuts for the wide avenues and lofty mansions of the well-to-do; limes and laburnums, and acacias for the middle incomes; unadorned macadam for the wage-earners." A society of established order must of necessity assign symbols of rank. "Within such limits, however, the occupiers themselves also had plenty of scope for little acts of symbolism, as, for example, in the furnishing of the front windows or the arrangement of the front garden." The corseted order of the Victorian garden pains us, but it told the Victorians much about that almost central question, the social rank of the occupants:

> The aspidistra half-concealed by carefully draped lace curtains,
> the privet hedge of carefully determined height, the geometrical
> perfection of the minute flower-beds edged with London Pride, the
> window-box trailing fern and periwinkle—these were some of the
> elements in one situation. Ivy-scaled walls, great round clumps of
> laurels, rhododendrons, lilac, and laburnum, lawns infested with
> sparrows and set with pedestalled urns, and gravelled drives—
> these were the elements of another. It would be a mistake to think
> of these features solely in terms of personal taste. They gave scope,
> it is true, for the outward expression of romantic idiosyncrasies,
> but they were equally emblems of different shades of respectability,
> some of suburbia's badges of rank, and their collective expression
> was a subtle acknowledgement of a locality's status in suburban
> society.[49]

The railroad brought the development of such housing areas as suburbs outside of London; they were more extensively developed there than elsewhere, but not very differently. In a society obsessed with class and fearful of

48. This and preceding details on the Victorian suburb are from ibid., pp. 185–88.
49. Ibid., p. 189.

misapprehension as to personal status, the housing combined an unbelievable timidity with just enough distinction to rank people as regards "respectability." The terrace of houses could shelter the gravediggers of northern Camberwell just as it did the barristers of the more select streets, but with the practiced eye of the class-divided society, there was no danger of stumbling blindly into inappropriate surroundings. The "little acts of symbolism" were fully as important as the fundamental act of providing shelter.

The Geographical Limits of Nonintercourse

We have considered the emergence of industry in Manchester and Britain in general; we now must look at the pattern of the city given to industry in other countries. The Industrial Revolution era witnessed the most salient of the changes in the city's morphogenesis. Writing in 1842, W. Cooke Taylor, a commentator on the evils of the Corn Laws, argued "that the geographical limits of non-intercourse established in Manchester are the greatest of the special evils connected with that town. The isolation of classes in England has gone far to divide into nations as distinct as the Normans and Saxons." His conclusion was echoed most effectively two years later when Disraeli published his *Sybil, or: The Two Nations*. Taylor saw this separation of the classes both as conducive to callous disregard for the welfare of the workers and as destructive of any acculturation process to be worked on immigrants to the city. Because Manchester required such massive in-movements of unskilled labor, it "does not afford a fair specimen of the factory population . . . and that outward aspect of the place affords a very imperfect test of the state of trade in South Lancashire. . . . There is always, and must necessarily be, considerable distress in a place where there is a large demand for untrained labour." In a caveat that Engels might well have practiced that same year as he observed Manchester life, Taylor noted clearly, "It is a very common error to attribute to the factories the evils which really arise from an immigrating and non-factory population." He continues, "I took some pains to ascertain the character of this immigrating population, and I found it such as to account, in a very great degree, for the high rate of mortality and the low condition of the morals in the township of Manchester. It appeared that peasants inadequate to the fatigues of rural toil frequently come into the towns with the hope of finding some light employment suited to their feeble strength, and that persons whose character is blighted in the country seek to escape notice in the crowd of the town."[50]

The "geographical limits of non-intercourse" combined with the implosion on the city of a rural population to contribute immeasurably to the deterioration of urban life. The in-migrants were not always of the best abilities and practices, and were so divided from the accomplished urban population in both the working and the middle classes as to be isolated from its improving influences. To demonstrate his point, and as well to serve

50. W. Cooke Taylor, "Notes of a Tour in the Manufacturing Districts of Lancashire: In a Series of Letters to His Grace the Archbishop of Dublin," 2d ed. (1842), extracted and rpt. in *The Idea of the City in Nineteenth-Century Britain*, ed. B. I. Coleman (Boston: Routledge and Kegan Paul, 1973).

almost as the text for our analysis of the impact of industrialization on American cities, Taylor takes note of the continuing mill villages standing self-contained outside the city center. First, those places were not flooded with the vast numbers of unskilled labor he notes in Manchester. In addition, those self-contained factory towns were characterized by the manufacturer serving two roles, that of factory manager and that of landlord for the housing of workers. Taylor reasons that in such a joint undertaking, the best interests of the landlord are served by as continuous a period of employment as possible, which he sees as considerably alleviating the rigors of industrial life, notably when some paternal relationship existed between the manufacturer and his workers. We may question the social wisdom of such a tie, but we need not question the practical benefits in housing to be gained from it. In essence, Taylor describes the situation before the generalization of housing that we have proposed as an essential analytical concept.

In sum, the Industrial Revolution in Britain brought about two new morphogenetic processes of great strength: geographical limits of social nonintercourse arose, creating at least the Two Nations that Disraeli discerned; in turn, housing was generalized within cities, thus abolishing the introduction of a subvention from the manufacturing process to housing. In any event, two distinct groups of capitalists were created with nonconvergent interests, in contrast to the traditional situation. Other morphogenetic processes have been discussed earlier; the forces exerted by the countryside and its social elite on the city led to the implosion of rural evictees on the city, the constraint of the physical spread of the city by aristocratic landowners, and the beggaring of the urban working class by high food prices artificially maintained by the rural gentry, prices that made it impossible for the urban working class to buy adequate housing for itself. Thus, the process of industrialization was only one of several forces shaping the city of the Industrial Age.

The Peculiar Case of the Industrial City in America

Until the shots were fired at Concord in 1775, most types of manufacturing were forbidden in the English colonies in America. The thirteen colonies had been set out with the notion of furthering the mercantile development of England. As a result, an active effort was carried on to stop or severely restrict any production of manufactured goods outside the mother country.

Not all production could be stopped; a few items, it was recognized, must be produced in the colonies for their own essential needs, or for the needs of England. From the beginning, elements of local handicraft were accepted, rather akin to those produced locally within the manorial or "natural" economy of the Middle Ages. Woolen cloth was woven in the home for family use; in Rowley in Massachusetts from the 1630s on, a modest quantity of this cloth was handwoven for sale in New England. Much of this manufacturing activity could exist in the obscurity of distance from the king's agents, but expansion of the scale of production beyond that intended for local consumption was difficult. Any noticeable flow of American goods to England or the Newfoundland or West Indian colonies would have brought anguished cries from the home manufacturers. In 1699 a Woolens Act "forebade colonial woolen cloth to be sold outside the place or plantation where it was woven; but as most rural families carded, spun and wove their own wool, this caused no hardship in America."[51]

The colonies were always permitted to process the agricultural products for which they were first set up. Molasses could be distilled into rum, though the Americans illegally imported molasses from the French colonies, where it was more cheaply bought than in the English islands. Tar and turpentine, barrel staves, box boards, and a number of other forest products were fabricated quite legally. Along with a booming trade in salt fish, flour, rice, indigo, tobacco, potash, and several other simply processed staples, America could support an active merchant community and the ships to carry its goods to the West Indies and Newfoundland, even on occasion to England.

But England's example was not lost on the colonial merchants who were fully as enterprising as, and perhaps somewhat more ingenious than, their English colleagues. They wished to try their hand at manufacturing just as they had at trading. The English sought to control the Americans' entry into manufacturing in several ways, of which the most effective was not the embargo placed by parliamentary acts, easily overlooked by those at such a distance, but instead the tight control that England exercised on the availability of specie (coined money) in America. The situation became so desperate that the legislature of the Massachusetts colony issued promissory notes to finance Sir William Phipps's expedition against Québec. These notes, with the possible exception of similar paper uttered in Sweden at this time, were the first paper currency ever issued and they did serve, though with certain awkward qualities.[52] The colonies found it difficult to operate in foreign trade or with England, where the balance of that trade was normally against the colonies, but internal to America the paper began to make possible the accumulation of bills of credit that became the main medium of exchange, in the end giving us our dollar "bill" in contrast to Britain's pound "note." With these bills, merchants could begin to assemble capital and look toward the creation of manufacturing establishments.

We cannot speak in detail of all of the early mills, but we may note their general use. Grist mills had existed from the beginning of the colonies, and from 1645 iron smelters were operating, beginning with one in Massachusetts.[53] Fulling mills, sawmills, and a few other simple waterpowered operations were carried on before the Revolution. But in general only the ironmaking industry showed much development. Until 1750, iron exports from America had been forbidden, though by then a number of smelters were at work in Massachusetts and the other colonies. The colonies had been self-sufficient in iron making perhaps as early as the beginning of the eighteenth century; certainly in 1750 when the British market was opened to colonial pig and bar iron, a surplus of around three thousand tons remained for

51. Samuel Eliot Morison and Henry Steele Commager, *The Growth of the American Republic* (New York: Oxford University Press, 1942), 1: 102.

52. Ibid., p. 104.

53. Peter Temin, *Iron and Steel in Ninteteenth-Century America* (Cambridge, Mass.: M.I.T. Press, 1964), p. 13.

export.[54] When that legislation had been adopted by the British Parliament, one of its provisions was that Americans could not develop any further works for producing finished products. Yet we know that such an embargo was largely disregarded. By 1775, "there were actually more 'furnaces' [where pig iron was produced] and 'forges' [where pig iron was resmelted into bar or wrought iron] in the Thirteen Colonies than in England and Wales . . . [and although] most of them were very small, employing but a few dozen hands at the most . . . the average annual production—300 tons of pig iron for each furnace, and 150 tons of bar iron for each forge—was about the same as in England."[55]

In 1700, the American colonies were producing around fifteen hundred tons of iron annually, about 2 percent of the estimated world production. In 1750, the figure had risen to around ten thousand tons annually, and then to thirty thousand tons in 1771. "In any case, the production of iron in America on the eve of the Revolution may have been as high as 15 per cent of world production, a proportion that was not again equalled until well into the nineteenth century. And while this high production was largely for domestic consumption, the colonies were net exporters of unfinished iron."[56]

Even from a very early time, at least as early as 1645, industry was not unknown to the new colonies, nor was it necessarily carried out on a trivial scale. But certain overriding conditions were imposed from outside that may have given American industry an unbalanced development during its first 150 years. We know that the English Parliament sought to ward off virtually all manufacturing in the thirteen colonies; we know as well that this effort was not wholly successful. Without such restraints, what would have been the amount of actual production? Only by looking at two facets of production—of iron and of textiles—can we guess. On the basis of existing bits of evidence, we can assume that certain industries in America would have developed on a large scale well before the Revolution if the English Parliament had not ruled otherwise. Distilling, shipbuilding, some basic kinds of textile production, and anything that would have benefited greatly from cheap and vastly plentiful waterpower might well have grown up in the thirteen colonies, as did iron making. But in this realm of conjecture, we should not lose sight of the fact that to a point well in advance of what Parliament wanted, the settlers in the New World participated in Britain's emerging eighteenth-century Industrial Revolution.

Writing in 1917, Rolla Milton Tryon set out to study the nature of *Household Manufactures in the United States*. He proposed the notion of the "family factory," historically a peculiar concept, but one that helps us understand the great amount of manufacture done in America before the formal Industrial Revolution, as Phyllis Deane has shown there was in England.[57] Tryon shows that the scale of production in farm homes could be

54. Morison and Commager, *Growth of the American Republic*, p. 102.

55. Ibid., p. 103.

56. Temin, *Iron and Steel*, pp. 15–19.

57. Rolla Milton Tryon, *Household Manufactures in the United States, 1640–1860* (Chicago: University of Chicago Press, 1917). For a discussion of the English Industrial Revolution before

very impressive indeed—one family made more than eight hundred yards of textiles of various sorts in one year, as well as possibly other tools of agriculture and the general necessities of life. A distinctive unit of manufacture, the family sought both to maximize its product and to care for a diversity of needs. The agricultural implements were simple but usually sturdy and homemade, as were most furniture and household goods.

The process of self-provision, the Yankee commandment, prepared a fertile ground in which invention might germinate. Eli Whitney's visit to Savannah produced first the cotton gin and ultimately a vast social and economic transformation of the Western world. Immediate ingenuity, so typical of New England in the nineteenth century, created a flood of machines from a basically rural area in central Massachusetts, the valleys of western Connecticut, and the hill areas of Vermont. The cotton gin, effective and cheap firearms, the sewing machine, and a whole string of somewhat more complex textile machines came from what might seem a nonindustrial population. Yet when we look into their daily life, these inventors had always had to be builders of things to carry on the family factory. If that fact had been appreciated by the rather parochial English historians of technology, American technical accomplishment would not have broken upon England as such a surprise as a result of the U.S. displays at the Exhibition of 1851.

But the formal history of the industrialization of America usually begins only with Samuel Slater and the first cotton-spinning mill he set up in 1790 on the Blackstone River just outside the colonial port of Providence. We know that Slater had just completed a seven-year millwright's apprenticeship to Jedediah Strutt, Arkwright's partner, at Belper. As a trained millwright, he was freed of that indenture, but forbidden on pain of death to leave England, even for the English colonies—and certainly not for those that had just won independence. Yet Samuel Slater secretly set off for New York hoping to interest American merchants in furnishing him the capital with which to set up a mill. Manhattan proved a poor site for a waterpowered mill, so he accepted the offer of Moses Brown and other Providence merchants to come there and literally "set up shop," as it fell first to his lot to reproduce the machines he had worked with in Belper. This direct transfer of textile machines from the hearth of the English textile revolution suggests quite logically that America's industrialization was introduced by Slater, and was totally derivative of English technology. At best, that truth is only partial.

Slater did journey to America and reproduce the machines in use in England. But this act was not the birth of American industry, as is so commonly alleged. The United States was at that very moment producing something close to one-sixth of the world's iron output. In addition, the textile manufacture of the United States was a very large enterprise, despite the fact that most of it came from family factories. In 1790 the city of Providence and its vicinity produced 30,000 yards of woolen cloth, while in the first nine months of 1791 the city produced 25,262 yards of linen cloth, 5,858 yards of cotton, 3,165 yards of woolen cloth, 512 yards of carpeting,

1760, see the early chapters of Phyllis Deane, *The First Industrial Revolution* (Cambridge: The University Press, 1965).

4,093 pairs of stockings, 859 pairs of gloves, and 260 yards of fringe.[58] With respect to Manchester and southeast Lancashire, we have noted that only a well-developed domestic industrial district could take in and employ the product of a machine spinning mill such as Arkwright had established at Cromford and Belper, and Slater had brought to Providence (Pawtucket in later years).

The introduction of spinning machines into America came in a context rather different from the one found in Britain, both in legal constraints and in corporate controls. Gilds had never been effective in America, so corporatism was not a feature of American industry, and most assuredly not of the family factory. For this reason the family factory unit tended to handle all processes involved in the production of cloth, save perhaps for the act of fulling, which in the thirteen colonies as in England was the most difficult and unpleasant job, already "mechanized" in the late Middle Ages. Otherwise, the American family factory seems to have been based on the integration of processes within a single extended biological family residing on a single farm. I mean specifically to draw a sharp contrast with the conditions within the domestic textile industry of Lancashire, and only to a lesser degree of the West Riding. Because of this integration of processing within a single American farm, no dependence was placed upon merchants—later, factors—to organize and "put-out" the goods, as was found even in Yorkshire. Textile production thus became a universal feature of rural America, particularly in the area north of Maryland where free labor dominated. Those colonies dependent on slave labor tended not to be so heavily involved in this type of production, yet Tryon argues that during the American Revolution even slave labor was widely used in such household manufacture, reverting to field and servant employment once peace returned.

As household manufacture was so widely spread in the thirteen colonies, no specialized towns were given over to facilitating this manufacture. Instead, merchants in various towns bought or bartered for cloth and other textiles and sent them on for trade in cities, in the insular possessions of Britain in the West Indies and Newfoundland, but not in Britain itself, where these goods were strictly forbidden entry. In return for home-produced cloth, farm families and those city ones that made textiles gained the items of trade for which they had neither specie nor sufficient bills of credit. Thus, hand-woven textile products furnished a medium of exchange in a land starved, by England's antiquated economic practices, for a basic supply of coins for simple trade. Under such a circumstance, cloth making was both widespread and earnestly pursued.

Household manufacture did not require any charter of privileges as had so long been necessary in parts of England. Because England had failed after the mid-1640s to supply manufactured items to the American colonies in any quantity commensurate to their needs, people had had to develop certain types of manufacture in almost ubiquitous distribution. The notion of the specialized area of production, and consequent distant trade, was for-

58. Tench Coxe's report on manufactures, quoted in Tryon, *Household Manufactures*, pp. 133–34.

eign to American experience, save in the most important of raw staples—rice, indigo, tobacco, lumber, potash, fish, deerskin, furs, and the like—that were traded to England. But as the scale of export increased, notably in the Southern colonies, local self-sufficiency began to decline, and food began to move into the Southern area from elsewhere in the colonies.

Class distinction had always colored importation; the more pompous members of colonial society had traditionally favored imported English textiles over those produced in America. The very term *homespun* suggests a certain bucolic naiveté that would hardly flatter the self-esteem of the Boston merchant or the Virginia planter; they seem to have avoided those fabrics when they had their portraits painted, probably as well in most public places. But the country people and the working class did not shun naiveté, so most of the durable fabrics—the linsey-woolsey, jeans, duck, fustians, and the like—were made here well before 1775. In 1775 the patriots of any class rejected British textiles to such a degree that the trade virtually disappeared except in those areas held during the Revolution by British forces—New York City and parts of the coastal South. The effect was striking indeed when a nonimportation policy was introduced in 1774 and remained in effect until peace was near. For New England imports dropped from £500,000 in the period Christmas 1773 to Christmas 1774, to £71,000 in 1774–75, £55,000 in 1775–76, and nil until 1782–83, when, with the restoration of peace in 1783, imports quickly rebounded before Christmas to £200,000.[59]

After the war, the strong belief arose that if the nation were to survive economically, it must do two things that had immediate and vital bearing on the effort toward industrialization. First, it must integrate the thirteen separate local economies, previously firmly attached for the sale of staples and the purchase of manufactures directly to England, into a national economy now strongly excluded from the British market. Second, it must encourage the emergence of household manufacture from the family factory into full-scale factory development. With the lifting of the yoke of king and Parliament, the United States was free to engage in any manufacturing it could sustain, and to trade its goods to any port that would have them.

This political emancipation brought almost immediate industrialization. If we date the effective nation from 1789 and the adoption of the Constitution, we may perceive the clear foundation of a national industrialization several years before nationhood. This economically critical step could be taken so soon and so relatively surely because of the quantity of "quiet manufacturing" before 1776.

It was soon apparent to the American merchants trading now with the wide world that to practice their trade properly they needed access to manufactured goods to be exchanged for raw materials, which have always been the ballast, economic as well as physical, of any healthy merchant marine. The need for manufactures to exchange for needed raw materials combined with the general enterprise and ingenuity of the New England Yankees—there being really no other true Yankees—to encourage efforts to make use of that region's main factor endowment, the great disruption of its preglacial

59. Ibid., pp. 58–59.

Urban
Morphogenesis
in the
Industrial Age

river drainage by that relatively recent geologic event. Most places in New England had not, since the glacial age, drained properly. Water was plentiful in swamps and ponds of glacial origin, and streams were filled with rapids. These sites could be easily and cheaply developed into mill sites by building only small dams.

Waterpower was plentiful north of the southern limits of American glaciation, which reached southward to include all of New England and New York State and a thin fringe in northern New Jersey and Pennsylvania. That glaciated area had held the traditional water mills for sawing boards, grinding grain, and fulling cloth since the arrival of the English. Parenthetically, though the United States ultimately proved to be vastly rich in coal deposits even within the Appalachian states, at the close of the Revolution virtually no coal production had developed, and what soon developed came only in anthracite mining. Thus, though coal could subsequently shape the American economy, in 1790 it had yet to do so.

Waterpower had at first to furnish the muscle of any American Industrial Revolution. The nation was fortunate in its natural endowment beyond any level found in Britain. The glacier had disrupted the drainage in a hilly land with a moderately heavy rainfall—around forty inches a year—producing many natural reservoirs, as well as the rapids and falls at which the descent of water could be transformed into power. In fact, the very name given to North Providence when the site of Slater's Mill became a separate town—Pawtucket—was an Indian term for a place of falls. Later, the first true industrial city in America, Lowell, was set up by the Proprietors of Locks and Canals at the Pawtucket Falls of the Merrimac River in Massachusetts. With plenty of ponds and dam sites to be had, New England was an ideal physical location for an Industrial Revolution.

Such transformations of the economy also take place within a specific economic context that exerts a force toward scalar increase in production. The search following the Revolution for a national economy made industrialization desirable. Not only had the need arisen for domestic production of products for which the money would no longer be available to purchase from Britain, but also the nation strongly desired to secure domestically a group of staple manufactures—cheap and durable textiles, small metal products, wooden wares—that would provide trading commodities for exchange at the tropical African and Asian ports. Thus, as the merchants of the New England ports began fitting out ships to trade more widely than had been their privilege under British economic planning, they felt a strong need as well to secure an increase in American manufacture. To begin with, they could rely on the massive family factory production, but its competence to deal with an expanding trade was limited by the fact that such production was incidental to other occupations. In any event, that form of production was severely restrained by the small expansibility of handwork in a labor-deficient land.

American economic history has established the truth that the capital earned by the merchant shipowners of New England in overseas trade paid for the early factories, which came ultimately to make New England the first industrial district. Certainly the money that the Quaker Browns of Rhode Island had earned in the whaling industry paid Samuel Slater's costs in setting up his first mill. And the pocketbook of the Boston China traders bore the brunt of Francis Cabot Lowell's experiments at Waltham that created the first true factories found anywhere in the textile industry, in Europe as well as America.

The Early Textile Factories

The stage was set for the emergence of the New England industrial city by several false entrances. The earliest use of spinning machinery in America seems to have been in Philadelphia in 1775, "when probably the first spinning-jenny ever seen in America was exhibited in that city." This jenny was the earlier hand-operated one, not the Arkwright water-frame that Slater built in Providence in the fall of 1790. Mills were established in the Quaker City but they prospered no more than did one set up in Worcester, Massachusetts, in 1780. These efforts sought to tap British technology at a great distance and, in time of war with that country, hardly under the best of circumstances. "The first establishment, however, which can by any interpretation be considered a textile factory was erected at Beverly, Mass., in 1787. The legislature aided this enterprise. The factory continued in operation for several years, but its career as a cotton factory was brief, and it did not meet with much success."[60] In fact, that Beverly factory was more successful than is generally acknowledged, surviving until 1807 when it was put out of business by an embargo.[61] The modest pretensions of this factory show up clearly when we note that it produced only bed tickings.

The earliest phase of the Industrial Revolution in America was strikingly different from that epoch in England, as was the second phase. In England the earliest factory industrialization—at Cromford and Belper—was in the countryside, utilizing small groups of segmental labor and avoiding the legal constraints to innovation that existed in cities with their survival of medieval corporatism. In America the earliest factories were in the nation's largest towns—Philadelphia, Boston, Beverly, and Providence, all among the twenty largest places in the new nation—depending on one of the few pockets of segmental labor to be found in that overemployed land. But quickly each country shifted its locale for factories. Those in England grew up mainly in the towns, while in America factories sprang up mostly in the countryside, though often quickly developing a city outside their gates. Two main facts seem to account for this peculiar reversal. America had never experienced urban corporatism, so the city need not be shunned even in the earliest phase of industrialization. Also, America's general shortage of labor meant that the tiny available groups were more likely to be encountered in the city than in the countryside, where cheap land meant that wide ownership and full employment were possible.

The necessity of establishing this relationship with scarce labor led the

60. Caroll D. Wright, *The Industrial Evolution of the United States* (Meadville, Penna.: Chautauqua-Century Press, 1895), pp. 121–25.

61. Harold Underwood Faulkner, *American Economic History* (New York: Harper and Brothers, 1931), p. 298.

American factory system into a heavy dependence on segmental labor drawn ultimately from the land. Thus, given the growing need for waterpower, which could only in the very earliest phase be supplied in adequate quantities in or near port towns, the pull to the countryside came ultimately to be very strong in America, while it withered in Britain, because of an almost immediate eviction of any rural population that became surplus. Important as well were the poor waterpower resources of rural England. Only New Lanark, built by David Dale and Robert Owen on the upper Clyde, proved to be similar in locating forces to a hundred mill-dam sites in New England.

In America, a number of forces exerted pulls that ultimately resolved into a factory location. The availability of raw materials, power, labor, capital, markets, and transportation all entered into the decision. No doubt the availability of capital was initially most important, operating to cluster the earliest factories around the important trading ports where capital was being accumulated in trade. This geographical leash had considerable reach. Factories were set up within a day's journey of Providence, Boston, and Baltimore, so that the capitalists could exercise fairly direct supervision of their plants in a preelectronic era. The next question was, Where were sizable waterpower facilities available? Only when that question had been favorably answered would labor availability be considered. And once capital, power, and labor had been brought together, it was reasoned that further capital inputs would furnish transportation of raw material and finished product to the burgeoning factory city.

This formula worked. Several of its phases are of interest and importance to us in understanding the evolution of the tie of industrialization and urbanization in the United States.

American Industrialization and Urbanization

The first phase of industrialization-urbanization is represented by the earliest mills already noted. The large towns were all ports—Beverly was both a port and the nation's eighteenth "city" in population—where capital, potential market, available transportation, and small units of segmental labor were available. Power was in shortest supply, though initially, as in England, hand operation and the use of horses to turn machines masked that poverty. But in Providence and Baltimore, which both lay almost directly on the Fall Line, this first phase of industrial-urbanization could be extended over a longer period before recourse need be taken to a more inland string of factories. The Blackstone and Pawtuxet valleys adjacent to Providence and the Jones Falls valley at Baltimore became early homes to American industry. In New York City no first-phase industry based on waterpower gained much growth. Manufacturers had to look farther afield, by turning to the high falls of the Passaic River where, under the aegis of Alexander Hamilton, the Society for Establishing Useful Manufactures was organized in 1791 to develop the primary manufacturing town for the new United States. Using the fifty-foot fall as a power source, the society was authorized to lay out a "manufactory" within a six-square-mile reservation. The first plant to be built was for cotton textile production, but under governmental operation not much was accomplished. Only slowly, and along strange routes, did Paterson become an important industrial town, adding steam-locomotive production and silk weaving and dyeing in the 1830s, and subsequently many other forms of industry associated with the needs of a large metropolis.

Successful and continuing cotton textile manufacturing began with the factory Samuel Slater set up on the lowest falls of the Blackstone River in the northern part of the city of Providence. There, where previously a forge had been operated by waterpower, Moses Brown and William Almy financed and organized the firm that supported Slater's efforts. "In the years between Slater's arrival in America in 1789 and the passage of the Embargo Act, December, 1807, the industry adopted English machinery, imitated England in the type of labor employed, took advantage of the cheapened product of the cotton gin, and gained for itself a wide and expanding market. At each step the lead was taken by Almy and Brown of Providence, the first successful machine spinners in America."[62]

To understand the progress of the American cotton textile industry, we must distinguish among the three types of "machines" used in the earlier spinning efforts. The first developed, James Hargreaves's *spinning jenny* of 1764, did not lend itself to powered operation, as it had several somewhat discontinuous operations. This machine produced a soft yarn excellent for filling but not for use as the necessarily stronger warp threads. The second machine was the *water-frame*, which Richard Arkwright claimed he invented and which he patented in 1769. The process involved was continuous and could be carried out by mechanical power, producing a fairly stout yarn that was able to stand the strain of use for the warp in coarse fabrics such as those first produced in the Slater mills. The third type of spinning machine was the *mule*, so called because it combined features of the Hargreaves and the Arkwright machines. It was developed by Samuel Crompton in 1779. This mule could be hand-driven, and produced a stronger, finer thread that could be used successfully for the warps in fine cotton textiles. But the mule was such a heavy machine that it required the labor of strong men rather than children or women, who commonly operated both the jenny and the water-frame.

When Slater's first mill, built specifically as a "factory house" to avoid the inconveniences of the previous dwelling houses where Almy and Brown had experimented with cotton textile production, started production in 1791, it employed eight children and one adult supervisor. This use of child labor was a practice brought directly from Belper by Slater and widely used during the earlier decades of cotton production. Even as late as 1801, Slater was employing "over one hundred between the ages of four and ten" in his Pawtucket Falls mill.[63] This factory was so successful that it was producing great quantities of yarn that required ingenious selling to whatever market was available. In the early years this market was found in the small domestic shops of handweavers of woolen textiles. The early cotton threads spun on

62. Caroline F. Ware, *The Early New England Cotton Manufacture: A Study in Industrial Beginnings* (Boston: Houghton Mifflin, 1931), p. 19.

63. Ibid., p. 23.

the water-frame were fairly coarse and were desired mostly to provide the warp threads in mixed woolen-cotton fabrics. To sell from the Pawtucket mill, it was necessary to have the truly massive domestic market provided by the family factories.

Quickly following on his success in the first mill, Slater and his partners had a new building, specifically designed for cotton spinning, erected at the same falls. Fortunately, this 1793 mill building still stands, so from it we may gain a clear picture of what facilities were needed at that time. The descent from the New England barn is obvious; this two-story clapboard building is constructed with heavy timber framing and topped with an attic lighted by a clerestory, making three floors available for working. The waterwheel operated in a well just under the front door, with the power taken by belts to the several machines. At the front, a tower contained the stairs for the building and the ever-present bell loft, where the signal that began to regulate the lives of the worker, as never before, came to be hung. Within these buildings, real constraints were introduced both by the need to transmit power mechanically from the millwheel and by the use of wooden framing. In 1793 three cards and two frames with seventy-two spindles were at work in this mill. When more production was desired, the tendency was less strong to enlarge an existing mill than to build a second one. Thus, American mills tended to differ from English ones by being somewhat more spread out along feeder canals that brought the water to several individual mills with independent waterwheels, or later turbines.

Once the power at the Pawtucket Falls had been fully engaged, Slater and his partners looked elsewhere, developing true mill villages at some remove from Providence. In 1806 Samuel Slater and Company began the development of a town on the Branch River, a tributary of the Blackstone, which became Slatersville, one of the earlier of the "Arkwright Villages" that sprang up around Providence.[64] Yet the demand for cotton thread still increased. So in 1811 the company had to reach out even farther from

64. For a detailed discussion of these Arkwright Villages, see Vance, "Housing the Worker," pp. 304–7.

Providence, into the southern tier of Massachusetts at South Oxford, which became a separate town named Webster shortly after Slater developed his mill there. At Webster, "the property in 1817 consisted of one cotton factory of 2,000 spindles, a woolen mill, a grist and saw mill, 16 dwelling houses, and 700 acres of land." But even that establishment was not the limit to which the firm could expand, though mill owners had begun to see that the small increments to waterpower represented by the 1793 mill at Pawtucket, the mills at Slatersville and Voluntown (Connecticut), and that at Webster were becoming out of date. The large integrated factory was emerging, so the Slater Company looked outward and "purchased an estate consisting of a small cotton mill, several tenements, and a fine water-privilege at Amoskeag Falls, on the Merrimac River. This was the foundation of the great manufacturing city of Manchester, New Hampshire."[65]

The Congress sought a report on the cotton textile industry after it had been under way for a quarter of a century. "According to a memorial presented to the United States Congress there were reported to be at the close of the year 1815, 99 cotton mills in Rhode Island, with 75,678 spindles; in Massachusetts, 57 mills, with 45,650 spindles; and in Connecticut, 14 mills with 12,886 spindles; making a total of 170 mills operating 134,214 spindles. The average capacity of cotton mills at that time was only 500 spindles. The 'Old Slater Mill' (of 1793) at Pawtucket, up to this time the largest in the country, contained 5,170 spindles."[66]

The picture of the second phase of industrial-urbanization shows a number of relatively small mills scattered in the environs of the large colonial port cities at small waterpower sites that came normally to be surrounded by an Arkwright Village. In those villages, the manufacturer provided housing for workers recruited from the nearby countryside, in part by the offer of housing as well as employment for the entire family, down even to children of rather tender years. The Pawtuxet valley southwest of Providence still furnishes us with an example of this sort of settlement, which we might with some justice term village urbanization. The people taking up residence there were mostly from rural areas, gaining their first experience of urban life in small mill villages such as Hope or Lippet.

This second phase of village industrialization had followed on a first that, set at the edge of the port city, was little able to be expanded as the market increased. But like the first phase, the second was given over almost entirely to the spinning of yarn and thread for use as warps in handweaving. Under that narrow development of industry, the labor demands in any one place were reasonably met by attracting to the village a modest number of families from which the several classes of workers could be drawn. The men and older boys served often as mechanics, maintaining the machines and dealing with heavy loads. The wives worked as supervisors of machines and operatives of the more complex processes. The children from six to twelve or so could aid the machine tenders or tend their own.

65. Frederick L. Lewton, *Samuel Slater and the Oldest Cotton Machinery in America*, Smithsonian Report for 1926.
66. Ibid.

The Third Phase of Industrialization: Urbanization

Fundamental changes came in the third phase of industrial-urbanization in the United States, which are critical to our story. This third phase was a distinctively American Experience. It was the first period of industrial development in this country when true city forming and filling took place.

The first-phase mills at the edge of the colonial port had had only very modest impact on those places, mainly by supplying some trade goods to fill the holds of the burgeoning merchant marine at home in those ports. The Arkwright Villages of the second phase had greatly expanded the flow of goods, but they still lay sufficiently far from the city that they had doubtful impact on either its retail trade or its housing market. No doubt wholesaling in those port cities gained as this market for consumer goods in the surrounding countryside increased, but we should not overestimate the impact. Some evidence exists that the level of consumption of goods was then so small, compared with the present, that trade would have been mostly in food. And much of the food still came directly from the country into the villages without passing through the warehouses of the city wholesaler.

With the third phase came the creation of true industrial cities distinct to America. They stood as essentially self-contained new urban creations, because American technology and business organization were innovative and imaginative to a degree well in advance of Britain, and because they still had a large factor endowment of waterpower. When American industry sought to expand in the textile trade, it would still continue for some fifty years to turn to waterpower. In the third phase the search was for large components of waterpower, not so much because the spinning mills were becoming larger, which they were, but because in America a strong campaign was aimed at creating integrated factories for the production of textiles from raw material to fully finished product. Quite in contrast, in the textile areas of Britain, either in the cotton trade of Lancashire or the woolen trade of Yorkshire, complex urban integration—conurbation, as it came to be called in the 1920s—was needed to secure production. We have already examined this pattern at length.

In America no inheritance of established interest need be dealt with, so the sorts of process division found in the north of England—where towns had their time-honored specializations that carried over into the Industrial Age—could be avoided. Also, America's shortage of labor meant that mechanization was rather consistently held as a national goal. The whole resistance to machines—Luddism—that swept England in the early nineteenth century was absent in this country, where the family factory was a reality, not a totality. Those "factories" were located on family farms where basic support was provided by agriculture, so a decline in domestic textile production would not totally impoverish the workers. Industrialization of textiles into factories did affect the family factories; that effect led to the successful recruiting of segmental labor from just such farms into the factories that shaped the "Waltham System." But there was a difference. In America the part-time supplement to family support was wiped out by industrialization; in Britain the rural cottar's total livelihood nearly disappeared. In England a settlement and demographic revolution was wrought in the early nineteenth century, with the social and economic consequences that Engels witnessed and described. In America change came more by the industrialization of the countryside than by the full transformation of the national society and economy.

The Waltham System of Industrialization

The effort to create an integration of industry at one place was initially undertaken by a small group of Boston capitalists, most notably Francis Cabot Lowell and Patrick Tracy Jackson, brothers-in-law seeking to invest in local industrial development money earned in the shipping trades. Lowell went to Britain in 1811 to recuperate from an illness, found himself there when war broke out in 1812, and improved his time during the conflict by visiting cotton mills in Lancashire and Scotland. On those inspections he saw the earliest power-looms at work but was unable to purchase one, or even the plans therefor. On his return to America in 1813, Lowell set about building such a loom. With the help of a mechanic, Paul Moody, he successfully completed a power-loom that is commonly called the Waltham loom with power applied to the weaving frame through a cam action. Starting in 1814, he and Jackson organized the Boston Manufacturing Company, which immediately sought a site for a mill as close to Boston as possible, finding it at a five-foot fall on the Charles River nine miles west of the city at Waltham.

When the Waltham factory opened in 1814, it was the first of its kind in industrial experience; it was truly the world's first process-integrated plant. Starting with baled cotton bought from Southern dealers, Waltham workers carded, cleaned, roved, spun, and wove cotton into cloth, which in turn was finished for the market and transferred as a total product to a single wholesale dealer whose job was to sell and distribute. The Waltham company did not seek to match the finer products of Britain, turning instead to "plain, coarse, white sheeting made from number fourteen yarn which the power loom could turn out easily and which could be used for almost all purposes, especially by the western pioneers."[67] The market proved so good that by 1822 the investors in the Boston Manufacturing Company had earned 104.5 percent on their capital. Such a performance obviously courted envy and emulation, which assured that the Waltham System would find frequent competitors.

Fundamental to the Waltham System was the integration of the processes within a single plant, an act that led to the necessary clustering of a fairly large work force at one spot. No longer could casual segmental labor—Slater's eight children at Pawtucket—suffice. Instead, workers must be recruited, particularly while the use of waterpower often determined the establishment of the plant outside the existing cities. Even the Slater mill

67. Ware, *Cotton Manufacture*, p. 65. The smaller the number of the yarn (that is, the number of hanks per pound), the coarser it is. Number forty would produce a fine cotton, number fourteen would not.

had outrun its easily accessible labor, and had to seek large families and encourage their residence near the mill. In Waltham, conditions demanded both numbers and skills, so Lowell and Jackson devised a justly famous recruiting system. To tend their power-looms they found young women the most adept and reliable, usually between eighteen and twenty-two years of age. The city of Waltham had precious few candidates as the mills were increased in number ultimately to three, with a bleachery added, so recruiters were sent into the country areas seeking to hire young women for a determinate stint in the Waltham factory. Their success in gaining recruits was striking, but to understand the reasons we must look both at the treatment of those recruits in Waltham (the pull factor) and the eagerness of those young women to leave the farm (the push factor).

Massachusetts agriculture, and that of New Hampshire to the north, was beginning to show its limited future by the time of the War of 1812. Endless springtime clearing of stones from the fields seemed not to reduce the next year's stone crop, and the soils thus freed for cultivation were far from bounteous in production. The short summers did not foster too full an array of crops. In all, the New England farm seemed to produce more character than wealth among its cultivators. An increasing restiveness grew on those hill farms, which by the early nineteenth century were perhaps more "overpopulated" than any other section of America. The Yankee Exodus to the Middle West was one symptom, while the flooding of rurally born young women into Waltham and its successors was another.

Francis Cabot Lowell had observed English industry with an analytical eye and had come away determined not only to reproduce the factories but also to do it without the worst social features associated with them in the older industrial nation. His idea was to use a periodic labor force, which would maintain one foot on the farm while working for a few years to earn money in the factory. Caroline Ware believed "furthermore, about half of the workers, those in the group of largest mills, did not really move to the milltowns but maintained their connection with their home farms during the period of their work in the factory. Even the other group of workers who came to the mills with the intention to remain could never give up the possibility of returning to the land." In contrast to Britain, where landownership was narrow and aristocratic, in New England it was general and remained a constant refuge in times of economic difficulty. "Consequently mill labor became an impermanent group, as it often does where agriculture remains dominant while factories develop."[68]

Whether the outcome was fully planned or merely fortunate, in any event throughout much of the nineteenth century, industrialization was not associated directly with the creation of a permanent urban proletariat. Only in the years after the Irish famine and other agricultural collapses in Sweden, Germany, and elsewhere in Europe did the conditions change. The immigrants who went to work in the textile towns of New England could not find refuge in a destitute Ireland or in a socially rigid Sweden. They were an American proletariat produced not by native conditions but by the conditions of a Europe still weighted down by a feudal class system.

During their early years the factories of the Waltham System provided a novel, quite useful physical solution to the problem of periodic worker residence. The boardinghouse was established, built, and maintained by the factory owner, and kept a place of moral rectitude by carefully established rules. These houses were required for "a large body of unskilled labor continually drifting into the mills, forming a stream of fresh, vigorous country workers rather than a permanent factory class. The boardinghouse system of housing and controlling these workers was the skillful and popular adaptation which the early American manufacturers made to the limitations placed by the social and economic conditions which they had to meet."[69] As long as the recruitment of labor for the Waltham-type mills came through "factory nomads," this system of boardinghouses served quite well. However, with the turn to immigrant labor in the 1840s and 1850s, it became inadequate.

An important distinction must be made between the Slater- or Arkwright-type mills of Rhode Island and the ones under the Waltham pattern that spread across northern New England. The Arkwright mills were slow to progress to weaving as well as spinning, depending for many further years on putting-out of yarn to handweavers, who generally produced more complex fabrics—either finer in quality or with stripes and plaids. The soft weft yarns produced on the Arkwright frames were combined with fine, strong warp threads produced on hand-operated spinning mules to create a better class of fabric but one less cheaply manufactured.

What has this distinction to do with the evolution of the industrial city? Mule spinning required the labor of men, while water-frame spinning could be done by children, with the result that in and around Providence, where the Arkwright mills and Villages were clustered, the pattern was that of families living permanently in an industrial lifestyle. Because the water-power facilities available at any one place were small, the great integrated factories with their larger need for power did not develop. Perhaps this natural factor endowment kept the Providence textile development in the Arkwright rather than the Waltham stage. But with only a part of the industrial production clustered in factories—the weft yarn spinning—while warp thread production and actual weaving both remained domestic activities, the

68. Ibid., p. 13.
69. Ibid.

Urban
Morphogenesis
in the
Industrial Age

basis for urbanization was kept small. This industry was much closer to the English prototype than what came to be the American.

Providence was the great center of the textile dyeing and finishing industry in America and to it came gray cloth from the domestic looms fed by the nearby Arkwright Villages. Ultimately this area became the true Lancashire of America, with the same attractive force for the unfortunates of other lands and the same creation of an industrial proletariat. But the southern New England textile district languished in this second phase of industrial-urbanization for several decades in the first half of the nineteenth century, while the Waltham System spread over much of northern New England, creating the nation's first industrial cities.

The Waltham System was not merely one characterized by process integration and a particular source of workers living in boardinghouses. In addition, it was the first clear demonstration of the industrial multiplier effect. The Waltham company from the very beginning had manufactured most of the machinery used in its mill, and as a second and a third mill were built at the falls of the Charles, it constructed more looms and spinning machines. The company also initiated the practice of building such machines for others, thus establishing the strong tie that has subsequently existed between the manufacture of a consumer product and the making of machines for that production.

Lowell: The First American Manufacturing City

In Waltham the Boston Manufacturing Company entered upon an established town. The impact was obviously considerable in physical terms, but the town was not the product of the Industrial Age except in the rapidity with which it grew during the first quarter of the nineteenth century. But soon the needs of the market could not be met from the Waltham mills, nor could they be enlarged. All the power of the five-foot fall was employed in running the machinery of those three brick mills, "comprising eight thousand and sixty-four spindles, and two hundred and thirty-one looms." This machinery took the labor of "about four hundred persons, mostly females, working up seven hundred thousand pounds of cotton, and making two million yards of cloth per year."[70] But Waltham had met its limit as long as water was the source of power.

The Rev. Mr. Henry Miles has left us a starkly factual account of how America's first industrial city was born:

> In 1820, Mr. Paul Moody had charge of the Waltham Mills, and a
> friend of his, Mr. Ezra Worthen, a former partner in business, was
> connected with the manufacturing establishment at Amesbury.
> From his childhood Mr. Worthen had been acquainted with the
> neighborhood of Pawtucket Falls [of the Merrimac River] and when
> the profitableness of the [Waltham] manufacturing business led to

70. Rev. Henry A. Miles, *Lowell, as It Was, and as It Is* (Lowell: Powers and Bagley, 1845), pp. 21–22.

inquiries for water power, the immense advantages which this place held out soon struck his eye. While on a visit to Waltham, he expressed a wish to Mr. Patrick T. Jackson, one of the principal Directors of the company there, that they would set up works in some new place, and give him employment conducting them. Mr. Jackson replied that they would willingly do this, if he would find a good water power. Immediately Mr. Worthen named the Pawtucket Falls; and with a piece of chalk drew a map of the river and canal on the floor. The rude sketch was sufficient to give Mr. Jackson a favorable impression, who requested Mr. Moody to visit, with Mr. Worthen, the place which the latter gentleman had described. It was not long before they explored this whole neighborhood, tracing the course of the canal [around the falls built in 1797], surveying the adjoining land shores, and satisfying themselves that the place afforded great facilities for building up a large manufacturing town. Soon after the reception of their highly favorable report, the Directors of the Waltham Company resolved to procure this eligible site.[71]

This site was on the forty-eight miles of the Merrimac River between the New Hampshire boundary and the sea, in the course of which the water drops ninety feet; "a little more than one-third of the total fall occurred before the location of dams on the river, within a distance of about one mile at Pawtucket Falls, nine miles south of the New Hampshire boundary." Those falls were of a considerable potential as the "river has a mean discharge of 8,020 second-feet, producing in a descent of 30 feet a theoretical motive force equivalent to about 27,000 horsepower,"[72] something like four times the power produced by all the Boulton and Watt steam engines built during the eighteenth century.

To develop such a massive power source, a new form of industrialization had to come into existence. Initially, the Waltham interests had organized the Merrimac Company to buy the canal at the falls and the adjacent land in order to establish a new factory, but soon the scale of the waterpower was seen to be much greater than that needed for a single plant. In 1826 the Merrimac Company transferred all its holdings in machine shops, canals, waterpowers, and lands to the Proprietors of Locks and Canals, a separate company that subsequently furnished feeder canals and waterpowers to nine other major mills constructed in Lowell up to 1839. Unlike Slatersville or Waltham, this city was to have public utility waterpower as its foundation stone.

The mills built in Lowell could be more massive than any before seen, because little question of power shortage existed. To begin with, the mills were not too much larger than those at Waltham. Over the years, the buildings were heightened or extended until they became some of the larger structures in the country, running for hundreds of feet along the canals and

71. Ibid., pp. 22–24.
72. Margaret Terrell Parker, *Lowell: A Study of Industrial Development* (New York: Macmillan, 1940), p. 60.

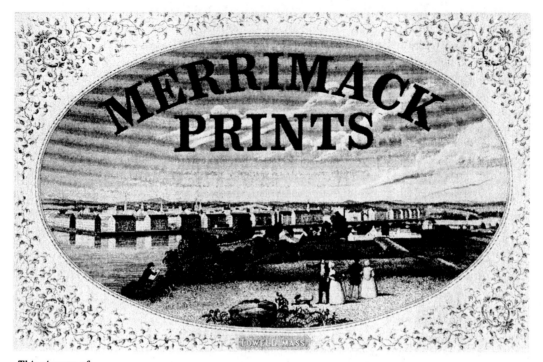

This vignette of Lowell shows the city in the mid-nineteenth century as it was represented on the label of the "Merrimack Manufacturing Company."

rising to five, six, or seven stories. Miles in 1845 described a typical mill yard:

> On the banks of the river, or of a canal, stands a row of mills, numbering, on different corporations, from two to five. A few rods from these, are long blocks of brick boarding-houses, containing a sufficient number of tenements to accommodate the most of the operatives employed by the Corporation. Between the boarding-houses and the mills is a line of a one story brick building, containing the counting room, superintendent's room, clerk's and store rooms. The mill yard is so surrounded by enclosures, that the only access is through the counting room, in full view of those whose business it is to see that no improper persons intrude themselves upon the premises.
>
> Thus the superintendent, from his room, has the whole of the Corporation under his eye. On the one side are the boarding-houses, all of which are under his care, and are rented only to known and approved tenants; on the other side are the mills, in each room of which he has stationed some carefully selected overseer, who is held responsible for the work, good order, and proper management of his room. Within the yard, also, are repair shops, each department of which, whether of iron, leather, or wood, has its head overseer. There is a superintendent of the yard, who, with a number of men under his care, has charge of all the out-door work of the establishment.[73]

73. Miles, *Lowell*, pp. 64–65.

The Continuing City

In 1845, thirty-three of these large mill buildings ranged along the canals and the bank of the Merrimac, making Lowell the largest cotton town in America and one of its few great industrial cities, with a population of thirty thousand. A full third of the population was engaged as operatives in the mills or their workshops, though female employment remained disproportionate, with 6,320 females and 2,915 males. Clearly, the Waltham System of recruiting women in the country was still operating, but soon thereafter the European immigration changed that pattern distinctly.

The boardinghouse built by the mill owner was a big part of these towns. The recruitment of labor required such a provision, and the siting of the factory cities at waterpower locations in the country left no alternative housing supply, as might have been the case in a port city. As long as boardinghouses were the manner of sheltering the workers, the quality of housing was probably equal to that beyond the narrow world of the mill yard, even though the supervision and moral policing must have irked anyone with a free spirit. The houses were normally of brick, built in rows along carefully laid-out streets. The crowding of the site was yet to come in its worst aspects. Short of the fact that individuals had relatively little personal space in these buildings, a condition found as well in the farmhouses of the time, few contemporary criticisms were made of the boardinghouses.

In 1834 Lowell already had a "main street," Merrimack Street, with shops for the sale of "clothing, shoes, dry goods, silks, shawls, linens and laces, china and hardware, West India goods, groceries, confectionary, drugs, books, and 'fancy goods,'"[74] to satisfy the needs of a population no longer self-sufficient. As Lowell's business community came quickly into existence, several hotels—the Merrimac House, the American House, and the Washington Hotel—were built. Contemporary observers noted that this burgeoning city had no office buildings, as the administrative functions—more elevated than those carried on in the counting room—were pursued in Boston, whence came the capital for the mills and the decisions that ruled the lives of those mills and their workers. Lowell exemplified for the first time an industrial city distinct from the center of long-distance trade that the colonial ports had been.

The newness struck Charles Dickens when he visited Lowell in 1842. "It was a very dirty winter's day, and nothing in the whole town looked old to me, except the mud, which in some parts was almost knee-deep, and might have been deposited there on the subsiding of the waters of the Deluge. In one place there was a new wooden church, which having no steeple, and being yet unpainted, looked like an enormous packing-case without any direction upon it. In another there was a large hotel, whose walls and colonnades were so crisp, and thin, and light, that it had exactly the appearance of being built with cards. I was careful not to draw my breath as we passed, and trembled when I saw a workman come out upon the roof, lest with one thoughtless stamp of his foot he should crush the structure beneath him."[75]

Dickens, despite his great contempt for America and dislike for its

74. Benjamin Floyd, *The Lowell Directory, 1834* (Lowell: The Observer Press, 1834), p. 131.
75. Charles Dickens, *American Notes* (1842; New York: Fawcett, 1961), ch. 4. As a lower-middle-class Englishman Dickens found it essential, and fun as well, to abominate everything American, but he was impressed by the Lowell mills.

people, still applauded the factories and by implication drew most flattering contrasts with Lancashire. "The rooms in which [the Lowell operatives] worked were as well ordered as [they] themselves. In the windows of some there were green plants, which were trained to shade the glass; in all there were as much fresh air, cleanliness, and comfort as the nature of the occupation would possibly admit of." Despite the heavy reliance on the Waltham System, factory labor had not the pathetic quality so common in Britain. "Out of so large a number of females, many of whom were only then just verging upon womanhood, it may be reasonably supposed that some were delicate and fragile in appearance: no doubt there were! But I solemnly declare, that from all the crowd I saw in different factories that day, I cannot recall or separate one young face that gave me a painful impression; not one young girl whom, assuming it to be matter of necessity that she should gain her daily bread by the labor of her hands, I would have removed from those works if I had had the power."[76]

Dickens abstained from drawing a direct contrast between the virtues he found in Lowell "and those great haunts of desperate misery" at home, arguing instead that "there is no manufacturing population in Lowell, so to speak: for these girls (often the daughters of small farmers) came from other States, remain a few years in the mills, and then go home for good." Certainly this was true. But would it not have been equally possible in England, save for the inhumane landowning system that shed so many social responsibilities from the account of the country where it belonged to the city, which could not possibly cope simultaneously with the sins of the English and Irish gentry? In New England a democratic society, which greatly irked Dickens by its crudity, unmannerliness, and general lack of understanding of "station," had dealt far better with its social responsibilities than had his own country. Thus, the early industrial cities of America demonstrate how successful urban life might be, if unencumbered by the responsibilities shed by the rural areas.

Only when great numbers of landless, destitute European emigrants—from Ireland, Britain, Sweden, Germany, and other countries where a rural aristocracy proved both cold-hearted and incompetent in dealing with the economic and social problems of the mid-nineteenth century—came in a flood did these American industrial cities begin to deteriorate. In place of the boardinghouse, tenements were built. These great wooden barracks occupied their lots so completely that in Lowell's neighbor, Lawrence, which developed at the middle of the century, women commonly hung their pots and pans on the wooden wall of the house next door to gain more space in their overcrowded kitchens. These tenements were the response to a need to house large families, any members of which would at least seek work in the factories and shops of the city, rather than the workers alone, as under the Waltham System.

Speaking of Lowell in its earlier years, Margaret Parker showed that "place of residence in the 1834 directory is indicated, in many cases, not by streets, but by corporations; '32 Hamilton corporation;' '7 Appleton corpora-

76. Ibid., p. 85.

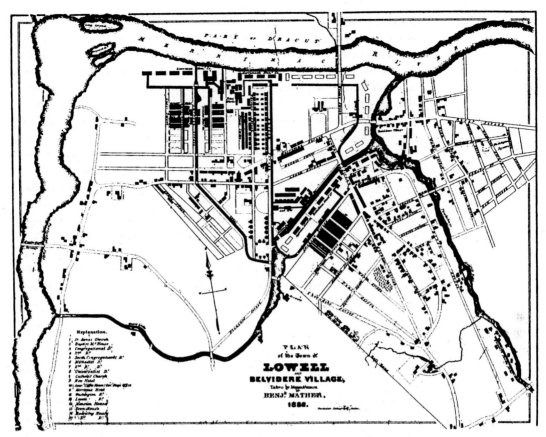

tion;' '2 Suffolk blocks,' '22 Carpet blocks' are typical addresses."[77] The securing of a job in one of the mills made housing provision available. "Each of the long blocks of boarding-houses is divided into six or eight tenements, and are generally three stories high. These tenements are finished off in a style much above the common frame-house of the country, and more nearly resemble the abodes of respectable mechanics in rural villages. They are all furnished with an abundant supply of water, and with suitable yards and out-buildings."[78] Some of the boardinghouses and apartmented houses were of brick, though as time went on wood seems to have become the common building material. In the boardinghouses, "the front room is usually the common eating-room of the house, and the kitchen is in the rear. The keeper of the house (commonly a widow, with her family of children), has her parlor in some part of the establishment; and in the same house there is a sitting-room for the use of the boarders. The remainder of the apartments are sleeping rooms. In each of these are lodged two, four, and in some cases six boarders." Although on the whole housing was satisfactory, the Rev. Mr. Miles found that "in many cases, these rooms are not sufficiently large for the number who occupy them; and oftentimes that attention is not paid to

The nature of the early mills with their yards and associated housing rows can be seen in this 1832 map of Lowell. From Proceedings of the Semi-Centennial . . . of Lowell (Lowell: Penhallow Printing Establishment, 1876).

77. Parker, *Lowell*, p. 73.
78. Miles, *Lowell*, p. 67.

Urban Morphogenesis in the Industrial Age

their ventilation which a due regard to health demands. . . . At the same time, it should in justice be added, that the evil alluded to is not peculiar to Lowell, and will not probably appear to be a crying one, if the case should be brought into comparison with many of the apartments of milliners and seamstresses in the boarding-houses of our cities." But despite this crowding, "the rents of the company's houses are purposely low, averaging only from one third to one half of what similar houses rent for in the city. In times of pressure a part of this low rent, and some instances the whole of it, has been remitted. There is no intention on the part of the Corporation to make any revenue from these houses. They are a great source of annual expense."[79]

Thus, the existence of the Lowell boardinghouse and its fellows in other Waltham System towns was encouraged by manufacturers, in a continuation of the medieval practice of assuming some social responsibility for workers. Self-interest was apparent; discipline in the houses made for better discipline in the mills, and the more healthy qualities of life there lent benefits to the employer as well as the worker. But doubtless the physical quality of life in these boardinghouses was probably not inferior to that in the country whence came the boarders.

The Boardinghouse in Nineteenth-Century America

The flood of migrants to the rapidly growing cities of the nineteenth century came commonly from rural areas where the extended family was perhaps the norm. Certainly in Europe, this large social grouping was standard, as it was in many rural sections of America. When they married, sons merely built ells on the family farmhouse, making it housing for several generations and several nuclear families. As daughters left for Waltham or Lowell, they would hardly have expected more than a boardinghouse-type accommodation. Similarly, as sons went to become mechanics, they would have eagerly sought these boardinghouses. At home they probably had relatively little individual space and certainly would in most cases have found living alone distasteful and impractical. Our present-day notions of the space needed by individuals and the virtues of privacy are recently acquired cultural traits that we should carefully avoid projecting backward into the last century. Then, people lived much together, in small space, with few physical possessions.

Because of that way of life, moving into the city commonly led individuals and even families to take up residence in a boardinghouse or, with more money, a hotel. Life in the nineteenth-century city was in a very literal sense "mobile"; people commonly moved on during their lives from one city to another, keeping their baggage to the minimum and living often in what we would think of as transient accommodations. A couple, even with children, might occupy one or two rooms in a boardinghouse or hotel. Certainly, for those without children such accommodations would be quite standard. Thus, when we read of these cities we find far more hotels than we would expect by their size, and boardinghouses in great numbers. The impact of

79. Ibid., pp. 68–69.

these rather dense housing forms on the city can be easily perceived. As long as conditions in the buildings were reasonable and large families were not crowded into spaces previously occupied by one or two individuals, an efficient form of city for the pedestrian era was provided. But as the flood of immigrants overpowered the physical form of housing that had been established for individuals or couples, the pedestrial city became a slum.

The Spread of Third-Phase Industrialization

By 1839, the ten textile companies that made up the main body of Lowell's manufacturing had been built. In addition, the Proprietors of Locks and Canals had grown from a beginning as a builder of textile machinery to the largest engineering works in the United States, building steam engines and steam locomotives among other forms of machinery. But Lowell had few resources other than power from water, and was not yet ready to supplement it with steam. This search for additional power had to come at other falls. Rather quickly in the fourth and fifth decades of the last century, factory cities were set up by Boston capital in Manchester and Nashua in New Hampshire, at Biddeford-Saco, Lewiston-Auburn, and Augusta in Maine, and at Lawrence, Chicopee, and Holyoke in Massachusetts. In most cases, fairly complex hydraulic works had to be established, distributing power by canal to several plants. Both Lawrence and Holyoke, particularly the second, were great waterpower cities. Interestingly:

> The mill communities which developed in northern New England as a consequence of the Waltham enterprise had their antithesis in the Providence region. Even though the Rhode Island mills had been denied the use of the Lowell loom, the southern region was not to be outdone in the matter of technological improvement. The adoption of the Scotch crank loom, which had been built by

William Gilmour, a Scotch immigrant, by a large Rhode Island concern already in 1817 showed that the manufacturers were keenly interested in vieing with their northern competitors. As a consequence, the contrast of systems of manufacture and industrial adjustments between the two districts is the more significant.

The major factor making for this distinction is geographic. The type of water power in the Rhode Island-Connecticut Region determined the make-up of these localities: small but numerous. But few of the communities had sufficient power wealth to serve more than one or two mills. The Blackstone Valley with its ninety-four cotton factories in 1844 illustrates the situation. Then, too, the ascendancy of Slater meant British rather than American practises should dominate. Thus, the constituency of the small factory villages was a collection of families dependent exclusively upon wages earned in the village mill, as opposed to the groups of young people recruited from the farm homes in the vicinity of Lowell and other northern mill towns.[80]

This, then, was the pattern in New England industrialization, the nation's nursery of manufacturing, at the middle of the last century. A continuation of the second-phase industrial-urbanization in southern New England produced regions of rather dense manufacturing population in a quasi-urban pattern of mill villages spread along a dozen separate river valleys, of which the Blackstone was merely the first and the most classic in its settlement pattern. These valleys with their mill towns encouraged the growth of the cities of Providence and Worcester through projecting upon them a diversity of demands for textile machines, engineering works of many forms, supplies of consumer goods, and food. Providence was the port where cotton was received and transshipped, first by canal up the Blackstone valley to Worcester and subsequently by the railroad net that developed in the area only some five years later than in Lancashire. In many ways this Rhode Island-Connecticut pattern of industrial-urbanization, the second phase, shared notable characteristics with the pattern of the north of England. Considerable specialization by towns occurred with respect to manufacturing processes and functions; the organization of the trade centered on Providence and, to a lesser degree, Worcester. Gray cloth moved about the area from one town to another; transportation needs were critical. Thus, the Blackstone Canal was opened in October 1828 to Worcester. But to secure that canal, water was diverted from the mills, and soon great conflict grew up between the demands for process and power water and that for lockage.[81] Finally, the Providence and Worcester Railroad, built between 1844 and 1847, solved this problem.[82]

80. Herbert Burgy, *The New England Cotton Textile Industry: A Study in Industrial Geography* (Baltimore, 1932), p. 27.

81. Edward Chase Kirkland, *Men, Cities and Transportation: A Study in New England History* (Cambridge, Mass.: Harvard University Press, 1948), 1: 85.

82. Interestingly, the Providence and Worcester disappeared into the New York, New Haven, and Hartford Railroad in the nineteenth century but emerged from it in 1973 when the owners of shares in the Providence and Worcester voted to end a long lease of the line and operate it

If the second phase of industrial-urbanization in New England led not to new cities but to an industrialized countryside, the third phase, as represented by the Waltham System cities, was fully urban. Perhaps the population was only periodically resident within the city, but the city itself was fixed and real. It differed from the older Atlantic ports mainly in the absence of the great mercantile functions. Office buildings were in Boston rather than Lowell or Lewiston, and most of the wholesale functions remained in Boston or Portland (Maine). But as money came to the workers, retail shops were opened in the Waltham System cities, and the towns became sizable by contemporary standards. In 1850 Lowell, with a population of 33,383, ranked twenty-third in the country in population, the same size as San Francisco and larger than Chicago, Detroit, or Cleveland. Boston was third, exceeded only by Baltimore and New York, while Providence stood seventeenth. Throughout the second half of the nineteenth century when the urbanization of America was rapid, New England, and Massachusetts in particular, showed the strong impact of early industrialization. With an area only slightly more than a third that of Ohio, the three southern New England states in 1900 had twice as many cities within the first fifty cities (eight) as did Ohio (four), commonly thought the state of the most good-size cities.

The Industrial City Comes of Age in America

By the middle of the nineteenth century, industry had become a sizable factor in American life, though we cannot determine its precise contribution until 1870, when the first census data on manufacturing employment appear (table 7.2). Then, 17.41 percent of the labor force was hired in factories, while still a full half was employed in agriculture. But despite the considerable changes that have occurred during the century for which we have data, manufacturing employment has increased in percentage contribution only from 17 percent to 24 percent in a full century. Thus, by the end of the Civil War, the general role of industry was well determined and its proportionate share in the national economic life established. For that reason, we may summarize the conditions about the time of the Civil War as the coming of age of the industrial city in America. Most subsequent changes affecting manufacturing workers were part not so much of an industrial-urbanization as of the general evolution of urban life and culture, and the physical transformation of the residential structure of cities. Finally, by around 1875, most cities had industry as an integral component of their support, so the actual process of industrial-urbanization became part of the general process of urban growth and evolution.

What, then, were the forms that industrial-urbanization took in the United States up to the close of the Civil War, when manufacturing became a general component of most American cities? We have already seen three stages of industrial-urbanization in New England, the last two of which were

themselves. As a result, the P&W was a tiny bit of line that survived in a solvent state the debacle of the Penn Central Railroad that had absorbed the New Haven when it merged the Pennsylvania and New York Central in 1968. Edward A. Lewis, *The Blackstone Valley Line: The Story of the Blackstone Canal Company and the Providence & Worcester Railroad* (Seekonk, Mass.: Baggage Car, 1973).

Table 7.2   Employment by Selected Industries in Five Census Years

Census Year	Total Labor Force in Thousands	Percentage of Workers Employed in Specific Industries				
		Agriculture	Manufacture	Trade and Finance	Transportation	Construction
1870	12,920	49.77	17.41	6.42	4.95	6.05
1880	17,390	49.51	18.23	7.02	4.95	4.77
1890	23,740	36.27	20.01	8.38	6.45	6.07
1900	29,070	36.84	21.81	9.49	7.22	5.71
1970	78,597	4.40	24.64	23.68	5.73	4.30

accompanied by the creation of distinct industrial organization cities, as in Providence for the second stage or Boston for the third. In these cities, the complex business and banking services were carried on; various goods were supplied by wholesalers to the largely industrial places. As time passed and industrial development within the textile towns matured, engineering functions initially carried on by the Boston Manufacturing Company in Waltham or the Proprietors of Locks and Canals in Lowell tended to become separated out. We find Lowell, Taunton (Massachusetts), and Paterson becoming important machine and metal-working centers. With the spread of markets for textiles, the financial and wholesaling functions tended to be located in larger cities.[83] Thus, with respect to the large cities, we must distinguish two phases of industrial-urbanization: the first when the administrative and financial functions of the factory era began to be expressed in large central cities grown from the colonial ports, certainly in the first several decades of the last century, and the second when actual industrialization of the port city itself took place, notably from the time of the Civil War on, when steam power became dominant. These two phases supply the last in our brief catalogue of expressions of industrial-urbanization.

Two forces were conducive to the large-city phases of industrialization: the introduction of steam power, and the large-scale immigration of Europeans into the United States at the middle and the end of the last century.

The United States is almost as old in the development and use of steam engines as Britain, with an independent line of advance running parallel in time with that of the Boulton and Watt engines. In America in the late eighteenth century, Oliver Evans began his ingenious efforts to develop a steam engine. He did so quite successfully, and with more courage and imagination than it had been done in Britain.

Caroline Ware tells us, "Steam did not come to supply energy for cotton manufacturing at all generally until railways made transportation of coal convenient and cheap after the Civil War." Samuel Slater constructed a

83. Allan Pred has written extensively on this period of American industrial-urbanization, expressing particularly the role that the great port cities played in this economic development. Allan R. Pred, *The Spatial Dynamics of U.S. Urban-Industrial Growth, 1800–1914* (Cambridge, Mass.: M.I.T. Press, 1966). The discussion here diverges genetically somewhat from Pred in viewing the first three phases of industrial-urbanization before turning to the large cities.

The Continuing City

"steam mill" in 1828, perhaps the first in the country, at Providence.[84] In 1839 the Naumkeag Steam Cotton Company was organized in Salem and remained in business until 1953, nearly bracketing the history of steam cotton production in New England.[85] Certainly as the waterpower at both the Arkwright and Waltham sites proved insufficient to meet the demands, coal would be brought in if at all possible and used to fire steam boilers. The Blackstone Canal carried a lot of coal and no doubt played a role in keeping some of the mills in the villages of the valley after water proved insufficient.

The great impact of the introduction of steam power came when the steam engine allowed any city to industrialize, even the large colonial ports, which until then had had to shun most mechanical production. We see the clearest case of this in southeastern Massachusetts, where New Bedford had been a major port in the early nineteenth century, depending on the whaling trade. Much given to enterprise and trade, the town had lacked the factor endowment to engage in the earlier phases of New England industrialization.

But in 1846, New Bedford men set about creating a cotton mill in a truly scientific fashion.[86] They sought by market and manufacturing analysis to determine what kind of cotton textile would best reward them and how its manufacture should be established. "They figured that they could make fine sheetings at a cost of twelve cents a yard and sell it for fourteen cents. 'All other calculations that we have made', their committee reported, 'show only from half to three-quarters of a cent profit.'"[87] Given this desire for fine sheetings, the proprietors needed mule-spun yarn, which in turn fairly determined what kind of mill establishment would be needed and where. We have already seen that throstle-spinning, as in the water-frame and its derivatives under the Waltham System, could be carried out by women, but mule-spinning, as in most of the Rhode Island mills, required male labor.

Thus, the incorporators of the Wamsutta Company in New Bedford faced a very different labor situation from that in the Waltham System towns. Men were critically needed; the city of New Bedford could be depended on to provide the segmental labor force of men more than women and children. An urban location with a generalized supply of housing was far more useful to their purposes than the boardinghouse system begun in Waltham. Basing its factory design on the Hope Mill in the Pawtuxet Valley of Rhode Island and its labor source on the city of New Bedford, Wamsutta became highly successful and showed the way toward the large steam cotton mill that depended on the cheap fuel and massive labor available in a port city, particularly one of declining sailings. In contrast, when Lowell sought at the same time to expand, it reproduced itself and its parent, Waltham, at Lawrence, where at least in the beginning the boardinghouse became the norm. Most graphically, Lawrence and New Bedford, both industrialized in the mid-1840s, demonstrate the two distinct forms of industrial-urbanization produced by contrasts in power sources and in labor recruitment.

84. Ware, *Cotton Manufacture*, p. 82.
85. Dirk J. Struik, *Yankee Science in the Making* (New York: Collier, 1962), p. 304.
86. Burgy, "Cotton Textile Industry," p. 28.
87. Ware, *Cotton Manufacture*, p. 107.

Urban
Morphogenesis
in the
Industrial Age

Fall River followed on the New Bedford pattern, but only after a somewhat equivocal start as a waterpower town. On the site, the Quequechan River falls over 130 feet in less than a mile and a half between a good natural reservoir in the Watuppa Ponds and tidewater. Hardly a better congregation of factor endowments could be envisaged. The first mill was established in 1811, depending on one of the several falls, and others were set up with fair rapidity. Fall River came to specialize in calico printing, and also undertook the manufacture of a distinctive set of textile machines for that trade. As skill improved, and the basic cloth that had begun the Waltham factory in 1814 began to lose customers in favor of the fancier printed goods, Fall River continued to expand until the Quequechan could no longer power the city.

In 1859, a radical change occurred in the local industrial pattern. Steam was introduced as a power source, and the mills moved away from the river and onto the shores of the several local ponds where boiler water of good quality could be secured from reservoirs produced on a granitic surface by glacial disruption and damming of preexisting drainage. At the same time mills were spread along the waterfront, where the coal could be discharged directly from coastal schooners to the coalyard of the mill. "Localization in Fall River is thus primarily due to the tidewater location which made possible the receipt of cheap fuel. The situation of the city, however, in a region where manufacturers had a propensity for textiles, and its accessibility by water to markets were accessory in establishing its pre-eminence."[88] And preeminent it indeed became. By 1875 Fall River had a third of all the spindles in Massachusetts, and stood the largest textile city in the country.

The National Pattern of Industry

As in New England, nationally the first three phases of industry had revolved around the availability of waterpower, initially at small dam sites near Baltimore and Philadelphia and other colonial mercantile towns, next near larger falls on the Mohawk River or the upper Hudson, and finally at large "waterpower cities" such as Paterson and Rochester. In the Middle Atlantic states the use of steam was early and more rapid in coming. Industry in the New York-Brooklyn-Jersey City-Newark area, in southern New Jersey, and in eastern Pennsylvania was heavily reliant on steam power long before the older and more industrialized New England had to turn in that direction. And in the fourth phase, when steam power was introduced, the focus in the Middle Atlantic states was more heavily on the industrialization of the port cities: (1) New York, Brooklyn, Jersey City, and Newark, (2) Philadelphia and the numerous suburbs it had already swallowed up by 1854, (3) Baltimore, and (4) the growing nexus of industrial-urbanization around Pittsburgh at the forks of the Ohio.

The concentration of steam-powered industry in the large cities was certainly a response to the opportunities for long-distance trade available there, as well as the very considerable local market they furnished. Pred has cited a number of forces that encouraged "Urban-Size Growth," among them

88. Burgy, "Cotton Textile Industry," p. 34.

"endogenous natural increases" in population, the "absolute increase of wages and real buying power" in the second half of the nineteenth century, urban "agglomeration economies" not yet matched by sharp rises in the cost of urban factory sites that would in our time force manufacturing into the suburbs or industrial satellites, and a mass of "circular and cumulative growth processes" that encourage the expansion of the city as a market for manufacturers.[89]

The Great Immigration and Industrialization

To the forces of urban growth Pred cites, we might add another of great significance: the great flood of immigrant labor into the port cities, which for the first time in the late 1840s and succeeding decades made labor fairly plentiful and thus somewhat less costly in relative terms, and certainly easier to assemble in large blocks. The notion of untapped local segmental labor pales before the onslaught of great masses of immigrants wherein all members of the group were seeking work and were, in a particularly striking way, footloose as to the site of that employment. Nonetheless, the immigrants were initially found in the port cities, or in their environs, and there they were most likely to remain, all things being equal. Some groups, particularly the Germans and the Scandinavians, were moving toward distant ties in the Middle West, in a much more directed migration than affected the Irish and the Italians, and later the Russian Jews. Those three groups found themselves arrived in coastal cities rather bereft of an onward objective, and tended to remain there unless they had specific individual ties to persons of the same ethnicity in more distant cities. Unlike the Scandinavians and the Germans, the early influx of Irish and Italians had not gone to the interior, thus their ties were less likely to be there.

The scale of migration to the United States was changing during the nineteenth century (table 7.3). From an annual average of just over eight thousand immigrants in the period 1821–25, the numbers rose consistently to ten times that figure in 1841–45. But the late 1840s witnessed a flood of desperate Europeans unheard of in any previous migration, reaching a yearly average for the period 1846–50 of 186,868, and in the next five years of more than 250,000 a year. Perhaps no other statistic from the last century shows more graphically how badly European social policy had failed, most notably in Great Britain and Ireland; the western isle had always been the largest source of migrants in every period up to 1855, but Britain took over and stood at the head until the 1880s, when Germany came to lead the pack.

I emphasize these figures for two reasons. First, they go far toward explaining the fourth stage of industrial-urbanization in the United States. Second, they serve as concrete evidence of how complete was the collapse of the traditional feudal-rural social structuring of Europe that took place at the middle of the nineteenth century, however much the failure of the revolutions of 1848 may have seemed to argue otherwise. The effort to maintain a rural and aristocratic dominance in Europe could continue for another sixty-

89. Pred, *Spatial Dynamics*, pp. 41–46.

Urban
Morphogenesis
in the
Industrial Age

The clustering of workers' residence by ethnic congregation is clearly shown in this map of Lowell. The dominant French Canadian population is shown as occupying the traditional "rows" adjacent to the older mills.

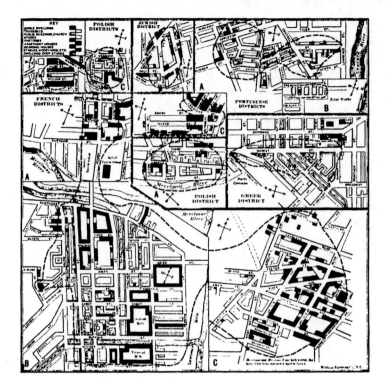

six years, until 1914. Political power rested with the landed aristocrats, who could use the emerging industrial cities of Europe as a dumping ground for social and economic problems first nurtured in the country. America existed as a safety valve for overpopulation and underproduction. Those weary of the defunct but not replaced social system that Europe had inherited from the Middle Ages could go there. By going to America this mass of emigrants from Europe took the same course that the new settlers in the medieval bastides had done seven hundred years earlier. Europe's history had been one of "repression in the country," as the German aphorism has it. *Stadtluft macht frei* recounts the medieval escape from serfdom to the city, later to the bastides in the twelfth and thirteenth centuries, and the vast flood to American cities in the nineteenth century. A commonly held European notion has been that the nineteenth-century migration was simply a dash for economic gain; it was that, but freedom in the nineteenth century required money most critically, as the intellectual and political freedom of Europe's upper classes showed so clearly. And whatever intellectual advance Britain's higher social classes made came more from their leisure than from their genes.

The Fourth Phase, Coming in the Great Cities

The rapid growth in size of the immigrant force, which came particularly after 1845 as the figures in table 7.3 show, went along with the switch to steam power to allow the larger mercantile and transportation cities to become industrial places as well. The history of American urbanism shows this

Table 7.3 Immigrants Arriving in the United States, 1821–1900

Years	Total Immigration	Yearly Average	Country of Emigration				
			Great Britain	Ireland	Scandinavia	Germany	Italy
1821–25	40,503	8,100.6	8,890	12,926	97	1,394	251
1826–30	102,936	20,587.2	16,189	37,798	163	5,367	158
1831–35	346,631	69,326.2	32,182	72,257	693	45,592	1,895
1836–40	346,627	69,325.4	33,628	135,124	1,562	106,862	358
1841–45	430,336	86,067.2	80,186	187,095	4,909	105,188	674
1846–50	1,279,915	255,983.0	186,858	593,624	9,533	329,438	1,196
1851–55	1,748,424	349,684.8	235,981	694,683	15,511	647,273	3,668
1856–60	849,790	169,958.0	187,993	219,436	9,169	304,394	5,803
1861–65	801,723	160,344.6	247,089	176,359	16,738	233,052	3,448
1866–70	1,513,101	302,620.2	359,807	239,419	109,654	554,416	8,217
1871–75	1,726,795	345,599.0	329,793	295,179	119,688	508,394	27,060
1876–80	1,055,395	211,079.0	178,250	141,692	123,328	209,868	28,699
1881–85	2,975,683	595,136.6	784,636	345,399	352,334	709,390	109,504
1886–90	2,270,930	454,186.0	422,719	310,083	344,160	492,950	197,805
1891–95	2,123,879	424,775.0	195,362	227,202	244,599	397,640	288,235
1896–1900	1,563,685	313,737.0	76,172	161,214	126,913	107,512	363,658

trend strikingly when we discover that large components of the growth in population of cities in the nineteenth century came from the great increase in a few very large places—New York, Philadelphia, Chicago, Boston, St. Louis, Baltimore, and their environs—fully as much as from the spread of city growth through the nation. The advantages of concentrated population for labor, consumption, superior transportation connections, and readily available capital all plumped for the big city to be the site of the fourth phase of industrial-urbanization. We can think of the Northeast, Middle Atlantic, and eastern Middle Western states as the region dotted with mercantile cities dating from before 1850. In those cities and their environs, manufacturing concentrated. In the second half of the last century, a new settlement form arose, that of the industrial satellite, which should be distinguished from the residential suburb.

An industrial satellite was a town, fairly close to a major administrative city, where the specific manufacturing processes were carried on, usually under the financial or corporate control of the central town of the industrial complex. Lowell was clearly an industrial satellite of Boston in the same way that the Arkwright Villages of Rhode Island were of Providence. A region centering on a mercantile-transportation city—most commonly a colonial port—commonly had these satellites spread around it for a distance of fifty to one hundred miles. These satellites were served by the central city's wholesaling establishments both for the needs of the people and for those of the plants, provided with financial, medical, legal, and other services by the dominating city, attached to the outside world by railroads converging on that city, and generally in the orbit of that place in terms of political control, newspaper publication, and what small number of cultural events were made available. In truth, the fourth phase had two settlement components: the dominating mercantile-transportation hub, now heavily industrialized and vastly expanded in population as the city of assimilation for a massive immigration, and the surrounding industrial satellites, connected to the hub by rail and ties of corporate control. Along with its metropolitan role in cultural, political, and servicing matters, the central city maintained an integrated system of dominant city and industrial satellites.

The American Industrial City in 1860

At this point in history, industrialization had become an aspect of most larger towns, particularly those of great size or long standing, and it was commonly assumed that the extended industrialization of the metropolis would care for most of the manufacturing needs of the nation. A dichotomy no longer existed between the city and the factory town: cities were industrializing and factory towns were fast becoming urban, at least on a limited scale. Just before the Civil War, a number of regional centers already available to serve the various parts of the United States rose to true metropolitan importance. This rapid growth came in part from quickening of industry related to a fast-spreading network of rail lines, the continuing flood of European migrants, and the increase in America's trade with the rest of the world. The "cities of the United States" had previously been on the East and Gulf coasts or aligned along the Ohio River; now, truly metropolitan places were growing up in the Middle West and the Far West.

Initially, the cities of the East Coast and the Ohio River grew to metropolitan size, but by 1860 railroad towns with important components of manufacturing (Chicago and St. Louis) had risen to that status. In the three censuses taken after the Civil War in the nineteenth century, the common advance of population and industrialization was clear (table 7.4). In 1870 the cities were important regional transportation centers, but they were as well heavily industrialized for their time and region. Only Washington, no doubt a metropolis as a result of the growth during the war, stood in a different category. The cities to reach full metropolitan status in 1880 were so dominantly industrial as to need no further explanation. By that year the necessity of an industrial base for rapid urbanization was accepted; only as industrialization spread to other regions did metropolitanism also arrive there. In 1890 most of the newly arrived metropolises were in, or more precisely on the edge of, the Great Plains, where meat packing, the handling of grain, and the carrying out of transportation functions brought workers and the growth of cities. In the latter part of the last century, the status of metropolitan city virtually always implied also the role of major manufacturing center.

With the advent of that correspondence, we need no longer think in terms of the city during the Industrial Revolution. As cities were industrialized, urbanization was largely an outgrowth of two forces: mercantilism, which shaped the urban revolution of the seventeenth century, and indus-

Table 7.4   Census Year in which Cities Reached 100,000 Population

1820	*1890*	Nashville	Duluth	Montgomery
New York	Denver	Oakland	Elizabeth, N.J.	Phoenix
1830	Indianapolis	Portland, Ore.	El Paso	Savannah
Philadelphia	Kansas City	Richmond, Va.	Erie	Shreveport
1840	Minneapolis	Seattle	Evansville	*1960*
Baltimore	Omaha	Spokane	Flint	Albuquerque
New Orleans	Rochester	*1920*	Ft. Wayne	Beaumont, Tex.
1850	Scranton	Akron	Gary	Columbus, Ga..
Boston	St. Paul	Camden	Honolulu	Greensboro
Cincinnati	*1900*	Dallas	Jacksonville	Hammond, Ind.
1860	Columbus, Ohio	Des Moines	Knoxville	Jackson, Miss.
Chicago	Fall River	Ft. Worth	Miami	Lansing
St. Louis	Los Angeles	Hartford	Oklahoma City	Lincoln
1870	Memphis	Houston	Peoria	Lubbock
Buffalo	New Haven	Kansas City, Kan.	San Diego	Madison
Louisville	Paterson	New Bedford	Somerville, Mass.	Newport News
Newark	St. Joseph	Norfolk	South Bend	Niagara Falls
Pittsburgh	Syracuse	Reading	Tacoma	Portsmouth, Va.
San Francisco	Toledo	Salt Lake City	Tampa	San Jose
Washington	Worcester	San Antonio	Tulsa	St. Petersburg
1880	*1910*	Springfield, Mass.	Wichita	Topeka
Cleveland	Albany	Trenton	*1940*	Torrance
Detroit	Atlanta	Wilmington, Del.	Charlotte	Tucson
Jersey City	Birmingham	Yonkers	*1950*	Wichita Falls
Milwaukee	Bridgeport	Youngstown	Austin	Winston-Salem
Providence	Dayton	*1930*	Baton Rouge	
	Grand Rapids	Canton, Ohio	Corpus Christi	
	Lowell	Chattanooga	Little Rock	

trialization, which wrought an even more profound change in the nature and size of cities during the nineteenth century. Since that time the fundamental form and structure of the city has not experienced any radical upheaval and transformation such as took place during those two periods. Subsequent to the Civil War, and in other countries to a similar degree, the changes in cities have come largely from increases in the scale of trade and manufacture, from growth of population, and from fairly radical transformations in the technology of transportation. Thus, in the next chapter we may view the city of the present not largely as a fundamental transformation of past cities, as has been the case up to now, but rather as the evolution of the Industrial Age city that came into full form about the middle of the last century. For this reason our method of looking at that modern city may change. We no longer need deal with periods and historical procession; instead, we may seek a process model to explain the structure and utilization of the modern city, particularly in America, but generally in Western civilization.

Urban
Morphogenesis
in the
Industrial Age

Urban Form in the Modern World

The Emergence of the
Complex City, 1845–1945

The antiquity of cities, widely understood, tends to hide from us a clear perception of the physical structure of the modern metropolis. The misunderstanding comes from a failure to give sufficient attention to the processes at work in the shaping of cities. For three thousand years urban places have housed a variety of activities—the religious function of the acropolis was almost immediately joined by governmental and trading activities and ultimately by educational, social, legal, and cultural undertakings that would controvert any notion of the single-purpose city. At the same time urban morphology remained remarkably simple. There were specialized buildings—the stoae and basilicas for public gatherings, *horrea* for storing goods, and *cenacula* for housing extensive populations, for example—and even discrete clusterings of buildings as in a forum, but in virtually all cities there was a seamlessness to the fabric given by the common dependence on pedestrial movement for transportation. Distinctions existed, particularly those given by social division of clan, class, and religion, but they did not bring forth a morphologically complex city. Only where walling had been undertaken, to be succeeded by unsecured construction beyond the gates, was there clear diversity, giving us our first morphogenetic division into *urb* and *suburb*—that incrementation beyond the walls of the city. The clear distinction between the polar extremes of city and countryside was maintained and the ambiguity of the suburb was commonly resolved after a relatively short time: physically by the building of a new and more encompassing wall, and legally by the concept of a politically expanded city—the *contado* of the city in Italy or its liberties in England. Society and the structure of its largest artifact tended toward simple, if all-powerful, distinctions between city and countryside, with cities gaining a special importance from the small portion of the national population living within them.

The change in the role of cities was not instantaneous, as few evolutions are, but the shifts came in a sufficiently rapid fashion to allow us to look upon the hundred years after 1850 as a great transformation in urban geography leading to the creation of the complex *city*, diverse in morphology as much as in economy, society, and culture. The driving force of this transformation was the great increase in the scale of urbanization, leading to, among other things, a level of geographical specialization to match the much older building specialization begun in classical times. That spatial division was engendered by the rapid increase in size of cities and was given a structure by the rapid increase in the complexity of transportation available for the use of city people.

The city of pedestrial movement by citizens had, of necessity, to be as small in area as possible. Not all such places were as compact as might be desirable. Classical Rome, medieval Milan, late-Renaissance Paris, and Restoration London were all larger than was convenient, and each had to lean heavily on water transport to bring in the food its people needed, in

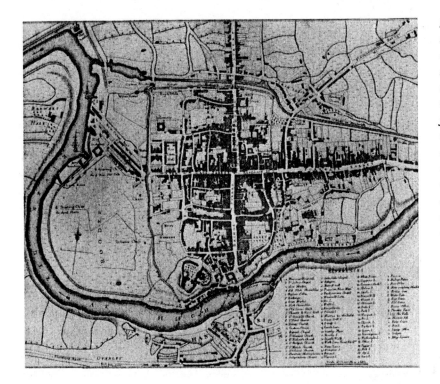

In 1794 Chester still
showed the medieval
development of a
Roman castrum,
with the cardo and
the documanus
forming the medi-
eval high streets
and burgage plots,
clearly suggesting
centuriation of
Roman times. The
Roman wall,
transformed only
moderately over
the centuries, can
still be seen, and
the small change in
the scale of the city
over nearly two mil-
lennia is evident.
From John Aikin,
A Description of
the Country from
Thirty to Forty
Miles Round Man-
chester (London:
Stockdale, 1795).

quantities beyond the provision of the immediate vicinity. It seems reasonable to argue that these cities, giant for their time, could not have existed
without a cheaper and more comprehensive form of external transportation
than was available within their city bounds. Thus, their absolute populations
could increase well beyond the common value for cities of their period,
forcing great crowding within those bounds as no effective substitute for
walking in internal transportation had yet been found. We cannot say that it
was only in the middle of the last century that cities were seen to be ham-
pered by the absence of effective alternatives to pedestrian movement; we
can say that the problem then became so exaggerated in a few large cities
and so widespread with the growth of many sizable cities that more earnest
efforts were made to find practical alternatives.

Evolution of Transportation and the City

In the seventeenth century in Paris, and the eighteenth in London,
experiments had already been undertaken in a search for vehicular transportation. The results were successful enough to show the considerable utility of
such movement but not cheap enough to permit broad use of the horse-drawn
vehicles involved. It was only in the nineteenth century that much success
was obtained in creating truly public urban transportation. The development
of the omnibus, first in Nantes in 1825 and then in Paris three years later,
began the democratization of urban transport that was a generation later to

The Emergence
of the
Complex City

365

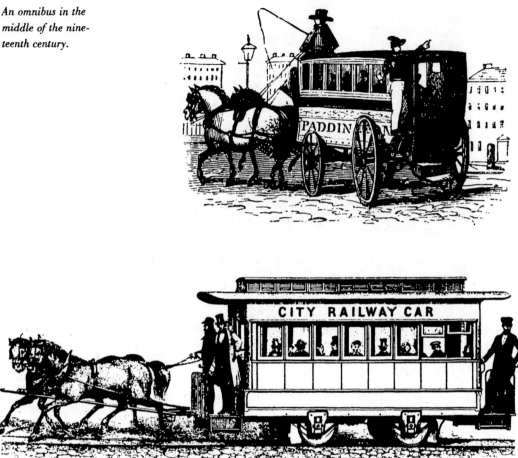

An omnibus in the middle of the nineteenth century.

The horsecar became le chemin de fer Américain *because it was developed and so widely used in the United States.*

transform the structure of cities. New York City added the next improvement, the horse-drawn streetcar, which in 1832 broadened the class-utilization of transport, demonstrating the wide geographical field open for development. Although the omnibus had been taken up rapidly, the more commodious, and thereby cheaper, streetcar took twenty years to gain very wide utilization. Only in the 1850s were many American cities served with horse-car lines and did the technology reach Europe through *le chemin de fer Américain* launched in Paris in 1853, the beginning of the era we here consider.

Before we take up the transformation of the traditional structure within the urban bounds, it is necessary to consider the contemporaneous answer to a nearly timeless question: what were the differences between the city and the countryside in the matter of transportation? Until the nineteenth century both areas had been basically served by pedestrial movement. In the countryside, where animals were a necessary element of most agriculture, draft animals could be used for haulage, but they were perhaps not much more available to the common country folk for riding than they would have been in the city. The curious and the enterprising seeking to reach the horizon did so mainly on foot.

The quickening of economic activity—consequent upon the Mercantile Revolution of the seventeenth and eighteenth centuries—reshaped cities as merchants' towns and ports; it also remade much of the countryside and in doing so forced a Transportation Revolution there as well. Larger markets of a mercantile empire, such as England's in America, India, and Africa, called for a larger product of even fairly traditional industries such as the country woolen manufacture of Gloucestershire, East Anglia, and the West Riding. Iron was demanded in greater tonnages. Cotton was introduced and quickly became the staple for a burgeoning textile industry, particularly in Lancashire. Much of this growth took place in the countryside, where some unused or at least purchasable waterpower could be found and where changes in agriculture were making workers available for enlarging factories. Although the United States was not the seedbed of this industrialization, due in considerable part because of the restrictions that a mercantile Britain placed on such activities in its colonies, country manufacture was a hidden presence before independence and a critical national goal after 1783. After that date there was as urgent a push to provide the infrastructure for manufacture in the New Republic as there had been in the former metropolis. And that creation of facilities looked particularly to the shaping of a transportation more efficient than the plodding of draft animals and the trudging of people.

In this effort a striking contrast emerged between the republic and the former mother country. In Britain it was a shortage of waterpower that forced industrial growth into cities, where the various processes involved in creating textiles and metal products could be undertaken in separate steam-powered factories. This medieval practice, which saw the "mysteries" of a single process in a chain of fabrications restricted to a distinct gild in its particular occupation quarter of a city, became a force in shaping the industrializing city. Where in the Middle Ages gilds, each with its specific process, had had different quarters, though commonly adjacent one with the other, in the emerging city of the Industrial Age that process-distinction was maintained but now in separate, if adjacent, towns. Parts of an industrializing town such as Manchester or Birmingham, or later industrial satellites nearby, became the home for a particular process, rather than the full fabrication from raw material to finished product. In the United States there was no such medieval practice in most instances. During the colonial period most industrial activity had been illicit, and the point need not be tortured that in that circumstance the fine distinctions of custom and traditional practice tend to be forgotten. Pragmatism emerges in control where the constraint of custom and common law are absent within a surreptitious pursuit. Simply stated, in the United States manufacturing had tended to undertake to carry out all the processes in the creation of a product within one household when such activity had to be clandestine; when manufacture became legal, there was no tradition or law to obviate the joining of all processes in a single plant. The slavish copying of British practice by Samuel Slater in the 1790s had interrupted what might be seen as the

"American practice" of carrying on process-clustered production, but with the advent of the Boston Manufacturing Company in Waltham in 1814 we resumed our tradition.

Returning to the question of the transportation infrastructure for industrialization, both Britain and America greatly needed improvement in transport within the countryside, though for somewhat different reasons. In Britain the shortage of waterpower forced additions to industry to come near the alternative source of power, that is, coal for the operation of steam engines. With an inheritance of mercantile towns from an earlier period and a considerable history of manufacture even in the Middle Ages, the successor steam-powered factories tended to be located near sources of orders for goods (mercantile towns) and investment capital (then largely mercantile in origin). The towns near coal fields gained an edge: Manchester became the metropolis of the new cotton-textile trade; and the West Riding of Yorkshire held on to its role as the heart of one of the English woolen districts. Possessed of coal fields that East Anglia and Gloucestershire lacked, the West Riding became the metropolis for English wool. From its medieval iron trade, Birmingham with its Black Country came to dominate all metallurgy in Britain. Canals and later railroads were built to bring coal to these industrial metropolises, allowing cities and their industrial satellites to burgeon.

In the United States waterpower was plentiful throughout the Appalachians, though New England seemed initially favored because glaciation had provided ponds and lakes that tended to even out the flow of streams in the face of seasonal contrasts in rainfall. And, as in Britain, the Yankees had both the mercantile towns to furnish the requisite orders for the product of factories and the mercantile capital for the building of those plants. In New England water was an even more dispersed source of power than Britain's coal had become. To make use of it, however, the same improvement of transportation was required. Manufacture was similarly tied to the availability of power, but with waterpower—before the development of electricity—it was necessary to take the plants to the power rather than the power to the plants, as in Britain. For this reason it should not surprise us that the earliest canals in America came in New England and that the first network of railroads was developed there.

This industrialization in the early years of the last century caused great improvements in the infrastructure of rural transportation in the English Midlands and North, and in New England and the northern Appalachians. By 1850 a comprehensive network of railroad lines was available in each area, such that industrialization and urbanization could approach a scale never before thought possible, let alone reached. Through the much enhanced rural transportation—initially sought by canalbuilding and canalization of rivers, though ultimately accomplished through the much more adaptable construction of railroads—a new system of urbanization became possible. Britain experienced two major changes: the growth of vast cities of complex economic structure and great areal extent, which came in this century to be called conurbations, and the considerable enlargement of what had been medieval market towns to become cities with industry as well as

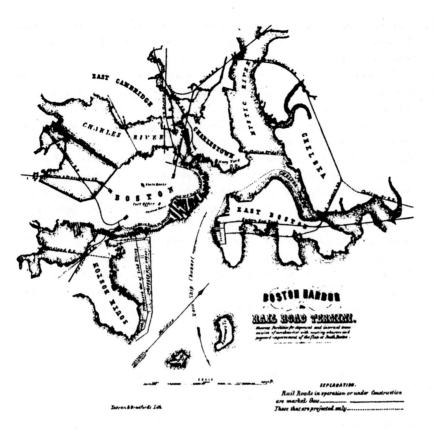

trade. In the United States the railroad allowed the growth of two types of settlement not found in colonial times: the industrial satellite, which at first tended to spring up near the mercantile ports that supplied its market and the capital for the construction of its factories, and suburbs that became the location for the residential incrementation to the older traditional cities. Suburbs had existed in medieval cities, on a very small scale, and they sprang up around Paris and London after 1830, when the omnibus provided intra-urban transportation. It was in America, however, that the suburb was seen as the normal and desirable form of urban residence made possible by the building of railroads. Those lines had not been constructed to bring suburbs into existence, though once lines were laid out they allowed suburbs to burgeon in what had been rural villages located along the rail line.

The geographical pattern of suburbs differed between Europe and America. Around Paris, London, and several other large European cities suburbs came mainly in the form of "villa districts" built close to the borders of the traditional city and first engendered by the construction of large and expensive houses for those possessed of private carriages. The coming of the omnibus made such locations as St. John's Wood and the other areas north and west of Paddington in London possible residential sites for an upper middle class not always possessed of carriages. The developments were seen as somewhat pastoral, but the morphology of the additions tended to be

The Emergence
of the
Complex City

369

similar to that found in the Georgian housing estates; the main distinction between them was found in the architecture, which tended to be rather more eclectic in the suburbs. European suburbanization was tightly angular in form, with a parsimonious use of land, a continuity of structure outward from the city center, and a much more characteristic use of attached or continuous building form.

In North America, both the United States and Canada, the suburb was clearly the creation of the railroad, which gave it its characteristic morphology. Carriages and omnibuses were capable of frequent, almost individual stops, but trains were not. Even the earliest locomotives took time to be halted and considerable effort to get under way again. Thus, stops—halts, to the English—had to be spaced out, causing the growth of suburbs to be discontinuous in geographical pattern. What resulted were bead-pattern strings of suburbs originally divided one from another by remnants of the open rural ground in which they sprang up along rail lines. The fundamental contrast between Europe and America probably came at first from the service characteristics of the transportation that initiated suburban development. But the openness of American suburbanization, as contrasted with the European compaction, undoubtedly represented the differing conceptions of land found on opposite sides of the Atlantic. Europeans viewed land both as scarce and as the foundation for social distinction. Landowners in Britain sought to make available for suburban building small, compact tracts that would still leave grounds and fields for the "big houses" that gave families social status. On the Continent the agricultural and social values attaching to rural lands were such that a similar meanness of suburban provision existed. It was only in North America that suburbanization took place in an environment of a generous land provision. In the United States social status did not depend on landownership in those parts of the country that were rapidly suburbanizing; and the vast stretches of virtually empty land in North America led to the view that there might be a democracy of space. The dispersed and privately owned farms of colonial New England had impressed on the American mind the virtue of private, detached, and individual ownership of housing. This strong cultural inclination was reinforced by the early transportation improvements that allowed suburbanization. The rejection of narrow ownership of land by the Massachusetts settlers of the 1630s had laid the cultural foundation for the American suburb; the railroad allowed it to grow without serious legal and spatial transformation.

Systematic Change with the Coming of the Railroad

To understand the nature of the large city at the middle of the last century, we must remind ourselves that the development of railroads worked a fundamental morphological shift. The traditional city that stood as the core of the emerging metropolises was compact in the best of cases and horribly crowded in the worst. In the 1840s Britain and other industrializing European nations became aware of, and greatly concerned by, the crowding in cities. Even in basically rural Denmark, Copenhagen had developed some of the most cramped and fetid of tenement areas, a condition equally characteristic of Naples far to the south. The form of the traditional city of Europe can be thought to have reached a limit of traditional growth by 1850. Studies such as that of the British Royal Commission Studying the State of the Large Towns and Populous Places in the 1840s clearly perceived the problem; they were less effective in conceiving solutions. The problem, we now realize, lay in the exhaustion of the ability of traditional urban morphology to care for the demands of greatly burgeoning populations and increasingly complex cities. As long as city people had to get about by walking, there was within traditional morphology no way out of the noisome growth of the larger places. The obvious solution could be seen to lie in a transformation of that longstanding physical structure in one of two ways: the buildings themselves could be transformed by pushing upward the limits of construction, or the city itself could be enlarged in geographical extent in some fashion by providing a new form of transportation that would allow people, and goods, to move easily over a wider area.

Each of these possible solutions was actively experimented with in the 1850s, allowing us to view that decade as the initial one of the great "urban transformation" that changed both the prince's capital and the merchant's town of the seventeenth and eighteenth centuries into the modern metropolis. Before taking up that transformation, we should look back for a moment to what had been happening during the first half of the last century. We have already noted the coming of the railroad, which almost immediately transformed the countryside about the city by encouraging the growth of industrial satellites—equally in England and New England—and before midcentury the railroad suburb had emerged around larger places possessed of a network of rail lines. Boston was the first to have such a pattern, lending a historical justification for viewing the Hub as in many ways the birthplace of the complex city in America rather than the large European cities with well-developed rail systems and similar experiences. New York's transformation was rather different, because its insular location made the ramification of rail lines awkward. There, instead, it was ferry connections that began suburbanization, a situation shared with San Francisco in the shaping of the Bay Area City. These early railroad and ferry metropolises grew in reflection of the articulation of their characteristic transportation.[1]

But those industrial satellites and suburbs at first possessed a geographical isolation that gave to them a morphological distinction. None was a literally continuous extension of the traditional city form; rather, each was an entity located in space in relation to the city but tied to it by rail lines or waterways that left open space as an integral and internalized part of the growth pattern. Large cities of the early to mid-nineteenth century, be it Boston or Hamburg, took on a "planetary system" morphology, with a focus on the traditional city—port, capital, market town, or strongpoint—and the ranging around it of satellites and suburbs. As in heavenly planetary sys-

1. For a discussion of the emergence of the railroad-shaped metropolis, see James E. Vance, Jr., "Labor-Shed, Employment Field, and Dynamic Analysis in Urban Geography," *Economic Geography* 36 (1960); for a similar view of the emergence of a ferry-shaped sympolis, see James E. Vance, Jr., *Geography and Urban Evolution in the San Francisco Bay Area* (Berkeley, Calif., Institute of Governmental Studies, 1964).

*The emergence of
suburbs in the Lon-
don region is well
shown by this map
of the provisions for
suburban rail service
by the Midland
Railway after it
built into London
in 1867.*

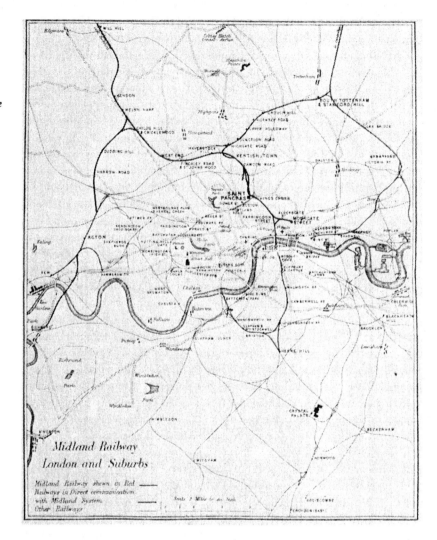

tems, gravitational attraction held this open morphology together, but unlike
the heavens, the modern metropolis had direct physical ties, attaching the
parts together along rail lines and waterways.

The limitations on movement introduced by the primitive technology of
the railroad forced these components of the planetary system to remain
initially apart. It was clearly evident to contemporary observers that the
space originally built into the system introduced problems and costs that
would ideally be avoided. The industrial satellite could not very effectively
make use of central-city institutions, stores, or housing; the suburb could
not provide housing for the lower economic classes working in the traditional
core because of the relatively expensive nature of early rail travel. This latter
point is accentuated when we look at the Bay Area City, or New York. In each
of those places suburbanization became more economically democratic than
in the railroad metropolises because ferries could make better use of the
primitive steam engines of the time, thus lowering the cost of that propulsion

and allowing it to be applied to vehicles of such size that masses of people could be carried.[2]

The nature of early suburban development—essentially beads of growth at railroad stops in the adjacent countryside—and of industrial satellites served only partially to relieve the crowding of the traditional city. As long as those places remained the reception area for migrants to the city, as they did in the great ports where most of the overseas immigrants landed—Boston, New York, and Baltimore in America, and Liverpool and Glasgow (with respect to Irish immigrants) in Great Britain—crowding probably increased. The general growth of activity in these core areas, consequent upon the increase in manufacturing and trade, put pressure not merely on the housing provision but on that for shops, warehouses, and offices as well. It was in this context that the central-city transformation took place. Still depending heavily on pedestrial movement, the heart of the emerging metropolis had somehow to be enlarged in a way that would permit it still to function with people moving on foot. The answer to this was great density of land use but without actual additional crowding within buildings, as these were physically enlarged now through the construction of taller structures. The general height of city-center buildings began to increase using traditional building technology, stairs for access to upper floors, and masonry walls to carry the additional stories. Obviously each of these aspects of incrementation had its faults. Too many flights of stairs were thought intolerable for all but the most disadvantaged—the origin of the concept of the garret for the poor—and more stories borne by masonry walls meant that those had to be thickened to such an extent the ground-floor space was sharply reduced.

The Rise of the Skyscraper

The solution began to appear in the 1850s with the first use of elevators and the early efforts to create what came to be known as skyscrapers. It has been argued that the skyscraper was distinguished from earlier tall structures, such as the spire of Ulm Cathedral, which rose above five hundred feet even in late medieval times, by the possession of three structural characteristics. The first, "well-above-average height" was, of course, shared by all tall masonry structures of the Middle Ages and Renaissance, but two were distinctive to the skyscraper and very much the product of the middle of the last century: the installation of the passenger elevator and "the employment of cage and curtain-wall construction."[3] It is impossible here to detail the adoption and evolution of these structural features beyond merely noting that around 1850 these two elements began to come into large-city construction, particularly in New York. But with the rebuilding of Chicago after the fire of 1871, a more innovative adoption of the form was undertaken, and by the end of the century the skyscraper was viewed as a distinctively American

2. For a discussion and analysis of the relative cheapness of ferries, and thereby their mass use, see Bion J. Arnold, *Report on the Improvement and Development of the Transportation Facilities of San Francisco* (San Francisco, March, 1913).

3. Winston Weisman, "A New View of Skyscraper History," in *The Rise in American Architecture*, ed. Edgar Kaufman, Jr. (New York: Metropolitan Museum of Art and Praeger, 1970), p. 131.

creation and certainly the *signum* of the modern city as yet to be adopted in Europe.

To make possible the architectural—as opposed to geographical—solution of the space problem in cities, the elevator was the key to open the first lock inherited from the past. In 1850 in New York a manufacturer, Henry Waterman, made the first use of an elevator, essentially the hoisting machine that dated back at least to the late-medieval cranes found in places handling heavy commodities such as the salt of Lüneburg and the cargoes of Antwerp. Waterman transformed these ancient lifting machines to provide vertical transportation between two floors of his factory by attaching a platform to the cables of the hoist. Quickly thereafter, in the hands of Elisha Graves Otis who had installed such a primitive lift in a bed factory where he was employed, improvements were worked out that made the elevator safe against cable failures. With that perfection the passenger elevator was available and several were installed in New York City buildings in the 1850s.[4] In 1859 came the first installation in a hotel. It was of an awkward screw propulsion, rather than Otis's later cable-drawn improvement. The Haughwout Store—also in New York, built in 1857, and only five stories high—had a similar installation. From these beginnings the great utility of the elevator became evident, and rather quickly further adoptions were made in public buildings. Once the elevator had come into use, architects were emboldened to increase the height of buildings beyond the modular five stories that had come to be seen as the greatest height to which people would willingly climb on foot.

The urge to reach to higher levels, made possible by the elevator, came to be constrained by masonry construction. The problem was that weight-bearing walls had to be thickened to carry more stories, and that enlargement encroached upon the most valuable space in a building, the ground floor. This additional lock on expanding the size of building through increasing height was opened by the adoption of cage and curtain-wall construction. Again, the decade of the 1850s in America furnished the key. The earlier efforts were not aimed specifically at the construction of a truly tall building, but rather at the creation of a fire-resistant structure capable of supporting industrial activity. Such a structure was designed for Harper's, the publisher, in 1854 by James Bogardus, one of the earlier architects to use cast-iron components in construction. This Harper Brothers Building was only seven stories high, including the basement, but it was the first to employ wrought-iron beams—in place of wood, as in traditional building, or cast iron, which had been experimented with but not very successfully, because of its brittleness and poor resistance to fire. Wrought iron for use in tension, when combined with cast iron in compression, provided the first instance of successful all-iron construction. The Harper Brothers Building was not a full transformation of traditional construction; it used masonry exterior

4. John W. Oliver, *History of American Technology* (New York: Ronald Press, 1956), p. 404. In 1941 a U.S. Army bomber flew into the side of the Empire State Building in New York, severely damaging an elevator and causing the car, with its operator, to fall eighty stories. The operator was badly injured but not killed. In instances of equipment failure, rather than direct aerial attack, American safety elevators have proved most worthy of their name.

walls, but its interior structure of iron was far more fire-resistant than had previously been possible, and it proved to be much lighter than older construction.[5] That lightness of dead load became a critical feature soon thereafter when iron construction was carried to its logical limit with the creation of the cast-iron façade and then of iron-post-borne party walls. The iron cage within the building joined to, and bracing, an iron post-and-infilling exterior finally created the condition whereby (1) the dead load weight of the building per story was considerably reduced over masonry construction, and (2) that weight could be concentrated on a set of columns opening up the sides of the building to better fenestration and the ground and lower floors for use without thick and continuous masonry walls. The iron-cage building became a reality with the Equitable Life Assurance Society (subsequently Equitable Insurance) Building in New York of 1868–70. Although only five stories high, that structure is considered by several students of the skyscraper to be

5. W. A. Starrett, *Skyscrapers, and the Men Who Build Them* (New York: Charles Scribner's Sons, 1928), pp. 20–22.

The Emergence
of the
Complex City

the first one in existence because it had an iron-cage construction and the first elevator found in an office building. Thus, all the elements critical to the building of truly tall buildings were in place, to become the pandect for the experimentation that produced obvious skyscrapers in the early 1890s. Independent footing of the piers for the columns was devised in Chicago after the bad experience of the Federal Building there—finished in 1880, and placed on a "continuous foundation on soggy soil"—showed that deeper piles reaching to firm ground or bedrock were required to support the newly enlarged buildings. The increasing weight of additional stories was reduced when Balthasar Kreischer, a New York manufacturer of fire brick, found the solution of both dead load and fire protection in the hallow tile, which he patented in 1871. Finally, in 1884–85, the best material for constructing the cage, which supported the building and on which the walls were hung, was found in structural steel, first employed for that purpose in the ten-story Home Life Insurance Company Building in Chicago. With it the skyscraper became a reality in a form that has changed only in detail, not in fundamentals, for a full century. During that period in the Windy City the height has risen from little over a hundred feet to nearly fifteen hundred, but the engineering structure has remained fundamentally the same, with the main difference showing up in the severe problems of wind force encountered in constructing buildings more than a quarter of a mile high.

The architectural solution to the problem of packing more people into the heart of the city was thus in hand soon after 1850. A truth quickly assailed urban society, however, that the cost of such vertical accommodation was such that many activities and large components of society could not be cared for through tall buildings. Obviously, heavy industry could not be carried on in structures of considerable height. Similarly, the poorer classes, which had throughout history been sheltered for the smallest possible cost, could not be housed in expensive buildings. By the middle of the last century it was obvious that an architectural solution could not care for most of the exigent demands. Instead, those seeking to facilitate the increases in industry and trade, which supported the cities that came with the maturity of the American Republic, had to turn toward a geographical solution to the problem of the city's growing economy and population. And in Europe, where the American skyscraper was adopted only very slowly, virtually complete provision for growth had to be placed on the physical expansion of the metropolis. Only in the last generation has the tall building been further transformed, as we shall see in the next chapter, and with that change the architectural solution to the crowding problem has been reasserted.

The Geographical Solution to City Growth

The increase in the average height of buildings in the traditional core of metropolitan areas, which obviously added far more space than did the more exceptional skyscrapers found in only small numbers even in the largest cities, could care for only part of the spatial needs of the growing urban centers. Experience showed that five or six stories was the natural modular height of city buildings until automatic elevators and reinforced concrete construction were introduced after World War I. Thus, the core area became more accommodating of growth, but not infinitely so. This was especially the case with respect to housing, which could not accept the costs of higher-building construction, and to industry, which needed the strength of low and spread-out structures. Starting in the 1840s, the railroad had encouraged the growth of industrial satellites—at waterpower sites in New England and in the environs of such traditional industrial towns as Birmingham and Manchester in England—and was beginning to permit the creation of bead-pattern suburbs at the stops along the rail lines adjacent to the larger cities. Those suburbs, however, could only be used by the upper classes in England, leaving the vast body of city people crowded in the traditional core of those cities. In the United States conditions were somewhat more democratic, both because of the cheaper cost of housing in suburbs and of railroad tickets, available in weekly, monthly, or even season versions, and because of the relatively higher wages of labor in the United States. Still, even here there were a great many city people who could not afford to live in a railroad suburb while remaining employed in the traditional core. Crowding of central housing increased as economic growth led to ever-expanding employment there.

The decades of the middle third of the last century witnessed a great growth in city population in the United States, but it was concentrated in the larger metropolises and in the hearts of those now giant places. Thus, the crowding problem was exaggerated by its concentration in a relatively small number of cities—Boston, New York, Brooklyn (then separate), Philadelphia, Baltimore, Pittsburgh, Cincinnati, Cleveland, Chicago, St. Louis, New Orleans, and San Francisco. Elsewhere, the American city was still of small enough size that the traditional urban fabric could provide adequate housing depending on rail transportation for long distances and walking and horse-drayage for local movement.

In the largest cities—New York, Brooklyn, Philadelphia, Chicago, and Boston—the longstanding morphological solutions were so hard-pressed by the final third of the last century that great efforts were made to shape a geographical expansion of the city to match the architectural one we have noted. This search came particularly in housing, where the need to secure reasonably priced incrementation was great. The physiological limit of five or six flights of stairs put a lid on housing expansion in the traditional city. In the years just after the Civil War the "elevator apartment house" was devised in New York, mainly for the wealthy who wished to ape the style of life of contemporary Paris, where large *appartements* were piled one on another rather like a stack of what the ancient Romans had called *domus*—that is, large and complete dwellings occupying one story (in ancient times, the ground floor) in a taller building housing other families. The elevator apartment had first appeared in New York City just after the Civil War when J. C. Cady designed the Aurelia and Richard Morris Hunt the Stuyvesant, the latter an "Apartment house complete with a *concièrge* living on the ground floor."[6] These socially as well as structurally elevated buildings demon-

6. John Burchard and Albert Bush-Brown, *The Architecture of America: A Social and Cultural History* (Boston: Little, Brown, 1961), p. 112.

The Emergence
of the
Complex City

The five levels of Parisian life (by Edmond Texier in 1854) portray an interesting urban morphology. Before the introduction of elevators, the "French flat" had come into existence in Paris as the ancestor of modern apartments, but it was vertically stratified in such a way that social class declined sharply with increasing elevation—just the reverse of the situation when elevators were introduced into housing at the end of the century.

strated graphically how it was possible to pile people up in the city without reducing the space or amenities available to them. The price, however, was so great that this architectural remedy could serve the needs of only a small upper-income group.

The Railroad Suburb

The same was true, though not in quite so restrictive a fashion, of the earlier railroad suburbs. What was obviously needed was a form of transportation that could bring into the built-up city the wedges of undeveloped land lying between the several radiating railroad lines as well as that land that remained too far from their suburban stations to be used for development. With railroad suburbanization there remained much open land between the beads of growth at the outlying railroad stations. These two types of open land enclosed within the boundary of the railroad suburbs would furnish a sufficiently large increment to the area of the traditional city to allow a massive increase of modest and low building for housing, thus keeping the costs down. We should not forget that an area of a basically circular form increases geometrically with the simple arithmetical lengthening of the radius. The traditional city, which even in the larger places extended only two to three miles from the center, could gain a considerable enlargement of its built-up area through suburbanization without, initially, much increase in the radial journey from the city center, where most employment was to be found. Thus, a geographical solution to the crowding problem of the Industrial Age city through full use of all land within the outer radius of the railroad suburbs represented a powerful remedy, and one that could benefit the lower middle and blue-collar classes as well as the wealthy.

The latter point must be made because the early suburban dwellers tended to be the rich, who moved out of the early-nineteenth-century city as much for health reasons as for the aesthetics and social cachet of living beyond the city's edge. The causes of the frequently recurring epidemics in the cities of the last century were not fully understood, but observation had shown that there was less contagion in rural areas. Those who could afford to had already begun to send their families away from the coastal cities during the hot summer period, partly for the greater comfort in the countryside but also partly as a preventive measure against disease. It was a short step from this seasonal departure from the city common among the upper classes before the Civil War to the permanent movement of those classes to the outermost fringe of the metropolis. In this way there grew up in the United States a logical association of the edge of the city's residential fabric with the home of the socially elevated. Only where industrial satellites were in existence within the broad suburban band was this class association of the edge of the city interrupted.

Generational Shift in Suburban Residence

There were never so many truly wealthy families that a complete annular ring of their housing might surround a city. The result was a class-striping at the edge, with a few truly wealthy suburbs, usually located where the environmental amenities were perceived to be highest, interbanded by middle-class suburbs located either where transportation to the central city was superior in speed, or adjacent to industrial satellites where those of the middle class living in that band might find employment. The appeal of the true edge of the city seems consistently to have gripped the members of the upper classes. For that reason there was a generational shifting in the residence of the younger additions to the fortunate classes. The rich moved outward each generation, unless they had such an open suburbia that their estates permitted scions to build new residences on family lands. The middle class also followed the outward shift of the suburban frontier, introducing the process of handing down parents' properties to those a little less able to buy the desired spot. Sociologists have looked upon this process as one of "invasion and succession," but that term is commonly a poor description of what is going on. Except where there is extreme pressure induced by ethnic segregation erected in the face of a rapidly expanding ethnic population, the economically less favored population does not force itself upon the more fortunate. What happens is a generational shifting toward the periphery, which became the main social-geographical process in American cities in the first half of the last century: the children of middle-class or upper-class parents, who themselves join their natal class, generationally find new housing at the edge of the city. When their parents die, the children commonly find the environmental qualities of their own housing preferable to that of their parents, leading them to sell off the family house, normally to a person of a slightly lower economic class. This slippage in social class of the residents of an area comes normally from the fact that the chosen, the "in," place to live at a particular time is not where the parents resided but rather where the current upper middle class tends to live under a generational shift of residence.

This generational shift exists as well in European cities, though its operation is far less clear and observable. The narrow ownership of land, its treatment as the symbol of social distinction, and the much greater reliance on relatively immutable morphologies of housing—such as the *appartement* in France and elsewhere on the Continent and the row or terrace house in Britain—all slow down the handing down process. The massing of these partible ownerships into conjoined structures has tended to create vast areas of relatively consistent environment and architecture that do not change with the succession of generations. In America, where the detached single-family house is the module, changes in both environment and architecture can come more rapidly and effectively with each generation.

Generational shift and the handing down process have been the most widespread forces at work in the shaping of American cities. A major reason for this near ubiquity is to be found in the transportation underpinnings of these social and economic practices. The growth of suburbia, which is a critically necessary element in the working of generational shift, has entailed a dependence on transportation since early in the nineteenth century, when larger cities had grown too extensive to be reached in all parts by walking. Thus, disregarding in the modern context the small suburbs of medieval and early mercantile cities, we may make the basic point that the form, use, and location of a suburb tends to be conferred by (1) the common form of transportation at the time of its inception, (2) the age of the individual suburb, and (3) the changes in transportation that have come since the suburb's initial development.

With respect to the location of suburbs, there is an annular succession shaped by transportation. The very early suburbs of the Industrial Age city were few in number, small in size, and approached by the small groups that had access to carriages for moving around the city. In the second quarter of the last century, with the establishment of omnibuses, these germinal extensions of the traditional city expanded considerably, though still in a relative rather than a truly extensive sense. Now "villa areas" were developed, frequently in handed-down areas of suburban estates that were newly practicable for subdivision into generous lots for villas. In this context the truly rich could, because of their probably more leisured status, continue to move outward, bequeathing both their former estates and a remnant of their social

cachet to the upper-middle-class suburbanites who were constructing large, detached, but not land-surrounded houses in these new omnibus-served suburbs. Omnibus suburbs would, of necessity, cling to the edge of the traditional settlement, leaving the rich with their carriages as the only group that might wander farther afield from the traditional city.

It was the coming of the railroad that changed the situation wherein only the generally leisured could move any distance outward from the traditional city. The railroad was not initially constructed to aid suburbanization, but once in existence it served that purpose. It seems to have had its main influence on the housing of the solid middle class, those families in which the husband had the money to commute to the city from the suburbs, if mechanical transport were available. The result was that a bead pattern of suburbs grew up at a spacing of two to three miles along these rail lines, the operating characteristics of the locomotive determining the intervals. Because steam trains were relatively cheaper per passenger than omnibuses, certainly for the distances covered, the houses built in these bead-pattern suburbs were more numerous than in the earlier villa districts, though still quite substantial and of single-family occupancy. Lots tended to be fairly compact, perhaps eight to ten or twelve thousand square feet in area, because the composite journey-to-work involved walking to the suburban rail station from the houses clustered fairly efficiently around it. Once the limit to comfortable walking distance had been reached by residential construction, it was physiologically better to move to the next outward train stop than to walk an excessive distance within the slightly closer suburb. This sharp

The Emergence
of the
Complex City

constraint on the individual suburb size was one of the major forces in the continuing search for a more geographically comprehensive form of transportation to supplement the railroad.

The Rise of the Horsecar

Not only the gaps in the bead-pattern housing structure but also the increasingly wide open sectors between the radiating rail lines encouraged that search. A still different force urging on the efforts at the geographical improvement of rail transport came from the concentration of rail service largely on radial movement to and from the city. The main interconnection among railroads came at or near the center of the city, so the various sectors reached by rail could be interconnected only near the core. Circumferential transport—that from one outlying area to another located on a different vector—was poorly served by rail. Not only was there the desire for improved public transport leading to the central city from within the sectors between rail lines, but also there was the need to create some form of circumferential service that could interrelate the several radial lines without recourse to the crowded junctions near the core of the metropolis. Thus, what was sought was the creation of a more comprehensive and ramified network. The steam railroad did not furnish such a network as it then operated any more than it does today.

The search for a more fine-meshed public transport in the suburban band was less intense than the effort to find transport with a higher density of service within the traditional city. Omnibuses had begun the introduction of true public transport in the central city just after 1825, but their high operating costs had limited the size of the group that might use them. The contemporaneous development of the steam railroad as a mechanized form of transport for long-distance movement suggested an obvious way to bring to the city a form of transportation that could carry far more people, and thereby make possible increasingly economical working. Efforts were made to introduce trains to street running, but the results were highly unsatisfactory. The mass of the steam train was such that it could not be stopped quickly, making it dangerous to operate amid pedestrians and horse-drawn vehicles. In addition, trains were slow to accelerate and their locomotives tended to spew sparks on those nearby. By the early 1830s the street-running experiments were seen as a frontier expedient not acceptable within a major metropolis.

The heart of Boston could be reached by rail because large tidal flats surrounded the city's small peninsula and became the site for railroad embankments separated from the city's street net. But in New York the solution was particularly difficult. At the time the only practicable access to Manhattan Island was from the north, with a crossing of the narrow Harlem River and a line carried down the long north-south axis of the island. City growth had come in that same axial alignment, so the edge of the built-up city was particularly far removed from the business core south of Wall Street. The railroad promoters would have built southward to that colonial limit of the city, but the municipal government would not have it. Twenty-third Street was as far as they would countenance steam's running: south thereof any trains would have to be horse-drawn. The promoters did not face this constraint for the first five years of the railroad's existence, as horse traction was used throughout the line's entire length until 1837. At that time the railroad extended from Prince Street to Harlem, but steam working stopped at 14th Street, with horse traction employed south thereof. This "street railway," commonly considered the world's oldest, is thus rather ambiguous as a model for latter constructions. It was intended as a true railroad, to use steam, but for its first five years the narrow geographical scope—the charter limited construction to Manhattan Island—encouraged horse working. Only when steam was belatedly introduced was a functional division of the New York and Harlem River Railroad struck. With the adoption of steam, a station was established on Fourth Avenue between 26th and 27th streets, with the line thence to the heart of the city being worked by horses, confirming the status of this section (26th Street to Prince Street) as that pioneering horsecar line. But steam traction always disturbed the Common Council and mayor of New York. In 1844 they forbade steam operation south of 32d Street, and in 1858 south of 42d Street. That latter action finally led the New York and Harlem Railroad—as its name was by then spelled—and its tenant, the New York and New Haven, to adopt 42d Street as the terminal for standard railroad operation when Commodore Vanderbilt's merger of the Harlem, Hudson River, and New York Central lines created the need for a new station in New York. Opened in 1871, Grand Central Depot at 42d Street stood for forty years as New York's main and only important station.[7]

The early development of the street railway in New York City suggested the practicability of the medium—it was adopted for use in a somewhat analogous situation in New Orleans within two years—but there was then nearly a twenty-year gap before the horse-railway systems became common in the United States. It was only in the 1850s that most of the larger cities adopted street railways: Brooklyn at the beginning of the decade, Paris in 1853, Boston in 1855, and most other large cities by the outbreak of the Civil War. These operations had been encouraged by the New York demonstration that street railways were practicable, though they were delayed in installation while a distinctive horsecar technology came to be worked out. The wheelbase of the cars was shortened, permitting the rounding of tighter curves, something also facilitated by the adoption of a narrower gauge than the railroad's standard. Lighter cars with a more restricted loading gauge not only made street running more practicable but single-horse traction more effective. Thus, it was only about 1850 that the true street-railway era begins, again supporting the notion that it was only during a fairly short period at midcentury that the rapid transformation of the city to a modern form was accomplished.

7. William D. Middleton, *Grand Central, the World's Greatest Railway Terminal* (San Marino, Calif.: Golden West, 1977), pp. 11–25.

The Emergence
of the
Complex City

The Streetcar Revolution

The street railway had an impact on urban morphology not previously witnessed in such a short period. The walking city had, save in a small number of giant—and awkward—cities, been a place whose radial extent from the center of the town was seldom more than a mile. With the advent of the horsecar lines the outward limit could be, and was, pushed up to about two and a half miles, thereby vastly increasing the area of the city from little more than three square miles to just under twenty. This rapid areal expansion became an omen for street-railway cities; and compact growth could be maintained because the horsecar lines were so easily ramified, wherever the street for development was at hand, that a circular and fully developed city resulted. For a generation this vast land incrementation permitted the housing of a working-class population, at a generally reasonable cost—more so in America than in Britain because lines were much more common and extensive in American cities, and because wages were that critical bit higher here to permit more democratic use of street railways. On the Continent, particularly in France where the street railway came to be called *le chemin de fer Américain*, greater use than in Britain was made of this mode of transport, probably in some measure because continental city housing was in tall structures of small tenements and *appartements*, which created a very compact built-up area even in a city as large as Paris. Thus, a place was created that was practicable for horsecar service without the undue ramification of lines that made operation expensive. In contrast, American cities with large amounts of single-family housing developed at such a relatively low density that the practicable outer limit of horse traction was being reached and strained within the generation that followed the Civil War, and before the giant population growth that came with massive European immigration had fully begun.

It was in this immigrant-crowded metropolis that the next innovation in intra-urban transportation was sought, again most earnestly and effectively in the eastern part of North America. Before we look at that development, recognition should be made that the Germans were carrying out similar experiments with electricity and the French—given their cardinal role in the evolution of chemistry—with compressed air and the use of gaseous reactions. But it was the American-Canadian solution that was truly successful, becoming the model the rest of the world adopted in short order during the final decade of the last century.

Steam had not proved a satisfactory motive power for urban use. Nevertheless, efforts had been made to adopt steam traction, accepting the fact that it could not effectively intermesh with street traffic. The solution, obviously a compromise, came through the separation of the steam-drawn lines from the streets, with those public systems carried either in tunnels below ground level or on tracks elevated above the street. In London in 1863 the first subterranean line was opened as the Metropolitan Railway extending from Paddington Station in the northwest to Farringdon Street at the edge of the City. This was a costly project whose extension was further limited by London's general lack of straight and wide streets in which a trench could be

cut and subsequently be roofed over to allow street traffic to return. Only slowly and at great expense was the Metropolitan Railway extended into a circular line that eventually interconnected most of the railroad stations located on the north bank of the Thames. Even at this slow pace, none of the "cut-and-cover" underground lines passed through the true heart—either shopping or financial—of London. In New York in the late 1860s almost the obverse solution to the problem of using steam in the city was sought. There, the elevated railway was experimented with and lines were developed northward on Broadway. In due course in the 1870s and 1880s elevated lines were rapidly extended toward the north end of the island, and as well within the shopping, if not the financial, district. There were numerous environmental objections to these steam-drawn elevated trains, but the speed with which their routes might be expanded and their greater proximity to the office and shopping objectives of most intra-urban travelers overcame objections to their construction. But the underground and the elevated were big-city projects, too costly to be used in smaller places. It was in the eastern part of North America, where there were a number of medium-size cities, that the search for a solution was continued.

That solution became fairly apparent in the 1870s when the work of Edison in the United States and the Siemens brothers in Germany made electrical generation and transmission practical. In 1879 Germany held an Industrial Exposition in Berlin for which Werner Siemens developed and installed an electric railway of a rather primitive sort. He followed up on this with short electric lines in Germany and Northern Ireland built during the early 1880s. The scientific and engineering communities were very much aware of the potential for electric traction; what remained to be done was to work out the system of transmission from the generating station to the motors in the car. When tried out on the streets of Berlin, Siemens's system of third-rail operation was found dangerous from the shocks it administered to horses making a misstep. This third-rail system could function reasonably well when employed on a separate right-of-way, as it was at Lichterfelde and at the Giant's Causeway in Ireland; but it was not the solution to street running in cities.

Edison was also interested in this problem, but at the same time he was wrapped up in the experiments that would lead to the invention of the phonograph. It fell to the lot of one of his assistants, Frank Sprague, to pursue the matter of electric traction for street railways to a successful conclusion. Sprague, originally a graduate of Annapolis interested in electricity, resigned from the Navy to work at Menlo Park with Edison but soon found that the electric locomotive project captured so little of the great inventor's interest that he left to found his own company to engage more actively in the experimentation. In this work he was far from alone. Edward Bentley and Walter Knight had electrified part of the East Cleveland Street Railway in 1884 through the use of a third rail carried below street level in a conduit rather like a cable-car cable. In the mid-1880s Leo Daft, who had installed a third-rail line in Baltimore and in East Orange, New Jersey, had also experimented with two overhead wires to create the electrical circuit. In 1886 Charles Van Depoele gained the right to electrify the Capital Street Railway in Montgomery, Alabama, thereby earning the honor of having created the first fully electrified system in the United States. From a historical vantage point, however, we now realize that each of these systems had serious technological failings that would have made wide adoption unlikely. It remained for Sprague to put all the necessary pieces together successfully and to shape the installation in Richmond, Virginia, that opened in the spring of 1888 to become the model quickly adopted not only in North America but worldwide.

What Frank Sprague accomplished was to devise a system of electric supply that was cheap, easily extended, and highly successful. This was distribution on a single overhead wire, using the track as a return "ground," from which power was taken by a spring-controlled, underrunning trolley pole. In addition, he developed an excellent traction motor, ingeniously held in geared contact with the actual car axles by a wheelbarrow mount that compensated for poor and rough track. Finally, Sprague contrived a simple and effective controller that easily handled the problem of increasing and decreasing the flow of electricity to the motors, regulating the speed of the car. It was found that the traction motors might be used as brakes, greatly facilitating the rapid stopping of the car. This early work also brought out the superior qualities of the electric traction motor in gaining rapid acceleration. With fast stopping and starting, a much reduced mass compared with the steam trains, an efficient and cheap supply of power, and an already developed right-of-way furnished on streets, either by existing street railways or by new construction for which no more than a franchise to occupy part of the street area was needed, the electric traction system became the first truly effective instrument of the geographical expansion of cities. Thus, the year 1888 represents a great turning point in the matter of urban morphogenesis.

Richmond was hardly large or important enough at this time for its

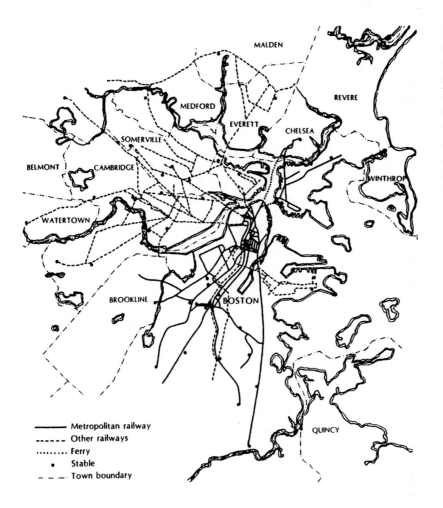

The horsecar lines brought together as the Metropolitan Railway in Boston in the mid-1880s created the world's largest horsecar system and the first major installation of Frank Sprague's trolley system.

activities to transform urbanization so radically. But Boston was, and it was Henry Whitney, president of the world's largest and most successful horse-car company, the West End Street Railway of Boston, who began the change. Whitney had been interested in the Richmond electrical experiment by one of his associates. Soon after the line was opened under electric traction, Whitney went to the former Confederate capital and Sprague conducted an experiment for him—when in the middle of the night he put all the Union Railway Company's cars on the line and managed to start them one after the other in close file (by dint of firing the boilers to the maximum at the generating station and putting as much current in the line as could be secured from his generators). This convinced the Bostonians that their much more densely used lines could be operated employing the Sprague system, which they immediately ordered to be done. Thus, Boston was the first large metropolitan city to adopt what had come to be known as the trolley, gaining its name from the original overrunning electric pickup, which seemed to be trolled along the two wires then employed.

The Emergence of the Complex City

Boston: The Laboratory for Electric Traction

In the period of fifteen years after Henry Whitney's decision to electrify the West End Street Railway, Boston probably did more to evolve electric traction than any other city. This was the case not merely technically but economically as well. I believe this important role grew out of Boston's very early adoption of the geographical solution to urban crowding, allowing us to look upon the Hub as the laboratory of the suburb as much as of the electric railway. Boston had stood as the world's first railroad hub, having the service of three radiating railroads before London had any mainline connection and before Paris had any rail service at all—the first was in 1837 to Saint-Germain, followed by Right- and Left-Bank lines to Versailles in 1839 and 1840. That Bostonian railroad provision combined with the distinctive political structure of New England—with established and geographically defined rural towns—to encourage the creation of perhaps the earliest bead-pattern suburbs to be developed. Ultimately, Paris gained a fringe of such places, high in social status, with a concentration toward the northwest in the direction of Versailles where the earliest rail lines had been constructed by the Rothschilds and the Periere brothers, but Boston had such suburbs both earlier in time and more broadly occupied in class terms.

By midcentury there was active commuting from blue-collar as well as middle-class suburbs into Boston, creating the practice of suburbanization on a relatively greater scale than in perhaps any other large city. During the last 150 years Boston has normally been the American city where the suburbs bulked relatively largest in numbers of people and importance. It was in Boston's first suburb, Brookline, that the great apostles of suburbanization—H. H. Richardson, who found the first widely adopted architectural idiom for the suburb, and Frederick Law Olmsted, who developed the first conscious morphology for suburban layout—lived and worked. We should appreciate that America made two fundamental contributions to world urbanization in the last century, the skyscraper and the suburb; it was in New York and Chicago that the architectural model for coping with urban growth was shaped, but in Boston that the urban-morphological contribution was worked out to a mature form.

In the late 1880s, when the West End Street Railway was being electrified, that system stood as the leading horsecar line in America, the largest street railway system in the world, and the only example of a unified system serving an entire large city. The west of Boston was well developed in the suburbs of Brookline and Newton. The first was so close to Boston, though socially, politically, and culturally distinct from the city, that the horsecar lines could provide it with intra-urban service. Newton lay too far away for horse traction, so the Boston and Albany Railroad took up the burden of tying the numerous suburban "villages" that grew up there to the center of employment in the Hub, through the construction of its Highland Branch wandering through the two premier Boston suburbs, dotting them with stations designed by Richardson or his disciples, and bordered by parks and estates from the drawing board of Olmsted or his pupils. But all of this transportation was radial from downtown Boston, leaving movement within the suburban band in an awkward state. The safety bicycle, introduced in the mid-1880s, helped along those lines, but the electric cars held out hope for a more effective and universal solution. It proved much easier to create suburban networks of trolley lines in those places where the railroads could, at best, provide only a multiplication of radial lines, as in the Highland Branch. This was particularly important to women seeking to move about the suburbs rather than to commute to the city, as did their husbands. In addition, what we would today call the service trades found the trolley service valuable in getting about the suburbs. And as the suburban band expanded, it engulfed some older industrial satellites, creating therein the desire on the part of the more prosperous workers to move out of the mill towns toward a new working-class suburbanization that might be facilitated once networks of suburban trolley lines, particularly those circumferential to the traditional city, could be opened.

The history of the West End Street Railway greatly encouraged the early adoption of electric traction. Boston had begun developing horsecar lines in the 1850s and during the next thirty years had created a number of different companies normally serving separate sectors outward from the downtown. By 1885 these had been merged into four major companies. That same year a Boston shipowner, Henry Whitney, whom we have already met, decided to engage in a large suburban development in Brookline adjacent to Boston where he and his investment group bought some five million square feet of land. They hired Frederick Law Olmsted to lay out a new, landscaped and divided boulevard along Beacon Street, only to realize that to develop this land successfully they needed not merely a horsecar line but an electric operation, because the distance from the city core was too great for effective horse traction. The resulting West End Railway could not easily undertake electrification, because the company's access to the downtown had been granted by the state legislature over the tracks of other companies, which had no interest in facilitating their competitor's business by agreeing to his mechanization schemes. It became evident to the Whitney group—which, interestingly, included Albert Pope, America's premier bicycle builder, who fully understood the need for transport in the suburbs—that the only way to get the mechanized line to downtown Boston was by merger with one or several of the existing horsecar companies. "In early 1887 Whitney and his associates began to purchase the stock of the established lines, and by June Whitney had control of all four. . . . Rationalization began almost immediately. With more than 3,700 employees, 1,700 cars, 8,400 horses, and 200 miles of track, the West End was a gargantuan outfit for its day." In organizing this massive company Whitney pioneered the corporate structure that was later to be adopted by most of the larger city transit systems. "Fares were standardized and some free transfer points established. At Whitney's urging, the West End abolished zone fares and established a uniform nickel charge for any ride *regardless of length*. The flat fare provided a simple method for handling a high volume of traffic moving in diverse directions. It was also a definite saving to long distance passengers at the expense of short haul travelers. Additional conveniences awaited mechanization. Crosstown lines and a universal transfer system only became feasible when a new

The Emergence
of the
Complex City

motive power made longer routes possible."[8] The earnest nature of Whitney's visit to Sprague's Richmond installation is easily understood in this context.

The West End decided to undertake an experimental electrification on the Sprague system of a stretch of its track. Proving highly successful, in contrast to the essential failure of another experimental stretch using the Bentley-Knight system of electric conduits, Sprague's overhead trolley wire was adopted for all lines, and all were to be electrified. Passenger totals increased 59 percent to 137 million in 1894; crosstown lines became common, thereby facilitating the movement about the city without recourse to downtown junctions; and the lines were ramified to virtually all parts of the metropolitan area by 1895.[9] Still, the trolley network of Boston, the most extensive in the world, extended only some five miles from the heart of the city. Anyone wishing to commute a greater distance could do so in a practical way by turning to suburban train services. Even so, the lengthening of the lines and their ramification, when joined to a very rapid growth of suburban housing, had so built up traffic that the heart of the city was becoming "blockaded" by trolley cars.

The Geographical Impact of the Nickel Fare

Before we look at the solution to that problem, we should note the impact of Whitney's decision to adopt a flat nickel fare. This was done because the operating superintendents were convinced that it would be cheaper to operate the electric cars that were being substituted for horse traction. These cars were considerably larger than the horsecars they replaced, were capable of continuous operation over very long days—horses could work for only a few hours each day, requiring time-consuming replacement—and could be run closer together on the track. The West End Street Railway reasoned that there would be such an increase in traffic that more was to be earned by encouraging a mass transport than an expensive but rather exclusive one. All of this because of the considerable initial costs of electrification of the lines, which in Boston ultimately averaged about $86,000 per mile.[10] With such investments to amortize, it seemed essential to develop a large clientele for the trolleys.

The geographical impact of the flat nickel fare was dramatic. For the first time a form of transportation came into existence that reduced the economic cost of distance, if not its time demands. Once one had boarded the trolley, it cost no more to ride to the end of the line, even using transfers to other lines, than it did to go only to the next stop. The relatively low cost of electric-car travel, added to this geographical comprehensiveness, meant that most elements of the working population could envisage using the trolley in a journey-to-work. Once that assumption was made, the location of worker

8. Charles W. Cheape, *Moving the Masses: Urban Public Transit in New York, Boston, and Philadelphia, 1880–1912* (Cambridge, Mass.: Harvard University Press, 1980), pp. 118–19. Emphasis supplied.

9. Ibid., p. 120.

10. Ibid.

housing was freed from what had been a longstanding constraint. Fatigue was considerably overcome in the journeying to and from work and the continuing extension of the electric lines allowed an ever-increasing area to be brought within the potential residential area of a major urban labor-shed. In effectively doubling the radius of commuting, from two and a half miles to five miles, the area open to housing was raised geometrically. Because Boston shared with Chicago a true port site, with only around half the circle of environs lying on land, the outward spread was unusually lengthy for the population growth. Still, the geometrical increase in the suburban area with lengthening of the radial journey was such that enough land could be added to the suburbs to assure plentiful land for development. This supply kept the prices down, making suburban lots much cheaper than those near the core and encouraging workers to move outward in their search for relief from the core-area crowding problem. As long as the extended journey toward the edge of the metropolis cost no more in money, there seemed a great economic advantage to the lower-income groups to move out of the central city. If the housing they secured there were no larger than they had had in the center, then it would be cheaper. And if as dear, it was likely to be considerably more roomy. By the time of the trolley it was becoming clear to urban Americans that open, green, less dense housing areas tended to be more healthful. Although seldom formally propounded, this idea was widely held and encouraged a general, democratic suburbanization of American cities. The low and flat fares of American trolley systems, in which practice Boston was merely the pioneer, made American suburbanization a quite different thing from that of European cities, where only the rather well-to-do managed to move into suburbs.

By the time the trolley systems were fully developed, just before World War I, North American metropolitan regions had vast areas of blue-collar suburbs. The traditional city was considerably drained of its working-class residents, reducing the pressure for residence and permitting a more efficient reassignment of core-area land to nonresidential purposes. The suburban train and trolley services still focused strongly on the downtown of cities, most particularly in Boston, though the electric cars tended to have, in addition, lesser foci at outlying road junctions where radial and circumferential (crosstown) routes came together and interchanged passengers. For the first time there might be a number of transportation nuclei in metropolitan areas, rather than the single original nucleus at the heart of the traditional city. For several generations the suburban journey had been a rather simple one, from the port, industries, counting houses, and shops of the old core to and from the new housing areas. But with the trolley and its subsidiary junctions, much more varied and complex journeys outside the core became possible. For the first time it was practicable to move from one suburb to another, without entering the downtown, or to commute to and from the outlying industrial satellites that had frequently become embedded within the rapidly expanding suburban belt. In this way the satellites could expand their industrial production, through hiring additional workers, without having to create an enlargement of the mill towns that had earlier had to be set up as a support for satellitic development.

Morphological Changes Brought by the Trolley

A number of industrial satellites expanded in the Boston area. Waltham, the true hearth of integrated manufacture in the world as well as in America, grew industrially in the late nineteenth century by becoming a significant outlying trolley hub. The same was true of Framingham, Quincy, and Lynn. These towns lay far enough from Boston to have good steam railroad service, but until trolleys provided a large labor-shed of workers they could not easily grow industrially. Eastern Massachusetts demonstrated more graphically than anywhere else how the trolley could provide labor and working-class housing to support large industrial towns. Brockton, Salem, Lowell, Lawrence, North Andover, Haverhill, and Newburyport grew to become major American manufacturing cities in the trolley era. Not much farther from Boston, and still very much supported by a trolley network, were New Bedford and Fall River, the latter at this time the world's largest cotton textile factory town. By the time of World War I eastern Massachusetts had the greatest density of trolley lines of any region in America, considerably the result there of an intimate, widespread interaction of the trolley and the factory. Only in southern Belgium did Europe have a similar trolley-industrial landscape. But the early adoption in Massachusetts of the low, flat fare was the premier example of freeing distance of an "economic cost" and its impact on the lives of the blue-collar class.

The signal success of the trolleys in stimulating suburban growth, while still tying the suburbs mainly to the employment and shopping facilities of the traditional core city, worked somewhat ironically to bring about a great transformation of the traditional city's morphology. Discussion of that striking change must wait for a more general analysis of urban morphology. Here, however, in the specific context of Boston we must acknowledge some of that evolution. The trolley lines were intended to be a dense and diverse network within the closely built-up city and its suburbs. To accomplish such a service pattern, junctions became frequent and the more encompassing of these became potential sites for shopping in a wider context than the small bead-pattern suburb that had come earlier.

Such junctions in Brookline, Newton, Waltham, and other close-in towns and cities of the suburban-satellite band became important sub-metropolitan shopping centers with quite large stores, even some small department stores. The trolley made conflux on these outlying town centers possible. Even more, it opened all parts of the suburban-satellite band to transit to downtown Boston at all times of day and at a low cost. Much as the metropolitan area was becoming more complex and not so exclusively core-centered, the easing and cheapening of access to downtown Boston for women living in the suburbs encouraged the growth of shopping in the Hub. We now know that the trolley era (1890–1940) was the time of downtown supremacy in shopping of a specialized, infrequent-demand sort. Food and common, frequently sought goods might be bought in the suburbs, but large, distinct, special items would come from the heart of the metropolis. The trolley made that domination possible.

Because of the often quite specialized nature of those demands, shops selling those particular goods had to stand in the center with its easiest overall access to the total metropolitan population. In geographical terms this meant that the central business district had to develop the most encompassing and efficient network of transportation ties. Further, it meant that the shopping core, to provide the specialization of goods impossible elsewhere in the metropolitan area, had to have the best of the best. This showed up in an important separation of core-area functions that began with the advent of electric traction, though suggestions of the split can be seen earlier in the time of the horsecar lines. This was the division between the strongly office-oriented functions of the downtown and those of the shopping sort. In Boston the two developed through a separation that left them neighbors: State Street became the core of the office-financial district, Washington Street that of the department stores and their handmaidens. Partly because the offices had drawn workers into commuting travel before the department store had developed enough to woo the wives of the office workers to customary shopping in the central city—that is, because offices came before the advent of the trolley, whereas department stores were mainly contemporaneous with electric traction—the traction lines tended to focus on the shopping district and to burgeon with the development of the central shopping district. This co-evolution of the shopping district and electric traction perhaps began in Boston, the city that practically invented the American department store, giving its name to half a hundred such institutions spread from the shores of Massachusetts Bay to San Francisco Bay, and certainly introduced the trolley to America and the rest of the world's big cities.

The Boston Subway

In Boston the trolleys converged on Washington Street, the colonial "high street" and thereby a narrow, winding thoroughfare, and subsequently on Tremont Street, the next street to the northwest. These two streets became increasingly clogged with "sparkers," to the point that by the early 1890s they were almost impossible for other wheeled vehicles to use and certainly difficult for pedestrians to cross. Further expansion of the suburban street railways was stymied by this clogging of the center. The Bostonians themselves began to look upon this as the "barrier or blockade" problem, for transverse movement was becoming very difficult. Some measure of the rapid increase in riders with the advent of trolleys is given by the fact that Boston's per capita ridership of streetcar lines (horse traction) was 118 in 1880 and 175 in 1890, when electric lines were fast replacing the horse.[11] Between the year of the adoption of electric traction by the West End and the turn of the century, the outer edge of the contiguously built-up city expanded from four to ten miles. The growth was so rapid that traffic shot up a quarter in the four years after Whitney's decision to electrify.[12]

Bostonians came to the same conclusion as had Londoners and New

11. Ibid., p. 125.
12. Ibid.

Yorkers in the 1860s, that the only way to solve this blockage problem was to rise above it or burrow under it. The West End had proposed building a subway through the heart of downtown Boston in 1887, but a decision made that year to consolidate all street railway companies and one made the next year to electrify them put off the actual crisis for several years. In 1891 a joint state-city commission was established, including among its five members John F. Kennedy's grandfather, then a Democratic congressman from Boston, and Henry Lee Higginson, the staunchest of Brahmins and the founder of the Boston Symphony Orchestra. Congressman Fitzgerald was greatly taken by Berlin's Stadtbahn, an elevated line, and he led a faction opposed to subways as unpleasant and unhealthful in an era of widespread pulmonary disease. The 1892 report of the Rapid Transit Commission continued this interest in solving the blockage problem, but it was rather equivocal, favoring a solution to the transit problem by such things as consolidating the city's railroad terminals into two union stations, but not coming down strongly in favor of a specific plan to remove the trolley blockages. In the aftermath of this inconclusive document, the West End and others proposed building an elevated line or, failing that, a trolley line across Boston Common to keep down the costs. The outcry of Proper Boston was uncharacteristically shrill, even engaging the stern attention of Julia Ward Howe, whose *Battle Hymn of the Republic* seems all the credentials she needed as a defender of patriotic ideals.

A clogged and crowded Boston had to do something, so the city stepped in and undertook to build a subway that would be observant of the local pieties yet progressive in its unclenching of the stranglehold that the West End company's successful electrification had set upon the heart of the city. Perhaps the most geographical aspect of the problem was that the traditional city wanted the subway while the emerging suburban band, partly within the municipal limits but increasingly extending outside them, wanted more urgently some increase in the speed of travel to and from that to-be-improved core. The rapid outward extension of the closely built city—from a radial width of some two and a half miles to more than five miles—accomplished during the first few years of trolley operation had begun to make commuting from the suburban area of most active residential incrementation progressively more time-consuming. The economic cost of the journey-to-work may have been constrained by a commutation of daily fares to weekly and even monthly charges and by a single flat fare, but the time taken each morning and evening was not equally reduced. In Boston the outer suburbanites gained an ally in Captain Joe Vincent Meigs, the inventor of a rather unusual tubular steam-powered monorail—an experimental section of which had been erected in East Cambridge—who had initially sought to promote this system in particular; when the system ultimately showed technical problems, he pushed for elevated lines in general. Boston, the largest example of a medieval organic town on North American shores, was notably unsuited to elevated railway construction within the heart of its traditional city core. It was that fact perhaps above all others that determined that it should have the New World's first subway line. But even when agreement was reached on the necessity to burrow under the heart of the city rather than steaming above it on a viaduct, the problem of speeding up service to the suburbs remained. Thus, in the Hub we may observe the first effective solution to these two problems within what was to become the standard technology of a modern metropolis, the use of electric traction. London had a considerably older subway, thirty years before Boston; New York had an older elevated line, again thirty years before the Yankee metropolis. But these were steam-operated lines when Boston was examining the general subject of rapid transit. Odd bits of experimentation elsewhere had employed electric traction: the City and South London Railway opened in London in 1890 had used electric traction, but in such a mean and eccentric fashion that no one ever followed its lead; Liverpool had electrified a short but very specialized stretch of dockside elevated line in 1873; and Glasgow had opened a subway in 1896 but operated it with cable traction until the 1930s. But for a complexity of reasons it was in Boston around the turn of the century that what came to be the standard technology of urban electric railways was worked out in practice.

There is little doubt that Boston's pioneering role in subway and rapid transit technology was due to the fact that the city was the first large place to set about electrifying its street railways. With electric traction in hand, the problems that had beset such tunneling elsewhere were considerably reduced. The steam and smoke that continued to make a ride on the Metropolitan Railway in London a trial could be avoided, while the overhead wires made the development of a street-running electric feeder system practicable. There might be aesthetic objections to trolley wires, but there were few of those that were practical considerations as well. Thus, it was easy to carry the trolleys underground, tying together the best solution yet found for urban mass transit (electric traction) with what had to be the future solution to funneling the greatly increasing numbers of passengers to and through the downtown areas (subway construction). This first "Boston solution" was soon enlarged, again in Boston as we shall see, and has been joked about for generations by New Yorkers amazed by trolleys underground. Only in our day, and mainly in Europe, has the trolley tunnel come again into its own as the latest in planning techniques.

The Tremont Street Subway, as it was called when it opened for service in 1897, was the fourth line to follow on London's example of the 1860s, but definitely the first of wider significance. We have already noted the short and idiosyncratic line of the City and South London Railway. And Glasgow's subway, completed just before Boston's, was a single ring, entirely underground—without even surface connection save by elevator—and was operated by cables until the 1930s. Even older was the short stretch of cut-and-cover subway completed in Budapest for the 1896 Hungarian Millennial Exposition. This line led to the fair site through a real estate development associated with the exposition. When that fair concluded, the Andrassy Street Subway remained to connect this bourgeois area with the heart of Budapest's business district, though it was never expanded beyond a couple of stops at its outer end, and its small original cars remained in use until the 1960s. Thus, Boston's was the first electric subway that was expanded using its original technology.

Construction on the Tremont Street Subway began in 1895. The project called for access to the tunnel, as it was first termed, at three points, two in the south and one in the north, where ramps would lead from the surface down to the subway, carrying trolley cars underground. Up to 285 of these cars could be handled in an hour without crowding, because most of the route had four tracks, one of the first instances of multiple trackage underground. The total length of the tunnel was two and two-thirds miles reaching from Haymarket Square, adjacent to the railroad station in the north, to Shawmut Avenue in the south and Boylston Street at the Public Garden in the southwest. The utilization of the subway was much advanced through the adoption of multiple-unit operation, under which several cars could be joined and run as a unit by a single motorman, allowing more cars per hour to move safely through the tunnel. This device had been developed by Frank Sprague for the South Side Railway in Chicago (an elevated) and was installed there earlier in 1897. This "M-U" operation became the basis for heavy rapid transit, because it for the first time permitted the running of trains on these urban lines that were equivalent in passenger capacity to those on the steam lines.

The opening of the Tremont Street Tunnel in September 1897 immediately relieved the blockages on that route and on Washington Street, which paralleled it through the downtown. The speed-up of access to the suburbs, however, remained a problem in the general context of introducing cheap mass transit to metropolitan areas. Chicago and New York had made an expedient solution to that problem by constructing elevated railways through the city center and outward to the fairly distant suburbs. These had originally been steam-drawn and only at the time of Boston's experiments in the late 1890s did Chicago seek to electrify its El lines. New York waited a few more years before doing so. But Boston could not envision taking an El line across the downtown, so it was there that the experiments that finally demonstrated the greatest practicable technology were carried out and resolved. With the Tremont Street Tunnel open, the Meigs group of elevated-railway promoters pushed for the construction of elevated lines intended to connect through the city core via the newly finished tunnel. To accomplish that goal, the Meigs group gained control of the West End company and merged it into a new corporation, the Boston Elevated Railway. Then the subway was reequipped to handle heavy rapid-transit cars of the sort created for Chicago's electrified Els. Because there were four tracks, it proved possible to run both trolleys and rapid-transit cars through the tunnel, though using separate platforms, low-level for the trolleys mounted by steps and high-level for rapid transit entered directly at platform level. The arrangement, however, greatly reduced trolley capacity, so there was strong pressure brought to bear by the city to construct a separate heavy-traction subway parallel to Tremont Street, as was done on adjacent Washington Street. This was the first example of what has become the standard technology for very large cities, worked out tentatively in 1901 when the Boston El trains first used the Tremont Street Tunnel, and fully developed when construction of the Washington Street and Dorchester-Cambridge lines was commenced soon thereafter. As if these experiments were not enough for one metropolis, Boston also pioneered a subaqueous tunnel, at first carrying trolley cars, to connect under the harbor to East Boston. This line, which opened in 1904, was soon to be repeatedly copied by New York in gaining the interconnection of the five boroughs that had been joined into one city in 1899.

The development of the multiple-unit heavy rapid-transit car carried in a subway at the heart of the city, usually fairly coterminous with the extent of the traditional city, and on an elevated structure outside that core, became the turn-of-the-century state of the art for metropolitan transit. New York used the split in level between Manhattan and the outlying boroughs, even elevating the lines in northern Manhattan. Hamburg followed this American metropolitan practice directly. Philadelphia, slow in adopting rapid transit, did carry its generally elevated line through the center, under Market Street, when service began in 1908, though there was little expansion of the system for a generation. Chicago, a leader in El development, stuck to that form until it opened its first central-city subway in 1943, to be doubled by a parallel line in 1951. No doubt part of the delay came from that city's low-lying site and severe storm drainage problems. By the time of World War I there had been general acceptance of the three principles that Boston had established in 1901: (1) transit in a metropolitan city must conform basically to the existing arterial-street pattern and be electrified, (2) the system must be carried underground through the traditional core because of the crowded nature of that area and its largely prevehicular street net, and (3) high-speed rapid-transit lines outside the traditional core would be provided through elevated or surface rights-of-way that reduced the capital cost of the system to a manageable level.

This brief look at Boston's transit evolution is intended to bring out the forces shaping the ultimate design and broad historical timing of its individ-

In Chicago the focusing of intra-urban transportation on the downtown was so extreme that an elevated line around the core, the Loop (shown here on Wabash Street), had to be constructed. Note the electric streetcar line on the street under the elevated. Photo: Chicago Elevated Railway.

ual stages. Because Boston was the American, and in some instances the world, pioneer in those technical adoptions, this examination provides us with the most succinct picture to be had of that technological evolution. What we must now add are the basic changes in urban morphology that stemmed, at least in part, from this evolution of urban transportation, changes that, along with the characteristic urban transit at the outbreak of World War I, largely remain with us even today. There has been great incrementation to this modular pattern, but it has come primarily at the edge of the 1914 metropolis and supplemental to its standard of transportation. Obviously, in cities of less than a million people, rapid transit normally was not developed; the urban area was seldom extensive enough to provide the requisite market or, for that matter, the absolute need for such considerable private investments, as they first were. In those medium-size cities only the first of the Bostonian principles applied, that the street railways would be fully electrified. In all likelihood, as in most rapid-transit systems, there would be the adoption of Boston's economic practice of the flat fare, traditionally a nickel, so in all levels of urban places up to and including the giant metropolis, the "economic cost" of intra-urban travel was unitized, and at a low level, at the same time that this complex electric traction was being devised.

Urban Morphogenesis in the Electric-Car Era

We are immediately confronted by two aspects of urban morphogenesis that we must distinguish. The first is the re-ordering of space within the traditional city and the second is the elaboration of spatial patterns in the suburban-satellitic band. Up to this point we have been concerned largely with the role of electrified transit in facilitating the journey-to-work, and thereby encouraging the suburbanization of metropolitan residence. This undoubtedly was the most radical transformation that the trolley era brought, but we should appreciate that moving one function away from the traditional core tends to free central space for other activities to begin there, or at least to provide space for the expansion of land uses already found there. Initiation of new activities or expansion of existing activities will lead to a fundamental transformation of a morphologically established area. In terms of the great mid-nineteenth-century problem of crowding in traditional cities, electric traction created a great geographical solution. Particularly the democratization of the suburban shift through electrification and the nickel flat fare opened large areas previously required for housing to other and more economically productive uses. Retail and wholesale commerce and industry might spread within the core, not only because housing pressure was reduced there but as well because workers might now be recruited from the much wider labor-shed of the metropolis as a whole. In commerce, there was a great lift to retail trade due to enlarging metropolitan population tied by a dense electric-traction system focusing on the city center. The cheap fares, the frequent trolleys even during the day, and the greatly ramified street-railway system all served to encourage suburban women to begin shopping downtown, or to make far more frequent journeys to those precincts. The massive scalar rise in transit passengers between 1890 and World War I confirms this, as well, of course, as the massive growth in the size and number of downtown department stores catering to that trade. Even wholesale commerce was aided in a general way by electric traction, through a greater ease in securing qualified workers, the creation of an intensive network of mechanized transport in the core city, and even the use of trolleys for the distribution of the package freight so much the outflow of a wholesaling operation within a large metropolitan area. We shall take up these specific land uses and their transformation in the time of the trolley, starting as seems logical with the evolution of the location, scale, and function of retail trade during this period.

The Transformation of Retailing

It is difficult for us today to appreciate how recently the conditions of medieval trade were transformed into what we all accept as modern practice. In 1850 that transition was only beginning, but it began to pick up speed in the period between the Civil War and World War I. In 1850 the provision of goods to purchasers still partook heavily of the medieval practice of artisanal production—the geographically dispersed handmaking of goods, often only in response to orders previously placed by the purchaser. Because any artisan could produce only a small volume of goods during a year, it is clear that geographical dispersal of the workplace by such handworkers was possible, and probably desirable for their support. They might easily dominate a market, admittedly a quite small one, if the purchaser had to count on several visits to the workshop to secure the finished good.

The Emergence
of the
Complex City

399

Contributing to this parochialization of production was the simple absence of standards of size, construction, and taste in many goods. Before the Civil War there was no statistical information on the size distribution of the population, men or women. Any making of clothing for general use tended to produce only ill-fitting garments rejected by the fastidious in favor of tailor-made garments, which required the geographical proximity of the artisan and the customer. The Civil War did change things somewhat for men, because that conflict produced the first mass conscription, the first giant armies, and, for clothing those men, the first extensive anthropometry (obviously only of men). From those measurements, and based on the needle trades brought into being after 1861, ready-made men's clothing became practical and reasonably successful. Even such standards, of course, did not totally suffice, and in recent decades an extension of mensuration has come in "big and tall" clothing for men, though oddly not "small and short" clothing, as does exist for women. Women's clothing had to wait until the close of the period under discussion before ready-made garments were widely accepted. How the standard measurements were arrived at has always seemed a mystery, there never having been conscription of women until the establishment of the Israeli state in 1948.

It is only in our time that modularity and standard sizing have been established. Differences among the products of individual manufacturers were common, even in the items produced by a single worker over time. The semicircular roofing tile was traditionally produced by slapping clay on a worker's thigh—thus making the desired taper—but one can easily envision that the tiles shaped by youths, workers in their prime, and old men would be different products. In historical geography it is possible to regionalize many things, particularly building materials, clothing materials, food, and drink, the most important of consumption items. Raw materials were normally of local provenance, so considerable variation among goods could take place. As long as human society was guided by local practice rather than "style," the geographical dispersal of production was protected by local taste. But with migration, internal and overseas, taste tended to become interwoven and thus lost to a style one gained more commonly from a distance. To facilitate such external provision of goods, which was likely to follow on outside shaping of taste, standardization of size for particular items seems to have been important. It is hard to sort out, but the geographical extent and anthropometric diversity of the New Lands may account for the fact that in the United States men's shirts may be bought in different sleeve lengths, though that is impossible in Britain (as is finding a narrow shoe there).

As with most human actions, there was a circularity to this matter of standardization. Having established some general agreement on taste and sizing, centralized shopping might become common. And once common, then its style would tend to dominate, reinforcing the appeal of the center against the artisan production and sale in the small town. It was for these reasons that the central shopping district gained ascendancy during the fifty-year period between America's earliest large-scale wars. That growth of centralized shopping before the late 1880s put increasing pressure on the horse-drawn street railways, and after that time caused electric traction to be introduced and initially well rewarded. It is hard to imagine the central business district in its halcyon days without the contemporaneous development of the trolley, and then of rapid transit. This association of shopping with transit development is well demonstrated by the impact of rapid transit on cities. Boston's Tremont Street and Washington Street subways fixed the heart of the shopping district, concentrating the location of department stores in a fairly tight clustering at the intersection of the two true rapid-transit lines at Washington and Summer-Winter streets. This process Walter Firey observed a generation ago in Boston, and we may see it at work in other large cities.[13] Although he did not make a specific point of the matter, we should add to his analysis of the location of the central retail district the progressive nature of this concentration with the adoption of heavy rapid transit. In the horsecar and trolley eras, downtown Boston had gained a unique status within metropolitan retailing, but it was with the building of the subways and their outward extension along separate rights-of-way—or even more elevated lines—that the central intersections of the system gained their most dominant position. The earlier railroad stations had not so concentrated the location of the general-merchandise (department store and variety store) shopping. It waited on the arrival of the subway.

Why did the rapid-transit development lead to a concentration of the city's general merchandise retailing? The answer lies, I believe, in the difference between steam-train commuting and rapid-transit travel. Even when Firey was writing in 1947, the rapid-transit system extended only about seven miles from the major intersections at Park Street and Washington and Summer-Winter streets. Subsequent extensions have considerably increased that distance, but in a time when downtown shopping has radically declined. It seems fair to say that during the palmy days of the central retail district the rapid-transit train moving over a fairly short distance was the greatest force in concentrating retailing. The horsecar radius was something around two and a half miles; the trolley probably doubled that distance. Rapid transit did not so much extend it, only a couple of miles in Boston's case, but it so speeded up movement over those seven miles that further incrementation to the tributary area of central business districts came from adding on trolley and bus connections made at the outer termini of the rapid-transit lines. The entrance figures for the Boston Elevated Railway in 1943, quoted by Firey, bear out this conclusion. The busiest subway-elevated entrances were four in the downtown shopping district and four termini of the radiating rapid-transit lines. Obviously, there had to be a great conflux of surface-transit passengers on those termini to raise their receipts as high as or higher than those of the downtown destinations.[14]

The cheapness and ubiquity of mass transit in the heart of the metropolis—the seven-mile radius of the rapid-transit lines plus an outward connection by trolley and bus that is harder to determine, though it probably added

13. Walter Firey, *Land Use in Central Boston* (Cambridge, Mass.: Harvard University Press, 1947), pp. 229–61.

14. Ibid., p. 237.

The Emergence
of the
Complex City

401

little more than another five or six miles—made it the nearly universal means of access to the shopping district in the center. In the case of Boston, only those suburbs lying more than twelve miles or so from the core area probably depended mainly on steam-train service for downtown shopping trips by public transit. Within the metropolitan area, the 1920s witnessed a small but in the long term significant variation in this vastly normative pattern of public-transit access to the central business district. That change came in the emergence of an income-class divide in the form of transportation used in the journey-to-shop, with some incrementation by occupation. The upper middle and upper classes by this time had seen the rapid rise of women drivers, because many families owned two cars and even in one-car families the husband often commuted to work by train from the outer suburbs, leaving the car at home for the wife's use. As we shall see, this rise in cars available for the wife's use during the day began the growth of suburban town-center shopping for other than the most basic necessities, when a few of the more socially distinguished towns began to house shops of a sufficient style to encourage women to think it safe, in terms of taste, to shop there away from the established arbitration of taste to be expected in the downtown stores. In the 1920s, once driving came in these outlying clothing-store clusters, it appears that women became emboldened to drive to the edge of the central city and there carry on a somewhat more specialized purchasing of clothing and household items. In the case of Boston, this led to the creation of the Back Bay shopping area clustering around the Ritz-Carlton Hotel and along Newbury Street. Other cities had a similar outlying but still core-city high-priced specialty shopping area, such as that near Forest Park in St. Louis, on the Near Northside in Chicago, and on Wilshire Boulevard in Los Angeles.

There was as well a more democratic development of shopping peripheral to the downtown but still well within the core of the metropolis. Sears, Roebuck and Company led the way in this development by constructing its special form of the department store clearly at the distant edge of the downtown where free parking could be provided. The rationale for this location was expressed as a response to two aspects of specialized shopping: that Sears was in a real sense a "man's department store," and that by the late 1920s most men had access to a car if they wished to use it for shopping. The success of these large but clearly branch department stores at the edge of the downtown, which were opened in the 1930s for the most part, was such that other firms gained the confidence to follow in similar locations. The range of stores was, however, still somewhat limited, restricted mainly to household goods (furniture, linoleum, rugs, paint), automotive needs (new and used cars, parts, painting), building supplies, and other types of selling that could benefit from large and fairly cheap space, free adjacent parking, and automotive transport by the customer of the purchased goods. Let it be emphasized at this point that these edge-of-the-downtown shopping areas were an extension of that metropolitan-core retailing area, not a true outlying shopping center, which we shall consider in due course. What these peripheral shopping areas represented was an automobile extension of the central business district, as well as an increase in locational specialization within the core-area retailing structure.

Re-Sorting of Functions at the Center

Inside the central business district the advent of the trolley, and even more of rapid transit, had begun this re-sorting and real extension of functions. More shoppers could reach the downtown at a reasonable price in money and time, and with the fall in artisan production and its replacement by factory production of the same basic items, the central business district gained additional trade. This growth came from the simple fact that under artisan production the pay of the artisan is normally joint, part coming from the manufacturing act and part from that of selling. Under retailing divorced from manufacture, the profit must come entirely from the selling operation. To reach an acceptable entrepreneurial profit, the scale of sales must be enlarged to make up for the full cost of the return for manufacture, and probably as well for the introduction of "new" costs of shipment from a greater distance and more critical reliance on wholesaling. It seems likely that in the period around the Civil War, and possibly for several decades thereafter, manufacturing did not totally depart from major metropolitan regions. What had been produced by artisans now was likely to be produced by small manufacturing plants dispersed among a nation's major metropolitan areas. We appreciate this geographical pattern in the early years of the automobile industry—with its factory-based but not greatly agglomerated production. As time has passed there have been mergers, and failures, in most industries that have led to an increasing geographical concentration of manufacture. That spatial contraction obviously has forced the transportation and wholesaling of goods that were previously locally made and available to retailers directly from the plant, rather than through an intermediate wholesaler's warehouse.

Thus, the scale of selling had to increase first with the artisan-factory shift and subsequently with the local-national plant shift. To encompass these new costs, which might be considerably counteracted by the economies of scale in factory and then giant plant concentration, stores that might tap an entire metropolitan market had to be developed. To accomplish that business goal, there was essentially only one geographical location that might be adopted under train and electric-traction transport: at the convergence of all lines of those forms of transport within a metropolis, in the central business district. As long as mass transport was public transport, there was no alternative to locating many kinds of retailing—those requiring metropolitan-wide markets—at the core of the traditional city in the central business district.

Within that district the specialization of products sold in particular shops was reflected in an internal geography of retailing. Before the middle of the last century, even the larger cities of the United States, mainly the ports established by European settlers in the sixteenth and seventeenth centuries, were characterized by what we might think of as commodity-combining shops commonly operated as a joint wholesale-retail establishment. These were frequently the businesses of merchants whose interests included commerce as well as shipping. Ships were financed, sent to distant destinations, there to trade in local goods that were distributed in trade by the merchant on the ship's return to home port. Thus, the selection of goods

the merchant might be handling at any one time was likely to be determined more by where the ships had been, what items they had secured at a good price, and when they returned to home port than by established demands of the local populace. Advertisements in early newspapers confirm this pattern of trade and make clear that only by combining both wholesaling and retailing and various commodities was mercantile activity profitable in the first half of the last century.

The geography of this early retail trade reflected its strong tie to shipping and wholesaling. Shops were normally located on streets leading up from the wharves on which these foreign goods were landed. Even when the American Industrial Revolution began early in the last century, it seems to have been common practice for manufacture to be tied to the colonial ports, in being undertaken as near to those places as waterpower was available and, perhaps more important, in being financed by the mercantile capital that had begun to accumulate in the larger ports. The tie also took the form of having selling agents, commonly drawn from the same merchant group that provided the capital, owned and dispatched ships, and traded in a diversity of goods, designated to handle the entire product of the new American factories. The tie between Samuel Slater's textile mill and the Almy, Brown, and Tiffany merchant families in Providence is well known, as is the role of the "Boston Associates" of former China traders and shipowners in the shaping of the great textile towns such as Lowell, Manchester, Chicopee, and Holyoke. The counting houses of these merchants-turned-manufacturers at first clung to the docks, bringing the retail trade there in what might be seen as a dependent location.

As the provision of goods from the United States began to overtake and surpass that from outside the country, the wharf-head location became decreasingly functional, particularly after the mid 1830s when the railroad and the American factory, in harness, oriented the receipt of goods in the city to a different site, the environs of the railroad station where freight cars could be spotted on side tracks for unloading into wagons for transport to nearby wholesale-retail establishments. These "team tracks" (referring to the tractive force used) became a magnet around which the filings of retailing and wholesaling were attracted. Still, the link of the two forms of trade tended to be maintained because manufacturers commonly had agents established in the nearby city to handle the sale of their goods on a wider scale, and they might engage in some local retailing of those products. And in more distant cities an intermediary wholesaler might equally undertake retailing within his local market while serving as distributor in bulk to a much wider area. The firm of Field and Leiter in Chicago was just such a business, one wherein the split between wholesaling and retailing was to take place only late in the last century when the name Marshall Field took on totally retail connotations.

Once rail transport of goods became the dominant means of getting products to market, the geography of retailing in American cities came to reflect the point of connection of that urban place to the emerging railnet of America rather than to the docks of colonial times. In Boston, for example, the shops moved toward the northern rail terminals (of the Fitchburg, Eastern, and Boston and Maine railroads ultimately joined in a Northern Union Station just beyond Haymarket Square) and toward the southern rail terminals (of the Boston and Albany, New Haven, and Old Colony railroads later brought together in a Southern Union Station). The wharf-head site tended thus to be abandoned by retailers and to be taken over by more clearly mercantile-financial establishments. As State Street, this abandoned wharf-head site became Boston's financial district, a district that played perhaps the dominant role in the financing of railroads in the United States and one nearly as significant in the shaping of American industry. But the shoppers went elsewhere, particularly to the streets leading toward the southern station. Parenthetically, we might note here that this siting of retail shops seems to have become permanent, because once the trolley and rapid-transit developments began, they were constructed to the shops, rather than the other way around.

The New York Example: Rule by Rapid Transit

In New York a very different history was experienced. The original merchant shipowners and wholesaler-retailers were located adjacent to the docks, particularly those on the lower East River. This siting became extremely eccentric, as residential growth had to take place in a narrow vector northward from the Battery, causing the large retailers to move away from the port but not truly toward the railroad, as in Boston and many other cities. Admittedly, the railroad was closer to the retailing district that grew up on Lower Broadway than it had been to the wharf-head site where retailing began in New York. But the late arrival of the railroad in New York and its untypical form with horse-traction on its southern extensions made the geography of commerce there unusual. The elevated lines of the 1870s were built in considerable measure to make the far-downtown location of retail shops economically viable. But as a test of the strength of the general principle that the dominant retailing district would grow up near the railroads, the opening of two new rail connections to Manhattan with the construction of Pennsylvania Station and its tunnel connections both to New Jersey and to the Long Island suburbs put in service in 1910 worked a major translocation of Manhattan retailing, drawing department stores northward from Lower Broadway and Eighth Street to the vicinity of Penn Station at Herald Square (34th Street).

We may then take as a general geographical principle that by the middle of the last century, when railroads were coming to most American cities—though Boston had had them fifteen years before and thereby had begun its shift of shops in response to the station magnetism somewhat earlier—the main source of goods for a city's shops was rail. As long as the linking of wholesaling and retailing persisted, the source of goods probably played the dominant role in determining the siting of the commercial establishment; but once that tie began to weaken, retailing might potentially respond to different locational forces. Thus, we must first look at the divorce between the two scales of commerce. It is impossible to do so in detail here, so I shall attempt to summarize more extensive conclusions on this split that I have presented elsewhere.[15]

Retailing seems to have hugged wholesaling in location as long as the inconstant supply of goods and the problematic quality of the local market made attaining an acceptable level of entrepreneurial profit from retailing alone a matter of doubt. Merchants with the desire to see their business grow were likely to find the geographical flexibility of wholesaling, with its ability to summon orders from afar without the same necessity to force customers to gravitate to their doors, appealing as the way to gain that growth. While cities, even the oldest of them found in the colonial ports, were relatively

15. James E. Vance, Jr., *The Merchant's World: The Geography of Wholesaling* (Englewood Cliffs, N.J.: Prentice-Hall, 1970).

small and movement from even the near countryside to them was infrequent and often difficult, wholesaling would have seemed the dynamic partner in this commercial embrace. With the growth of cities during the first two-thirds of the last century—due to industrialization and the enlargement of transport and mercantile functions to support that activity—local markets were greatly enhanced. New York had become a city of a million people, and other ports had grown in kind, while inland industrial cities such as Pittsburgh, Cincinnati, and Cleveland were expanding rapidly. More and more cities seemed to be reaching a population where a specialization in retailing became feasible economically. This shift was further encouraged by the industrialization of the society itself. The number of people, even the percentage of the population engaged in nonfarming pursuits, was growing with sufficient rapidity that many of the household sources of goods characteristic of an earlier America were disappearing. Those living in tenements could not normally grow their own food or make their own textiles. They might still make much of their clothing, but they could not spin and weave the cloth for it. Furniture, pots and pans, and many things that might have been home-fashioned in the eighteenth century were now purchased. Another important change had come in the matter of supply. With domestic American manufacture now tied to urban markets by reliable train transport and the electric telegraph, in place of overseas sources that were months away by sailing vessel in an era when there was no electrical communication, the supply of goods could now be nearly continuous, certainly rapidly replenished in case of unusual demand. All these conditions quite simply made the embrace of the two components of commerce less essential. A retailer might logically expect to gain a reasonable entrepreneurial profit. Similarly, the wholesaler with the enlarged market, the access to telegraphic communication, and the reliance on domestic rail transport rather than sailing vessels to distant shores could expect to gain by putting a more concentrated effort into the distribution of goods to a large number of retailers located in an array of small towns.

Divorce of Retailing from Wholesaling

The divorce of retailing from wholesaling was normally amicable, with in many cases an agreed on sharing of the capital but a subsequent concentration of attention in two different lines of trade. The retailer gained one very considerable advantage: he could tap a greater variety of wholesalers and thereby gain a diversity of goods, which might be expected to enlarge his trade. From this elaboration of lines was likely to come a larger total of business and quite probably some increase in the intensity of the use of the space he occupied. Translated into geographical terms, this meant that the retailer seeking to expand his trade became increasingly dependent on the conflux of customers. In the coupling with wholesaling, access to customers was not so vitally important, though still desirable. Wholesale trade has always depended, obviously, on mass sales. Even in the era when country merchants had to go to the city to select the goods they would buy in moderate volume, they tended to visit established connections, because of the credit relationships that commonly existed. Having gone to the city on a major, normally infrequent, search for goods, the country retailer could be expected to go wherever in these still modest cities his wholesale connection was located. This greater spatial flexibility of the wholesaler with respect to customers was counteracted by the extreme dependence of those same merchants on finding a location that was favored by rail connections to distant suppliers of their goods. We shall in due course take up the location of wholesaling, so it is sufficient for now to emphasize the point that the desirable location for wholesaling and that for retailing began to diverge sometime around the Civil War, leaving the retailers to experiment with new locations and to turn to dependences other than the steam railroads that so strongly determined the location of wholesalers' warehouses.

How did the retailers move in this context? To answer, we must begin by noting that it was the easy access to a large and probably inconstant body of small purchasers that now mattered. Even ties of loyalty that might be created by long association and the extension of charge privileges could not supply the constant need for replacement brought on by the mortality of established local retail customers, in contrast to the frequent corporate immortality of wholesale customers. Survival depended on easy access, growth on easier connection, and domination on easiest conflux. In these terms the retailer came to see location as of the greatest importance to business success, and thus a charge to be accepted willingly. Soon after the Civil War it became obvious that retailers were willing to pay the highest land rents of any occupier of land, in either absolute or relative terms. Per square foot of land, per foot of sidewalk frontage, and per square yard of building space, the retailer became dominant, with the most successful retailers the kings of the land-rent mountain. In that situation it was the locational judgments of the leading retailers that gave shape to the land use of the heart of the traditional city.

Going back for just a moment, we should fix in mind that the siting of the city, its point of settlement initiation and thereby the historical heart of the traditional city, was determined by external conditions, by its ties to a wide trading system that was planting a trading entrepôt on distant shores. As the city grew, the wholesaling part of commerce generally continued this exogenic dependence, with its elevation of the use value of sites in the heart of the traditional city. But for retailing the dependence was geographically different: it was internal to the city and its possible metropolitan extension. Few places received many retail customers from afar, and even those that did, such as New York, St. Louis, New Orleans, and San Francisco, still received such a small proportion of retail customers from external origins that the shopping district was located not in response to this minor component but in reflection of the geographical origin of the great mass needed to make a retail business successful—that is, the metropolis itself. This transformed geography of the retail component of commerce induced a fundamental shift in the downtown business district, causing it to expand in volume of business space used in commerce and in area of land taken up by trade. As we shall see, there was with morphogenesis an architectural-geographical split of the sort we have noted in the solution to the general

crowding problem in cities. To architecture and landscape architecture fell the lot of providing new building forms and spaces to care for this transformation, while to geography came the responsibility for finding the large functional areas needed to permit the metropolis to evolve. The split between wholesaling and retailing was only one of three such sunderings placing greatly increased spatial demands on cities. Industry was increasingly being separated in space from the housing of its workers, and the central city was becoming ever-larger as a workplace while relatively smaller as a place of residence. In all these cases, it was proving that the divorced functions took far more space once split than they had immediately before while coupled.

These splits afforded to each form of land use what seemed to be appropriate economic solutions to growth. Retailers, as kings of the land-rent gradient, had the most money to spend per unit area, permitting them to preempt land in or near the core that had previously been in other uses, particularly those of residence. It appears that in most cities the retail district experienced its incrementation on its boundary with housing, though there were much less common experiences of growth of shopping facilities into industrial areas. There might be residuals of retailing still within the quarter it had previously shared with wholesaling, but these were remnants of the past rather than any advance party of change. The departure of retailing, for the most part, from this older combined commercial district opened up space for the growth of the residual wholesaling. That activity could also economically preempt the low economic class of housing that tended to be built adjacent to the railroads, the artery giving life to warehousing. Thus, expansion within wholesaling tended to come in situ or outward from the original wholesaling district but parallel with major rail lines, rather than perpendicular to them, as was the common case for retailing.

The Emergence
of the
Complex City

Industry's demands for space tended to be rather large in relative terms, while once freed of dependence on securing nearby worker housing it might move anywhere on the periphery of the metropolis where spacious and cheap sites were available alongside rail lines. The spread of factories thus came on relatively cheap sites at the physical edge of the city. There might be remainders of plants in the older traditional core of the metropolis, but the only growth there tended to be in those industries for which central location, and its greater call on all routes of distribution within the metropolis, was critical. Newspaper publishing, baking, brewing, and some other perishable-food production found great value in the availability of intra-metropolitan transport within immediate reach of central sites. Most industry gained little advantage from core location once workers secured intra-urban mobility from the trolley. Factory owners found the lower capital, and often construction, costs of peripheral location useful in conserving invested capital for experimentation, advanced mechanization, and marketing effort. As the railside sites increased in size and number with outward shift, the type of rail transportation that mattered to manufacturers became more easily available if they moved toward the edge of the metropolis rather than remaining in a cramped and expensive central location.

The common single-family residence was purchased by those with the smallest ability to extract economic advantage from a specific location, particularly when intra-urban transportation tended to be spatially uniform because of the flat nickel electric-traction fare. The main economic gain that might be secured from a specific housing site was cheap land costs, a fact that greatly encouraged those with relatively modest incomes to search out lower-income suburbs, commonly recently built on the cheapest land at the edge of the metropolis. The only other place where such cheap housing might be available would be in areas abandoned by those seeking more pleasant environments for residence. These districts of abandonment and succession were frequently found in housing areas intermixed with older industrial, wholesaling, and transportation land uses, where environmental conditions could be undesirable both physically and socially. There was commonly a social factor in this choice between relatively cheap housing at the edge of the city and similar provision in environmentally undesirable districts nearer the core. Those with casual jobs requiring daily or at least very frequent rehiring or those of recent immigrant status, and thus commonly living within groups speaking their language and practicing their social customs, tended to opt for the core, whereas those with only a modest income but who had been acculturated to the city commonly selected the outlying lower-income suburbs. This division tended to be reinforced by the continuing employment of the now native population in the factories, transportation installations, and trades and services of the suburban-satellitic band. The lower-income "reception area" of the central city might offer no cheaper housing than the cheapest suburbs, but until the wage-earners secured reliable and continuing jobs in that outer band, those suburbs were impossible territory for residence. It commonly took immigrants time to secure those reliable jobs, so the reception areas remained a functional necessity to the recent arrivals. Environmentally, the central areas were poor and to keep rents down the crowding was great, but unlike the case before the advent of good, cheap mass transit, the core tenement area was no longer the only solution to blue-collar housing. It was a social necessity for recent ethnic migrants but not a true economic necessity for the whole working class. And with cheap transit, core-area businesses could be served by a labor-shed coextensive with the denser built-up part of the suburban-satellitic band.

Commodity-Combining Contrasted with Specialty Selling

The location of various urban activities in terms of land-rent paying ability has been accepted as the main land-assignment practice at work within North American cities since at least the turn of the century. We have considered it first in its broadest aspects, those that determine which of the major land uses will occupy what parts of the major components of the metropolis. We may now refine this broad analysis in order to examine how land rents sort individual retail functions within the shopping districts. To begin with, it is essential to distinguish between gross rents and those charged per unit area. Gross rents will reflect the establishment size, itself considerably a measure of the various commodity lines combined in a single firm's store. Within the history of retailing we find a significant distinction between commodity-combining and specialty shops, with a complex cycle observable. The earliest shops, those created as an adjunct to wholesale merchants' activities, tended to be reasonably specialized, though perhaps the oldest were more subject to variation because of the indefinite expecta- tions of returns from long trading journeys to very distant ports. As these mercantile voyages became more routine, with established contacts in the Hong trade or with Liverpool, the lines of retail trade in the attached retail shops would tend to become more defined and reasonably limited. This sort of wholesale-tied retailing would, of course, be mainly limited to the largest towns, the colonial ports. Once in the newer, and normally smaller, cities, retailing would have to stand somewhat more on its own. In doing so the firm, to gain an acceptable level of entrepreneurial profit, would tend to combine a greater range of commodities. In these smallest places, this was the origin of the general store; in somewhat larger places, it would be the basis for the grocery, hardware, dry goods, and housewares stores of specifically focused but wide-ranging lines. Only in the largest cities might there be specialty stores—say, chinaware alone—unless smaller places took on such a strong wholesaling role that they might gain the specialization possible in a retailing-wholesaling coupling. Chinaware wholesaling in Kansas City led, for example, to a retail shop specializing in china soon after the Civil War.

The importance of this commodity-combining and specialty split in the matter of urban morphogenesis shows up in the early geography of the central shopping district. To begin with, specialization became the posses- sion of only the largest cities, with the wholesale-tied specialization already noted standing as the main exception. The central district of very large cities became the locale of what specialized shops there were in America before the Civil War. At that time it took the largest local markets available, plus the conflux of a smattering of customers from more distant places, to support specialization. Boston, New York, Philadelphia, Baltimore, and Montréal were the first North American cities to witness such specialization based on local market and visitors. As St. Louis, Chicago, New Orleans, San Francisco, Toronto, and Winnipeg grew they began to develop a lesser array of specialty shops backstayed more by their wholesaling functions than a local market, which was still small by comparison with those in the colonial entrepôts. These early specialty shops dependent in part on visitors would show a clustering near the terminals of longer-distance transportation. We still find this, for example, in the clustering of camera shops near New York City's rail terminals. In contrast, those shops combining many lines, which might be little more than larger versions of the same thing in lesser cities, would show a particular orientation toward the conflux of local transportation. Because these commodity-combining stores would tend to be larger in size, they would tend to occupy extensive premises and must do so quite close to the nexus of local transport, though perhaps not always directly on top of it because of their considerable spatial extent.

Here we find an interesting split within specialty shops. Those of great specialty, where there might be no more than a single shop in a metropolis and its extensive hinterland, could be located peripheral to the central shopping area, often toward the rail depots, while those specialized in trade but frequently enough visited to permit several examples in a city would tend to seek a site as close to the focus of local transportation as possible. The antiquarian bookstore might well serve as an example of the first and a shoe store of the second. The bookseller could easily operate anywhere within the central shopping district, but the shoe store owner could not. He must be at the conflux of local transport, commonly adjacent to the most important cluster of clothing stores. There is the classic question of where two ice-cream cone sellers on a beach would locate; the answer has consistentlybeen stated, "Side by side in the middle of the strand." Applying this concept to the city, where specialization led to several competitive establishments, they would be likely to locate close together and at a point logical for the conflux of customers of their particular sort and coming from the entire metropolis to that central point.

The Rise of the Giant Commodity-Combining Establishment: The Department Store

The locational requirements of the commodity-combining shops were in contrast to those of specialty selling. We have seen that commodity combiners were the pioneer merchants in most smaller cities and country towns. They also played a major role in the larger cities, but in those places their appeal was quite different. In smaller places the commodity-combining shop was there because only by lumping a number of submarginal profits gained from individual lines could an entrepreneurially acceptable total profit be reached. In the larger city the rise of the department store, in simple terms another form of commodity-combining operation, came not from an interest in lumping profits to gain a threshold profit, but rather from the desire to gain

a competitive edge over specialty shops by charging a lesser unit profit on each item sold in order to sell the goods more cheaply. Such a policy could only prove successful for the merchant who gained such a large volume of trade that a vast number of smaller individual profits could be totaled to form a substantial entrepreneurial profit. Having said that, we easily understand that the department store needed to be in a place where access could be had to a large block of customers likely to shop in it.

The department store is generally agreed to have come into existence in Paris in the middle of the last century. There the Bon Marché, whose very name signaled its emphasis on low prices, began operation on the Left Bank in 1852, drawing customers from a much wider segment of the population than had the previously existing specialty shops. Quickly the Right Bank

The Emergence of the Complex City

413

came as well to house several competitors in what might be thought the primordial state of the department store. Aimed at a working-class as well as higher-income group, these early department stores, those founded before the wide availability of public transportation, showed a regionalization within the largest metropolitan areas. In Paris the major department stores came to be located in four different districts, three on the Right Bank where the greater population resided. In London, they were spread fairly widely within the city. Boston, which had one of the earliest American department stores, Jordan Marsh, because of its smaller size had less dispersal, but still some. It was only when the subways were constructed in the 1890s that the first dispersed pattern within the downtown began to contract, an eventuality that Eben Jordan clearly anticipated when he became a staunch supporter of the first subways, two of which intersected in front of his store.

In Paris the size of the city population, and perhaps its continuing occupational and class complexity, has allowed department store dispersal to remain even in this century when the Métro has furnished probably the finest urban transit in existence. Further support for the argument that class-consciousness may encourage department store geographical spread is to be found in London, where the Underground, less dense in pattern than the Métro but still adequate to overcome extreme urban districting, has not drawn all large stores to one place. Over time the more working-class examples toward the east in London have disappeared, but the posh shops to the west have not gravitated to Oxford Street, the transportation nexus that has become the site of the largest department stores. Further support for this weighing of the relative force of transit and class in the location of department stores is found in New York, where the traditional site for department stores on or near Lower Broadway began to be abandoned soon after Penn Station was opened in 1910, though the last "downtown" department store, Wanamaker's, did not close until the early 1950s. The superior conflux of subway services near 34th Street worked this major geographical shift. During the last twenty years a further northward shift has taken place as subway service to the Upper East Side has been improved and the practice of suburban residents flowing into Manhattan to shop, often by commuter train, has declined. Currently, the major complex of department stores in New York is adjacent to the intersection of Lexington Avenue and 57th Street, leaving the Herald Square stores, Macy's and Gimbel's Herald Square, as the largest establishments in the metropolis but no longer the goal of the greater number of shoppers. They go to more local department stores, dominantly in the suburbs but within the core as well at 57th Street. This sort of replication of department stores could come about only because in the United States the department store tended to avoid a narrowing of tributary population by too strong a class orientation. With the continuing rise of urban populations, these basically popular department stores could branch out without losing their acceptable entrepreneurial profits in each branch. This development further bore out the dominant role of transportation in the location of American department stores. The greater role of class in Britain, for example, tends to keep the department store as a downtown phenomenon or else, as in the case of the rather snobbish Harrod's, as a neighbor to the wealthy.

The location of department stores certainly reflects public transportation, and shifts therein, but the precise placing of these often huge establishments creates a seemingly magnetic force drawing other shops within its strong field, in a normative pattern that we see repeated in most large cities. This replicative pattern is clearer in North American cities, from Montréal to San Diego, than in European ones, where contrasts in history, morphology, and society contribute to a somewhat more varied geography of commerce. Thus, in order to state some general locational principles that apply to a large number of cities, I shall talk about North American cities, with only very short references to a few overseas cities.

The critical quality of the department store is its role in shaping a normative magnetic field that permits us to talk in general terms about central shopping districts. Before the advent of these great stores, in that critical half-century of peace after Appomattox, central areas seem to have responded more to the needs of wholesaling than to those of retailing, often leaving the sorting of commercial functions to the needs and desires of extrametropolitan customers. With the advent of the department store, the metropolitan needs gained ascendancy, the divorce from wholesaling took place, and the pedestrian became the dictator of choice. The latter fact may seem contradictory, so much having been made of the role of the trolley and, later, rapid-transit lines in the location of the central shopping district. To understand the point, however, it is only necessary to make a distinction between access *to* the shopping district and access *within* it. Electrified public transit did provide the major part of the access to the district from other sections of the metropolis, with steam railroads—and in a few cities steam ferries—providing virtually all the rest. Thus, the site of the central shopping district was given by these broad alignments of public transit. Once sited, however, the internal ordering of the shopping district, then as today, came from the realities of pedestrian movement. Because people have changed little over the last century, their increased height only fractionally enhancing their speed of walking—perhaps to be countervailed by a smaller dependence on their legs, such that they lack in stamina what they may gain in speed—the nature of that internal structure has changed little geographically. It has, however, changed greatly architecturally. As central business districts have experienced greatly increasing demands for space, they have not been able to add great geographical blocks to the core save in one of two ways.

The Rise of the Office: The Elevator

The first incrementation to the city came through the specialization of use by sector within the central business district. Originally, these districts had seen shops on the ground floor with offices, even of banks, on the second and other upper stories up to a total of no more than five stories. With that height limit established by human stamina, and to a lesser degree by building techniques, growth could come only by separating these office and store functions, introducing two functional units each capable of growing to its own "pedestrian limit," a distance of no more than a few hundred yards. What resulted was an office "walking zone" a few hundred yards across, normally served by railroad stations where workers could arrive on commuting trains and out-of-town business visitors by regular long-distance trains. Adjacent to it, and commonly away from the nexus of distant and outer-suburban transportation, there would be an additional walking zone for shopping, commonly later in development and more related to intra-metropolitan transit than the first zone, now commonly called the financial district. Each of these zones had a lid of around five stories placed on it until the elevator came into common use in the years after the Civil War.

Experience with the elevator varied between these two zones. For the financial district that mechanical lift was of critical importance, because much of the movement tended to be internal to a rather clearly defined group of employees in a single organization or in a modest number of commonly related organizations. In that situation the walking zone limits could be reached within a few adjacent buildings, as in the structures built to house a legal community, a medical one, or even a single very large insurance company. To allow this repeating circulation by employees, the elevator afforded the main improvement that could be secured in "transportation." It seems to me not at all a matter of chance that the earliest skyscrapers to be built, those in New York and Chicago, were constructed predominantly for

The constant increase in the scale of office functions required frequent enlargement of office buildings. In this case we see the 1886–87 enlargement of the Equitable Building at 120 Broadway in New York (the earlier form is shown on page 375 for 1875).

The
Continuing City

416

insurance companies and were among the earliest buildings to be equipped with elevators. Large metropolitan newspapers were other early entrants into the construction of skyscrapers, again finding a great advantage in piling large numbers of workers on top of each other and thus, by elevator, being able to secure rapid personal intercommunication.

Within the office zone the elevator and the emergent skyscraper served quite well between the wars to afford the growth in space needed. Even so, in the largest cities, particularly those major colonial ports or great railroad junction cities—Boston, New York, Philadelphia, Baltimore, St. Louis, and Chicago—there was a tendency for separation of functional groups even within the so-called financial district. The lawyers herded together; the brokers clung to the environs of the stock exchange as closely as did legislators to the call of the voting bell; and shipping companies looked down on the head of the wharves as they had done when that locale was the near totality of the city commerce. Association of those in a particular trade was repeating, and time was important even before computers. To associate quickly and frequently meant a separation of office functions into subunits within the financial district. There might be an occasional association of sorts among most of the subunits, but it would likely be much less frequent than that working within the subunit itself. What clustered the units together was probably not, in fact, this often rather infrequent association among subunits but rather a shared dependence on the railroad station, as the destination of commuters and the place where distant customers and clients arrived and departed. Also, for those office functions that were so distinctive as to avoid great interaction with others of the same precise occupation, there would be quite localized service establishments—law offices, banks, telegraph offices, and the like—that would set up shop in the financial district as the place most convenient to the greatest number of their customers. In gaining access to those services, and to distant clients coming to the city to visit such an individual office, office buildings constructed for general rental would also seek to be within such a financial district near the railroad station.

If the elevator, and the skyscraper it made practical, transformed the financial district during the final twenty years of the last century, its impact on the shopping district was quite different. The question was one of "establishment scale" and the nature of clients and customers. Offices frequently were highly internalized institutions, dealing with fellow office workers and often with a relatively small number of people per day. The elevator served well in this situation. For the customers of a large store, the service was more difficult, though the lift did permit the expansion of the department store above the five-story ceiling of its early decades. It is impossible to establish what the new ceiling was once elevators were introduced, but the experience of hundreds of department stores around the world bears out the general conclusion that eight to ten stories seems to have been the practical limit. There are a few examples higher than that, but the highest stories were commonly occupied with office and other divisions of the operation that required less access by customers than the selling floors. And for firms other than the department store, where the combination of many lines of merchan-

This etching of South Station, Boston, shows the conflux of public transportation that supported most large-city business districts. Shown are the station (then the busiest in the world), the elevated railway, and the subway system (the first in the Western Hemisphere). Margaret Philbrick, 1937. Used by permission.

dise in a single establishment was an entrepreneurial necessity, the ceiling on retailing seems to have been considerably lower. Furniture stores, with their huge space demands, and some specialty stores in New York and Chicago, where space was scarce and expensive, seem to have been the only other examples of retailing carried on much above the second or third floor. For most of the land within the shopping zone at the center, the height of retailing was no more than three stories and in many places only a single story. Upper floors, if they existed in a building, were likely to be taken up with storage.

Geographical Growth of the Central District

What this tells us is that the elevator had a much less emancipating role within retailing than it had in office activities, hotels, apartment houses, hospitals, and other "residential" functions. For that reason the architectural expansion of the shopping district was less than the general growth in retailing required. In that situation, as in most other problems facing metropolises, if architecture could not suffice, then geography must. In seeking a geographical solution to the expansion of the shopping district, retailers faced the same pedestrial constraints as those seeking to expand the financial district's office space. The notion of the walking zone persisted within the shopping district, limiting the overall extent of a fully integrated area. A generation ago it was shown that around four hundred yards was the greatest distance that shoppers could be confidently expected to walk in their shopping peregrinations.[16] Thus, if the shopping district needed to be more geographically extensive, in light of its being kept wide-ranging by the rather low building ceiling characteristic for retailing structures, that greater extent must be gained by an internal separation of retail functions among several walking zones, each given over to a specialized cluster of shops. The inherence within a cluster would come from the common association in customers' minds of that particular grouping of shops such that in a search for a good or service those customers would logically look toward that particular walking zone. Thus, in women's fashion clothing, say, there would be great advantage attaching to a location near the largest magnet drawing women to the city, that is, the department stores, if an establishment sought to present its fashion clothing to women in general.

The walking zone division of the shopping district would have these tracts of inherence but they, unlike biological cells, would not be morphologically and functionally exclusive one from another. Logical, and commonly the case, would be the situation that toward the edge of one tract there would be an element of integration with the establishments and functions located in an adjacent tract. For example, in looking for the location of men's clothing stores within the American city before World War II, those stores were commonly intermediate in site between the general fashion clothing tract—the home of the department stores and women's fashion clothing shops—and an office tract within the financial district. For this male-oriented clothing area, much of its custom would come from the large number of white-collar workers in adjacent office tracts. A test of the validity of this assumed association by adjacency has been provided by the considerable rise of women's fashion shops within, or closely adjacent to, office districts during the decades since World War II, the operative principle being that women have risen considerably both in numbers and in pay scale within office institutions since 1945. Thus, in seeking to understand the location of various retail establishments we must consider several functional principles: the existence of the walking zone tract of related activities; the interaction with adjacent tracts that will be found in the land use at the edges of these units; and the dependence of all core-area tracts on public-transport networks to support their existence, often dependence on different forms of transportation by specific activity. Retailing has, since the turn of the century, been most intimately tied to rapid transit, whereas financial district offices have leaned much more heavily on rail commuting wherever it is available, and wholesaling has relied on public freight movement, originally by rail but increasingly by motor truck.

16. Raymond E. Murphy, James E. Vance, Jr., and Bart J. Epstein, *Central Business District Studies* (Worcester, Mass.: Clark University, 1955). This work, for which I was the main field investigator, forms the basis for the initial conclusions of this section, revised by some thirty years of further observation of shopping districts on five continents.

A Model of the Central Shopping District

If the location of retailing responds to general forces, we may then attempt to establish a common model of store location within a modular central shopping district. Obviously, the very large and the very small cities—those among the latter that possess true shopping districts—will tend to depart from this model, but its presentation allows us to summarize many relationships in a small compass.

The traditional fulcrum on which all central shopping district functions are balanced is the former or present intersection of major electric-traction lines, even in cities that no longer possess such traction, having substituted buses for trolleys of one sort or another. Where the trolleys met, even if they no longer do so, tends to be the anchor of the district. Around it stores would be ranged in response to a fairly simple system of land rent, but itself often the summation of a complex set of interacting forces. The matter of walking distance we have already considered. Along with it went a special form of distance decay under which building lots well removed from the conflux of transit routes that sites the district in space had fewer pedestrians passing on their front, to the point that pedestrians were likely to disappear from the fronting sidewalk that some three to four hundred yards from that transit anchor. As virtually all movement within the shopping district was in the past, as now, largely on foot, a location too far from stops on public transit was effectively ruled out for retailing, save for those types of trade so specialized that they might depend on the uncommon use of individual transport—horse-drawn cabs in the nineteenth century, taxis more recently, and cars today for the prosperous who can afford high central-area parking charges.

Other factors that determine land rents in addition to this distance decay are the nature of retailing carried on in the walking zone, proximity to the financial district, adjacency to hotels, and association with high-rent, high-density housing structures. What this says is that land value comes from relative location and from developed use of land. The initial value may come from the location, but that figure is then inflated or deflated by the use that comes into existence on the lots. Not all land similarly far from the fulcrum has an equal value, even though part of the value of any site stems from its distance from the conflux of transport.

The department store, as the magnet drawing the greatest number of shoppers to the district, will be located near that fulcrum, either because the proprietors of these great stores had no funds to occupy such choice sites or because they created the neutrality that came to surround their stores. No doubt in some cases the presence of the department store, particularly several in close proximity, shifts the value to the site. The clustering of department stores near Lexington Avenue and 57th Street in New York has greatly enhanced the land values in that location even within the last generation, when transport has not changed greatly but land use has. Once a major department store has become fixed near the heart of the shopping district, where the peak flow of pedestrians on the sidewalks is likely to be, land values reflect that concentration and a peak land value intersection is normally to be found there. Land values drop off absolutely in all directions, but not at the same rate, because the land uses, and possibly the access, vary by vector of movement away from the peak value intersection. If the terrain is difficult, or railroads, highways, parks, or other obstacles to movement of shoppers intervene, the decline in land values will be much sharper. Where an adjacent financial district or a hotel cluster occurs, the large temporarily resident population tends to enhance pedestrian flow and to provide likely shoppers, thus keeping land values higher and producing a slower decline along that vector.

Once pedestrian flow has become relatively fixed in its various routes and volumes, the major determinant of land values has been established, giving a pricing to space in the shopping district. It might seem that price is the only determinant of the location of shops, with those best able to pay rents preempting the most central lots, as general theory has it. But price is only one of several forces at work. Association becomes very important in some instances, such as the locational interaction of shoe stores and women's clothing shops with the department stores. In that instance, high price of space and intimate association go together. But in other cases, such as the interaction among antiques shops—it seems they are on occasion the best customers for each other—or camera, book, and sporting-goods shops, the important association may come well down the price slope at some distance from the peak value intersection, even when they may be highly profitable establishments. The control of this form of associational location comes from the practice of comparison shopping, which grew up with the enlargement of shopping areas and increases in tributary population such that several shops selling the same line came into operation and thrifty customers would search in each before making a purchase. These associations of shops created clusters within the shopping districts, with their location in relation to the peak value intersection determined by a dichotomous situation: some of these clusters, such as those for women's clothing, were intimately linked to the department stores, and thus would have to pay high land rents to gain the competitive or supplemental association they needed; others had no considerable linkage to the truly core functions, and thus would tend to pay lower rents, though they must cohere one with another in just as strong a cluster as any other specialty. Sometimes that specialization comes from access to adjacent land users not located withing the shopping district, say to apartment dwellers in nearby housing areas or to office workers in a proximate financial district, as in the furniture stores and delicatessens near tall apartment blocks and the stationery and office-supply stores near the financial district.

What this says is that the oversimplification of store location—frequently presented in any purely economic analysis of the shopping district—needs revision. Money counts, but other things do as well. The limits of the walking zone, the values of association, and a further factor—social evaluation—enter into the location decision. Certain types of retail and service activity have come to be seen in customers' minds as being undertaken in particular places. High-style specialty clothing for women has gained geographical connotations. Although Paris invented the department store, haute couture in the City of Light is not to be found in the department stores, or even as near neighbors to those massive magnets.

Instead, the Faubourg St. Honoré, close to the longstanding socially prestigious part of Paris, became the most approved site for designers and their intentionally exclusive products. In this case geography gave prestige, as it often does in the city. As high fashion spread more widely, with the establishment of fast verbal and graphic communication within Western society, the same geographical separation of haute couture from the department store complex came to be found in New York, Boston, Chicago, Los Angeles, and other large and prosperous places. By the 1920s Fifth Avenue, without a subway or an elevated, and thus more exclusive in access, had taken over the high-fashion role in New York. Boston had made of Newbury Street a smaller though no less esteemed shopping cluster adjacent to the Hub's distinctive in-town but not downtown suburban railroad stations, rather than to the convergence of the rapid-transit lines, though the ramp leading down to the Tremont Street subway was quite close. Chicago shaped its Miracle Mile, the first of what ultimately came to be a pretty mongrel breed, when emulation gave the term to serried used-car lots most distinctive for their massed lumens. On Michigan Avenue north of the Chicago River, high-style specialty shops lined a major boulevard adjacent to, but not within, the central shopping district. Los Angeles modernized the Faubourg St. Honoré for the Los Angeles scene by locating stylish shopping along the Miracle Ten Miles of Wilshire Boulevard all the way to, and beyond, Beverly Hills.

The trolley and rapid transit had made downtown shopping possible for the entire metropolis; the automobile at first concentrated high-style shopping on the edge of the downtown, but ultimately permitted, as we shall see, the dispersal of that exclusive merchandising toward the highest-income suburbs. Again, it was a social evaluation that did the deed more than any measure of land rent. Los Angeles demonstrates this point well. By the 1970s its central shopping area had gained a negative social evaluation in terms of clothing shopping, leaving Broadway as an obvious "ethnic" marketplace, dependent on the conflux of buses in a city without surviving electric traction. Customers for haute couture, even for its cheaper copies, do not ride the bus. In Chicago a similar fate seems possible despite the great efforts on the part of the city that brought two subway lines through the heart of the central shopping district after 1940. The growth on the Miracle Mile of North Michigan Avenue has been so great that even the epitome of the American department store, Marshall Field and Company, has opened a branch there within a mile of its downtown State Street store. Social evaluation is lowering the status of State Street, while in a rather isostatic movement North Michigan Avenue is gaining a scale of shopping development such that it is the area of appeal for the high-style component of metropolitan shopping.

The Social Evolution of Shopping

Today most large American cities demonstrate a striking reversal of the conditions that brought the central shopping district into being after the Civil War. Then, it was the creation of a mass-appeal shopping area, aided by and in turn aiding electric traction, that allowed the diversification of the lines of merchandise that might be sold within the metropolis. Only at the center could an adequate market for many lines of goods be obtained.

With the advent of the automobile as a vehicle for the shopping journey of women, certain outlying convergences of highways became possible sites for mass-appeal shopping of the sort associated with the department stores and the type of shops clustering around it. After World War II much of this mass-appeal shopping was effectively moved away from the center when department store firms began opening branches in what came to be known as regional shopping centers on large tracts of open land within the suburban band. In due course we shall examine that development, but here it is essential only to note that much of the downtown shopping gravitated away after 1945. This left the central shopping district as the local shopping center for the population resident in the traditional city. That population was strikingly varied: it included some extremely well-off people who could afford to buy comfort and high amenities within the expensive and crowded core, and a much larger group of poor, often recently arrived and occupying the housing abandoned by the blue-collar classes once they had gained the necessary mobility to move to the suburbs. The sort of shopping that has developed along Broadway in Los Angeles exemplifies the local shopping center for the working classes living in the traditional city. The sort of shopping found from the 1920s onward along Newbury Street, North Michigan Avenue, and Wilshire Boulevard served first the prosperous of the inner parts of the metropolis. The reversal of the nineteenth-century conditions shows up in the decline of the central shopping district as a mass-appeal seller. Although absolute sales may have held up, this is not always the case in small and medium-size cities such as Grand Rapids or Tulsa, where there has been a virtual abandonment of the central district by retailers of clothing and other items traditional to the central shopping district. In all metropolises, the share of the center in total metropolitan sales of general and clothing merchandise has plummeted since World War II.

It is in the matter of specialized high-fashion clothing that the metropolitan core has held its role as merchandiser to an extensive urban region. In cities where the downtown department store may have shrunk or even departed for the suburbs like Wanamaker's in New York City, that same place may have experienced healthy growth in fashionable retailing. Boston's Back Bay seems fast to be overtaking the Washington Street district as the dominant as well as the more burgeoning of retail districts. Good rapid transit plays its part, though the conflux in the Back Bay is minor compared with the intersection of Summer-Winter and Washington streets. What seems to make the difference is the practicability of large parking structures such that the core upper-income trade can be greatly magnified by the continuing cityward movement of prosperous suburbanites, mainly by car, to make this the fashion center for the whole metropolis. In massive and very style-conscious urban regions, such as New York-northeastern New Jersey and Los Angeles, it seems that even very fashionable stores have begun to disperse, taking what had been the Wilshire Boulevard function to several much more peripheral shopping centers surrounded by a market of sufficient size to keep them in business.

The Emergence
of the
Complex City

423

The necessity of carrying our discussion of the forces at work shaping the central shopping district somewhat beyond 1945, the end of the period here considered, grows out of the desire to show the way in which social evaluation and shifts therein have tended to increase the component of high-style and highly specialized sales in the core area at the same time that mass-appeal selling there was declining heavily. This situation seems to be true of only the largest metropolises; in medium-size and smaller cities, the relative decline of the core tends to take place across the board. The conclusion is obvious: urban population has grown and metropolitan incomes have risen, so this decline can only have come about through geographical shifts in retailing. The integrated outlying shopping center is the patent cause. But because those centers have grown to national importance only since the end of World War II, it seems desirable to leave discussion of them until the next chapter. Here, however, it seems appropriate to anticipate the known evolution of the central shopping area by making it clear that the classic core shopping district developed progressively, and in response to the several forces here noted over a period of about fifty years (1890–1940), the time of the trolley and its rapid-transit elaboration. Subsequent rapid-transit developments, as in Toronto, Montréal, San Francisco, Atlanta, and several smaller places, particularly Calgary, Edmonton, Vancouver, and Sacramento, have all taken place in the era of automobile domination. In the Canadian examples, a complexity of conditions—the lower per capita disposable income in Canada (which has maintained the relative position of the downtown area in mass-appeal shopping), the more severe winters (which make driving less appealing for much of the year there), and the more arbitrary nature of planning in Canada resulting from the absence of a due process clause in the recent Canadian Charter—has allowed the new rapid-transit systems to be more like the prewar ones in their morphogenetic impact than those built since 1960 in the United States. By now, however, all North American cities seeking to create railed transportation must do so with full recognition of the continuing domination of even intra-urban transport by the automobile. The morphogenetic forces are now so transformed that not only the incrementation of the city formed in this automotive context—the suburban and exurban bands—but also the pretransit traditional core has seen a radical transformation of the prewar structure. The number of sizable cities with virtually no central shopping district today—Phoenix, Albuquerque, Grand Rapids, and Tulsa, for example—is considerable. They were not originally shaped that way; rather, they have been shorn of previously existing functions. The nature of that change will be considered in some detail in the next chapter. Here it is sufficient to note that the time span of this chapter, the half-century before the outbreak of World War II, saw the flowering of those central shopping districts. Even where they have survived, they show little new growth and have a distinctly autumnal quality.

Wholesaling, the Land Use of Mobility

Wholesale trade is a peculiarly obscure aspect of American economic life, given the fact that it is critical to the functioning of any advanced society and that its volume considerably exceeds that of retailing. This was not always the case; as we have seen, until the middle of the last century retailing and wholesaling were commonly joined in a single mercantile establishment. When retail trade seemed to require different skills and a separate location from wholesaling, there were as well sound reasons for wholesale trade to become independent. The geographical fields of endeavor of the two types of trade were sufficiently contrasted to require quite distinct forms of commercial intelligence, as well as contrasting times of entrepreneurial anticipation. The most common wholesalers had to find their market spread over an extensive region, a region much larger in the last century than the metropolis because that settlement form was just coming into existence and was frequently too small in trade to support an active entrepreneurial merchant. Distant retailers buying from wholesale establishments might supply an appraisal of what they wished to purchase at a particular period of time, but they could hardly present an encompassing view of the larger market or often of the long-term demand for goods likely to be found within it. It was skill in anticipating the answers to these two sets of questions, and on the basis of those answers seeking to establish a continuing and timed flow of goods to meet demands as they arose, that taxed wholesale merchants and rewarded them when they found the correct response. For retailers, there were similar questions of volume and timing of goods, but they operated (then) within a confined geographical sphere wherein commercial intelligence had to be far more detailed. The wholesaler had dozens or hundreds of customers; the retailer hoped for thousands or great multiples thereof. The retailer then had little concern for transportation. People shopped and took most of their goods away with them. The wholesaler not only had to deliver goods, commonly in large volumes, to customers, but had to arrange their shipment from manufacturers to a warehouse long ahead of expected sale and frequently from a great distance. Then as now, the wholesaler could not seek their delivery to the receiving dock too far ahead in time lest vast capital be immobilized over an unproductively long period. The wholesaler's establishment, thus, became almost entirely dependent in location on the lines of distant transportation. Only those wholesalers whose market would be largely restricted to the city or the metropolis—produce merchants and the wholesaling aspect of commercial banking, for example—had to give much thought to the transportation available internal to the city. It was this peculiar concern that placed produce-wholesaling districts very central to the city, so that restaurant chefs and the owners of small food stores could call for and carry away their lettuces and tomatoes. But even these types of wholesaling dependent on customer calling still normally required access to a regional or national transportation network by which they could secure perishable products quickly, cheaply, and reliably. Thus, it was the external connections leading to and from the city that sited the wholesaler's warehouse, while it was the flow of customers to the retailer's shop that placed that establishment within the city.[17]

17. This section is based heavily on my book, *The Merchant's World: The Geography of Wholesaling* (Englewood Cliffs, N.J.: Prentice-Hall, 1970), one of the very few monographs dealing with wholesale location and the forces that shape it.

We have seen that transportation played a major role in siting the central shopping district, but pedestrian movement was the critical force in the internal organization of that district. In wholesale trade, organized transportation was always the dominant force, with pedestrian movement of little or no importance. Thus, we seek the explanation of the characteristic placing of warehouses and other wholesaling establishments in the patterns of long-distance transportation. The waterfront in the colonial ports and the early-republican river towns was the first location of warehouses in North American cities. Only as railroads reached these older cities was there any limitation of that generalization, and even then not so great a relocation of warehouses as might be thought, because railroads tended to go to existing centers and to be built on graded routes along river valleys. Only as the volume of wholesaling in a city expanded was there the likelihood that the newer establishments, or expansions of older firms, would be commonly found along the rail lines coming into the city, away from the river as well as along it. Because sites available, even on the landward side of riverine cities, were fairly limited—within practical reach of the center—warehouse construction tended to be multistory. A strong influence on this architectural morphology was the perfection of the elevator, for freight as well as people, already discussed. In simple truth, for most of the second half of the nineteenth century the technology of goods handling was more advanced vertically than horizontally. Boxcars were still unloaded by hand, with crates and boxes moved by human muscle-power. Only when raised to higher floors was mechanical assistance of much use. Thus, piling up stories, so as to limit the horizontal spread of a warehouse, was advantageous, with the ceiling on height imposed primarily by current building technology, which depended on weight-bearing masonry walls. Massive structures emerged, such as Marshall Field's Wholesale House, covering a large lot to a height of seven stories, and on cramped sites sometimes to as many as ten stories. The introduction of iron- (later steel-) cage construction encouraged this lofty development during the twenty years before World War I.

Examining the remains of warehouse construction at the turn of the century, we find that it showed a congregation of structures such that we might at first think there was a strong associational value in wholesaling, just as there obviously was in retailing. But further investigation clearly demonstrates that the clustering in wholesale trade has an additional component beyond gaining access to the same customers as one's competitor. That addition comes from the operating characteristics of North American railroads at the end of the last century. Freight trains brought loaded boxcars to the city from afar, and the process of separating the train to deliver individual cars was quite specific. Railroad companies established so-called yard limits within which cars would be spotted on a firm's siding without additional charge beyond the long-haul rates. To make this system work, the company sidings had to be reasonably placed in relation to the freight yards, normally then as near the city center as possible. In addition to this necessary location within the yard limits, there was an even more geographically constraining force, that exercised by the out-shipment of goods from the wholesaler's warehouse. Normally, wholesalers received their goods in carload lots, that is, in full boxcars sent by the manufacturer to a single wholesaling warehouse, where the goods would be promptly unloaded and stored against future orders from the merchant's customers. Those orders were frequently, though not always, for considerably smaller amounts of goods, such that out-shipments were commonly in less-than-carload lots (LCL) of a single item. The wholesaler sought to lump LCL items to be sent to a distant customer so as to make up a full carload shipment, which might then be dispatched by rail in a full boxcar loaded at the merchant's warehouse. But frequently the exigencies of time, which do enter into wholesaling even if less urgently than in retail sales, meant that the wholesaler must dispatch a smaller shipment, not waiting to make up a full carload. Under the operation of railroads in the era before the introduction of the motor truck in long-distance transport, which comes mostly only after World War I, these LCL shipments had to be handled by transportation companies specially organized for that purpose. Freight forwarders rented boxcars from the railroads and sought to solicit wholesalers and other shippers for package freight sufficient to fill those cars for specific destinations within a short period of time. In that way individuals could gain a use of the railroads for small shipments in the era before package mail was introduced, by the great department store owner John Wanamaker, who was postmaster general in the Harrison administration (1889–93). Where freight forwarders were unavailable or circumvented, the railroad companies commonly maintained a "freight house" in a city where LCL freight might be assembled into carload lots. In this era when package mail was not available or just starting, there were as well a number of express companies—Wells Fargo and American Express started in this activity—that handled small shipments in an expeditious way. They, in turn, had taken over from a very informal arrangement inaugurated on the railroads of southern New England early in the American railroad experience, whereby passenger train conductors agreed to accept packages or letters for deposit at a city at the end of their run. The freight house and the express office could serve as a point of assembly of package freight only by standing near the center of the city, obviously alongside the railroad. Given that location, wholesalers, who were heavily dependent on package freight for shipments to their smallest or most impatient customers, had to be as close to these structures as possible.

The scale of the wholesaler's operations, the need to be at a railroad siding for the in-shipment of goods, and the value of being near the freight houses and express offices joined to shape a characteristic location for warehousing once wholesaling and retailing had become separate, as they commonly were by the turn of the century. That location was along the rail lines adjacent to the central shopping district. When the separation of retailing from wholesaling had begun, the former tended to move away from the previous joint residence, leaving the district adjacent to the railroad station to warehousing, save only along the one or two streets leading from the office and retail districts to the station to be occupied by specialized retailing intended to capture the impulse buying of commuters walking to and from that station. Bakeries, wine shops, candy and flower shops, tobacco- and newsstands, bars, cobblers, and other enterprises intended to catch the attention and trade of the vast flow of pedestrians using the station to gain access to the city core could benefit from this human river. Once beyond its banks, however, this band along the rail lines would be given over to the wholesaling that benefited from the easy access to freight-handling facilities.

In the traditional wholesaling structure that evolved in the second half of the last century, there were agents facilitating this trade who dealt in orders rather than the physical holding of goods. These were manufacturers' sales agents whose job it was to enlarge the sales of particular factories by being readily available in a major city to provide information on the goods, to speed up their ordering and shipment, and to engage in the active promotion of sales within the urban region. These were operations dominated by the needs of personal access, particularly for those likely to come to the city by train from some distance. The result was that such sales agents tended to seek to occupy office space not far removed from the station, perhaps most commonly in the upper stories of buildings along the arterial routes leading to the station, leaving the first floors to the shops seeking the impulse sales mentioned above. In large cities, particularly the colonial ports and the early river entrepôts, a considerable proportion of the office space might be rented out to such agents, contributing a major component in the filling up of an office district and providing a considerable clientele to the city hotels that tended to cluster around the station and onward toward the office district. In the masculine gratification of the times, this area transitional between wholesaling and office functions adjacent to the hotels and not far from the central shopping district became the location of the better, and fully ample, restaurants that came into being in American cities after the Civil War. These strongly masculine institutions, not infrequently refusing to serve women in certain rooms or at certain times, took on much the function that the coffeehouses of London had served in the seventeenth and eighteenth centuries, and that Lübeck's Schiffergesellschaft has held from 1535 to the present. These restaurants, normally with a most active bar, became the venue for business meetings, as described in Thomas Mann's account of Thomas Buddenbrook's lunches at the last noted restaurant.

The Rise of Interurban Trucking

The rather tight clustering of wholesaling in the period before World War I began to change at the close of that conflict when many motor trucks were first adopted by city business firms. The war had proved the strength and utility of trucks that could operate on any road, carrying a load sufficiently smaller than a boxcar to make them useful in the delivery of goods to the ultimate customers of wholesalers and retailers. This modification of transportation began a transformation in land use that has continued down nearly to the present. First, it was particularly in the onward shipment of goods from wholesalers' warehouses that the truck proved itself, but initially only in delivery to those customers within the city and its metropolitan area. In part that constraint was a reflection of the poor state of rural roads even in the more densely settled parts of the country. It was only in the 1920s, when states pushed their efforts at road building and the federal government commenced the active financing of arterial roads, that the horizon for trucking moved farther from the city. By the late 1920s most eastern cities were tied to other urban places in the region by organized truck routes, as was also the case in California and the West Coast in general. There was little or no transcontinental trucking and no heavily used network of subcontinental lines. But as most wholesalers served a region considerably below the level of subcontinental extent, the impact of trucking could be significant in this first decade of the motor transport industry.

The introduction of trucking made possible the casting adrift of one of the two anchors that had greatly constrained the movement of warehouses before the war. No longer were the freight houses and the express offices so important to these large-scale merchants; instead, importance attached increasingly to access to the arterial highway system emerging as the significant state and federal routes took their place. But access to those routes was, by its linearity, far less confining than the railroad yard limits had been, permitting warehouses to be set up anywhere it was possible to establish a siding within easy reach of a major highway. The railroads found that to continue handling these incoming shipments, particularly where they moved over regional but not larger distances, they must accommodate the wholesalers by moving the yard limits outward, sometimes to the physical edge of the city.

This outward movement of wholesaling also made land for potential warehouses much cheaper, because the increase in the available space was so greatly expanded with radial departure from the city. Cheaper land encouraged merchants to construct lower buildings that could be built more cheaply because of lesser loads to be borne by the foundations and columns. The adoption of truck transport for shipments from the warehouse encouraged the use of large outlying sites where it was easier to maneuver and park large trucks. The shift in the geographical morphology thus led to a fundamental change in the architectural morphology associated with wholesaling. Up to the outbreak of World War II, this siting of warehouses mainly at the interface of rail and road transportation became the American standard, demonstrating that the advantages gained in handling large volumes of goods outside the core could be obtained once trucks distributed wholesalers' wares, and that warehouse employees could manage to reach these peripheral sites using cars of their own.

While the great warehouses were being shifted outward, the office aspects of the trade remained heavily in the center, though changes began to be discernible. Manufacturers' sales agents, whose trade depended on providing services for customers who were heavily concentrated within the metropolis, began to shift to locations on the arterials leading from the central district, where they could easily be visited by a local population using cars and trucks. The same rationale that caused Sears, Roebuck and Company to set up its "men's department stores" on the outskirts of downtown caused the National Cash Register Company, the Hobart food machinery firm, and appliance and business machine wholesalers providing repair services to cling in an elongated band strung outward on these major metro-

The harbinger of a transformed retailing structure in cities was the automobile-oriented men's department stores opened by Sears, Roebuck and Company in the 1920s. Shown here is the Lawrence Avenue store opened in Chicago in 1925. Note the tower that remained the attracting symbol of these stores until well after World War II.

politan arteries. In this way the wholesaling pattern of the metropolis just before World War II had three basic elements: the remnant of the much older, entirely rail-oriented warehouse district at the very center; a thin line, commonly intermixed with automobile-oriented neighborhood retailing extending out along several heavily trafficked arteries; and a large and rapidly expanding string of massive warehouses located between rail lines and major regional highways, well toward the edge of the built-up city and frequently beyond the corporate limits of the germinal city that had brought the metropolis into existence. Although there have been major changes in this pattern during the last thirty years, discussion of the transformation will be reserved until the next chapter where the "modern city," that of the post–World War II years, will be considered in its complexity.

Geographical Revolution in Industry

The Industrial Revolution of the early nineteenth century began the shift of industry away from the colonial ports, where it had previously been concentrated until the introduction of machinery elevated the availability of waterpower to dominance in industrial location. The mill towns might be close by the cities, as Pawtucket was to Providence and Waltham to Boston, or sufficiently removed to become important cities in their own name, as Lowell, Lawrence, Manchester, and Fall River became. At least until the time of the Civil War, this distinction between mill town, later industrial city, and the traditional core of the larger metropolises was maintained. The tendency was for the large industrial undertakings to be sited in these satellites and factory cities, leaving to the traditional core city a vast array of smaller industries not requiring great components of power. With the shift to steam power, which came in the United States around the time of the Civil War, the necessity to carry on heavy and extensive industry away from the core was considerably reduced. The city could grow industrially, as it in fact did, sopping up much of the rapid increase in urbanization in the United States in a small number of large metropolises that were becoming workshops of a thousand productions. With the advent of steam, all a metropolis needed were good, practicable sites for factory construction and an expanding labor force of the sort made available by massive European migration to this country. The recurring waves first of Germans, Scandinavians, English and Irish, and then of Bohemians, Poles, and other Slavs, and finally of southern Europeans provided the workers; and the great reception areas for in-migration were the now vastly grown colonial ports and river and Great Lakes entrepôts. Boston and the colonial ports of southern New England— Newburyport, Salem, Providence, New Haven, and Bridgeport—filled rapidly with a great diversity of increasingly large industrial undertakings. Some individual factories were still sited on or adjacent to the docks, where coal for steam raising and raw materials for manufacture might most cheaply be secured; where the scale of consumption of raw materials and fuel was less massive, no more than a rail connection might suffice. In the earliest phase of this burgeoning of industry in the metropolises themselves, from midcentury to perhaps the 1880s, growth was probably greatest fairly close to the core and the tenemented housing that had grown up there, which might be used to house the flood of immigrants who would help fill the industrial jobs. But with the trolley, the intra-urban transport available to the blue-collar group, industry could begin to look toward larger, and often cheaper, sites away from the traditional city.

It was at that juncture that we may begin our discussion of the geographical pattern of industry within metropolitan cities. Because Americans had been forbidden by England to engage in manufacture in colonial times, with the major exception of the production of bar iron, there was relatively little industry in cities when the American Industrial Revolution commenced in 1790. And as noted, that campaign to gain industry for this country led at first to the shaping of industrial satellites at a remove from the traditional cities. Within those cities there was, of course, some accompanying industrialization, such as shipbuilding which had to be carried on in a port, and ship fitting and repair, which had to be undertaken in working ports where such services were greatly needed. As cities grew in population and economic activity, with the development of a national economy to replace the colonial one, all sorts of initially small productions began, commonly in factories interspersed with port and wholesale functions. The advent of steam, which came before the middle of the last century, though of course it grew much more quickly after that date, made it possible to expand these many germinal manufacturing undertakings without leaving the center of the city. In cities such as Providence, there was rental steam power from some of the larger factories to the smaller firms. The multifarious productions of the ports, combined with the ingenuity fostered by need and experience, provided further factories, commonly small in the beginning but very rapidly growing if the need they filled was widely felt. The growth within individual firms as well as the increase in the number of discrete firms was such that by the time of the Civil War, industrial crowding within the older cities was increasingly felt.

The growth in scale of firms meant not only that they must look for larger space but also that they normally had reached such a size that they could afford to provide their own steam power and could attract a labor force for which the employment provided by the firm would determine the family's residential choice. The freedom offered by these two changes was such that satellitic sites might be chosen where previously only a location in the heart of the traditional core would have served. When factory operations were moved away from the center, that site was left for at least another generation to provide a seedbed for later arrivals on the industrial scene. At the same time, the increasing size of the firms that moved to the satellites meant that the large-scale incrementation to the industrial labor forces was likely to take place there. Changed market conditions can cause rapid expansion in firms employing hundreds or even thousands of workers or, in times of depression, equally rapid contraction. But as the American economy was in broad terms growing rapidly between the Civil War and World War I, the industrial satellites of large cities became one of the more important components of urbanization during that half-century.

At first the outward shift was not over any great distance; factories were constructed at or near the edge of the built-up city, but seldom far into the countryside unless controlled by some localized resource, either waterpower for electrical generation or a mineral occurrence. In the Pittsburgh region, factories were strung along the deep and winding valleys of the tributaries of the Ohio River, not because the location conditions were right in relation to Pittsburgh and its market, but instead because local coal moved on rails, normally built in the valleys, as did iron ore brought in from farther away, and water—the most voluminous component of iron- and steelmaking, as well as most forms of manufacturing—was most available there. In this situation, as in the early waterpowered textile industry around Providence and Boston, an extensive industrial region grew up, with the factories spread outward from the core city for as much as a hundred miles, but also with strong control of these factories and their operations exercised by the mercantile and financial community of the core city. Boston effectively dominated the New England textile industry down to the time of its massive shift to the South in the 1920s and 1930s, just as Pittsburgh was the center of control of the American iron and steel industry, which ranged even more widely from mines in Michigan and Minnesota to ironworks in Baltimore and Birmingham.

Industry proved particularly amenable to this sort of corporate conglomeration, to the extent that any discussion of the geography of industry American cities must take note of this administrative and market-establishment function. Corporate control was often all that was left within the original center of the industry after technical improvements had led to the departure of the factory activities. Boston became the center of the American woolen industry while that trade was mostly conducted in New England. Boston remains the place where the auction price of wool is largely determined, even though there is little manufacturing left in nearby satellites. In similar fashion, New York came to establish the prices and the organization of sugar refining, coffee roasting, and cotton manufacture, a role it continues even though only a relatively modest portion of the American industry is anywhere near Gotham today. Pittsburgh has this role in iron and aluminum, Chicago in grain and meat, Houston and Calgary in oil, and

Buffalo and Minneapolis in flour, even when in several instances the city is no longer the dominant or even a particularly important processor, as is the case for Chicago and the meat industry. Once a manufacturing commodity market has been established, there is a tendency for longevity, which results from the fact that in creating an auction market where prices are set, experience, availability of speculative capital, and physical proximity among the traders are essential. Chicago has demonstrated the need of all three of these attributes in the recent attempt by its Board of Trade to add to its longstanding trading in grains, pork bellies, and other agricultural products the establishment of an auction market, where prices are set on all sorts of negotiable paper such as stock options and other arcane forms of corporate remuneration.

The Advent of the Flat Factory

The decade following World War I was the time of the great shift in factory locations. The manner of growth before that time had commonly been to build taller and taller and longer and longer structures for manufacturing at or near the original location of the firm. The enormous buildings for the American Woolen Company strung along the banks of the Merrimack at Lawrence, their cotton peers at Manchester for Amoskeag, large carpet mills at Enfield Falls, Connecticut, and Amsterdam, New York, and the early car factories such as Ford at Highland Park, Michigan, were examples of this traditional giantism. Expanding trade was handled by enlargement of manufacturing facilities, at first only in the traditional way. But Henry Ford's adoption of the assembly line in 1913, to expand production of the first mass-produced car, his Model T introduced in 1908, began to change things. Although the first assembly line was installed in a multistory building at Highland Park, it soon became clear that the technology would be simplified and made less costly by the adoption of the flat factory, one on a single level where the flow of assembly could be essentially continuous. Even in firms building items far smaller and less complex than cars, there began to be an awareness that many types of manufacturing could be speeded up and cheapened by location in flat factories. But to build these at any reasonable cost, outlying sites were required. It was the rapid rise of motor transportation, both by truck and by car, that came right after World War I that supported this shift. Workers could converge on an outlying site when they drove themselves to work. Components of manufacture could be trucked in from nearby, rather than having to be produced at a distance and arrive only periodically by freight car, or else made on site, thereby further crowding the plant layout. And increasingly, trucks could be used to distribute the finished product within the urban areas and its neighboring regions. In automobile manufacture, this was the period of dispersal of assembly plants to various parts of the United States, further encouraging a new morphology of factories in what was by then America's largest industry. The rise of radio, electrical appliance (refrigerators and ranges), and several other mass-consumption industries during the 1920s lent further dynamism to the rapid shift to the flat factory on a peripheral site.

San Leandro, California, south of Oakland, became the site of a great amount of wholesaling after World War II when the flat factory or warehouse became nearly universal with the introduction of pallets and forklifts. Photo: R. L. Copeland, 1977.

That shift to the edge of the city, or at least to areas that had not as yet been divided up into blocks, came not merely because of the increase in production that was being experienced, but as well because the space per worker was growing. Data are not readily available on the space per worker before World War I, but we do know that it was smaller than even in the early 1920s. Most older industries had been highly labor-intensive, with fewer and smaller machines, thus gaining increased production mainly by crowding more workers together. Since mechanization was generally greater in America than in Europe decade for decade, and factories perhaps more generously built in a country of cheap land and cheap building materials, crowding was somewhat relieved, but still intense by modern standards. Power was universally distributed mechanically, along shafts and the belts that they moved, so pushing everything together not only increased production but also made mechanization more practicable; in mechanical transmission of power from a waterwheel or a steam engine, loss through friction was considerable and greatly increased by small elongations of the shafts and belts. The development of electricity as a source of power, through the use of dispersed small electric motors, came at the turn of the century, encouraging the greater use of machines. Those machines took up more space, even though they reduced the number of workers needed in production because the speed of machines could be greatly increased, yielding higher production per hour. In this situation it also was possible to apply power at so many separate work stations that the assembly line became possible, not only further increasing the desire for space but even determining the sort of space needed. Linearity became a critical component of production, to the point that some plants had to expand beyond the modular

The
Continuing City

434

size of blocks in most American cities, which were divided almost universally into fairly regular, rectangular street blocks.

This combination of greater space needs per worker and specialized form for the emerging factories forcefully projected new industrial development out of the core of cities. What remained in those traditional sites were either small, often moribund firms surviving from the past, or productions so strapped for labor or low rents as to be encouraged to occupy less than ideal space. The aging multistory factories near the core also served as a seedbed in which fledgling industries might begin with the least financial risk. But if they succeeded, they were likely to move promptly to purpose-built factories at the periphery of the city where volume and productivity could be increased. With this ever-recurring desire to move out of the core into roomier plants, the space needs went up. In metropolitan New York it is figured that the pre-1922 plants stand on 1,040 square feet of plot space per worker, while those constructed from 1922 to the close of World War II occupy 2,000 square feet and those built during the first ten years after the war 4,550 square feet of plot space per worker.[18] This trend has continued during the subsequent quarter-century, obviously much enhanced by the increasing use of robots.

By the 1920s many factory designs were so enlarged, particularly in at least one dimension, that construction within the normal grid pattern of the city was virtually impossible. And increasing dependence on self-transporting workers made large areas of employee parking essential. It became the practice to provide such parking free of charge, so firms have never been able to shift the economic cost of parking space to employees as they have done with the cost of housing since it became generalized during the first half of the nineteenth century.

The Model of the Factory before 1945

The trends of the 1920s continued in a fairly consistent fashion until World War II. Space usage continued to grow, car commuting became more nearly universal, and the creation of larger factories and more mechanization persisted. The rapid increase in the size of manufacturing operations tended to be reflected in ever-larger assemblages of factory buildings, to the extent that truly giant factory complexes, sometimes employing tens of thousands of workers, were created. The River Rouge plant of the Ford Motor Company, constructed mainly in the 1920s, was the first of these giants, but others were to follow in the automobile, locomotive, and aircraft industries. Shipyards, initially during World War I, became such mass-production facilities, though the cycles of construction were such that they tended to have surpassing booms and virtually lethal busts. All these giant industrial complexes introduced a different urban morphogenesis from the ones we have been discussing. No site short of the countryside well outside the city could be examined for new developments of the sort. These were

18. Data presented in Edgar M. Hoover and Raymond Vernon, *Anatomy of a Metropolis: The Changing Distribution of People and Jobs within the New York Metropolitan Region* (Cambridge, Mass.: Harvard University Press, 1959), p. 31.

factories without houses; the workers had to commute over considerable distances, with residential communities in the vicinity of the plant growing only slowly to match the jobs available. The industrial expressway had to be devised to tie these great complexes of production to the complexes of housing and business needed for the workers. The Arnold Industrial Expressway in the eastern part of the Bay Area and the Willow Run Freeway built in Detroit during World War II were such connections to deal with a situation where the scale of production required a truly detached and specialized satellite provided with workers by the existing metropolis. This seems to have been the culmination of the continuous evolution of the factory from the small workshop of mainly hand labor at the fringes of the early-republican traditional city to the integrated plant that was a geographical as well as an entrepreneurial entity. As we shall see, in the post-1945 period that integration tended to decline, but for now we may consider the pattern of industrial land use only in the pre-1945 city.

Any model of the industrial structure of the prewar city would show little survival of the original core-fringe factory area. The growth of the central shopping district, the office-financial area, and some aspects of wholesaling were normally such that the oldest factory quarter had been obliterated. Somewhat farther out along rail lines, and intermixed with surviving wholesalers' warehouses, would be found multistory factories from the first half of the hundred years we have under consideration. These tall but relatively confined buildings would be in use for the sorts of manufacture found in most cities—machine-shop operations, small metal fabrication, shaping of builders' needs, and various food-processing activities among them. By 1940 most operations with markets wider than the metropolis would have moved out of such traditional-city quarters, taking up larger units in areas that had not yet been plotted into street blocks by the time of World War I. There, mass-production facilities, with linear assembly lines and increasing use of heavy machinery, were constructed—as time passed, more commonly in single-story factory buildings and surrounded by parking lots for employees. By this time the geographical link between factory and worker housing had been sufficiently weakened that the minority of workers probably lived in fairly close proximity to the factory. The improvement of arterial roads during the superhighway era of the 1930s permitted this stretching of the still integrated fabric of the metropolitan city. The now extensive factories reached by these arterial roads were still physically contiguous to the central cities, and their workers tended to use the normal street system of the metropolis to reach their workplaces.

Throughout this evolution between the wars there had been an element that ultimately reshaped the broad urban morphology: the giant factory complex. These were never present in great numbers, but their size and the crowds of workers they gave employment to assured them great individual importance. The rapid build-up of industry in the late 1930s—the American attempt at "preparedness" for possible war—brought these huge complexes into being. The anticipated scale of production under preparedness was even insufficient for the actual needs of the early 1940s. Shipyards, tank and truck plants, airframe and airplane-engine factories, and other facilities needed for the conduct of the first global war were at a scale never before envisaged, save in the automobile industry, where Henry Ford, that peculiarly narrow prophet, had started building his giant River Rouge plant even during World War I. The great industrial complexes of the early 1940s had to be constructed away from the built-up city and to become linked with it by industrial expressways that served the pendular movements of workers, three shifts a day during wartime conditions. No such giant plant could have been constructed save on the outskirts of a major industrial metropolis, as the tens of thousands of workers employed there could be secured and cared for only by the existing commercial, residential, and public-institutional structure of such a metropolis.

The giant exurban plant demonstrated clearly that the physical integration of the factory and the city had become elastic, functional but not necessarily confined within a continuous morphology. Just as the evolution of the factory from the upstairs workshop near the port to River Rouge, or even more Willow Run, had led to the creation of a distinct and specialized architecture for industry, the growth in the scale of manufacture, facilitated by developments in transportation, led to a new urban morphology of factories. The industrial plant had become a separate, commonly freestanding structure sited in response to a number of location forces but with little reference to either the morphology of the general metropolis or its working-class residential areas. The large scale of the industry and the great personal mobility of workers combined to allow a new level of geographical abstraction in the matter of industrial location within a broad urban region. The postwar decades have seen that this quality can cause not merely the broad movement of factory location within the urban region, but also interregional shifts in industrial location such that a new sectionalism has arisen in the United States, pitting the smokestack belt against the rest of the country.

The American Solution to Worker Housing Provision

Up to the middle of the last century, housing in American cities largely followed the medieval practice of a close association with workplaces. Within cities, those who worked in retail and wholesale establishments lived either in the buildings employed for the trade or in housing within walking distance of them. As the greater part of industry was then based on water-power, the hydraulic town or city built to develop the power potential of a fall became certainly the most characteristic location for factory-worker housing. In Waltham after 1814 the boardinghouse had sheltered the unmarried workers, and in Lowell after 1825 those with families were resident in row houses ranged closely around the mill yard. These residential facilities were frequently constructed directly by the mill owners or, if not so directly, by investors drawn commonly from the same classes. In the countryside, hydraulic cities—such as Lowell, Lawrence, Chicopee, and Holyoke in Massachusetts; Manchester, Nashua, and Rochester in New Hampshire; Saco, Lewiston, and Auburn in Maine; Amsterdam and Rochester in New York; and Paterson in New Jersey—joined residence closely with industrial development. In the emerging metropolitan areas, the industrial satellite—

such as Pawtucket near Providence, Waltham near Boston, and Ellicott City near Baltimore—grew up with the same form of close morphological association of factory and worker housing. But practices changed after 1850, and housing was generalized within metropolitan cities as well as within the hydraulic cities. Housing thus came into existence often through the efforts of small investors constructing tenements or row and cottage houses for rental to factory workers.[19] From midcentury on, city housing tended to be rental in nature and increasingly multiple-occupancy in style. As we have already seen, the tenement and the apartment took over as the typical elements of true city housing.

It was only the development of the trolley that changed that modular structure, shaping the blue-collar suburb to join the older but far smaller railroad suburb of the middle and upper classes. From around 1890 on, the sober and skilled working class could begin to aspire to these suburban houses. In the larger metropolitan cities those outlying residences might come in multifamily units—such as the three-deckers of southern New England cities, which frequently combined the flat of the owner with two for rental, ranged normally one above and the other below the owner's flat. The location of factories brought about, as well as reflected, this suburbanization of worker residence. The trolley made possible the move of the blue-collar workers to the suburbs, while at the same time the outlying residence of that group—combined with the efficiencies of the larger factory on a flatter plan—led factory owners to move their works toward the edge of the city. Up to the time of World War I this worker housing was heavily rental in nature, mainly because at that period mortgage funds were hard for blue-collar workers to obtain; they normally were given for only a modest part of the construction cost, and then for only a short period of years, six to ten, requiring sizable repayments. The small builder constructing for his own account, the modest investor seeking a stable and consistent return by having one or a few housing structures built, and the occasional worker whose family had managed to save the rather large down payment, were the main sources of this blue-collar suburban housing, leaving the main body of workers to rent these facilities.

The Rise of the Middle-Class Suburb

As long as the trolley remained the main form of transport available to working suburbanites, this physical pattern tended to be repeated with each decade's addition of housing to the metropolis. Only the middle and upper classes departed from the common pattern, both by being better able to finance their own housing and, around 1910, by taking up the nascent automobile to secure movement within the suburban band. Well-to-do suburbanites could move away from the suburban railroad stations into the countryside farther away, using cars to provide access from their houses to those outlying commuter railroad stops. The men commonly worked in the

19. For a discussion of the generalization of housing, see James E. Vance, Jr., "Housing the Worker: The Employment Linkage as a Force in Urban Structure," *Economic Geography* 42 (1966): 294–325.

The elevated began first with steam power, as shown here on the Lake Street line in Chicago in 1893. Using such relatively expensive technology meant that the first suburbs tended to be more for the middle class than for the masses. Note that the streets were unpaved, though sidewalks were, probably because those traveling had to walk from the elevated station to their homes. Photo: Chicago Elevated Railway.

traditional city, but women increasingly used cars for shopping in the clusters of shops located within the suburban band. Thus, there was a good historical background for the American development of the station wagon—licensed as a "suburban" in several states—to serve just this need, though ultimately its human milieu was broadened to include most social classes, if not all morphological components of the metropolis. With this newly introduced complexity of suburban transportation there came a further split in the economic-class structure of the band. Even before the station wagon was introduced, the very wealthy had been able to move beyond a walking radius from the commuter stations by normally having access to the horse-drawn vehicle, with a driver to operate it, to pick them up at the station at night and return them there in the morning. This transportation separation within suburbia introduced the thin belt of "estates" found even in the last half of the nineteenth century. But only with the coming of the automobile, soon to be refined into the station wagon for middle-class suburbanites, could the group able to live beyond walking distance from the outlying station increase significantly in numbers. Most of these families could not afford estates, but they could buy the roomy houses on large lots that began to fill out comfortable tree-shaded and lawn-encompassed subdivisions toward the edges of the bead-pattern towns that had grown outward from the city along the commuter lines. The number of middle-class purchasers was considerable but still sufficiently limited that the normal practice appears to have been for real estate developers to hedge their risk by engaging in subdivision of large parcels into lots, but seldom undertaking the actual construction of speculative houses on those lots. Instead, individuals bought lots and contracted with a builder to construct a house thereon for their residential occupancy. Occasionally, in the more active middle-class markets small builders would buy a few lots and then set about, serially, constructing houses for these middle-class purchasers until the subdivision had become filled with these basically individually constructed houses.

The Emergence of the Complex City

The Morphology of the Suburbs

It seems useful here to review briefly the state of housing in the suburban band at the close of World War I. The first dwellings in that band would have been remnants of earlier farm housing, few in number and frequently not conveniently located with respect to the suburban railroad stations that were developed along the rail lines constructed out of cities starting in the 1830s. Much more important as the germ for subsequent "suburbanization" (in the precise sense) were the clusters of houses built by middle- and even upper-class pioneers moving away from the city in the period when the only way to do so efficiently was to settle in one of the bead-pattern towns ranged around the railroad stops between Boston and Framingham on the Boston and Albany Railroad, Philadelphia and Paoli on the Main Line of the Pennsylvania Railroad, San Francisco and Palo Alto on the Southern Pacific Peninsula Line, and other such potentially suburban stretches of railroad. It was from these clusters of nucleated settlement at closely spaced stops within the countryside adjacent to the older cities that those seeking to build true suburban estates on larger blocks of former farm land set out for their domains. That sprinkling of large units of basically suburban residence served to push the outer edge of the metropolis well into the countryside, transforming an agricultural into an urban residential economy. These estates signaled the future by bringing in a nonagricultural service-trades population, improving the commuter rail service, and generally ripening the land for suburbanization. The blocks of land not contained in estates would, because of their proximity to high-income-class housing, tend to gain a cachet of desirable social location such that the next outward wave of suburbanization would tend to move into that quarter. Eventually, as wages were raised, most estates became too expensive to provide with servants and workers, and even the wealthy tended to trade the amenity of a handsome bank balance for that of a designedly pastoral and feudal environment. The early rail-age estate came eventually to be a bespoke housing subdivision for the middle class, a golf course, or, among the generous, a park for the ordinary folk.

The great change in the suburban pattern came when this middle- and upper-class residential morphology, with a few small inliers of blue-collar housing for those serving the needs of the prosperous—shopkeepers and their clerks, suburban town employees, servants on the estates and, in smaller numbers, in the larger middle-class houses, and others of modest means but needing to live among the prosperous—was joined by a much more massive morphology of more modest housing for the blue-collar classes. The working-class spread to the countryside came when the steam railroad was joined by the electric-car line, commonly with low and unit fares that made access to the suburban band by the working class practicable and, finally, a flood. The locale for that blue-collar in-migration was found in the bounds between the radiating railroad lines, where the countryside remained untransformed by the suburbanization that had reached land much closer to the traditional city, and in odd bits in and around the bead-pattern railroad suburbs where the land was socially or visually less attractive and had thus been passed over by the earlier swells of middle-class suburbanization. The flood of migration along the trolley lines was so large that all morphological gaps tended to be filled with this modest suburban housing, spreading a seamless carpet of residential land use out from the traditional city. There would be the peaks of social esteem represented by the former estate districts, with slopes of some social elevation occupied by the middle class. But underlying it all would be great expanses, a plinth, of modest family housing now served by trolley lines. Because the construction of those light rail routes depended ultimately on some vague expectation of eventual profit to undertakers, there was a gentle constraint on the outward spread of the trolley wire. The "trolley city" remained a compact one; in fact, trolleys increased compaction of urban morphology because they served to fill in the gaps of previous suburbanization with patches of modest worker housing. At the close of World War I, this was the normal pattern in a North American metropolis. The quiet and calm of these suburbs belied what became a wrenching generation of suburban transformation between 1918 and 1940. That transformation was divided into two unequal periods, the first from World War I to 1934, and the second from that year to the outbreak of World War II.

Suburban Transformations after 1918

The first transformation of the pre-1918 residential provision came with the rapid decline, during the 1920s, of the trolley as a medium of intra-urban transport. It is unnecessary here to sketch in full detail the background of that decline beyond noting that throughout the early years of the trolley era (1890–1910) there was always the expectation that profits would improve once the construction phase was completed and a larger part of a railway's earnings could be dedicated to maintenance of way. In those early years receipts rose rapidly—additional lines were being added and numbers of riders were growing rapidly—so there was little careful accounting as to the actual return on the capital invested; the burgeoning money flow seemed to make such figuring unnecessary. When war broke out in Europe in 1914, goods became more expensive, as did labor once the United States approached the war. The cost of repair and even operation rose rapidly just at a time when replacement of the original infrastructure was needed. During the four years of the war the unrealistic returns on capital invested in electric traction became quite clear. It was discovered that most of the later—that is, outer-suburban—additions to urban trolley systems were not truly economic. As pressures increased in the companies, it became natural that they should first think of abandoning those outer extensions to bring fare receipts into closer approximation with operating and maintenance costs. Starting in 1918 electric-traction mileage began to decline with abandonment of lines, to the point that by the end of the 1920s many people living in the suburban band were beginning to experience difficulty in moving around that area by electric traction. The depression that began in 1929 greatly aggravated the situation, leading to further abandonment of lines and curtailment of service on those that remained in use.

This abandonment of the trolley lines hurt in two ways. The first was the obvious one of simple loss of service, such that persons living in certain parts of the suburban band were denied rapid and reliable service in intra-urban journeys. Buses were slowly substituted for most abandoned trolley lines, but their speed and comfort levels were so low that those stranded along the abandoned trolley lines commonly found it preferable to try to provide for their own suburban transportation by purchase of a car. The second painful consequence of trolley abandonment came in the matter of fares. We saw earlier in the chapter that the flat-rate nickel fare reduced the economic cost of distance within the metropolis to a low, and frequently uniform, charge. Endowed with that low cost, many lower-income families moved well out into the suburban band while still keeping their transportation costs under control. When the traction companies began to realize that their low rates could not be continued, a conclusion reached around 1917, they began to raise fares, thus creating a problem for the lower-income suburbanites. When trolley service came to be given up a decade or so later, those who replaced it with automobile commuting found quickly that the costs of living in the suburb could be high. If high fares must be paid on the remaining public transport, there seemed to be no benefit at all; the same transport that had been cheap was unchanged, yet now far more expensive. But by turning to the private automobile to provide suburban transportation, some return was gained from the increased costs in that the family would now have a car to use outside of working hours, so shopping expanded in suburban towns where prices tended to be higher than in the larger places, particularly the centers of industrial satellites now surrounded by the expanded suburban band. It is not surprising that many families opted for the car even if its total money cost might be greater per year than that for public-transit fares.

Once the automobile became democratized, a shift aided greatly by Henry Ford's mass production of the Model T such that these cars were sold in the early 1920s for as little as $285, a new dynamic for suburban housing was in hand. Whereas until then only the fairly well-to-do could move away from fixed transit lines, now an increasing population could do so, in fact had to do so. Land that had lacked the amenities for higher-economic-class residential development could now be envisaged as potential housing sites for blue-collar families. That trend was aided by the flexibility that car transportation offered, such that several members of a family might find work, the head of the household possibly in the traditional city—reached from the end of a trolley line in the inner part of the suburban band—while older children or even the spouse might find employment within those parts of the suburban band approachable only by car. The combination of family incomes might thus make the income total gained from the collective use of a car great enough to cover its increased cost over public transport. By the late 1920s the automobile suburb was a reality in American cities, and the more than twenty million cars registered in the United States made mass housing in the suburbs as possible as it had been under control of the trolley wire. But to make the system work with increased transportation costs, it was critical to keep the rental costs of housing under stern control by assuring a large supply of modest-price suburban housing and access to it for people not possessed of any appreciable amount of capital.

Solving the Housing Problem

The 1920s were a time of prosperity but not one when the blue-collar class had much accumulated capital. Savings were modest for that group and not particularly likely to enlarge in a time when a number of useful but relatively expensive household machines were being offered for the first time. The car was the most obvious and appealing example, but the refrigerator, radio, washing machine, electric stove, and self-feeding furnace were other important introductions that tended to appeal particularly to the servantless working classes. In the late 1920s more of the blue-collar class were able to think about buying their own houses, a need because the shift to the suburbs was notably a move from the rental residential area of the traditional city to the owner-occupied residential area of the suburbs. What made the situation particularly difficult was the high need for capital for working-class entrants to these areas. The necessity to purchase a house in order to live there, a car to survive there, and a number of household appliances to be happy there put great pressure on many families if they sought the suburban solution to the continuing housing problem. Before we take up the question of how to solve the problem of housing, we should recognize that there existed a severe constraint of capital availability for even skilled and continuously employed workers and their families. If the common practice of the higher-income groups—residence in owner-occupied, single-family, detached suburban housing—were to become a general form of housing provision in America, some effective way must be found to make increments of capital available to the many substantial workers' families seeking to move to the suburbs.

The housing problem had almost certainly always existed in cities. Rome was crowded and noisome in parts, medieval cities even more so because of their constriction within narrow walls. The rapid growth of urban population consequent upon the Commercial Revolution of the sixteenth and seventeenth centuries and the Industrial Revolution of the eighteenth and nineteenth centuries brought the matter of housing provision to national attention. Government investigations at the middle of the last century delineated the scale and urgency of the housing problem, but effective remedial action was delayed by the absence of any existing practice to deal with it. Only toward the end of the last century, and first in Bismarck's Germany, was it perceived that adequate housing was a national concern. There had been earlier rather piecemeal attempts at public housing, as for example early in the nineteenth century at Verviers in Belgium. One of the more fundamental concerns that led to the formulation of Robert Owen's initial "socialist" proposals in the 1820s was the belief that there must be governmental acceptance of responsibility for provision of adequate housing regardless of family income. As that socialist thought spread, it was taken up primarily in cities where individuals and some local governments sought a public provision of housing with charges geared to the ability to pay rather

This aerial view of Sonoma, California, shows the further transformation of a Laws-of-the-Indies town (compare with figure on page 216) during the rapid growth of automobile-based suburbanism and exurbanism after 1945. The forty-acre small holdings shown in the earlier plan of the town can still be seen in the grain of the housing tracts laid out a full century later. Photo: R. L. Copeland, 1981.

than the amortization of the cost of the housing. This became in essence the European solution to the problem of providing adequate housing. Britain followed Germany in the late 1880s, first in London but later in most cities, and eventually even in the countryside where most agricultural housing was of a rental nature. By 1940 it was established practice in most of Western Europe that working-class housing was heavily subsidized in its construction phase. That general solution to the housing problem was worked out in a characteristic morphological context. Land tended to be narrowly held in Europe, or else so split into tiny peasant holdings that it was difficult to change. These landholding practices inhospitable to the easy spread of the city were further reinforced by the nearly universal dependence in the pre-1939 period in Europe on public transit for moving workers in the journey-to-work. Trolley lines were numerous, but because they were most commonly built and operated directly by municipal corporations, they were not distantly ramified beyond the traditional city's boundary. Working-class housing might be subsidized in its construction, but it was only so supported within a narrowly confined area, that of the municipal corporation that provided the funds and built the transit that moved ordinary people about the city. The era of widespread ownership of cars in Europe had to wait at least for the 1950s, and even later in some countries.

In North America contrasting geographical conditions seem to have induced a quite different solution to the common housing problem. There was normally a very wide ownership of rural land, and that in fairly large blocks because colonial efforts to introduce feudal landholding practices to North America had, in the main, failed. As housing pressure in the traditional city grew, the North Americans, both Canadian and American, sought urgently to use this cheap and extensive endowment of land for working-class as well as upper-income housing. There were commuter railroads at work in dispersing the more well-to-do to suburbs by the time of the Civil

War. During the generation after Appomattox, a large amount of North American ingenuity was turned toward adding a democratic component to city transportation, to be realized in the late 1880s with the phenomenally rapid spread of trolley lines. Both in Canada and in the United States, this spread was almost wholly the work of private investors, who operated under franchises to occupy the streets of a particular city. These grants might be assembled from several adjacent municipalities, so it became common in Canada and the United States for trolley systems to extend well beyond the limits of the central, traditional city, opening up large tracts of normally fairly cheap land for housing development. With the low, often unit fares charged by these North American trolley systems, the blue-collar classes could join their white-collar counterparts in seeking housing on thesenumerous blocks of cheap development land.

This geographical solution, contrasting with the architectural one used in Europe to solve the housing problem, created the metropolis that came to be dominated by the suburban band that emerged as the North American city. While inordinately cheap suburban transit was being provided—through an odd and generally unrecognized subsidy from private capital to families of modest income—a surprisingly large spectrum of urban people could seek the suburban solution to the housing problem. But with the collapse of that "capitalist subsidy" when electric-traction companies were forced to raise fares and curtail services during World War I, practices even more in evidence in the decade that followed, the housing problem became more difficult of solution. The widespread adoption of automobile commuting overcame the impending catastrophe resulting from the abandonment of trolley service to the outer parts of the suburban band, but it did so only at a price that began to disrupt the stability of the North American solution to the housing problem.

Turning specifically to the United States so that we may deal with its particular remedy in this disrupted housing provision, we should note that the final straw that broke what had been an entirely private, capitalist solution to the general housing problem came with the Great Depression of the 1930s. That economic debacle led to an even more rapid program of abandonment of trolley lines, and rises in fares, that put increasing financial pressure on the ordinary family in the suburbs. Their incomes tended to decline with the onset of the Depression, their costs rose with the removal of the capitalist transportation subsidy, and their own capital tended to shrink disastrously with the collapse of the stock market. The suburban housing market fell into desuetude. The American solution to the housing problem was in a shambles by the time Roosevelt assumed office in 1933.

The New Deal Revision of the American Solution to the Housing Problem

The New Deal, though at the time viewed as radical in many of its programs, proved to be part of what by 1934 was a longstanding American solution to the urban housing problem. That solution was the use of private investment applied to relatively cheap land to provide an individual house to families owning and occupying those structures. That goal in the mid-

In the years immediately after 1945 the demand for housing was extreme, and it was satisfied by two mechanisms—veterans' loans and veterans' housing tracts. This is San Leandro, California, south of Oakland (shown in the background), where cucumber and cabbage fields were rapidly transformed into tracts with houses sold for no money down and a total cost of under $5,000. Photo: R. L. Copeland, December 21, 1947.

nineteenth century had led to the construction of rather tightly packed small houses, often in rows with party walls, and sited on rectangular blocks at the fringes of the traditional city where land, though cheaper than at the center, was still relatively expensive. The small lot grew out of that land-cost factor, whereas the small house came from the modest capital available to the working class. When the trolley arrived on the scene in the 1890s, the land provision became much more ample, so new lots grew in size and the row house was abandoned (save in a band of territory extending from around Albany in the Hudson Valley southward along that river to metropolitan New York, thence across middle New Jersey to the Delaware valley, along that stream including much of adjacent eastern Pennsylvania, between Philadelphia and Harrisburg, southward to include metropolitan Baltimore and westward in an interrupted fashion to include the cities of the Ohio valley below Pittsburgh and metropolitan St. Louis on the Mississippi, with a distant outlier in San Francisco after the Gold Rush). Trolley-era housing tended to be more open, with larger lots but not much more ample buildings, at least for the laboring classes. This was the beginning of true blue-collar suburbia, which came to cover great areas in the larger metropolises. With the forced shift to automobile commuting during the late 1920s, the land base for an even more massive provision of modest housing was in hand. What was missing was the capital to bring about its construction. After five years of the Hoover Depression, the collapse of the private housing market was nearly complete, bringing distress to those already owning houses in the suburbs and preventing much further outward movement of ordinary families.

To perpetuate the use of the largely unconscious but certainly traditional American solution to the housing problem of industrial society, the Roosevelt administration set about finding a way to amplify the capital available to those of modest income. The way found was to guarantee the repayment of mortgages taken out to cover the construction of housing. This federal guarantee of repayment was combined with a strong pressure to reduce the down payment, from as much as half the construction costs to a rather minor percentage, and to reduce the repayment charges by stretching out loans, from the six to ten years previously common to as much as twenty-five years, thus making purchase of housing little more expensive than the payment of rent. A final component of this New Deal housing plan was the assurance of reasonable quality in the structures built, through the establishment of basic standards of architecture and construction. As enacted in the Federal Housing Administration (FHA) legislation of 1934 and following years, FHA loans were available for new construction of lower- and middle-income housing both in single-family, owner-occupied houses and in apartment developments of moderate size. The latter provision was rather little used, so we have come to view the FHA as having brought about a major transformation of the residential structure of American cities through the addition of vast tracts of automobile suburbs. That was the way it worked out in practice, but when proposed, the legislation was seen as not taking sides between the apartment housing within the traditional core city and the single-family units at the outer edge of the suburban band. In fact, along with FHA financing went a second federal program to provide cheap loans for the repair of existing housing that had fallen into a bad state.

The ultimate dominance by the suburban rather than the traditional-city housing provision must be understood in terms of the collapse of the trolley and the rise of the automobile, not just in California as was first thought, but everywhere outside of New York City and, to a lesser degree, Chicago. The rise of the car had suggested a further transformation of the morphology of residential areas for ordinary families, but the collapse of the housing industry in 1929 had put off its realization. The availability of FHA financing starting in 1934 had allowed the change to come about. Only the relatively short time between the enactment of the New Deal's housing policy and the outbreak of war in 1939—and America's entrance in 1941—limited what became a major urban transformation to match that worked by the trolley in the 1890s. Little more than five years intervened before all nonemergency housing construction was stopped. Even so, the nature of the transformation was visible by 1940, even if the scale of change could not at that time be predicted with confidence.

Before we take up that evidence of a new kind of metropolis, it is worth noting that the New Deal also envisaged the development of publicly owned housing in the United States. This was to be in housing projects built by separate authorities in cities and rented at subsidized rents to the lowest-income groups. This represented a new departure for America. Germany in Bismarck's time, Britain in Gladstone's, and other countries of industrialized Europe had begun to provide public rental housing, often with ready acceptance thereof by the tenants and no stigma different from that of general social class. But in the United States the late adoption of public housing, only in the 1930s, and its unplanned involvement in the acculturation of recent immigrants to the city—blacks, Hispanics, and Asians mostly—produced a very stigmatized situation. To live in public housing came to be associated with permanent status in what has come to be called the underclass, that part of American society seemingly permanently consigned to poverty, family disintegration, social disorder, the lowest occupations, and a violence bred at least in part of a sense of hopelessness. Perhaps for the remainder of the 1930s public housing was still so experimental that it had an open future, but by the post-1945 period public appraisal of that housing had become so scathing that the United States has only reluctantly engaged in further construction. Public housing in the United States has smacked of the dead end—socially, economically and morphologically—ever since.

A 1939 Model of Suburban Morphology

The emergent pattern of widely accepted housing in the United States at the entrance of this country into World War II was almost exclusively suburban. Only that eternal exception in American experience, New York City, continued to maintain the morphological practices of the past. Boston, the birthplace of the American suburb, adopted the new form virtually without dissent by the late 1930s, and most other metropolitan areas marched in the same column. For the first time there were virtually no class distinctions, save for the publicly housed underclass mentioned in the previous paragraph. The rich had been suburban for a century, the middle class for at least half that time period, and the sturdy working class at least partially so since the turn of the century. Now all marched together, if to varying destinations within the suburban band. The wealthy still tended to occupy the most attractive part of the suburban band, often on its outer fringe where the thousand-year English association of the gentry with the countryside gave automatic "class" to the morphology and its "address." The middle classes similarly tended to locate where association gave a cachet, one seemingly earned by living next to the housing of an earlier generation's social leaders. Homer Hoyt in the late 1930s discerned this tendency toward sectorial spreading, guided by class, when he wrote on his sector theory of city structure, a work commissioned in part to help guide the lending practices of the FHA program.[20] As the wealthy and the middle class preempted the countryside adjacent to their parents' neighborhoods, the blue-collar groups had to take what was left, which tended to be those areas with fewer natural amenities, and often in the open countryside surrounding the now embedded nineteenth-century industrial satellites. Thus, all classes were on the edge, but the specific vector from the core of the traditional city at whose pioneering edge they resided was determined largely by class divisions already established by the middle of the last century.

There is little need here to expand on the morphology of the residential areas built up even in the late 1930s for the rich and middle classes. Those areas showed little change from earlier times except in a diminution of house size. With the general rise in wages, the servant became relatively more expensive, such that even the rich had to economize a bit. And the middle classes pretty much gave up having servants. Instead, those prosperous

20. Homer Hoyt, *The Structure and Growth of Residential Neighborhoods in American Cities* (Washington, D.C.: Government Printing Office, 1939).

families turned to machines for comfort in the home. Two cars freed both spouses of geographical constraint. Electric household appliances made the wife's job generally shorter and less taxing. Without servants, however, smaller housing was in order. Seldom was the lot size reduced, but certainly by the outbreak of the war the newer houses for this class were somewhat compacted, if better supplied with bathrooms and mechanized aids to housekeeping.

The Industrialization of Housing

It was in the lower-middle-class and working-class suburbs that the major transformation of the late 1930s became most observable. The federal program of mortgage guarantees so opened the market to the masses, at least by comparison with times past, that a new form of construction could be employed. Where even as late as the 1920s the most common form of suburban development had been the subdivision of blocks of land into a plat of lots, which were then sold to individuals for their personal use or to small builders who might construct, serially, a small number of houses that would be sold over a period of time to individual purchasers, in the late 1930s the housing tract with the industrial production of houses came into wide use. The market was now larger, more clearly defined by FHA regulations— which even served to influence the architecture that was favored by lenders—and seemingly more predictable as to the rate of purchase. Given the lowering of the threshold for entrance into the suburban housing market— by the opportunity to build on cheap land afforded by the use of automobile commuting and by the reduction in down payments and the spreading out of mortgage payments afforded by FHA financing—a never-before-available mass of buyers was on hand. To keep prices down, and thus obtain or even expand that potential market, builders began experimenting with what we have come to realize was the industrialization of housing provision. Houses within a tract tended to become standardized to a single model, or at most a few, contributing that modern pejorative *tract house* to our language. The nineteenth-century technical shift, begun in the United States, away from the skilled post-and-lintel construction in wood toward the more simply built balloon frame—introduced at the beginning of the period under consideration—was changed by a further shift toward the preassembly of major components of a house. Roofing trusses, side panels, bathroom plumbing units, and kitchen cabinet groupings could all be built repetitively at a workshop or assembly yard on the building site. Eventually, whole walls were so constructed, to the point that an individual house could be assembled from these massive components in a few days with very little skilled labor. To gain the advantages of this system large tracts were desirable, and to secure those at a reasonable cost the focus of builders' attention turned toward the physical edge of the city. By the late 1930s the dispersive forces in existence in the metropolis were strong indeed; only the outbreak of war in Europe in 1939 stalled what could be seen as a major technical shift in housing construction. The course of that conflict magnified the postwar transformation, as we shall see, by further elaborating the industrial production of housing, induced by the need to construct large Army camps, shipyard

As the influx of people to cities continued to surge, ever-greater provisions in real estate developments were called into existence. By draining and regulating the tidal flow of marshes on San Francisco Bay, a "new town" of Foster City was shaped to provide housing for commuters from San Francisco (shown at top right), as well as San Francisco International Airport, the second largest employment center in the metropolitan area (middle background), and the various industries of Silicon Valley behind us. Photo: R. L. Copeland, April 21, 1978.

housing tracts, and housing projects for war industries in previously little industrialized areas. In addition, the return of general economic prosperity during the war was such that the scale of the postwar market was much greater than that possible in 1939.

The industrialization of housing shaped a new morphological component of the metropolis, the vast housing tract as a modular unit for accretion. The importance of this module lay in its very scale, one sufficient to permit the construction of a planned component of retail and service activities to care for the needs of a large population quickly introduced to what had previously been quiet rural land. The planned shopping center did not have its precise beginnings with the FHA-financed tracts. That had come in 1923 in Kansas City, when the J. C. Nichols Company had laid out a major real estate development on the southern outskirts of that city called the Country Club District. Within it was constructed a shopping cluster, Country Club Plaza, first for the service of those living in the development's apartment houses and some individual housing, but second intended to draw customers from other suburban areas to the branch department and other "downtown" stores ultimately built in the plaza. That name probably stemmed from the Nichols Company's adoption of Spanish colonial architecture, then very much the rage as a result of the Pan-Pacific Exposition in San Diego held in 1915 and built in that style. Although subsequent "plazas" in the suburban band have seldom followed Spanish colonial architecture, the generic term for an integrated shopping center in the outer portions of the suburban band has become *plaza*.

It seems appropriate at this point to leave any further discussion of tract housing and its associated land uses to the next chapter, where we shall consider postwar urban morphogenesis. The trends were established in the six years after 1934 but were held in abeyance during the course of World War II. At this point it is sufficient to take firm note of the arrival of several new morphological components of the metropolis: the housing tract, the shopping plaza, and all sorts of service and support facilities of what were in truth virtual "new towns" springing up at the edge of the metropolis. New forms of school construction, new types of industry and office buildings, and many features of modern America grew out of this first major transformation of the housing structure to be introduced since the early nineteenth-century shaping of the American suburb.

The Transformation of Roads to Cope with Automobile Commuting: The Superhighway

It seems that the road has been with us since the beginning of human settlement, as of course it has in a very basic sense. But until the beginning of this century, most of those roads were earth roads, the natural surface of the ground little more than cleared of brush, trees, and stones. Even in cities most streets were earth, the more important ones perhaps graveled, and a truly minute mileage was paved with stone or wooden blocks. It is only in this century that city streets have been consistently paved with asphalt or cement. Even that paving was normally merely a coating of the earlier surface, with little or no reengineering of the alignment, grade, or width. With the advent of the automobile, the pressure for extending pavements, first felt in the 1880s with the rise of the use of safety bicycles, increased, but the emphasis continued to be mostly on spreading the hard surface rather than on creating roads for modern mass automobile movement.

The wrenching shift from trolleys to private automobiles, which came in the 1920s, led to a rapid extension of hard-surface roads so that by around 1930 road improvement could turn to examine the nature of the route beyond the matter of its simple surface. As the 1920s wore on, the increasing use of cars for commuting and for recreational driving began to create traffic jams, which led in turn to calls for enlarging roads so that a greater and faster flow of traffic might be obtained. It was early in that last prewar decade that the proposal for superhighways was advanced in earnest. By then it was appreciated that two driving conditions created much of the congestion being felt: the conflict of cars and trucks operating on two-lane highways of necessity or choice at differing speeds, with the slowest holding up the fastest if any great amount of oncoming traffic made passing impossible; and the conflict of two streams of traffic where major roads and highways intersected. To overcome the first conflict the multilane highway, dangerously three or more wisely four lanes, was designed so that there might be two, later three, lanes of traffic moving in the same direction but at varying speeds. To overcome the conflict of crossing traffic streams, the grade separation was devised, carrying one over the other so that free flow on both might take place simultaneously. To transfer traffic from open road to its intersecting route, the cloverleaf junction was devised, first in New Jersey but rapidly put in use in

Massachusetts and California. In Britain "gyratory traffic control," the rotary circle in America, was fervently adopted in the attempt to solve this conflict at intersections, but virtually no non-Briton finds these "roundabouts" an effective solution to the problem.

Whatever specific features of traffic engineering were used, their intent was to enlarge the capacity of designated roads to deal with a rapidly increasing demand posed by the democratic adoption of the car. In cities this became a particular problem, for congestion was not merely a weekend or seasonal phenomenon; it came about every working day because the common roads of the past could not care for the volumes of traffic introduced by daily mass use of cars in a densely built-up area. The need for the creation of an automobile-era highway system was first felt within metropolitan areas and in the penumbra of rural territory surrounding them, which was subject to frequent city-based journeys. And it was there that virtually all the effective changes worked before World War II were to be found. Even as late as 1939, in a government report called *Toll Roads and Free Roads*, which contained the first national traffic count, it was shown that only fairly close to large cities, or intermediate between two sizable cities located near one another, could superhighways be justified under contemporary thinking.[21] As Franklin Roosevelt noted in his summary of the recommendations, this report "shows that there is a need for superhighways, but makes clear that this need exists only where there is congestion on the existing roads, and mainly in metropolitan areas. Improved facilities, needed for the solution of city street congestion, are shown to occupy a fundamental place in the general replanning of cities." Thus, when we consider the birth of the automobile road, we must do so in the urban region.

Two problem situations emerged beginning in the early 1930s. The first came from the clogging of arterial roads leading to and from cities and the outer edge of the suburban band; the second lay beyond that boundary and prevailed for the distance outward that daily traffic converging on the city remained dense or weekend and holiday traffic spreading out of the city overtaxed the normal rural road system. The first situation arose from daily commuting and the intracity movement of trucks; the second from those coming from outside to the metropolis or from the traditional core to the surrounding countryside. It was in the heavily urbanized Northeast that the arterial street and highway problem was first attacked. This region had been the site of an extensive system of toll turnpikes constructed in the early nineteenth century, just before the coming of the railroad, intended to facilitate transportation between the colonial ports and their economically developing hinterlands. Much of southern New England, New Jersey, eastern Pennsylvania, Maryland, and Virginia east of the Blue Ridge were served by these straight and newly located roads. Their virtual abandonment once the railroad arrived in the period between 1830 and 1850 meant that these now toll-less turnpikes were frequently direct in course but so little used that they had not been constrained by roadside development. They might be widened to three or four lanes without excessive land-taking costs.

21. *Toll Roads and Free Roads*. Message from the President of the United States to Congress, April 27, 1939 (Washington, D.C.: Government Printing Office, 1939), 132 pp.

The Newburyport and Worcester turnpikes in Massachusetts were rebuilt in the early 1930s as a new form of superhighway, four lanes in width throughout most of their length, with a separation of opposing traffic flows by median strips, and with grade separations where designated arterial routes intersected them. In Rhode Island, Connecticut, southern New York, New Jersey, and on southward to Washington, these enlarged roads came into being and were rapidly filled with traffic, proving the point that improved facilities seemed to generate a use larger than what had preceded them. The environs of Chicago, Detroit, Los Angeles, and Oakland-San Francisco witnessed similar superhighway construction, but without the early-nineteenth-century turnpike relics to locate them.

The impact of this construction was quickly felt in the cities from which they extended. Motor trucking was considerably speeded up, thereby made more economical, and under those circumstances greatly expanded in use. Factories could be moved farther out of the traditional core or even away from the metropolis itself but still have rapid access to the city for securing raw materials and ultimately for the sale of their product. Wholesaling was fundamentally transformed, at least in its more innovative components, by making its final break from the core of the traditional city, moving often to the edge of the metropolis where the geographical approximation of rail facilities for receipts from manufacturers and arterial superhighways for shipments to retail customers was easiest to obtain. And these superhighways unclogged and speeded up the journey-to-work to the city core and to other employment in the suburban band and its embedded industrial satellites, thus encouraging additional and more distant suburban commuting. In this context the large tracts of FHA-style housing on cheap land at the edge of the metropolis became both possible and popular where superhighways radiated from the core.

Although the superhighways were relatively few in number, they did begin to shape a new urban morphology—as had the railroads in the 1850s and the electric-traction lines at the end of the century. The rudiments of the automobile era were in place by 1940, and the signs could be read. But the cessation of construction other than for wartime needs froze those signs for a

The Emergence of the Complex City

period long enough to transform the scale of their ultimate implementation, but not the form.

The other problem, that found beyond the metropolitan boundary caused by conflux on the city from elsewhere and an afflux of city people seeking recreation in the countryside, also received attention. The urge for getting out of the city for recreation was already appreciated in the last century. Frederick Law Olmsted, that patristic figure in the American suburban revolution, in the 1880s had devised an elaborate system of carriage roads in a girdle surrounding Boston. He accomplished similar massive structures for recreational movement within metropolitan Chicago and Kansas City. The Westchester County suburbs of New York City came also to be threaded by parkways constructed for the early car recreation at the time of World War I. In the late 1930s that Westchester system was being extended northward in the ten-mile strip of the Empire State lying east of the Hudson and in adjacent Connecticut, where the Merritt Parkway, opened in the late 1930s, became the showpiece of recreational highway construction—partly for its engineering, which carried the superhighway to its logical development as the totally limited-access highway, and partly for its imposition of tolls to pay for it all. That seemingly easy way to gain the latest form of automobile road through the collection of user tolls was also employed on the first longer-distance automobile road to be opened, the toll turnpike from King of Prussia just west of Philadelphia to Irwin just east of Pittsburgh completed in 1940. The latter was more a truck than a recreation road, but it, along with the all-automobile Westchester and Merritt parkways, formed a model of the highway of the future, one that had to wait for nearly a decade to gain reasonably widespread recognition.

At this same period in the late 1930s Los Angeles was similarly becoming clogged by daily traffic. To deal with that situation the California Highway Department planned and constructed an urban arterial, fully grade-separated, and with limited access and multiple lanes divided by direction of flow. But unlike the situation in the East, the Golden State had dedicated all its user taxation derived from motor vehicles to highway expenditures. Thus, the Arroyo Seco urban highway became the first freeway, both because of the unrestricted flow of vehicles and because of the absence of any toll on the route between downtown Los Angeles and Pasadena. Like all other pioneering automotive roads of the late 1930s, the Arroyo Seco Freeway remained the only freeway until well after 1945 when civilian construction could resume. Only in quite specialized circumstances, as in the Willow Run Industrial Freeway built from Detroit westward to the vast Willow Run defense plant, constructed during World War II, was the model copied until peace returned.

Morphogenesis of the American City in the Industrial Era

During the hundred years that ended with the American entry into World War II the relative balance among the three major morphological components of the American metropolis shifted strikingly. At the middle of the last century the core city, what I have here called the traditional city, was strongly dominant, housing most of the population in the urban area, then hardly a metropolis as we now use the term. The traditional city was one that grew up largely within the control of pedestrial movement, in the journey-to-work and other repeating urban movements. Beyond the limit so imposed lay only a few nuclei of settlement, those around waterpower sites where industrial satellites had come into existence and those strung as beads of suburban residence along the inner reaches of the railroad converging on the traditional city. These nuclei formed the base on which, during a century, the vast suburban band of the modern metropolis was shaped and filled out to become a massive and continuous city of great morphological complexity. Most of the growth came in the residential dispersion to this band, leaving the traditional city as the home for a few very wealthy and a great mass of recent arrivals in the city, as yet not fully acculturated and economically almost an underclass. Until the time of World War I it was mostly housing that filled out the emerging suburban band, but after 1918 both industry and wholesaling increasingly became located in the parts of the suburban band best served by extrametropolitan transportation routes, rail and then road. With that outward shift of employment opportunities, the earlier separation of residential from workplace functions in the suburban band began to become less distinct. No longer was the dichotomy between industrial satellite and suburb so precise; the arrival of the automobile as a means of commuting meant not only that suburban dwellers might seek employment in other than the closely adjacent satellite or the central city, but also that those suburbanites might seek employment anywhere within the metropolis, in the traditional core, any satellite, or even in previously entirely residential suburbs, some of which were becoming modestly sprinkled with factories, warehouses, and shops.

The trolley had spread the fabric of the traditional city, making it larger both by additions and by the stretching out of the initial fabric. The car and the truck changed its nature, leading to a rapid relocation of many previously central functions to new sites within the suburban band. Industry began to leave the city, taking jobs with it. Wholesaling perhaps even more distinctly turned away from its traditional core sites. And in the suburbs themselves changes were coming in the dependence on particular shopping facilities. The central business district maintained itself, but the seeds of change were seen in the rise of specialty shopping facilities within the suburban band. That rise came more quickly when the FHA programs were initiated in 1934, bringing a socially wider spectrum of residents to the suburbs. The numbers of potential suburbanites grew rapidly, and only the onset of World War II slowed down the pace of change.

World War II was not so long as to obliterate the strong trends of the late 1930s, but it was total enough to assure that once normal growth and expansion of the metropolis resumed, it would do so with a clear break from the past. For that reason it seems best here to close the century of the industrial metropolis and to pick up its successor in the next chapter. That successor was certainly not a nonindustrial one, but by comparison with the metropolis that evolved between 1845 and 1945 it was a far more comprehensive city with a far more complex morphogenesis.

Urban Morphogenesis since 1945

The Rise of the Complex City

Events obviously foretell fundamental transformations in human societies as well as in nature. The rise to dominance of the automobile (in the matter of movement within metropolises) and the successful New Deal rejuvenation of the American solution to the housing problem (through the continuing incorporation of "cheap land" into that metropolitan structure) suggested the most likely nature of American urban morphology after the close of World War II; but they did not foreordain that structure, as the contrasting European experience demonstrated. National practice and public policy could strongly affect the nature of the change. In the interwar years Britain had used both public housing and government-supported private development to improve residential conditions, as had the United States by the late 1930s. But by 1945 wartime events had left the two countries quite different. In America the New Deal had lost its urgency, and in 1946 a Republican, and conservative, Congress was elected while no enemy destruction had been visited on American cities. In contrast, Britain's traditional social structure had been shown to be archaic by the fully democratic demands placed on Britons during the warfare, leading to the election of a Labour government in the summer of 1945. And that government immediately faced the problem of rebuilding cities badly damaged by German aerial bombardments, including that by the first major rocket weapons. Elsewhere in Europe physical conditions were much closer to the British than the American, and a socialist political philosophy, Christian or secular, was nearly universal.

For this reason it becomes hard to talk about "Western cities" as a class and increasingly necessary to distinguish between North American and European. Here I shall mainly talk about North American cities in the postwar period, because the conditions in the New World reflected long-term processes that became observable in Europe only after its cities had been reconstructed to make up for wartime damage. Ultimately, we may properly talk about a new Western urban morphogenesis, but for some fifteen to twenty years after 1945 North America and Europe had to pass through separate periods of experimentation to find the logical application of the prewar processes to this quite radically transformed time. In Europe public planning and construction dominated well into the 1960s, whereas in the United States a private, market-oriented postwar construction boom commenced by 1947. Each was massive in impact and ultimately radical in its influence on urban physical structure.

As would logically be anticipated, the growth to American cities in the first few years after 1945 picked up where processes stood at the U.S. entry into the war in 1941. New civilian automobile production recommenced in 1946, but only in 1947 did masses of cars become available. In similar fashion the shortages of building material consequent upon the shift from national defense to civilian construction delayed the ability of builders to meet market demand until the late 1940s, and even then only after the full development of industrialized house production was worked out in its pre-

liminary form. Wartime experience gained in the building of wooden barracks in army camps and emergency housing for shipyard and other war
workers quickly advanced the system of organizing this mass production of
major subassemblies used in the construction of hundreds or even thousands
of nearly identical single-family houses on a single tract of land. Kitchens,
bathrooms, roofing trusses, and other major components of a house were
preassembled in erection yards to be trucked to the individual house lots,
themselves graded in mass numbers by bulldozers, the major earth-moving
machine to grow out of the vast construction demands of World War II. With
Federal Housing Authority (FHA) financing already in place, supplemented
by legislation at the close of the war whose G.I. Bill of Rights entitled
veterans to low-interest loans for mortgages on houses, by the late 1940s the
speed of house building outdistanced any prewar experience. Before 1939
there had been small experiments in the construction of housing tracts
where—unlike the earlier normal practice of mass subdivision of lots with
individual or small-builder construction of one or a few houses on those
lots—builders not only divided the land but also built all the houses to
occupy the resulting lots, sometimes as many as a hundred or more. After
the war the housing tract became not merely the norm but in some places
virtually the exclusive morphological unit by which cities expanded their
residential land use.

The significance of the tract should be clear, for many of us have lived in
or adjacent to it for almost a half-century. Now we should look at the house
that evolved. Single-story, nonbasemented houses—those built on a slab
rather than a cellar—gained a dominant position because the bulldozer
favored such a foundation, and the combining of prefabricated subassemblies suggested concentrating most such joining in the final phase on a
single, ground level. Because this physical form of the house was different
from that built by small contractors and master carpenters before the war,
the new form was given a cachet of quite different geographical origin, in
truth largely apocryphal. Called ranch houses or California ranch houses,
these were built in the greatest number in the East. Probably they should
have been called process houses—though who would have bought a structure so named?—because they owed their morphology, hardly to be dignified as architecture, to the exigent quality of the housing demand and its
solution through industrialized processes. By imputing their style to a
ranch, those houses gained a bit of the romantic background they certainly
lacked in history. Ranch buildings tend structurally to be of the simplest
form, most easily constructed by the amateur builder, commonly a shed
using post-and-lintel framing and board-and-batten siding. The ranch house
had neither shed construction nor a rural setting; there is no question,
however, that to those accustomed to the individually constructed prewar
house it had a different and highly amateur look, without historical reference
or style. Being low, squat, and seemingly vernacular, it could be imagined to
have a historical precedent only distant and not widely known. Probably it
was the motion-picture representation of the ranch house that was known at
all widely. So it is probable that we should join the postwar ranch house with
the low, dented-crown cowboy hat as part of Hollywood's shaping of an

**The Rise of the
Complex City**

American cultural geography, drawn more from movie entertainment than from geographical exploration.

Obviously not all houses after 1945 were built in the stylelessly basic box form of the ranch house. As more expensive structures became available, they usually had more architectural qualities, but two things distinguished these houses of the 1950s from earlier times: there was a much increased turning away from historical "styles" toward a seemingly "modern" look that again was most commonly single-storied; and even quite expensive houses tended to be built by developers in tracts of a considerable number of houses rather than by master carpenters to the design of architects and on individual lots. In geographical terms this shift of the modular unit of accretion from the house to the tract worked great changes. These may be summarized to begin with before we examine a few in detail.

A Geography of Suburban Tracts

As we have seen in earlier chapters, the Commercial Revolution of the seventeenth century and the Industrial Revolution of the late eighteenth and early nineteenth centuries began the economic-class partition of the city. But there remained a scalar constraint on that separation: cities were still quite compact geographically, and economic-class numbers—save at the bottom—remained small. Thus, economic classes still resided fairly close together. In the post-1945 period American society was further revolutionized, not so much by occupation—as Western society as a whole had been in recent centuries—as by economic class. Wages for blue-collar employment grew sharply in some trades, and the white-collar components of general employment were the growth industries of the postwar years. The results were several: white, native-born Americans became increasingly middle-class in their economic status; and in consequence that specific economic class grew massively as a proportion of the whole. The narrow economic-class separation of the prewar city was now replaced by a separation into much more massive units that of necessity became more geographically isolated one from the other. There was, as well, a shift in the center of economic and political power from the traditional core to the suburban band, a movement encouraged by the increasing distances that were now internalized within the metropolis. It seems that fewer and fewer members of the urban elite remained resident in the traditional core city, so the population that continued to reside there was increasingly isolated from the more powerful elements of society. And the introduction of the modular unit of the tract meant that even between the middle, upper middle, and upper classes the class separation became increasingly geographical. The adventitious element introduced by growth through construction of housing on individual lots, often scattered openings in a largely built-up area, was largely removed from American urban social geography. Tracts were unlikely to produce such cross-income class neighboring, while at the same time the isolation of the more fortunate economic groups was now far removed from the central city. The "monolithic" suburb emerged as the structure into which people were sorted.

A New Social Geography

This rise of a distinct, integrated, and self-conscious suburban culture is certainly one of the two major aspects of postwar social geography in metropolitan areas. The other, the transformation of the core city into a dominantly recent-immigrant reception area, tended in fact to exaggerate the more evolutionary change within the suburban band. What grew up was a striking contrast between the polycultural traditional city and a "nativist" suburban band. Of these two cultural and morphogenetic regions, the suburban was the more visibly apparent, because it was in a state of construction throughout much of its extent and thus physically reflective of the culture of the group resident there. In contrast, the influx of rural people into the traditional city—by blacks from the rural American South and by Hispanics from the rural areas of Middle America—was not immediately reflected in the form of the place. Instead, the changes were more muted there; the color of paint on the trim of tenements and row houses; the visual nature of local retailing; the storage of items of possible future use on stoops, balconies, and fire escapes; and, finally most dominantly, the surface transformation of the outside of buildings built in a different culture, the painting of murals and graffiti on any plane surface. Certainly the individual graffito might serve to delineate the turf of an urban gang, but the multitude and complexity of the paintings on any plane surface was more than this direct assertion of territoriality, it was as well a means by which one culture's urban morphology could be given a new culture's gloss. In Toronto the row houses of the inner city's Chinese quarter are by form indistinguishable from others of the turn-of-the-century city, but the use of very Chinese reds and greens even to disguise the common brick has given the district at least the suggestion of Orientalism.

What we learn from all of this is that cultural groups seek to give to their residential areas a cultural identification. In the postwar metropolis the increasingly "nativist" suburbs, including numbers departing from the ethnic identity of the Little Italy or the Chinatown of the traditional core, have gained an urban morphology that suggests cultural assimilation, with a substitution of a suburban identity for an ethnic one. The ranch house architecture, the automotive transportation for all local needs, a conscious horticulture of established design, the family focus of sport and recreation, and a number of other recent innovations have distinguished the suburb for all residents of whatever original ethnicity. The Chinese quarters of San Francisco, owing considerably to the continuing influx of immigrants, have the Oriental gloss; those of suburban El Cerrito in the East Bay at most indicate the houses of Chinese-Americans by a bonzai or two next to the carefully swept sidewalk and the Mercedes in the driveway. The simple truth is that in most suburban situations what residents seem to seek is geographical rather than ethnic community, to be distinguishable from the metropolitan mass by income class and the cultural and material attributes thereof rather than by ethnic origin.

Ethnicity Shapes the Core City

In contrast is the situation in the traditional core city, where economic class plays its part but there is as well a strong component of isolation from a native culture. Those living there might be seen as having two constraints on their inability to melt unobtrusively into the family-structured middle-class life of the suburbs have restricted residential integration even where formal segregation has been abolished. And, unfortunately, that attempt to exclude black families from suburban areas is still strong in metropolitan areas. The result is not that blacks are totally restricted to their original reception area in the traditional core, though far too many seem hopelessly lodged there, but rather that their difficulty in gaining acculturation and a social form of security in the general suburbs persists. For that reason blacks have tended to seek socially specialized suburbs, those largely populated by other blacks. Black American subculture is carried outward into the suburban band intact affording to that group a social sense of security that many formerly "ethnic" groups find otherwise when they are able to become immersed within the nativist general suburb where geographical community comes to replace that of race and ethnicity.

areas. The result is not that blacks are totally restricted to their original reception area in the traditional core, though far too many seem hopelessly lodged there, but rather that their difficulty in gaining acculturation and a social form of security in the general suburbs persists. For that reason blacks have tended to seek socially specialized suburbs, those largely populated by other blacks such that black American subculture is carried outward into the suburban band affording to that group a social sense of security that many formerly "ethnic" groups find when they are able to become immersed in the nativist general suburb where geographical community comes to replace that of race and ethnicity.

Obviously, this distinction between the black suburb and the more culturally general one is neater than full truth. Where any large grouping of families drawn from a once strong ethnicly identified cluster moves into a nativist suburb, there will remain an ethnic or specific cultural system that operates culturally alongside that geographic community. In the case of El Cerrito, California, already noted as a large center for Chinese-American suburbanization, there seems to be a geographical community—that of a general suburbanization with its associated urban morphology and material culture—as well as a number of intersecting cultural systems, of probably declining force, that tie individual families in the town outward to earlier reception areas where geographical community and cultural system are coterminous. In El Cerrito's case those reception areas were both Oakland's Chinatown and San Francisco's. What this tells us is that there are two aspects of suburban location: that precise one of geographical community and often as well one of "location" within a more spatially extensive cultural system. If history is a guide, the impact of geographical community will, over ensuing years or even more generations, strengthen whereas that of cultural system will tend to decline.

Geographical Community and Cultural System

At this juncture it seems desirable to point out that the cultural practice of urbanization has always had these two elements at work, geographical community and cultural system. In traditional societies they have tended toward a uniformity in the impact of cultural system, with the main distinctions among cities showing up in the geographical community, which clearly is distinct to each major city. Only as cultural systems that originated outside that traditional society are projected within it does cultural system come to produce differences among cities of a single country. Thus, in strongly traditional cultures, such as France, contrasts among the nation's cities were largely geographically rather than culturally induced. But in recent decades the large but geographically selective influx of Arabs from North Africa has created greater cultural diversity in cities where they converge, such as Paris and Marseille; most French metropolises are still traditional in social complexion, but a few have become quite polyglot. Britain was also throughout most of its history a country of traditional culture in the cities. But in the nineteenth century a large Irish in-migration began to change some of those larger places, particularly Liverpool, Manchester, and Birmingham. Since 1945 that introduction of a cultural system with external roots has grown both in complexity of sources and in numbers. West Yorkshire has become tied to an Indian-Pakistani cultural system; Bedford and parts of the Home Counties to an Italian source region; and much of Scotland, surprisingly, to an American cultural system.

It has been characteristic of this introduction of externally based cultural systems that the first impact has come in cities rather than the countryside. Only in the New Lands of the nineteenth century—most dominantly in the United States but as well Canada, Australia, and South Africa—was there much intrusion of external cultural systems in rural life. Canada was particularly distinctive in this matter because of its adoption of the notion of group settlement advanced in the years at the turn of the century by the interior minister, Clifford Sifton. On the Prairies large blocks of land came to be associated with external cultural systems, most notably the Ukrainians but also the Mennonites, the Icelanders, and great numbers of Americans. With the closing of the settlement frontier, by 1890 in the United States and by the late 1920s in Canada, there has been little chance for subsequent floods of immigrants to shape such rural culture regions. All immigrants, whether in the countryside or in the city, bring with them such cultural systems but they tend to preserve them only where clustering of families from a particular cultural system takes place. In the city any persistent clustering within the reception area usually preserves elements from the external system, as was the case where group settlement took place in the countryside. Once families move to the nativist suburbs, however, most ties to an external cultural system decline, and residents there come increasingly to adhere to their geographical community with its composite culture.

Not all suburbs, fundamentally a morphological designation, show this dominance of the geographical community over the externalized cultural system. Where the geographical community is coextensive with a single

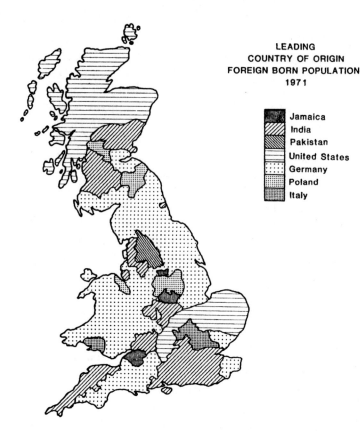

The clustering of immigrant population, particularly around international airports, is demonstrated on this map. Elsewhere in Britain the principal immigrant group is either American (where NATO forces or petroleum workers are involved) or German (where relatively prosperous and skilled worker migrants have come).

**LEADING
COUNTRY OF ORIGIN
FOREIGN BORN POPULATION
1971**

Jamaica
India
Pakistan
United States
Germany
Poland
Italy

cultural system, as is commonly characteristic of black and Hispanic-American suburbs, this adherence to the composite suburban culture is far less rapid or complete. For that reason we should distinguish between the two expressions of suburbanism: the general, nativist suburb and the specialized, normally ethnic suburb. The geographical community affects both, but far less strongly the specialized areas. Thus, in the general comments about suburbs to which we now turn, the impact on specialized suburbs will be much reduced or even absent.

The Postwar Suburb: Phase One, Up to 1960

For some fifteen to twenty years after the close of World War II, the American metropolis was in a highly transitional state; the automobile had effectively revolutionized the morphology of housing in those cities, whereas the location of economic activities changed at a more deliberate pace and in a more evolutionary way. Because housing had shifted so radically, even with a much less transformed workplace pattern, the automotive journey-to-work had become vastly widespread. Once large numbers of families lived in postwar suburbs—those built without any geographical reference to public forms of transportation other than, possibly, the expressways hammered together in the late 1930s and again in the late 1940s—most employed members of those families had to depend on driving to get to work.

**The
Continuing City**

It takes little imagination to see that once workers are converging on a workplace by private, commonly individual cars, the former constraints exercised on workplace location by public transportation decline in force. But it takes time for the balance to shift. At the beginning of the postwar period there was still a large enough group using public transit to have a bearing on the pattern of worker convergence. The geography of both the labor-shed and the employment field would reflect the formerly commanding role played by public transportation.[1] But as the numbers of those driving to work increased, any plans to enlarge or modernize a manufacturing or wholesaling establishment would be likely to raise the question of movement to open, peripheral, larger sites normally unserved by public transit. Were such a shift to be made, all workers would then be forced to adopt automotive commuting to maintain their employment, and the dominance of the car in the suburbs would have become yet more complete.

The increasing use of the car for commuting meant that all working members in a family were likely to own one, further distinguishing the suburban lifestyle from that of persons living and working in the traditional city core. Once employers could count on individually mobile workers, many firms found that their labor-sheds now excluded the potential working population of the traditional core. Once employers could count on individually mobile workers, many firms found that their labor-sheds now excluded the potential working population of the traditional core. In this way what had begun as a morphologically induced supplement to the traditional lines of daily movement in cities had come to dominate, in the long run putting those living in the traditional city at a great disadvantage in securing jobs. At this juncture we can see that what had begun as a transition had come to rule as the dynamic force in cities. At that point the fully evolved city of our experience came into existence, and we may perceive in sharp focus not only a second phase of the postwar suburb, but a second phase of the geography of economic activity in postwar metropolitan areas.

The Immediate Postwar Model of the Central Business District

A considerable transformation had occurred by the close of this transition stage, extending from 1945 to the early 1960s, but the overall form of the metropolis had been maintained. That form was still quite intelligible in terms of the interwar model of metropolitan morphology outlined at the conclusion of the last chapter. There was one dominant center of business activity, still very truly a central business district, which comprehended both the most diverse and largest shopping area in the metropolis and the vastly dominant cluster of office buildings conjoined with any financial district that the city might possess. This central business district still lay at the point of initiation of the city, adjacent to its port or original railroad station, and was surrounded by a frame of wholesaling and light industrial buildings.

1. For a discussion of the nature and evolution of labor-sheds and employment fields, see James E. Vance, Jr., "Labor-Shed, Employment Field, and Dynamic Analysis in Urban Geography," *Economic Geography* 36 (1960).

Radiating from the core there were commonly sectors of higher-income housing that had declined in social cachet, and land value, to become a seedbed for various types of shops and offices. These were the ones gaining financial advantage from locating at the site of reasonably available customer parking on or adjacent to a major arterial street leading between the outlying middle-class suburbs and the downtown. In the sector extending outward to the higher-income suburbs, there was likely to be a lot-by-modular-lot substitution of several-story apartmented houses for what had previously been large individual-family houses. Also within the core frame, and in the wake of the shift of the boundary of the central business district as it moved caterpillar-like in the direction of the higher-income suburbs, were reuses of what had been central retailing and wholesaling activities. Because this zone of abandonment lay in the direction of the city's point of initiation, it was here that the earlier hotels and wholesale-retail establishments lay. These tended to be other sites and structures abandoned by their original proprietors, being sold to those who might still operate a business in a zone of decline. Hotels there became little more than cheap rooming houses, while stores descended in style, class of goods, and general quality. Army-and-Navy stores selling work clothing replaced moderate-price but style-conscious clothiers. Housewares and dry goods stores were replaced by establishments selling on credit cheap furniture, fire-damaged goods, and other distressed merchandise. Because the frame surrounding the city core was by location a zone of transition—from higher to lower uses in the wake of the shift in the central business district boundaries and from residential to commercial in the van of that movement. The period after 1945, when the fundamental geographical structure of the metropolitan area as a whole was being reshaped, was a time for which it is hard to establish a representative model of land use. At the beginning of the transition period and for perhaps a decade (1945–54) there seems to have been active assimilation of land in the van of the central business district shift for that set of land uses benefiting from easier parking and still cheaper sites than in the heart of the district. In turn, the land given up by the more important central district uses still seemed to find renters who could maintain themselves in business in these economically inferior sites. During this period the sites within the heart of the central business district seemed to maintain their value, for there was no widely held view that the central business district was about to lose much of its importance for general-merchandise shopping.[2]

The complex and, in the early 1950s, stable structure of the American central business district attested to the functional health of that land-use district. Most cities of a hundred thousand or more population had two or even three downtown department stores and a considerable choice of specialty shops ranged between and around them. It proved possible to estab-

2. This and the following paragraphs are based on an extended period of field research on that I carried out as the principal investigator in a project, with Raymond E. Murphy, to establish the nature, extent, limits, and internal structure of the central business districts of American cities. Raymond E. Murphy, James E. Vance, Jr., and Bart J. Epstein, *Central Business District Studies* (Worcester, Mass.: Clark University, 1955); also available in article form in *Economic Geography* 30–31.

lish normative relationships for the district surrounding the "100 percent location," the point within the district where land values were highest because it was there that pedestrian flow was greatest. The stores precisely at the 100 percent location were commonly small in size and most highly dependent on impulse shopping drawn from persons within the peak flow of shoppers. Cigar stores, men's shirt stores, candy shops, newsstands, and other small but intensely patronized stores were placed as close to the pedestrian peak as possible, substituting extremely high rents for newspaper advertising costs. It was the department stores that brought shoppers into the center, both by their size and diversity and by their very heavy advertising budgets aimed at bringing in shoppers for a particular good and garnering their attention for many other goods. It was this magnet quality of the department store that tended to give a modular physical form to the central business district.

In that modular form the department stores and the shops associated with them lay at the heart of the shopping district. Shoe stores, women's dress, skirt, and blouse shops, five-and-ten-cent stores, and other general-merchandise stores occupied a number of blocks clustered tightly around the 100 percent location.

The Office Subdistrict

The second major focus in the downtown was an office subdistrict. In the late nineteenth century shops tended to occupy the ground floors in the city's heart, whereas offices occupied several stories above the ground floor. But just as shops became larger, particularly those that were becoming department stores, so did office firms and the structures built to house them. With the widespread adoption of elevators after the Civil War—in part when the hydraulic plunger lift was developed that permitted relatively low lift but with big cars capable of holding numbers of people—department stores in particular grew to five to ten stories in height, and some other shops began to occupy several upper stories. At that point the piling of offices on top of shops became impractical, except in the smaller cities. The result was the creation of a bicentric central business district.

Once office districts began to develop, those quarters gained an internal structure of their own. The highest land values remained within the shopping quarter, but within the office quarter there was a secondary peak, commonly at a major intersection and rapidly becoming the site for the larger and more prestigious banks of the city. Because banks were permitted to count their buildings as part of their assets, those structures were commonly large, impressive, and prominently located. This quality of prominence and prestige could earn further money for the bankers involved if they built an office building above their banking room, using the ever-improving elevators to gain access to upper-story offices. Once recourse was made to elevators, the meaning of "location" in the heart of the city was transformed. At first only a few hundreds or thousands of square feet were provided in office buildings, but by the time of World War I the first truly large buildings were being attempted, and were proving good investments. In 1908, when the southern

In 1973 the twin towers of the World Trade Center replaced the Hudson Terminal and other structures at the site of the terminal of the Hudson-Manhattan Tubes (later PATH). At 110 stories these are the world's second tallest and, at 9.5 million square feet, largest office buildings. In the right foreground is the Woolworth Building, which at sixty-two stories was the tallest in the world from 1913 till 1930. The great difference in bulk of the signal buildings of these two eras is clear. Photo: Port Authority of New York and New Jersey.

tunnels of the Hudson-Manhattan Tubes were being completed, two massive office buildings at 30 and 50 Church Street in Lower Manhattan were completed, connected by bridges above the street and housing an office population of some ten thousand workers. These connected structures, the Hudson Terminal Buildings of 1909, were perhaps the first giant office erections made possible by the large site on which they were raised, which had been cleared to facilitate the construction of the southern Hudson-Manhattan Tube for the use of travelers to and from the ranked railroad terminals housing the "western" railroads that then reached only to the New Jersey shore of the Hudson River. With twenty-two stories above ground and four below, this was one of the earliest structures to contain more than a million square feet.

Such massive buildings had been anticipated by H. H. Richardson's seminally important design for a wholesale house for Marshall Field in Chicago, built between 1885 and 1887. But because cities had grown rapidly during the second half of the nineteenth century, large sites, such as that made available through the construction of the Hudson-Manhattan Tubes, became very scarce. Instead, an increase in the rental space of a structure tended to imply the adoption of an ever-increasing height for a building constructed on a fairly traditional lot, or at most several adjacent traditional lots. The test of this notion is, in fact, provided by the fate of the Hudson Terminal Buildings. When the Port Authority of New York and New Jersey took over ownership and operation of the Tubes in the postwar years, that superdevelopment agency appreciated that the fifty-year-old buildings were no longer prime rental structures. The site remained commodious, but a structure of twenty-two stories was out of date in Lower Manhattan. By the years after World War II, the accommodation provided in financial districts was more vertical than horizontal. The 22-story structures were replaced by another pair, the World Trade Center, but this time 110 stories in height and themselves covering a much smaller proportion of the lot made available by the razing of the Hudson Terminal Buildings. As opened in 1974, the World Trade Center buildings comprised more than four million square feet, far more than the massive turn-of-the-century buildings they replaced, and with much more open usage of the site.

The Modular Lot and the Skyscraper

Because the financial and office section of the central business district commonly occupies a significant part of the traditional city, or even all of it, the platting of blocks and lots there tends to perpetuate the urban modality of the first decades of a city's existence. American cities, as we have seen, have largely followed the speculator's pattern as first worked out in detail in Philadelphia at the end of the seventeenth century, a model that tended toward the creation of myriad small lots. Thus, any simple replacement of older by newer buildings has forced upon the substitute a smaller modular ground plan than its owners might have wished. Even where the assemblage of those smaller lots was undertaken, the trouble introduced by that small module meant that the chance of obtaining truly extensive parcels was slim. In most cases it would be far easier to develop building technology to expand the size of buildings rather than attempt to secure larger ground sites. The key was, of course, found in the development of a safe and practical elevator. Elisha Graves Otis accomplished that feat in the 1850s, and in 1857 the first relatively safe passenger elevator was installed in the H. V. Haughwout store in New York. With this easier access to upper stories, for some thirty years the increase in the height of buildings relied almost entirely on the pushing of traditional masonry construction to its limits, probably reached in the 1880s when Chicago witnessed the construction of several "ultimately" tall masonry office buildings. The Montauk Building of ten stories was opened in 1881 on what would have been a fairly modest traditional lot of seventy by ninety feet. In this construction the fundamental technical advance was made—the creation of a "floating raft" beneath the structure's foundation to carry the heavy dead load brought on by high and thick masonry walls—that permitted the Chicago skyscraper to emerge. In 1891 the apogee of masonry construction seems to have been reached with the completion of the still-standing Monadnock Building of sixteen stories. The great nineteenth-century architect Louis Sullivan called it "an amazing cliff of brickwork, rising sheer and stark, with a subtlety of line and surface, a direct singleness of purpose, that gives one the thrill of romance. It is the first and last work of

The Monadnock Building in Chicago, built in 1891, shown in this gravure published ca. 1893–94, was the tallest office structure built with weight-bearing walls and, at sixteen stories, the culmination of millennia of traditional building practice. It fortunately survives. By permission of the Chicago Historical Society.

its kind; a great work in its day."[3] But unfortunately, on the small lots of Chicago's Loop, with its poor bearing soil of deep clay, heavy masonry could be carried no higher, thus limiting the size of buildings at a time when both investors and occupants wished for larger structures. The floating raft improved on the foundations by increasing the bearing capacity, and it waited upon a lighter substitute for solid masonry to allow structures above some sixteen stories.

The Steel-Cage Structure

The problem of height was twofold: masonry weight-bearing walls had to become increasingly thick in the lower stories to carry the massive dead load of many upper stories (five hundred or more feet), but they were little more than almost solid columns of building stone with little usable interior space. The office building could hardly be that. The ground-floor walls of the Monadnock Building were seventy-two inches thick, restricting the interior space in a building occupying a rather modest traditional lot. But already there was a technology that could help solve these constraints. William Le Baron Jenney had, six years before, designed the Home Insurance Building,

3. Quoted in Harold M. Mayer and Richard C. Wade, *Chicago: Growth of a Metropolis* (Chicago: University of Chicago Press, 1969), p. 130.

a structure that introduced the iron and steel cage to construction. When the building was opened in 1884–85, it was ten stories high on a lot 148 feet on La Salle Street and 96 feet on Adams Street, reaching to a height of 160 feet.[4] With some hundred and thirty thousand square feet of floor space, the Home Insurance Building was one of the larger office buildings in the United States in the early 1890s. Even more, its structure was radically innovative with an interior iron and steel cage of posts and beams enclosed from the elements by no more than a hung curtain wall. A contemporary commented that "while [Jenny] felt he was contributing to the making of new architectural forms, that was not his motive. . . . His main purpose was to create structural features which increased the effective floor areas and made it possible to secure more daylight within the building"[5] (because the mullions between the windows could be reduced drastically, since they did little more than give stiffening to the curtain wall). These mullions now bore no weight other than that of the vast structure's skin.

It was this steel-cage "Chicago building" that set the stage for a fundamental transformation of the financial and office district in cities. Not only did that technology allow the economic use of far more of the enclosed space than had masonry, but it also allowed for the subsequent heightening of the

4. *Industrial Chicago: The Building Trades* (Chicago: Goodspeed, 1891), p. 183.
5. Quoted in Mayer and Wade, *Chicago*, p. 129.

structure, as was accomplished in the Home Insurance Building in the 1890s. From the freedom this technology offered from interfering with the established foundations of adjacent buildings a further advantage: concentrating the weight bearing of a building on piers interior to the structure. Now the periphery of the structure was cantilivered out from its interior and could be almost as easily attached from inside as constructed from outside. It was now possible to envision a city of closely packed tall buildings permitting a reasonably spacious accommodation of numbers previously thought impossible.

Chicago went on to shape the logical economic response to its pioneering of foundations and weight-bearing steel skeletons. As a recent architectural historian has noted, "The new buildings of Chicago were not constructed by the city, by religious organizations, by educational institutions, or by private groups as palatial edifices. They were built by businessmen and they were built for profit. Even the Auditorium, which was the civic and cultural center of Chicago for many years, was built to make money. It was a civic center, a hotel, and an office building. It was financed like any other business venture on the expectation of profit."[6] It was in what the last century was called the Garden City that the modern office building, in its technical and economic qualities, was worked out for others to copy.

New York Adopts the Skyscraper

Common parlance has frequently called the modern office building the "Chicago skyscraper," and that it certainly became, but in the beginning it was not so much the distinction of height that compelled the type of structure as much as it was the demands for economically viable construction in the densely occupied and traditionally parceled core. The world's quintessential nineteenth-century city, Chicago, produced this profitable office building, an element of urban morphology unknown save for governmental structures before the last century. That the office building became in the end a skyscraper required more than the Chicago experience, important as it was. New York City—particularly in its financial and office district, which essentially came to occupy the full area of the colonial city—was more characterized by small and somewhat irregular lots at the core than was the Prairie metropolis with its regular speculator's grid of the 1830s. Thus, when New York City grew with the rest of the country in the first half of the last century, owners of central lots there envisioned gaining more rentable space by adding more floors of offices. New York had been the nursery of the elevator and now, possessed of the idea of steel-cage construction learned from Chicago architects, it began to work out the evolution of a "skyscraper." At first there was little difference between the two cities. Chicago had its ten-story Home Insurance Building in 1884–85 and New York its eleven-story Tower Building at 50 Broadway in 1889. New Yorkers seemed to lack the courage of the residents of the city of the large shoulders: Bradford L.

6. Hugh Dalziel Duncan, introduction to Arthur Siegel, ed., *Chicago's Famous Buildings* (Chicago: University of Chicago Press, 1965), p. 8.

Gilbert, the architect of the Tower Building, had to occupy the top floor of his structure to convince New Yorkers that his design was safe.[7] No case can be made for the birth of the skyscraper in New York, but certainly the morphological component had its adolescence there, just as it now has its maturity in what has come to be called the Windy City.

What gave that adolescence to New York was probably the traditional colonial layout of the office district. Small lots meant that height was first introduced mainly to gain more units of rentable space. But in the competitive market of office-building rental, height came rapidly to have its own justification. Particularly where there was a direct tie between a specific building and a particular tenant, or owner, the general sales appeal of having a taller or the tallest building caused competitive incrementation. The Tower Building in New York retained its ultimate distinction for only a short time, allowing the decades bracketing the turn of the century to become a time of sometimes annual shifts in the distinction of being in the tallest building in New York, and commonly the world. In 1890 the *New York World* Building on Park Row gained the title of world's tallest with twenty-six stories and a gold dome in the finely dressed form that came to be associated with its architect, George B. Post. By the late 1890s a less elegant St. Paul Building, again by Post, with twenty-five rental stories, became the tallest. The pace continued: in 1908 the Singer Sewing Machine Company's narrow tower pushed height over area, reaching to 612 feet to become the world's tallest, only to lose that distinction eighteen months later to the Metropolitan Life Tower, 693 feet, finished in 1909. In 1913 Frank Woolworth gained a long hold on the title

7. Gerard R. Wolfe, *New York: A Guide to the Metropolis, Walking Tours of Architecture and History* (New York: New York University Press, 1975), p. 12.

(for seventeen years), until the thousand-foot office building arrived in the early 1930s, with Cass Gilbert's sixty-story, 729-foot Woolworth Building. Meanwhile, a considerable number of buildings of five hundred feet or more were constructed in New York City, with a few elsewhere. This race for height tended to produce buildings that were distinctively tall and narrow, commonly built on fairly small sites.

The original Equitable Building in Manhattan, at 120 Broadway, represented a large building for its time (1870) at five stories, and was the first office building anywhere to be served by an elevator to reach its upper stories.

In contrast was the more massive building, often quite high but more notable for sheer bulk. The classic example was the Equitable Building in New York City. The second Equitable Building, one of the first large structures associated with the insurance industry, as well as the investment of the large funds these companies controlled, was built in 1872 with masonry-supported walls and the first elevator ever installed in an office building. When the building burned in January, 1912, the now much larger company replaced it in kind with a forty-two-story structure without any setbacks, using the entire one-acre lot to house a 1.2-million-square-foot office building, some thirty times the lot area. Today, even in New York City the ratio can rise only to twelve times, the result of the public outcry engendered by the Equitable Building.[8] Whereas the skyscraper had first been introduced to gain more rental space for structures built on small lots, it subsequently became an instrument of gaining prestige as "the tallest." But with the adoption of height limits beginning about the turn of the century, it became as well a device for trying to stave off the charge of excessive crowding onto

8. Ibid., pp. 9–10. In Boston the Westminster Hotel, which exceeded the height code adopted at this time, was forced to remove its top story to fall within the height limits of a hundred feet. Col. W. A. Starrett, *Skyscrapers, and the Men Who Build Them* (New York: Charles Scribner's Sons, 1928), p. 102.

After a fire in 1912 destroyed its earlier building, the Equitable Insurance Company constructed a new building of forty-two stories. Opened in 1915, it reshaped American cities. This massive sheer-sided building of 1.2 million square feet, thirty times its ground area, so shocked observers that New York City adopted the notion of setbacks and the ziggurat outline for skyscrapers. This outline became the American norm for the next thirty-five years.

lots by putting significant increments of space in narrow towers that avoided the perception of such overcrowding.

Physical Evolution and Geographical Spread of Skyscrapers

The setback, essentially a design device to overcome the sense of mass and the cutting off of light by walls rising forty or more stories on a small lot, gave to buildings built after World War I a characteristic ziggurat outline rising commonly to a tower of uninhibited height as long as it occupied no more than a quarter of the lot size. The result of 1916 legislation in New York City was a city of stereotypical towers with any sense of mass limited to fairly low structures that did not rise above the first mandated setback height. In such a configuration the tower became the *signum urbis* for the modern American city. But to obtain quite high towers, those rising above thirty to forty stories, larger lots had to be obtained. Thus, in the 1920s and 1930s the new tall buildings became somewhat less concentrated than they had been along the streets of the financial district, Park Row, and Bowling Green. A new siting factor, the availability of larger-than-average lots, began to play a role in the gross morphology of the skyline. Sites in the emergent

The Rise of the
Complex City

Midtown Manhattan office district—brought into more active development by the completion of Pennsylvania Station in 1910 and the opening of a vastly transformed Grand Central Terminal in 1913—were of nineteenth-century origin, and thus were somewhat more regular and capable of collection into larger development parcels than had been the parcels in Lower Manhattan first laid out in colonial times. Particularly where extensive earlier buildings stood, or clearances for railroad improvement took place, these larger nineteenth-century sites were more common. The depression of railroad tracks on both the New Haven-New York Central line to Grand Central and the Pennsylvania-Long Island line through Penn Station eventually afforded a number of extensive sites. The first Waldorf-Astoria Hotel, at Fifth Avenue and 34th Street, was to be replaced by a larger and taller second Waldorf built over a full block on Park Avenue at 49th and 50th streets, a large site made available as "air rights" over the new-covered tracks at a newly electrified Grand Central Terminal. The site of the first Waldorf then could be developed as the location for a new, very tall office tower, for even with setbacks it permitted an economically viable skyscraper.

The 1920s saw very active development in most larger American cities, and even fairly small cities began to have their one "skyscraper" of twenty to twenty-five stories, usually built by a bank and topped out as a fairly small tower. New York City was where most of the innovation in office buildings was occurring. In the Lower Manhattan financial district, sites tended to be smaller as well as far fewer in number. Still, what set out to be in 1929 the world's tallest building, the Bank of Manhattan Company Building (40 Wall Street), topped out at 927 feet when the Chrysler Building then under construction seemed to stop at 925 feet. The Wall Street structure had seventy-one stories as completed, but suddenly after the die was cast for that project the architects for its Midtown rival began erecting a stainless-steel spire above the seventy-seventh floor, which gave it an additional 122 feet and the distinction of being the "world's tallest" building.[9] In these economically overheated times, such a distinction became transitory. The promoters of a tower on the site of the old Waldorf-Astoria on Fifth Avenue had adopted a third locale for a monumental skyscraper—to go along with Wall Street and the immediate environs of Grand Central Terminal where the Chrysler Building had been erected on 42d Street. This was the neighborhood of the then fairly new Pennsylvania Station. The Empire State Building was designed to rise eighty-five stories, gaining a clear edge over not merely 40 Wall Street but also the auto company's entry. And to gain further insurance against a short tenure of the coveted title, measured only in months for the Chrysler Building, a seventeen-story tower was added to the top of the 34th Street project. Topped out at 102 stories, 1,250 feet, in 1931 the Empire State Building was to hold the title for more than forty years. The Depression of the 1930s so shrank the market for office space that almost no tall buildings were built for twenty years. And when the construction of skyscrapers

9. Wolfe, *New York*, pp. 39, 256.

A great race for height broke out in New York City around 1930, when an effort was made to exceed the Woolworth Building as the world's tallest. In 1929 the 40 Wall Street Building (Bank of Manhattan) was completed at 927 feet, outdistancing the Woolworth's 792 feet. By 1930 the Chrysler Building, originally announced at 925 feet, was raised through a stainless steel spire to 1,047 feet, making it the tallest for nine months. But then a columnar top was added to the Empire State Building then under construction, heightening it to 1,250 feet. The Empire State Building held the record between 1931 and 1973, when the World Trade Center towers reached to 1,350 feet, all of it real office space. Architect's drawing, Chrysler Corporation archives.

The Rise of the Complex City

The long history of the Equitable Insurance Company's headquarters is a microcosm of skyscraper history. In 1961 those headquarters were shifted to 1285 Sixth Avenue, where a 750-foot "international style" tower had been constructed, now in the new corporate row of the Avenue of the Americas.

resumed after World War II, it was carried out under quite different geographical and morphological controls.

New York was not the only city to witness this contribution of summitry to the shaping of the office district. After holding the role of innovator in the 1880s and 1890s, Chicago seemed to take a back seat until the 1960s. At the outbreak of war in 1941, the tallest building in Chicago was the Board of Trade at 605 feet, and the last 81 feet of that was no more than a *symbolic statue*. But this city of muscularity did maintain its traditional function of setting goals for wholesaling structures. The eighteen-story Merchandise Mart, completed on the north bank of the Chicago River in 1929–30, was the largest building constructed before the Pentagon in Washington, built early in World War II. With more than four million square feet, the Mart demonstrated that the modern city has the need for large units of space so integrated that it can house a vast cluster of related offices and showrooms.

Most of the larger American cities had twenty- to thirty-story buildings before the war, but only a few reached above that height. Certainly New York and Chicago did. Cincinnati had its Carew Tower of forty-eight floors (574 feet); Cleveland the tallest building outside New York in the fifty-two-story Terminal Tower (708 feet); Hartford the Travelers Insurance Company Tower of thirty-four floors (527 feet); Minneapolis the Foshay Tower of thirty-two stories (447 feet); Pittsburgh the University of Pittsburgh Cathedral of

Learning of forty-two stories (535 feet); and Seattle its 500-foot Smith Tower with forty-two stories. Most of these structures were true towers, a large number of individually rather small floors piled up to considerable heights mainly to create a building of distinction and symbolic importance. In four states that chose to replace their state capitols in the decade of the 1930s—North Dakota, Nebraska, Louisiana, and Oregon—all but the last settled on a skyscraper capitol to do so. There seems to have been the clear perception that, not only symbolically but also functionally, the tower building served well to bring a considerable amount of space into a configuration that was highly efficient for office use.

The Postwar Skyscraper

In the period under broad consideration here, the years after 1945, the skyscraper was one of the components of urban morphology that experienced fairly radical transformation, both in specific architectural expression and in geographical location. Geographically the skyscraper has become much more widely distributed, both within a metropolitan area and in the country as a whole. We have seen that not very many American cities had truly tall buildings before 1945—less than ten had buildings over five hundred feet tall. Since the war, the number of places with at least one five-hundred-foot building as grown considerably. Now there are thirty-six cities in Canada and the United States with office buildings over 500 feet high; seven with buildings over 750 feet (Boston, Chicago, Dallas, Houston, Los Angeles, Minneapolis, New York); and three with office buildings more than 1000 feet tall (Chicago, Houston, and New York). And even more significantly, these buildings are not always located in the core-area financial and office district.

If we accept that the earliest skyscrapers, up to just after the turn of the century, were tall mainly because they represented a way of piling more rental space on a relatively small traditional lot, or of providing a rather commodious building for organizations that needed large units of space within the traditional downtown, then it was within that downtown area that all skyscrapers were to be found. In the second phase of high construction—characterized by the erection of tower buildings such as the Singer, Metropolitan Life, and Woolworth buildings in New York, the Foshay in Minneapolis, the Smith Tower in Seattle, and the Travelers Insurance Tower in Hartford—height in and of itself seems to have been the objective. In several instances these towers were constructed peripheral to the heart of the city and in areas where sites were extensive, certainly ample enough to permit the same interior space to be provided in a lower building. But still, in all these cases the towers were in or directly adjacent to the traditional downtown areas of a particular city. In fact, throughout most of the period of tower building construction—that is, down to the outbreak of World War II—skyscrapers and traditional centrality were closely related, even if the newer structures were built more commonly at the edge of the downtown than at its heart, as would have been the case if simple land values had been the controlling factor, as many still believe.

The Tall Building as a Morphological Need: Skyscrapers outside the Center

The first skyscraper construction outside the downtown began in New York City just after World War I. Then the Midtown section, stretched diagonally between Pennsylvania Station at 32d Street and Seventh Avenue and Grand Central Terminal at 42d Street and Lexington Avenue, rapidly gained importance for the myriad office functions not directly associated with stock-brokering and banking. Company headquarters, publishers, advertising agencies, railroad regional offices, and a wide range of other often large-scale office institutions could gain easier access for themselves in Midtown than they now had in Lower Manhattan, where the appeal had been suburban connections in an era when they were more easily secured by ferryboats than by trains. But after the completion of the Pennsylvania Railroad tunnels to Midtown Manhattan, the building of Penn Station, and the electrification of the New Haven-New York Central lines to the new Grand Central, the newer, and thereby more distant, suburbs were more easily reached by commuter trains directly from Midtown. The rise and growth of this second office district in New York City demonstrated that the constraint of tall buildings to the downtown was a function of where the first tall buildings came into existence rather than any actual functional limitation.

Other cities began very tentative experiments with nontraditional locations for skyscrapers. In Chicago the Wrigley Building, followed by the Tribune and Palmolive towers, showed that the Near Northside on North Michigan Avenue could support tall structures. Boston's Back Bay gained the New England Mutual Insurance Building at this same time, while in Hartford and Springfield, other important insurance centers, very large but somewhat lower insurance company headquarters were constructed away from the heart of the city. Particularly in regard to insurance company headquarters, it became apparent that any considerable height these buildings were given in these outlying locations came more from the desire to cluster together very large units of office space than from the advertising uses of a tall building, as in the Travelers Tower in Hartford, the Metropolitan Life Tower in New York, or the Sun Life Building in Montréal. Certainly by the years after World War II most large insurance headquarters had abandoned the downtown, as had Connecticut General in Hartford, Fireman's Fund in San Francisco, and State Mutual in Worcester, in these cases constructing massive but relatively low office buildings even in rather open country. This trend in the 1960s and 1970s carried many corporate headquarters to suburban or even exurban locations, as for IBM and General Foods in Westchester County north of New York, and a great many manufacturing and retailing companies that had so many branches that the headquarters and manufacturing or selling functions were of necessity separate in location.

The skyscraper spread throughout much of the metropolis. Not merely the central business district but also major subcenters could anticipate having the same sort of single dominant building that small cities might have expected before 1945. When one overlooked a postwar metropolis from the air or an adjacent mountain, ten- to twenty-story buildings became somewhat scattered in their geographical spread, certainly with the dominant cluster in the central business district. The rationale for this scattering seems to have contained two elements: some of the outlying taller buildings were located in the subcenters already noted, while others were somewhat more randomly sited, gaining their height and bulk not from where they stood but rather from the fact that they housed a particular office institution requiring a large block of space conveniently assembled into a single compact building. As those corporate demands for space grew, so did the number of compact skyscrapers built to fulfill that market.

The Advent of the Large Compact Building

The compact office building is not necessarily low in height: rather, it is relatively proportional in height and area per floor. Large buildings might be low, but in the postwar years they were large in area per floor regardless of their height. This situation was the result of a fundamental change in building configuration first worked out in New York City in the 1960s when Lever House and the House of Seagram Building were constructed using a new formula to guard against excess piling up of building volume on a single lot. This was the substitution of open space on the lot for setbacks in the profile of the building. If a sufficient open plaza was left at ground level, a straight-sided structure of considerable height and individual floor areas could be built. In essence the compact building had been substituted for the tower building. With these open plazas it was assumed that the passage of light and air among tall buildings would more than equal that among ziggurat-like structures shaped by setback regulations. As rather large blocks of interior space were now envisioned by most developers, they sought larger lots so that the structure might contain a commercially viable amount of office space. In more recent buildings built in New York City, the floor area of the building must be kept under twelve times the plot area, whereas the Equitable Building of prezoning times (1915) contained more than thirty times its plot size in interior space. [10] Thus, the nine million square feet of the World Trade Center in New York can be contained in two 110-story buildings, each of great internal size, because they occupy a project area of sixteen acres, are separated from their neighbors by a five-acre central plaza, and are buffered by three low structures in the same project.

The creation of the compact building has changed American cities in a little-appreciated way: the volume of office space in our cities has grown much more than the general experience of the central business district would suggest. In the earlier decades of this century, we tended to measure the relative importance of a city by the absolute height and number of taller structures. Even the most massive and tallest of tower buildings of the prewar years, the Empire State Building, had only somewhat more than two million square feet of interior space. Now a good number of cities have million-square-foot office buildings, some of which are not widely known

10. Ibid., p. 10.

The massiveness of office buildings in the later 1980s is shown by the comparison of the Wool-worth Building at the extreme right, the two World Trade Center towers at the center, and the World Financial Center buildings on the waterfront to the left. Photo: Port Authority of New York and New Jersey.

because they are not particularly tall. The tower buildings were the norm for the prewar years, but one structure in particular managed to be different, the R.C.A. Building in Rockefeller Center. Built on a two-acre site, the Empire State Building was forced into adopting a low, five-story plinth surrounding the tower in order to gain the sense of height that the eighty-five-story shaft gave. Even so, about one-third of the interior space of 2,158,000 square feet had to be taken up with elevators and other services. On the more ample twelve-acre site of Rockefeller Center, the R.C.A. Building of 850 feet could rise almost uninterruptedly seventy floors, giving so much space that this structure—known familiarly as the Slab—became the world's largest office building in 1939.[11] It was the R.C.A. Building that further amplified the awareness that truly large structures could be rented, even in specialized activities and in noncentral locations. And in addition, this slab of a structure began the architectural shift away from the tower toward the powerful image of the great compact structure of truly massed interior space.

Technology Encourages the Compact Building

A number of technological and architectural changes that came about in the postwar years encouraged the increasing use of great slab-sided struc-

The Continuing City

11. Federal Writers' Project, *New York City Guide* (New York: Random House, 1939), p. 336.

tures rising in boxy buildings from the ground to flat, and generally un-adorned, roofs. The glass curtain wall was, when first used, a dramatic expression of height and bulk, though it ultimately became a jarring cliché before its use declined with the rise in energy costs in the 1970s. New steels, greater use of reinforced concrete members, almost universal installation of air conditioning and fluorescent lighting, which permitted "daylight-like" conditions deep within the interiors of massive buildings, and the adoption of an open construction with modular verticals widely spaced leaving floor-space use very flexible—all made the "big" as well as the "tall" building economically rewarding. The World Trade Center, already mentioned, was not so very different from much lower structures save for the fact that with its considerable bulk and its great height, 110 stories of equal floor space from ground to roof, special wind bracing was required that was secured in the actual exterior structure of the two towers. The bracing members were mas-sive enough that the fenestration of the towers appeared as relatively small holes seemingly punched into the great slabs of the four simple sides of the buildings. In the currently tallest building in the world, the Sears Tower in Chicago, wind was also a problem, in this case overcome by making the building a bundle of smaller tower-like structures bound together to give the whole structure lateral stability and the tallest of these towers, at 1,454 feet, sufficient wind resistance.

The Rise of the
Complex City

Today's pinnacle, the Sears Tower in Chicago at 1,454 feet. Photo: Hedrich-Blessing, from Sears, Roebuck and Company.

Outlying Office Clusters

The two postwar transformations of the office structure—toward much bulkier buildings and away from absolute concentration within the downtown office and financial district—joined to reshape the geography of office functions. In a number of metropolitan areas major outlying office centers grew up. In St. Louis outlying Clayton, the county seat of St. Louis County, which does not include the city but does basically surround it, there arose an impressive cluster of medium-height office buildings and hotels, located with good access to Lambert Field, the area's main airport, and central to the Missouri core of the metropolitan area. In Buckhead near Atlanta, at several places in Orange County outside Los Angeles, and in Concord and Walnut Creek east of Oakland, truly suburban office districts with tens or even hundreds of thousands of square feet have emerged, providing space for offices of regional or national concerns. The key to their location is usually to be found in superior transportation facilities, freeways for Clayton, Buckhead, and Orange County, the Bay Area Rapid Transit (BART) rail system, as well as freeways at Concord and Walnut Creek, and commuter railroad service in Stamford, Connecticut, and Metropark, New Jersey. In the context of radical transformation of metropolitan structure, which came with the shift toward multicentered and complexly approached functional areas, offices ceased to have one dominant set of location factors, gaining instead such an array of potential locations that even fairly small metropolitan areas would be likely to have several office districts, only one of which would remain in the traditional downtown.

National Spread of Tall Buildings

The same diversity of locations found within the metropolis has also come to characterize the nation as a whole. At the turn of the century Boston, New York, Philadelphia, Baltimore, Cleveland, St. Louis, and Chicago were home to most of the offices serving regional or national functions. Today the range of locations is much greater: San Francisco, Los Angeles, Denver, Seattle, Houston, Dallas, New Orleans, and Atlanta have become nationally important office centers, now with truly tall, and often massive, office buildings in the core, and often with important outlying clusters of such structures as well. If we rank North American cities by the simple measure of the height of their tallest buildings (see table 9.1), we find that in 1985 thirty-five cities in North America had one building or more of five hundred or more feet in height, three hundred buildings in all. If we lower the threshold to four hundred feet in height, normally at least thirty stories, we add another twenty-two cities and some two hundred buildings outside of New York City. That means, again outside New York, that there are about four hundred buildings that would be considered quite tall, and many of the newer examples are also quite commodious. A building of half a million square feet of interior space is no longer highly unusual, any more than one of four hundred feet in height. In addition to the cities listed in table 9.1, Baton Rouge, Dayton, Des Moines, Edmonton, Fort Wayne, Hamilton, (Ontario), Kansas City, Las Vegas, Little Rock, Memphis, Miami, Nashville, Newark, Oakland, Omaha, Providence, Richmond (Virginia), Salt Lake City, San Antonio, Toledo, Vancouver, Winnipeg, and Winston-Salem have such office structures.

It is in the great regional or national financial centers that the very big tall building has found its place, no longer just in New York and Chicago, though they are still the quintessential office metropolises along with Houston, Los Angeles, San Francisco, and Boston. Nearly as important for office functions are Toronto, Dallas, Pittsburgh, Denver, Atlanta, and Montréal. Beyond this dozen cities where the office function takes on national, or at least very major regional, importance come some forty cities with considerable significance to their regions and even in exceptional cases to the national pattern of office activity. Examples of the latter case are Oakland, where the Kaiser Corporation in the 1950s built the largest building then west of Chicago, and subsequently added two more structures twenty-five to twenty-eight stories high considerably for its own occupancy. In Boise in similar fashion several large national corporations have their headquarters in extensive clusters of office space. In large cities the rental market for office space is so large that vast office districts come into being at the core and outlying districts may have hundreds of thousands of square feet in office structures. In smaller cities there may be less demand for rental space, but there may be large institutionalized offices for a single company that re-

The Rise of the
Complex City

═══════════

Table 9.1   Tallest Buildings in North American Cities

City	Tallest Building of 500 Feet or More	Number of Buildings of 500 Feet or More
Chicago	1,455	39 Rank 2
New York	1,350	117 Rank 1
Los Angeles	1,017	13 Rank 6
Houston	1,002	26 Rank 3
Seattle	954	8 Rank 9
Toronto	952	10 Rank 7
Philadelphia	940	8 Rank 9
Dallas	939	18 Rank 4
Hartford	878	4
San Francisco	853	15 Rank 5
Pittsburgh	841	9 Rank 8
Atlanta	825	8 Rank 9
Boston	790	13 Rank 6
Minneapolis	775	6
Miami	764	3
Indianapolis	728	4
Detroit	720	2
Denver	714	6
Cleveland	708	3
New Orleans	697	4
Calgary	689	5
Tulsa	667	4
San Antonio	656	2
St. Louis	630	4
Des Moines	630	1
Kansas City, Mo.	626	3
Milwaukee	625	1
Columbus, O.	624	6
Montréal	624	3
Albany	589	1
Louisville	580	1
Charlotte	580	2
Tampa	577	2
Portland, Ore.	546	3
Litle Rock	546	1
Fort Worth	546	3
Jacksonville	535	1
Buffalo	529	1
Oklahoma City	500	1

361 buildings over 500 feet spread over 39 cities

Source: Newspaper Enterprise Association, *The World Almanac and Book of Facts* (1989), pp. 640–47.

The
Continuing City

quires accommodation, as in Tulsa and Calgary in the oil industry, Hartford and Dallas in insurance, and most cities in banking.

Office functions have certainly grown because of increasing population and economic activity in the United States. Offices also have become far more widespread within metropolitan areas, and in the United States as a whole with the creation of a much clearer regional balance in this country in the years after 1945. In Canada that balance is evolving, though it is still obviously absent in Atlantic Canada, and the national support is sufficiently reduced in size that the scale of office functions calls for fewer and generally smaller buildings. But with the increasing relative position of service activities and trades joined to that greater regional balance, the office function has gained considerably in rank in the use of space in individual cities and has spread widely geographically, becoming a much more significant support for individual cities, and for cities in general.

The Kinesis of Retail Trade since 1945

Each of the functional components of land use in the city has been fundamentally transformed as to location since 1945. We have just seen that even the large office structure has become much less concentrated than it was in its location in the prewar years, leaving us with office clusters or even districts in many places in a large metropolitan area. It should not surprise us, then, that there has been a similar spreading out of the sorts of retailing we previously associated with the downtown areas of cities. In some cities it is still accurate to talk about the central *business* district, but in others what was once so designated has now become more descriptively the central *office* district, with retailing much reduced, often to very specific types of selling associated with office activities and the personnel working in them. Fairly important medium-size towns, such as Mobile, Tulsa, Phoenix, Grand Rapids, and Tacoma, which once had active and extensive areas of downtown retailing—in clothing, general merchandise, and specialty selling— now have been largely abandoned by shops seeking to appeal to the general populace. Even in those medium-size cities still maintaining some downtown general-appeal shopping—Salt Lake City, Sacramento, and Worcester, for example—the relative position of the downtown in total metropolitan sales has dropped radically. In fact from New York City downward there has been this radical transformation, not always to the virtual extinction of core-area selling as in Phoenix, but to the point that any metropolitan area is characterized by a loosening and stretching of the fabric of retail trade as much as it is for other land uses. The major differences found among types of land use are summarized by the statement that for manufacturing and wholesaling the core area has essentially been abandoned, for residence and shopping it has been more abandoned than maintained, and only for office activities has the major mass remained in the center, though even there in all but the few financial-center cities—Boston, New York, Chicago, Seattle, etc.—there is probably more office space outside the downtown than in it.

The view of the central business district as a shopping area presented earlier reflects that land-use district at the summit of its importance. The years since the early 1950s there described have seen the massive relative decline in the area as a shopping district, and in most cities a very considerable absolute decline in retailing land use. Only the very large expansion of financial, service, and legal activities in most downtown areas has kept that part of the city from becoming one of the great open spaces of the metropolis. The number of department stores left in central business districts is greatly reduced. Many traditional firms have simply gone out of existence, often unable to make the investment needed to continue to serve a metropolitan market from a half-dozen or more suburban branches, when before World War II they could serve that market from a single downtown store. Here we should distinguish between the *oriented* movement of retailing, characteristic of the modern history of trade until World War II and the *kinetic* movement since 1945. The peak land-value intersection, the 100 percent location to merchandisers, has moved slowly in cities, commonly starting at or near the original point of attachment of the city to an extensive system of mercantile trade of national or international scale. That attachment came near the docks or the railroad station in inland cities, and as other forms of transportation have been developed the peak intersection has tended to shift slowly in a resolution of forces, one exerted by the point of attachment, others based on the spatial growth of the city, the location of the more prosperous suburbs, the evolution of intra-urban public transportation, and the adoption of individual transport by private car. But the movement of the absolute core of the central business district has been slow, exceptional to that district, and propulsive of the district as a whole. As the core has shifted, so have there been two attached components of this single district, a *zone of discard* in the wake of the shift, which has left areas abandoned by central business functions to go over into skid roads, degraded ad hoc housing, and other indicators of land that has been walked away from by metropolitan-wide retailing. In the van of the shift of the advance of the central business district, in its slow and oriented movement, there has grown up a *zone of assimilation*, where traditionally land was being shifted from residential into retailing and office uses. This zone of assimilation commonly lay on the side of the central business district closest to the upper-income housing areas, that is, in a boundary zone where the generational shift of higher-value housing outward was normally taking place. New kinds of retailing and highly specialized shopping were often found in such a zone of assimilation.

Since the dynamism in central-area retailing largely disappeared—that is, since the early 1960s—this zone of assimilation has changed its function. No longer is assimilation likely to include expansion of retailing. The abandonment of retailing within the entire central business district has been sufficient that new forms of selling can easily find rental space within the central business district. Specialized types of retailing can now afford such central business district space, and find themselves more benefited by the uniqueness of the district than does general-merchandise selling to the metropolitan-wide market. In the past it was at the core that mass selling took place, particularly during the earlier decades of the establishment of the money economy when low and fixed costs of food and shelter tended to take up all but a bit of the family income. Today, with a money economy refined, expanded, and made more diverse over a number of generations, living in that economic fashion, and with a vast physical and morphological metropolis as the home of city people, mass selling now is largely carried out in the suburbs, both for the city people and for those from rural areas turning thence for any diversity of goods.

The Rise of Mass Selling in the Suburbs

The development of the first railroad suburbs at the middle of the nineteenth century introduced retailing into those areas. The simple, repeating, everyday needs had to be satisfied by shops in these emerging residential areas, leaving to central-city trips the securing of goods in less frequent demand and of a more specialized nature. There were corner grocery stores in the city, and there had to be town-center groceries in the suburbs. As commercial bakeries came into use in the late nineteenth century, replacing home baking, both city neighborhoods and suburban town centers gained them. Such was the history for most frequent-purchase sales as they were separated out to become the main business of hardware dealers, dry goods merchants, druggists, and the like. Thus, the evolution of mass-appeal selling of a great variety of goods encompassed both city and suburb. But until the years after World War II a considerable range of mass-appeal goods—those merchandisers tended to call shopping goods as opposed to everyday convenience goods—remained available mainly in the city core. Public transportation was firmly footed on a double base, of commuting to central-city employment from housing in the suburbs and occasional shopping trips to the central business district. As long as women, in particular, had infrequent access to automobiles, this journey-to-shop in the city core was the main way in which suburban families secured clothing, style goods, housewares, and a number of other items usually lumped together as general merchandise.

Cars were already becoming available in the suburbs in the 1920s, perhaps first for husbands shopping on Saturdays, but eventually for wives shopping on weekdays. At first each group may have continued to go to the central business district or its edge, where Sears Roebuck began to build retail stores with adjacent free parking—men's department stores—in the late 1920s. It was the congestion that cars introduced into downtown shopping that began to suggest to merchants and land developers the wisdom of reexamining to geographical mechanics of the whole operation. In seeking to enter the retail store business in the 1920s, Sears Roebuck was doing so from being a major mail-order seller to farms in particular. In that trade Sears had particularly concentrated on sales of machinery, hardware, household and farming goods, work clothing, and similar low-style utility items. The result was that men as much as women engaged in this shopping by mail. When the company sought to supplement mail-order selling with stores, it did so in an era when most men, even those on farms, had access to a car, so the combination of retail store and free off-street parking seemed a natural drawing card for those shoppers and their wives, who might be expected to shop with them. Sears was still quite conservative in its geographical think-

The Rise of the
Complex City

489

ing. The company chose to locate its department store branches at sites with parking but still at the edge of the central business district.[12] The success of this operation encouraged emulation, but in terms of morphogenetic change a more innovative model played an even larger role in reshaping our cities.

Country Club Plaza and the Arrival of the Outlying Shopping Center

That role was the one chosen by a Kansas City real estate developer, Jesse C. Nichols, who better than any other American fully understood the American suburb as it came into being before World War II. Nichols had begun at the turn of the century as a general American entrepreneur, characteristically while still a student at the University of Kansas. Using the money he had earned as a hawker and a newspaper stringer, he spent a summer in Europe, arriving there in archetypal fashion as a hand on a cattle boat. This brought urban morphology to his attention, giving to him a lifelong interest in the complexity and interrelatedness of city life. When he graduated from college, he was given a one-year scholarship to study at Harvard, and there he was influenced by a series of lectures on land economics given by O. M. Sprague. Returning home, he soon managed with others to buy a tract of land at a bankruptcy sale in Kansas City, Kansas. With that start in 1904 he went on to develop over the years much of the area southwest of downtown Kansas City, Missouri, creating the largest integrated private land development in the country. This Country Club District was at first in the typical mode of the time, large tracts of single-family detached houses attached to the downtown by emerging trolley lines. Kansas City had been one of the earlier places where the "sparkers" had been introduced and that, along with the even earlier adoption there of Olmsted's notion of the suburban parkway with its ample width and conscious planning, meant that there was good pre-automobile arterial road development there. It is not surprising, therefore, that the core of the city was being crowded by cars by the time of World War I.

Nichols fully understood what was happening, and that in the future shopping was likely to be increasingly carried out by car. He began quietly buying up land to develop a shopping district located some four miles south of the central business district. It was deliberately not located on a trolley line but it was to be surrounded by apartment houses, which ultimately housed some fifty thousand people, as insurance of localized support for his shopping district, Country Club Plaza, which gave the generic term *plaza* to us for such facilities. In this development 46 percent of the space was taken up with streets and parking facilities, including one of the first parking garages ever built. Country Club Plaza was located at the nexus of a very considerable network of roads, some one hundred miles, that Nichols had had constructed over the years to serve his ever-spreading housing developments. The overriding principle he applied in the development of the Plaza saw him retaining control of the land, which he viewed as a basic resource.

12. Boris Emmet and John E. Jeuck, *Catalogues and Counters: A History of Sears, Roebuck and Company* (Chicago: University of Chicago Press, 1950).

Only through this control would it be possible to bring about good design and direct growth.

Country Club Plaza was officially announced in June 1922, and construction thus began on the first integrated outlying shopping center in American history, and the oldest prototype of what has become widespread in Canada, parts of Latin America, France, and other places in the industrial democracies. Nichols believed,

> Wide streets, squares, and plazas are needed in these days of parking. In many developments of this kind the streets are made almost of uniform width, and as a result in some places there is too much street and in other places too little. We [at Country Club Plaza] make a distinction between a side street, a street and a traffic way. Main traffic ways should have great width, but byways should be wide enough only to give capacity to go from one traffic way to another. . . . The shops are built around a square or plaza . . . and the main streets in commercial areas are 100 to 200 feet in width. [13]

Thus, the distinctive feature of Country Club Plaza, and what gives it such importance in the study of urban morphogenesis, was its full acceptance of the automobile as the fundamental means of getting to and from shopping, for specialty shopping as much as convenience goods. For the former others were very slow in applying that thought to the location and design of mass-appeal shopping facilities beyond the range of daily or frequently repeating demands. This Kansas City shopping center was designed to house some

The first integrated outlying shopping center was opened by the J. C. Nichols Company of Kansas City in 1923. Based on the rapid rise of automobile ownership in the 1920s and the construction of a major real estate development of apartments and houses nearby, Country Club Plaza gave the world both the form and the noun that have come to characterize these centers in the United States and elsewhere. Photo: J. C. Nichols Company archives.

13. Quoted from a speech given by J. C. Nichols to his company associates in 1934. The material in the previous two paragraphs is summarized from the same speech. Source: J. C. Nichols Co.

The Rise of the Complex City

250 shops, and to include one and then several branches of department stores, thus creating direct competition for the shopping facilities in the central business district.

It was only after 1945 that the integrated shopping center in an outlying location became common. In the 1930s department store branches were built in some of the more prosperous suburban town centers—Wellesley and Belmont outside Boston, White Plains and Garden City outside New York, on the Main Line in Philadelphia, and at San Mateo on the San Francisco Peninsula. These were, however, simply accretions to older town cores and, as in the core, individual buildings were commonly owned outright by the department store firm. They did not follow J. C. Nichols's notion that the shopping area should be developed by a single real estate firm, which would continue to own the center in order to control its character. During the early postwar years centers with that nature began to spring up, less in the high-income suburbs where the 1930s department store branches had stood but rather more at points of arterial highway conflux in the middle of the larger increments of tract housing. The suburban band of metropolitan areas increasingly became the home of the general-merchandise shopping that had formerly concentrated in the central business district.

This was not simple substitution of one shopping district for another; instead, it was the substitution of a number of submetropolitan centers for a single district at the center in the traditional core of the city. Where one "main store" had previously sufficed to care for the needs of a metropolis, often in an enormous store with half a million square feet or more of selling space ranged over five to ten stories, after the late 1940s four, six, or even more branches were needed to sell to the same, possibly enlarged metropolitan area. At first the notion was one of substituting the dominant outlying center for the dominant core district—in fact, Omaha had an integrated shopping plaza, called the Center and located according to Christalleran principles near the population center of the metropolitan area, which sought to make such a direct substitution. But experience proved by the late 1950s that seeking to care for shopping-goods selling in the suburbs of necessity introduced the need for a number of shopping centers rather than a single dominant one. By 1960 it was clear that there would be many outlying integrated centers in a large metropolitan area, that they would vary from one to the next reflecting the economic-class orientation of their realm within the metropolis, that they would be merchandised differently from the central district stores, and that they would dominate an area no more than ten miles across.[14]

Postwar Shopping Centers

After World War II a pattern of specialized shopping emerged such as there had been for seventy-five years, but that pattern was now one of limited dispersion of the activity rather than concentration, as had been the case in

14. James E. Vance, Jr., *Capturing the Horizon: The Historical Geography of Transportation since the Transportation Revolution of the Sixteenth Century* (New York: Harper and Row, 1986), pp. 503–18.

the first century of the Industrial Era. Though separated from housing, wholesaling, and manufacturing, shopping was now dispersed in a fairly direct proportion to the geographical spread of residential population. The impact of that general situation on shopping in the central business district was considerable. There was not too large a resident population in the traditional core, and increasingly those living there tended to be recent immigrants to the city, often members of what came to be called the economic underclass, those persons and families living on welfare payments or even the underground economy of petty theft and participation in illicit activities. There was as well in the heart of the metropolis a large daytime population of workers in offices who were potential customers at lunchtime and after work. These two highly polar groups commonly are the consistent support for downtown shopping, producing a notably skewed mix of shops—those selling the cheapest and most basic goods, and those selling the most expensive and specialized—a polarity that has tended to make the central business district a poor site for good middle-class department stores, leaving a number of cities without any example of the traditional magnet that anchored the district for three-quarters of a century. The survivors in the central business district have tended to be highly ethnically oriented or specialty-goods shops selling to downtown white-collar employees. That latter group has in a small number of tourist- and convention-oriented cities—such as San Francisco, Denver, Chicago, Atlanta, Miami, New York, and Boston—received added market weight from tourists and convention goers, enhancing the upper-income-group specialty sales.

The Nature of the Integrated Outlying Shopping Center

The more than forty-year postwar commercial development has meant that by now the location of mass-appeal goods selling is dominantly in the suburbs. It is impossible here to note the hundreds of integrated outlying shopping centers beyond stating a few general characteristics of those places. At first these were built on the long-term arterial streets that had risen to prominence early in the automobile era. Now with the introduction of federal funding for freeway development *within* a metropolitan area, which came with the Interstate Highway Act of 1954, the newer integrated outlying centers tend to be located adjacent to major freeways, desirably at the intersection of two such routes. As noted, the centers do show economic-class orientation to the general economic class of the area in which they are found. Because these centers are controlled by developers who maintain ownership and seek to maximize their returns by sharing in the gross earnings of the shops, low-volume or low-profit shops tend to be weeded out, leaving many kinds of specialty selling in suburban areas to cheaper commercial strips or semiabandoned older town centers. The integrated outlying shopping center houses the middle of the market in types of goods and in price classes. Only in very affluent sectors of the metropolitan area would any specialty shops of unusual nature be found in organized centers. Finally, those centers tend to be the purlieus of the chain store, whether of books, drugs and sundries, shoes, greeting cards, or youth clothing. Because of this

The Rise of the
Complex City

the shopping center has produced not merely a sameness in selling within one metropolis but also a sameness across the country. A few are distinct, as in the West Edmonton Mall with its amusement park, wave-churned swimming beach, "resort hotel," and Parisian street (where they do have *café au lait*, but serve it in a glass). Most malls and plazas within the bounds of North America are the same. It is a specialized land use but a seemingly ubiquitous culture, and the merchandise seems to go with it. [15]

Wholesaling at the Edge of the City

The motor truck came out of World War I as a sturdy and relatively reliable transporter of heavy loads by road. It was the roads that were lacking, so most intercity freight continued to move by rail. Only as a national system of roads was designated and improved through federal investment beginning in the early 1920s did trucking take on any important role in long-distance haulage. But by the 1920s city streets had already been sufficiently improved to permit the distribution of goods and packages within a city or its immediate environs. For that reason it was in this localized environment that the first shifts in the location of wholesaling took place.

The traditional location of wholesaling in the city, since the arrival of railroads, had been near the initial station on the line that first reached the place. The key to that setting seems to have been its role as the easiest place to unload goods arriving by rail, particularly those that might arrive in fairly small shipments filling less than a full boxcar. These less-than-carload lots commonly reached the city in the cars of freight consolidators, those who would lump many small shipments passing between two cities into units sufficiently large to make economic use of a full boxcar. These normally were received at freight stations maintained by the railroad company to which the teams and wagons of the forwarder, or of the local wholesaler or retailer, could go easily to pick up their shipments. In the case of more urgent shipments there were express companies—Adams, American, and Wells Fargo Express the best known among them—which usually maintained their own express offices and even wagons for taking those packages to the consignee within the city. It was this clustering together of freight and express offices, along with possible sidings where full boxcars could be spotted for direct unloading—either on team tracks where those not having sidings could have their car spotted and their wagons and crews come to unload it, or on actual warehouse sidings used only by a specific company—that served to locate the wholesaling district in a city. In the case of wholesalers distributing goods to merchants and institutions outside the city as well as in it, it was important to be near this transportation conflux both for receipt of goods and for further shipment outside the city. As long as wagons had to handle wholesale trade that activity tended to be tightly clustered around the transportation conflux where, to gain more space, they normally built up-

15. This section represents a summation of a paper of mine, "Emerging Patterns of Commercial Structure in American Cities," *Proceedings of the International Geographical Union Symposium in Urban Geography*, Lund Studies in Geography Series No. 24 (1960), pp. 485–518.

ward in height. In the great wholesaling towns of the middle Missouri River valley, along the Richmond and Danville Railroad on its extension to Atlanta, and in the port cities on the Ohio River and Great Lakes in the Middle West, such wholesaling districts were filled with massive buildings sometimes rising to ten stories with masonry-supported floors. The rise of the elevator in the second half of the last century had encouraged this piling up of wholesale trade; the rise of the motor truck after World War I began its dispersion.

It was in those wholesaling operations where intracity distribution was the dominant function that change could first be seen. Goods would be shipped out from the wholesaler by truck, even if those goods that came from beyond the city still arrived at the warehouse by freight train. There were some cases where goods produced within the city were largely distributed within that same city as well. In such a situation trucking became the main form of transportation, leaving the wholesaler free to choose a nonrailside site if he wished. Similar in dynamics was the department store warehouse, particularly for furniture and other bulky items from which purchases must be delivered by the store to the ultimate customers. Thus, in the 1920s there were experiments at nonrailroad locations for wholesalers' warehouses that proved the possibility of a greater choice in location for such establishments than those sited traditionally along the rail lines. During the 1920s and 1930s these truck-based wholesaling sites became more common, though they tended still to depend on the rail shipment of incoming goods. There was some latitude in the siting of warehouses—they might be anywhere within the frame surrounding the city core—but they could hardly stray very far from that core with its convergence of rails and the earlier arterial highways.

After 1945, however, the dynamics changed quickly and radically. By the 1930s intercity motor freight had already taken on some importance. And during that period the superhighway began to make truck distribution from manufacturers to wholesalers increasingly common. With both receipts and dispatches moving by truck, the warehouse in the center had become conditionally unstable in location by the outbreak of the war. After 1945 several changes that had taken place during the war—the vast development of earth-moving machinery during the conflict, the general substitution of truck for rail transport, and the spread of industries out from dense multi-level structures in the traditional core city to single-story factories in the satellite-suburban band—created such a state of disequilibrium in those wholesaling firms remaining in the traditional core area that the outward shift of firms in the first twenty years of post–World War II America was nearly complete. Only office-type wholesaling and that restricted in its customers to those working near the center of the city, or most easily served by customer conflux on the core, remained in that area.

When we seek at this juncture to explain where wholesaling is carried out today in metropolitan areas, we can begin to understand the fundamental role of two location factors: transport by truck, and the new technology of materials handling by pallet and forklift. Much as the truck had gained its first acceptance for haulage during World War I, much wider usage came

The Rise of the
Complex City

495

during World War II when the forwarding of materiel to the front came mainly in great truck convoys. Earth-moving machinery and road-building vehicles were much perfected during the years of the war. Thus, in 1945 the stage was set for a great increase in over-the-road shipment. That change obviously further encouraged the outward movement of trucking firms and of the wholesalers they served so considerably. Junctions of major arterial roads near the edge of the built-up city became common foci for these terminals and warehouses, now increasingly located without specific relationship to rail lines.

At those peripheral sites the buildings themselves were greatly transformed. In the same period when trucks and earth-moving machines were being fundamentally improved the forklift was introduced, the use of which aided in the placing and storing of goods on pallets. The two sturdy horizontal surfaces of a pallet are held apart by narrow cross-pieces that support a load off the floor on the upper surface. A vehicle can insert a tongue-like, tapering beam—usually two, for stability—between the upper and lower surfaces. The vehicle can then lift the pallet load, move about with it, and even raise it to some height and stack several loads. For efficient use of this technology, warehousing had to be reduced to a single level, even though pallets might be stacked to a considerable height. The result was the spatially extensive, single-story warehouse that might cover several acres of land, or even more. Sites for such structures were most easily found, and were cheapest, at the edge of the built-up city.

With trucking and forklifts providing the main mobility in moving goods, the labor input in materials handling was greatly reduced, not only allowing wholesaling to be cheaper to conduct but also allowing it to be carried on peripherally where laborers were not usually very numerous. Those workers themselves now universally had access to private cars for use in their journey-to-work, further facilitating this move to the edge of the metropolis. From having been a quite central land use before the truck and forklift,

wholesaling became characteristically a land use at the edge of the country-side.

There were various types of wholesaling, each with a typical location. Only a few of those may be cited here.[16] Where there had to be a conflux of small merchants on the wholesale establishment—as in purchasing fruits and vegetables by small shop owners or restaurateurs, of records by record dealers, of plumbing fitments and fixtures by independent plumbers, and of auto parts by repair mechanics, for example—the establishments tended to remain in the central area, adjacent to the central business district. As the conflux from the burgeoning suburbs might be quite extended, these stockroom-type warehouses have tended to be replicated in the suburban band as it widens toward the country. Now there are several nuclei for stockroom wholesaling, the outer ones commonly in industrial satellites that have become embedded in this thickening of the suburban band. Much that is wholesaling involves the transfer of mainly the titles to goods, more than the actual commodities themselves. These wholesaling and manufacturers' sale agents tend to cluster in office buildings, the purlieus of office functions. With the rise of supermarket chains the traditional produce wholesaling districts have commonly been abandoned, being replaced by much more peripheral but still organized market developments where fewer customers may congregate but individual orders tend to be greatly enlarged. Today, many goods arrive by air—flowers; fish; soft fruits; specialized replacement parts for cars, trucks, planes, and other machinery; computer supplies; pharmaceuticals—and the wholesalers handling these have tended to cluster near airports.

When we seek a generalization to explain the current location for wholesaling, we find four characteristic locations: of titular wholesaling in general office districts; of stockroom wholesaling in various often one-establishment

A massive nexus of transportation. Here in Oakland were located the termini of two transcontinental railroads: the Southern Pacific in the middle foreground, and the second Western Pacific (now Union Pacific) at the right at the entrance to the Alameda Estuary. One of the major container ports on the West Coast lies before us, as well as major Army and Navy supply depots. Dipping beneath the Seventh Street Container Pier (foreground) is the transbay line of the Bay Area Rapid Transit system. Photo: Port of Oakland.

The Rise of the Complex City

16. For a detailed discussion of wholesaling location, see James E. Vance, Jr., *The Merchant's World: The Geography of Wholesaling* (Englewood Cliffs, N.J.: Prentice-Hall, 1970).

locations spread throughout a large metropolis; of large-scale general wholesaling near freeways toward the edge of the metropolis; and of specialized wholesalers either near the terminus of the transportation bringing in the goods or near a cluster of corporate customers when the goods may be fairly narrowly purchased.

Industry beyond the Satellite

The general outward spreading of land uses that has become common in recent decades began much earlier for manufacturing than for any other activity. In the earlier years of the Industrial Revolution, the need for power forced manufacturing into rural areas, but as close to cities, notably ports, as that power could be found. Thus, as suburbanization got under way in the last century, there was some intermixing of suburban residence and satellitic industrialization. But now there is a genetically quite different form of peripheral industry: that that gravitates to the edge to gain not power—it is much more ubiquitous in this era of electrification—but rather to fullfil other resource requirements more readily available there. As the scale of American manufacturing increased, particularly just after the turn of the century, site demands increased even more. Factories in the nineteenth century, even at waterpower sites, tended to be relatively tall, three to five or even more stories. The reason was that early factories were disproportionately dependent on labor. Machines, though adding to the productivity of the worker, did not do so to the degree that we are used to. Machine tenders, often called tenters in England, had to be numerous, and it was necessary for them to work long hours at low wages if they were going to compete effectively with skilled handworkers. In this situation labor availability was both difficult and critical. Cities tended to afford groups of segmental labor that might be recruited for factory work.[17] As the constraint of power was somewhat relaxed with the substitution of steam for waterpower, the demand for large numbers of tenders drew late-nineteenth-century factories to pools of workers, found more in cities than in the countryside. Combined with the necessary assemblage of materials by rail, this meant central-city factory locations.

Conditions changed when Henry Ford introduced the assembly line in 1913. Prior to that introduction even large automobile factories had been multistory and were commonly found in closely built-up areas. But an assembly line had of necessity to be linear, perhaps turning corners within a huge plant but not rising and descending over many different levels. The flat factory was the result in operations where the assembly line became a critical element in production. By the 1920s electric factories—those employing small electric motors in place of the older, and often cumbersome, plants run by belts and pulleys from a central rotative power source at a large steam engine—became the norm. Those steam-operated factories had to be

17. For a discussion of these earlier periods of industrialization and the concept of segmental labor, see James E. Vance, Jr., "Housing the Worker: Determinative and Contingent Ties in Nineteenth Century Birmingham," *Economic Geography* 43 (1967): 95–127.

made blocky in structure, reducing the linear distance from the single "prime mover" to the various fabricating machines. The individual electric motor and the assembly line meshed very well to permit both the increase in machine use and the single-story factory with its ease of installing machines. Labor productivity went up, wages could rise, and workers could begin to commute more easily to work. In large cities industrial areas sprang up near the edge, in outer Queens in New York City, in Framingham and Lynn near Boston, and at Cicero and East Chicago around Chicago.

Once the factory had arrived at the edge of the city, the motorized journey-to-work became extremely common in factory employment. Workers expected free parking, which added further to the space demands of a large industrial establishment. The drop in the price of cars in the 1920s led to that motorized worker, further strengthening the peripheral spread of factories by making labor plentiful even toward the edge of the city. The adoption of FHA financing for small, suburban, single-family houses further aided this spread of industry in metropolitan areas, because the place where FHA housing could be built most economically because of cheaper land was, similarly, next to the countryside. By the late 1930s almost no new industries were being opened in the traditional factory district toward the center of the city, and many that were there were being shifted to the outer part of the suburban-satellitic band.

Much had to be placed in abeyance during World War II, but industry did not suffer that deferral; where a particular type of production might be deemed nonessential, the firm engaged in it in most instances simply shifted to an essential production. Thus, factories grew, gained new machinery, and in general came out of the war in better condition than when they entered it. That improvement often came from the displacement of the industry into newer and more efficient quarters commonly on an open peripheral site. The only constraint seemed to be the difficulty that workers might have in getting to work when cars and gasoline were in short supply; usually buses or even new trolley lines came in to reach to the new industrial districts.[18] And after 1945 as cars and gas became widely available these outlying plants became the dominant location for manufacturing in the metropolitan area, often as established firms in older traditional factory districts took over wartime factories at the edge that would no longer be needed for war industries.

World War II had a second massive impact on industrial location. Just as it contributed to peripheral spread within the metropolis, the war also led to the dispersal of industry into areas that had lain beyond the manufacturing belt in 1939. The South, Southwest, Far West, and even the Plains area gained plants serving national markets. The nonmanufacturing city increasingly became the exception: all metropolitan areas tended to have significant plants in some industry or other, meaning that the agricultural service center, government city, or wholesaling place largely lacking other economic

18. In the Bay Area the Kaiser shipyards at Richmond were located at the northern edge of the Oakland metropolitan area, while workers' housing had to be found in Oakland and Berkeley as well as in temporary housing built near the yard. To carry those workers to the yards, cars and rail from recently abandoned elevated railway lines were laid down on San Pablo Avenue between Oakland and Richmond, a route previously only of auto travel.

The Rise of the
Complex City

Industry after World War II moved out along freeways. Boston's early circumferential highway, Route 128, became one of the two preeminent centers of high-tech in the United States when it began developing in the 1950s with the factories shown here at Waltham and Weston, Massachusetts. Photo: Massachusetts Department of Public Works, 1985.

activities became quite uncommon. Those previously nonmanufacturing cities, of course, do not have traditional factory districts, but they normally have modern factories at one entrance or another to the metropolitan area. Today, factories show more functional interaction with rail lines than any other land use save those directly related to the operation of rail transportation. But that tie is only very partial. Many kinds of manufacture handle such small quantities of goods, either materials coming in or products leaving, that they can be operated with truck transport. Because of that fact, in the postwar period there have been a number of so-called industrial parks, places with lots of part of an acre or a few acres that could be used for light manufacturing. These divide between developments supplied with rail sidings and those depending entirely on trucking. This distinction exists between those industrial parks that truly house industry and those that are the sites, instead, of wholesaler's warehouses. Where industry of any volume and size of product takes place, it is likely that rail access will be important; where production of little items, possibly with small volumes, and wholesaling dominate, rail access is usually far less necessary. In those industries where trucking serves for transportation, the location conditions of factories and wholesaling warehouses are normally essentially identical. Thus, the industrial park is in actual practice a wholesaling and light industrial development.

Because so many industries today can get by without rail access, their possible locations within a metropolis are legion. Wherever local authorities can be influenced to zone land for industry seems to be a potential site. Old gravel pits, quarries, river flood plains, forest clearings in New England, the edges of small towns in the Middle West, and sagebrush plains near cities in the Southwest all have come to provide industrial space. Labor is assumed to be reasonably mobile—traveling sometimes fifty miles or even more each way in the journey-to-work by car. As farming has given full employment to fewer and fewer families, the farmer himself, his children, and even his wife have come to be employed in factories spread from the edges of the city, through small towns, even into truly open areas. As long as residential areas are located no more than an hour or an hour and a half away from a plant, now individually mobile workers almost universally fill the jobs that are made available.

That worker mobility combines with the postwar decline of regional domination to produce a situation wherein industry is now a national economic activity. This spread has meant that no longer does one section of the country contain most of that manufacture. The rise of the Sunbelt as a factory site has of necessity been accompanied by a similar creation of a Rustbelt in the former manufacturing belt, not so much because all is obsolete there as that, under a greater regional balance, what national production there is will be spread throughout the country rather than restricted to the area bounded by southern Maine, southeastern Minnesota, central Missouri, and Hampton Roads in Virginia, as it was before 1939. Much as the American population has continued to grow and until recently the standard of living has had a long-term rise, that growth has tended increasingly to leak away, not supporting American industry. The improvement in communications and long-distance transportation has meant that just as the formerly "dominated area" of the United States, that section exterior to the manufacturing belt delimited above, has become a home for industry to service the American market, now low-labor-cost areas in other parts of the world, and competing areas of high technology in Japan, France, and Germany, have joined what is now an international manufacturing belt for the American market. To understand this shift, all one must do is reflect on what would happen in Munich, Stuttgart, and a dozen cities in Japan if the American market for automobiles were to be closed to imports. There has been a dogmatic assertion that the United States must seek as much free trade as possible to survive economically. Like a number of economists' assertions, this is an "established truth" that may well be neither established nor true. If there is one group that seems uninformed on geographical realities, it seems to be economists. But for our purposes here it seems that dispersal of industry has been so radical since 1945 that wherever we have urbanization, we now have industry. Even small towns have gained factories, not as they did in the early decades of the Industrial Revolution because of power provision, but rather because of the provision of less costly labor, which has gained a dominant role in the location of domestic industry because communications and transportation have made it so easy to shift that industry "overseas." And economic doctrine has greased the rails for such an international dispersal.

The Rise of the
Complex City

The Loosening of Urban Structure

It is clear that the years since World War II have been characterized by a loosening of the urban fabric to the extent that the real growth of the city has been considerably greater even than the demographic growth, healthy as that may have been. No longer does the term *city* very accurately represent what urban places are like, unless we redefine *city* to include vast suburban, and even exurban, bands of space. A rigid definition of the city including only the incorporated area of the traditional central city would leave us with large numbers of aging and ailing places hardly reflecting the ever-increasing, prospering urbanization of American life. The same would be true of many of the world's cities, as much in Western industrial societies as in the cities of the less developed countries. Cities in most areas are growing strongly; they have quite simply abandoned their traditional form, taking on a radically new one. The real legal structure of urban fabric demonstrates the transformed functional relationships to be found there. Basic land uses remain much as before—there are retailing, wholesaling, manufacturing, and many geographical limits of the now greatly extended city—but their present interactions and characteristic locations are much more geographically dispersed than they were before 1945.

There has been vast area growth, which even without massive population increase has probably caused at least the doubling of the area of most built-up cities. In that more encompassing urban area several fundamental changes in the functional structure have taken place. Most notable of these is the rise of a city of "urban realms" to replace the more characteristically single-centered metropolis of prewar decades. Such a realm is a largely self-contained extensive area within which a mix of land uses is such that daily life can be carried on without normal resort to external locations in other realms. There will always be a turning to other realms for some purposes by those living or working near the boundaries between realms. And for un-usual demands, which can be met only in a single place even within a large metropolitan area, there will be gravitation from all the clustered realms to that specialized location. But for most daily purposes, the realm is that self-sufficient area that cares for an individual's needs. What this says is that increasingly most residents of large metropolises do not make use of the entire urban area, save for exceptional needs; instead, they live and operate within a realm that is geographically confined enough to allow them to function relatively efficiently in spatial terms. Of course, there are always exceptions to such a generalization. There will be individuals who move very widely, who may even commute great distances each day. They prove the existence of a set of realms by standing as notable, and noted, exceptions to the general pattern of daily movements.

The Urban Realm

It is somewhat difficult to determine the order of the introduction of the dynamics of the realm or of the dispersal of functions from their initial locus of development in the city. Certainly, to permit realms to come into existence, with their necessary range of activities sufficient to permit enclosure within a boundary of a daily action system, there had to be a dispersal of formerly central-area functions. Retail trade of general merchandise and shopping goods had to increase in the suburban band to the point that the mass-appeal goods that most families would normally have sought would have been available within the outlying realm. In addition, numerous jobs would have had to be available in that band. The outward shift of wholesaling and manufacturing would have served, along with retailing and office functions, to provide that employment. These necessary preconditions for the successful creation of realms—through the enlargement of once highly dependent suburban and satellitic bands to the point that there was a sufficient "suburban" population to create self-sufficiency in daily activity within several discrete realms—certainly seem to have followed on the original stages of functional dispersal within the whole metropolis.

In 1964 when the notion of urban realms was first proposed,[19] that dispersal had been strongly under way for nearly twenty years, though without any formal acknowledgment of its morphogenetic consequences. In the succeeding twenty-five years, evidence of the existence of urban realms has been found in a number of places, suggesting that the general dispersal of functions throughout the metropolis has caused this evolution of the geographical unit of daily living—the urban realm—to emerge in cities large enough to have several realms. That threshold population figure has never been established through empirical research. General evidence would suggest that populations of more than a quarter of a million within a physically extensive metropolitan area would be required for the emergence of realms. In this preliminary phase of our understanding of the geography of urban realms, there would then be the suggestion that a population figure of perhaps 175,000 to 250,000 is the threshold for a realm. In contrast, the upper limit of population for the realm can be assumed under Walter Christaller's central-place theory, wherein once threshold markets are reached, further subdivision into even smaller and more convenient market areas can be assumed as population grows; in the shaping of realms, the control would seem to be more geographic area than realm population. It seems likely that Manhattan (New York County) is a single realm, even though an equivalent population in a smaller isolated metropolitan area might support several distinct realms. There is no established area, or radial extent, that obtains in all, or even a majority of, urban realms. One may ultimately be discerned. Until it, is the soundest generalization as to area we can come up with is that it seems unlikely that realms will be less than ten to fifteen miles across in flat, open country.

The Early Centers of Urban Realms

The bearing that the rise of urban realms has on land uses within metropolitan areas is direct: once a realm has emerged, there will be a very

19. James E. Vance, Jr., *Geography and Urban Evolution in the San Francisco Bay Area* (Berkeley, Calif.: Institute of Governmental Studies, 1964).

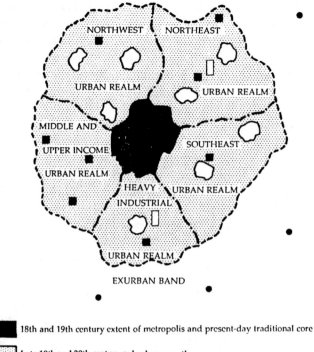

18th and 19th century extent of metropolis and present-day traditional core

Late 19th and 20th century suburban growth

Initially outlying industrial satellite now surrounded by suburbs, often serving
     as administrative center for realm

Post World War II integrated shopping centers

Major professional sports facilities

Free-standing small town

- - - - Edge of built-up metropolis

—·— Inter-realm boundary

strong tendency for each of those realms to have examples of all the major
land uses, even those that in the era of the single-centered city were located
at a single place within the metropolitan city. Thus, the spread of central
business district–like shopping centers in a number of places within the
metropolis should have been anticipated, and can now be explained. As the
formation of realms has progressed, it is significant that such integrated
outlying shopping centers have grown in size and complexity. The first
generation, say 1948 to 1965, saw facilities larger than the suburban-
shopping town centers (such as Wellesley or San Mateo), but not notably so.
Branch department stores had fifty to a hundred thousand square feet, and
there were fairly standardized associated specialty stores selling shoes and
other clothing accessories, as well as a branch general-merchandise store of
the five-and-ten type. In the last twenty years the size and complexity of the
larger realm centers has increased. Two or more department stores are
essential in the regionally dominant center, specialty shops have become
more diversified in retailing, and office functions have taken on increasingly
important roles. These realm centers have in this way come closer in function to the traditional central business district, differing from it in two

important ways: the realm centers have a rather different morphology, being functionally disaggregate, and they serve not the entire metropolis, as did the central business district, but rather the entire realm in less populous examples or a major segment of a realm with a very large population. The disaggregation of buildings has resulted in the specific morphology of the store, reflecting its function and distinguishing retailing structures from office ones.

Given the historical evolution of central business districts, there was an intermixture of shops and offices. Even in the last century crowding in the city core became sufficient that when a retailing function needed only the ground floor, there was a strong likelihood that a second or third floor above a store would be given over to office, or even hotel, use. These "walk-up" facilities have tended to become obsolete, particularly with the secular decline of the central business district as a retailing area. In many cities upper stories other than those of formal office buildings have tended to become relics, with dirty or broken windows and a depressing sense of abandonment. Turning to the early integrated outlying shopping centers, we find that during the first generation of their construction this walk-up component was jettisoned, and most structures within the center were of a single story—except within department store branches where convenience of shopping called for sales on several floors, with escalators bringing that space easily together.

The Mature Outlying Shopping Center

In the second phase of outlying center development, during the last twenty years, and particularly with the emergence of the realm centers, the space within those centers has grown so massively—to be measured in terms of a million or more square feet—that no longer does the spread-out, single-story pattern of shops make much sense. In the central business district there was great resistance to walking more than three or four hundred yards from the peak value intersection; therefore, it should not surprise us that spread-out shopping malls found that the more peripheral shops simply did not do well. To overcome that problem, the two- or even three-story mall, with interconnecting escalators, was introduced. Again, we encounter one of those instances of circularity that is hard to resolve genetically. The multistory mall, which had been fully anticipated by the shopping arcades of the early nineteenth century—such as the splendid Arcade still found in downtown Providence—created more exposure to inclement elements than did its flat predecessor, if unroofed. It took ingenuity to envision covering the now less areally extensive center and, in an era of climate control, air conditioning the whole thing. That move not only made shopping more pleasant, but it finally accomplished the ultimate objective of opening up the fronts of stores so the goods therein might make a direct appeal to passing shoppers. In the 1930s all sorts of curved windows had been used to cut out reflection from plate-glass planes, giving the visual impression of such an opening; in the covered shopping mall, no illusion had to substitute for reality.

In these covered and climate-controlled realm-size shopping malls, the several million square feet of selling space involved did introduce locational differences. Some sites would have more passersby, just as did those near the 100 per cent location in the traditional central business district. But as carefully planned developments, the malls established the practice of putting the strongest magnets for customers, the several department stores, at the ends of the enclosed mall, seemingly arguing that they would be able to draw shoppers to themselves wherever located in the development and, given the common use of comparison shopping among the department stores, would also draw customers the full distance to a second department store, even at the other end of the development. Certainly, this practice of terminating malls with department store branches did force upon their designers some upper limit to the linear distance shoppers could be asked to walk, forcing the adoption of multistory structures with small shops ranged on several levels. The climate control and the ability to have two or even three "street-front" levels reached by galleries—for the first time since medieval Chester in England and the covered arcades of nineteenth-century Brussels, Providence, and London—meant that upper floors beyond the department stores gained retailing value. There probably would have been a separation of retailing and office functions in any event; this emergence of the several "street-front" gallery levels assured that division.

The Rise of Offices in the Suburban Band

There had been offices in the town centers in the suburban band even in the last century. Upstairs over shops there had been physician's, dentist's, attorney's, and other types of offices intending to house professionals serving the local population. With the great reliance on fraternal organizations to provide some primitive form of social security before the coming of Social Security under the New Deal of the 1930s, the rooms of Odd Fellows, Masons, Foresters, and a considerable array of other "orders" helped to fill out these local centers with equally local organizations. Events have conspired to change much of this, leaving the earlier town centers nearly as technologically relict as the central business district. But offices have come to the suburban band in much the form they have evolved into in the core city: now there are often specialized office buildings, with no ground-floor shops even, which rise to a considerable height. The twenty-story office structure in the suburban band is not legion, but, equally, it is not wildly exceptional. As most growth in cities that are economically and socially healthy has come in that suburban band, it should not surprise us that in some metropolitan areas the building of office structures in the outlying realm centers has come at such a rate and with such a size that now there can be more square-footage of offices there than in the remnant central business district. Southfield, Michigan, a twenty-minute drive by freeway from downtown Detroit, now has more office space than that traditional core district.[20]

The rise of these outlying, often realm-center, developments has in the

20. *The New York Times*, August 22, 1986.

quarter of a century or more of evolution made them huge centers of what were the traditional downtown functions. Peter Muller has shown that the Post Oak area of Houston would be the ninth largest "downtown" in the country if it were in a downtown location.[21] In some of these realm centers, such as that at King of Prussia twenty miles west of Philadelphia, where the Pennsylvania Turnpike, the Schuylkill Expressway, and three other arterial highways come together, there are now six department stores—more than in any central business district today. By now it is thought that more office space is to be found in outlying areas than in the downtown areas of American cities. As recently as 1983 the divide for office space was 57 percent downtown and 43 percent outlying, though the majority is now suburban. Rents and availability of qualified workers seem to explain the shift. With space in Manhattan averaging almost $40 per square foot for offices, realm centers and other massive outlying office districts can gain a considerable edge, even with companies serving national markets, not just those from the realm in which they are situated. Returning to Southfield, Michigan, it is found that eighty of the top Fortune 500 companies have offices in that one major outlying center.[22] With twenty-one million square feet of office space, to Detroit's seventeen million, in 1986 the suburban office cluster had two million square feet of space in eleven buildings under construction, whereas none was under way in the core of Detroit. Of course, Detroit had an exceptional and eccentric location for the core of a metropolitan area. Lying on the Detroit River, and thus the international boundary, downtown Detroit had to seek most of its customers in little more than half a circle, the southeastern third lying in Canada. Southfield, lying fifteen miles northwest of downtown Detroit, has access to a full circle of tributary area. While transport by rail ruled, downtown Detroit could remain healthy, but once automotive transport became dominant, an outlying "core" well away from the "blind side" of the Canadian border would gain a great advantage.

Southfield is by no means unique. Clayton outside St. Louis emerged as a realm center earlier in time. The Washington Metro has given Bethesda in Maryland this quality, as BART did a decade earlier in Walnut Creek and Concord in the East Bay. And Southborough, thirty miles west of Boston, gained this realm-center quality not from rapid-transit developments but from lying near the interchanges of the Massachusetts Turnpike, the outer circumferential highway for metropolitan Boston, and the historic Worcester Turnpike already laid out in the first decade of the nineteenth century. The truly large clusters of formerly central-area activities that make up the largest realm centers do emerge where unusually good transport access is at hand. The ordinary realm center will have some offices, certainly more than required to serve the realm itself, but the Capital Beltway, Metropark, Route 128, and other rail-sided outlying megacenters, like the highway-sited ones previously noted, demonstrate that for the truly exceptional realm center to develop, there needs to be good access to more than the realm itself. In truth these megacenters literally replace, or at least replicate, the downtown,

21. Ibid.
22. Ibid.

The Rise of the Complex City

gaining access to long-distance transport as well as local. From a metropolitan airport, say Lambert Field outside St. Louis, it is commonly as easy to reach the megacenter as to reach the downtown—sometimes easier. Thus, business travelers can conduct their business in Clayton fully as easily as in downtown St. Louis. Today it is hard to draw a significant concrete distinction between a Clayton and a St. Louis. In this way we can see how far the evolution of urban realms has come in no more than a quarter of a century. Any notion that urban morphogenesis has lost its impact is fully belied by such events.

Complex Structure of the Suburban Band

In the 1960s it was particularly fashionable among social critics to decry the monotony and regimentation of "life in the suburbs." The denizens of central-city districts largely populated by single-person households, or those of two adults without children, found the prospect of living in family-oriented suburbs socially arid. It was assumed that women held captive in the suburbs during the daytime must suffer great deprivation, and men returning in the evening must do so with no lift to their spirits. The child-centered existence was envisaged as a state as near to puerility as adults were likely to be reduced to. Diversity thus found its refuge in the somewhat bohemian districts of traditional central cities.

This extremely dated and somewhat mythical view of the suburban band tells us how different the realms of the city found in the suburban band are today; also that they were most likely not half as uniform or bovine as the social critics believed them to have been even in the past. Auditoriums for the performance of classical music, and particularly for modern youth music, have been built in this vast band of urban territory. The New York Philharmonic plays in Concord, California, in the East Bay as much as in San Francisco. The branching of state universities and the founding of state colleges and junior colleges have brought higher education to the part of the city where the vast majority of its citizens live. Even in the nineteenth century the railroad suburbs were well provided with colleges—in the environs of Boston, Philadelphia, Chicago, San Francisco, and other large cities. State universities were most commonly first located in the more bucolic environs of a city. It was the middle class that tended to send its sons and daughters to college, and for that class the suburb was the typical home for solid Americans. From 1636 on the American college had more characteristically lain in suburban and small-town America than in its more urban and urbane places. Only in the late nineteenth century, with the rise of true graduate universities—Johns Hopkins, Clark, and Chicago, for example—was there any important reliance on city locations for innovations in education. But on the whole what were or did become suburbs came to house by far the larger number of great universities—Cambridge, Princeton, Pasadena, Palo Alto, and Berkeley serving as examples.

It is in the emergence of a "lifestyle" structuring of residential geography that diversity in the suburbs has become adamantine. There is a widespread misperception that the suburbs arose particularly after World War II. Numerically that notion has some validity, but genetically it has none. We have already noted the railroad suburbs of the middle of the last century, the trolley ones at the turn of this century, and the FHA-automobile suburbs of the 1930s. Thus, even within the suburban band there was a diverse morphology available for potential residents. Even though the largest increments to American suburbia have come since World War II, that growth was never as uniform as the critics would have had it. The price range among housing tracts was always great. Because the generational shift in housing affected the rich upper middle class as well as all segments of the population, new houses of large size were as characteristically found in the suburbs as the small ones of the threshold entrant to suburbia.

The Lifestyle Basis of Suburban Residential Geography

The increasing emphasis on lifestyle has meant that within suburbia there are quite distinctly different groups with particular ways of living. Certainly the family-oriented working- and middle-class housing tracts cover vast areas, though even for these there are variations. Ethnic origin is reflected, without in any way being mandated. Families still tend to buy where their friends and relatives live, narrowing their choice for housing. Churches and schools assume great importance in this strongly familial group, further distinguishing "right" from "wrong" housing decisions. Suburbs may have particular sectors favored by ethnic and religious groups. Most American metropolises have vectors of Jewish settlement radiating outward from the parts of the inner city that were the reception areas for Jewish immigrants at the turn of the century. Some, such as San Francisco, do not have such vectors, leaving us with the interesting question of why. It is easy to argue that discrimination and segregation account for any ethnic vectoring to be found in our cities. It is hard, however, to find that sort of forced location of housing in the patterns of German or Scandinavian housing in the Twin Cities, or in the location of housing clusters for socially and economically dominant groups in other cities. People may have been forced to buy housing in particular areas in the past; but today such clustering is more commonly the geographical expression of a desire within an ethnic group for a particular clustering. This practice, which elsewhere I have referred to as congregation, seems the most widely expressed dynamic in the location of housing throughout North America today.

Congregation, Separation, and Segregation

We now must contend with three forces at work in the location of housing for specific families: there is *congregation*, a clustering of the like-minded, which is certainly the most widespread determinant of where families come to live; *separation*, a force only partially related to ethnicity despite the emphasis in social-geographic writing in the 1980s on "white flight" and other possible explanations of our housing patterns; and *segregation*, that traditional practice, now illegal in the United States, of excluding certain ethnic groups from particular housing locations. Living near families or churches or particular schools, when a voluntary choice, constitutes congregation. It bulks largest as a force shaping housing, because not only does it shape what are strictly social decisions, it also comes into play when we find choices among special "environments" as places to live. Most metropolitan areas today have marina developments, places where natural waterways, or those the products of bulldozers, provide a waterfront site for housing and a place where an individual may have a boat for recreational use. Similar in form are the metropolitan Wyomings, areas on the edges of the metropolis where local zoning and health laws permit the ownership and stabling of horses. There are country-club developments near most cities wherein lovers of the Celtic sport, or at least of its post-competition relaxation, can live on the links.

If congregation dominates our housing choices, clearly separation and segregation are much lesser forces, declining in that order. Separation is probably most evident in the matter of the isolation of economic groups one from another. Starting in the nineteenth century the well-to-do moved out of the heart of the city, probably dominantly to avoid the seemingly intractable scourge of pandemic disease. The rise in an understanding of the nature of disease, and great strides in its control, have made public health separation less of a force today. Instead, separation almost certainly gains its force from a great concern by many people to flee the personal insecurity they see in central cities, particularly as those areas have become the reception area for immigrants and the refuge for groups adopting what are often seen as antisocial lifestyles. Drugs, robbery, theft, and assault reside, in the popular mind, in the traditional core of the metropolis; therefore, protection from them is to be found in separation, in a move to the suburbs, often to those perceived as being highly inhospitable to those groups of individuals seen as practitioners of such antisocial behavior. There are other separations as well—from industry to avoid its pollution, from noise or ambient light, from children as in "adult communities," and from still other things.

Segregation has been known for so long, but now is so rapidly declining, that little can be said about it. Most assuredly segregation did shape a city's housing pattern until very recently, and thus the inheritance remains. Families of blacks live where they do because they were previously made to. That is outright segregation. But when children of those families live in adjacent, outward-trending housing tracts where no segregation has ever been practiced, the force at work is not segregation but rather congregation.

Much more could be said of these three forces generally shaping the residential areas within suburbia. Here it is sufficient to note their existence, and to emphasize that the operation of the three, along with all the other forces of diversification here discussed, means that the suburban band today is as strongly characterized by complexity as is any traditional core of any North American metropolis.[23]

23. For a more detailed discussion of these three forces, see James E. Vance, Jr., "The American City: Workshop for a National Culture," in *Cities of the Nation's Historic Metropolitan Core*, vol. 1, *Contemporary Metropolitan America* (Cambridge, Mass.: Ballinger, 1976), pp. 1–49.

Generational Shifting of Residence

The separation within cities introduced by generational shifting of residence has been carried to a logical extreme in the years since 1945. For the full period of commuting, now more than a hundred years, young couples beginning the formation of a household have often had to move away from the residence of their parents in order to find housing for themselves and at a price they might be able to pay. Thus, there was a generational separation for each commencing generation, obviously mainly among the young. In the postwar decades a similar generational separation has tended to be attached to those reaching retirement age. That statement, though it reads rather simply, is in fact more complex than it seems. The point to be emphasized is the word *retirement*. Until the time of the New Deal, the 1930s, large groups of workers never retired in the sense that we use the term today; they just got old and at some point became physically unable to work. Then, without income in many cases, the elderly had to be cared for by others; those with extended families commonly were thrown upon public, club, or denominational charities. Towns and cities maintained Poor Houses or Poor Farms to care for the old, and fraternal organizations or religious denominations undertook to provide alms for the elderly.

With the advent of Social Security under the New Deal, retirement as a normative element in American life was introduced. Thus, retirement frequently came earlier, when retirees were still active, and able and willing to care for themselves. But in view of the retired person's reduced income, the usually much smaller family at home, and a declining ability to care for real property, a specialized form of residence was increasingly indicated. In the 1930s small apartments, often created by the ad hoc subdivision of large older homes, were the form of retirement housing most commonly found. With the addition of nearly a decade to life expectancy since the early 1930s, the notion of separate retirement communities has grown, often encompassing the relocation of retirees from the metropolitan areas of their working life. Florida, California, and Arizona began to fill with the elderly from other regions, and where such extreme translocation did not take place, nearby retirement developments or towns came to house many of those living beyond their working years. Perhaps the first instances of this creation of development tracts for the retired was in the edge-of-the-suburbs ring where most incrementation to the urban housing supply was to be found. But with little passage of time two newly typical sites came to house the elderly. Those seeking to remain within the broadly extended city commonly moved into a retirement building, frequently operated under a condominium arrangement and located, in a number of cases, adjacent to the now static central business district. Those willing to leave the urban milieu commonly moved to "adult communities" or "retirement communities" built beyond the standard commuting boundary of the metropolis, but still within a reasonable distance for a one-day trip back to a former home. Visiting seldom fills an entire day, so the outer limit for the day visit can be much farther out than that for a daily commute to work. The introduction of retirement thus created at least four new elements in urban morphology. It shaped first the small retirement

Rossmoor, a geriatric housing community near Walnut Creek, California, represents the increasingly common generational housing separation, in this case an enclave physically divided from the normal suburban incorporated towns of Lafayette to the right and Walnut Creek to the left, and protected from intrusion by a suburban housing development with a normal age structure.

apartment as an introductory phase of retirement. This was followed by the rise of retirement suburbs, usually of small houses or low garden apartments. With the ultimate freedom to move away from the location of their life's work, retired persons could take up a new geographical existence, either in small towns somewhat removed from the metropolis, or in another part of the country where there might not be much opportunity for large populations to earn their living but where, through transfer payments, large numbers of retired people might live. In all of these a new morphology of small housing units, commonly with shared, organized recreational facilities, came into being. Many of those small units came to be in the elaborate mobile home that became the ultimate form of the rather flimsy travel trailer of the 1930s.

This shift out of the city was not introduced by the institution of retirement, but it was encouraged in a way that had previously been impossible. To understand what was happening, we need turn our attention to the general practice of creating urbanism and urbanity beyond the morphological edge of the metropolis.

Urbanism beyond the Edge of the City: Exurbia

For more than two thousand years—in fact, since cities first came into existence—Western society has been characterized by a strongly dichotomous attitude toward settlement. In fact, this attitude is doubly divided: there has been a perpetual separation between urban morphology and that of country settlement, and there has been an equal division between metro-

This villa of the Visconti family, located near Abbiategrasso on the Naviglia Grande *outside Milan, was a fifteenth-century* ex urbia.

politan and Arcadian cultural attitudes. In our times, however, these previously almost immutable distinctions have changed fundamentally. Throughout its long history dating back to classical times, the suburb has of course always tended to demonstrate some degree of transition between town and country. The test of suburbanization, however, has been a morphology closer to the city than the country and a culture with the urban component dominant. In geographical terms, beyond the outer edge of the suburbs there might be germs of urbanity in cultural terms, but there seemed to be no morphology suggestive of the city. In the *contado* of medieval Italy and the Home Counties of England, and in large houses elsewhere as well, the urban culture could be found as an exotic element in a native rural life. The Venetians found this pastoral setting for urbanity on the Brenta Riviera, the Parisians along the Loire, and the English in the Dukeries and on the Cheshire and Lancashire Plain. But such tiny germs of intermixture in rural areas hardly transformed rural life for more than a few; fundamental dichotomy ruled most people's lives, in the city as in the countryside.

It was in the nineteenth century that people other than a relict feudal nobility began to enjoy at least the seasonal removal found in the rural-urban dichotomy. It was the artistic community that pioneered the turn by city people to the countryside. Artists and writers in Paris turned first to Passy but later to Barbizon near the Forêt de Fontainebleu, to the Seine Valley below Paris, and to the coast of La Manche. In the United States a similar bohemian quality attached to the seasonal intrusion of city people into rural life. The Hudson Valley, the coast of Maine, Florida, and California all supplied a "sublimity" that painters then sought, and Concord, the White Mountains, and the Berkshire Hills all seemed to provide inspiration to writers. In view of the romanticism so widespread among artists and writers in the last century, it is assumed that suggestive landscapes should draw professional romantics out of the city.

It seems that an additional factor may have influenced this seasonal migration from the city, even in some cases a persistent one throughout the year. The professional artist and writer were among the very small number of persons in the last century who might engage in highly urbane work without living permanently in the city. In modern terms, they were the primordial exurbanites, those who are part of urban society but not geographically tied to the city. The literary community in Hartford—Harriet Beecher Stowe, Mark Twain, Charles Dudley Warner, and others—could exist in this geographical context just as did the Concord sages and the Berkshire persons of letters from Melville to Edith Wharton. Publishers might function in New York and Boston, but good train service between there and literary exurbia provided adequate access for the occasional visits required of published authors. If the countryside and the small town were desirable environments, and they seem to have been from Amherst to Carmel, then authors could write and support themselves in them.

This Barbizon phase of exurbanism was joined by another: the country craving of the wealthy, who clearly could live wherever they wished without worrying about whence the money would come. As early as colonial times some prosperous Boston merchants had had seasonal houses in Milton and other country towns. The building of railroads had made such country-house living possible for a somewhat larger group. The north shores of Long Island and of Boston Bay, the Main Line west of Philadelphia, Westchester and Rockland counties north of New York City, Lake Geneva northwest of Chicago, and the Santee Hills above Charleston all were adopted by the elite of nearby cities for exurban residence. Perhaps the most distinctive of these urban country communities was Tuxedo Park in Rockland County, New York, where Pierre Lorillard spent several million dollars beginning in 1885 to create a "park" for gentlemen with hunting, fishing, one of the older golf courses in America and a four-story "country club" designed by Bruce Price where a modified version of New York's Society could be carried on in the country. Part of that modification came when the formal evening suit of a tail coat was simplified into a shorter black jacket and black velvet vest that came to comprise, with the same trousers, a tuxedo, giving a geographical name to what the British still rather lamely call a dinner jacket, as if a fully formal suit never appeared with food.

Thus, it was the rich and the artistic who began the shaping of a settlement form well removed from the edge of the suburbs but still fully intended for the housing of people periodically needful of the cities' services and institutions and quite culturally tied to things urbane. Time has, as it will in a democracy, simply expanded the group able to have the pleasures of the countryside while still remaining tied to the occasional services of the city and the high level of civilization—the urbanity—that urban places of great size give to their culture.

A number of changes that have taken place since 1945 have widened the group able seasonally to live within the urban economy but still reside for a time beyond the physical limits of the metropolitan area. The summer house or cabin, the so-called second home, has become possible for a larger proportion of the population, both because, at least until the beginning of the 1980s, there has been an improvement in the North American standard of living, and because transportation and communications have been improved. The Interstate Highway System in the United States was put under construction beginning in 1954, creating a long-distance highway network that permitted faster and easier approach to those second homes located outside of metropolitan areas. Telephone communication was well in hand at the beginning of the period, but the elaborated form—using computers interconnected on telephone lines, or sending tapes or disks by mail—is quite recent in development. As long as the country houses of city people remained purely recreational, as they dominantly were in the early postwar years, there was little change in function from what began with the summer resorts of the mid-nineteenth century and the winter resorts developing toward the end of that century.[24] In the postwar years, however, a number of persons began to spend an increasing portion of their time in these country residences, undertaking productive work there in addition to any recreational use they might make of the property. In some occupations this was fairly easily done, as among freelance workers of all sorts—illustrators, editors, writers, researchers, various forms of analysts, composers, and a great number of the self-employed; where they did their actual labor was often open to wide personal choice, though at the same time they had to have occasional access to the central part of the metropolis where those employing them had their offices. Airline pilots and other personnel, who tended to have short and bunched hours of actual work, could also take up a largely exurban life. We cannot here specify all the types of work that could be exurban. It is sufficient to note that the numbers so employed were now of sufficient size to introduce a new component of urban land use into the countryside.

The radical change came when it had to be acknowledged that one could not always tell either the edge of the "city" or the definite nature of its morphology. The colonial farmhouse in Bucks County, Pennsylvania, might as well house a Broadway actor as a Pennsylvania chicken farmer. The same was true for most of Connecticut, much of the Berkshires of Massachusetts, and the counties within a hundred miles of New York, either to the east on Long Island or to the north in the Hudson River Valley and its bordering highlands. A subsection of American fiction came to concentrate on this area—work by John Cheever, John Updike, and Peter De Vries, for example—and a national magazine to chronicle its life, the *New Yorker*, which in precise terms should be *Mostly the New York Suburbs and Exurbs*.

---

24. For a discussion of this emergence of resorts, see James E. Vance, Jr., "California and the Search for the Ideal," in, *Regions of the United States*, ed. John Fraser Hart (New York: Harper and Row, 1972), pp. 185–210. (A reprint of the June 1972 number of the *Annals of the Association of American Geographers*).

Exurbanization of Employment

At first those exurbs were clearly anchored economically in the great metropolis—and in some others such as Boston, Washington, Chicago, Los Angeles, and Oakland-San Francisco—but increasingly the anchor became less fixed. Perhaps from the experience in the first decade after 1945 it came to be realized that activities that had traditionally been concentrated in the core of great metropolises might more easily be carried on elsewhere. In the 1960s and 1970s a number of corporate headquarters of national firms—IBM, General Foods, and others—moved from Manhattan to the outer suburbs of New York, and a similar shift took place in other metropolitan areas. With corporate headquarters at the edge of the suburban band, it obviously became possible for employees to live well beyond the edge of the suburbs and still maintain a reasonable commuting distance to work. The high-level executives of firms had always had more latitude in where they lived; now lower-level employees might enjoy greater freedom. These early experiences in the 1960s and 1970s seem to have encouraged still a different morphogenesis, that of the outward movement of what came to be called backroom activities from the central city. With the computerization of banking and other financial supervision functions such as insurance, it came to be appreciated that most of the routine clerical and fiscal functions could be carried on by workers in the outer suburbs just as readily as those "downtown." In Hartford and other insurance centers these functions were moved from the center. In large financial-center cities a similar shift came for oil companies, mercantile firms, company headquarters, research facilities, and a range of offices employing considerable numbers of people. Space is much cheaper in the suburbs than downtown. With the completion of the Interstate Highway System, the first federal program to spend any appreciable amount of money on metropolitan highways, there were now extensive systems of urban freeways facilitating the conflux of workers on sites other than at the core, where the traditional road system had converged since the time of the founding of the city. In an era of mainly automotive transport in the journey-to-work, these new subfoci, the hearts of the several urban realms as they evolved after 1945, could function; they would not have been able to do so in the rail era. Buses began to be available within the suburban band so women and youthful workers without cars could commute to outlying locations. And with increasing standards of living it came to pass that in states like California most adults had access to a car to get to work.

This rise of suburban employment was slow in being recognized. Even when the new rapid-transit facilities—such as BART mainly in the East Bay City—were being designed, planners tended to think the critical need was for access to and from the traditional city center. Although normally not planned to develop outlying employment centers, the train must run both ways in either rush hour, which meant that good transportation was available outward as well as inward at the rush hour. Taking the Bay Area as an example, we find that BART had its eastern terminus at Concord in Contra Costa County east of the bay. Since BART opened in the early 1970s, very large office buildings have been constructed at both Walnut Creek and

Concord on this line, creating what are very significant employment centers toward the edge of the suburbs. Other new transit systems seem either to have encouraged this trend or, now, to be planned to accomplish that end. The Interstate Highway System, with its urban components, and any existing new rapid-transit system seem to have had their primary urban morphogenetic impact in this creating of a balance between the traditional development in the core and a new diverse development in the realm centers toward the edge of the metropolis.

Small Town Urbanity

The shift toward the edge of the metropolis has encouraged the rise of exurbia. The nuclei for that exurban development have been the scattering of small towns in what was originally the agricultural penumbra around most large cities. Just as the railroad bead-pattern town centers became the nuclei for suburban development, the small town centers on railroads or arterial highways became the germ around which exurbia could collect. No longer was the railroad a necessity. Those towns with railroads, in the years after 1945, were unlikely to have any local passenger services, so the operative force in essentially all cases was the use of personal commuting by car, with a few instances of bus commuting. The nineteenth-century suburbs had had to start in a bead pattern at suburban stops on the rail system; now all that was needed were reasonable long-distance roads that could speed up the increasingly long commute into the metropolitan area. Once in exurbia, individuals could leave the stream of traffic on any intersecting country road and find potential housing wherever the fancy struck them. Initially, most housing was sought with architectural, or at least environmental, distinction. The old house, the house on a hilltop, the house on a lake or river, or the house with old trees shading it was the first objective of the exurbanizing persons. But as time has passed and the number of exurbanites has grown, it has been necessary to build anew the various "distinctions" sought. Ponds have been created, antiquity built from plans, and orchard areas taken over

The Rise of the
Complex City

for their shade rather than their fruit. Exurbia, as suburbia before it, has grown in density, though eschewing anything like the density of its predecessor. To do otherwise would be to give up the conscious environment that brought exurbia into being.

Rise of the Conscious Environment

It was that consciousness of environmental distinction that first brought exurbia into being. The old house in the pastoral landscape of Bucks County, the Hudsonian landscape of Rockland County, the seascape of Essex County north of Boston—the literary landscape of some of John Updike's writing—and other distinctive environments were the magnets that drew city people outward. When all such landscapes inherited from the past were "used up," the demand did not abate; instead, it was met by design. Marinas were constructed; Royal Barry Wills and his successors in design created a new colonial morphology in the 1930s, this one with garages internal to the original construction. Exurbia can be created, but it could not have arisen as a concept and a geographical objective had there not been a real organic landscape of the desired sort inherited from the past.

The landscapes of the past were normally nearly as much the creation of human beings as of nature, and it became clear to thoughtful observers that their new geographical freedom of choice as to where to live conferred an aesthetic and environmental freedom of choice impossible in urban areas. The pull that caused many people with urban economic support to become exurban was this new opportunity to select their desired, conscious environment. Because the spacing of residence in that exurban band was so much greater, the chance for choice in the conscious environment was facilitated. It was very hard to make a Philadelphia suburb from the row house, or a Boston one from the three-decker. But out of sight of the next house, design freedom was vastly enlarged. A New England version of Wyoming could be had on a ten-acre site as long as you were willing to accept maples or old-field pine in your paddocks. Exurbia became the locale of the conscious environment, and exurbia made that conscious decision a possibility.

Certainly today the main bases for exurbia are two groups of people: those who can live outside the metropolis but still remain a functioning part of its economy by making occasional visits to the city, and those whose income is totally independent of place of residence. There have been recent efforts by some to find a way to support themselves in the extensive penumbra of the metropolis by working at home. A number of firms have established a modern "putting-out" system under which piecework is periodically supplied to residents of the countryside and collected from them when finished. Needle trades have pioneered in this, but more recently various forms of computer entry and manipulation have similarly been put out to workers in their homes, which obviously may be in the countryside as well as the suburbs. The State of California has recently been experimenting with such a program of computer usage at home with the purpose of reducing commuting traffic. Using the catchword *telecommuting*, this program introduced by the California Department of General Services hopes to reduce commuting by seven billion passenger-miles per year. There also would be some saving in the eighteen million square feet of office space currently planned for the state. The potential is not small, even as matters stand. Out of an American labor force of around a hundred million, fifteen million do at least some work at home.[25] To the extent that domestic production and office work expands, the potential for the expansion of the urban life without specific urban morphology is enhanced.

The modern city thus has a very complex morphology and an ever-expanding body of morphogenetic processes. We may continue to talk about the traditional core of the city with its quite specific pattern of streets and buildings. Surrounding it are the complex physical and functional features of the suburban band, recently gathering to itself a wider diversity of functional activities and being divided internally into a set of urban realms, often with increasingly important realm centers where replication of the central business districts grows by the year. And beyond the physical edges of the metropolis there lies an ever-expanding penumbra of land that has growing economic, social, and demographic ties with the metropolis but that maintains either an original or a reproduction of the widely diverse conscious environments that first drew city people into the metropolitan frame of the countryside. As efforts continue to make this exurban band less dependent on the labor carried out within the metropolis, the country frame of the city gains population, economic strength, and relative importance. Such a tripartite "city" of traditional core, suburban band, and exurban penumbra must be seen and analyzed as one of increasing complexity, often with new constituents such as the urban realms that have become the daily unit of active life for most city people.

In this complex evolution we may trace the search for the continuing city, which has been the core of civilization for more than three thousand years of human effort.

25. *Christian Science Monitor*, August 29, 1986.

Index

Illustrations are indicated by boldface page numbers and tables by italic page numbers.

Abandonment, and succession, 320
Absolutist's city, 29
Accretion, in medieval cities, 169
Acropolis, 48, 49
Adams Express, 494
Adaptation, morphological, 20
Agde, 185
Agora, 51, 53, 55
Agriculture, in New England, 342
Aigues Mortes, 180
Airport and traffic circle (Camden, N.J.), **456**
Alban Hills, 74
Albany, N.Y., 446
Alberti, Leon Battista, 230, 233
Albert Memorial, 36
Albi Cathedral, 231
Albuquerque, N.M., 424
Alkmar, 227
Almy, William, 337, 405
Alnwick, 185
Amalfi, 117
American colonies, imports to, 333
American Express, 494
Amoskeag Falls, Merrimack River, 339; mill, 433
Amsterdam, 226, **227**, 229, 230
Amsterdam, N.Y., 433, 437
Angevin Empire, 117
Annapolis, Md., 271, **272**, 273
Antwerp, 161, 226; medieval, **156**
Apartment house, elevator in, 377
Appartements (France), 380
Aquitaine, 203; Basin, 182

Arcade (Providence, R.I.), 505
Architecture: functional, 123; high, 233; history of, 11; of New England towns, 261; vernacular, 6
Ardennes, 115
Aristocracy, 147; in Industrial Revolution, 294
Aristotle, on Hippodamus, 47
Arizona, 511
Arkwright, Richard, 289, 309, 310; "Arkwright Village," 338, 339, 343; machine, 337; mills, 343
Arles, 124
Arnold Industrial Expressway, 436
Arno River, 142
Arroyo Seco Freeway, 454
Artisans, in medieval London, 164
Artisans' and Labourers' Dwelling Act of 1868, 319
Ashton-under-Lyne, 292, 298, 311
Assemblage in medieval cities, 168
Assembly line, 433
Association of Retail and Wholesale Trade, 406
Athens, 35, 52, 58
Atlanta, 424, 485, 493
Atrium House, 65
Auburn, Me., 437
Auditorium building, 472
Augsbourg, 161
Augusta, Me., 351
Australia, 463
Austria, 119
Automobiles, 402
Autun, 143

Back Bay (Boston), 423, 480
Bacon, Francis, 219, 220
Bacon's Rebellion, 271
Bailyn, Bernard, 255
Baltic trade, 226
Baltimore, Md., 373, 377, 412, 417
Bank of Amsterdam, 230
Bank of Manhattan Co. Building, 476
Barbarian invasions, 119
Barbizon, 513, 514
Bar Harbor, Me., 271
Bari, 182, 204
Bar iron production, 329
Basilica, 9, 131
Bas Quercy, 188
Bastides, xiv, 13, 28, 177, 178; absence
   of servile tenure in, 197; agriculture in,
   197, 204; census of, 189; characteristic
   names of, 198; consuls in, 191; eco-
   nomic role, 179; economy of, 181;
   equality in, 184; interaccessibility in,
   188; location of, 181; and New World,
   200, 259; occupations in, 194; plan,
   187; preconceived, 180, 188; recruits
   to, 192; refugee villeins in, 191; rela-
   tionship to New England towns, 261;
   settlers seeking, 183; shapes of, 187; in
   southwest France, **179**; wine produc-
   tion in, 182; wine trade and mercantil-
   ism in, 198
Bastidors, as pioneers, 182
Bath, England, 18, 271
Baton Rouge, La., 485
Bavaria, 210
Bay Area Rapid Transit, 484, 507, 516
Bayonne, N.J., 117, 202
Beaumont-en-Perigord, **190**, 200
Beebe, Lucius, 65
Belgium, 296
Belper, 332
Bentley, Edward, 386
Beresford, Maurice, 180, 189
Berkeley, Calif., 508
Berkeley, William, 271
Berkshire Hills, Mass., 515
Berlin, 385
Beverly, Mass., 335
Béziers, 121, 185
Biddeford-Saco, Me., 351
Bidonvilles, 229
Birmingham, England, 30, 316, 463
Blacks, in American cities, 37
Black Sea, 47
Blackstone Canal, 351
Blackstone River, 331, 337, 351
Block assemblages, in Philadelphia, 267
Bloomsbury, 247

Boarding houses, 343, 350
Board of Trade Building (Chicago), 478
Bogardus, James, 374
Boise, Idaho, 485
Boissonade, P., 112
Bolton, 292; duke of, 272
Bombay, 10
Bon Marché (1852), 413
Bordeaux, 117, 204
Boston, 255, 257, 262, 297, 371, 373,
   377, 382, 383, 388, 393, 395, 412,
   417, 422, 430, 432, 479, 485, 487,
   493, 508; beach layout, **259**; Franklin
   Simon Reuses Museum, 21; horsecar
   lines, **387**; industrial cluster, Route
   128, **500**; laboratory for electric trac-
   tion, 387; medieval town, 268, 395;
   new city hall, 21; public garden, 396;
   railroads, **369**; subway lines, 397;
   symphony orchestra, 394; trade with
   China, 335; trolley, 387
Boston (Lincolnshire), 115
Boston and Albany Railroad, 388, 405,
   440; Highland branch, 389
Boston Elevated Railway, 397, 401
Boston and Maine Railroad, 405
Boston Manufacturing Company, 341,
   342
Boulevard des Italiens (Paris), **404**, 413
Boulevard Montmartre (Paris), **404**
Boulton, Mathew, 284
Bourg, 124, 148, 177, 193
Bourg-faubourg theory, 124, 155
Bourges, 141
Bowman, Winifred, 298, 311
Bramante, D'Angelo, 233
Brasilia, 34
Bridenbaugh, Carl, 251
Bridgeport, Conn., 431
Brighton, 271
British class system, 327
British railways, 318
British working class, impoverishment of,
   296
Broad Street (Philadelphia), 263
Brockton, Mass., 392
Brookline, Mass., 388, 392
Brooklyn, N.Y., 356, 377, 383
Brothels, Roman, 68
Brown, Arthur, Jr., 21
Brown, Moses, 331, 337
Brunelleschi, Filippo, 230, 233
Brussels, 117
Buckhead, Ga., 484
Bucks County, Pa., 515, 518
Budapest, 8, 396
Buffalo, N.Y., 433

Buildings: cast iron, 374; foundation problems, 376; large compact, 481; in New York City, **482**; spread of tall, 485; tallest, 477, *486*; technology, 482; tower, 482
Burgage plot, 128
Buxton, 271
Byzantine cities, 27

Calgary, 424, 432
Calico printing, 292
California, 452, 453, 511, 513, 518; Central Valley, 16
Calvert, George, 256
Camberwell, **323**, 324, 325
Cambridge, England, 508
Cambridge, Mass., 258
Camden, N.J., **456**
Canada, 252, 424, 463; British sovereignty, 254; charter (1981), 424; conquest of (1763), 253; urban transportation in, 445
Canaletto, Antonio, 222
Canals (Amsterdam), 229
Capital accumulation, 34
Capital Beltway, 507
Capitals of Middle Ages kings, 112
Carcassonne, 185
Carcopino, Jérôme, 68
Cardiff, 30
Cardo, 61, 365
Carew Tower (Cincinnati), 478
Carmel, Calif., 64
Carson House (Eureka, Calif.), 5
Cartwright, Edmund, 289
Castra, Castrum, 13, 178, 212, 215
Cathari, 121
"Cathedral of Learning," 478
Cavendish-Harley family, 242
Cenacula, 66, 364
Cens, 180
Censitaires, 183, 253
Central business district, 400, 420, 488, 505; contractualism in, 401; geographical growth, 418; office subdistrict, 467; pattern in 1950s, 466; post-1945 model, 465
Central London Railway, 322
Central-place theory, 75, 113, 147
Chamberlain, Joseph, 316
Champlain, Samuel de, 252
Charlemagne, 24
Charles River, 341
Charleston, S.C., 269, 270
Chartres Cathedral, 231
Cheever, John, 515
Cheltenham, 271

Chemin de fer Américain, 366, 384
Chequers of Salisbury, **195**
Chester, **365**
Chicago, 373, 376, 377, 412, 417, 422, 432, 433, 447, 453, 454, 478–80, 487, 493, 508; birthplace of the skyscraper, 471; electrified El, 396
Chicopee, Mass., 351, 437
Child labor, 339
China, ancient, 45
Chinese districts, 461
Christaller, Walter, 147, 210; and central-place theory, 75
Chrysler Building, 476, **477**
Churchill, Winston, 4
Cicero, Ill., 499
Cincinnati, 276, **277**, 377, 407; as archetype of American cities, 279; Carew Tower, 478; industry, 279; land speculation, 278; layout, 278
Cities, 12, 44; American, reaching 100,000 population, *361*; chartered rights of, 117; class distinctions in, 174; classical, xiii, 9; colonial, 10, 255; divine location of, 42; after 1850, 364; eternal verities of, 7; European–world domination, 10; expansion of, 44; growth of, 376; heretical, 122; organic, 22; orthogonal, 47; periods of adaptation, 26; in pioneer life, 279; preconceived, 22; *radio-concentrique*, 155; reason for existence, 42; role and purpose of, xiii; Roman, xiii, 27, 61; security in, 510; stages of development of, 18; streetcar pattern in, 384; transformation of role of, 364; in trolley era, 455
City-country relations, medieval, 146
City and South London Railway, 395, 396
City of Factions, 133
Civil war, 399
Clark, George, 219
Clark University, 508
Class assembly, 166, 236, 327
Clayton, Mo., 484, 507
Cleveland, 377, 407
Clifton, Bristol, **250**
Cloaca Maxima, 68
Cluny Abbey, 121
Clyde Valley, 292
Coeur, Jacques, 141
Colbert, Jean-Baptiste, 219
Colchester, 115
Colonization at home, 177
Colosseum, 68
Commerce, 69
Communal government, in medieval cities, 176

Index

Communes, 28, 118
Concord, Calif., 484, 508
Concretion, in medieval cities, 169
"Conscious Environment," 518
Constantinople, 9, 125
Constitution of 1789, 333
Construction: cast iron, 375; highway and trucking, 429; iron cage, 375, 426, 471; of industrial satellites, 432; mass, 449, 459; post-and-beam, 127; steel-cage, 471; structural steel, 376; terracotta, 376
Contado, 119, 364, 513
Contrat d'Hostice, 195
Contrats d'Hostice et d'Accensement, 199
Conzen, M.R.G., 185
Copenhagen, 370
Cordes, 204
Corfu, 120
Cornières, 190, 194
Corporation Street scheme, 316
Cotswolds, 285
Cotton, 297, 337
Counter-reformation, 210
Country Club district (Kansas City, Mo.), 450
Country Club Plaza (Kansas City, Mo.), 490, **491**
Cours-la-Reine, 224
Covent Garden, 240, 242
Croker, John Wilson, 242
Cromford, 289, 332; mill, 310
Crompton, Samuel, 289, 337
Crusades, 28; Albigensian, 27, 119, 137, 181; fourth, 125
Crystal Palace Exposition (1851), 331

Daft, Leo, 386
Dallas, Tx., 479, 485
Dark Ages, 9
Dayton, Ohio, 485
Decumanus, 61, 365
Deffontaines, Pierre, 201
Delaware River, 263
Delft, 227
Democracy, origins of, 174
Denver, Colo., 485, 493
Department stores, 308, 413; development of, 412; location of, 420; men's, 402, 430
de Poitiers, Alphonse, 183
Derbyshire, 289, **295**
Des Moines, Iowa, 485
Dessau, Germany, 19
Detroit, Mich., 436, 453, 507
De Vries, Peter, 515
Dickens, Charles, 249, 347

Dickinson, Robert, 201
Dioecism, 75
Disraeli, Benjamin, 302, 327
Districts: Chinese-American, 462; in English cities, 316; ethnic, 461; London housing, 236; nativist, 461
Domme, 188
Domus, 65
Dordrecht, 228
Drake, Daniel, 278, 280
Drake, Isaac, 279
Drumlin, 258
Duc de Sully, 220
Duke of Gloucester St., 273
Dukeries, 513
Duties, feudal, 120
Dyos, H. J., *Victorian Suburb*, 323

East Anglia, 286
Eastborne, 271
East Boston subway tunnel, 397
East Cambridge, Mass., 395
East Chicago, Ind., 499
East End of London, 321
East India Companies of Europe, 210
"Edge-City," 484
Edison, Thomas A., 385
Edmonton, 424, 485
Elbe-Saale frontier, 201
El Cerrito, Calif., 461, 462
Eleanore of Aquitaine, 205
Elephant's child (Kipling), 38
Elevated railways, 385; Berlin, **385;** Lake Street, Chicago, **439;** Lower Broadway, 406; and suburbanization, 439
Elevator, 378, 417, 467; invention of, 374
Elizabeth I, 234, 240
Ellicott City, Md., 438
Elne, 185
Empire da mar, 120
Empire State Building, 476, 481
Employer-worker conflict, medieval, 144
Employment: exurbanization of, 516; in selected industries, 354
Emporium, 72
Enfield Falls, Conn., 433
Engels, Friedrich, 301, 305, 311
England, 28, 202, 210; medieval, 119; segmented labor in, 284
English East India Company, 211
"English Nation," 210
Entrepôt, 156, 252
Equitable Center (New York City), 483
Equitable Insurance Company Building: 1870, **474;** 1875, 375; 1886–87, **46;** 1915, 474, **475**, 481; 1961, **478**

Eton College, 242
Etruria, 59, 74
Etruscan cities, 27, 58, 59
Etruscan Gate (Perugia), **60**
Euston Square, 321
Evelyn, John, 245
Everyman, 6
"Expansible city," 123, 239
Exurbanization of employment, 516
Exurbia, 381, 512, 514

Factories: Ashton-under-Lyne, **287;** in
    English cities, 316; without housing,
    436; model before 1945, 435; in 1930s,
    436; and trolleys, 438; and warehouses,
    434
Fall River, Mass., 356, 430
Families, occupational, 153
"Family factory," in America, 330
Faneuil Hall (Boston), 22
Faubourg, 124, 193
Faubourg Ste. Honoré, 422
Federal Hill (Providence, R.I.), 261
Federal Housing Administration, 445,
    447, 459
Feudalism, 269
Field, Marshall, 405
Field and Leiter (Chicago), 405
Fifth Avenue (New York City), 422
Fireman's Fund Building (San Francisco),
    480
Firey, Walter, 401
Fitchburg, 262; railroad, 405
Fitzgerald, John, 394
Flanders, 115, 117, 143, 145
Flat factories, 433, 434
Florence, 135, 144, 176, 233
Florida, 511, 513
Fondaco, 140
Fora (Rome), 62
Ford, Henry, 433, 442
Ford Motor Company, 435
"Foreigners" in medieval cities, 170
Forest, medieval, 127
Form and function, 19, 20
Fort Wayne, Ind., 485
Forum Julium, 63
Foshay Tower (Minneapolis), 478
Foster City, Calif., **450**
Fourcés, 29
Framingham, Mass., 440, 496, 499
France, 28, 210, 252, 296, 463, 501; me-
    dieval, 119; southwestern and bastide,
    178
Freeways, 454, **517**
Freighthouses, 429
French Canadians, rustification of, 255

French colonization in America, 252
Fressia, 145
Furnaces and forges, 330

Gallia Narbonensis, 185
Gascony, 202
Gaul, 71, 124, 145
Georgia, 275
Georgian city, 234
Georgian houses, 250
German new towns, 201
Germany, 119, 190, 298, 501; east of
    Elbe, 178
Ghent, 143
Ghettos, 163, 170
Ghibellines, 132, 134
Ghiradelli Square, 121
Giant's Causeway Railway, 386
Gilbert, Bradford L., 473
Gilbert, Cass, 474
Gilbert, Humphrey, 211
Gildhall, 151
Gilds, 144, 145, 148, 151, 285
Gimbel's (Herald Square), 414
Glasgow, 373, 395
Gouda, 227
Governor's Palace, Jamestown, 273
Grand Central Depot, 383
Grand Central Terminal (New York City),
    476, 480
Grand Rapids, Mich., 424, 487
Grant, Ulysses S., 7
Great Eastern Railway, 319
Great Northern Railway, 321
Great Western Railway, 318
Greece, 45, 77
Greek cities, xiii; anticipate New England
    villages, 56; commerce in, 54; common
    elements in, 49; functional simplifica-
    tion, 57; houses in, 44, 55; internal
    structure of, 44, 52; open systems, 61;
    preconceived, 27; stoa, 54; walls of, 57
Greek city-states, 26, 45
Greek *polis*, 18
Greek revival architecture, 19, 43
Grosvenor family, 242
Guelphs, 134; and Ghibellines, 132
Gutkind, E. A., 197

Haarlem, 227
Hadrianopolis, 58
Hamburg, 371
Hamilton, Alexander, 336
Hamilton, Ontario, 485
Hammond, J. L. and Barbara, 293
Hanover Square, **248**
Hanse, 162, 226

Hanseatic League, 120
Hadrian's Villa, 75
Harper Bros. Building, 374
Harrisburg, Pa., 446
Harrod's, 414
Harrowgate, 271
Hartford, Conn., 514
Haufendorf, 201
Haughwout (Department) Store, 374, 470
Haverhill, 392
Heerschildordnung, 211
Hellespont, 47
Henri IV, 223, 242
Henry the Navigator, Prince, 208
Higginson, Henry Lee, 394
"High and Far-Off Times," 39
Highways, 436, 453, 454; interstate, 515
Higounet, Charles, 189
Hippodamus, 47, 51, 57
Holland, 210; Land of Cities, 9
Holmes, Urban, 119
Holyoke, Mass., 351, 437
Holy Roman Empire, 24
Home counties, merchant movement to, 169
Home Insurance Building, 25, 470, **471**
Hong Kong, 10, 297
Hooke, Robert, 245
Hope, R.I., 339
Hope Mill, 355
horrea, 71, 364
Horrea Epagathiana, 73
Horsecar, **367**; in Boston, **387**; in New York, 382, 383
Hôtes, 195
Household manufacture, 332
House of Seagram Building (New York), 481
Houses: Amsterdam, 228; back-to-back, 313; Barbados in Charleston, 269; generalization of, 309; Georgian construction, 249; Greek, 50; in Lowell, 349; Mediterranean, 135; New Netherlands, 268; northern development of, 152; ranch, 459; Roman, 64; in Rome, 69; row, 313; in Savannah, 275; tall northern, 153; terrace, 324; tract, 449; tower, 133, 134; Victorian suburban, 324
Houses, medieval: English, 155; origins, 126; size of, 129; wooden, 126; in Ypres, **161**
Housing: American, 458; construction costs, 460; country club, 510; economic class partitioning, 460; European and American differences, 458; exurbanization of, 516; factory-tied, 437; Georgian estates, 370; in Great Depression, 445; industrialization of, 449; London estates, 322; in Manchester, 301, 305; mass-production style, 460; and nickel-fare, 390, 410; problems with, 443, 445; reception area for migrants to city, 410; rental in Middle Ages, 142; technology, 460; and trolleys, 446; for workers, 310, 437, 460
Housing, public, 443, 444, 447
Houston, 432, 479, 485
Howe, Julia Ward, 394
Hoyt, Homer, 448
Hudson-Manhattan tubes, 468
Hudson Terminal Building, 469
Hudson Valley, N.Y., 16, 513
Huguenot, 200
Hungarian Millenial exposition (1896), 396
Hunt, Richard Morris, 377
Huss, John, 121
Hyde Park, 248

Idiograph, 15
Illiteracy, 4
Îlot, 196, 197
Immigration, 463; in British cities, 327; and factory labor, 431; flow of, 357; Great Britain population, **464**; Irish, 373; labor in New England mills, 343; U.S., 357, *359*
Industrial cities, 30, 344, 353; nature of, in U.S., 360
Industrialization: England, 10, 367, 368, 370; France, 10; fourth phase, 358; third phase, 351; in U.S., 10, 333, 336, 340, 368
Industrial revolution, 23, 293; Britain, 328; first stage, 285; Manchester, 285; narrow ownership of land, 294; in New England, 30; second stage, 286; shaped geography outside London, 284; in U.S., 30, 328, 431
Industrial satellites, 369, 377
Industry: in cities, 284, 430; development of, 367; location in nineteenth-century city, 410; in parklike areas, 500; post-1945 location, 499; beyond satellites, 498; segmental labor in, 336; U.S. pattern, 356
Innocent III, Pope, 27
Inns of Court, 237
Insula, insulae, 66, 196
Iron manufacture, 432
"Isolated city," 298
Italy, 117, 119

J. C. Nichols Co., 491
Jackson, Alan, 321
Jackson, Patrick Tracy, 341
Jamestown, Va., 272, 273
Japan, 501
Jenney, William Le Baron, 470
Jersey City, N.J., 356
Jerseys, 253
Jews, 162, 185
Johns Hopkins University, 508
Jones, Inigo, 241
Journeys, 33
Julius II, Pope, 233

Kamerzell House (Strasbourg), **154**
Kansas City, 454, 485; China selling in, 411
Kellett, John, *The Impact of Railways on Victorian Cities*, 317
Kensington, 247
Keutgen, Friedrich, 118, 119
King of Prussia, Pa., 507
Kings Cross, 321
Knight, Walter, 386
Knossos, city form, 44
Korea, 297
Kraters, 5
Kreischer, Balthasar, 376

La Rochelle, 117, 200, 209
Labor: high wages in U.S., 377; scarcity in American industry, 335; surplus, 284; worker mobility, 501
Labyrinth, 44
La Manche, 513
Lambert Field, 508
Lancashire, 299, **300**
Land: and frontier, 281; market, medieval, 166; modular division of, 48
Land assignment, 33; in bastides, 192; late medieval, 166; Marxist, 8
Land rent, 142, 409; in Manhattan, 507; medieval, 167; in merchant's town, 225; for retailing, 507
Land speculation, 235, 280
Land use separation, 57
Languedoc, 27, 119, 203
Las Vegas, Nev., 485
Latium, 71, 74
Lavedan, Pierre, 51, 58, 195
Law, commercial, 257
Law merchant, 257
Law of symmetry, 4
Lawrence, Mass., 351, 355, 392, 430, 437
Laws of the Indies, 211–18
League of Twelve Cities, 58

Leasehold, and shoddy construction, 311
Leiden, 227
Le Marais, 223, 242
Les Tournelles, 223
Levant, 28
Lever House (New York), 481
Lewiston-Auburn, Me., 351, 437
Libri Ritualis, 58
Liège, 115; county of, 30; as market town, **148**
Lippet, R.I., 339
Little Rock, Ark., 485
Liverpool, 296, **317**, 373, 463
Lombard, 162
London, 119, **222**, 369; commercial road, 20; estates, 241, **243**; of Fitzstephen, 164; Georgian, 234; Great Fire, 222, 237, **238**; houses in piazzas, 241; housing for poor, 236; merchants, 167; metropolis of mercantilism, 235; new road, 20; planning, 36; rail termini, 318; suburbs, 369, **372**; twelfth-century, 164; underground and department stores, 414; West End, 240, 247
London and North Western Railway, 320
London Metropolitan Railway, 384
"London Rebuilt," 239, 245, 250, 263
London River, **165**
Long-distance trade, 208, 209, 296
Loop (Chicago), 470; the El, **398**
Los Angeles, 422, 453, 479, 485
Louis XIV, 224
Louisbourg, 254
Louisiana capitol, 479
Louisville, Ky., 276, 277
Louvain, 117
Lowell, Mass., 334, **346**, 347, **349**, 392, 430, 437; boarding houses, **351**; Francis Cabot and, 335, 341; ethnic communities, **358**; history of, 344; mill yards, 346
Luddism, 340
Luifel, 228
Lynn, Mass., 499

Macedonian cities, 48
Macy's, 414
Maguelonne, 185
Mails, 229
Maine, 513
"Main Line" of Pennsylvania Railroad, 440, 514
Manchester, 30, 296, **282**, 297, 463; canals, rivers, and roads, **299**; conurbation, 302; in 1840, 307; in 1843, 302,

Manchester *(cont.)*
303; Engels on the working class, 301; marketplace, **306**; as village of manufacture, 292
Manchester, N.H., 351, 430, 437
Manhattan: Island, 382, 507; midtown, 476, 480; office district, 476
Mann, Thomas, 428
Manufacturing, 328; domestic, 284; household, 332
Marketplace: Manchester, **306**; medieval, 129
Markets, medieval, 158
Market square: Bruges, 159; Nuremburg, **145**
Market Street (Philadelphia), 263
Market towns, 148
Marmande, 204
Marseilles, 463
Marshall Field and Co., 422; wholesale house, 426, 468
Marx, Karl, 302
Maryland, 253, 256, 271
Marzebotto, **59**
Mas, 201
Massachusetts, 257, 329, 452; turnpike, 507
Massif Centrale, 201
Mass production, 433
Mass selling, 403
Mass transit, 401
Matlock Bath, 289
Mayer, Harold, 470
"Mayfair," 242, 247
Mazarin, Cardinal, 219
Maze, Greek, 50
Medemblik, 227
Medieval cities, xiii; absence of class areas, 174; anticlerical nature, 122; factionalism in, 132; as legal districts, 176; nature of, 112; north of Alps, 143; organic nature, 122; shaping forces, 125; south of Alps, 136
Mediolanum, 22, 62
Meigs, Capt. Joe Vincent, 395
Melville, Herman, 514
Memorial Opera House (San Francisco), 21
Memphis, Tenn., 485
Mercantile cities, 29, 219; enlargement of buildings in, 221; model of settlement, 114; revolution of fifteenth century, 194; system of Rome, 72
Mercantile model of settlement, 252
Mercantilism, 218, 219; in colonial America, 329; creation of mass markets, 286; financing, 334

Merchandise Mart (Chicago), 478
Merchant's Hall, 154
Merchants: British in North America, 254; in Middle Ages, 149; as organizers of trade, 160
Merchant towns, 28, 210, 221, 245; form of, 224; rise in Middle Ages, 165
Merrimack River, Falls, 334, 345, 433
Merritt Parkway, 454
Metropark, N.J., 484, 507
Metropolitan Life Tower (New York), 480
Metropolitan Railway: Boston, 389; London, 322, 395
Miami, 485, 493
Middle Ages, 9, 208
Midi, 201
Milan, Milano, 22, 24, 121, 364, **513**
Miles, Henry, 344
Miletus, **46**, 47, 49, 52
Mills, steam cotton, 354
Minneapolis, Minn., 433, 479
Mírabel, 204
"Miracle Mile" (Chicago), 422
"Miracle Ten Miles" (Los Angeles), 422
Mitty, Walter, 5
Mobile, Ala., 487
Model T, 433, 442
Modular units, 163
Monadnock Building (Chicago), **469**, 470
Monorail, 395
Monpazier, 13, **14**, 180, **196**
Mons, 117
Montauban, 204
Montauk Building, 470
Montclair, N.J., 204
Montgomery, Ala., 387
Montréal, 16, 254, 412, 415, 424, 485
Moody, Paul, 341
Moorfields, 264
Morocco, 209
Morphogenesis: American cities in industrial era, 454; evolutionary vs. revolutionary, 8; processes of, 6; as synthesis, 38
Morphology, 4, 392
Moses, Robert, 35
Moudon, 143
Mountain of Buereu (Liège), **206**
Movement, pedestrial, 364
Muller, Peter, 507
Mundus, 59, 60
Murphy, Raymond E., et al., *Central Business District Studies*, 419, 466

"Natural settlements," 113
"Near Northside" (Chicago), 402
Nantes, 366

Naples, 144, 371
Napoleon III, 36
Narbonne, 119, 121, 185
Narragansett Pier, 271
Nashua, N.H., 351
Nashville, Tenn., 485
Natick, Mass., **496**
National Cash Register Co., 429
Nation state, 9
Naumkeag Steam Cotton Co., 335
Netherlands, 119, 226
Newark, N.J., 356, 485
New Bedford, 355
Newbury Street (Boston), 402, 423
Newburyport, 263, 392, 431; turnpike, 453
Newcomen, Thomas, 290
New England, 253; agriculture, 342; in colonial times, 260; geographical pattern, 266
New England towns, 257; functional design, 268; organic growth of, 262; point of initiation, 262
Newfoundland, 258, 332
New Hampshire, 257
New Haven, Conn., **262**, 431
New Orleans, 377, 408, 412, 485
Newport, R.I., 64, 261, 271
Newton, Mass., 392
New World, 192; discovery of, 209; points of attachment, 10; settlement, 200
New York and Harlem River Railroad, 383
New York Central Railroad, 480
New York City, 16, 331, 333, 336, 356, 366, 370, 373, 377, 383, 388, 407, 408, 412, 417, 422, 446, 447, 472, 479, 485, 487, 493; department stores, 414; the El, 396; rapid transit, 406; suburbanization of factories in, 435
New York World building, 473
New York, New Haven, and Hartford Railroad, 405, 480
New Yorker magazine, 515
Nichols, Jesse, 490
Nicholson, Francis, 272
Nîmes, 124
North Andover, Mass., 392
North Dakota, capitol of, 479
North London Railway, 322
North Michigan Avenue (Chicago), 423
Norwich, 115
Nottingham, 30
Nuttall, Zelia, 213

Oakland, Calif., 453, 485; port of, 497
Oglethorpe, James, 275

Office buildings, elevators and, 174
Offices, 467, 506
Office zone, 417
Old Colony Railroad, 405
Oldham, 292
Old State House (Boston), 260
Olmsted, Frederick Law, 388, 454
Omaha, Neb., 485
Omnibuses, 320 **366**, 382
"One Hundred Percent Location," 467
Orange County, Calif., 484
Organic growth, 42, 48, 175; in Athens, 57
Orleans, 117
Ostia, 160; apartment houses, 66, 67; decline of, 72; entrepôt for Rome, 70; port for Rome, 71; streets, 70
Otis, Elisha Graves, 374, 470
Owen, David Dale, 336
Owen, Robert, 336, 443

Pac-Pacific Exposition (1915), 450
Paddington Station, 322
Palace Green, 273
Palais de Jacques Coeur, 141
Palazzi, palazzo, 65, 135, 139
Palazzo Ricardi Medici (Florence), **139**
Palo Alto, Calif., 440, 508
Paoli, Pa., 440
Paréage contracts, 35, 180
Paris, 36, 117, 229, 364, 369, **378**, 383, 463; Faubourg Ste. Honoré, 422; Place des Vosges, **244**; planning, 36; suburbs, 369; urban railroads, 388
Parker, Margaret T., 345, 348
Parks, public, 229
Parkways: Arroyo Seco, **517**; Westchester County, N.Y., 454
Pasadena, Calif., 271
Passaic River, 336
Paterson, N.J., 354, 437
Paul, Lewis, 288
Pawtucket, 332, 334, 345, 430, 438
Pawtuxet River, 244
Pax Romana, 74, 124
Peak district, Derbyshire, 310
Pearson, Charles, 318, 321
"Peninsular line," Southern Pacific Railroad, 440
Penn, William, 263, 267
Pennsylvania, 253
Pepin, Denis, 290
Pericles, 7
Periere Bros., financiers, 388
Perigord, 188
Persian wars, 26, 467; in Athens, 57
Philadelphia, 255, **265**, 335, 377, 417,

Philadelphia *(cont.)*
485, 508; land sales, 266; model, intent of, 266; pattern, 267; residential squares in, 263; scale of blocks, 265; in 1681, 263; speculators' town, 264; squares, 264
Philbrick, Margaret, 418
Philip II of Spain, 212
Philip of Macedon, 26
Phoenix, Az., 424, 487
Piazza del Duomo (Florence), 142
Piazza della Signoria (Florence), 142
Piazza Maggiore, 132
Piazzo del Campo (Sienna), **130**
Piepowder Courts, 149
Piraeus, 57
Piranesi drawing of Roman architecture, **40**; map of classical Rome, **76**
Pirenne, Henri, 146, 176, 188
Pittsburgh, Pa., 276, 377, 432, 446, 485
Pius IX, Pope, 144
Place d'armes, 157
Placea, 196
Place des Vosges, 223, **244**
Plague, 137
Planning: in bastides, 184; in London, 36; in New York City, 35; in Paris, 36
Plantation, 45, 252
Planted town, in Europe, 177
Plaza, 217, 450
Plots: bastidor's, 189; burgage, 365
Plutarch, 51
Po Basin, 115
Polis, 18
Pomerium, 59, 60, 121
Pompeii, 64
Portland, Me., 262
Ports, 235
Portus, 124, 148, 156, 177
Portus, second port of Rome, 71
Portus Augusti, 71
Post, George B., 473
Post-industrial city, 31
Post Oak (Houston), 507
Prague, 8
Pred, Allan, 354
Priene, size of, 55
Prime movers, 434
Prince, Hugh, 320
Prince's capital, 209
Prince's towns, 221
Princeton, N.J., 508
Processes, urban, 24
Production, process-clustered, 368
Proletarianization of English labor, 295
Propontis, 47

Provence, 27
Providence, R.I., 260, 261, 331, 335–37, 343, 351, 430, 431, 485; Arcade, 505
Providence and Worcester Railroad, 352
Pubs, 315
Pulaszki Skyway (N.J.), **453**
Puritan consociated churches, 262
Putting out system, 285
Puylaroque, 188
Puymirol, **172**

Quaker capitalism, 265
Quarters: factional, 139; industrial, 141; occupation, 151; of tolerance, 162
Queens, N.Y., 499
Québec, **253**, 254, 329
Quincy Market (Boston), 22

Rabastens, 204
Ragusa, 120
Railroads, 368; in Boston, **369**; intra-urban, 321; shipments, 327; team tracks, 405; in Victorian cities, 318
Railways, electric, 385
Rasmussen, Steen Eiler, 240
RCA Building, 492
Realm centers, 507
Renaissance, 231
Renaissance cities, 29, 230; social distinctions in, 232
Reps, John, 263, 265
Residence, generational shifting of, 511
Retailers, 408, 409
Retailing: after Civil War, 399; commodity combining, 411; medieval, 158; in Middle Ages, 159; specialty selling, 411; and wholesaling, 404
Revere, Paul, 200, 258, 261
Rhode Island, 257
Rhodes, 120
Ribauz, 120
Richardson, H. H., 388, 468
Richmond, Va., 386, 485
River Rouge plant, 435, 437
Rochester, N.Y., 437
Rockland County, N.Y., 437
Roman architecture, 40
Roman colonies, 185
Roman countryside, 74
Roman empire: death of, 8; reaches New World, 212
Roman houses, 64, 67
Rome, 144, 231, 364; irregular pattern of, 61, 62; tall houses, 66; urban explosion, 77; wheat imports, 71

Index

Romulus, 62
Roosevelt, Franklin Delano, 445
Rossmoor (Walnut Creek, Calif.), **512**
Rotary traffic circle, 452
Rothschilds, financiers, 388
Rouen, 117, 209, 297
"Roundabouts," 452
Route 128 (Mass.), **500**, 507
*Royal Commission Studying the State of
    the Large Towns and Populous Places,*
    313, 371
Rörig, Fritz, 132, 145
Rugby School, 242
Rural economy, 303
Rural implosion, 118, 151
Russell, John, 241
Russell, Josiah Cox, 168

S. Spirito (Florence), 233
Saco, Me., 437
Sacramento, Calif., 424, 487
Sacred furrow, 59
St. Albans, 143
St. Denis, 157
St. Germain, 388
Ste. Honoré, 224
St. James Park, 248
St. John's, 258
Ste. Livrade, 204
St. Louis, Mo., 377, 408, 412, 417, 446,
    507, 508
St. Malo, 209
St. Paul Building, 473
St. Peter's Basilica, 231
Salem, 258, 261, 392, 431
Salisbury Cathedral, 231
Salt Lake City, Utah, 485, 487
Salvation, 122
San Antonio, Tx., 485
San Francisco, 16, 21, 370, 377, 408,
    412, 424, 446, 453, 485, 508
Sanitation, Roman public, 68
San Leandro, Calif., **434, 446**
San Mateo, Calif., 504
Santee Hills, S.C., 514
Savannah, Ga., 269, **274**
Savery, Thomas, 290
Savoy District (London), 190, 235
Saxony, 145
Schiffergesellschaft (Lübeck), 428
Schuylkill River, 263
Sears, Roebuck and Co., 402, 429, **430,
    484,** 489
Sear's Crescent, 22
Seattle, 485, 487; Smith Tower, 479
Segmental labor, 285, 336, 342

Segregating processes, 53
Segregation, 36, 169, 509
Seigneuries (Canada), 253
Separation, 509
Septimania, 27, 185
Serfdom, 146
Shopping, 225, 422, 423, 496
Shopping centers, 225, 423, 450; outly-
    ing, 487, 489, 493, 505; social evolu-
    tion of, 422; suburban, 492
Siege castle, 254
Siemens, Werner, 385
Sienna, 117, **137**
Sifton, Clifford, 463
Signum Urbis, 475
Simmons, Jack, 319
Simon, André L., 202
Singapore, 10
Singer Sewing Machine Building, 473
Site and situation, 16
Sixteenth century, changes during, 208
Sjoberg, Gideon, 31
Skyscrapers, 417, 469; in Chicago, 470;
    definition of, 373; first, 25; and modu-
    lar lots, 469; as morphological need,
    480; in New York City, 468, 472; physi-
    cal evolution of, 475; postmodern,
    483; post-1945, 479; ziggurat shape,
    475
Slater, Samuel, 331, 337, 367, 405
Slater's Mill, 331, 334, **338**
Slatersville, 338, 339
Slums, in Manchester, 308
Smith Tower (Seattle), 479
Socialism, and post-war housing, 458
Social Security, 511
Sofia, 8
Sonoma, Calif., **216, 444**
South Africa, 463
Southern Pacific Railroad, 440
Southfield, Mich., 506
South Station (Boston), **418**
Spain, 211, 275
Speculation, in land, 35
Spinning: Arkwright machine, 337; en-
    gines, improvements in, 289; introduc-
    tion of steam, 289; Jenny, 289, 337;
    water-frame, 337
Sprague, Frank, 386
Squatting tenure, 258
Stadtluft macht frei, 255
Stahlyard, 140
Starrett, W. A., *Skyscrapers and the Men
    Who Build Them,* 474
Star pattern, New England towns, 260
State Mutual Insurance (Worcester), 480

Index

Stations: Northern Union (Boston), 405;
    Pennsylvania (New York City), 406,
    476; Southern Union (Boston), 405
Steam engine, 290
Steam power, rental, 431
Steelyard, London, 169
"Steelyards," 210
Stoa, 54
Stow, John, 164
Strand, the, 223
Strasbourg, **153**
Strassendorf, 201
Stratification, social, 322
Strawberry Banke (Portsmouth, N.H.), 262
Streetcars, 384
Streets, 130, 401; Athens, 58; classifica-
    tion, 246, 263; Greek, 50, 51; grid pat-
    tern, 51
Structures: flexible use in Middle Ages,
    171; gothic, 129; steel-cage, 470;
    weight-bearing wall, 469
Strutt, Jedediah, 289, 331
Suburban band, complex structure, 508
Suburbs: annular shape of, 380; bead pat-
    tern, 370, 440; black, 462; blue collar,
    391, 438; created by railroad, 370; eco-
    nomic democracy, 372; generational
    shift in, 379; invasion and succession,
    379; of London, 372; middle class,
    438; morphology, 448; after 1918, 441;
    post-1945, 464; railroad, 326, 369,
    378, 381; roads for, 452
Subways, 394; cut and cover, 385; origins,
    384
Sultan Street (Camberwell), 209
Summerson, John, 234, 237
Summer-Winter and Washington Streets
    (Boston), 423
Sun Life Building (Montréal), 480
Superhighways, 451, 495
Switzerland, 190
Sybil, or The Two Nations, 302, 327
Synoecism, 56, 73, 75, 77
Syracusa, 130
"Systematic Settlements," 113, 114

Tacoma, Wa., 487
Taiwan, 297
Taunton, Mass., 354
"Telecommuting," 518
Temple, 43
Temple, William, 227
Tenements, 407, **409, 473**
Terminal Tower (Cleveland), 478
Testut, Lucfen, 200
Textiles: early American factories, 335;
    manufacture, 136, 432; mills, 340;

plants, 340; in U.S. Census (1815), 339
Thames Street, 246
Three Rivers, 254
Thrupp, Sylvia, 166
Tiber River, 72
Tiffany, merchant family, 405
Tivoli, 75
Toledo, Ohio, 485
Toll Roads and Free Roads, 452
Toronto, 424, 461; city hall, 22
Toulouse, 119, 121
Tournon d'Agenais, **199**
Tout, T. F., 178
Tower Building (New York City), 472
Tower Houses, 133, 134, **135**
Towns: bastidal, 257; common, 260;
    growth, 150; Norman, 122; orthogonal,
    260; restored Roman, 124; south of the
    Alps, 120; in U.S., 268
Trade: American, 334; feudal centuries,
    113; general merchandise, 492; growth
    of, 366; in Holland and England, 211;
    long-distance, 72, 113, 403; in New-
    foundland, 332; originating in Europe,
    116; retail, 488; split of retailing and
    wholesaling, 407; Venetian medieval,
    125; in West Indies, 332; wholesale, 72
Traders, necessity in Middle Ages, 160
Trading: alliance, 115; facilities in cities,
    221
Traffic circle, **456**
Trains, multiple unit operation of, 397
Trajan's Column, 5
Transportation: automotive, 489, 491; in
    Bay Area City, 373; changes in, 452;
    class division in, 439; democratic, 445;
    evolution, ix, 365; horsecar, 366; im-
    provements, 221; pedestrian flow, 421;
    relationship to settlement, ix; revolu-
    tion, 366; streetcar, 384; trolley era,
    392; trucking, 495, 496, 500; walking
    district, 419; water, 365
Travelers Insurance Building (Hartford),
    478, 480
Trees, in Victorian suburbs, 326
Tremont Street (Boston), *394*, 396
Trier, 124
Trogir, 120
Trolley lines, 442; in Boston, 393, early
    work on, 386; expansion, 391; and
    shoppers, 393
"Truck" System, 314
Trucking, interurban, 428
Tryon, Rolla Milton, 330
Tulsa, Okla., 424, 487
Turino, stages of, 7
Turner, Frederick Jackson, 199

Index
========

Turnpike: Pennsylvania, 454; Worcester, 496

Turpe lucrum, 167

Tuxedo Park, **381,** 514

Twain, Mark, 514

Unit fare, 389

United Nations, 21

United States, 296, 463; immigration in, 357; industrial belt, 501; national pattern of industry, 356

University of Chicago, 508

University of Pittsburgh, 478

Updike, John, 515

Urb and suburb, 364

Urban history, 8

Urban initiation, 32

Urbanity in small towns, 517

Urban morphogenesis, xiii, 4; in electric car era, 398; Great Revolution in, 386

Urbanization: social, 118; U.S., 250, 336

"Urban realm," 502, 503, **504**

Urban-rural balance, 10

Urinals, Roman, 68

Utopian, morphology of Savannah, 275

Vaison-la-Romaine, 68

Van Allen, William, 477

Van Depoele, Charles, 386

Vance, James E., *Capturing the Horizon,* 492; "Emerging Patterns of Commerical Structure in American Cities," 494; *Geography and Urban Evolution in the San Francisco Bay Area,* 371, 503; "Housing the Worker," 310, 438; "Labor Shed, Employment Field, and Dynamic Analysis in Urban Geography," 34, 371, 465; "Land Assignment in the Pre-Capitalist, Capitalist and Post-Capitalist City," 193; *The Merchant's World,* 297, 406, 425

Vancouver, 424, 485

Venice, 161

Versailles, 112, 232, 388

Verviers, 297

Verviers, Belgium, 443

Vienna, 124, 138

Village aggloméré, 201

Village de route, 201

Villages, Arkwright, 343

Villefranche de Rouergue, **125,** 197

Villeneuve d'Agen, 204

Villeneuve-sur-Lot, 182, **183, 191**

Villeréal, **203**

Virginia, 253, 271, 274

Visconti Villa, **513**

Vitruvius, 211–18; *Ten Books of Architecture,* 5

Voluntown, Conn., 339

Von Thünen, 275; "Isolated state," 75

Wade, Richard, 470

Waldorf-Astoria Hotel, 476

Walnut Creek, Calif., 484, **512**

Waltham, Mass., 335, 392, 430; system, 340, 344, 350, 437

Wamsutta Cotton Co., 355

Wanamaker, John: and Co., 423; as postmaster general, 427

Ware, Caroline F., 337

Warehouses: flat, 434; location of, 426; after 1945, 429

Warner, Charles Dudley, 514

Wars, between Holland and England, 211

Warsaw, 8

Washington, D.C., 22, 34; metro, 507

Wastelands, in medieval Europe, 175

Water-frame spinning, 337

Waterman, Henry, 374

Water-power, 334

Watt, James, 284; improvements in steam engine, 290

Weaving, 288, 300

Weber, Max, 261

Wellesley, Mass., 504

Wells Fargo Express, 427, 494

Westchester County, New York, 480

West Country, 286

"West End" model, 247, 250, 271

West End Street Railway, 389, 390

Western world, 74

West Indies Trade, 332

Westminster, 112

Westminster Hotel (Boston), 474

West Oakland transportation nexus, **497**

Weston, Mass., 500

West Riding of Yorkshire, 287, 291

Wharton, Edith, 514

Wheatley, Paul, 42

Whitney, Eli, 274, 331

Whitney, Henry, 387, 389

Wholesaling: in central business district, 429; location of, 425; in Middle Ages, 160; after 1945, 494; and railroads, 426; railroad sidings and, 427; and retailing, 404; shifts in location of, 425; towns, 495; traditional structure of, 428

Williamsburg, 271, 274

Willow Run freeway, 436; plant, 437

Wills, Royal Barry, 518

Wilshire Boulevard (Los Angeles), 402, 423

Winchester, 157

Winds in Greek cities, 56

Wine, 202

Index

Winnipeg, 485
Winston-Salem, N.C., 485
Woolen industry, evolution of English, 286
Woolworth, Frank, 474
Woolworth Building, 468, 474
Worcester, Mass., 260, 262, 335, 351, 487; turnpike, 453, 496
Working class, British, impoverishment of, 296
Workingmen's trains, 319
World trade, America enters, 334
World Trade Center (New York City), 469, 481, 483, **468**
World's Tallest Building, 484

Wren, Christopher, 245, 246
Wright, Frank Lloyd, 20
Wrigley Building (Chicago), 480
Wycliffe, John, 121

Yamassee War, 271
Yerkes, Charles Tyson, 322
Yorkshire, **291**
Young Women Operatives, 341
Ypres, Belgium, 161
Yucatan, 45

Zone of Assimilation, 488
Zone of Discard, 488

Index

Designed by Martha Farlow

Composed by The Composing Room of Michigan, Inc.,
in Bodoni Book and Poster Bodoni

Printed by The Maple Press Company, Inc., on
55-lb. Glatfelter Offset Smooth Eggshell finish